OXFORD MEDICAL PUBLICATIONS

Clinical psychology and medicine

Clinical psychology and medicine

AN INTERDISCIPLINARY APPROACH

FRANK JAMES VINGOE

Principal Clinical Psychologist,
University Hospital of Wales, Cardiff.
Lecturer,
Welsh National School of Medicine,
Cardiff

with contributions
by

IAN TAYLOR

Senior Clinical Psychologist,
University Hospital of Wales,
Cardiff

OXFORD
OXFORD UNIVERSITY PRESS
NEW YORK TORONTO
1981

Oxford University Press, Walton Street, Oxford OX2 6DP
OXFORD LONDON GLASGOW
NEW YORK TORONTO MELBOURNE WELLINGTON
KUALA LUMPUR SINGAPORE HONG KONG TOKYO
DELHI BOMBAY CALCUTTA MADRAS KARACHI
NAIROBI DAR ES SALAAM CAPE TOWN

British Library Cataloguing in Publication Data

Vingoe, Frank James
Clinical psychology and medicine. – (Oxford medical publication).
1. Medicine and psychology
2. Clinical psychology
I. Title II. Series

610'.1'9 R726.5 80-40973

ISBN 0 19 261219 0

Typeset by Oxprint Ltd, Oxford
Printed in Great Britain at the University Press, Oxford
by Eric Buckley,
Printer to the University

To W. Leslie White, Headmaster, and Alfred, Mary Ellen, Grace, Sylvie, Lisa, Wendy, and Michael Vingoe for their understanding and support

Preface

This book, which is written primarily for medical students in their clinical years and for general medical practitioners, should also be helpful to those preparing for the Diploma in Psychological Medicine and the Membership examination for psychiatrists. It will also be of interest to clinical psychologists and those other health professionals who need to have a basic knowledge of clinical psychology. Most readers will find this book self-contained and will not find it necessary to consult another text in order to understand it. However, it is assumed that the reader who needs to develop his knowledge of basic experimental and theoretical psychology in more detail will consult more extensive works in psychology while reading this text.

Psychologists are able to contribute much more in the area of general medicine than many health professionals realize, and it is hoped that this book will help non-psychologists to recognize problems or situations in which the expertise of a clinical psychologist may be beneficial. In some cases, the clinical psychologist may be able to suggest ways in which the doctor or other professional could apply certain techniques. In other cases, perhaps when the doctor's time is limited, referrals for psychological help will be made to the clinical psychologist, who will be directly involved in treatment planning. To what extent psychological methods may be of help in a given situation is best determined by the doctor in consultation with the psychologist. This book is written in the hope that it will encourage interdisciplinary approaches to problem solving, and encourage interdisciplinary teaching, where students of medicine and psychology share various seminars related to general medicine. An example of an area which would benefit from the multidisciplinary approach is the study of pain. At the same time the limitations of the psychological approach must be recognized by the psychologist and explained to other health professionals.

This book aims to show that man's behaviour is determined by many factors and that most forms of maladaptive behaviour, whether in the behaviour of an individual or an organization such as a medical ward, are best treated by an interdisciplinary team which takes advantage of each health worker's particular expertise. It is recognized that a book can do little more than suggest increased interprofessional co-operation. It falls to the various workers in the field of health actively to encourage communication. While initially the involvement of various professionals may seem time-consuming, in the long run an increased interdisciplinary involvement will be more productive, reduce interdisciplinary friction, and increase the overall effectiveness of health personnel.

This book could not have been completed without the help of many colleagues. Parts of the manuscript were read by Joy Abbati, Maurice Driver, Alex Kellam, John Pathy, and Ian Taylor, all of whom were helpful in providing constructive criticisms regarding the text and illustrations. I am especially grateful to Ian Taylor, who wrote Chapters 8 and 19 of this book.

I am also grateful to Ralph Marshall, and the staff of the Department of Medical Illustration, for preparing the figures. I should also like to thank many librarians, especially those of the Psychology Department library at the University of Wales Institute of Science and Technology, Cardiff; and the Welsh National School of Medicine library; but above all, Brenda Harding, librarian at the Post Graduate Centre, Whitchurch Hospital, Cardiff.

Deserving my thanks for performance above and beyond the call of duty is Maureen Cowie, who deciphered and typed various drafts of the manuscript, and who provided moral support when it was sorely needed; and Hazel Spencer whose help in the typing of the manuscript is also much appreciated.

The dedication of this book expresses my indebtedness to my headmaster, who well remembers my attempts to write; to my parents; and to my family, who gracefully sacrificed or postponed many activities while I was involved in writing this book.

Cardiff 1980 F. J. Vingoe

Acknowledgements

The author would like to thank the following for permission to reproduce figures and tables: Fig. 2.1: J. F. Schadé and D. H. Ford and Elsevier/North Holland Biomedical Press; Fig. 2.2: C. Blakemore and G. F. Cooper and Macmillan (Journals) Ltd.; Fig. 3.1: Tavistock publications; Figs 3.2 and 3.3: Pergamon Press, Ltd.; Fig. 4.6: John Wiley and Sons, Inc.; Figs 4.7 and 4.8: Elsevier/North Holland, Inc.; Fig. 4.9: Harcourt, Brace, Jovanovich, Inc.; Fig. 4.10: Elsevier/North Holland, Inc.; Fig. 5.1: W. B. Saunders Co.; Figs 5.2 and 5.3: Lochem: De Tijdstroom B. V.; Fig. 5.4: McGraw-Hill Book Co.; Fig. 5.5: W. B. Saunders Co.; Figs 7.1 and 7.2: Dr M. V. Driver; Fig. 7.3: De Erven Bohn, Amsterdam; Figs 7.4 and 7.5: Holt, Rinehart, and Winston, Inc.; Fig. 7.6: H. D. Roffwarg and Holt, Rinehart, and Winston, Inc. (modified version); Fig. 10.1: Psychological Corporation; Fig. 17.1: Paul 't Hoen and Waverley Press; Fig. 18.1: D. G. Mackean and John Murray; Fig. 18.2: Dr M. V. Driver; Table 1.1: John Wiley and Sons; Table 2.1: Methuen; Tables 3.1. and 3.2: Dr Rosalyn Saltz and the Baywood Publishing Co., Inc.; Table 5.1: John Wiley and Sons.

Contents

1
Introduction: clinical psychology in perspective

Truth, which only doth judge itself, teacheth that the inquiry of truth, which is the love-making or wooing of it, the knowledge of truth, which is the presence of it, and the belief of truth, which is the enjoying of it, is the sovereign good of human nature.
Francis Bacon: *Of Truth*

This book is written for medical students, doctors, clinical psychologists in training, and other professionals who work in hospital, clinic, or other medical setting. Although some workers may overstress the psychological component of physical disease, it is generally agreed that many patients presenting to their doctor for what may be perceived as a medical problem are in need of some psychological assistance. It is clear in many cases that emotional factors are serving to exacerbate the physical problem, and, indeed, what appears to be a medical problem may be completely solved by one or other psychological approach. This book will be helpful when it comes to deciding which particular professional should take the role of the major therapist: physician, psychologist, social worker, occupational therapist, or other professional. In other words, are there specific problems which should be directly referred to a psychologist, or is the medical practitioner or social worker quite able to treat the patient using certain psychological methods? Frequently, of course, after initial consultation with the clinical psychologist, the decision taken will involve close co-operation between a number of different professionals.

After briefly tracing the historical background of clinical psychology, I shall discuss in this chapter models in clinical psychology and medicine, and then outline the various roles of the clinical psychologist in assessment and evaluation, in treatment procedures, and in research. In relation to research, there will be a short discussion of the development of single-case experimental designs which are increasingly used in behaviour therapy and studies using biofeedback. The clinical psychologist's role as consultant and administrator will also be discussed, with some emphasis on the psychologist's relationships with other professionals.

THE HISTORICAL BACKGROUND TO CLINICAL PSYCHOLOGY

Most psychologists would agree that psychology originated, as did many other sciences, in the field of philosophy. Boring's (1950) *A history of experimental psychology* is acknowledged to be the text *par excellence* in this area. However, for those whose time is limited, Keller's (1973) text is highly recommended, particularly Chapter 12 on the development of learning as an area in psychology. Boring traces the rise of modern science in the seventeenth century, laying particular stress in the first chapter on physiology and physics. The first six chapters are devoted to what would now be termed physiological psychology and provide an excellent historical background for the student of psychology or physiology. While the title of this book might suggest some narrowness of outlook, a number of chapters relate closely to the early development of clinical psychology, such as the mental-test movement. Although the mental-test movement began with tests of reaction-time and colour blindness, etc., it later broadened to include measures of more extensive practical application. Alfred Binet (1857–1911) in his studies of intelligence in schoolchildren provided the basis for much that came later in the field of psychological measurement. But it was the mental tests devised for the armed forces during and after the two world wars that gave the impetus for the development of clinical psychology as a profession. In selecting people for general military service, general-ability or intelligence tests were desperately needed to select-out those who were unfit. In addition, with new scientific developments, specialized tests of numerical ability, perceptual ability, mechanical aptitude, etc., were needed to select people for new highly specialized jobs such as operating radar, sonar, and fire-control systems.

There is general agreement that the field of clinical psychology began with the mental-testing movement, and that assessment or evaluation still plays a significant role in clinical psychology. However, this particular role has broadened in nature, and with the increased involvement of the clinical psychologist in therapeutic, research, and other activities, such as training and various forms of consultation, the percentage of his time spent on this activity has considerably decreased. For those interested in training programmes in clinical psychology, the requirements for entry into American and Canadian programmes may be found in *Graduate study in psychology* (American Psychological Association 1980–1) and for British programmes in *Regulations for the British Psychological Society Diploma in Clinical Psychology* (British Psychological Society 1974) and *Postgraduate qualifications and courses in psychology* (British Psychological Society 1976).

MODELS IN CLINICAL PSYCHOLOGY AND MEDICINE

Simon and Newell (1963) defined the term 'model' as 'a synonym of theory', while Lachman (1963) noted that the model 'brings to bear an external organization of ideas, laws, or relationships upon the hypothetical propositions of a theory or the phenomena it encompasses. This external organization or model contributes to the construction, application, and interpretation of the theory'.

Although theory, or model-building, is not particularly stressed in this book, it is important for the mental-health professional to be aware of the influence of his theory or model on his behaviour as a professional or scientist. The early chapters of Part IV of this book discuss therapeutic points of view or models (a further discussion of this topic can be found in Barber (1976)). Although some people insist that they do not follow a model or theory, it is probably true to say that most if not all of us do so to a certain extent, implicitly if not explicitly.

As noted by Davison and Neale (1974), in 'formulating a medical model of mental disorder . . . certain concepts are taken from medicine and applied, by analogy, to a new domain, abnormal behavior'. Obviously, the way one conceives of abnormal behaviour is based upon the particular model one holds. Davison and Neale discussed the statistical, medical, psychoanalytic, and behavioural models of abnormal or deviant behaviour.

The statistical model of abnormal behaviour conceives of the term 'abnormal' as meaning 'statistically infrequent'. This model is limited in its application, however, because many desirable behaviours are statistically infrequent yet not considered as abnormal or deviant in the pejorative sense. For example, a high level of creativity or intelligence is generally seen as highly desirable. However, a person who exhibits a low level of intelligence tends also to be limited in his behavioural capabilities such as self-help skills. He is therefore usually classed as abnormal.

In very general terms, the *medical model* views disturbed behaviour as symptomatic, with the actual disease process or pathology underlying the symptoms. Some mental-health workers even suggest that the aetiology of accidents is to some extent psychological, i.e. underlying predispositions may lead to an 'accident proneness'. Thus, from the medical model viewpoint, only the symptoms are observable and the disease or psychopathology (psychic conflict in psychoanalytic terms) is inferred from the symptomatology. The patient is unaware of the underlying pathology and may be said to be 'unconscious' or unaware of it.

On the other hand, the *behavioural model* views the behaviour or observable 'symptoms' as the actual psychopathology. The behavioural model does not assume an underlying pathology and is concerned mainly with the 'here and now', rather than focusing extensively on past events. For example it looks at the difficulties the patient may be having in his environment (in his family, with his friends, at work, etc.) and what can be done to help the patient eliminate or decrease the anxiety that arises in specific situations, for example, to increase his assertive behaviour.

The particular model adopted has implications for treatment. For example, those who subscribe to the medical model tend to view the treatment of symptoms as a palliative only. In order to cure the disease (psychopathology) the basic disease process must be uncovered. If symptoms alone are dealt with *symptom substitution* may be expected to take place, and far more dangerous symptoms may be substituted for those removed. The issue of symptom substitution is discussed in Part IV.

Those who subscribe to the behavioural model would not deny that a patient's problems may be partially based on incidents that occurred during his childhood, but there is relatively little emphasis on investigating these incidents. The emphasis is on treating the problems that exist for the patient at the present time, and on identifying the stimuli (situations, 'significant others', etc.) that may be controlling and maintaining the person's maladaptive behaviour. It is assumed that the patient has learned to behave in ways which cause him difficulty, just as he has learned the behavioural patterns which facilitate his mental health. Thus, it is reasoned, if maladaptive patterns of behaviour are learned, they can be unlearned or extinguished.

The medical model may be appropriate in the understanding and treatment of physical illness, but it is of no use in understanding maladaptive behaviour. When the actual social-learning history of maladaptive behaviour is known, principles of learning appear to provide a completely adequate interpretation of psychopathological phenomena, and psychodynamic explanations in terms of symptoms underlying a disorder become superfluous (Bandura, 1969).

It would be an exaggeration to say that psychologists always subscribe to the behavioural model and medical professionals to the medical model, although a number of textbooks give this impression.

While many refer to the medical model as if it was one single view of disease or disorder, the medical model can view disease in three ways (Davison and Neale 1974):

(1) infectious disease: such as the common cold or hepatitis;
(2) systemic disease: non-infectious diseases, such as diabetes;
(3) traumatic disease: disorders resulting from physical assault or through the ingestion of a poison.

Some applications of the medical model is abnormal psychology may be seen in Table 1.1.

Davison and Neale pointed out that:

> the traumatic disease model has . . . been widely applied within the field of abnormal behavior. The behavioral abnormality resulting from a severe blow to the head is a somatogenic traumatic disease. Moreover, just as a systemic disease may be the malfunctioning of a psychological process, so may external trauma be psychological rather than physical and assault psychological processes rather than physical organs. Psychogenic traumatic disease models have been adopted by behaviorally oriented psychologists.

TABLE 1.1
APPLICATIONS OF THE MEDICAL MODEL IN ABNORMAL PSYCHOLOGY

Medical disease	*Definition*	*Applications to abnormal psychology*
Infectious, e.g. pneumonia	Invasion by microorganism	Paresis
Systemic, e.g. diabetes	Organ malfunction not caused by external agent	Biochemical theories of schizophrenia Autonomic theories of neuroses
Traumatic, e.g. broken arm	External agent produces malfunction	Psychological stress theories

(From Davison and Neale 1974.)

They went on to say that the adoption of a particular model results in a selective view of the kinds of data that will be collected and the particular type of interpretation of the data which will be used. They therefore recommended that in order to obviate overlooking (a) certain types of data, and (b) possible explanations, 'the only reasonable way of looking at the data is to assume multiple causation. A particular disorder may very well develop through an interaction of learning and biological factors'.

McKeachie (1967) discussed the case for the use of multiple models in clinical psychology. While he agreed with other psychologists that models other than the illness or medical model of mental disorder need to be developed, he felt that the medical model should be used where appropriate while these 'other models that may prove more useful' are being developed. He concluded that he could not agree with Albee, who felt it was necessary to abandon the medical model, and instead believed that in problem-solving generally and in dealing with human problems particularly, good solutions were more likely to be found if many alternatives are available.

Clearly, social mores and attitudes are significant factors in one's definition of behavioural abnormality. Thus, the definition of what is considered abnormal varies from culture to culture and from time to time in the same culture.

ROLES OF THE CLINICAL PSYCHOLOGIST

Assessment and evaluation

The perceived role of the clinical psychologist has traditionally been that of administering psychological tests, but this perception has expanded very significantly in the last two decades. Only a limited amount of individual assessment with psychological tests is now used to help decide which treatment procedure to adopt. Although the measurement of intelligence and the assessment of various specific mental skills may be useful to the occupational psychologist in attempting to help an individual plan his vocational future, these procedures may be of little or no help to the clinical psychologist in deciding what psychological treatment may be most appropriate for a particular patient. More extensive evaluation procedures may be helpful in the determination of the effectiveness of various ward programmes such as a *token economy*. In addition, they may be useful in assessing the effectiveness of treatment procedures on response to operations, response to pharmacological treatment, and on attitudes to other medical interventions. Many behavioural programmes involve almost continuous assessment of response to treatment. Thus, the perceived role of the clinical psychologist in assessment has broadened considerably from an individual mental testing approach to a more general programme approach. Behavioural analysis is discussed in Chapter 15.

Treatment procedures

There has also been an expansion or broadening of the clinical psychologist's involvement in treatment procedures. Some time ago the idea was prevalent among many psychiatrists that psychotherapy (treatment of personal and emotional problems through the use of interviews) should be carried out only by qualified medical practitioners, and that psychologists, social workers, and other health personnel were ill-fitted for this treatment procedure. It was apparently felt that a significant component of severe emotional problems was medical or physiological in nature and thus the therapist must necessarily be medically trained. However, the trained clinical psychologist consults the patient's GP or a specialist where necessary. An overlapping of roles has developed between the psychiatrist and clinical psychologist and between the latter and the social worker. The exchange of information and ideas between the psychologist and doctor is particularly fruitful, benefiting from the medically trained person's knowledge of organic disease and the psychologist's knowledge of principles of learning and other psychosocial factors in emotional disorders.

The research role

Readers who are unfamiliar with research in the behavioural sciences should find Agnew and Pyke (1978) a very readable and informative book. The psychologist is particularly well trained for research work, both in a technical sense and in recognizing areas of potential research application. Again, collaboration between doctor and psychologist may result in the development of creative ideas. One of the most common types of research in the clinical setting involves determining the effectiveness of one or more treatment procedures; for example, determining the effectiveness of personal-effectiveness (self-confidence) training in a group of patients in a ward over a specific period. The research role usually involves the psychologist in assessment and therapy of some sort as well. For instance in the above example in order to determine the efficacy of the personal-effectiveness training it is necessary to obtain a non-biased or objective measure of each patient's personal effectiveness, before and after the training. In order logically to conclude that changes in personal effectiveness are actually based on (i.e. result from) the specific treatment intervention, the use of a control group of patients who are exposed to all procedures except the specific components of the personal-effectiveness training should be included. If patients are randomly assigned to the two groups, experimental and control, and it is reasonably certain that the groups are equal in respect of all other variables which might have an influence on the results, the researcher would expect to be able to determine unequivocally the effect of the specific treatment programme. If the study takes place on a ward, it will not be surprising to find that the non-treatment or control group also show improvements in personal effectiveness, in that members of the treatment group may very will increase their interaction with members of both the treatment group and the control group. However, since both groups would normally be assessed on the components of personal-effectiveness behaviour prior to and after the intervention, one would readily become aware of this 'confounding' effect.

Design of clinical studies

Historically emphasis has been placed on research using the randomized-groups design in psychology, but recently the value of the single-case study has been promulgated.

In the group-type of experimental design a group which receives treatment is compared to a non-treatment or control group. The researcher is interested in obtaining differences between these groups, which are assumed to include subjects who are essentially equivalent in the characteristics which may influence performance on the criterion or dependent variable. In some cases the subjects in the control group are actually matched to subjects in the treatment group on variables thought to be related to variation in the dependent variable, such as improved social-skills behaviour. However, the researcher may also be interested in using subjects as their own controls, i.e. a within-subject design. An example of a pertinent variable in a programme which emphasizes an improvement in social skills is extroversion. It clearly would not be appropriate to use an extremely introverted group as control for an extremely extroverted treatment group.

The practical difficulties in using group designs with clinical populations has led many to publish uncontrolled case studies which, however interesting and suggestive they may be, neither lead to reliable conclusions nor to confidence in applying the methods they advocate. An *uncontrolled case study* or *anecdotal case report* does not involve systematic data gathering, and there is no control over variables other than the defined active treatment or independent variable. Thus, one is uncertain what factor or factors may account for any change in the target behaviour or dependent variable from pre- to post-intervention. Fortunately an increasing number of *systematic case studies* are appearing, particularly in the behaviour-therapy literature. Blanchard and Young (1974) and Blanchard and Miller (1977), reviewing the literature on clinical biofeedback research and the psychological treatment of cardiovascular disease respectively, systematically divided the publications they reviewed into specific categories of scientific merit. The studies reviewed were categorized as 'anecdotal case reports', 'systematic case studies', 'single group outcome studies', 'single-subject experiments', and 'controlled group outcome studies'.

The usefulness of single-case studies in psychotherapy research has been emphasized by Shapiro (1966). However, he stressed a correlational clinical approach, in contrast to Leitenberg (1973), who preferred the experimental analysis of the single-case and the objective measurement of clinically relevant target behaviours. The use of single-case experimental methodology ensures that one may validly attribute changes in behaviour to the methods used to produce these changes.

Although the design of treatment studies is important, the technicalities will not be discussed in detail here. Rather, where an explanation of a particular design is valuable, it will be provided in conjunction with the presentation of a case study.

Sequence in studying behaviour

Psychology is usually defined as the study of behaviour. The observation of directly visible behaviour has tended to receive a great deal of attention, but there is now a trend away from a strict behaviourism, which deals only with observable behaviour, and towards unobservable, covert variables such as attitudes, feelings, and emotions. These variables must, of course, be inferred from the behaviour which is observable, and this behaviour may vary from the responses to a questionnaire or observations made during an interview to various psychophysiological measurements obtained on a polygraph, such as skin resistance, forearm blood flow, and heart rate, as well as electroencephalographic variables such as the density of alpha rhythm (9–12 Hz). Clearly, the interpretation of these various behaviours is based upon a process of assessment or evaluation. It is clear that therapeutic procedures as well as the assessment and measurement of various factors involve *objective observation*. There is then an attempt to *evaluate* or *understand* what has been observed, which, in turn, leads to the *prediction and the control of behaviour*. This sequence in studying behaviour is not only pertinent in the experimental laboratory, but also in carrying out clinical work of various kinds, for example therapeutic procedures. Therefore the psychologist attempts to evaluate his own work continuously so that he does not continue to use techniques whose efficacy is not supported by the conclusions of adequate research programmes.

Consultant and administrative role

The psychologist can advise on measurement techniques or by helping with the experimental design of a research project. For example, there are many sources of bias, of which doctors may be unaware, where patients rate themselves on various behaviours, attitudes, etc. Sometimes a little consultation can go a long way towards improving what might have been a less than adequate research project.

The role of the clinical psychologist as programme administrator, or, in some cases, ward administrator varies from setting to setting and from firm to firm. Steward and Harsch (1966) carried out a survey on the extent to which psychologists participated in various administrative tasks from feeling free to refer patients for music therapy to administering a hospital ward. None of the psychologists extended his administration to strictly medical matters. However, one psychologist reported that he acted as superintendent of a mental hospital for a six-month period. This study indicated that a high percentage of psychologists felt free to initiate new therapeutic methods (e.g. patient government, ward projects). The psychologist's authority on the ward was frequently seen as equal to the physician's authority, and psychologists were often responsible for conducting ward-staff conferences about general ward problems, as well as the treatment of individual patients. A very important point made by Steward and Harsch was that the delegation of authority to a particular psychologist was often the result of an especially good working relationship between the psychologist and his medical colleagues. Thus, while the great majority of trained clinical psychologists are fully qualified to carry out research projects and certain ward programmes, again it is clear that the relationship between medical staff and the psychologist is extremely important when deciding to what extent a particular psychologist is able to carry out non-medical administrative tasks which in the past have been the province of the doctor.

The majority of clinical psychologists work in hospitals and clinics, a smaller proportion working in prisons and in various community agencies. In these settings they are able to relate social, organizational, and environmental variables to emotional and physical problems. Views differ on the work of the educational psychologist as compared to that of the clinical psychologist, and it is my opinion that there is much overlap in function, and that co-operation between the clinical and educational psychologist is to be encouraged. (See the *Bulletin of the British Psychological Society* (British Psychological Society 1978) for a recent Division of Educational and Child Psychology inquiry on the psychological services for children.)

Part I
Psychology of the life-span

INTRODUCTION TO PART I

Chapter 2 of this book considers the development of the organism from conception to adolescence, and Chapter 3 discusses the life-span of the individual from maturity to old age.

The initial section of Chapter 2 considers the genetic aetiology of various disorders, and, after a discussion of maturation, reviews the interesting literature on environmental stimulation. The assessment of language, intellectual, and emotional–social factors are then discussed. In the section on the assessment and treatment of mentally retarded and autistic children, a behavioural approach to treatment is emphasized, and some important issues are raised related to the generalization of treatment effects. Chapter 2 is completed by a short section on adolescence.

The first section in Chapter 3 is devoted to a discussion of various conceptions of maturity. This is followed by a section on the much-neglected middle years, during which many people tend to assess their accomplishments in life and to consider what the future holds for them. The general problems of the elderly person are discussed in the third section, while the fourth section discusses bereavement, grief, and attitudes towards death. This section includes a summary of some attempts to desensitize people towards what has been, for many, a taboo topic. The final section of Chapter 3 discusses the psychotherapeutic and behavioural approaches to the care and treatment of the elderly.

2
Psychology of the life-span: (conception to adolescence)

The child is father of the Man
Wordsworth: *My Heart Leaps Up*

The area of developmental psychology has grown significantly during the last twenty-five years. *Carmichael's manual of child psychology* has now expanded to fill two large volumes (Mussen 1970) rather than one. In general, developmental psychology has changed from being a largely descriptive endeavour, with an emphasis on developmental stages, to a more experimentally-based developmental psychology. More specifically there has been an expansion of research in the area of cognition and learning; a great increase in research on cognitive development based on the concepts of Piaget (1952); a proliferation of studies in *behavioural modification*, and an increase in the research on the extent to which parents and other non-professional groups can be trained to carry out treatment procedures with children.

THE NATURE–NURTURE CONTROVERSY

The *nature–nurture issue* or controversy within the psychological field is concerned with the relative contributions of genetic and environmental factors in determining individual differences in such characteristics as general intelligence, extroversion, and various other cognitive and personality factors. In addition, the aetiology of various psychiatric conditions such as neurosis; schizophrenia; and manic-depressive psychosis, has been investigated and attempts made to determine the degree to which there may be genetic predispositions to develop these particular conditions. The work on the genetics of the *psychotic disorders* can be found in a number of texts, such as Claridge, Canter, and Hume (1973); and Slater and Cowie (1971).

Genetic factors

Most researchers are consistent in assigning a larger proportion of the variance of general intelligence to genetic factors. For example, based on the Otis measure of intelligence, the *H value* (value which indicates the percentage of the variance in a particular variable attributable to genetic factors) is 0.62. However, when it is suggested that there are so-called 'racial' differences in intelligence which are genetically based, emotional reactions may predominate, especially among those who have not read the relevant literature. The *Zeitgeist* has much to do with how far the genetic point of view is accepted in psychology and psychiatry at a particular period. To a large extent the *Zeitgeist* has been opposed to genetic research in psychopathology in the twentieth century, particularly perhaps in the United States, since many American political documents even two centuries ago stressed that all men were created equal. In addition, behaviourism has held sway in American psychology. As far as the nature–nurture issue is concerned, American psychology was *environmentalist* is attitude. However, on the other side of the Atlantic a more biological and genetic viewpoint has been prominent. Ernst Rüdin, the father of psychiatric genetics, founded a genetics research institute early in the second decade of the twentieth century in Munich and concerned himself with studies of manic-depressive psychosis and the disorder which was later to be called schizophrenia. Unfortunately, ideas regarding the 'Master Race' developed in Germany at about the same time, and, particularly when the atrocities carried out during the Second World War became known, many people tended to be suspicious and distrustful of hereditary points of view. About a quarter of a century after the war the controversies concerning intelligence and race were to surface in response to the words of Jensen (1969) in America, and Eysenck (1971) in Great Britain. Incidentally, reports concerning genetics were not the only type of psychological work which resulted in the generation of much emotional heat. For example, the studies of obedience completed at Harvard by Milgram (1963) in which people 'followed orders' in administering electric shocks to human subjects for failure to learn in an experiment were said by many to recall the tactics employed by those who carried out orders in Nazi Germany.

A great deal of research has been done on the genetics of mental illness. Research findings on the relative incidence of schizophrenia in families, for example, led many in the mental-health field to consider the role of genetic transmission in the development of this disorder. Simultaneously many investigators explained the development of schizophrenia on the basis of learning, since it was found that the family environment was basically that provided by schizophrenic parents, and the degree to which children learn through imitation has been well documented. This confounding of psychological and hereditary variables in the interpretation of the aetiology of schizophrenia thus resulted in further widening the cleavage within psychology and psychiatry.

Brown (1942) has written on the genetics of *psychoneurosis*, and has rightly pointed out the great difficulties involved in such an endeavour. Much of this difficulty was due to uncertainty about the homogeneity of the symptoms subsumed under the names of specific neurotic conditions. Brown found that several conditions may become confounded under one specific diagnostic label. He studied 104 neurotics by interviewing about 500 relatives. Relatives were categorized in terms of their psychiatric abnormalities. It was found that while 81 per cent of control subjects had normal parents, this was true of only 47 per cent of patients characterized as having *anxiety states*. This difference was statistically significant. In addition, the analogous differences for the *hysteria* and *obsessional* groups were significant. While admitting the impossibility of attributing differential variance to environmental and genetic factors, Brown was of the opinion that, in the development of the neuroses, genetic factors were as important as factors related to the environment. It is difficult to draw specific conclusions about the genetics of neurosis, because of the few studies undertaken, the unreliability of diagnostic procedures, and the difficult nature of determining the role of environmental factors.

The status of the genetic nature of neuroticism could be considered as being similar to that found by Gottesman for the Minnesota Multiphasic Personality Inventory (MMPI) variable in psychesthenia (Pt) (Dahlstrom, Welsh, and Dahlstrom 1972). Gottesman (1963) used 68 pairs of adolescent twins, half of whom were monozygotic and half were dizygotic. The MMPI and High School Personality Questionnaire (HSPQ) (Cattell, Beloff, and Coan 1958) were used for assessment purposes. Gottesman's conclusions based on *hereditability* estimates for the MMPI scales were that as far as the psychesthenia and schizophrenia scales were concerned appreciable variance was accounted for by heredity but that environment predominated. Interpretations of the diagnostic features of schizophrenia are not the same on both sides of the Atlantic, but Gottesman's results concerning depression and psychesthenia also indicated that heredity and environment contributed equally to these two MMPI scales. Thus, until more conclusive results are forthcoming, it would seem best to view neurotic disorders as determined equally by hereditary and environmental factors.

Slater and Shields's (1968) discussion on genetic aspects of anxiety and Gottesman and Shields's (1973) article on genetic theorizing and schizophrenia are particularly recommended to the clinician. A lucid discussion on the relatively well understood genetic disorders which the clinician sees from time to time. such as *Turner's syndrome, Klinefelter's syndrome,* and *Diabetes mellitus* is found in Rosenthal (1970). Other more frequently encountered conditions such as *Huntington's chorea, Down's syndrome* (mongolism), and *phenylketonuria* (PKU) are also considered. The psychological reaction of the patient to one of these conditions often results in a referral to the psychiatrist or clinical psychologist, and therefore it is advisable for the therapist to become acquainted with sources on genetic counselling such as Fuhrmann and Vogel (1969) or Stevenson and Davison (1970). While it may be argued that genetic counselling *per se* is better accomplished by the medically trained, psychological treatment can be very useful in helping the patient or relative of the patient to adjust to the disorder and to accept its implications in a realistic way. However, it is clearly important here that inter-disciplinary consultation be encouraged and maintained.

The idea that heredity determines a norm of reaction or fixes a reaction range, the specific *phenotype* being determined by the particular environment which the *genotype* encounters, is here accepted. However, it must be remembered that 'the most probable phenotype of some genotypes may be such a deviant one that even the most favourable of currently known environments would not suffice to bring it within the normal range' (Allen 1961).

Maturation

The concept of *maturation* or level of neurological development is an important aspect of the examination of the individual child, as problems of developmental delay may have implications for motor, linguistic, intellectual, and social–emotional adequacy. It is clear that certain unlearned behaviours (i.e. innate behaviours) must await the maturation of the central nervous system and other functional units of the organism. For example, a baby is unable to hold his head upright without support until certain head and neck muscles and specific neural connections from the muscles to the cerebral cortex have developed. This child is quite unable to learn a skill until the specific neural connections have developed which are necessary for the behaviour that is involved in the performance of the particular skill. Prenatally the increase in the protein and nucleo-protein content of the cells as cell differentiation increases is important. The changes which occur after birth are initially concerned with maturation (growth, protein synthesis, and myelinization). There is an emphasis on cell size increase with age and the *pyramidal* cells of the second and sixth layer of the cerebral cortex exhibit the greatest rate of size increase in the first three months of life. Interestingly, it has been found that at birth the dendritic pattern of the human newborn cerebral cortex is not much more complex than that of the rat and it does not begin to approach the adult state until 24 months. Even then it is somewhat less complex that than of the adult (Schadé and Ford 1973). Since maturation is markedly depressed by hypothyroidism and starvation, the importance of endocrine factors and diet in the normal development of synaptic connections must be emphasized.

In 1977 Davidson re-emphasized the importance of nutrition by stating that malnutrition during the first two years of life could result in irreversible intellectual deficit. In addition, other factors have been shown to cause intellectual deficit, for instance untreated phenylketonuria (PKU) and non-disjunction during meiosis, which appears to be the basis of Down's syndrome (mongolism) in the vast majority of cases (Lejeune 1970; Rosenthal 1970). The early diagnosis of those who are irreversibly subnormal, and, perhaps more importantly, those for whom intervention can successfully prevent intellectual and other deficits, is clearly of high priority.

Fig. 2.1. Ontogenesis in fusiform cells in man. The last two drawings show the difference between a two-year-old and an adult. (From Schadé and Ford 1973.)

Hetherington and Parke's (1975) text on child psychology contains an excellent chapter on prenatal development. These authors divided prenatal development into three periods: (1) that of the *ovum* (conception until the implantation of the zygote on the uterine wall); (2) the *embryo*, approximately from the end of the second week to the end of the eighth week of pregnancy, which is a period of rapid development; and (3) the *foetus*, the period from the end of the second month until birth. They noted that it is during the period of the embryo that environmental intrusions caused by such things as maternal disease, faulty nutrition, and drugs may result in devastating, irreversible deviations in development. The highest rate of spontaneously aborted embryos also occurs during this time and it is reported that most of these have genetic and chromosomal defects. The time at which various diseases are contracted is extremely important. For example, if rubella occurs during the first month of pregnancy, there is a 50 per cent occurrence of deviations. However, after the third month, rubella has a near nil association with abnormalities. Fortunately there is an increasing awareness of the influence of drugs on the development of the intra-uterine organism. Hetherington and Parke consider this problem and provide an interesting discussion of the influence of thalidomide on the foetus. The influence of maternal smoking on birth-weight is now well established. The maternal emotional state is important in that it may influence autonomic variables such as adrenaline level, which in turn may affect the foetus. It is reported that women with severe emotional problems have more difficulties during pregnancy than normal women.

Early diagnoses can be accomplished biologically during prenatal life, as in *amniocentesis*, or postnatally, as in testing for PKU. There is controversy regarding the use of amniocentesis in diagnosing such conditions as Down's syndrome and *spina bifida*, particularly in disorders which in some individual cases may not result in gross deformities or in intellectual retardation. For example, in the case of spina bifida, if surgery is completed within the first two days of life, there is a marked reduction in subsequent disability. Lejeune (1970) stressed the need for physiological research into Down's syndrome by noting that 'In contrast to the case of amniocentesis, . . . a physiological understanding of trisomy could save many lives without destroying any'. However, Queenan (1970) reported that the risks involved in amniocentesis were small if carried out by experienced doctors at the appropriate time, and if the abdominal rather than the transvaginal approach were used. Littlefield (1970) stressed the degree of savings possible if all pregnant women of 35 years of age and older were to be examined by amniocentesis. Although much of what I have discussed above is medically orientated, I feel that more clinical psychologists could usefully involve themselves in research concerning problems of pregnancy, such as counselling those who are considering an abortion or those who present with a deformed or defective child. The psychologist should learn about the medical aspects of such problems and be ready to consult with the medically trained when necessary. A useful handbook prepared for the general practitioner, but also useful to the psychologist working with the mentally handicapped and his family, is available from the American Medical Association (1965).

Environmental factors

Post-natal environmental conditions can also have an important effect on development. A great deal of research has been carried out on the effects of early experience on physiological and psychological development. These studies tend to be either studies of deprivation of stimulation or specific experiences, or comparisons of impoverished versus enriched environments. Obviously, the better-controlled research has involved animals; but in animal research there is always the question of how far the findings can be generalized to the human population. Deprivation studies have found that the behaviour of both young animals and babies implies that they actively seek stimulation. This conclusion has been confirmed to such an extent that a scale has been developed to measure the *sensation seeking motive*. This scale and some of the studies in which it has been used is discussed later in Chapter 11.

Somewhat paradoxically, some stress stimulation is probably necessary for normal development. It has been found, for example, that the deprivation of stimulation, including stressful stimulation, may lead to psychological and even physiological disorders. Levine (1960) studied three groups of newborn rats, a group which was regularly picked out of the nest, placed in a cage, and given a mild electric shock, a control group placed in the shock cage without receiving shocks, and a group which remained in the nest and received no handling. Contrary to Levine's expectations, the group which was not handled demonstrated deviant behaviour on the attainment of adulthood. The behaviour of the shock group and the control group was not perceivably different from each other. Levine has replicated this experiment and obtained the same results. He concluded that it was invariably the non-manipulated 'controls' that exhibited deviations of behaviour and physiology when they were tested as adults. The deviant behaviour exhibited included crouching in a corner in the test box and a limited willingness to explore the environment. There was a tendency for these animals to defaecate and urinate frequently, a much used indicant of emotionality or stress response. Reminding us that during stress there tends to be an increased volume of adrenal steroids in circulation, Levine pointed out that there was a significant difference between the stimulated and non-stimulated animals in stress response, in that the non-stimulated group were slower to respond to stress as measured by adrenal steroid secretion, and, in addition, maintained their stress response for much longer. Levine concluded that the prolongation of the stress response could have severely damaging consequences such as stomach ulcers, increased susceptibility to infection, and eventually death due to adrenal exhaustion.

Levine noted that the maturation of the central nervous system might have been accelerated by stressing these animals. This conclusion was based on an analysis of brain tissues which showed a higher cholesterol content, suggesting that there had been a greater development of white matter. In addition, it was reported that the manipulated animals opened their eyes earlier, gained weight more rapidly, and were earlier in developing motor co-ordination. Thus, it seems that both structure and function may be affected in stimulated rats. In discussing his results, Levine refers to the research carried out on children who have been brought up in institutions, such as orphanages. While some have attributed the developmental retardation found in children growing up in such environments to maternal deprivation, Levine is of the opinion that the critical variable is lack of stimulation. The concept of maternal deprivation, while it has had its usefulness in generating research, is too vague and should now be abandoned. Noting that no differences were found in those animals who received painful forms of stimulation and those handled in a more gentle fashion, Levine ended his paper by indicating that some degree of stressful experience in infancy could be necessary for successful adaptation of the organism to the environment it encounters in later life. Obviously, the definition of 'stress' has considerable importance. It could be hypothesized that many problems of adulthood, such as agoraphobia and anxiety states, may in certain cases be partially accounted for by a lack of stimulation in childhood. On the other hand, it would seem that what might appear as an 'overstimulation' as in 'overprotective' mothering can also contribute to various forms of neurotic handicap.

It is critically important to specify what type of stimulation may be necessary for specific maturational processes. An example of this is the work of Riesen (1965) on the effects of a lack of visual stimulation. Riesen reared chimpanzees in total darkness and found that they afterwards suffered from various perceptual defects and difficulties in problem-solving; the normal experience of patterned vision was a critical variable in this research.

Noting the research of Hirsch and Spinelli (1970), which related changes in the organization of neurones of the visual cortex of cats to early visual experience, Blakemore and Cooper (1970) exposed kittens to normal binocular vision in an environment made of only horizontal or only vertical stripes. After being reared in complete darkness for the first two weeks of life, the animals were placed in this monotonous environment for five hours a day while the visual field was limited to approximately 130°. These experimenters extended this regime to the age of 5 months, which was well beyond the 'critical period' in which total visual deprivation causes physiological deficits. From five months, the kittens were exposed to a normal visual environment and their reactions observed. The animals were noted to be extremely inept, and to lack visual place and startle response to appropriate stimuli, although their pupillary reflexes were normal. After only 10 hours of normal vision they showed normal startle responses and visual placing. However, there were permanent defects such as clumsy, jerky following-responses and responses indicative of poor perceptual distance judgments. The kittens also showed differential behaviour responses to vertically and horizontally striped rods. In addition, those kittens exposed to vertical lines were found to have developed many visual cells sensitive to vertical contours and a relative absence of others. The analogous development occurred in those kittens exposed to horizontal lines.

These authors concluded that:

> the visual experience of these animals in early life has modified their brains, and there are profound perceptual disturbances. But we do not think that there is merely passive degeneration of certain cortical neurones because of under-activity. . . . It seems instead that the visual cortex may adjust itself during maturation to the nature of its visual experience. Cells may even change their preferred orientation towards that of the commonest type of stimulus; so perhaps the nervous system adapts to match the probability of occurrence of features in its visual input.

Rosenzweig and his colleagues have carried out a great deal of research relating both anatomical and behavioural variables to differential experimental factors (Rosenzweig, Bennett, and Diamond 1972). The animals used have included different strains of rats, laboratory mice, and gerbils. Typically, the animals used have been randomly assigned to one of three conditions: (1) standard laboratory colony cage with a few other rats; (2)

Fig. 2.2. Blakemore and Cooper's experiment on the effects of early visual experience. The visual display consisted of an upright plastic tube, about 2 m high, with an internal diameter of 46 cm. The kitten, wearing a black ruff to mask its body from its eyes, stood on a glass plate supported in the middle of the cylinder. The stripes on the walls were illuminated from above by a spotlight. The luminance of the dark bars were about 10 cd m^{-2}, and of the bright stripes about 130 cd m^{-2}: they were of several different widths. For this diagram the top cover and the spotlight have been removed from the tube. (From Blakemore and Cooper 1970.)

enriched environment in which several rats live in a large cage with various play objects which are varied from day to day; and (3) impoverished environment in which the rat lives alone. After a certain experimental period, the animals are sacrificed in order to analyse their brain tissue.

They found that larger neurone cell bodies and an increased RNA to DNA ratio were present in rats reared in the enriched environment. Both of these factors are indicative of higher metabolic activity. The greatest difference found in the animals who experienced enriched versus impoverished environments was in the occipital lobes; and the most consistent finding was in cortex/subcortex weight ratio. The differential effects of the three environments resulted in significant differences between all groups in cortex/subcortex ratio. Rosenzweig and his co-workers experimentally ruled out factors other than learning and memory affecting their results. Handling, stress, maturation, or isolation were not significant factors in differential brain changes, although stress produced significant increases in adrenal-gland weight.

While many readers of Rosenzweig's research reports may hope that similar enriched environmental experiences may lead to similar brain changes in humans, Rosenzweig and his colleagues devoted significant space to cautioning those who may generalize the findings in lower animals to the human being. They noted that while experience in an enriched environment may improve subsequent learning, this facilitation was often only temporary.

Hetherington and Parke (1975) provided an excellent review of the widely publicized monkey deprivation studies of the Harlows (Harlow and Harlow 1972), and reviewed some of the reports on the early deprivation experienced by the human infant through 'institutionalization'. Both groups of reports dealt with a general lack of stimulation, but the monkey studies were most concerned with the deprivation of social stimulation. In the Harlow studies animals were either placed in a situation of total or partial isolation from birth, in some cases for six months, in others for one year. In the condition of partial isolation, the animals were reared alone, but they were able to see and hear other infant monkeys in nearby cages. However, no physical contact was possible between them. Thus these monkeys were denied the normal social stimulation obtained through interacting with other monkeys, particularly from their peers. Hetherington and Parke concluded that:

> Total isolation involving reduced sensory and perceptual stimulation, as well as no contact with other animals, was more debilitating than partial isolation. . . . The impairment in social behaviour increased as the length of the deprivation increased, with one year of total isolation producing a total social misfit. Deprivation immediately after birth was more damaging than deprivation after a period of social experience. Intellectual capacity was not affected by the deprivation experiences if the monkeys were adapted to the testing environment before intellectual assessments began. . . .

In reference to the studies involving institutionalization, Hetherington and Parke pointed out that some orphanages and other institutions in which children were cared for in the 1930s and 1940s provided environments which provided little stimulation. Some children appeared to have difficulty in forming meaningful relationships with others, while others seemed to behave in a very dependent way, needing excessive amounts of attention and affection from others. Deficits in IQ and abstract thinking, and delay in language development have been reported. In addition, extremes in activity level, such as withdrawal, apathy, or aggressive over-activity, have been noted.

In order to determine if intellectual and other deficits produced by these depriving environments could be reversed, Skeels (1966) took advantage of a situation in which, to avoid overcrowding, a group of children were transferred from the depriving environment of an orphanage to an institution for the mentally retarded, which, in comparison, could be described as enriched. Typically each child was given an adult or older girl who served as a surrogate mother. About 18 months after transfer a reassessment indicated a very significant increase in IQ for the transferred children, while the IQ of the children remaining in the orphanage decreased quite significantly. In a later follow-up it was demonstrated that the gains made by the transferred children were maintained. Much later, when the subjects were between their mid-twenties and mid-thirties, it was found that the transferred group were equivalent in status to those children who had grown up in the homes of similar socio-economic status without having experienced institutionalization (Skeels 1966; Hetherington and Parke 1975).

It has been reported that the effects of six months' and twelve months' isolation can be reversed in the rhesus monkey by exposing the 'patients' to 'therapists' who are much younger than themselves and thus less socially demanding (Hetherington and Parke 1975).

Although the reports of Skeels (1966) and Harlow and Novak (1973) both report successful therapeutic progress in the development of social–emotional behaviour and in IQ after initial deprivation conditions, it should be noted that the therapy or 'enriched' environmental conditions were introduced relatively early in life, at twelve months in the infant monkey, and at an average of nineteen months in the human infant. It would seem far less likely that such successful intervention could take place at much later ages in either a rhesus monkey or in a human child. Thus, while the above research forces a revision of earlier views regarding the non-reversibility of the effects of social deprivation, it should not be interpreted too idealistically or generalized outside the limits imposed by the obtained data. Having said that, however, the importance of screening babies and young children for psychological and other disorders takes on added significance. Psychological screening will be considered in the next section.

Summary

This summary represents the author's view of the nature–nurture controversy. At conception an infinite number of hereditary predispositions come into existence. While it is generally agreed that hereditary factors limit the individual's ultimate level of physical and psychological development, both the intra-uterine and post-uterine environments are important factors influencing the development of the individual's potentialities. For example, during pregnancy, various diseases, disorders, dietary factors, and maternal emotional factors may affect the development of the intra-uterine organism. Factors in the post-uterine environment, such as exposure or non-exposure to certain perceptual patterns, a poor or enriched intellectual environment, adaptive or non-adaptive family relationships, may also maximize or minimize the probability of developing particular abilities and personality traits to their potential levels. Figure 2.3 presents a hypothetical illustration of a person's psychological development at the age of 18. The figure suggests that the discrepancies between a measured ability or trait and one's potential

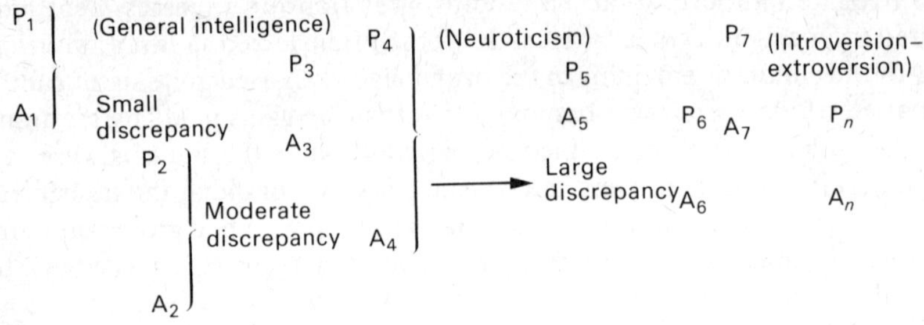

Fig. 2.3. Hypothetical illustration of a person's psychological development at the age of 18. Discrepancies between potentialities (P) (hereditary predispositions) and present abilities (A) as a function of intra-uterine and post-uterine environment; *n* in P_n and A_n indicate that there are an infinite number of potentialities.

in the particular area may be small, moderate, or large, depending upon environmental factors, and the time at which the measurement is obtained.

Not only does the individual have certain potentialities (which may be interpreted as both assets, e.g. general intelligence, and liabilities, e.g. neuroticism) but he also is motivated in certain ways. The interaction between motivation and the present level of development of a certain trait or ability is therefore extremely important in one's understanding of the individual.

PSYCHOLOGICAL SCREENING OF CHILDREN

The policy of screening pre-school children and schoolchildren for physical or medical disorders seems fairly well accepted, although in sparsely populated areas medical practitioners may have a very limited amount of time for this task. In addition, some families have not established the habit of consulting a doctor about their children's health. For these and other reasons, many disorders may remain undiagnosed and untreated. Often psychological problems remain undiagnosed and untreated because there is a shortage of, or even an absence of, psychologically trained staff. Unfortunately, in the absence of educational or school psychologists, a child-guidance clinic, or other psychological resources, a child may easily be misdiagnosed by untrained but otherwise well-meaning staff. It is often difficult to determine if a child's primary assessment should be for mental retardation or emotional disturbance, to use rather broad categories. Thus, well-trained psychologists with both educational and clinical training are indispensable.

Psychological diagnosis may be categorized in a number of ways. There are diagnostic schemes such as that of the American Psychiatric Association (1968), the General Register Office (1968), or the World Health Organization (1957), or one can carry out a *behavioural or functional analysis* (Kanfer and Saslow 1969). It is sometimes argued that some mental-health professionals place too much emphasis on diagnosis, but some system of classification is necessary for epidemiological and research purposes. Many difficulties have been encountered in a research context when one finds that a particular label, for example, 'early infantile autism' (EIA) has been applied based on diverse criteria, by different workers, making it extremely difficult, if not impossible, to compare research results.

The inadequacies in the procedures used in psychological screening and psychological diagnosis and assessment have been stressed for some time now by psychologists and other mental-health workers. Some psychological tests used for diagnostic purposes have proved to be unreliable, and when people are categorized according to information obtained from interviews the results are often inconsistent.

A number of trends have led to a resurgence of psychiatric classification as a topic for debate: (1) a sociological focus on the effects of 'labelling'; (2) the rapid development of behavioural modification as a source of polemical attacks on the medical model and associated classification system; (3) criticisms regarding the poor reliability of the various standardized schemes of classification; and (4) the realization that psychiatric classification problems have much in common with problems of biological classification. The taxonomic literature suggests that classification is undertaken for five main purposes: (1) as a basis for communication within a science; (2) for information retrieval; (3) as a descriptive system for the objects of study in a science; (4) to make predictions; and (5) as a source of concepts to be used within a scientific theory (Blashfield and Draguns 1976).

It is important to remember the unreliability of some psychological tests as diagnostic procedures when assessing both children and adults, particularly when attempting to assess younger children (i.e. those below the age of six or seven), since the *predictive validity* of many psychological tests at this age is even more limited. During the first two years many test scales rely on sensorimotor items which do not correlate highly with the larger percentage of verbal items which tend to be used at higher age-levels and are more related to academic performance in schools.

General developmental assessment

Sheridan (1975) was concerned with the early diagnosis of physical, mental, and emotional–social deficits or handicaps, and developed procedures for the screening or evaluation of children up to five years of age. Her manual included the Stycar sequences, which are based on early developmental schedules such as those of Bayley (1969) and Gesell (1954). The Stycar sequences enable the paediatrician to carry out early diagnosis and clinical management of younger handicapped children. The Stycar sequences are most useful to the doctor, but the psychologist and others who work with young children will also find Sheridan's manual of interest. Sheridan also felt that these procedures could be used as a basis for advising the parents as well as the teachers of handicapped children. She pointed out that the developmental charts were not quantified as is the typical psychological scale. The charts include the following age levels: 1, 3, 6, 9, 12, 15, and 18 months, and 2, 2½, 3, 4, and 5 years. The examination includes four main areas of functioning: (1) posture and large movements; (2) vision and fine movements; (3) hearing and speech; and (4) social behaviour and play. Sheridan provided some useful guidelines for the interpretation of these tests, being careful to point out the limitations of basing a diagnosis on one administration. Her tests are most useful in assessing progress.

In order to assess young children the psychologist may wish to use the Griffiths Mental Development Scales (Griffiths 1971), which include the following sub-scales: locomotor, personal–social, hearing and speech, eye and hand co-ordination, performance, and practical reasoning. The Griffiths scales measure areas of functioning similar to those examined by the Stycar sequences, but they are the only quantified test of their type which has been developed and standardized on English children. A mental age and a developmental quotient may be calculated for each subscale in addition to a general quotient.

Language development

Providing as it does the basis for much later learning, language is perhaps man's greatest asset. Therefore, screening for delays in language development and other language disorders is of critical importance. The development of both receptive (verbal comprehension) and expressive language may be measured by the Reynell scales (Reynell 1969). These functions may be assessed separately from the one-year to the five-year age levels and the advantage of the comprehension scale is that it does not require speech. One is able quantitatively to compare the comprehension and expressive language levels of a handicapped child to those characteristic of children who demonstrate normal language development (Reynell 1970). The Illinois Test of Psycholinguistic Abilities (ITPA) (McCarthy and Kirk 1961) is used extensively to assess linguistic maturity. The test consists of nine subtests, the results of which may be shown in a linguistic psychograph or profile, so that an individual child's comparative performance on the nine scales may readily be seen (Mittler 1970). Mittler believes that the most promising application of the ITPA lies in its use for diagnostic purposes, and as a basis for the design for an appropriate remedial programme and the selection of an appropriate learning situation.

Intellectual assessment

Many clinical psychologists prefer to administer the Stanford–Binet Intelligence Scale (S–B L–M) (Terman and Merrill 1960) or the Wechsler Intelligence Scale for Children (WISC) (Wechsler 1949) in order to obtain a reliable indication of general intelligence. Both the Stanford–Binet and Wechsler scales of intelligence (Wechsler 1949, 1955, 1967) provide a measure of general intellectual ability, and the Wechsler scales provide a 'verbal intelligence quotient' (VIQ), a 'performance intelligence quotient' (PIQ), and a 'full-scale IQ' (FSIQ) which is considered to be a useful aid to differential diagnosis or assessment when, as is frequently the case, the tester is interested in more than the general intellectual level. For example, the determination or specific delineation of brain damage in the child or adult is often carried out by the use of one of the Wechsler scales as a screening instrument, to be followed by more specialized tests. Clearly, the use of *computerized axial tomography* (CAT) may obviate the use of intelligence tests in the general assessment of cortical or subcortical damage in many cases. However, it is in the more specific assessment of psychological deficits that intelligence scales and other more specialized tests involving language and memory functions, etc., may be found particularly useful as a first step in the treatment or rehabilitation of those patients who are expected to benefit from psychological intervention.

The (S–B L–M) can be administered from the two-year-old age level to adulthood, and the WISC can be administered from the five-year to the fifteen-year level. The Wechsler Pre-school and Primary Scale of Intelligence (WPPSI) published in 1967 was designed to assess children from four to six-and-a-half years of age. It is, in general, similar to the WISC and provides verbal IQ, performance IQ, and full-scale IQ. Wechsler (1967) discussed *standardization, reliability,* and inter-correlations of subtests extensively.

There is a critical need for the intellectual screening of pre-school children, and the demand for such screening increased with the development of 'Head Start' programmes in America. Because the task of screening all pre-school children is so enormous, a relatively short, reliable, and valid test is needed. In the attempt to select such a test or test battery, Kordinak, Vingoe, and Birney (1968) initially used the Peabody Picture Vocabulary (PPVT) (Dunn 1959) with a group of migrant children of Spanish–American background. However, it was found that because these children were bilingual, interpretation of many of their responses was difficult. The conclusions of the Vingoe *et al.* (1969) study of Head Start children suggested that the WPPSI was a useful screening device for pre-schoolers, in that it incorporated in one test the essentials of the screening battery recommended by Riley and Epps (1967), whose used the PPVT, the Gesell Developmental Designs, and the Draw-A-Person Test (DAP). Contrary to Riley and Epps's (1967) findings, the DAP did not prove to be a valuable screening device, as the performance of most children was unrealistically low on this instrument. Thus, it was suggested that the DAP be restricted to the building of rapport and interest in the pre-school child. Therefore, the WPPSI is recommended as a screening device for pre-school children. If time is limited, the DAP used to establish rapport, together with an abbreviated WPPSI and a short parental interview provide useful screening.

Various other tests or test batteries have been used for screening purposes, such as the Full Range Picture Vocabulary Test (FRPVT) (Ammons and Ammons 1948) or Raven's Progressive Matrices (Raven 1956). A fairly comprehensive discussion of intellectual assessment is provided by Savage (1970).

Assessment of emotional–social factors

A number of behaviour-rating scales have been developed for use in the classroom for both research purposes and for purposes of psychological screening. For example, Conrad and Tobiessen (1967) have developed kindergarten behaviour-rating scales in order to predict learning and behaviour disorders. These scales are referred to as the Schenectady Kindergarten Rating Scales (SKRS) and are used to screen large numbers of children, so that remedial action can be taken very early on. There are fourteen scales altogether and the scales can be administered within ten minutes. Three of the ratings involve play and peer relationships, four involve manipulative or motor activity, four concern speech or verbal activity, and the remaining three consist of ratings of 'fearfulness', 'frequency of anger towards adults', and 'frequency of anger towards children'. Teachers are able to administer the scales with minimal training, and adequate inter-rater reliability has been demonstrated. The validity of these scales is discussed in Tobiesson, Duckworth, and Conrad (1971).

The Science Research Associates publish a Rating Scale for Pupil Adjustment which measures personal and social adjustment in the classroom for children aged between about eight and fourteen. Children are compared to others of their own age on twelve variables which include: 'tendency towards depression', 'tendency towards aggressive behaviour', introversion–extroversion', 'emotional security', 'impulsivity', 'motor control and stability', and 'social maturity'.

The instruments that assess social–emotional maturity, the Vineland Social Maturity Scale (Doll 1953), and the Gunzburg Progress Assessment Charts (Gunzburg 1974*a*) are used with subnormal populations. Other screening instruments, particularly for specific populations, are discussed in the very comprehensive manual edited by Mittler (1970).

PSYCHOLOGICAL PROBLEMS OF CHILDREN

The previous section suggests that many of the problems of childhood can be classed as: (a) problems of developmental delay; (b) problems involving disorders in the reception or expression of language; (c) problems of backwardness in intellectual or academic skills; (d) problems involving mental retardation or intellectual deficit and; (e) emotional–social problems—

though of course a child may have problems in a number of these areas at the same time.

This section is mainly concerned with mental retardation or subnormality, and early childhood autism. Children in these two categories may exhibit certain specific maladaptive behaviours which will need to be treated in their own right, for example, self-injurious behaviour, such as head-banging, eye-gouging, scratching, digging or burning of the skin, etc. Other types of undesirable behaviour include excessive aggression towards others, enuresis, encopresis, and social withdrawal.

Coleman, Burtenshaw, Pond, and Rothwell (1977) analysed the pre-school referrals in a British inner urban area. They noted that the problems in most cases involved symptoms of a pattern of stress or disturbance which involved the family as a whole. They therefore concluded that the child's problem could only be understood as an environmental one, in which such factors as the parent's marital situation, poor housing, the father's violence, or the adults' unrealistic expectations of the child might all play a part.

Coleman and his co-workers categorized their primary referral problems into: (a) management problems; (b) neurotic disorders; (c) problems of developmental delay; and (d) social stress. In analysing the referrals by age, sex, and category it was found that while only 11 per cent of the girls were characterized as management problems, 42 per cent of the boys were placed in this category. However, in terms of neurotic disorders there was a greater preponderance of girls. There seemed to be an approximately equal proportion of boys and girls characterized as problems of developmental delay, while a somewhat higher proportion of the girls (32 per cent, compared with 21 per cent of the boys) were placed in the 'social stress' category.

In South Wales a home advisory service for young children with problems of developmental delay has been in operation for a number of years. This programme, based on the Wisconsin Portage Project, involves weekly home visits in which the home adviser carries out an in-depth assessment and teaches responsible members of the family how to help the child complete various tasks between visits. Thus, there is an extensive behavioural assessment initially and a continuous assessment on progress made. In teaching the family to carry out the treatment at home the problem of the generalization of treatment is obviated (Clements, Bidder, Gardner, Bryant and Gray 1980).

The subnormal or mentally retarded child

There are two main handbooks or manuals on mental retardation, one edited by Clarke and Clarke (1974) in Great Britain, and the other edited by Ellis (1963) in America. The major purpose of this section is to provide a brief overview of the area, including the assessment of the subnormal person and some discussion of the techniques used in training the handicapped person in specific skills such as those included under the heading 'socialization' and 'self-help'.

It is important to differentiate children who are backward from those who may be classed as mentally subnormal. Backwardness does not necessarily involve below-average intelligence. For example, many people who have a very low reading-age are of average intelligence. It is easy to make the mistake of thinking that those who are backward in some areas are also mentally retarded, but deficits in one or in even a number of specific areas does not necessarily signify an overall intellectual deficit.

In addition to the potential confusion between backwardness and mental retardation, many people, including professionals, may fail to discriminate between the mentally retarded and the autistic child (see the next section). This potential confusion is perhaps understandable when one observes the limited ability of the autistic child to communicate and the extent to which there may be overlap in specific problems such as self-injurious behaviour, or aggression towards others.

Assessment

Twenty-five years ago the mentally retarded were primarily classified through the score they obtained in an intelligence test, those obtaining an IQ between 50 and 70 being considered 'educable' and those between 50 and 25 IQ being classed as 'trainable'. Those in the latter category were regarded as management or custodial problems, although in a number of states in America special-education classes were available for them. Some school districts developed separate special-education classes for those handicapped in various ways, such as the hard-of-hearing, the cerebral palsied, and the emotionally disturbed. Difficulties in diagnosis were exacerbated when the child exhibited multiple handicaps, particularly of a sensory nature. However, through the development of behaviour-modification techniques, the chances of teaching the trainable, or the more severely retarded child competencies for living outside an institution—although in some cases working in a sheltered workshop—have been considerably improved.

Today, some psychologists question the wide use of intelligence testing with the mentally retarded. I feel that in certain cases, particularly with the less retarded, their use may be helpful. However, in terms of training or management, a much more specific and functional analysis is necessary. Gunzburg (1974*b*) said that: 'Systematic teaching of social competence is a legitimate task of education and appreciable achievements in that area are more vital to the mentally subnormal person's happiness and emotional adjustment than proficiency in the conventional areas of education.' Gunzburg, however, warns us that too narrow an interpretation of social competence is inappropriate.

The use of the Vineland Social Maturity Scale and the Gunzburg Progress Assessment Charts to assess social–emotional maturity has been mentioned above. Both of these 'scales' may be used to assess assets and deficits in socialization, etc., and the Gunzburg assessment procedures have been extended recently. Gunzburg's Progress Assessment Chart of Social Development (PAC) was designed for the use of teachers of mentally retarded children and adolescents. It is important to realize here that the term 'teacher' is a broad term including ward personnel and others involved in training. The dimensions assessed through the use of PAC charts are listed in Table 2.1.

TABLE 2.1
FOUR DIMENSIONS ASSESSED BY THE PROGRESS ASSESSMENT CHARTS

Dimension	*Type of behaviour assessed*
1. Self-help	Dressing, washing, eating
2. Communication	Receptive and expressive language, use of money, reading, writing
3. Socialization	Interaction at home or institution; interactions outside home or institution
4. Occupation	Manual activities, leisure occupations

(Modified from Mittler 1970)

Specific behaviours are checked by a person who has had an adequate opportunity to observe the child and can determine whether or not the child typically performs the particular behaviour.

Gunzburg (1974*b*) stated that the assessment provided the opportunity for designing a tailor-made programme of remedial action for the individual pupil. He has developed four versions of a Progress Evaluation Index (PEI) (Gunzburg 1969), which correspond to the four forms of the PAC; the PEI gives an opportunity for comparing the individual qualitative PAC records with 'average attainment levels', and this procedure enables the teacher to identify the 'backward mentally handicapped child with reference to the 'average' and 'above average' functioning mentally handicapped child (Gunzburg 1974*b*).

Watson's (1975) Global Evaluation Scale, which is a checklist for assessing self-help skills, may be found useful in working with the retarded. Many other helpful checklists in training the retarded and the psychotic child are also discussed in his book.

Training/treating the retarded

Many of the procedures used to develop a wider behavioural repertoire or eliminate undesirable behaviour in the retarded, as well as in other people, are based on operant techniques, one of the most basic being the appropriate application of reinforcement contingencies (see Chapter 15 for a discussion of operant conditioning). Many of the techniques such as '*Time-out*' (TO) '*Overcorrection*', and the *shaping* of social–recreational skills are discussed in Watson (1975). Margolies (1977) reviewed the use of many of these behaviour-modification techniques in the treatment of the autistic child (see the next section). One of the most important tasks involved in training the retarded is breaking down the skills to be learned into their component parts before training begins, so they may be taught in a piecemeal fashion. Since the treatment of the retarded is a very time-consuming and continuous process, it is important that the staff should be patient and tolerant. More specific details on training procedures are provided in Clarke and Clarke (1974).

Some recent research on the treatment of the retarded

Young (1977) treated three severely subnormal adolescents for *stereotypy* (specifically complex hand movements). He noted that the subjects he used were functionally similar to an autistic group. Young was interested in the psychophysiological concomitants of complex hand movements, in particular cardiac arrhythmia. Both overcorrection procedures (Foxx and Azrin 1973) and the reinforcement of *antagonistic (alternative) activities* have been used to treat stereotypic behaviour. Young found that the frequency of complex hand movements significantly increased in a small restricted environment and that they were significantly reduced when alternative activities were available, engaged in, and reinforced. He suggested that the latter technique was more effective than the overcorrection procedures of Foxx and Azrin in reducing the frequency of complex hand movements. An association was found between complex hand movements and decreased cardiac arrhythmia. On the other hand, there was an association between rocking behaviour and increased cardiac arrythmia. It was suggested that differential cardiac arrythmia was associated with differing types of stereotypic behaviour.

Although stereotypic behaviour considered by many as fairly innocuous, potentially interferes with other more useful behaviour, self-injurious behaviour must be viewed more seriously. Schneider, Ross, and Dubin (1979), for example, treated a 32-year-old institutionalized female named Ellie whose 'specific mutilative behaviour included head banging, eye gouging and eye tissue damage (to the extent that she had completely detached her right eye), cutting and burning her skin, and ingesting excrement and other objects which induced choking and was life threatening. At the time of her transfer to the unit, Ellie was completely bald, had an artifical right eye, and was covered with 44 separate skin lesions from her self-injurious episodes'. Ellie was also prone to tantrum behaviour which was followed by self-injury when she was not given attention. She was treated by gradually training her to 'sit' on command when a tantrum occurred. Token reinforcement for appropriate behaviour was used, which could be exchanged for cigarettes, a commodity high on Ellie's reinforcement list. The training was carried out in such a way that Ellie would even respond to unfamiliar voices giving the command 'sit'.

In the experimental condition the maximum duration of tantrums was 10 seconds and no self-injurious behaviour occurred, whereas in the control condition tantrums lasted up to 600 seconds and were consistently followed by such behaviour. A follow-up indicated that the alternative response procedure was still effective in eliminating the self-injury and there was evidence of greater generalization. Similar results were found one year after the initial treatment. The authors suggest that the procedure used may be helpful in treating other problematic institutional behaviours.

Peniston (1975) carried out a project in which he treated fourteen male mental retardates for their disruptive and hostile behaviour in a 'closed'-ward. The procedure used included '*time-out*' and '*contingent positive reinforcement*'. Eleven of the patients were reported as severely or profoundly retarded. Tokens were used, as rewards for desirable behaviour. These tokens could be immediately exchanged for a *primary reinforcer*. There were four target behaviours to be eliminated or reduced: (1) physical aggression; (2) psychotic-like behaviour; (3) verbal aggression; and (4) rocking behaviour. Token exchange was gradually postponed until the end of the morning or afternoon. Both token withdrawal and time-out were used as *negative reinforcers*. Specifically, the time-out procedure was put into operation when the patient displayed disruptive behaviour, and consisted of placing the individual in a 'time-out' room (4 ft × 4 ft) which was located near the dayroom away from the main activity area. A modified *over-correction technique* was used to eliminate the rocking behaviour. The results indicated the value of 'time-out', or withdrawal of tokens, in reducing the verbal aggressive behaviour and the psychotic-like behaviour. In contrast, the physically aggressive behaviour decreased 'whether or not the "time-out" was contingent upon it'. The undesirable rocking behaviour did not respond to the over-correction technique, although the rate decreased. All in all, Peniston's project was a successful one: three of four target behaviours were successfully modified over a period of five months.

Summary

Provided a detailed functional analysis is carried out to determine the individual's deficits, it may be safely stated that the behavioural methods developed over the last twenty years or so have been shown to be effective in helping the mentally retarded person. There is now convincing evidence that the child who is generally classed as subnormal or mentally retarded can be trained in self-care tasks and other activities and that his disruptive or aggressive behaviour can be modified to enable him to live outside institutions in hostels or in some cases with his parents. Many of those people who would have spent their lives institutionalized a quarter of a century ago can now be trained to live a productive life with the understanding of those around them. We have the technology! Do we have the other conditions to accomplish the training, treatment, and placement that is so badly needed for the mentally retarded population?

We turn now to a consideration of autistic behaviour, and as will be seen, many of the techniques already discussed are also used to treat the autistic child.

Early infantile autism (EIA)

Two of the major monographs on the topic of childhood autism are by Rimland (1964) and Wing (1976). A specifically behavioural approach is reported in Hutt and Hutt (1970). The syndrome of *early infantile autism* (EIA) has long been, and continues to be, a diagnostic, aetiological, and treatment problem (Ward 1970; Margolies 1977). Campbell, Dominijanni, and Schneider (1977) reported a case of monozygotic twins concordant for infantile autism and recommended further genetic twin studies in this area, but there is no firm evidence for genetic determinants of this syndrome.

Diagnostic difficulties

The differentiation of autism from childhood *schizophrenia* has been the concern of many theorists. Ward noted that both types of children have poor object relations, poor contact with reality, and poor body images. Drawing from Kanner (1943), Ward regarded the schizophrenic child as one who had been able to form relationships earlier in life, while he regarded the autistic child as one whose aloneness had been evident from birth. Seemingly, then, the schizophrenic child regresses to a lower level of adaptation, while the autistic never develops an adequate relationship with his environment. Ward wrote that although both

> EIA children and schizophrenic children display poor reality contact, the schizophrenic child manifests the deficit via an extremely vivid and distorted fantasy life, delusions, hallucinations, etc., while the EIA child displays a narrow focus of attention upon stereotypic physical activities (rocking, twiddling, slapping, screwing, rolling, etc.) to the exclusion of the rest of the external world.

Margolies (1977) referred to the De Meyer, Churchill, Pontius, and Gilkey (1971) report which concluded that when four popular scales of autism were used with the same group of 44 children, the degree of correspondence reached only 35 per cent. Margolies, quoting from Lovaas, Koegel, Simmons, and Long (1973), indicated that childhood autism had not been an especially helpful diagnosis, in that there was little agreement on when the label of autism was appropriate; it was related neither to a specific aetiology nor to a specific treatment outcome.

Having noted the general lack of agreement in the diagnosis of EIA, it is nevertheless useful to note Ward's conclusions about the diagnostic criteria that seem to represent the consensus of opinion of the workers in this field.

Kanner (1943) initially isolated and labelled this syndrome. Both Ward (1970) and Margolies (1977) point out that while Kanner originally used twelve criteria to delineate the syndrome of EIA, he later (Kanner and Eisenberg 1956) reduced these to two characteristics in that the majority of the original criteria could be associated with other types of childhood psychopathology.

Ward added two other criteria (3 and 4 below) to those of Kanner and Eisenberg. He suggested that these four criteria would differentiate the EIA child:

(1) lack of object relations from birth;
(2) maintenance of sameness via stereotypic behaviour;
(3) lack of use of speech for communication; and
(4) lack of neurological dysfunction.

In spite of the definitional differences, Wing (1976) reported some confidence in reports on age-specific incidence of the partial or complete autistic syndrome of 4–5 in every 10 000 children. The prognosis for these children was not particularly good and most autistic children would live out their lives being quite dependent upon others.

Margolies discussed prognosis and referred to the De Myer, Barton, De Myer, Norton, Allen, and Steel (1973) 12-year follow-up study of 120 autistic children, which indicated that only 1–2 per cent had recovered to a level of normal functioning; 16–25 per cent were reported as functioning at a fair level, and the remainder were either on a poor or a borderline level. Of the total, 42 per cent were still institutionalized. However, Margolies pointed out that these data were obtained at a time when behavioural treatment was rarely undertaken.

Margolies went on to discuss the aetiology of the disorder and included such diverse views as seeing the disorder as a dysfunction of the central nervous system, as resulting from sensory deprivation, as a reaction to overstimulation, as resulting from approach–avoidance conflict, or as resulting from the reinforcement patterns applied by parents. Margolies concluded that the aetiology was based on the interaction of multiple factors having differing degrees of importance in leading to the condition.

Ethological analysis of autistic behaviour

Hutt (1975) presented an interesting ethological analysis of autistic behaviour. The children used in his research essentially satisfied the four criteria listed by Ward (1970) and were between 2½ and 6 years of age. The variables selected for study by Hutt included social interaction with particular emphasis on *gaze aversion*; stereotypies, and the physiological concomitants of these behaviours. Hutt noted that approach gestures towards adults were normal with the exception of the child's gaze aversion. Hutt demonstrated that while the autistic child gestures appropriately in other ways, across a wide variety of situations he will simply avoid looking the adult in the face. 'Efforts to make the child look at the adult's face . . . result in tears and anguish.' In a study by Hutt and Ousted (1966) cardboard models of faces were used as stimuli in order to investigate gaze aversion in six autistic and six non-autistic children, all of whom were patients in a psychiatric hospital. The stimuli included a happy face, a sad face, a blank human face, a monkey face, and a dog face. The results showed that the autistic children spent most of their time looking at the environmental stimuli (room fittings such as taps, light switches, etc.). And while they spent about as much time looking at the blank face and the dog's face, they avoided looking at the happy face. They spent much more time on the environmental stimuli than on the faces, and avoided *exploring* the faces. In contrast, the non-autistics showed the least interest in the blank face, but looked at the other faces for about equal periods of time, and examined each face in turn. Hutt concluded that the results of this preliminary experiment suggested that the smiling human configuration is least approached by autistic children, but most approached by non-autistic children. In discussing the effects of the autistic child's behaviour on others, Hutt noted that the descriptions of these children's behaviour as aloof, detached, impersonal, or withdrawn said more about the effect that behaviour has on us than about how the children actually behaved; and that just as in adult social discourse, for example, gaze fixation denoted inclusion in the group, gaze aversion would denote social exclusion. In interactions with peers the autistic did not exhibit *territoriality* and if another child went off with a toy belonging to him he did not attempt to recover it, but withdrew. Gaze aversion was functional in terms of being a stimulus for non-aggression, and it inhibited any aggressive or threat behaviour on the part of other conspecifics.

Hutt defined *stereotypies* as 'repetitions in an invariant form of motor patterns which appear to have no observable goal'. He carried out a study in which the frequency of the initiation of stereotyped behaviours and time spent in stereotypic behaviour was related to the complexity of the environmental situation. The situations were as follows: (a) an empty room; (b) the room with a box of blocks present; (c) a passive adult present, and (d) the active adult engaging the child in play. The results showed that time spent in stereotypic movements was directly related to increasing environmental complexity. However, the presence of an active adult appeared to inhibit these apparently purposeless movements. Hutt suggests that in view of a greater inhibition of stereotypic movements when an active adult was present, there might be a greater need to perform these movements in this more complex environment.

The EEG records in association with the autistic child's behaviour led Hutt (1975) to hypothesize that both behaviourally and cortically the autistic child was in a state of heightened arousal. Engaging in both gaze aversive and stereotypic behaviour were seen as functional in lowering the heightened arousal of the autistic child. The main competing neurophysiological theories of autism were actually reconcilable. However, Hutt's conclusion based on neurophysiological and behavioural evidence was that the hypothesis that autistic children were chronically hyper-aroused was more likely than its main rival, the hypothesis that such children were in a state of REM sleep.

Behavioural treatment of the autistic child

Two relatively early reports on the behavioural treatment of autistic children were those by Davison (1964, 1965). Basing his procedures on Ferster's (1961) *functional analysis* of autistic behaviour, Davison (1964) demonstrated that non-professionals (undergraduates), after having trained in the principles of social learning, were able through the use of *operant techniques* to gain control over an autistic child's behaviour and that there was a significant increase in responsiveness to adults in general. Davison defined therapist-control as the percentage of commands obeyed by the client without the use of *reinforcement*. He also found that by the end of the programme, activities which were not carried out initially, even with reinforcement (sweets), were carried out without reinforcement by the end of the programme. Further, various undesirable and avoidance behaviours were seemingly eliminated, and pro-social activities were able to be substituted for the undesirable behaviours. The second case study reported by Davison (1965) involved a nine-year-old boy whose diagnosis as an autistic was verified by Rimland. The child's mother was motivated to try a *social-learning therapy* programme and was introduced to the type of therapy that would be used, via a lecture and demonstration-training film (Davison and Krasner 1964). An unemployed teacher was employed by the parents to spend about five hours with the child each week-day in carrying out the procedures such as setting up *reinforcement contingencies*, depicted in the film. Davison noted that after the elimination of tantrum behaviour, control over the child was achieved through frequent association of chocolates with the presence of the teacher for obeying many instructions. The child also became aware of others and was much more responsive; he learned to write a number of words, including his name, he was beginning to read, and had reduced his stereotypic twirling behaviour. In general, Davison was very optimistic about the use of operant procedures in the treatment of autistic children.

More recently, Yule, Berger, and Howlin (1975), focusing on language deficits and accepting the importance of biological factors, recommended behavioural modification procedures. They emphasized a behaviour analysis and the use of the *reversal technique* (see the next chapter).

Margolies (1977) reviewed the behavioural treatment approaches used with EIA children. He noted that traditional forms of psychotherapy had had little success with infantile autism. He pointed out that *primary reinforcers* were used in the initial treatment of autistics because the autistic child usually lacked the ability to gain through the use of *secondary reinforcers* such as verbal approval. The second stage usually involved the pairing of secondary reinforcers with primary reinforcers. Margolies noted that Jellis (1972) recommended that the reinforcers chosen should not divert the child's attention away from the task (e.g. toys were often distracting), should not interfere with the time intervals between stimulus presentations (e.g. food could do this), and should not be subject to rapid *satiation*. In view of the high distractibility of autistic children the use of a specially constructed distraction-free learning booth (Hewett 1965; Margolies 1977) was recommended. Some of the reinforcers found to be effective included tokens, the visual patterns of a kaleidoscope, and the visual display of a colour organ.

Margolies discussed the use of behavioural methods in the modification of the following undesirable behaviours: distraction; self-destructive behaviour, such as head banging; tantrums; aggressive and disruptive behaviours; and self-stimulation behaviour, such as rhythmic rocking. He also discussed reports on toilet training, developing eye-contact, imitation, increasing peer interaction and pre-social behaviour, the modification of classroom behaviour, and developing verbal behaviour and language skills.

In reviewing studies on verbal behaviour and language skills, which included mute autistics, *echolalics*, and children who used *psychotic speech*, Margolies noted that although verbal and language training were appropriate targets for behavioural intervention much of the data presented had been in case-study form and that experimental inference as to the effectiveness of various components of the intervention was not possible at this level of analysis. It was questionable to what degree meaningful language had been taught as compared to a more mechanical speech utterance. Margolies quoted Lovaas (1970) who basically admitted the limitations of progress in teaching the older and mute autistics.

Margolies pointed out the limitations of much of the research reviewed both from an experimental and from a treatment-outcome point of view, but also said that the large volume of pre-experimental data supporting the effectiveness of behaviour modification could not be taken lightly, and that although one case study suggested little, a large volume of pre-experimental reports confirming the utilization of behavioural intervention did suggest that something positive might be occurring. However, it would take better-controlled experimental work to confirm this assertion. In referring to the *base-line condition* of these children he suggested that behaviour modification had produced real change. Maladaptive behaviours (e.g. tantrums, self-destructive, and disruptive behaviour) had been reduced or eliminated in a number of reports; the repertoire had been expanded (e.g. toilet training, some functional speech) in still others.

Kinsbourne (1977) seems to support the view that there should be an emphasis on the individual autistic child, rather than on invariant characteristics of autistic children. He noted that the most crucial problem in infantile autism from a behavioural point of view was the variability of its manifestations and the determinants of this variability. Those determinants, he said, must be identified if one's emphasis was on behavioural change so that we can then (by means of environmental or pharmacological change) maximize adaptively appropriate states. He pointed out that the classical model of psychometric and neuro-psychological research was inadequate since it looked for invariants in the behaviour of the affected population. Thus, while research should attempt to determine the sources of this wide variation in the characteristics of autistic children, treatment of necessity should be based on an adequate behavioural analysis and thus focused on the individual. Clearly, Margolies's (1977) review article would support this individual approach to the autistic child.

Summary

Some autistic children can be helped in language development, but the degree of help is limited. The diagnosis of early infantile autism is not consistent and a great deal of further research is necessary in order to determine which techniques are effective with which specific problems. However, the behavioural approach to treatment appears promising, although the reversal procedure and other systematic case studies are needed.

SOME ISSUES IN PSYCHOLOGICAL TREATMENT

Part IV of this book is devoted to psychological treatment procedures, and many of them may be used equally as well with children as with adults. The purpose of this section, however, is briefly to discuss some of the issues in psychological treatment which have led to the use of parents and other non-professionals in behavioural programmes of treatment.

Three major issues relevant to treatment stand out. The first is the fact that there is a lack of trained therapists. It is clear that in the foreseeable future there will not be enough mental-health professionals available to treat those children and others in need of psychological help although some would argue that people should learn to treat their own psychological problems (see Chapter 19). A related issue is the suggestion that people with limited training can successfully carry out therapeutic programmes. A third issue is the failure of treatment successfully carried out in the clinic or hospital to be adequately maintained in the home, at work, etc.

There is evidence that the personal characteristics of the therapist are the important elements in effective treatment rather than an extended degree of professional training. Some might argue that, in fact, the traditional training of the clinical psychologist ill fits him to be a successful therapist, and that much of the training given by graduate departments of psychology tends to produce qualities which are somewhat antagonistic to the performance of an adequate therapist.

There has been a strong trend in recent years that may go a long way towards correcting for the lack of therapists and which should help to prevent the frequency and extent of relapse that occurs when a person is treated in an environment which is considerably different from his usual habitat(s), and no provision is made for the tendency towards relapse. This trend, is, of course, the extent to which parents, college students, and senior citizens have been trained to provide treatment for children who are emotionally disturbed or who lack adequate social–emotional stimulation in their environment.

It is true that professionals of certain theoretical persuasions have always encouraged parents to treat their own children, but the recommended procedures were hardly experimentally based. Recent work based on experimental principles of learning has been concerned with training parents in behavioural principles (Reisinger 1976; Reisinger and Ora 1977; Reisinger, Ora, and Frangia 1976). As Baer and Wright (1974) have pointed out, although behavioural modification approaches as applied to children have been non-developmental in outlook, some highly successful results in changing certain behaviours have been reported.

(Reisinger *et al.* 1976) noted that therapeutic gains made in the clinic or professional setting were unlikely to be upheld outside without some extension of the therapeutic programme. Most would agree that a significant factor in the relapse rate is the failure to take into account the environmental or community setting to which the patient returns after treatment. The behaviour of significant others such as teachers, parents, peers, etc., outside the hospital or clinic must frequently be changed in order to maintain therapeutic gain in the patient or client. It has been found that parental support is essential both in maintaining desirable behaviour and in the alleviation of undesirable behaviour in children. Parents have been successfully trained in managing their children by utilizing reinforcement contingencies (Reisinger *et al.* 1976). Aggressive and destructive behaviour, tantrums, hyperactivity, speech deficits, and fire-setting behaviour have been some of the conditions successfully modified by behavioural methods in which parents were the main agents of change. An example of a relatively early report in which parents successfully modified their child's tantrum behaviour is provided by Williams (Ullman and Krasner 1965). Through an *extinction procedure* (i.e. simply withdrawing attention) to the child when he exhibited bedtime temper tantrums, and providing attention when he exhibited appropriate behaviour, his undesirable behaviour was eliminated (see Chapters 15 and 16 for an extended discussion of behaviour therapy).

Reisinger *et al.* (1976) found that most studies which involved parents had concentrated on middle-class families. It had been found that lower-class families were less enthusiastic and efficient in reacting to intervention programmes. However, lower-class parents under certain conditions could be trained successfully to change the behaviour of their children. Additional reinforcements, such as hairdressing appointments, china, and money, had helped maintain participation in intervention programmes by lower-class parents.

While concluding that parents could be trained effectively, Reisinger *et al.* were right to point out the difficulties which result from organizational constraints in which 'children's treatment formats are established far more on the bases of professional convenience and politics than on any evidence in regard to parents.'

While space does not permit a more extensive discussion of the use of parents and others in treating maladaptive behaviour in its natural setting, enough evidence is avilable to support the theory that parents and other non-professionals can effectively carry out behavioural programmes. Psychologists should be more willing to train appropriate people to carry out such programmes. In this way the relapse rate could be significantly modified and a greater emphasis could be directed towards teaching the individual self-control procedures as discussed in Chapter 19.

ADOLESCENCE

Cultural anthropologists have pointed out that in many societies adolescence is a relatively non-stressful period of development, but in industrialized societies such as in Europe, America, and elsewhere, the adolescent years are considered to be years of considerable stress for many individuals. There are many textbooks on the topic of adolescence, of which Conger (1973) and Horrocks (1976) will be found to be particularly readable and informative. For those who would like a shorter overview of adolescence, Froese (1975) has written an interesting and up-to-date article.

The period of adolescence is generally considered to range from the onset of puberty (pubescence) to adulthood (characterized by physical and, it is hoped, psychological maturity). Thus, the span of this period varies from 10 or 11 to 20 or 21 years of age in girls, and from 11 or 12 until 22 in boys. Clearly, psychological difficulties may be associated with an early or a relatively late onset of puberty in either sex. The definition of maturity may, of course, vary widely (see Chapter 3).

The main problems of adolescence concern:

(1) the achievement of emotional independence from parents or parent surrogates (some authors have called this emancipation);
(2) attaining economic independence;
(3) coming to terms with one's own sexuality; and
(4) the achievement of ego-identity.

The adolescent is faced with many conflicts which must be resolved if mental health is to be maintained, and it may be optimistic to refer to the adolescent period as an opportunity to learn how to take decisions. Douvan (1970) has referred to adolescence as 'the age of self-exploration'.

The achievement of identity

Erikson (1963), considered that the major problem of adolescence was in achieving identity. 'Ego identity gains real strength only from wholehearted and consistent recognition of real accomplishment—i.e. of achievement that has meaning in the culture'. He contrasted the child training methods used by an Arizona Indian group with those of modern industrial society. Referring to the Indian way, he noted that:

The essential point of such child training is that the child is from infancy continuously conditioned to responsible social participation, while at the same time the tasks that are expected of it are adapted to its capacity.

Such training might do much to prevent the development of an adult feeling of *helplessness* or *uncontrollability*, as discussed by Seligman (1975) (see Chapter 4), and would instead bring about a feeling of accomplishment and control.

Erikson suggested that some of the difficulties that children got into when 'they seem to us to "interfere" with' the adult world was indicative of their 'wish to demonstrate their right to find an identity in it'.

Erikson referred to American adolescence as 'the standardization of individuality and the intolerance of "differences"'. He was concerned about the 'ego qualities which emerge from critical periods of development—criteria . . . by which the individual demonstrates that his ego, at a given stage, is strong enough to integrate the timetable of the organism with the structure of social institutions'.

Erikson is well known for his 'Eight Ages of Man' which refer to developmental or life stages. These ego qualities or life stages are: basic trust vs. basic mistrust, autonomy vs. shame and doubt, initiative vs. guilt, industry vs. inferiority, identity vs. role confusion, intimacy vs. isolation, generativity vs. stagnation, and ego integrity vs. despair. While the stages which precede it are important, the critical stage for the adolescent is '*identity vs. role confusion*'. Erikson noted that where this was based on a strong previous doubt as to one's sexual identity, delinquent and outright psychotic episodes were not uncommon. He interpreted the clannishness of the adolescent 'as a defence against a sense of identity confusion. For adolescents not only help one another temporarily through much discomfort by forming cliques and by stereotyping themselves, their ideals, and their enemies; they also perversely test each other's capacity to pledge fidelity.' The next stage '*intimacy vs. isolation*' produces problems for some adolescents for whom intimacy is threatening. The normal 'young adult' is ready 'to commit himself to concrete affiliations and partnerships and to develop the ethical strength to abide by such commitments, even though they may call for significant sacrifices'. While intimacy is a goal of this stage of development, Erikson pointed out that not only can 'avoidance of contacts which commit to intimacy' lead to problems but some partnerships 'amount to an isolation *à deux*, protecting both partners from the necessity to face the next critical development—that of generativity.'

Female adolescent problems

What difficulties do females encounter during adolescence that males do not? There have always been differences between the sexes in terms of the particular areas of conflict during adolescence, but it is hypothesized that with the recent changes in woman's rights and the expansion in the acceptable roles women play in Western society, for some women, at least, the degree of conflict may be heightened.

Douvan (1970) has written an informative chapter on conflict in females at adolescence. She wrote that everyone agreed that the changes of puberty initiated the quest for identity and that radical pubertal changes both stimulated and endangered the process of self-discovery. Referring to the menstrual cycle, with its accompanying changes in mood state, Douvan believed that because of the variability and instability of internal cues associated with the menstrual cycle the girl would come to rely more heavily than the normal boy on external cues and the expectations of significant others—on feedback from an audience—as anchors for her self-definition. Citing the work of Kagan and Moss (1962) Douvan noted that the boy's masculine self-concept was based at least in part on skills that were measurable and pleasurable aside from social feedback but that the girl's self-concept was almost entirely dependent on social skills that could be measured or proven only by the response of an audience.

Douvan noted that experienced gynaecologists usually considered dysmenorrhoea as a psychosomatic condition. She also referred to the clinical literature which tended to support the hypothesis that amenorrhoea and irregularity in menstruation are symptoms of 'a basic rejection of feminity'.

The almost exclusively female problem of anorexia nervosa is primarily a problem of adolescence which includes amenorrhoea, in some cases primary amenorrhoea, as one of the defining symptoms (Crisp 1973, 1974). The other symptoms of anorexia nervosa include loss of appetite and weight-loss which cannot be attributed to any primary physical or psychiatric illness. Crisp (1973) referred to the adolescent who had decided to stay thin and exhibited a 'fear of and need to avoid normal adolescent weight . . . as an "adolescent weight phobia". Crisp (1974) found that in severe form, anorexia nervosa was found in approximately one in every 150 girls of between 16 and 18 years of age. Eighty per cent of the cases have their onset in the mid-teens. While the incidence of this disorder may be considered relatively low, the mortality rate has been reported as about 10 per cent, and Crisp felt that with the increased emphasis on weight control, the incidence might be increasing.

Problems of students

Blaine and McArthur (1966) agreed with Blos, that 'neuroses in early adult life represent adolescent conflicts "kept open indefinitely"'. Erikson (1966), in his introduction to Blaine and McArthur's book: *Emotional problems of the student* wrote that 'Colleges offer young people a sanctioned interim between childhood and adulthood. Such a moratorium is often characterized by a combination of prolonged immaturity and provoked precocity.' Bojar (1966) discussed the psychiatric problems of medical students which seemed to focus (in the United States at least) on academic achievement, and for some, on whether or not they had chosen the appropriate professional field of study. Those medical students who were financially supported for example by working wives might feel inadequate or resentful. Some of the wives might seek psychiatric help for themselves because they felt neglected and rejected in competing with their husbands' books for attention. Many of the problems of medical students are also characteristic of students in other fields. For some students who continued into post-graduate work some of the typical problems of adolescence might not be resolved until they married and started work.

Some mental-health professionals argue that the process of achieving identity and becoming a psychologically mature person might involve a much longer period of time than many people would care to admit. In the next chapter we shall discuss various views of maturity.

3
Psychology of the life-span (maturity to old age)

A pale consumption was the fatal blow,
The stroke was certain but the effect was slow,
'Twas God that gave the warning long and kind,
He's called above, his partner left behind
With two small children for to remain,
Till God is pleased that they shall meet again.
West Cornish Epitaph, Sennen Churchyard, 1800

THE ATTAINMENT OF MATURITY

Although it is relatively easy to define physiological maturity, attempts to formulate a definition of psychological maturity frequently lead to sharp differences of opinion and even heated argument. Some people equate psychological maturity with the achievement of some well-defined status, such as the completion of one's formal education, entry into the full-time job market, or marriage. However, for others it is not only the achievement say, of economic independence from one's parents, but also, and perhaps more importantly, the achievement of emotional balance, so that one is able to be flexible in adapting both to the anticipated critical periods of the life-span, and to the unexpected crises that may occur from time to time. First, let us briefly see what some of the major personality theorists have had to say about *psychological maturity*. We will then discuss the measurement of maturity and conclude this section by reviewing some of the pertinent research.

Theoretical views on maturity

In the view of most personality theorists, maturity is roughly equated with mental health. Thus, for Freud, with his emphasis on developmental stages, the final or 'genital' stage represents the stage of maturity (see Chapter 13). In the *genital stage*, there is much more emphasis on the *ego, 'secondary process thinking'*, and on rationality in general as compared to the more immature stages where more *intrapersonal conflict* is present and a balance has yet to be achieved between the major components of personality. As noted by Blum (1953):

The ability to attain full satisfaction through genital orgasm makes the physiological regulation of sexuality possible and thus puts an end to the damming up of Instinctual energies . . . . It also makes for the full development of love and the overcoming of ambivalence. Furthermore, the capacity to discharge great quantities of excitement means the end of reaction formations and an increase in the ability to sublimate. Emotions, instead of being warded off, are used constructively by the ego as part of the total personality.

According to Erikson (1963), in order for a person to become a mature adult, he must, to a sufficient degree, develop all the ego qualities, so that 'a wise Indian, a true gentleman, and a mature peasant share and recognize in one another the final stage of integrity'. He goes on to say that ego integrity implies an emotional integration which permits participation by 'followership' as well as acceptance of the responsibility of leadership.

Carl Rogers emphasizes the development of the self-concept in his 'self theory' of personality (see Chapter 14). Rogers (1951) said of his personality theory: 'It pictures the end-point of personality development as being a basic congruence between the phenomenal field of experience and the conceptual structure of the self—a situation which, if achieved, would represent freedom from internal strain and anxiety, and freedom from potential strain; which would represent the maximum in realistically oriented adaptation.' There is great emphasis in Rogers's theory on self-actualization, which is a basic tendency for the person to maintain and enhance himself. Maslow (1962), among others, held the view that man is always in the process of *becoming*, i.e. through the process of *self-actualization* man not only tends to maintain *psychological homeostatis,* but to achieve what Maslow termed '*peak experiences*', which may also be termed emotional highs or 'happiest moments, ecstatic moments, moments of rapture, perhaps from being in love, or from listening to music, or suddenly "being hit" by a book or painting, or from some great creative moment'. Maslow continued: 'The emotional reaction in the peak experience has a special flavor or wonder, of awe, of reverence, of humility and surrender before the experience as something great.' The interested reader is referred to Maslow's book for his existential ideas and a full description of self-actualization and peak experiences.

On the basis of the above discussion, the views of Maslow and Rogers in regard to psychological maturity seem to be more fluid than those of Freud or Erikson. In other words, the impression one obtains from reading Rogers and Maslow is that one is always in the process of becoming—the development of psychological maturity does not stop at a certain age or stage, but continues throughout all or most of one's life-span. It may be that this difference is more apparent than real. However, Rogers and Maslow are certainly much more future-orientated than Freud or Erikson and seem less structured in their ideas regarding what may be considered as psychological maturity.

Measurement of maturity

Can psychological maturity be measured? Certainly, various tests or scales have been constructed which purport to measure an aspect or aspects of this variable. For example, there are the various scales of the California Psychological Inventory (CPI), such as 'self-acceptance', 'achievement via independence', psychological-mindedness', etc. Thus, some would say that the person who obtains a psychograph or personality profile at or above the mean on an inventory such as the CPI, or within the normal range of scores on the MMPI would be classed as normal and psychologically mature. However, a definition of maturity based only on inventory responses may be unacceptable to those who think of maturity as a condition allowing for flexibility in adapting to new and unique situations which are met with throughout the life-span. While it is true that one of the scales of the CPI measures 'flexibility', and that, for example, the M scale of the 16-Personality Factor Questionnaire (16-PF) (Cattell, Eber, and Tatsuoka 1970) measures an 'imaginative vs. practical' factor or orientation to situations, the isolation of pure factors which make up psychological maturity is, to say the least, exceedingly complex, if not beyond our present capabilities. For example, one person who obtains a relatively high score on the M scale of the 16-PF or on the Psychopathic Deviate (Pd) scale of the MMPI may be engaged in criminal activities, be reputed to have a poorly developed conscience or super-ego, and to have difficulty in delaying gratification, etc., whereas another person with the same score may be a highly respected policeman, a successful businessman, or an effective psychologist.

Research

For both Rogers and Maslow there is an emphasis on what Maslow terms *growth motivation*. Much of the research which has been related to Rogerian ideas has been concerned with the congruence between present self-concept and the so-called self-ideal, which refers to the person one would like to be. Turner and Vanderlippe (1958) found, for example, that better adjustment was related to the degree to which present self-concept was congruent with ideal self. Adjustment was measured by greater participation in extracurricular activities, better academic performance, higher ratings of adjustment on the Guilford–Zimmerman Temperament Survey (Guilford and Zimmerman 1955), and higher sociometric ratings by fellow students. Vingoe (1968) found that the higher the congruence between self and ideal ratings the greater the self-acceptance as measured by the CPI (Gough 1957). A number of criticisms of self-ideal congruence as a measure of adjustment, mental health, or psychological maturity have been made. A discussion of these appears in Chapter 14, where the 'self-concept' approach is considered in more detail. It will suffice here to consider the criticism of most relevance to this section. While earlier discussions of the ideal self considered it as relatively stable (Turner and Vanderlippe 1958), later formulations by those who emphasized self-actualization and growth motivation have indicated that a complete or near-complete congruence between self and ideal concept suggests a relative lack of psychological growth. In other words, it is suggested that if we have nothing much left to strive for (high self–ideal congruence), then we are no longer motivated to achieve psychological growth and reach a plateau or a condition of stagnation.

Can one logically expect to construct a measure of psychological maturity that is global in nature, that is one that can adequately measure maturity in all people, at all times, in all situations? Many psychologists would prefer to think of maturity as a function of behaviour exhibited in a specific context or situation; i.e. they may prefer to accept psychological maturity as analogous to honesty, in that honesty has been shown to be situation-specific. Various research projects have focused on maturity in a certain area, such as academic achievement or religion. For example, reviewing the social psychology of education, Getzels (1969) referred to Lavin's (1965) work in school which found that 'better achievement is related to positive self image, less defensiveness, and greater interest in particular content areas'. However, Getzels cautioned against placing too great a value on these correlations, which are relatively low and often inconsistent. In discussing 'becoming', Allport (1955) noted that a mark of maturity seemed to be the range and extent of one's feelings of self-involvement in abstract ideals. Allport felt that religion could help man to integrate all aspects of his being, while protecting him against anxiety, doubt, and despair. Dittes (1969) reported on the work of French (1947) who was interested in differentiating those with more mature religious sentiments from others. Her report, based on interviews, tests, and autobiographies, concluded that the more mature were more likely consciously to 'recognize and accept both strengths and weaknesses as part of their selves.'

Heath (1965) has examined a construction of maturity within both an ego psychological and self-organizational context. He noted that a mature person was not necessarily to be considered a normal nor adjusted person. However, he considered psychological health and maturity to be synonomous terms. A mature person was not free of internal conflicts and might exhibit evidence of this disturbance in his behaviour. The term 'mature' referred to psychological development and to an approachable ideal type but not an achievable end-state. It seems that Heath agreed with Allport (1955), Maslow (1962), and Rogers (1959) that man is always in the process of becoming. A mature person has learned and is continuing to learn how to cope with various forms of stress encountered during the life-span. At times regressive behaviour will be exhibited by a mature person. However, this *regression* would be '*regression in the service of the ego*', a term introduced by Ernst Kris (1952) and defined as 'a partial temporary, controlled lowering of the level of psychic functioning to promote adaptation. It promotes adaptation by maintaining, restoring, or improving inner balance and organization, interpersonal relations, and work', (Schafer 1958). (A more extended description of the concept 'regression in the service of the ego' is provided in Chapter 13.) The experimental and theoretical literature suggested to Heath that there were minimally five genotypic developmental dimensions which served to define a maturing person. The 'maturing person becomes more stably organized, integrated, allocentric, autonomous, and more of his internal and external experiences become symbolized and available to awareness'. However, an eventually rigid, inflexible person is not suggested by the phrase 'more stably organized'. Rather, there is increased stability in the sense of a greater integration of past experiences which serve the individual in his adaptation to the stresses of everyday life, be they encountered during adolescence, the middle years, or during old age.

ADJUSTMENT IN THE MIDDLE YEARS

Many psychologists agree that of the main periods into which the life-span is typically divided, it is the middle years or so-called middle age that has been most neglected. During this phase of the life-span one can both look as far forward as back in terms of evaluating one's life; one can assess the successes and failures of the previous years and take decisions regarding the future.

Peck (1973) discussed the second half of the life-span. Referring to Erikson's work on developmental stages (Erikson 1963), he felt that the last forty or fifty years of life were described by Erikson's eighth stage: '*ego-integrity vs. despair*'. However, Peck thought that it was sensible to divide the last half of life into a 'middle age' and an 'old age' period, realizing that different stages might occur in different orders within the two above periods.

Orientations towards life

On the basis of personality analyses of thousands of business men of middle age, Peck classed middle-aged people into four different bipolar orientations towards life. First: '*valuing wisdom vs. physical powers*'. Peck tended to divide people who valued physical powers as a major mode of coping with life, from those who valued wisdom or the use of mental powers. He noted that those who clung on to physical powers in the face of inevitable decline of these powers as they grew older tended to become depressed and otherwise disenchanted with their lives. He felt that this non-functional mode of coping was one of the major aetiological factors of middle-age depression. Therefore Peck's advice would be for those who have based their self-concept on physical powers to change to a mental or wisdom orientation. The second orientation discussed by Peck was related to the male sexual climacteric or menopause, '*socializing vs. sexualizing in human relationships*'. He stressed that social relationships should take on more importance than the sexual aspect of heterosexual interactions. He felt indeed that if this transition could take place successfully potentially interpersonal relationships would possess a greater depth of meaning than before. Thirdly, Peck argued for '*emotional flexibility vs. emotional impoverishment*'. Emotional flexibility he defined as: 'the capacity to shift emotional investments from one person to another and from one activity to another'. Peck noted that such flexibility was particularly important at this stage of life since this was the time that relationships were dissolved or weakened owing to the deaths of relatives and friends and to children leaving the home, etc. Those who are unable to establish new interpersonal relationships, change jobs, or change their life-style, may become extremely impoverished in the emotional sense. For example, a patient with whom the author recently became acquainted had been a publican for twenty or so years and had been encouraged to sell his pub some years before retirement age. Very soon after this he became depressed, since he had invested his life in this particular pub and its customers, and was apparently quite unable to make the necessary changes to replenish his impoverished emotional life. While some may suffer like the publican others are apparently more than ever before in a position to develop relationships of a rich and varied kind. The fourth orientation is: '*mental flexibility vs. mental rigidity*'. Peck noted that ' "too many" tend to grow increasingly set in their ways, inflexible in their opinions and actions, and closed-minded to new ideas, as they go through the middle years'. To some degree this flexibility–rigidity seems to be related to the '*locus of control*' variable discussed in detail in Chapter 4, and to the factor of '*uncontrollability*', which Seligman (1975) related to depression. Basically, one tends to be more flexible if one holds an *internal locus of control* orientation in that one has the attitude that one has control over one's reinforcements. On the other hand, those who hold an *external locus of control* orientation are fatalistic in that they feel that whatever they do they have no essential effect on their reinforcements. The externally-orientated person, then, would subjectively experience a lack of control over his life.

Peck went on to discuss three orientations during the 'old age' period: '*ego differentiation vs. work-role preoccupation*'; '*body transcendence vs. body preoccupation*'; and '*ego-transcendence vs. ego preoccupation*'. He noted that the stage of '*ego differentiation vs. work-role preoccupation*' may occur during the 'middle age' period for many women since 'their "vocational" role as mother is removed by the departure of grown children'.

Research

Neugarten (1973) noted that the prevailing theme of middle age was a reassessment of the self. This, as well as other conclusions regarding the middle-aged, was largely based on a highly selective sample of people in this age range. Neugarten's sample of 100 people was drawn from lists of university graduates, professional directories, and in some cases from more selective sources such as *Who's who in America* and *American men of science*. Clearly, this sample was a highly intelligent verbal group who had attained a fair degree of success in life. Thus, while Neugarten's interview results are not questioned, it is well to keep the highly selective nature of her sample in mind when considering the extent to which the results may be generalized to different groups.

Neugarten noted that those in middle adulthood tended to feel psychologically closer to the elderly than to the young. It was not that the middle-aged group felt old, but rather that they realized that the elderly had already gone through much of what they themselves were going through, whereas young people did not have the same background of experience.

Neugarten found that whereas men perceived a close relationship between age and career-line, women related middle-age to events within the family, such as the launching of children into the adult world. Men tended to focus on discrepancies between career-aspirations and actual career attainments. Neugarten suggested that biological factors were more salient for men than women. Perhaps, contrary to stereotype, Neugarten's findings suggest that women are relatively unconcerned about the various manifestations of the climacterium. Neugarten found that there was a greater concern over their husbands' physical functioning. Men began to note that their physical performance in recreational activities was not what it had been, they were perhaps particularly aware of heart attacks in some of their contemporaries. Their health became a much more salient subject to them than it had been previously. It was also found that most women in this sample felt that the sense of increased freedom was 'the most significant characteristic of middle age'.

Neugarten was:

> impressed with the central importance of what might be called the executive processes of personality in middle age: self-awareness, selectivity, manipulation and control of the environment, mastery, competence, the wide array of cognitive strategies.

Middle age is perceived as the time during which the person is at the prime of life, and able to take decisions with greater ease to cope with many contingencies which would have been found threatening earlier, but it is also the time when a person begins to structure his life in terms of the years still remaining to him. It is suggested, to some extent based on Peck's (1973) discussion on orientations towards life, that middle-aged samples not as intellectually able as Neugarten's sample are more likely to be aware of their physical self. Thus, they may be more prone to focus on the limited time available to them to satisfy any remaining ambitions they have. Clearly, further research with widely differing samples is needed to test this and other hypotheses regarding the middle-aged groups in Western society.

GENERAL PROBLEMS OF THE ELDERLY

Pearce and Miller (1973) estimated that the population of Great Britain would be approximately 60 000 000 in 1980, of whom 7 000 000 would be over

65, the retirement age for the majority of males in Western countries. Bromley (1974) pointed out that 25 per cent of the admissions to hospitals involved people over 60 years of age and about 10 per cent or more of these appeared to have sustained some degree of brain damage. According to Pearce and Miller, of the estimated 7 million people who would be 65 or over in 1980, approximately 10 per cent or 700 000 would be categorized as demonstrating organic dementia. Thus, if the above figures are at all accurate, the National Health Service will need to be prepared to cope with considerable numbers of our senior citizens and to consider alternatives to hospitalization where possible. However, many old people will need to be in hospital or some other institution and will become what Goffman refers to as 'inmates'.

Institutionalization, stigma, and problems of identity

The 'inmate' of an institution usually lives in a situation in which definite tasks are performed at definite times and in definite places. In other words, there is a great deal of regimentation. Institutionalization is said to take place when the patient becomes

> apathetic, habit-bound and intellectually deteriorated. Patients with . . . serious mental illnesses are unlikely to improve under routine hospital conditions. . . . 'Nowadays, efforts are made to keep such patients active and interested in things and to return them, whenever possible, to community care . . . the adverse effects of institutional routines are clearly observable in geriatric wards and homes for the elderly. These effects are compounded by physical infirmity which limits mobility, and by an apparent decrease in activities requiring psychological effort' (Bromley 1974).

Goffman's book: *Asylums* (1961) graphically portrays the situations that tend to result in institutionalization, and in *Stigma* (1963) he discusses the factors that contribute to a patient or other inmate losing his personal identity, a loss which contributes to the development of so-called *institutional neurosis*. While inmates may have some personal possessions with them, their home, together with its furnishings, such as a favourite armchair, are no longer available. In addition, the inmate's spouse and other relatives to whom he is adapted are absent. These factors and others lead the inmate either to seek people with whom he can relate, or perhaps to withdraw from others. Because of the nature of the institution, the geriatric patient is highly likely to regress to an earlier mode of adjustment. While his mobility and self-help behaviour may have been poor before admission, he is likely to appear less able in the institution. Owing to shortages of staff, and in the interests of 'efficiency', conformity is likely to be reinforced. With the increased level of dependence leading to more child-like behaviour, the patient is likely to perceive people caring for him as parent-figures. Since each nurse or therapist must care for more than one patient or inmate, several patients may vie for more attention, just as several children in a family may develop so-called sibling rivalries. Patients may misbehave by throwing temper-tantrums, by whining, or by sulking in order to get the attention they feel they deserve. Depending upon their pre-morbid personality, some may express paranoid ideation, becoming convinced that others are working against them in some way.

Neugarten (1971) found that most people hold many erroneous beliefs about the so-called aged which may lead to a fear and a dislike of this group. Perhaps many of us even tend to stigmatize the aged (Goffman 1963). Goffman, in noting that the framework of *stigma* is used in reference to ever new categories of persons, refers to 'Fears and Defensive Adaptations to the loss of Anal Sphincter Control', a topic of some pertinence to the aged. Goffman's basic theme throughout his book on stigma is that those with stigmata, particularly if clearly observable, tend to develop problems of identity, since the various losses or deficits of old age are related to the individual's self-concept. Neugarten sees old age as a period which brings new situations and problems, such as various illnesses, retirement, widowhood, and the awareness of approaching death, all of which are coped with as a function of the individual's personality—what the person has been and what he is at the present. Thus, she sees ageing as a part of a continuous life cycle which is influenced by the particular individual's childhood, adolescence, and adult years.

Neugarten's comments are of great importance in regard to the general mode of response of the individual to the ageing process. In other words, if the individual has been well adapted and flexible in his coping mechanisms during the earlier stages of his life, he will generally be expected to respond more adaptively to the inevitable changes associated with the ageing process. Therefore, while ageing is a fact of life, one's relative acceptance of memory deficits, reduced psychomotor speed, poor sensory acuity, etc., is important as a function of the relative rate of decline in these areas. Let us first examine the main physical and psychological effects that take place during the ageing process.

Effects of the ageing process

While there are both physical and psychological changes associated with the ageing process, the main emphasis here will be on the psychological effects of ageing.

The various physical changes which are associated with the ageing process include thin, dry, wrinkled skin, white hair, and thickened and brittle nails. However, it is the changes in skeletal and muscular systems that produce most of the disabilities associated with old age. Muscles atrophy; gait and other movements are slowed. Post (1965) indicated that more severe mobility disorders, such as rigidities and tremors, are caused by central nervous system changes which border on the pathological. Pathy (1978), noted the controversial nature of clinical tremor in later life. However, he felt that tremor was uncommon in healthy old age. There are decreases in cardiac output, renal blood flow, and in basic metabolism rate and oxygen consumption of the body as a whole. However, it is important to note that there are large individual differences in these changes. Post emphasized the fact that the decrease in general adaptability was significantly more important than the functional changes in the bodily organs. He noted that the recovery from various stresses was significantly more prolonged in the aged, and since specific hypothalamic cells govern endocrine and metabolic activities of the body as a whole, neuronal deterioration and death were thought to play a leading role in senescence. Referring to studies carried out by Himwich and Himwich (1959) and Himwich (1962), Post concluded that the results of this experimental work suggested that the typical reduction in the brain's oxygen utilization was linked to neuronal loss.

Psychological deficits of old age and their assessment

The typical psychological changes associated with ageing include a reduced psychomotor speed and manipulative ability which may be partially accounted for by a greater 'decision-taking' time (as in a reaction-time task) and partially by physical factors such as increased muscle tone or rigidity. Tremor can be a problem. In addition, memory may be deficient and learning difficult. If deficits, particularly in these last two areas, are severe or extreme, the neuropsychologist may be led to conclude that mental deterioration is profound and a diagnosis of organic dementia may be indicated. The definition of dementia is no easy task (Pearce and Miller (1973)). After discussing some of the factors which have been associated with dementia, such as 'social decline', *global intellectual impairment*, specific deficits in intelligence and memory, presence of *senile plaques* and *neurofibrillary tangles*, and intellectual decline associated with age, Pearce and Miller concluded that the best attempts at defining dementia had resulted from 'a multidisciplinary concept of dementia as a symptom'. Pearce and Miller's working definition of *dementia* was as follows:

> Dementia is a symptom arising from cerebral disease, often progressive, which is characterized by a decline of intellect and personality which reflect a disturbance of memory, orientation, the capacity for conceptual thought and often of affect.

Assessment

Patients suspected of dementia may be diagnosed neurologically through the use of a typical neurological assessment procedure, which may include abbreviated mental tests emphasizing orientation and memory factors, the assessment of reflexes, and so forth. Computerized axial tomography (EMI scan) is very helpful in detecting dilated brain ventricles and cortical atrophy and may obviate the use of psychological tests for general diagnostic purposes. However, where rehabilitation or management of the patient is concerned, psychological testing will determine the specific assets and deficits in mental abilities of a particular patient. The two main types of test employed by psychologists in this context are measures of intelligence and measures of memory functioning. Although personality functioning is obviously an important consideration, and may be assessed using some of the scales discussed in Savage, Gaber, Briton, Bolton, and Cooper (1977), such as the 16-Personality Factor Questionnaire, this particular aspect of the individual can often be assessed through the interview or by observation on the ward by staff, observations at home by the patient's family, or possible observations in a work or other situation by the patient's associates.

Intelligence or general mental ability

Most psychologists use the Wechsler Adult Intelligence Scale (WAIS) (Wechsler 1955) to assess intelligence and as a general screening instrument which may suggest specific defects. The WAIS is a test consisting of eleven subtests, measuring specific abilities, six of which make up the 'verbal scale' and five of which are included in the 'performance scale'. Details of standardization, reliability and validity, etc., may be found in Wechsler (1955), and the research on the WAIS and other Wechsler scales is reviewed by Matarazzo (1972). The WAIS provides a 'verbal intelligence quotient (IQ)', 'performance IQ', and a 'full-scale IQ', which is roughly the average of the verbal and performance measures. Wechsler's definition of intelligence includes a composite of different abilities, some of which are relatively insensitive to the ageing process while others tend to deteriorate with increasing age. For example, one's vocabulary tends to remain relatively intact with ageing, as does one's fund of information. However, tests which involve psychomotor speed, visual perceptual abilities, and short-term memory tend to show a deterioration. Since the WAIS verbal scale includes more subtests which measure those functions relatively insensitive to the ageing process, while the performance scale measures many of those factors which tend to decline with ageing, the psychologist typically finds quite significant differences in verbal and performance IQs in the demented. Thus, to some extent assessment is based on differential performance on Wechsler's verbal and performance scales. In very general terms, verbal subtests are *left-hemisphere dependent* (in right-handed people in whom the left hemisphere is dominant), while performance subtests are right-hemisphere dependent. It should be stressed that, as in many other areas, different neuropsychologists prefer different assessment procedures.

As is pointed out above the fact that certain functions decline more rapidly with age and are more affected by neuropathology than others is taken into account in the assessment of deterioration and dementia. Taking the age factor into consideration, a number of procedures are used by psychologists:

1. *Wechsler's 'deterioration quotient' (DQ)* is determined by the following ratio:

$$DQ = \frac{\text{'Hold' tests} - \text{'Don't hold' tests}}{\text{'Hold' tests}}.$$

The term 'hold tests' refers to specific WAIS subtests, which tend to be little influenced by age and neuropathology. Wechsler's DQ has been much criticized (see for example, Savage 1971).

2. *The new Kendrick Battery* consists of an object learning test, and a digit-copying test. Through statistical procedures one may determine the probability of deterioration or dementia as compared to the presence of an affective disorder (Gibson and Kendrick, 1979).

3. *Mill Hill vocabulary* (Raven 1958*a*) minus the score on the *Standard Progressive Matrices* (Raven 1958*b*), a non-verbal intelligence test.

There are a number of other possibilities. However, the previous experiences of the patient must be taken into account; and one should proceed with caution and avoid taking short cuts in the assessment of deterioriation or dementia.

Recognition of declining abilities may lead to depression, which tends to complicate diagnosis. Clearly, depression may be the primary diagnosis but the depressed mood state typically involves *psychomotor retardation* and a picture of *confusion*. *Ruminative, morbid thoughts* frequently interfere with an adequate performance on cognitive tasks and the individual may be suspected of being demented. Thus, the patient may be primarily depressed, demented, or even both. A full history and assessment should be carried out in order to avoid a misclassification. In general, if a non-demented, depressed patient is treated as if he is demented, his condition is very likely to deteriorate. Larner (1977) looked at groups of elderly depressives, dements, and physically ill subjects using a 'false recognition technique' (FRT), the 'synonym learning test; (SLT) from the older Kendrick Battery (Kendrick 1972); and the 'digit span forward' subtest (Wechsler 1955), a short-term memory task. As noted by Larner and others, the SLT can be seen as a very stressful task by many patients and can preclude accurate assessment. Kendrick (1975) was aware of this problem and he and his colleagues have recently reported on a substitute for the SLT (Kendrick, Gibson, and Moyes 1979).

In the FRT the subject must discriminate between target words (words previously presented to him) and *distractor words* (presented for the first time, but with an association value in relation to the target words). The extent of previous *encoding* is based on acceptance of distractors. Larner found that, compared to the depressives and physically ill groups, the dements were less able to discriminate between the distractor and target words, and evidence of a severe encoding breakdown was found. Larner was able through use of a cut-off score on the FRT to correctly classify 90 per cent of both demented and depressed patients. Qualifying his conclusions in terms of the preliminary nature of his study, Larner found that 'the FRT could offer considerable discrimination between senile/arterio-sclerotic dementia and depression in the elderly.† It is considerably less time-consuming and stressful than the SLT, and is more directly related to the memory breakdown in these states.'

Memory

A general discussion of memory may be found in Chapter 10. Therefore, only a brief discussion is included here, with reference to ageing.

Memory processes are reputed to decline with increasing age beyond the attainment of maturity. Talland (1971) noted that *registration* seemed to be affected more than the ability to perform either *recall* or *recognition* tasks. The reasons given for this deficit include 'reduced motivation, a negative attitude to novelty, a reduced general state of arousal or its opposite, heightened arousal, with a consequent enhancement of interference from the autonomic system'. In reference to the latter two difficulties implicating degree of arousal, M. W. Eysenck (1977) suggested that it was probably unlikely that differential arousal levels between young and old subjects was a major factor in differential ability to learn. However, he noted that 'it is clear that more research should examine carefully the hypothesis that one source of age-related differences in memory lies in uncontrolled variations in arousal level as a function of age'. Eysenck concludes his chapter on 'Ageing and memory' by stating that 'the evidence is most consistent with the hypothesis that deep and elaborate encoding occurs decreasingly among older people, and that this is the prime cause of age-related deficits in secondary memory).‡

The aetiology of many forms of dementia is unknown and restorative treatment may not be possible. However, it is important to ascertain whether treatment is feasible, and if so to begin it as soon as possible. In some cases some interactive psychological process may be occurring. For example, the early, relatively slow development of dementia associated with a depressive condition tends to exacerbate the dementia and to make any treatment difficult, in that the patient is not particularly motivated to improve. In fact, one of the major priorities of those working on a management or rehabilitative basis with the elderly is the maximization of the person's motivation for performance, whether that performance involves paying attention to news broadcasts or engaging in social activities.

BEREAVEMENT AND ATTITUDES TOWARDS DEATH

The topic of death has been, until recently, taboo for many people in Western society (Averill 1978). Most people still feel uncomfortable when confronted with someone who has recently lost a loved one. However, there

†As indicated by Pathy (1978) many now believe 'arteriosclerotic demention to be multi-infarct dementia and that arteriosclerosis *per se* does not lead to dementia.

‡Essentially equivalent to long-term storage (see M. W. Eysenck 1977, pp. 6–7).

are signs that the situation may change as we gradually learn that 'death is a fact of life' and as opportunities to discuss death become available.

The University of Cincinnati provides a course entitled 'The Psychology of Death and Dying' which is designed for those in medicine, nursing, psychology, and sociology, but which is also open to those from other departments. Bluestein (1976*a*; 1976*b*), who conducts the course, notes that high schools, universities, professional schools, adult education classes, and even some pre-school religious classes are including material on death and dying in their programmes. The majority of students in Bluestein's course are within the 19–25-year-old age range and Bluestein reports that '85 to 90 per cent . . . have experienced strong emotional reactions to death themselves' (Bluestein 1976*b*). The content of the course includes suicide, ageing, funerals, euthanasia, the psychology of grief and bereavement, the psychosocial aspects of widowhood, counselling the dying, and teaching children about death. The course includes field visits to morgues, funeral homes, etc., and there are many guest speakers. The initial approach is an intellectual one, but there is opportunity for emotional involvement through group discussion and other activities, and counselling is available for the student should the need arise. Many students report at the end of the course that their previous morbid fear of dying has disappeared, and nursing students have claimed that their effectiveness with the terminally ill is greater. Bluestein feels there is a growth that arises from the confrontation of death. She notes that her students have reported the experience of 'anticipatory grief' for themselves and others and indicates that there 'is some evidence that the grief reaction is less severe and shorter in duration among those . . . who have had an opportunity to engage in "grief-work" prior to the actual death of someone close (as in the case of a long-term terminal illness)' (Bluestein 1976*a*). A similar course, specifically designed for the aged and for the middle-aged children of the elderly, is briefly discussed below under the heading 'Management and treatment of the elderly patient'.

Parkes has carried out a great deal of research in the field of bereavement and produced an excellent book in this area (Parkes 1972). He noted that one of the most severe forms of psychological stress was the loss of a spouse, and it was a stress that was inevitable for many of us. Parkes believed that grief was a process which involved three stages: (1) numbness; (2) pining; and (3) depression; and recovery could not really be expected until the bereaved person had gone through the depression stage. He emphasized that many secondary losses often followed a bereavement. For example, a widow might have to cope with a considerable loss of income, of emotional support, of companionship, of a sexual partner, etc. She might have to seek employment and learn new or re-establish old roles and she might need to make many adjustments based on these changes in her life. Much of a person's behaviour exhibited during a grief reaction might be interpreted as 'searching' for the lost one. It is as if the bereaved cannot believe that the loved one is no longer alive. Parkes listed the following components as being characteristic of the bereaved person's behaviour:

(1) alarm, tension, and a high stage of arousal;
(2) restless movement;
(3) preoccupation with thoughts of the lost person;
(4) development of a perceptual set† for that person;
(5) loss of interest in personal appearance and other matters which normally occupy attention;
(6) direction of attention towards those parts of the environment in which the lost person is likely to be;
(7) calling for the lost person.

Aspects of this searching behaviour may persist for years in some people, and one might very well argue that in certain cases this behaviour is adaptive in helping to make the bereaved person's present life situation more bearable. For example, there was one patient who had been emotionally closer to her brother than to anyone else in her family. When she visited the cemetery where her father and brother were buried she would always find herself walking straight to her brother's grave, and forgetting to stop at her father's. When feeling depressed she would often feel that her brother was by her side comforting her, more than a decade after his death.

Parkes noted that 'grief work' was a necessary process in adapting to a personal loss: grief work involved the repetitive worry concerning the loss, and behaviour which suggested that the bereaved person felt that the deceased was still recoverable. According to Parkes (1972) the components that are involved in the process of grief work include:

(1) a preoccupation with thoughts of the lost person,which derives from the urge to search for that person;
(2) a painful repetitious recollection of the loss experience, which is the equivalent of worry work and which must occur if the loss is not fully accepted as irrevocable;
(3) an attempt to make sense of the loss, to fit it into one's set of assumptions about the world (one's 'assumptive world') or to modify those assumptions if need be.

Anger and guilt are emotions characteristic of some widows during the recovery from a bereavement. Writing about a study of London widows, Parkes (1971) noted that anger and irritability were associated with the 'early (yearning) phase of grief and that loss of aggressiveness occurs in the later (despair) phase'. He suggested that there was support for the view that ideas of guilt and self-reproach were greatest in those bereaved people who later went on to develop psychiatric illness. He indicated that pathological

†The bereaved person's perception is strongly influenced by her thoughts and fantasies regarding the loved one. This 'perceptual set' acts as a filter through which all sensations are processed.

grief has a higher probability of occurrence in those who exhibit (a) identification symptoms; (b) extreme guilt; and (c) delay in the onset of grief exceeding a fortnight.

Parkes (1972) referred to the current research which was concerned with identifying those bereaved people who are at 'high risk' so that appropriate interventions such as counselling could be offered to those in need. Parkes cited Gorer's comments about mourning as perceived by contemporary Britons, who treat mourning as 'a weakness, a self-indulgence, a reprehensible bad habit instead of a psychological necessity' (Gorer 1965; Parkes 1972). Parkes's text is highly recommended to those who are working closely with the elderly, particularly in a counselling relationship. The chapters: 'Gaining a new identity', and 'Helping the bereaved' will be found especially helpful.

Pertinent to Gorer's comments above is the discussion on the social functions of grief and mourning by Averill (1978), who felt that while mourning practices were group- or societally prescribed, certain individual benefits might accrue from the articulation of grief within acceptable limits. Averill noted that mourning practices might provide support for the bereaved by allowing a recognized period of withdrawal and by setting a time-schedule for the reorganization of behaviour. He illustrated these benefits by describing the mourning practices of the Kotas of southern India (Mandelbaum 1959) which consisted of two funerals, the first of which was dramatized through cremation of the deceased in the presence of others, so that denial of death was not possible. The second 'funeral' which helped the bereaved to reorganize her life, was an eleven-day, very elaborate, ceremony. Initially, complete expression of grief was encouraged and gradually 'activities became less somber'. The ceremony ended with widows and widowers engaging in sexual intercourse, a practice which symbolized the bereaved person's return to a normal life pattern. Averill felt that if the bereaved was helped to understand the reasons for the grief reaction he might more adequately cope with the pain of grief, and the chance of pathological complications ensuing were thereby decreased.

Many health workers and perhaps even 'the man in the street' would consider the period immediately after a bereavement to be a very critical one for the bereaved from a psychological point of view. It is also generally thought that the mortality rate increases during this period. If one examines the burial records from the nineteenth century or earlier, it is frequently found that many widows and widowers seem to have died within a short time of their spouse's death. In fact, Parkes reported twentieth-century data concerning the death rate of all males over the age of 54 in England and Wales whose wives died during two specific months of 1957 which supported this suggested higher mortality rate among these widowers. Figure 3.1 shows that the mortality rate during the first six months of bereavement was 40 per cent higher than the expected rate based on national figures for married men

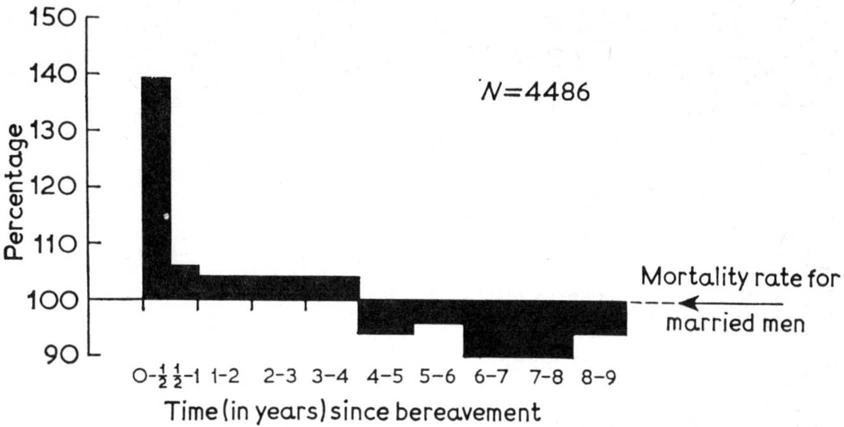

Fig. 3.1. Mortality rate of widowers aged over 54 as a percentage of the rate for married men of the same age. (From Parkes 1972.)

of the same age.

One might expect that there would have been a higher mortality rate for widows since traditionally wives have been more 'dependent' on their husbands in earlier generations and the *Zeitgeist* has supported the idea that 'a woman's place is in the home'. However, it may be that widows are offered and accept more help from others during bereavement than is characteristic of widowers. In view of the greater acceptance of sexual equality and the increased tolerance for working wives, the mortality rate for widows may show a decline, particularly since women have a greater expectancy of becoming widows and may more readily prepare for widowhood than has been characteristic in the past. If a married male loses his wife at a relatively early age he is less likely to have been prepared for this event, and if he happens to have been highly dependent on her his chances of survival are correspondingly less. Clearly, the personality structure and maturity of the widow or widower are of considerable importance in reference to surviving and developing a new identity after the bereavement.

Raphael (1977) has carried out a controlled study to determine the degree to which post-bereavement morbidity could be decreased by preventative intervention. The symptomatology of the at-risk group included insomnia, depression, and general nervousness. The subjects considered to be at-risk for post-bereavement morbidity were given three months' treatment which included 'specific support for grief and encouragement of mourning'. The follow-up, 13 months after treatment, showed a significant decrease in morbidity in the treatment group. It is suggested that factors other than support for grief and encouragement of mourning might have been responsible for the significant results. Clearly, as recommended by Raphael, further research is needed to isolate the variables instrumental in decreasing post-bereavement morbidity.

MANAGEMENT AND TREATMENT OF THE ELDERLY PATIENT

Motivating the elderly for treatment is obviously best carried out by those health workers who have the closest and most consistent contact with the patient. Post (1965) stressed the importance of the psychiatric social worker and occupational therapy staff in placing a strong emphasis on various types of social and simple occupational therapy. He noted that where this had been done consistent improvement in behavioural rating scales had been found. Woods and Britton (1977) stressed the importance of determining idiosyncratic reinforcements, a point that must be considered in all treatment. However, as they point out, it must be remembered that while social reinforcement may be effective in motivating patients initially, patients may become satiated with staff approval so that it is no longer effective.

The rest of this section describes some of the therapeutic work with the elderly and is divided into two sections: (a) psychotherapeutic approaches and (b) behavioural approaches. However, it should be clear that this is a division of convenience in that there are many therapeutic programmes which include a number of approaches; making a strict interpretation of this categorization quite inappropriate.

Psychotherapeutic approaches

Chapters 13 and 14 provide an introduction to psychotherapy and an overview of the analytic and self-concept approaches to treatment.

Wolff (1971) reviewed some of the reports on individual psychotherapy with geriatric patients and discussed his own treatment of institutionalized geriatric patients using brief therapy as recommended by Goldfarb (1953). (Goldfarb stressed the importance of the therapist who supplied the patient with emotional gratification and increased his self-esteem.) Sessions were limited to fifteen minutes or less. Wolff found this brief method to be valuable in treating neurotic disorders in the aged, as well as those patients demonstrating acute and chronic brain syndromes. Essentially Wolff's report on the use of this brief therapy is consistent with that of Goldfarb. Wolff also found that individually oriented psychoanalytic therapy gave favourable results. While 8 of the 54 elderly patients treated were diagnosed as schizophrenic, they were able to communicate adequately and the results of their treatment together with the 46 neurotics were considered satisfactory. Interestingly enough, patients were described as exhibiting 'slight to moderate symptoms of the chronic brain syndrome with partial disorientation, slightly impaired memory for recent events and occasional confusion'. Therapy was directed towards achieving *insight* and *ego-strengthening* with the consequent diminishing of anxiety. While insight was not achieved by the schizophrenics, 44 of the remaining 46 patients were partially successful in this regard. Wolff found that underlying the surface symptoms of restlessness, anxiety, and insomnia was a 'profound fear of death' and because of high *resistance* to discussing this, an ego-supportive technique was substituted for the goal of complete insight. Wolff discovered that discussion concerning religion was quite helpful in decreasing the patient's fear of death. *Supportive therapy* emphasized increasing the patient's self-esteem by 'pointing out the patient's assets, his emotional maturity, the importance of experience in life and in work . . ., etc.'. While it is clear that Wolff's patients had become quite dependent upon the institutional environment, he noted that geriatric patients should always be reminded 'of the possibility of remaining effective, creative, and emotionally stable in spite of age'.

Butler (1973) discussed the '*life-review*' process which can be therapeutic to the elderly person, although it is probably best to carry out this process overtly in the presence of a therapist so that there will be therapeutic gain rather than a surfeit of depression, feelings of low self-worth, and other negative emotions which can result from an awareness and focusing on the inevitability of death and on self-perceived inadequacies of one's past life. Butler proposed that the 'life-review', which he defined as an inner introspective-like process in which the individual reminisces over his past life, was a universal process in older people. While most people tended to think of this process as non-functional and pathological, Butler pointed out that this need not be, and, in fact, the life-review could serve to integrate one's life and prepare the person for death. He noted that some writers felt that the process of *reminiscing* was beyond the older person's control, while others perceived the process as self-determined and as reinforcing. Butler conceived:

> of the life review as a naturally occurring, universal mental process characterized by the progressive return to consciousness of past experiences, and particularly, the resurgence of unresolved conflicts; simultaneously, and normally, these revived experiences and conflicts can be surveyed and reintegrated. Presumably this process is prompted by the realization of approaching dissolution and death, and the inability to maintain one's sense of personal invulnerability. It is further shaped by contemporaneous experiences and its nature and outcome are affected by the lifelong unfolding of character.

He presented a number of interesting case histories in which there was mainly an adaptive or constructive emphasis in the life-review as well as some in which there was a high degree of psychopathological emphasis. Butler felt that psychopathological manifestations such as anxiety, despair, and depression might be expected in those who: (1) placed great emphasis on the future, while tending to avoid the present; (2) tended to injure others with full awareness of so doing; and (3) might be described as 'pathologically arrogant and prideful' (Neugarten 1973).

Butler felt that the *endogenous depressions* in the elderly may arise from the life-review process and recommended research into the similarities and differences between depression and despair. He hypothesized that apparent deficits in recent memory might be related to the elderly person's avoidance of the present. The life-review process has to be considered in psychotherapy with the aged, although Butler noted that the dangers anticipated from the life-review process have been used as a rationale for the contra-indication for psychotherapy in the elderly. An important point for those health professionals working closely with the elderly was made by Grotjahn (1951). He stressed that it was important for the aged person to integrate his past life experiences as they have been lived, not as they might have been lived (Butler 1973).

Boylin, Gordon, and Nehrke (1976), working within the context of Erikson's developmental theory, reported on research concerned with relating reminiscence to ego-integrity in institutionalized elderly males. According to Erikson's theory psychological well-being in the aged is a function of reminiscence. In the author's words 'this reworking of the past will result either in the attainment of ego-integrity or despair'. The study utilized a modified form of Havighurst and Glasser's (1972) 'reminiscing questionnaire' to assess the frequency of reminiscing, the type affect (positive, negative, or neutral) demonstrated in the reminiscing, and the extent to which the reminiscing focused on particular periods of the person's life. The 'ego adjustment' measure was constructed to correspond to Erikson's stages: 'intimacy vs. isolation', 'generativity vs. stagnation', and 'ego-integrity vs. despair'. The prediction made was that there would be a significant positive relationship between ego-integrity and (a) frequency of reminiscing, and (b) positive affect of reminiscing. The results revealed a significant correlation between ego-integrity and (a) the frequency of reminiscing and (b) negative affect of reminiscing. The frequency of reminiscing was not correlated with 'intimacy' or 'generativity'. Thus, the results, which indicated that those patients who had achieved ego-integrity had an unfavourable view of their past experience, contrasted with previous research findings. Those subjects who were classed as frequent reminiscers seemed to dwell mostly on the period of early adulthood and to a lesser extent on their childhood years. The results suggested that negative affect was associated with the fifth decade of the life-span. Further research was suggested in order to determine whether subjects who had achieved ego-integrity through reminiscing had satisfactorily resolved their past lives and could accept death more easily. Erikson noted that:

> The lack or loss of . . . accrued ego integration is signified by fear of death: the one and only life cycle is not accepted as the ultimate of life. Despair expresses the feeling that the time is now short, too short for the attempt to start another life and to try out alternative roads to integrity.

Behavioural approaches

Chapters 15 and 16 provide a description of the theoretical basis of this general approach and some of the specific techniques used in the behavioural therapies. Perhaps the major assumption of the behaviour therapies is that both pathological and normal behaviour are learned and thus can be unlearned. Therefore, after establishing the various deficits, excesses, and assets of the patient through carrying out a *functional analysis*, the therapist is able to develop behavioural programmes in order that excess behaviour can be extinguished and deficits corrected through learning, or behaviours developed which will, in essence, enable the individual to maximize his *reinforcements* while more easily accepting those deficits which cannot be corrected. Clearly, the behaviour therapist does not suggest that all deficits, particularly if they are primarily biologically based, can be corrected. However, it has become clear that more can be done to help even those individuals with biological deficits than had previously been thought.

Preston (1973) described two student-teacher-type courses which were very positively orientated and emphasized a preventative approach. These courses were: (a) 'Ageing and retirement readiness', and (b) 'Learning to be mortal'. The students included the retired, near-retired, those long unemployed, and the middle-aged children of the elderly. While accepting the facts that the older person would have, in general, slowed down and that there would have been a decrease in learning rate, Preston noted that fear of failure contributed to the learning difficulties of the aged. She proposed that self-paced learning tasks could contribute to change in the elderly. Each student in the 'Ageing and retirement readiness' course was first asked to complete a questionnaire which assessed the student's ability in various practical aspects of everyday living, such as the handling of his financial affairs, use of leisure time, management of health, interpersonal relationships, attitudes towards approaching death, etc. Thus, teacher and student were in a position to use the results of this questionnaire to determine those areas of the student's life which needed discussion and change. Various procedures were used to increase attention span, to disrupt disturbing feelings, thoughts, and behaviour, and to treat anxiety and depression. Preston noted that she stressed methods of making and retaining friends, since the elderly were so prone to lose relations and friends through death. Specific practice was required of the students in learning new ways of behaving and in maintaining and extending old ones. Definite criteria were also set such as learning so many new words per week.

The course: 'Learning to be mortal' was most concerned with teaching people how to die. Again, the first task required of the student was the completion of a questionnaire on death and dying, the results of which aided in the selection of a project which might be designed to help him increase his awareness of himself, deal with suicidal thoughts, investigate the various emotions that he might experience, and so forth. The student might be encouraged to make friends with someone who was terminally ill and he might be given practice in the 'life-review' and asked to assess those life-time actions which have given him pleasure and those which have caused him regret. Group discussions on death and dying might be held, with various students taking different points of view. A further task for the student was composing an obituary, which encouraged the student to consider how he would like to be remembered. Preston's courses appear to be helpful to the elderly and the terminally ill, and to those who have close contact with the elderly and the dying patient, and such courses deserve to be emulated.

Ramsay(1977) discussed a behavioural approach, shown to be successful in treating phobias, which he applied to pathological grief reactions. Ramsay stressed the fact, echoed by many others, that everyone who suffered a significant loss had in some way to work through the grief. If psychopathology was to be avoided 'grief work must be done'. After reminding the reader of the sequence of events involved in the development of phobias from the learning point of view, Ramsay postulated a relationship between grief reactions and *phobias*. Critically important in the comparison was the avoidance response which occurred in phobias, precluding extinction of the conditioned response. The *incubation or 'Napalkov phenomenon'* (Eysenck 1967) is frequently put forward as an additional factor preventing the occurrence of *extinction*. While there is a relative lack of understanding of this phenomenon, which increases the strength of the conditioned response in the absence of actual conditioning trails, an increase in response-strength has been observed when, during *systematic desensitization* and *flooding*, strong *conditioned responses* are aroused for brief intervals. Ramsay proposed that some people were potential phobics in that they were characterized by a 'prepotent response pattern . . . to avoid confrontations and to escape from difficult situations'. This sort of person then, following Ramsay, 'will not tackle the "grief work" and will tend to get "stuck" in the grief reactions'. Ramsay indicated that if his reasoning was correct that some people classed as *reactive depressives* would exhibit patterns of life characteristic of the phobic, and, in addition, some phobics would suffer pathological grief.

Basically, the 'stimuli and situations which could get the grief work going, which could elicit the undesired responses so that extinction could take place, are avoided'. Referring to a number of single-case studies involving people with pathological grief reactions, Ramsay indicated that he and his colleagues found flooding and *prolonged exposure* to be highly effective as treatment procedures. Ramsay found *interpretative therapy* to be both unnecessary and much longer than his *behavioural approach* which could achieve success in about three weeks.

Jenkins, Felce, Lunt, and Powell (1977) studied the effect of introducing a regular recreation programme on the level of engagement in activity in two homes for the elderly. They reviewed the literature on the deleterious effect on the aged of a lack of activity and stressed that deterioration might be retarded by introducing programmes in which the activities involved were helpful in maintaining the elderly person's skills. In their experiment, *baseline data* on activity level was first obtained and then extra activities were provided, after which the *experimental intervention* of providing new activities was alternated randomly with baseline conditions for ten days. The experimenters' job was to assist residents to begin an activity if necessary, to make suggestions about choice of activity, to interact with the patients, and to provide social reinforcement for involvement. The results of this *reversal design* indicated that in both homes, the mean number of residents involved in activities over experimental days significantly increased over those involved on baseline days. It was noted that the mean number of residents present in the activity room (lounge) was similar under both baseline and experimental conditions.

It was found that the number of residents who used each of the different types of activity and the duration spent in each activity varied considerably. It was noted that only three activities (making pompoms, bead threading, and jigsaws) engaged at least two people at once for 25 per cent of the time. The graphic data presented showed that only three activities: looking at magazines, making pompoms from wool and cardboard, and polishing old coins, engaged up to four residents simultaneously. The low levels of resident involvement during baseline observations and the consequent increase with the presence of the experimenter who provided new activities and social reinforcement for resident involvement, suggested that an onus was placed on residential care staff to find ways to encourage and initiate activity. The authors concluded that rather than implicating the specific disabilities or characteristics of the subjects, 'low baseline levels are, at least in part, due to lack of opportunities to engage in the settings of the residential Homes'. It was noted that lack of funds, space, and staff time restricted the number of activities that could be made available and that selection of activities was more reliably based, not on verbally stated preferences but on observing the number of people who were present and participating. It was also recommended that owing to shortage of staff time more able residents or volunteers should be enlisted in initiating and running activity sessions.

Sachs (1975) used operant techniques in the attempt to increase walking behaviour, oral hygiene (toothbrushing), and social interaction in institutionalized geriatric patients. The results indicated success in each of the three applications, but we will only focus on the social interaction variable here. While there are those who suggest that a *disengagement process* is acceptable in maintaining life satisfaction (i.e. reduced activities, social and physical), the present study would support the *activity theory* in maintaining satisfaction. The subject in the social-interaction experiment was a 91-year-old male with a hearing loss, who was inactive socially. A reversal design (Hersen and Barlow 1976) (Baseline, Intervention I, Reversal, Intervention II) was used. Baseline observations were recorded during eleven 15-minute sessions. Both the number of social contacts and the durations of verbilization were recorded.

During Intervention I, the initiation of conversation and verbally responding to others were reinforced by social praise over 42 sessions. Reversal, in which reinforcement was not provided, took place over eleven sessions. Finally, Intervention II, in which reinforcement was again provided took place.

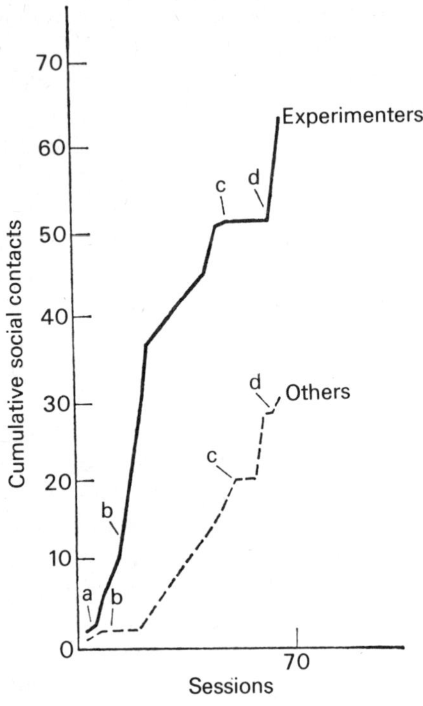

Fig. 3.2. Cumulative number of social contacts with the experimenters and with other residents and staff: 'a' indicates baseline; 'b' indicates initiation of reinforcement; 'c' indicates reversal procedures; and 'd' indicates the reinstatement of reinforcers. (From Sachs 1975.)

Figures 3.2 and 3.3 present the results in graphic form. The results in Fig. 3.2 indicate that there was little social interaction during the baseline condition. However, with the introduction of reinforcement in Intervention I there was a marked increase in the desired behaviour. When the reinforcement was removed the amount of social interaction levelled off. Figure 3.3 shows the increased amount of verbalization during social contacts and again the reversal procedure shows the levelling off of verbalization. The author concluded that 'Behaviors such as grooming, oral hygiene, social interaction and mobility are within the repertoire of most geriatric residents'. The term 'residents' was used in order 'to de-emphasize the passive patient role and increase behavioural expectations from them. The residents must alter their own expectations, but it is only when the staff alter theirs that behavioral change will occur.' Woods and Britton (1977) noted that consistent staff attitudes in regard to expectation and reinforcement were very important in therapy.

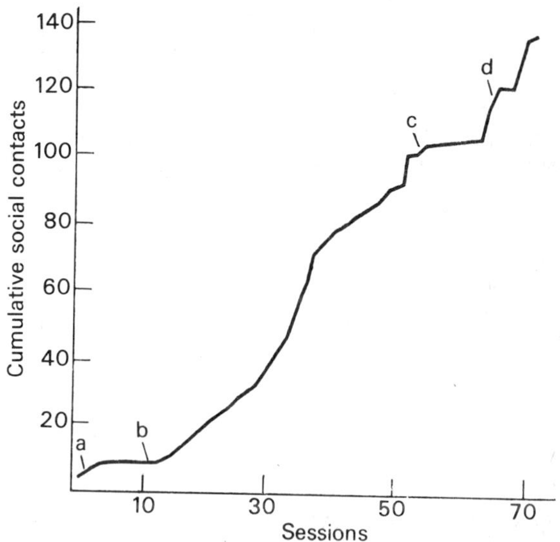

Fig. 3.3. Cumulative time spent in social interaction: 'a' indicates baseline, 'b' indicates initiation of reinforcement; 'c' indicates reversal; and 'd' indicates reinstatement of reinforcement. (From Sachs 1975.)

Saltz (1971) has reported on a so-called 'foster grandparent' programme which employed elderly people (above 60) in various children's institutions. These elderly workers were employed for twenty hours per week to provide personal attention and affection to infants and children who live in institutions. One of the major objectives was the alleviation of some of the financial and psychological problems which often face impoverished elderly people by providing them with interesting paid employment. The study included 37 foster-grandparents and 22 controls. The main procedure used to determine the effects of employment on the foster-grandparents was the 'foster-grandparent research interview schedule', which included an assessment of what the individual would need to be happy. Table 3.1 indicates the major factors mentioned by these people in order to be happy.

It can be seen that satisfying social contacts, good health, and financial security are mentioned by 50 per cent or more of the respondents. Table 3.2 indicates the increase in satisfactions found by the foster-grandparents after a two-year period.

It is clear that the programme was relatively effective in increasing life satisfaction for these elderly people.

Diesfeldt and Diesfeldt-Groenendijk (1977) studied the effect of exercise

TABLE 3.1
PERCENTAGE OF OLDER PERSONS GIVING VARIABLES AS A REQUIREMENT FOR LIFE SATISFACTION

'To be happy, I would need . . .'	Percentage mentioning variable
Purposeful activity	33
Independence	37
Feelings of usefulness	43
Financial security	50
Good health	69
Satisfying social contacts (family and friends)	83

(Adapted from Saltz 1971)

TABLE 3.2
INCREASE IN 'PRESENT SATISFACTION' AFTER TWO YEARS OF EMPLOYMENT AS FOSTER-GRANDPARENTS

	Per cent of those mentioning as a 'present satisfaction'		
Satisfaction with:	Pre-	Post-	p* <
Purposeful activity	4	42	0.01
Financial status	4	31	0.01
Health	31	58	0.10
Social relationships	31	62	0.05
Living arrangements	11	38	0.01

*χ^2 for change (1 d.f., one-tailed)
(Adapted from Saltz 1971)

on the cognitive performance of old people (average age 82) who were admitted to a nursing home because of various physical and mental handicaps. Twenty subjects were included in an exercise group, and twenty in a control group. The exercise group demonstrated a greater degree of free-recall than the control group. However, the other measurements: a recognition task, and a test of visuomotor co-ordination did not differentiate between the groups after a month's exercise treatment in the experimental group.

Grosicki (1968) stressed the degree to which the aged patient's life in hospital tended to be contingent on scheduled activities on the ward and how extensive their dependence on the staff could be. She noted that both incontinent behaviour and dependence on staff militated against returning the older patients to the community and maintaining them there. Previous research was cited as indicating that incontinence was the number one nursing problem and that the vast majority of incidents of incontinence had no physiological basis. Grosicki was interested in the extent to which incontinence could be modified through the use of operant techniques applied by nursing staff. The hypotheses were that incontinence could be significantly decreased in the treatment group as compared to a control group through the use of (a) *social reinforcement* and (b) *material reinforcement*. Further, that behavioural adjustment in the treatment group would improve significantly more than in the control group and that material reinforcement would produce a greater change than social reinforcement.

Baseline data included (a) the assessment of incontinence every half-hour, 4 hours per day for a fortnight, and (b) the completion of the MACC Behavioural Adjustment Scale by three independent raters. Scores were indicative of mood state, co-operation, communication, and social contacts. The *idiosyncratic reinforcements* of each patient were also determined. Intervention took place over a twelve-week period and included three minutes of social reinforcement when soiling had not taken place. Each patient was checked for incontinence hourly from 9 a.m. to 9 p.m. The social reinforcement involved talking with the patient or otherwise giving full attention to him. The control subjects were treated the same way except for the omission of reinforcement. Fourteen weeks after the end of the social reinforcement intervention, the material intervention was introduced. Whenever the patient eliminated appropriately without staff reminders he received two tokens; for eliminating appropriately with reminder, one token, and if found incontinent, he had to pay two tokens. The subjects were observed and treated in this way for eight weeks. During the last week of this period MACC data was again obtained. Frequency of incontinence was assessed three months after the cessation of social reinforcement and eight weeks after the cessation of material reinforcement. The results failed to support the hypotheses which proposed that incontinence in the experimental group would be decreased significantly more than in the control group, with a greater effect for the material reinforcement compared to social reinforcement. However, a significant decrease in the target behaviour was found in the control group. The hypothesis which stated that behavioural adjustment would improve was confirmed for three out of five behavioural variables during the social reinforcement phase of the study. Results of the follow-up indicated a significant increase in incontinence for the control group after both social and material reinforcement phases of the study. There were no significant changes in behaviour adjustment over the follow-up interval. Comparing the relatively negative results of the present study with the positively significant results of Carpenter and Simon (1960), Grosicki pointed out that in contrast to the earlier study, the subjects in the present study included people who were not only in the geriatric age range but also were organically dysfunctional. Grosicki suggested that the treatment group needed to cope with more changes and 'seemingly less consistency than controls'. It is suggested that these changes were perceived as a threat by the treatment group. Certainly many other authors have noted the threatening effect in the elderly of suggested changes (Wolffe 1971).

Bayne (1978) noted that confusional states in the elderly were common, difficult to diagnose as to underlying cause, as well as difficult to manage. There can be a high mortality rate arising from *acute confusional states*, and Bayne warned against considering only the age of the patient as a contra-indication for treatment. While the behavioural picture includes *delirium, stupor, disorientation, memory impairment,* and *restlessness*, the aetiology almost invariably involves an organic disease. If delusions and hallucinations are present, management is particularly difficult. Bayne noted that the risk of exhaustion is a real one, but recommended procedures which obviate the need for force, such as suggestion, to calm the patient. If this is unsuccessful then it may be advisable to use tranquillizers in order to control both anxiety and aggressivity. Until the aetiolgy is determined the patient should be kept under continual observation.

While general medical procedures are used to treat the underlying pathology, the recovery process can be accelerated by the staff's encouraging self-control and reminding the patient of their expectation of his recovery. Bayne noted that one should not rule out full recovery in the elderly simply because of a stroke or other condition entailing a long convalescence. However, full recovery 'does require a consistent, supportive, stimulating environment and a co-ordinated approach from all health professions involved'. Bayne went on to stress the importance of such factors as motivation, attitudes, alertness, etc., on the ability of the elderly to learn. He emphasized the value of prevention through an awareness of the general health of the aged patient. He recommended that neighbours visit the elderly frequently and that social or community nursing agencies be involved. Change should be avoided if at all possible by treating the elderly patient in his home and in other ways avoiding disequilibrium. If the patient should need to be admitted, a person familiar to the patient should be used to help in orientating the older patient to his new environment. While the utilization of a psychological consultation is not mentioned by Bayne, it would seem that many aspects of a patient's recovery from the confusional state are psychological in nature and research into rehabilitation procedures in this area is very desirable.

Woods and Britton (1977) considered treatment approaches to the elderly, while Miller (1977) reviewed the management of elderly demented patients. Whereas the populations considered are different, the differences are mainly in degree, with the demented demonstrating more severe psychological deficits than more general samples of elderly patients. Both Woods and Britton and Miller discussed programmes which involved: (1) stimulation and activity; (2) reality orientation (RO), and (3) behavioural approaches. Woods and Britton also reviewed 'milieu therapy'.

Stimulation and activity programmes are reputed to be based on the idea of some type of *sensory deprivation* process in the elderly. Woods and Britton reviewed the work on stimulation and activity as treatment procedures and found that many of these programmes were quite successful in improving orientation and cognitive functioning, although the findings on follow-up were questionable because of poor experimental design. The brief overview of the Diesfeldt and Diesfeldt-Groenendijk (1977) study given above supports the value of active participation in improving cognitive performance, although unfortunately no follow-up data is provided.

'Reality orientation' (RO) programmes (Folsom 1968) are based on the idea of a disorientation arising from 'loss of purpose and sense of identity'. These programmes attempt 'to re-orientate the patient to his current reality'. The procedure here is to emphasize teaching the patient information he tends to forget (e.g. to remind him what day it is, where he is, what he had for breakfast, etc.). Woods and Britton criticized some of the work in this area for poor design. However, they concluded that if RO programmes were carried on for a sufficient period of time and included therapist instruction and encouragement they could be quite effective. While reviewing management procedures with the elderly demented Miller suggested that merely providing a more stimulating environment was insufficient to maintain improvement. The patient must be actively involved in the situation. Miller also noted that the most encouraging response was shown by those patients who were less severely demented. That Woods and Britton were in agreement with Miller on this point was shown in their discussion on the value of active participation.

'Milieu treatment', in which patients are provided with social roles which allow them to participate in areas in which they can achieve a degree of success, was also reviewed by Woods and Britton. There is a de-emphasis on factors which maintain or tend to increase dependency of the patient on staff; and the responsibility for care and management is given to the patient as far as possible. While there is no hard data supporting such an approach, Woods and Britton in citing the work of Savage (1974) noted ward staff reports of less incontinence and a greater degree of responsivity to the environment by those receiving milieu treatment.

Woods and Britton in reviewing behavioural approaches to the treatment of the elderly found that operant procedures using tokens and material rewards had been useful in increasing within-group interaction in withdrawn and uncommunicative patients, in increasing verbal behaviour in elderly long-stay patients, in increasing exercise rate in elderly demented patients, and in increasing expected standards of behaviour such as personal appearance, constructive work, hygiene, and punctuality in elderly chronic patients. There was some evidence that *modelling* was a significant variable in at least one of the studies cited. Miller indicated that the behavioural approach might be of particular usefulness in patients who demonstrated deficits beyond those expected by their physical condition. Citing Looft (1973), Woods and Britton suggested that the approaches to treatment which included stress on cognitive factors were inappropriate for the elderly. It was suggested that environmental changes might be helpful, perhaps even producing 'improvements counteracting biological deterioration'. This environmental approach was echoed by Miller who stressed that an alternative to adapting the demented patient to his environment was the more feasible approach of making environmental changes consonant with the specific needs of patients. Miller also noted, in reference to the dissipation of intervention effects upon relatively long-term follow-up, that 'an alteration in the philosophy of intervention' was needed in working with the elderly demented. Miller again suggested that 'the main thrust should be towards manipulating the environment to suit the patient'. While Miller's suggestion is obviously a very valid one, some qualifications are perhaps in order. One can envisage geriatric wards and homes for the aged being designed by an architect in consultation with a clinical psychologist who advises on environmental structuring to match patient deficits, etc. The first qualification concerns the assessment of the patient for placement in such a changed environment. Both the capability and motivation of the patient are extremely important, and the relative lack of motivation on the patient's part might encourage staff to make many fewer demands upon him and to recommend placement in a less demanding environment. Thus, there would be a danger of succumbing to 'the easy way out' rather than encouraging and reinforcing those behaviours that the patient found difficult but was capable of achieving. Motivation is thus perhaps the most important aspect in the psychological treatment of the elderly patient. A changed environment would create few problems for those patients who remained in the hospital or old people's home for the rest of their lives. However, those who left this modified environment for a weekend, or more permanently, and had learned to depend on the 'less-demanding' hospital environment would encounter significantly more stress when confronted with the 'normal-environment'. If relations, friends, or community service agencies were able to provide sufficient help this problem could be overcome. However, at present this help does not seem to be forthcoming. If, however, Miller's ideas can be generalized so that elderly people can gradually modify their homes according to their deficits, then all well and good. Surely with the vast increase in the elderly population, government agencies can be encouraged to provide the support needed for research and development in this high priority area.

Part II
Basic psychological processes and their disorders

INTRODUCTION TO PART II

Part II emphasizes the value of psychophysiological concepts. Chapter 4 begins with an outline of some of the consequences of frustration and presents the main types of conflict; this is followed by a discussion of Neal Miller's conflict model. There is then a description of the work of Fenz and Epstein on the psychological and physiological responses of parachute jumpers during various stages of their training. The next section of the chapter discusses systemic and psychological stress, while the final section considers some of the important mechanisms used in coping with stress, with specific reference to surgery.

The main emphasis of Chapter 5 is on the psychosomatic disorders. The first part of the chapter considers the importance of arousal and cognitive labelling in the emotions. The second section discusses some of the main theories of psychosomatic medicine and concludes that the evidence seems to support a behavioural view as discussed by Lachman. The last section discusses some cardiovascular, dermatological, and gastrointestinal disorders and provides summaries of a number of treatment reports.

Chapter 6 is devoted to the psychology of pain, and includes sections on the concept of pain and on individual differences as well as an outline of the placebo effect; and the research on the personality and cultural factors of importance. The last section discusses the treatment of migraine and tension headaches.

Chapter 7 provides sections on the physiology of sleep, sleep-loss, and the main disorders of sleep—insomnia, somnambulism, and narcolepsy. Again, as in the previous chapter, behavioural treatment is emphasized.

Chapter 8, provides sections on the organization of perceptual processes, thinking, and on the abnormalities of perceptual experience. The chapter ends with an outline of current research on schizophrenia.

4
Conflict, stress, and adaptation

Full little knowest thou that hast not tried,
What hell it is, in suing long to bide;
To lose good days, that might be better spent;
To waste long nights in pensive discontent;
To speed today, to be put back tomorrow;
To feed on hope, to pine with fear and sorrow. . . .
To fret thy soul with crosses and with cares;
To eat thy heart through comfortless despairs;
To fawn, to crouch, to wait, to ride, to run,
To spend, to give, to want, to be undone.
Edmund Spenser: *Mother Hubberd's Tale*

Whether we consider man, or organisms lower on the phylogenetic scale, and whether we focus on 'primitive' or 'civilized' societies, life may be seen as involving a continuous, and at times, complex, interaction between organism and environment. A continuous process of adaptation takes place. The organism monitors and consequently appraises the environment in its efforts to maintain both a physiological and psychological homeostatis. The organism's behaviour then is based on its perception of this continuously changing organism–environmental complex. The organism may be frustrated and challenged at one and the same time. Conflict and stress are omnipresent.

These statements are not indicative of a fatalistic, or even a pessimistic, point of view, but rather are considered as a basis for a positive and optimistic outlook towards learning to anticipate and cope with life's many stresses. The purpose of this chapter is to discuss various hypotheses relating frustration to is consequences, to outline the generally accepted types of conflict situation, to discuss psychological stress with specific emphasis on the stress associated with surgery, and to present some of the research dealing with procedures for coping with stress.

FRUSTRATION AND CONFLICT

Although states such as frustration, conflict, and stress are highly interrelated for descriptive purposes they will be discussed separately here.

Everyone has experienced both frustration and conflict, although some people may appear to be more prone to frustration (i.e. have low *frustration-tolerance*) than others. *Frustration* is said to occur when a person is prevented from attaining, or delayed in attaining, a certain end or goal. This blockage in a person's behaviour may occur because of some physical or other readily observable barrier (e.g. real opposition from other people) which prevents him from moving forward towards the goal. On the other hand, the barrier may be psychological—perhaps some cognitive deficit or excess—or even a distorted perception of the total situation. In addition, there may be interference with covert activity: thought or imaginative activity. Thus, the factors which evoke frustration may be observable—objectively definable and in the individual's external environment—or subjective and perhaps based on faulty perception. Clearly, frustration may be evoked by a combination of these factors.

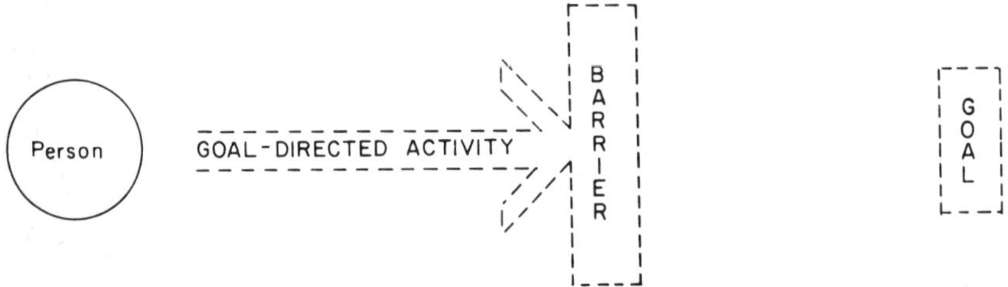

Fig. 4.1. Frustration: barrier against or interference with completion of goal-directed activity (overt or covert). The dashed lines indicate that the goal, barrier, or interference, and the goal-directed activity may occur covertly in thought or imagination as well as overtly in observable behaviour.

Cofer and Appley (1967) noted that in order for frustration to occur, two preconditions had to be met: (1) the presence of a drive or motive state which had not been satisfied, and (2) interference or thwarting of goal-directed behaviour, precluding satisfaction. Certain developmental crises or life events almost inevitably led to frustration. These included, for example, loss of love or security and support, forced independence in adolescence, and death of loved ones or anticipation of one's own death. Cochrane and Robertson (1973) have developed a 'life events inventory' based on an earlier instrument, the 'schedule of recent experiences' which is useful in assessing potential stress-inducing situations.

Conflict may be interpreted as a special case of frustration: i.e. being in conflict implies being frustrated. But before we go on to a discussion of conflict, it is perhaps appropriate that we discuss the major hypotheses concerning the effects of frustration.

Hypotheses relating to frustration

Cofer and Appley discussed frustration in terms of four major hypotheses which related frustration to its postulated consequences. None of these hypotheses was comprehensive; rather each of them considered only one type of consequent behaviour. The first was the well-known *frustration–aggression hypothesis* (Dollard, Miller, Doob, Mowrer, and Sears 1974). According to this hypothesis the occurrence of aggressive behaviour always presupposed the existence of frustration, and, conversely, the existence of frustration always led to some form of aggression.

The second hypothesis was the *frustration–regression hypothesis* of Barker, Dembo, and Lewin (1941) who found that 22 of 30 children who were frustrated in their play regressed to play that was less constructive. Cofer and Appley pointed out that in Lewinian terms, regression referred to a 'primitivization' or less differentiated level of organization. Cofer and Appley pointed to some evidence opposed to the hypothesis that regression always followed frustration by citing the work of Child and Waterhouse (1952, 1953), who showed that college students who were criticized on their performance on a variety of tasks (intended to produce frustration) produced either a decrement *or an increment* in performance as a function of the frustration-produced response interference.

The third hypothesis was the *frustration–repression hypothesis*, which was based on the work of Rosenzweig (1943). Using college students, he 'ego-involved' one group by telling them that they were having their intelligence measured, while another group—referred to as a 'need-persistive' group—was informed that the *tasks* were evaluated. It was found, in reference to the unfinished tasks, that significantly fewer tasks were recalled by the 'ego-involved' group. The failure of the 'ego-involved' group to recall unfinished tasks, was interpreted in terms of protection of self-integrity via repression of ego-threatening material.

The fourth hypothesis presented is the *frustration–fixation hypothesis*, which originated from Maier's (1949, 1956) work. Maier claimed that frustration-instigated behaviour was not motivational nor goal-oriented, and was not adaptive, and he thus set up a dichotomy between motivated (or directed) behaviour and frustrated behaviour which was *fixated* or *stereotyped*, abnormally resistant to modification, and without a goal. Maier's theory was based on studies in a restricted type of animal experiment, and it has been criticized mainly on the basis of the assumption that non-motivated behaviour resulted from frustration. In contrast to Maier's formulation, Cofer and Appley concluded that a clarification of frustration mechanism might show that extreme as well as moderate reactions were aspects of a complex self-regulating apparatus which was in essence adaptive.

Cofer and Appley implicated learning in the determination of frustration-instigated responses. This suggestion is supported by the work of Davitz (1952, 1969) who found, after reinforcing children to be either aggressive or constructive during pre-frustration play, that the type of training was a significant determinant of their particular reaction to later frustration. He concluded, however, that while the training used in his experiment was significant in influencing post-frustration behaviour, the total past history of the individual had to be considered in predicting and understanding his behaviour after frustration.

While all of the hypotheses noted have received some support in the literature, none of them taken in isolation can be said necessarily to follow frustration. However, when one notes aggressive, regressive, repressive, or fixated behaviour, one may not go far wrong to look for a frustrated desire, aspiration, or other thwarted drive or motive.

Types of conflict

It is generally agreed that conflict is produced when a person wishes to make two mutually incompatible responses simultaneously. Various types of conflict have been described. There are three main types of simple conflict situation. The simplest, probably most frequent, and easiest to resolve are *approach–approach conflicts*, in which there are two or more desirable goals which cannot be achieved simultaneously. For example, on a beautiful day, you may wish to visit the seaside and also to visit the mountains, both of which are a considerable distance away. You cannot visit both places in one day because of the distance. Usually this type of conflict is easily resolved, although some psychologists may agree that personality factors may differentiate those people who demonstrate a great deal of indecision in their behaviour from others who do not. When two incompatible response tendencies produce conflict, if one can be made stronger, then a resolution of the conflict will result.

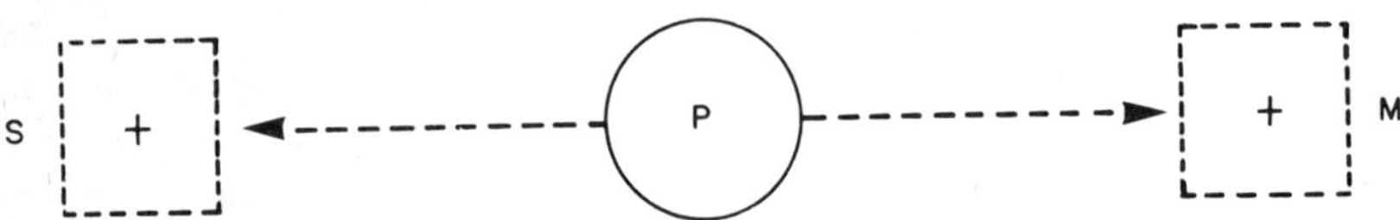

Fig. 4.2. Example of an approach–approach conflict. The single arrows indicate that the person is attracted to both positive situations. The equality of attraction is indicated by the equidistance of the person (P) from each goal. S = seaside, M = mountains.

In the case of the approach–approach conflict, as one moves towards one goal, this goal tends to become more attractive and the conflict is resolved by completing the distance (psychological or physical) involved.

The second type is the *avoidance–avoidance* conflict, which involves finding oneself between two equally undesirable goals or situations. For example, a bank employee is approached by a person who asks him for information regarding bank security. This person says that should he be refused, he will drop a note to the manager telling about the bank employee's homosexuality. Unfortunately for the employee, the manager is highly prejudiced against anyone who holds anything other than conservative ideas regarding sex. Thus, the bank employee perceives himself as being caught between two equally undesirable alternatives. He wishes to avoid co-operating with the criminal element for fear of being exposed and possibly having to serve a prison term; yet, at the same time, he wishes to avoid being exposed as a homosexual, which he perceives as embarrassing in itself, but there is the additional fear of losing his job. In the case of an avoidance–avoidance conflict, the resolution may be reached by *leaving the field* and thus avoiding both negative situations. However, to the person involved this may not be perceived as a viable alternative. For example, the homosexual in the above example may consider leaving the area and moving to another job. After some reflection, he may think that it will not be easy obtaining another job, but, more importantly for him (unless he can be open regarding his homosexuality), he may believe that his 'criminal friend' will expose him wherever he goes. Thus, he finds himself in a position of *stable equilibrium*, in that, as he moves away from one negative situation, he finds himself closer to the other negative situation. The expected behaviour in this situation will be continuous vacillation between both negative goals with response blocking intervening.

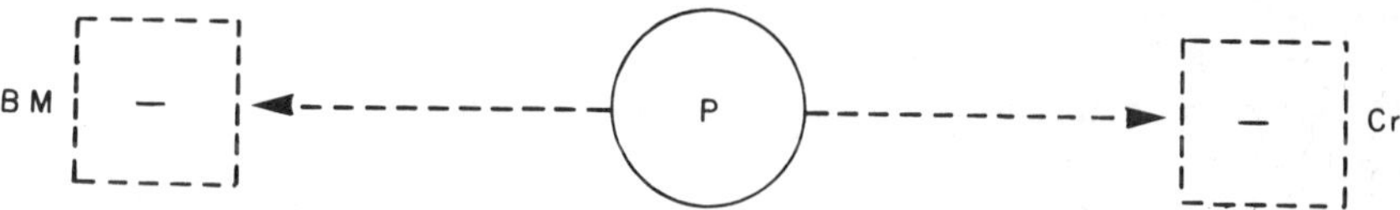

Fig. 4.3. Example of an avoidance–avoidance conflict. The single arrows indicate that the person is repelled by both negative situations. Cr. = criminal, BM = bank manager. There may or may not be a barrier preventing the person from leaving the field.

The third type of conflict is the *approach–avoidance*, and involves a situation in which one both wishes to approach a situation because it possesses positive characteristics, but at the same time, one wishes to avoid the situation because of perceived negative characteristics. For example, a medical student wants to prepare for tomorrow's examination to avoid failure, yet he also wants to invite an attractive member of the opposite sex to have dinner with him. A soldier is afraid and doesn't wish to be injured or killed and yet he does not wish to be perceived by others (or by himself) as a coward. Thus, he both wishes to be perceived as an adequate combat soldier and to avoid injury or death by leaving the battlefield.

This third type of conflict, the approach–avoidance will, like the avoidance–avoidance situation, produce vacillation. As the person approaches the goal, the negative aspects will appear more salient and he will retreat, this type of behaviour recurring until such time as the strength of the approach or avoidance movements change. For example, the medical student in the above example may decide that the young lady is not so attractive after all, However, the soldier in the second example above may not so easily resolve his conflict.

A more complex form of conflict which is frequently found in clinical work

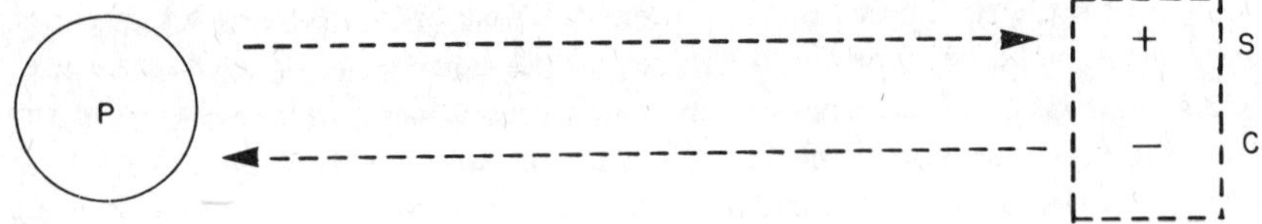

Fig. 4.4 Example of an approach–avoidance conflict. The arrows indicate that the person (P) is both attracted and repelled by the same situation or goal. S = safety from injury or death, C = being perceived as a coward.

is the *multiple approach–avoidance conflict*. Figure 4.5 illustrates an example of multiple approach–avoidance. This example depicts a man who finds himself ambivalent towards his mother, his wife, and his mistress. While he loves his mother, she makes inordinate demands upon him and seems rather insensitive to his feelings. He cannot leave his wife because he feels sorry for her, and thinks there is a probability that she will take her own life should he leave. He wants to leave yet feels compassionate towards her, even though the interpersonal relationship between them is very superficial and sexual relationships came to a halt some time ago. He wants to live with his mistress, but is of two minds here also, in that he sees in her many of the negative characteristics he sees in his mother. Unless there is a significant change in his situation or he receives psychotherapeutic help, he will probably remain vacillating between these three significant people in his life as he has done for many years.

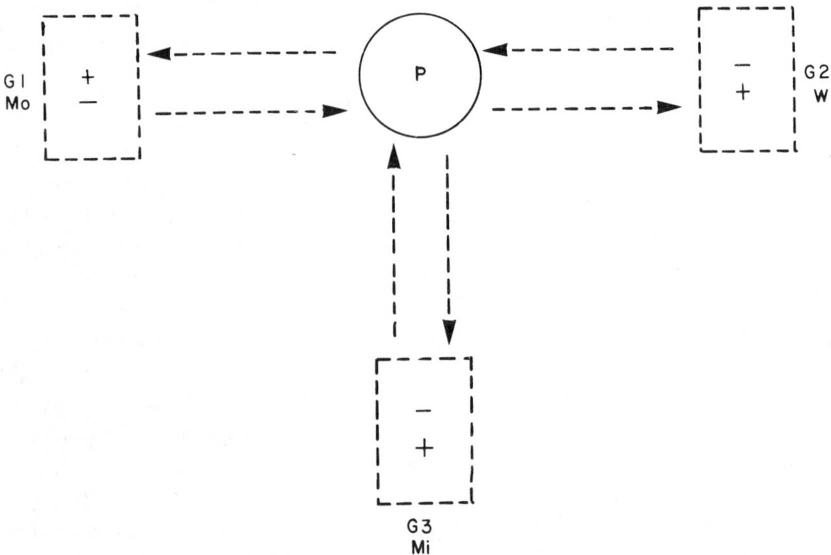

Fig. 4.5. Example of a multiple approach–avoidance conflict. The two arrows to each situation or goal indicate that the person (P) is both attracted and repelled by each. The degree of positive and negative value (valence) attached to each goal is theoretically equal. Mo = mother, W = wife, and Mi = mistress.

The concept of drive or motivation is important in making predictions about conflict resolution, since a person's behaviour is generally considered to be purposeful whether based on primary drives such as hunger, thirst, or sex, or on secondary drives or motives such as the need for achievement, need for power, need for recognition, etc. While psychologists of various theoretical persuasions have carried out research on conflict behaviour, such as Luria (1932); Lewin (1948), and Miller (1944, 1959), what follows will emphasize Miller's approach which is based on principles of learning and which forms the basis for many therapeutic techniques and for much of the experimental research in this area. There are a number of sources on Miller's approach to conflicts (Miller 1944, 1959, 1961, 1964; Miller and Kraeling 1953; Miller and Murray 1952).

Miller's conflict model

Miller (1964) regards conflict as a significant factor in many mental disorders. He presents a conflict model, which is based on a great deal of research and which is consistent with many clinical facts. The four main assumptions of Miller's model, which have been experimentally verified are:

(a) the tendency to approach a goal is stronger the nearer the subject is to it (gradient of approach);
(b) the tendency to avoid a feared stimulus is stronger the nearer the subject is to it (gradient of avoidance);
(c) the strength of avoidance increases more rapidly with nearness than that of approach (greater steepness of avoidance gradient);
(d) the strength of the tendencies to approach or avoid varies directly as the strength of the drive upon which they are based (increased drive raises height of the entire gradient).

Since the approach–avoidance and multiple approach–avoidance conflict situations are typically the most difficult to resolve, an example using Miller's model will be presented here. Many phobic situations may be viewed in terms of Miller's conflict model. A person who works on the seventh floor may be afraid of, and thus avoid, lifts. However, he may also wish to take the lift, particularly when going to work in the morning.

There are two ways to raise the height of the *approach gradient*, thus moving the point of intersection of the approach and avoidance gradients much nearer to the goal. (See strong approach versus moderate approach gradient in Fig. 4.6, where the fear goal is travelling in the lift.) The two methods of raising the approach gradient are: (a) by increasing the strength of the drive (motivation) to attain the goal, and (b) by increasing the amount of training (number of reinforced trials). Thus, in our lift example the co-operation of a colleague of our lift-phobic could be enlisted by asking this colleague not to walk up to the seventh floor, but to take the lift instead and to encourage the phobic person to accompany him in the lift. It is hoped that the wish to retain his colleague's company, with the consequent conver-

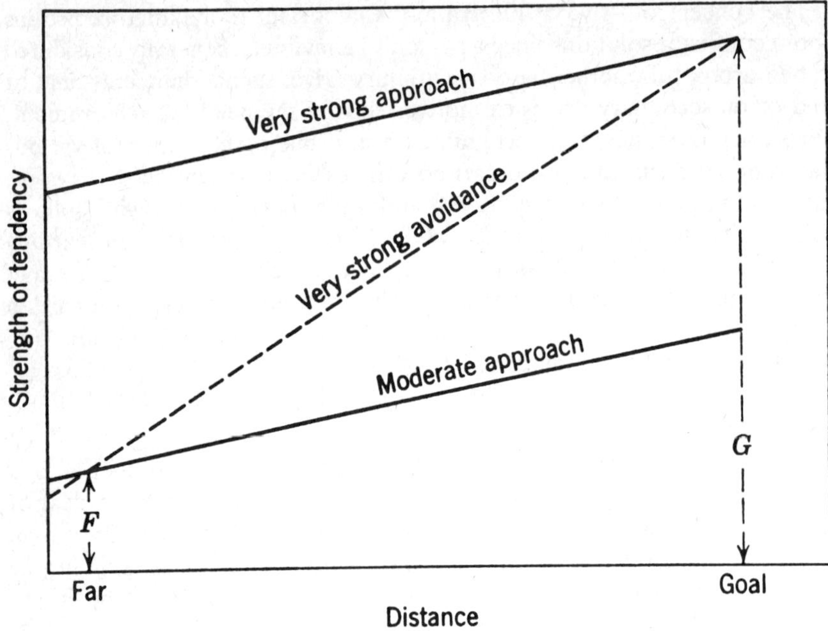

Fig. 4.6. When strong avoidance keeps the subject with moderate motivation far from the goal, very strong motivation is required to cause him to reach it, and going considerably nearer to the goal will produce a great increase (from F to G) in the amount of fear elicited. (From Worchel and Byrne 1964.)

sation, which is highly reinforcing, would be effective in raising the approach gradient and decreasing the strength of the phobia. If our phobic could be reinforced for each trip (trial) in the lift, then the probability of therapeutic success would be greatly increased. As will be seen in Chapter 15, the approach described here may also be interpreted as 'modelling', a behavioural technique of extensive value.

In discussing the method of raising the approach gradient Miller noted that the amount of fear elicited was important and that the above method would be successful only if the conflict were a relatively weak one. Thus, as shown in Fig. 4.6, the high level of fear elicited at the near point of intersection of the 'approach' and 'avoidance' gradients might be counterproductive, causing avoidance behaviour. However, in discussing relatively weak conflicts which are based on unrealistic fears, Miller noted that 'therapy can come about readily by natural increases in the drive to approach, or be facilitated by associates who use various means to enhance the attractiveness of the goal, encourage the subject, or even add motivation to escape mild ridicule to the other factors motivating approach'. In cases in which the conflict is a strong one, Miller recommended using the method of lowering the gradient of avoidance as a first step in therapy before increasing the strength of approach.

The steepness of approach and avoidance gradients is in many cases a function of experience. This has been demonstrated in various studies of parachute jumpers, in which both psychological (Walk 1956) and psychophysiological variables (Fenz and Epstein 1967) were considered. Fenz and Epstein noted that for the novice parachutist, the jump represented an acute approach–avoidance conflict, since on the one hand, there was the excitement and thrill of undertaking a new adventure, and on the other, the fear of injury and death. One of the advantages of these studies is that they are evaluating a real-life rather than a laboratory-induced stress. In addition, because parachute training involves repeated jumps, subjects may be used as their own controls and a high degree of experimental control can be obtained.

When asked to make self-ratings of fear in a period leading up to and including the jump, novice and experienced parachutists produced rather different results. While the experienced parachutists produced a fear curve which increased steadily from the week before the jump to the morning of the jump, the novices' curve of fear continued to rise up to a time just prior to the jump. Thus, the increase in fear for the novices was more extensive.

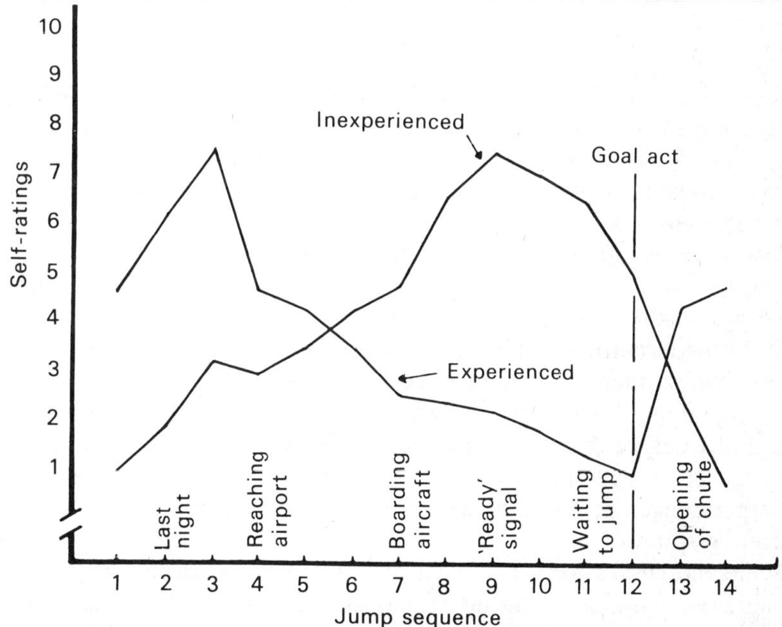

Fig. 4.7. Mean self-ratings of fear-avoidance for experienced and inexperienced parachutists as a function of a sequence of events leading up to and following jump. (From Fenz and Epstein 1967.)

At the moment of the jump, while the novices' fear curve began to decrease and continued to decrease until landing, the experienced parachuters' fear curve fell from the morning of the jump until the actual time just prior to the jump. In contrast to the novices' fear curve, the experienced parachuters' fear curve at the actual time of the jump began to rise and rose until the landing. The experienced parachutists' peak of fear response was much earlier than that of the novice. There are two adaptive consequences arising from this early peak fear response: (a) the experienced jumper is able to jump in a relatively relaxed state, and (b) the early peak can function as an early-warning signal. For the experienced parachutists the self-reported fear was lowest at the actual time of jumping, and this was interpreted as showing that a greater degree of inhibition of fear had occurred for the experienced parachutists before the jump. This theory is supported by the fact that there is an after-discharge of fear for that group alone.

Fenz and Epstein wondered if physiological measures of arousal, specifically heart rate, skin conductance, and respiration rate would parallel the fear self-ratings. The main purpose of their experiment was to determine if these parallels occurred. The subjects included ten experienced and ten inexperienced sport parachutists. It was found that the basal skin conductance curve for the novices increased up to the time the final altitude was reached just before the jump, while the analogous curve for the experienced jumpers increased until the aeroplane had lifted off, then it showed a steep decline. The heart-rate curve for the novices was quite similar to that for skin conductance, continuing to rise until the final altitude was reached. The experienced jumpers' heart-rate curve, when corrected for altitude effects, on the other hand, started to decrease somewhat at the end of the taxiing period, levelled off, and declined again between 1000 feet and the final altitude. When the final altitude was reached, the curve then increased rather sharply (see Fig. 4.8).

When the respiration-rate data was plotted it was found again that the novices' curve showed a continuous increase up to the final altitude, while the curve for the experienced parachutists began to change direction upon entry to the aircraft. Again, at final altitude the curve for the experienced men began to increase. There were similar overall relationships for the experienced and novice parachutists produced by the three measures, although the degree of correspondence for the experienced and novice parachutists varied with the physiological measure. The greatest degree of correspondence was found for skin conductance, followed in turn by heart rate and respiration.

While the curves for self-rated fear and the three psychophysiological measures were similar for the novice parachutists, this similarity did not hold for the experienced group. In the experienced group it was noted that over a prolonged period, during which there was a decline in self-rated fear, there was an increase in the physiological measures of arousal. The authors

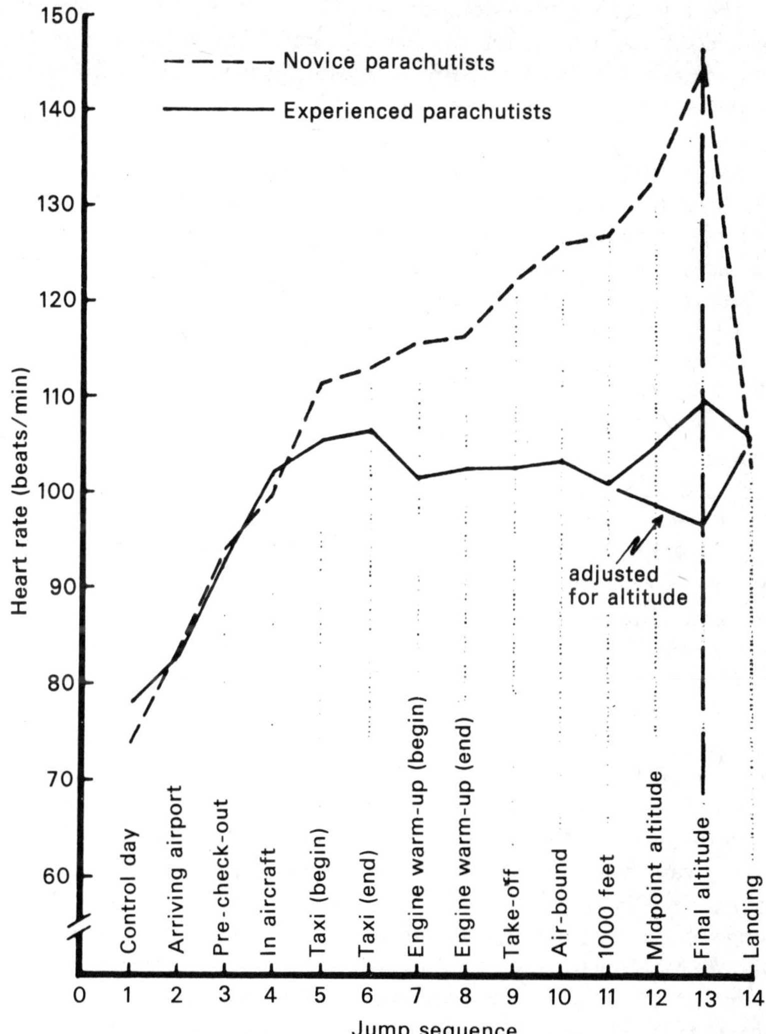

Fig. 4.8. Heart rate of experienced and novice parachutists as function of events leading up to and following jump. (From Fenz and Epstein 1967.)

concluded that 'psychological fear and physiological arousal are distinctive concepts'. It seemed that the experienced parachutists had learned to control their 'subjective stress' even though the three physiological measures taken alone would tend to suggest otherwise.

In reference to the relationships between the three physiological measures expressed as intrasubject correlations, it was found that these correlations were relatively high under conditions of moderate stress and that they were low under conditions of high stress, a finding with obvious implications for psychosomatic medicine. Chapter 5 provides a discussion of the interrelationships between various physiological measures of arousal as well as discussion of the psychosomatic disorders. In summary, it is clear that the experienced parachutists had learned: (1) to feel the greatest stress (indicated by the self-ratings) at the appropriate period in the jump sequence (i.e. their self-reported fear was more reality-based) and, (2) to develop coping mechanisms in order to inhibit their subjective stress. We will consider psychological stress in more detail in the next section, while a more extensive discussion of coping mechanisms follows.

ORGANISMIC STRESS

Frequently, when psychologists speak of stress they refer to some specific negative emotion such as a state of anxiety or fear. However, as has been implied to some extent already, the various negative emotions can be used contructively in order to prepare the individual both to perform various tasks adequately and to avoid emotional disorganization. There are a number of textbooks in this area, one of the most comprehensive is the text by Appley and Trumbull (1967), which considers stress from both a psychological and physiological point of view. Beecher in his book *The measurement of subjective responses* (1959) discusses stress from a psychopharmacological standpoint. The stresses of combat in Vietnam are discussed in *The psychology and physiology of stress* (Bourne 1969). Janis's book *Psychological stress* (1958) is of great importance to the medical profession, since he reports on his research on stress related to surgery. Janis has also reviewed this work in a later book *Stress and frustration* (1971). Lazarus gives an account of the processes used to combat psychological stress in *Psychological stress and the coping process* (1966). Finally, Torrence in *Stress, personality, and mental health* (1965) emphasizes the use of good mental functioning in coping with the stresses of everyday life. He notes that mental health is a way of coping with stress in a constructive way.

Selye (1952) was the first person to introduce the concept of stress into the biological sciences and has done a great deal to make the concept of stress a popular one. A number of reasons are given by Appley and Trumbull (1967) to account for this. First, there is the so-called 'bandwagon' effect. Stress has gained a great deal of attention and status as a research concept, and in many cases has been used as a substitute for various other terms, such as anxiety, pain, emotional distress, frustration, feelings of insecurity, etc. Secondly, research into stress has become popular since it is now possible to correlate psychological factors with their underlying physiological bases. Thirdly, there is a real interest in stress phenomena, particularly in relation to unusual environments such as those of space, the arctic, or under the sea. Appley and Trumbull also point out the possibility of linking traditional experimental research with the clinical and psychosomatic areas.

Selye's systemic stress

Before discussing psychological stress *per se*, the concept of systemic stress will be considered. The concepts of biological adaptation and homeostatis are very important in Selye's work; he sees stress as 'the state of the organism following failure of the normal homeostatic regulatory mechanisms of adaptation' or 'a state manifested by a syndrome which consists of all the non-specifically induced changes in a biologic system'. Systemic stress is manifested through the symptoms of a General Adaptation Syndrome (GAS) (Table 4.1). He refers to both the specific and the non-specific effects induced by a stressor agent. In considering the various disease syndromes, the greatest attention is usually paid to the factors which differentiate the various diseases, in order to make a diagnosis. However, it is those factors which the various disease syndromes have in common which make up the concept of systemic stress. Selye noted that after considering the specific characteristics of the various syndromes 'there remains a common residual response that is non-specific as regards its cause, and can be elicited with such diverse agents as cold, heat X-rays, adrenalin, insulin, tubercle bacilli, or muscular exercise. This is so despite the essentially different nature of the evocative agents themselves and despite the co-existence of highly specific adaptive reactions to any one of these agents.'

TABLE 4.1
THE GENERAL ADAPTION SYNDROME (SYSTEMIC STRESS)

Stage 1	*Alarm reaction* (a) Shock phase—lowered resistance (b) Counter-shock phase—mobilization of body (endocrines, such as pituitary and adrenals)
Stage 2	*Resistance* Continued adaptation on emergency basis (optimal adaptation)
Stage 3	*Exhaustion* Physiological and psychological adaptive responses decrease to point of collapse

(Modified from Selye 1952; 1956.)

Indirect psychogenic stimuli, such as the anticipation of pain, feelings of uncertainty, and anxiety-provoking situations, in addition to direct (surgical, pharmacological, or physical) intervention can induce a systemic stress syndrome. When adaptations to the particular form of the stressor are ineffective or when the stressor is non-specific, as in psychogenic stimulation, the GAS is invoked. As can be seen from Table 4.1 the first stage is the alarm reaction. This phase is made up of two parts, essentially a shock phase and a counter-shock phase. There is, first of all, a lowered resistance of the organism and this is followed by a mobilization of bodily resources, particularly from the sympathetic branch of the autonomic nervous system. The second stage, the stage of resistance, includes a continued adaptation of the organism on an emergency basis. A great deal of strain is thus placed upon the sympathetic system. Should this phase of the GAS be unsuccessful, the organism enters the third stage, the stage of exhaustion. During this state the organism has much lowered resistance in that adaptive responses decrease to the point of collapse. Clearly, the amount of time an organism spends in these various stages of the GAS depends upon the intensity and duration of the stress to which the organism is exposed, as well as the degree of resistance the organism has at its disposal.

Psychological stress

'Psychological stress' is a rather comprehensive term and includes Selye's idea of systemic stress. Cofer and Appley (1967) offer a definition of psychological stress as 'the state of an organism . . . in which the person perceives that his well-being (or integrity) is endangered and that he must devote all of his energies to its protection'. It is clear that the way one copes with stress takes many forms. In many cases psychopathology may result. Typically, stress stimuli produce a feeling of discomfort, anxiety, fear, dread, or terror in an individual. It can be seen that stress may refer to: (a) the particular stimulus or environmental situation to which an individual is exposed; or (b) the organismic state of an individual; or (c) the response the individual makes to the particular stimulus or situation. Equivalent environmental or organismic stimulation may be discomforting for some individuals yet non-discomforting for others. Thus, it can be concluded that both organismic variables and conditioning history determine whether or not a particular stimulus or situation is perceived as stressful or not. At the same time, a particular stimulus may be stressful under some conditions but not under others. For example, Beecher (1959) noted that it was not unusual for badly wounded men on the battlefield to refuse offers of morphine, while civilians who had sustained less severe physical insults cried out for medication. Clearly, the meaning of the injury is very important in the determination of the person's attitudes. On the battlefield the injured person knows that he will be removed from the front line to a much safer environment to recuperate, while no such feelings of relief can be entertained by the civilian casualty.

Most people who experience psychological stress do not demonstrate obvious tissue damage—at least at first—although in fact, tissue damage or the enlargement of various organs, such as the adrenals, may occur during the counter-shock phase of the alarm reaction. Many health professionals may have difficulty at first in accepting the fact that an individual is experiencing stress, if it is of a psychological nature, and may suspect that the patient is malingering. Psychological stress, whether based on distorted perceptions or not, may lead to maladaptive behaviour and, if untreated, may lead to actual tissue damage.

Stress is frequently provoked by frustrating events and situations involving conflict. There are also significant periods which occur during the life-span ('life events') which may, for some individuals, be characterized as having a high potential for evoking stress reactions. The first pregnancy and birth may be stressful for a fair proportion of women. Attending school for the first time may produce a stressful reaction, particularly in the child who has had little or no opportunity to explore his environment independently of his parents. The adolescent attempting to achieve independence may perceive his environment as stressful, especially if he has been 'over-protected'. The loss occasioned by the separation, divorce, or death of a significant other may result in considerable stress. Thus, it can be seen that stress is not a factor which one can avoid, it occurs frequently in everyday life and may be related to various life-events which all of us are likely to go through. Some people are able to pass through these various life-events with little disturbance, apparently having developed appropriate coping mechanisms so that their reaction to most of the various stresses of the life-span does not produce psychopathology. On the other hand, there are some who seem to have difficulty in responding to certain life-events which may evoke little stress in the majority of people.

We have seen that psychological stress results from an interaction of organismic variables, including the genetic and constitutional make-up of the organism, and environmental factors which may produce frustration and conflict and consequently have the potentiality of inducing a stressful state in the individual. Whether or not an individual is able to cope with the particular stress that may result from this interaction depends upon the coping mechanism he has learned.

MECHANISMS FOR COPING WITH CONFLICT AND STRESS

One cannot avoid the various stresses which tend to occur during the life-span. However, it is possible to predict the occurrence of many of these potentially stressful events, as well as some events which will inevitably be stressful, such as certain medical and surgical procedures. Before he is faced with potential or actual stress-producing situations the individual may be said to already exhibit certain personal characteristics, dispositions, or tendencies which are related to his ability to tolerate or cope with stress. In general, one would expect the mentally healthy person to be in a better position to deal effectively with stress and, therefore, that those of neurotic predispostion would be less tolerant and would possess less effective coping mechanisms. Plutchik, Hyman, Conte, and Karasu (1977) found that psychiatric patients reported a much higher level of stress, as indicated by a greater number of life problems and skin, muscular, and autonomic symptoms, than dermatology clinic patients and general medical patients being seen for screening purposes. In addition, a greater degree of dyscontrol, as measured by the Monroe (1970) scale, was reported by the psychiatric patients. Chapman and Cox (1977) found that the trait anxiety of abdominal surgery and renal recipient patients was significantly correlated to measures of post-operative pain, state anxiety, and depression. The reader may recall that trait anxiety is highly correlated with neuroticism. This neuroticism factor is discussed further below in reference to Janis's studies on surgical stress.

Another factor of importance is the *locus of control* variable. Basically, the extent to which an individual believes his behaviour relates to, or influences, his achievements, rewards, or the reinforcements he receives in life, is a very relevant factor in his self-perception, in his life-planning, and in the degree to which he engages in self-control activities, and in other behaviours that he expects to maintain or increase his positive reinforcements. Such variables as self-esteem, self-confidence, and assertive, positively-orientated behaviour would be positively correlated with an *internal locus of control*. An individual with this orientation would be referred to as an *internal*. On the other hand, if the individual believes that his behaviour has no relationship to the reinforcements he receives, and if he associates the reinforcements he receives to 'being lucky' or to 'fate', the individual would be classed as *externally controlled* or as an *external*. A great deal of research has been carried out on the 'locus of control' variable. Rotter's original monograph and many other articles on the locus-of-control variable have been reprinted in Rotter, Chance, and Phares (1972). Lefcourt (1972) has also published a review of this area of research. Lao (1970) noted that 'reactions to stress seem to be affected by whether or not the individual believes he can control . . . stress stimuli (that is, prevent or terminate pain). . . . Perceived control over impending aversive stimuli appears to affect whether a person will react by cognitively avoiding them or becoming vigilantly alert to them'. Butterfield (1964) found that external locus of control was significantly positively associated with *intropunitiveness* (a tendency to internalize hostility or feelings of aggressivity—see Chapter 11), and negatively related to constructive reactions to frustration. Erickson, Smyth, Donovan, and O'Leary (1976) found that externally orientated alcoholics reported more psychopathology than 'internals'. Internals appeared to differ from externals in their defensive style, using more avoidance-orientated defences. Additionally, significant relationships were found between external orientation and the Depression (D) scale of the MMPI and a measure of Projection respectively. The Rotter 'internal–external' (I–E) scale is reported as demonstrating adequate reliability

(Hersch and Scheibe 1967). These authors also found that externality was significantly positively related to the MMPI Psychesthenia (Pt.) scale, which was interpreted as measuring anxiety. Greater externality was also associated with lower scores on the CPI scales of 'well-being and 'tolerance' and the 'Adjective Check List' (ACL) (Gough and Heilbrun 1965) measure of 'dominance' (Hersch and Scheibe 1967). A more recent article by Rotter (1975) discusses some of the problems and misconceptions regarding the construct of internal–external control of reinforcement.

The concept of *helplessness* or *hopelessness* discussed by Schmale (1958) and developed by Seligman (1975) in his *behavioural theory of depression*, is an important factor in the perception of potentially stressful situations, one's stress tolerance, and one's ability to cope. Helplessness is similar to an external orientation in that one who is helpless believes that no matter what he does, he is unable to control his reinforcements. Operant learning principles (see Chapter 15) stress that our behaviour is modified by the consequences of that behaviour—that our responses operate on the environment, bringing us either positive or negative reinforcement. Thus, we tend to persist in those behaviours that are rewarding and to eliminate those behaviours which bring us punishment. Seligman noted that we can also learn that whatever response we make has no effect on obtaining reward, provided the situation or environment is 'arranged' to operate in this way. Thus, an animal or human can learn that there is no possible response that can be made that will make any difference, i.e. that will lead either to reward or to the avoidance of 'pain'. The concept of *controllability* is related to the locus-of-control concept, is similar to internality, and much discussed by Seligman with particular reference to depression. Controllability is considered at greater length in Chapter 11.

Thus, the above discussion would suggest that the possession of, or ability to learn to develop and acquire, adequate coping mechanisms would be related to a person's general mental health, to having an internal locus of control orientation and to being able to rate oneself toward the controllability end of an incontrollability–controllability continuum. The research would suggest that 'external' people could be helped to develop adequate coping mechanisms if their locus of control orientation could be shifted towards the internality end of the continuum. A similar point can be made in reference to the people who demonstrate a relative helplessness or hopelessness—people who feel (i.e. have learned) that they have no control over their environment or their reinforcements. While little research has been done in this area, Gutkin (1977) has used an operant programme which provided lower-class, black schoolchildren with both social and token reinforcement contingent upon 'appropriate behaviours'. A verbal statement was made which linked the reinforcement with the specific appropriate behaviour performed. Placebo classes obtained individual attention and non-contingent reinforcement, while control classes did not receive treatment. The contingent reinforcement children were found to be significantly more 'internal' compared to the other groups. In reference to increasing controllability, Seligman (1975) has suggested that we could inoculate people to avoid the development of helplessness. Thus, it may be possible to immunize people against stressful situations as suggested by Janis (1971).

Stress associated with surgery

Janis (1958, 1971) has reported extensively on his research concerning the stress associated with surgery. His first study involved intensive case studies of 23 patients before and after experiencing major surgery. He studied the relationship between pre-operative anticipatory fear and post-operative adjustment. His subjects were classed into three groups: low anticipatory, moderate anticipatory, and high anticipatory fear (see Fig. 4.9). Membership of these groups was then related to various measures of post-operative adjustment. The operations included lung or partial stomach removal—operations that could be dangerous and painful. The patients who fell in the

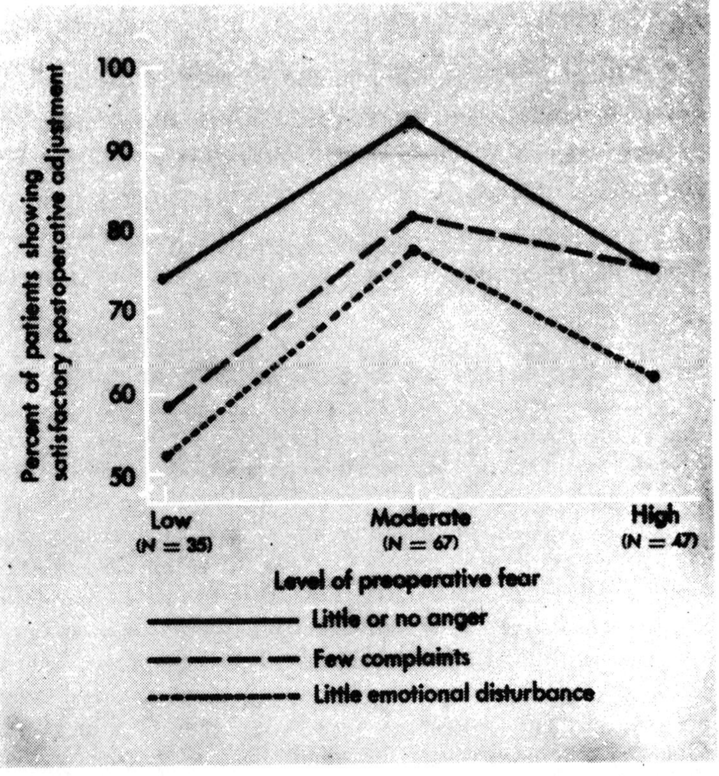

Fig. 4.9. Relation between pre-operative fear and post-operative adjustment. (Adapted from Janis 1958, 1968*b*.)

low anticipatory fear group appeared to use the defence of denial (major defence mechanisms are briefly discussed in Chapter 13). They denied any feeling of concern about their operations. They appeared to be relatively cheerful and optimistic, lacked signs of emotional disturbance, and did not exhibit insomnia. Those in the moderate anticipatory fear group requested and received realistic information about the operation and the recovery period from the staff. Their concerns were reported to be based on realistic threats. Apparently patients in this group could be reassured and were able to distract themselves from the anticipated stress. Finally, those patients in the high anticipatory fear group seemed unrealistically fearful in that there was a focus on body mutiliation and death. Members of this group included those with strong feelings of vulnerability. Sedation was typically used for problems of insomnia. Attempts to postpone the particular operation were more likely to come from people in this group.

The best post-operative adjustment was found in those who expressed moderate anticipatory fear, while both the low and high anticipatory fear groups tended to demonstrate relatively poor post-operative adjustment. The moderate group exhibited good morale and were quite co-operative with the hospital staff. The high group had a much greater tendency to be anxiety-ridden, to be emotionally over-reactive in response to routine treatment procedures during the recovery period, and demonstrated excessive fears of bodily damage. The low anticipatory fear groups were most likely to be angry and resentful toward staff. Complaints of mistreatment were typically made and routine post-operative treatments were, at times, not accepted.

Janis carried out a second study which involved a questionnaire survey of about 150 male college students who had recently undergone surgical operations. This second study essentially confirmed the results of the original study. Janis stressed the realistic approach of the moderately fearful group. He noted:

> Apparently, a moderate amount of anticipatory fear about realistic threats is necessary for the development of effective inner defenses for coping with subsequent danger and deprivation . . . They were motivated to seek and take account of realistic information about the experiences they would be likely to undergo from the time they would awaken from the anaesthesia to the end of the period of convalescence.

Although noting that some people who were members of the low anticipatory fear group might have been neurotically predisposed and probably needed intensive psychotherapy to overcome their tendency to use denial and projection of blame, Janis, nevertheless, was of the opinion that were this group to receive clear-cut information by a trustworthy authority, they would be capable of modifying their defensive attitude and becoming appropriately worried about what they would then realize was in store for them. Unfortunately, the high anticipatory fear group felt so vulnerable to body damage that they were unable to develop adequate coping mechanisms. The majority of patients in this group were found to have a history of neurotic problems.

Janis compared the patients who had been moderately worried with those who did not worry and found that the only significant difference between these groups was the amount of pre-operative information provided. Retrospective reports from those men who had received pre-operative information (51 men) and from those who noted a complete lack of information (26 men) revealed the following:

(1) the well-informed men were more likely to report that they had felt worried or fearful before the operation; and
(2) the well-informed men were less likely to report that they had become angry or emotionally upset during the post-operative period of convalescence.

On the basis of the above noted research Janis was led to suggest that if fear was not induced via pre-operative information or in some other way, the motivation to develop adequate inner resources in readiness for the anticipated danger or stress would be lacking. Therefore, the person's tolerance for stress during the actual crisis would be low. The importance of the 'work of worrying', a theoretical construct that emphasizes the potentially positive value of anticipatory fear was emphasized.

Janis noted that a failure to engage in the work of worrying could be expected whenever a stressful event occurred under any of the following three conditions: (a) if the person was accustomed to suppressing anticipatory fear by means of denial defences, by over-optimism, and by avoiding warnings that would stimulate the work of worrying; (2) if the stressful event was so sudden that it could not be prepared for; and (3) if an adequate prior warning was not given, or if strong but false reassurances encouraged the person to believe that he was invulnerable. The induction of moderate fear arousal by presenting realistic information about an anticipated stressful event was expected to serve as an 'emotional inoculation' by increasing both stress tolerance and by allowing effective coping mechanisms to develop. Janis cited Egbert, Battit, Welch, and Bartlett (1964) in support of his hypothesis. In this experiment about 100 surgical patients were randomly assigned to experimental and control groups. The patients were given similar treatment with the exception that 'experimental' patients received additional information about post-operative pain, reassurance about this pain, advice on muscle relaxation and movement, and an assurance that analgesics were available if needed. This additional information was also given post-operatively. The results of this experiment were that: (1) the experimental group requested about half as much sedation as patients in the control group; (2) on each of five consecutive post-operative days significantly less narcotic medication was required by the experimental group; and (3) the 'experimental' patients were discharged from hospital on average 2.7 days earlier than the control group. Janis concluded his discussion of stress associated with surgery by noting that 'A person will be better able to tolerate suffering and deprivation if he worries about it beforehand rather than remaining free from anticipatory fear by maintaining expectations of personal invulnerability'.

Cohen and Lazarus (1973) pointed out that many investigators who studied coping mechanisms appeared to divide them into *avoidance* or *vigilance styles*. The repression–sensitization scale of Byrne (1961, 1964) was mentioned as an example of this dichotomy. Cohen and Lazarus studied 61 surgical patients who were hospitalized to undergo the following operations: hernia (22 patients), gall-bladder (29 patients), and thyroid (10 patients). Patients were interviewed on the day before the operation and various tests were administered following the interview. The tests included a sentence-completion form which measured coping vs. avoiding styles. Notes were taken, and ratings of avoidant and vigilant coping mechanisms and anxiety were made. The post-operative dependent variables included number of days hospitalized, number of sedatives and analgesics, number of minor post-operative complications, and number of negative psychological reactions. The sum of these four measures constituted the fifth recovery variable. Cohen and Lazarus found, in apparent contrast to Janis's (1958, 1971) findings, that there was a trend for those patients who used avoidant modes of coping to do better than those who were classed by the authors as vigilant or as mixed in their use of coping mechanisms. However, only two recovery variables: number of days hospitalized and minor complications were significantly less for the avoidance as compared to the vigilant group (see Fig. 4.10). These variables did not, however, discriminate between the avoidance and the middle group. In addition, Cohen and Lazarus found that contrary to anything they expected from past research, those who knew the most about their operation—the vigilant group— showed the most complicated recovery from surgery. Cohen and Lazarus commented on the contrast between their findings and those of Janis: Janis's work had not been replicated and 'dealt only with relationships between pre- and post-operative emotional reactions, and did not examine modes of coping separately or look at medical recovery variables, as they did. They felt that the inconsistency between studies suggested the possibility that one might need to utilize different coping mechanisms for different types of stressful situation. In view of the number of statistical analyses performed they thought that their findings should be considered as suggestive only. In addition, they admitted that they did not control for individual difference within each medical condition—an important factor since some of the data they analysed suggested that the seriousness of the particular condition might have been related to the original coping classification and thus possibly to various recovery variables. Cohen and Lazarus thus recommended that in future research ratings of seriousness of medical condition might be desirable to determine the way individual medical factors could affect both

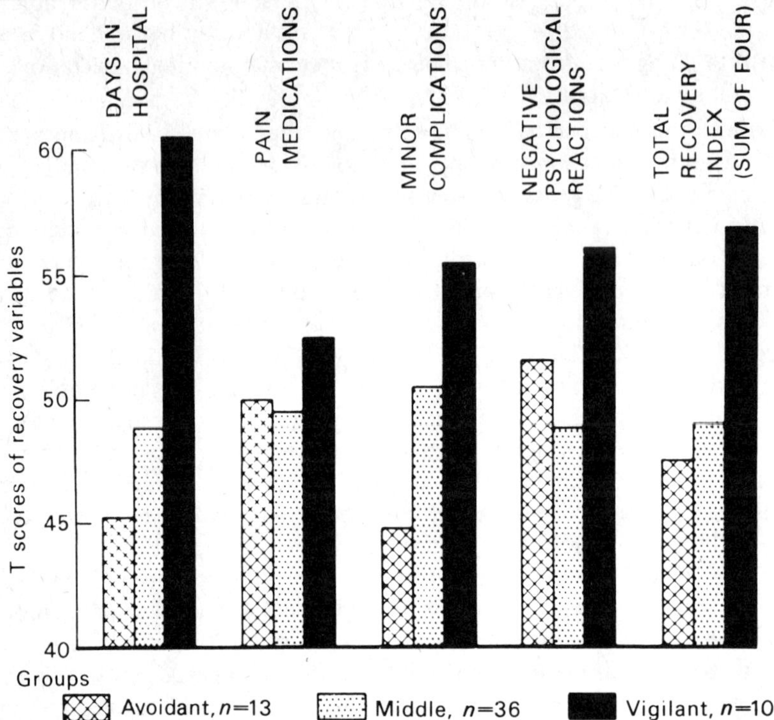

Fig. 4.10. Rate of recovery on 5 variables for groups differing in mode of active coping. (From Cohen and Lazarus 1973.)

recovery from surgery and mode of coping with its threats.

Langer, Janis, and Wolfer (1975) studied the modification of stress reactions via a cognitive control coping approach, which was compared with the provision of realistic information and reassurance omitting any explicit coping advice. These techniques were used with hospital patients for whom major surgery had been arranged. These operations were cholecystomies, 'D & C's, hernia repairs, hysterectomies, transuretheral resections, and tubal ligations. The cognitive coping approach involved teaching the patients to attend selectively to the positive or favourable aspects of the present situation whenever he anticipated or experienced discomfort, while distracting himself from the negative or unfavourable aspects. The purpose of providing the patient with realistic information was to produce emotional inoculation. Langer *et al.* noted that 'such preparatory communications are effective when they arouse a moderate level of anticipatory fear, which leads to constructive 'work of worrying', i.e. mentally rehearsing the impending threats and developing realistic, self-delivered reassurances that prevent subsequent emotional shocks, severe disappointment in protective authorities, and feelings of helplessness when the threats materialize'.

The patients were assigned to one of four groups in which a balance was kept in age, religious affiliation, sex, type of operation, and seriousness of operation. Shortly after hospital admission, each patient was given one of four types of interview according to his particular group assignment: (a) coping device only, (b) preparatory information only, (c) combination of preparatory information and coping device, and (d) control.

In (a) the coping device did not encourage denial but rather encouraged maintaining an overall optimistic view by taking account of the favourable consequences of the operation and reinterpreting the unfavourable ones. In (b) after assessing the patient's expectations during the preparation period, the preparatory information, which consisted of material typically available in nursing manuals on operative care, was provided. The same procedure was followed during the recovery period. In (c) the combined condition is self-explanatory. However, the same amount of time was spent with patients in this group, as other groups. Finally in (d) the control group compensated for the influence of psychologist–patient interpersonal contact.

Pre-operative ratings on anxiety and coping behaviour were obtained by the nursing staff before and after the psychological interview. Post-operative measures included an assessment of the behavioural indicators of stress, the number of analgesics and sedatives requested, and the length of hospitalization. Measures of blood pressure and pulse were taken on four occasions: before and after the interview, and one hour before, and one hour after the operation.

The results of this study showed that both the (a) coping and (b) coping plus preparatory-information conditions were effective in reducing pre-operative stress. The nurses' evaluation immediately before and immediately after the psychological interview indicated a reduction in anxiety and an increase in the ability to cope for patients in both of these conditions.

Table 4.2 presents the data on requests for analgesics and sedatives as related to the four treatment conditions in this study.

TABLE 4.2
PERCENTAGE OF PATIENTS WHO REQUESTED ANALGESICS, SEDATIVES, OR BOTH IN THE DIFFERENT TREATMENT CONDITIONS

Conditions	Analgesics	Sedatives	Both
Coping and preparatory information	73	67	67
Coping only	64	50	50
Preparatory information only	80	73	73
Control	93	93	93

(Adapted from Langer, Janis, and Wolfer 1975).

An analysis of the proportions of patients who requested analgesics, sedatives, or both revealed a significant effect for the coping strategy. The groups did not differ significantly on length of hospitalization. However, Langer and his co-workers discovered that the pattern of results was similar to that found for drug request data.

While Langer suggested that nurses could incorporate a similar coping procedure to that used in this study in their intake interview, he felt that it was also important to determine by analogue research in the laboratory whether the positive effects of the coping device were a function of the increase in the perception of control over the stressful event, the distraction, or some combination of the two, so that an even more effective strategy might be developed.

Discussion of surgery studies

In comparing the most effective coping procedure of the Langer study with that of the Cohen and Lazarus (1973) study, it may be noted that there is probably some similarity between the 'differential' coping procedure of the Langer study and the avoidant coping mechanism employed by the patients in the study of Cohen and Lazarus. Thus, Langer noted that 'Presumably, the patients' generally negative view of their physical condition, hospitalization, and the impending operation, were reinterpreted by directing their attention to the favourable aspects of their present situation'. The selective attention emphasized can very well be interpreted as at least differential or partial avoidance. While it is not suggested that the apparently discrepant results of those two studies can be fully resolved by this interpretation, it is felt that it merits some credibility.

As far as preparatory information is concerned, Cohen and Lazarus found that the most complicated recovery was shown by the vigilant group, who received most information. In apparent contrast, fewer patients in the preparatory information group in the Langer study requested analgesics and sedatives than those patients in the control group which suggested some positive effect. However, there is some suggestion that the addition of preparatory information to the coping procedure may have served to reduce the effectiveness of the coping procedure alone in reducing post-operative stress. Table 4.2 shows that while 50 per cent of those patients in the coping-only condition requested analgesics and sedatives, the analogous percentage of those in the coping plus preparatory information condition was 67. A further possibility which may go some way in accounting for the contrasting results of the two studies, is that Cohen and Lazarus's vigilant patients received too much information, thus increasing the number of interpretations that could be drawn from it. However, Cohen and Lazarus's admission that there was a lack of control for individual differences within each medical condition increases the difficulty in comparing these two studies.

In contrast to the results concerning the Langer drug request data, an analysis of blood-pressure and pulse-rate measures failed to reveal significant changes associated either with the psychological interview or the operation. Langer found that the changes in blood pressure and pulse did not correlate significantly with the behavioural measures of stress or with each other. Thus, the discrepancy in the blood-pressure and pulse-rate data, and the behavioural measures of stress would seem to support Fenz and Epstein's (1967) conclusions that 'psychological fear and physiological arousal are distinctive concepts'. In addition the lack of relationship between the physiological measures contained in the Langer study is consistent with the Fenz and Epstein finding that correlations between heart rate, skin conductance, and respiration rate were low under conditions of high stress. The physiological and behavioural indicants of emotional state are further discussed in the next chapter which is mainly about the so-called psychosomatic disorders.

SUMMARY

This chapter considers the role of frustration and conflict in reactions of stress. Four major hypotheses concerning the effects of frustration are outlined. These hypotheses relate frustration to aggression, regression, repression, and fixation. The approach–approach, avoidance–avoidance, approach–avoidance, and multiple approach–avoidance types of conflict are discussed. Neal Miller's conflict model is briefly presented with particular reference to psychological treatment. In an attempt to bridge the discussion of conflict and stress Fenz and Epstein's (1967) work on parachute jumpers is described. It is concluded that physiological and psychological stress reactions may not be correlated. For example, while the experienced parachutists had learned to control their psychological reactions, the physiological measures taken during the jump sequence would in themselves suggest a greater degree of experienced stress.

After a brief consideration of Selye's General Adaptation Syndrome there is a discussion of psychological stress. The various mechanisms for coping with stress, such as position on the 'locus of control' continuum and degree of controllability, are discussed.

Finally the stress associated with surgery is described with reference to the work of Janis (1971) and Lazarus and his colleagues (Cohen and Lazarus 1973), Janis stresses the importance of the 'work of worrying', which is associated with the presence of an adequate amount of anticipatory fear. He also studies the effect of information concerning the specific operation and the recovery period on the reaction to surgery. Cohen and Lazarus are interested in the avoidance and vigilance styles of coping with the stress asociated with operations. Finally, the report of Langer, Janis, and Wolfer (1975) is presented, which compares a cognitive-control approach and the provisions of realistic information in modifying stress reactions to surgical procedures.

5
Emotion and the psychosomatic disorders

Let not the sun go down upon your wrath
Eph. 4:26

THE RELATIONSHIP BETWEEN EMOTIONAL STATES AND PSYCHOSOMATIC DISORDERS

The emotional state of the organism is implicated in the development of the psychosomatic disorders. While infection or a structural/physiological aetiology is found in organic disorders, the aetiology in the psychosomatic disorders is psychological. The basis of psychosomatic conditions involves intense, frequent, and persistent emotional responses which ultimately lead to physiological and structural pathology. The typical example is the fact that in some individuals persistent high levels of anxiety or tension lead to an over-production of hydrochloric acid, which, in turn, leads to the formation of an ulcer. Table 5.1 presents distinguishing characteristics of organic illness, conversion reaction, and psychosomatic disorders. The conversion reactions, or hysterias, are functional disorders which include partial or complete paralyses, disturbances of the senses such as partial or complete blindness or deafness, or an insensitivity to pain stimuli. The aetiology is psychological and there is no, or very little, evidence of an organic basis for the particular disorder. In the assessment of patients suspected of a conversion reaction it is important to exclude organic factors. As shown in Table 5.1, motivation plays an important role in the development of the specific symptomatology. The behavioural view suggests that the patient is familiar with the symptomatology he exhibits and that by playing the role of a person who is paralysed in both legs, for example, he will be reinforced, typically by successfully avoiding some undesirable or feared task. The soldier who demonstrates these symptoms is likely to be removed from the battlefield, thus avoiding the threat of bodily mutilation or death. The 'hysteric' tends to exhibit an attitude of *la belle indifférence* to his difficulties. He appears to show little concern about his condition or its implications.

Some individuals show the development of a psychological disturbance which is based upon the presence of somatic pathology. Conditions which arise in this way are termed somatopsychological disorders. The psychological effect of the loss of a limb would be expected to be of greater significance in a person who placed a high value on physical prowess than in one who placed a much higher value on sedentary activities. The idea of the idiosyn-

TABLE 5.1
DISTINCTION BETWEEN ORGANIC ILLNESS, CONVERSION REACTION, AND PSYCHOSOMATIC DISORDERS†

Distinguishing characteristic	Organic illness	Conversion reaction	Psychosomatic disorder
1. Determinants:			
General	Physiogenic	Psychogenic	Psychogenic
Specific	Microorganisms Laceration Concussion Contusion	Difficult situation Earlier familiarity with symptoms	Stimuli provoking physiological changes (i.e. emotional reactions)
2. Structures involved	Any part of organism	Typically sensory or motor systems	Typically structures involved in or closely associated with autonomic nervous system innervations
3. Tissue pathology	Present	Absent	Present
4. Effect of suggestion	Pathology unchanged	Symptoms can be modified	Pathology unchanged (usually)
5. Effect of motivation on symptoms	Usually none obvious	Important: plays a determining or selective role	Usually none obvious
6. Reactions	Physical incapacity	Selective functional incapacity	Physical incapacity
7. Physical treatment	May have positive effect	Typically no effect	May have positive effect
8. Patient's typical attitude	Concern	*Belle indifférence*	Concern
9. Consistency and anatomical feasibility of symptoms	Anatomically consistent and dependent on nature of the damage	May not correspond to feasible anatomical patterns (e.g. glove anesthesia, shoe paralysis)	Anatomically consistent and dependent on the nature of the damage

† Terms such as 'usually', 'typically', or 'generally' should qualify each characteristic suggested, since there are occasional exceptions to almost every property indicated.
(From Lachman, 1972)

cratic perception of a person's organismic condition is generally accepted. A person's perception of, and mode of coping with, such a benign psychological insult as a fractured right arm, for example, is very much dependent upon the idiosyncracies of the person, which are usually subsumed under the rather global term 'personality'. The importance of self-perception and the relationship of perception to personality was considered in the text by Blake and Ramsay (1951). At the beginning of the Preface they noted that 'the study of perceptual activity provides a basic approach to an understanding of personality and interpersonal relations. Perceptual activity supplies the materials from which the individual constructs his own personally meaningful environment'. In considering the measurement of personality characteristics, a distinction is usually made between 'trait' and 'state'. As will be further discussed in Chapter 11 on mood states, a 'state' refers to a feeling or emotional condition of relatively brief duration, while 'trait' refers to a relatively enduring condition of the organism.

Emotion is much more in vogue in the psychological literature than hitherto, and the emotional state of the organism is considered to be crucially important in research, as well as in clinical work. Most people think of emotions as feelings and as involving organismic changes, as are expressed in 'feeling high, buoyant, or elated' or 'feeling low, blue, or depressed'. Whether one is considering a mood or a more enduring emotional state, two of the most important aspects are: (1) the *arousal level* of the organism and; (2) *cognitive labelling*. The structures involved in emotional arousal and expression include the reticular formation, the limbic system, and the autonomic nervous system. The second aspect involves the self-labelling of a felt change in arousal level, i.e. the subjective 'cognitive labelling' which, as Schacter and Singer (1962), and Konečni (1975), among others have demonstrated, is affected by various situational factors, such as the apparent mood of other people in the perceiver's immediate environment and specific stress stimuli.

Arousal

Autonomic nervous system indicants

Arousal is a concept which refers to the energy level of the organism, the degree to which the organism is mobilized to defend itself in a global sense or to escape from a stressful and potentially harmful situation. Physiologically, under high arousal conditions one would expect a relative dominance of the sympathetic branch of the autonomic nervous system, and a relative activation or increase in cortical activity. The organism would be alert, ready for some action, as opposed to being in a relatively relaxed or quiescent state. Autonomically, therefore, we would expect an increase in heart-rate possibly with an increase in heart-rate variability, and skin conductance would increase, as would respiration rate. The specific pattern of these reactions would, of course, vary depending upon the particular organism and the specific emotional state prevailing. More adrenaline would be available from the adrenal medulla, and more glucose would be available in preparation for the probably higher-than-average expenditure of energy. The vast importance of autonomic activity in states of arousal and in the emotions is shown in Fig. 5.1 which shows the various organs ennervated by the sympathetic and parasympathetic branches of the autonomic nervous system.

A more extensive discussion of autonomic activity may be found in Gardner (1968).

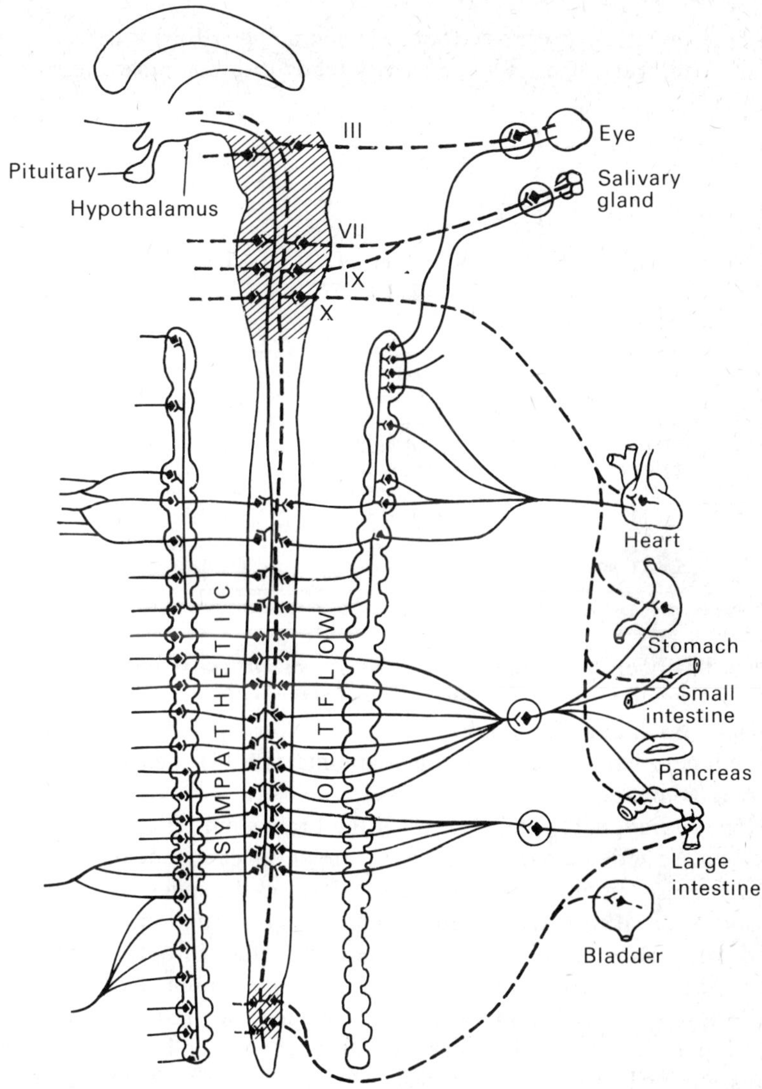

Fig. 5.1. The general arrangement of the autonomic nervous system. The projections from the hypothalamus to the pituitary gland have been omitted, while those to lower centres are shown in solid lines (sympathetic) and broken lines (parasympathetic). The portions of the brain stem and sacral cord from which the parasympathetic preganglionic fibres leave are indicated by oblique lines, and the sympathetic outflow from the thoracic and upper lumbar cord is labelled. Autonomic fibres to organs of the head and trunk are shown on the right side, while those on the left side represent the sympathetic outflow to blood vessels, sweat glands, and smooth muscle fibres attached to hairs. (From Gardner 1968.)

Central nervous system indicants
Arousal is indicated from electroencephalographic (EEG) measurements from the cerebral cortex. Faster activity tends to predominate, e.g. beta activity (see Table 5.2).

TABLE 5.2
SOME WAVE BANDS GENERALLY USED IN ELECTROENCEPHALOGRAPHIC INVESTIGATIONS

Hertz or cycles per second	Typical amplitude	Type record
More than 13	Mostly < 30 uV	Beta rhythm
12–14	Mostly < 50uV	Sleep spindles
7–11	Mostly < 50uV	Mu rhythm
8–13	Mostly < 50uV	Alpha rhythm
4–8	—	Theta rhythm
Less than 4	—	Delta rhythm

There has been an increased use of *evoked cortical potentials* (ECPs), which are used to measure the level of arousal typically obtained by auditory or visual stimulation. In addition, central nervous system arousal may be observed peripherally via electromyographic (EMG) measurement, for example, from the frontalis muscle.

Reticular formation The importance of the brain stem reticular formation (BSRF) in the activation or arousal or the organism cannot be overstressed. Neural impulses travel to and from the BSRF and the spinal cord, cerebellum, and cerebral cortex. The cells in the reticular formation which project to and from higher centres are extremely important in both normal and pathological changes in consciousness. For example, the changes which may be monitored electroencephlographically during the transition from the wake state through the various stages of sleep are governed by the ascending and descending branches of the reticular formation (RF). The maintenance of attention and vigilance while scanning the environment or engaging in cognitive activity are also dependent upon the normal functioning of the RF. The role of the RF in cortical activation was underlined by the research of Moruzzi and Magoun (1949). They found that electrical stimulation of the RF resulted in cortical activation as measured by the EEG.

Figure 5.2 shows the various brain areas with which the reticular formation interacts. Morgan (1965) noted that 'Reticular activation is a necessary, if not a sufficient, condition for emotional behaviour'.

Emotional behaviour has, however, been most linked to the so-called

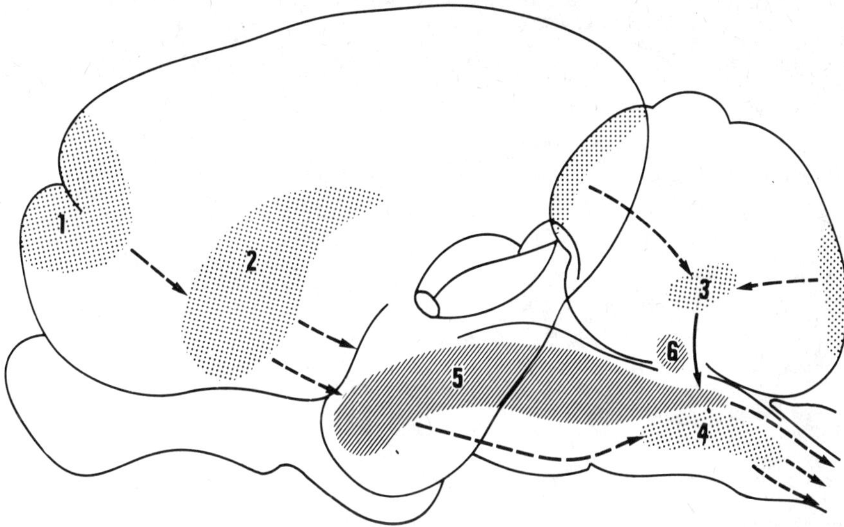

Fig. 5.2. Interaction of various brain areas with the reticular formation: (1) the cerebral cortex; (2) the basal ganglia; (3) cerebellar nuclei; (4) the medullary part of the reticular formation; (5) the mesencephalic part of the reticular formation; (6) the nucleus or centre regulating equilibrium or balance. (From Schadé 1968.)

limbic system. It is a ring of grey matter around and above the corpus collosum.

The limbic system The limbic system is particularly implicated in emotional reactions. 'The cortical part of the limbic system is the cingulate gyrus, which lies in the longitudinal fissure just above the corpus callosum. . . . The principal parts of the subcortical limbic system are the septal area, lying just under the forward end of the corpus callosum; the amygdaloid complex, or amygdala, which lies in the ventral surface of the brain not far from the temporal lobe; and the hippocampus, a structure shaped like a horse's tail . . . These various parts are interconnected with each other and with both the hypothalamus and mammillary bodies' (Morgan 1965) (see Fig. 5.3).

Morgan ascribed the mediation of emotional experience and expression to the limbic system as an integrated whole. He noted that 'experiment has established . . . that the limbic system is the central system in emotion'.

General significance of arousal

The utilization of arousal as an explanatory concept in psychology and neurophysiology has been well documented. For example, arousal has been related to the study of stress, learning theory and attention, vigilance, performance, sleep, heart-rate, and electrodermal activity in schizophrenics (see Greenfield and Sternbach 1972).

Many psychopathological conditions are reputed to be at least partially

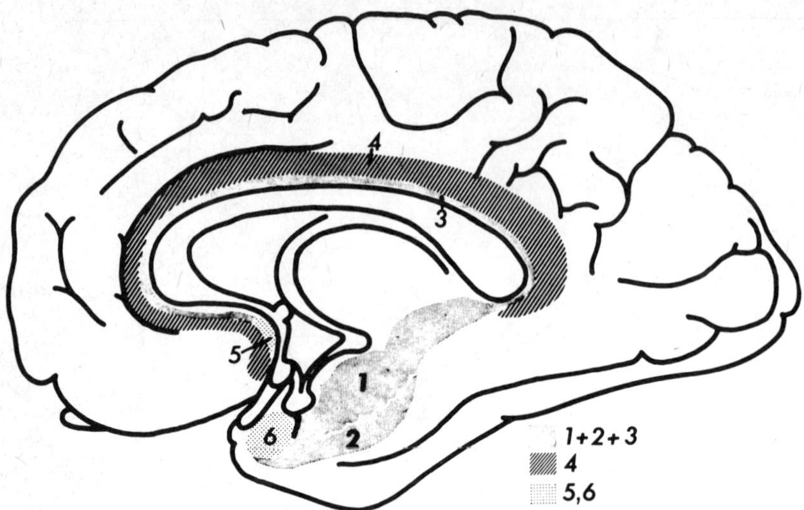

Fig. 5.3. Diagram of the areas of the brain included in the limbic system. (1) hippocampus; (2) area entorhinalis; (3) inducium griseum; (4) cingulate gyrus; (5) spetal area; (6) amygdaloid complex. (From Schadé 1968).

related to difficulties in under- or over-arousal or to an inflexibility in changing arousal level. Hare and Schalling (1977) considered arousal as an important concept in their studies of the psychopathic personality, while Shagass (1969) used the concept in his discussion of schizophrenia. Martin (1973*a*, 1973*b*) laid considerable stress upon the concept of arousal in her overview of somatic reactivity as applied to psychopathology.

In terms of arousal theory, Routtenberg (1968) presented an interesting 'two-arousal hypothesis' in which the reticular formation and the limbic system were posited as two mutually inhibitory mechanisms. Fiske and Maddi (1961) used arousal as a concept in the attempt to integrate the work on over- and understimulation, sleep, explorative and play behaviour, and so forth. They were of the opinion that each person had his own optimal arousal level and had the tendency to maintain this level. Both Maddi (1968) and Eysenck (1967) have developed the concept of arousal to such a degree that it has become an integral part of their respective personality theories.

Eason and Dudley (1971) used heart-rate and skin-conductance as dependent variables in an experiment involving three psychologically-induced levels of arousal. Response to these measures was as predicted with higher physiological responses (higher heart-rate and skin conductance) occurring with sequentially higher levels of induced arousal. Thus, the value of using autonomic measures, particularly heart-rate and skin-conductance, as indicators of arousal seems to be well established. The cortical measure most often used to assess the degree of arousal is, of course, the electroencephalograph (EEG). Table 5.2 presents the wave bands typically referred to in studies involving cortical arousal. The alpha, theta, and delta bands are particularly pertinent in sleep research and sleep disorders (discussed in Chapter 7). Alpha rhythm is of considerable importance in biofeedback and hypnosis research (see Chapters 17 and 18). Eason and Dudley (1971) used electrocortical potentials (ECPs) as a direct measure and EMG as a peripheral measure of central nervous system arousal. Significant differences were also found for these two measures corresponding to the three induced levels of arousal.

Eason and Dudley used 'reaction-time' (RT) as the behavioural dependent variable in their experiment and found RT to significantly decrease from moderate to high levels of induced arousal. Ham and Edmonston (1971) also used RT as a dependent variable in the comparison of the effects of a 'sleep-type' and an 'alert-type' hypnotic induction procedure. The results inducated that RT was significantly lower after the alert as compared to the 'sleep-type' induction.

The concept of arousal is thus an important one, which can be usefully measured cortically, autonomically, and behaviourally. It should also be noted here that biofeedback of autonomic and central nervous system activity has also become prominent in the literature and in clinical applications (Blanchard and Young 1974).

If arousal is implicated in emotional states one would expect that changes in emotional state would naturally produce changes in a person's level of arousal whether measured cortically, autonomically, or behaviourally. Normally, in the majority of people, a relative preponderance of alpha rhythm is found from the occipital–parietal channels of the EEG during a state of relaxed wakefulness. Figure 5.4 indicates the attenuating effect of

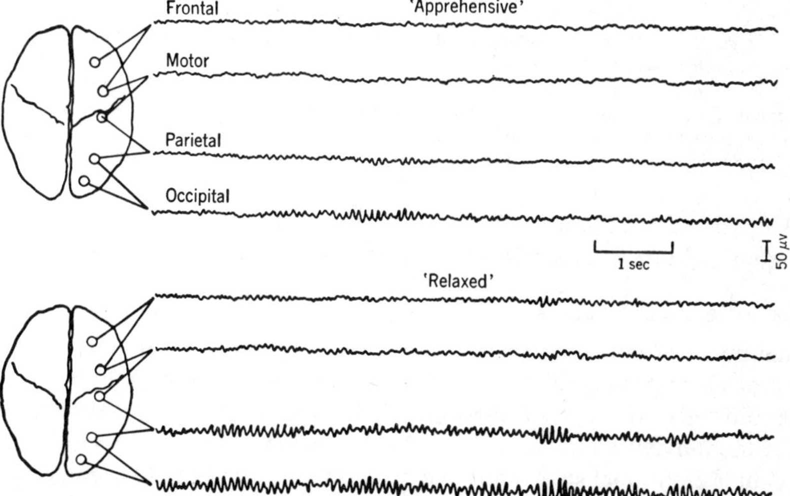

Fig. 5.4. Electroencephalograms from a normal subject during initial 'apprehensive' period and later 'relaxed' period. Note reduction or suppression of alpha rhythm during apprehension. (From Lindsley 1950.)

apprehension on alpha rhythm. In the 'apprehensive' condition, far less alpha rhythm is produced in the parietal and occipital channels.

Hebb (1966) has been associated with an activation theory of the emotions. He noted that too high a degree of arousal could have a disorganizing effect upon task performance. This was true whether the task was a complex mechanical one or one of maintaining a non-disruptive interpersonal relationship. Although relatively uncomplicated tasks which mainly require a mobilization of energy, such as running a race, or an over-learned response such as giving one's name, were able to be carried out at high levels of arousal, more complex tasks were optimally performed at a moderate arousal level (see Fig. 5.5). It can be seen that general arousal is an important consideration in emotional conditions.

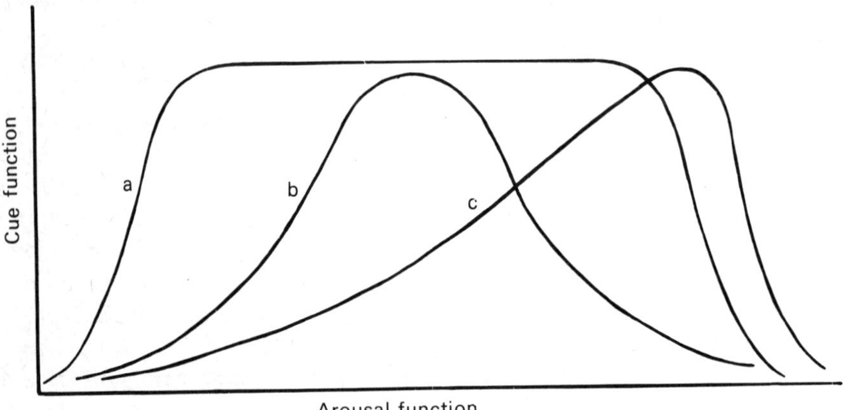

Fig. 5.5. Possible differences in the curve relating arousal to cue function or effectiveness of response, in three habits. In curve a, a simple, long-practised habit such as giving one's name when asked, maximal efficiency is reached with low arousal and maintained over a wide range; in curve b, a complex skill, the maximum appears only with a medium degree of arousal; and in curve c, a performance such as running a race which is relatively uncomplicated but demands full mobilization of effort, the maximum appears with higher arousal. (From Hebb 1966.)

We turn now to discuss two experiments in which there is an attempt to differentiate different emotions psychophysiologically.

Differentiation of emotions

A number of experimenters have been keen to differentiate between various emotions on a physiological basis. Typically an attempt is made to induce a particular emotion such as anger or hostility through the use of stooges or experimenter confederates, who treat subjects in ways meant to induce the particular emotional state while the subjects are 'wired-up' to a polygraph which is recording multiple physiological variables simultaneously. The emotional states most often associated with the development of psychosomatic disorders are fear and anger.

Ax (1953) reported on an experiment which was meant to differentiate between fear and anger. A large number of physiological parameters were monitored including respiration, skin temperature, blood pressure, and muscle tension. Subjects were informed that their only job in this study, which involved physiological differences betwen hypertensives and those without hypertension, was to relax. However, they were stimulated with 'a gradually increasing intermittent shock stimulus' which was insufficient to cause pain. However, when subjects commented about the sensation they felt, the experimenter expressed surprise and after causing sparks to appear close by the subject noted 'with alarm that this was a dangerous high-voltage short circuit'. This obviously produced an atmosphere of confusion and fear in most subjects. Anger was induced by using a polygraph operator who was said to be incompetent and arrogant, and who was employed at that particular time only because the regular polygraph operator was sick. This 'confederate' was very rude and unreasonably critical of the subjects for about five minutes. Thus, he became a very prominent target indeed in terms of felt hostility or anger. Ax included some comments made by some of the subjects which support the validity of the feelings induced.

> Just after the operator left the room following the 'anger' stimulus, one female subject said, 'Well! It's easy to see he is not an educated man.' A male subject said, 'Say, what goes on here? I was just about to punch that character on the nose.' Examples of fear reactions were also clearly genuine. One woman kept pleading, 'Please take the wires off. Oh! Please help me.' Another said during the interview that she had prayed to be spared during the fear episode. A man said, 'Well, everybody has to go sometime. I thought this might be my time.'

The induced fear and anger resulted in different patterns of physiological response. The fear profile was said to be similar to that produced by adrenaline injection, while the anger profile was more difficult to characterize in that it resembled that produced by a combination of adrenaline and noradrenaline.

Funkenstein (1955) also carried out work on the physiology of induced emotions, and has reputedly differentiated between externally directed anger and internally directed anger. His experiments suggested that outwardly directed anger was associated with noradrenaline secretion, whereas 'anger-in' (depression) and anxiety were related to adrenaline secretion. Funkenstein, basing his comments on work carried out by Von Euler in Sweden, suggested 'that anger and fear may activate different areas in the hypothalamus, leading to production of noradrenaline in the first case and adrenaline in the second'.

Thus, his work is consistent with that of Ax in associating anxiety or fear with adrenaline production. It should be noted that Oken (1967) has criticized both Ax's and Funkenstein's work on the basis of the complex physiological analyses necessary to arrive at their conclusions, and also from a conceptual point of view.

Another important factor to consider is cognitive labelling.

Cognitive labelling

Research seems to indicate that a given level of arousal may lead to differential emotional states or moods, depending upon the context in which the arousal takes place. According to Schachter (1964) the specific emotional label one gives oneself is determined by an interaction of cognitive (situational) and physiological (arousal) factors. According to Schachter 'the cognition . . . determines whether [the emotion] will be labelled "anger", "joy", or whatever'. Schachter and Singer (1962) injected adrenaline into student subjects who had been told that the experimenters were studying the effects of a vitamin supplement on vision. The adrenaline was expected to produce an increased level of general arousal. Half of the subjects were asked to wait in a room with a person (a confederate of the experimenter) who behaved in an 'angry', annoyed way. The other half were exposed to a person who behaved in a euphoric manner. This confederate made paper aeroplanes, danced, and sang, and generally seemed to be in a good mood. The results indicated that compared to control subjects who did not receive an injection of adrenaline (and thus were not particularly aroused), the subjects in the anger situation became more angry, while those in the euphoric situation became more euphoric. This research has not gone without criticism (Plutchik and Ax 1967). However, it would seem that provided one is unsure of one's mood or emotion, situational factors may lead one to label one's state accordingly.

We have discussed the concept of arousal, the areas of the brain of major importance in the regulation of arousal and emotional states, and situational or cognitive influences on the labelling of states of arousal. We turn now to a brief consideration of the theories of the psychosomatic disorders.

THEORIES OF THE PSYCHOSOMATIC DISORDERS

Introduction

Historically, the psychosomatic approach has tended to be psychoanalytic in emphasis (Kaufman and Heiman 1964), rather than behavioural. Those who are interested in a good overview of psychosomatic medicine in the nineteenth century may find Stainbrook (1952), reprinted in Kaufman and Heiman (1964) interesting. In more recent years, as noted by Claridge (1973), the number of psychoanalytically orientated studies in this area has markedly decreased, while there has been an increasing emphasis on laboratory research methodology. Whereas Maher (1966) included a behaviourally orientated chapter on the psychosomatic disorders in his text of psychopathology, Lachman (1972) appears to have been the first to have produced a book on psychosomatic medicine from a behavioural point of view. Lachman defined psychosomatic disorders as ' *physiological dysfunctions and structural aberrations that result primarily from psychological processes* rather than from immediate physical agents like those involved in organic disorders'. Lachman differentiated between psychosomatic disorders and the neurotic conversion reactions which might help the patient avoid engaging in behaviour which was threatening from a psychological or physical point of view. The typical physical example is the soldier who develops a functional paralysis of a leg, thus preventing him from returning to the battle zone. No tissue damage is involved in the conversion reaction. Table 5.1 (p. 103) differentiates between organic disorders, conversion reactions, and psychosomatic disorders.

Two of the major areas of psychological study which form the basis of an understanding of the psychosomatic disorders are learning and emotion. However, as in other disorders, it would be foolhardy to neglect other factors which may be of considerable importance. Clearly, as is true for other types of condition, the genetic–constitutional factor is of importance. Thus, for example, it may be hypothesized that a particular individual is especially susceptible to developing gastrointestinal pathology because through genetic aetiology or some form of constitutional weakness this system is more prone to be modified than other systems via emotional stimulation. The occurrence of significant life events has been mentioned in the discussion of stress in the previous chapter (p. 91). Factors such as the death of someone emotionally close, the loss of one's job, or a recent divorce or separation can be aetiologically important in the psychosomatic disorders. Thus the use of the 'life-events inventory' (Cochrane and Robertson 1973) may be useful in the assessment of those individuals suspected as being prone to, or likely to develop, a psychosomatic condition. Clearly, life events play a role in the development of other disorders such as depression and schizophrenia. While life events are generally important, it is the idiosyncratic perception and meaning of life events that is the crucial factor. Some individuals may be able to adapt successfully to a generally negatively perceived life event. In fact, Janis's idea of stress-inoculation may be quite pertinent in that those who have not experienced much stress lack experience, and are more prone to react non-adaptively. They have not received their inoculation.

Selye's General Adaptation Syndrome (GAS) has been briefly discussed in the previous chapter (pp. 89–90). However, Selye's ideas have been subjected to criticism. Basically, his idea is that prolonged stress will ultimately lead to physiological and psychological exhaustion, so that tissue damage and ultimately death result. Claridge (1973) noted that Cleghorn felt that the GAS applied well to animals but that its application with humans was limited. However, Claridge concluded 'that there does seem to be some similarity between the central nervous and somatic changes said by Selye to characterize the adaptation syndrome in animals and the response of the human organism to severe and prolonged threat as took place in concentration camps.' He noted that the concentration-camp syndrome 'is characterized by fatigue and apathy, difficuty in concentration, moodiness, sleep disturbances and vegetative lability'.

Certainly, genetic–constitutional factors are seen as important in the development of psychosomatic disorders. If one grants that emotional conditions are aetiologically important in the development of psychosomatic disorders, then frustration, conflict, and stress, as discussed in Chapter 4, are important variables. While the specific mechanisms through which stress affects the organism may be in dispute in certain cases, the importance of stress seems to be well accepted.

Whether the exposure of a particular person to a particular life event at a particular time increases the probability that the person will develop a psychosomatic condition may be related to personality factors. The specific coping mechanisms used may be related to a person's position on certain personality dimensions, or may be considered personality factors themselves. However, Mischel's (1968) cautions regarding the specificity of behaviour must be remembered. The context or situation is an important variable to consider in any attempt at prediction. Specificity and the state–trait distinction in personality measurement is discussed in Chapter 11.

With the above in mind, a number of the main theories of psychosomatic disorders will be briefly outlined.

The organic or somatic weakness theory

Through genetic factors, through accident, or through disease a particular system or part of a body-system may be more vulnerable than other systems or body parts to stress factors, which may lead to a psychosomatic condition. This theory is sometimes referred to as the 'weakest link' theory. This general theory would predict that if one's weakest system were, say, the respiratory system, one might be prone to develop asthma or some other psychosomatic condition of the respiratory system.

The personality-type theory

Helen Dunbar (1943) suggested that patients who exhibited similar psychosomatic conditions would also be found to have a similar constellation or syndrome of personality traits. Depending upon how general one considers the term 'personality', one may also include here the '*specific attitude hypothesis*' discussed at some length by Maher (1966). Basically, the hypothesis suggests that specific attitudes and specific physiological changes go together (Peters and Stern 1971). Probably this hypothesis has led to more experimental research than most others. Most of this research has been carried out by D. T. Graham and his colleagues (Graham and Kunish 1965). A good overview of the earlier research can be found in Maher (1966, p. 242–6). For example, the reputed attitude of those who suffer from hives is a feeling of being mistreated. The patient tends to ruminate about this mistreatment. The attitude associated with Raynaud's disease is also a feeling of being mistreated, but in this condition, the individual feels like retaliating in a hostile, aggressive way. With hives an increase in skin temperature is expected while with Raynaud's disease, a decrease is expected.

Gottleib, Gleser, and Gottschalk (1967) investigated the effects of suggestions of the hives and Raynaud's attitudes on skin temperature, pulse-rate, and blood pressure in twelve young men. The results indicated that the induced hives attitude produced an increase in skin temperature, but did not significantly affect the other variables studied. On the other hand, the Raynaud's attitude failed to produce a decrease in skin temperature. However, significant increases in systolic blood pressure and heart-rate were found. The specific attitude hypothesis was re-examined by Peters and Stern (1971) who obtained results contrary to earlier findings. Twenty subjects were hypnotized in one condition, but not in the other. A hives attitude was suggested in one condition, and a Raynaud's attitude in the other, while heart-rate, skin temperature, and peripheral blood volume was continuously monitored. Unfortunately, the effects of the suggestions were not significant. Thus, the theory of Graham and colleagues is not supported. Various differences in the design of these and similar studies were discussed, the most important one being a screening for hypnotizability carried out by Peters and Stern (1971). The authors noted that 'During the suggestion period, all three variables, temperature, blood volume and heart-rate, were significantly differentiated by the hypnotic factor or a hypnotic-time interaction'. Therefore, they recommend that the hypnotic factor be controlled in future studies.

Studies of personality correlates are discussed by Maher (1966). The connection that was sought here was one 'in which the personality of the patient reveals the presence of conflicts and ways of dealing with them which had predated the appearance of the psychosomatic symptom. Increases in the intensity of the conflict are accompanied by a worsening of the physical disorder. Resolution of the conflict is followed by disappearance of the symptom'.

Discussion

Lachman discussed the pros and cons of five types of theory relating to the psychosomatic disorders:

(1) the constitutional-vulnerability (weak-link) theories;
(2) the organ-response learning theories;
(3) stimulus-situation theories;
(4) emotional-reaction-pattern theories; and
(5) personality-profile theories.

However, he found little support for any of them with the exception of the organ-response learning theory.

Lachman noted that a study of the development of ulcers in rats had provided some basis for a genetic aetiology; thus giving some support to the 'weak-link' type theory.

We have already discussed aspects of personality-profile theory. As indicated above, Peters and Stern (1971) found no support for the 'specific-attitude hypothesis'. Many people, including GPs, hold that those who periodically suffer from tension and migraine headaches can be characterized by certain well-defined personality characteristics. However, as will be seen in Chapter 6, Phillips's (1976) study of headache patients failed to support this view.

While the earlier studies of Ax (1953) and Funkenstein (1955) appear to lend support to the stimulus-situation and the emotional-reaction-pattern theories, these studies have not been particularly well accepted. In reference to these two theories, Lachman noted that 'with few exceptions, the physiological reaction patterns of emotion are very similar in gross terms for a wide variety of differently named emotions and for different eliciting situations'.

We may summarize by noting that some support may be found for the weak-link-type theory. However, the evidence does not support either a stimulus-situation or personality-profile-type theory which predict that specific physiological reactions may be related to (1) specific emotional situations, and (2) different patterns of physiological reaction in emotion. That is, there is little or no reliable evidence that specific psychosomatic disorders are related to specific types of emotional stimulus conditions or emotional states. Finally, it has been difficult to find evidence supporting the personality-profile-type theory.

Lachman suggested that the organ-response theory was the most acceptable. He noted that there was ample 'evidence for a general paradigm of autonomic learning', and so followed an emotional or autonomic learning theory approach.

Emotional or autonomic learning theory

Lachman noted that his theory 'emphasizes the role of learning in the development of psychosomatic aberrations without minimizing the role of genetic factors or of nongenetic predisposing factors'.

He distinguished three types of psychosomatic phenomena:

(1) constructive psychosomatic reactions;

(2) destructive or pathological psychosomatic reactions; and

(3) psychosomatic diseases.

The first type of phenomenon is clearly adaptive in the sense of including reactions that help combat the development of some disorder. Lachman provided a number of examples, one being a 'reduction of internal haemorrhaging resulting from patterns of visceral vascontriction and peripheral dilation in response to emotional stimulation'.

The destructive type of psychosomatic reaction results from intense emotional stimulation that is persistent over time. Lachman noted that these reactions may sometimes be completely or partially reversible. The following examples of this type of psychosomatic reaction are given: hypertension, cardiac dysrhythmias, and asthmatic attacks.

The psychosomatic disease type of reaction involves actual tissue pathology. As Lachman noted, there is relatively permanent structural change of a maladaptive kind—duodenal ulcers, permanent cardiac dilation, or colonic abrasions resulting from physiological reactions to emotional stimulation are examples of psychosomatic diseases.

Lachman's central thesis was that: 'Emotional behaviour—intense internal reactions that initially in the history of the organism were aroused via receptor stimulation—may lead to conditions of chronic physiological activation or may produce more or less permanent structural changes—psychosomatic manifestations'.

He goes on to discuss the importance of classical conditioning, emotional redintegration, stimulus generalization, and the roles of symbolic stimuli and ideation in the emotional or autonomic learning process. *Classical conditioning* and *stimulus generalization* are dealt with in Chapter 15 (pp. 267–8), where the development of a conditioned emotion reaction (the case of Albert) is described. *Emotional redintegration* refers to the remembering of a total emotional situation on the basis of perceiving some element or part of that situation, or, through stimulus generalization, perceiving some stimulus or cue that is similar to some elements of the previously encountered emotional situation.

Symbolic stimuli (a form of semantic generalization) which represent some element of an emotional situation may be enough to trigger off an emotional reaction with its own concurrent physiological changes.

Ideation stresses that even the thought of an element of an emotional situation, or one that has been associated with an emotional situation, may be enough to lead to an intense emotional response.

The process involved in an emotional reaction may include aspects of a number of the factors described above. For example, a person while climbing a cliff alone falls and hurts himself. He has been exposed to the elements for a considerable period before help arrives and has become fearful and concerned over his survival. He reports later that the sight of a shape that was similar to that of a rock-formation on the cliff close to where he had fallen results in an intense feeling of fear with palpitations and disturbed respiration, etc.

Lachman also discussed the emotional learning that took place operantly through differential reinforcement (see Chapter 15 for a discussion of operant learning). The critical point here is that '*rewarded autonomic responses may be selectively learned*'.

Although not specifically mentioned by Lachman, observational learning or modelling may also be important in the development of the psychosomatic disorders (see Chapter 15 for a discussion of observational learning).

SOME PSYCHOSOMATIC CONDITIONS

We will limit our discussion to some cardiovascular, dermatological, and gastrointestinal conditions.

Some cardiovascular disorders

In his discussion of the psychosomatic cardiovascular disorders, Lachman includes psychosomatic coronary disease, essential hypertension, angina pectoris, and migraine. Since migraine headache is discussed in the next chapter on pain and in a later chapter on treatment, it will not be discussed here.

Birk (1973) has edited a book *Biofeedback: behavioural medicine* which provides discussions of a number of cardiovascular disorders. In it for example, Engel discusses the cardiac arrhythmias, while Weiss and Engel discuss the operant conditioning of heart rate in patients with premature ventricular contractions. Hypertension is discussed by Schwartz and Shapiro, and the biofeedback treatment of Raynaud's disease is discussed by Surwit.

Coronary disease

Lynch (1977), in a very readable book on cardiovascular conditions, showed that psychological factors associated with loneliness were very much related to the high death rate attributed to cardiovascular disease. He noted that 'an entire generation has been raised to believe that dieting, exercising, inoculations, and other forms of preventative care are *the* means to avoid disease and premature death. The idea that another crucial element influencing well-being is the ability to live together—to maintain human relationships—seems strangely "unscientific" to our age. Yet . . . loneliness and isolation can literally "break your heart"'. Lynch found that approximately 55 per cent of all deaths in America were attributable to cardiovascular disease, including strokes.

In commenting on the Framingham studies (begun in 1945) undertaken to determine the causes of heart diseases in America, Lynch pointed to the unreliability of some of the conclusions made. While the social structure of Framingham was an important variable, the results of the study, which had omitted the consideration of social and psychological variables, were overgeneralized to apply to communities vastly different from Framingham, areas in which an unstable family structure was the rule rather than the exception and where violence and crime were common.

Lynch found that the development of coronary heart disease seemed to be related to five factors:

(1) elevated blood pressure;
(2) elevated serum cholesterol;
(3) cigarette smoking;

(4) electrocardiographic evidence of left ventricular hypertrophy;
(5) glucose intolerance.

He noted that many inappropriate conclusions were drawn from the Framingham data which, in essence, led to the conclusion that emotional stress factors were unimportant in the development of coronary heart disease. The point made by Lynch was that relatively few stress factors existed in Framingham in that the divorce and crime rate were quite low, and 'all-in-all Framingham was a very peaceful and socially stable town'. Therefore it was difficult to implicate emotional stress factors in the development of heart disease with data drawn from such a community. Since that time, as pointed out by Lynch, emotional stress has been implicated in higher levels of serum cholesterol, elevated blood pressure, smoking, and obesity, and subsequent studies have led to the suspicion among medical scientists that social and psychological factors may not only significantly influence the course of heart disease—they may be the most important of all risk factors!'

Raynaud's disease

Raynaud's disease is defined as 'a functional disorder of the cardiovascular system: that is, it involves no observable organic pathology in its early stages. Its symptoms consist of intermittent, bilateral vasospasms of the hands, feet, and rarely the face, which can be elicited by cold stimulation and/or emotional stress. During an attack, the affected area usually goes through a three-stage colour change, first blanching, then turning cyanotic blue, and finally becoming bright red as the spasm is relieved and active hypermia sets in' (Birk 1973).

Jacobsen, Hackett, Surman, and Silverberg (1973) treated a patient with Raynaud's disease via hypnosis and operant techniques. The patient was trained to increase the temperature of his hands. He was successful in increasing his hand temperature by as much as 4.3 °C. There was also marked symptomatic improvement that was maintained at a seven-month follow-up. Blanchard and Haynes (1975) also reported the successful treatment of a patient with Raynaud's disease via biofeedback procedures. Hand temperatures were significantly increased from pre- to post-treatment. The authors reported that the actual feedback training was the most important part of the treatment and that the booster feedback training at follow-up periods of two, four, and seven months was fairly encouraging.

Hypertension

Schwartz and Shapiro (1973) noted that the treatment of hypertension via feedback procedures was successful only in regard to systolic blood pressure. Birk (1973) felt the relative lack of success of biofeedback in reducing diastolic blood pressure was probably due to 'the irreversible deteriorative anatomical changes that occur within the walls of blood vessels when hypertension has been long established'. In spite of this somewhat gloomy report,

Jacob, Kraemaer, and Agras (1977) who reviewed the literature on the relaxation treatment of hypertension, concluded that provided patients regularly practised relaxation, the clinical use of relaxation was promising. The authors cautioned however, that 'Although the clinical potential of relaxation therapy in hypertensive treatment seems well established, it should not be concluded that it can replace pharmacologic therapy'. Jacob *et al.* recommended that 'when an optimal blood pressure . . . [cannot] be obtained by medication alone, or when side effects from medication would make a reduction in dose desirable' relaxation treatment should be used to complement pharmacological treatment.

Blanchard and Miller (1977) have reviewed the psychological treatment of cardiovascular disease including hypertension, cardiac arrhythmias, coronary artery disease, and peripheral circulatory disease, including Raynaud's disease. Together with Surwit (1973), Blanchard and Miller feel that a viable psychological treatment for Raynaud's disease is temperature biofeedback. It is, however, pointed out that motivation is extremely important in carrying out biofeedback training. Attendance for formal treatment and the willingness to practise regularly at home are both important.

Blood-pressure feedback, electromyographic (EMG) feedback from the frontalis site, biofeedback of galvanic skin response (GSR), and systematic relaxation training were all found to be useful in the treatment of hypertension.

We turn now to a brief discussion of some skin conditions which may be influenced by emotional factors.

Some dermatological disorders

Many skin disorders may be affected by emotional factors, but those considered to be exclusively emotional in origin include dermatitis actifacta, trichotillomania, cutaneous hypochondriasis, and delusional symptoms referred to the skin (Knight 1979). Occasionally patients exhibiting other skin conditions are referred to the clinical psychologist or psychiatrist because emotional factors may be exacerbating the condition (e.g. hyperhydrosis) or interfering with treatment in some way (e.g. lichin planus, alopecia areata) in cases where viable medical treatment is available. Sometimes, general reassurance may be of some help to the patient suffering from a skin disorder in which emotional factors are significant. More frequently, the patient may feel quite inadequate and assertion therapy or social skills training may be recommended (see Chapter 15). The treatment of trichotillomania will illustrate some of the treatment procedures used in this area.

Trichotillomania

Trichotillomania or chronic hair-pulling may be considered as a serious problem for children, since the condition of the child's scalp can elicit teasing and ridicule from other children, which may lead to withdrawal and even absence from school. Obviously, it may be no less a problem for the adult whose appearance may be especially important if his job primarily involves interaction with other people. While in some cases social interaction may be a problem to begin with, in others the frequency and degree of interpersonal contact may decrease dramatically as a consequence of the patient's appearance.

There have been a number of recent reports on the behavioural treatment of trichotillomania (Evans 1976; Levin 1976; and McLaughlin and Nay 1975).

Evans (1976) treated a child who had begun hair pulling at ten months of age while in a cast after orthopaedic surgery. When treatment began at 8½ years of age, she was almost bald and her siblings and other children were habitually ridiculing her. Previous treatment efforts had included medication, ignoring her hair pulling, and reprimanding and shaming her. While her academic work was described as average, she was reported as quiet and withdrawn. Hair pulling occurred at least once daily. A home programme was developed which required minimal professional time. During the first phase the mother reinforced the child with a star (later to be exchanged for one cent) if she abstained from hair pulling for a designated period. If the child was observed in hair-pulling this contingency would result in five minutes *time-out* in the child's bedroom. After seven weeks the hair-pulling decreased to zero. After fourteen weeks phase two commenced in which the *reinforcement interval* was increased to one day. Following twelve weeks of phase two the programme was withdrawn. At the three-month follow up there was no evidence of a relapse and significant others were socially reinforcing the child for her appearance.

Levine (1976) treated a young man of 26 for trichotillomania using *covert sensitization* (see Chapter 16). Basically, after an explanation of the technique and the use of relaxation a situation was described in which the patient was pulling his hair. After imagining this situation, the patient was asked to imagine that he had pulled out part of his scalp which was leaking blood and hot pus. He was further asked to imagine being nauseous followed by vomiting. These aversive scenes were followed by *aversion-relief scenes* which were in contrast to the previous aversion scenes and involved situations in which the patient had no desire to engage in hair-pulling. After six weeks of treatment he was symptom-free and this condition was maintained at the three- and six-week follow-up. Additionally, impulses to pull his hair were absent. Levine stressed that the felt positive control experience by the patient was probably a very significant factor in treatment success.

McLaughlin and Nay (1975) treated a seventeen-year-old female who pulled both scalp hairs and eyelashes. Her symptoms which were of six years duration resulted in an absence of eyelashes and baldness over the front third of her scalp. She reported that when she was anxious her hair-pulling seemed to increase. The first step in treatment required the client to monitor her hair-pulling. Following this two-week 'baseline' period she was asked to place all hair pulled during the week in an envelope and to post it to the therapist. A contract between the client and therapist was drawn up which included the following steps: (1) when tense the client was to practise *systematic relaxation procedures*; (2) the client was to practice *self-reward* consisting of the imagination of 'one of a number of predetermined positive cognitions' such as imagining herself with normal hair; (3) the client was to use *response-cost* whenever she engaged in the to-be-extinguished behaviour. The response-cost involved the detailed recording of all the conditions, etc. associated with her hair-pulling. After eighteen weeks of treatment hair-pulling has decreased to zero and her hair had grown from nil to two inches in length. This progress was maintained at the three-month follow-up. Her hair length had increased, although her eyelash growth was still limited. As was true of Levine's client, McLaughlin and Nay (1975) reported that their client noted how positive she felt about achieving control during treatment. The client also indicated that the relaxation, response-cost, and the use of positive imagery were particularly helpful. Finally, McLaughlin and Nay stressed that a warm interpersonal relationship between therapist and client was a significant element in treatment success. Lachman (1972) discussed some of the other skin disorders such as neurodermatitis and urticaria.

Some gastrointestinal (alimentary tract) disorders

If one considers psychosomatic-type conditions of the alimentary tract then obesity, anorexia nervosa, pathological vomiting, duodenal ulcer, various types of colitis, gastritis, and chronic constipation and diarrhoea, etc., may be included.

Obesity

Obesity is a major health problem. A great deal of money is spent every year on special diets, slimming clubs, etc., by those attempting to lose weight. Many of those who lose weight fail to maintain the weight loss. The psychoanalytic approach associates problems of obesity and anorexia with the oral stage of development. However, there is little evidence of treatment success using the analytic method.

The behavioural approach focuses on the situational factors that lead to and maintain the overeating response. The importance of self-control is difficult to over-emphasize. However, since the self-control of obesity is discussed extensively in Chapter 19, limited space will be devoted to this treatment procedure here.

Leon (Leon 1976; Leon and Roth 1977) has provided us with two recent reviews of the literature on the aetiology, theory, and treatment of obesity. Leon and Roth outline Schachter's view on obesity, and discuss the research bearing on its validity. Basically, Schachter (1971) discovered that, in contrast to the findings with normal subjects, 'there is little correspondence between gastric motility and self-reports of hunger'. Schachter suggested that for the obese, eating seemed to be controlled by external rather than internal cues. He summarized his previous research by noting that 'eating by the obese seems unrelated to any internal, visceral state, but is determined by external food-relevant cues such as the sight, smell, and taste of food'. As noted by Leon and Roth, Schachter and his colleagues have more recently expanded the externality hypothesis 'to include externality as a general personality trait rather than a trait specific to eating behaviour'. Much of the research on obesity has involved college students and others who may be somewhat overweight, but would not necessarily be called obese. Leon and Roth felt that the term obese should be reserved for this individuals who were 50 per cent or more above ideal body weight; and they observed that conclusions regarding 'obese' people were difficult to make, since there had been varied definitions of 'obese' and because of the age, sex, and socio-economic differences between the different samples used.

After reviewing the pertinent studies Leon and Roth concluded that 'the support for Schachter's externality theory of obesity appears to be equivocal at best'. In addition, they noted that Stunkard and Fox's (1971) report did not support the idea that 'the obese are less sensitive than persons of normal weight to internal cues of hunger'. They then went on to discuss various other factors which had been related to obesity, including psychodynamic issues. The main conclusion from their review of the available evidence is that obesity cannot be considered as a unitary syndrome. They noted that research efforts would be more profitable if the type of obese person being studied were carefully specified.

Leon's (1976) report on the treatment of obesity basically concluded that behavioural modification techniques showed a great deal of promise. Traditional approaches were not considered very effective, while intestinal-bypass surgery could be dangerous, although it could produce significant reductions in weight. Leon stressed the importance of those behaviour techniques which placed emphasis on 'learning how to permanently change one's eating pattern'. Self-control procedures aimed at maintaining weight reduction are discussed in Chapter 19 of this book.

We turn now to discuss in some detail an interesting case of pathological vomiting.

Psychosomatic vomiting

Vomiting of emotional origin may occur as a psychological reaction to parental demands to eat more, in general, or more of a particular food. It may occur in adolescent girls who feel that they are overweight or may become overweight if they do not restrict their food intake. Many of these girls may either be classed as borderline anorexic or actual cases of anorexia nervosa. For approximately ten per cent of this latter group, the condition becomes fatal.

Perhaps the most dramatic, relatively recent, report on the psychological treatment of an alimentary tract disorder is that of Lang and Melamed (1969) who described their treatment of a case of pathological vomiting in a nine-month-old boy. This boy's life was actually in danger by the time psychological treatment has begun after a lack of success with other non-behavioural procedures. Lang and Melamed noted that 'clinical workers have described an apparently 'psychosomatic' vomiting in children which is generally accompanied by a ruminative re-chewing of the vomitus'. The condition is frequently interpreted analytically as a disturbance in the mother–child relationship. Lang and Melamed felt that emesis and rumination may be considered as learned habits and thus amenable to treatment via 'counterconditioning', since a number of studies had demonstrated that vomiting was a conditional response. However, apparently only one study (White and Taylor 1967) actually used conditioning procedures in the treatment of a case of ruminative vomiting. Electrical aversion conditioning was the actual treatment used by Lang and Melamed. The child had been hospitalized three times previously for persistent vomiting after eating, and a lack of weight gain. 'Vomiting was first noted during the fifth month, and increased in severity to the point where the patient vomited 10–15 minutes after each meal. This activity was often associated with vigorous thumb-sucking, placing fingers in his mouth, blotchiness of the face, and ruminating behaviour'. Difficult relationships between the child's mother and the maternal grandmother were reported during a number of weeks when the family were living with the grandparents. A marginal marital relationship was suggested by a social worker.

Despite various tests, including gastrointestinal fluoroscopy and an exploratory operation, no organic basis for the disorder was found. The use of special diets, antinauseants, etc., did not improve the child's condition. Neither the prevention of thumb sucking nor the provision of a close friendly one-to-one relationship was helpful.

From a weight of 17 pounds at 6 months of age, the patient's weight had fallen to 12 pounds at 9 months and a nasogastic pump was being used to feed him. 'The attending physician's clinical notes attest that conditioning procedures were applied as a last attempt, "in view of the fact that therapy until now has been unsuccessful and the life of the child is threatened by continuation of this behaviour"'.

Observation over two days indicated that within ten minutes after feeding the child reliably regurgitated most of his food. Lang and Melamed also monitored EMG activity from three sites related to the sequence of activities during vomiting. The monitoring indicated that accompanying the onset of vomiting were 'vigorous throat movements . . . in contrast with quiescent periods and periods where crying predominated'.

Sucking and vomiting behaviour were clearly differentiated on the EMG record. At the first indication of reverse peristalsis, shocks of 1-second duration and 1-second interpulse interval were administered until the vomiting response terminated.

In general, the nurse would signal as soon as she thought an emesis was beginning. If EMG confirmed the judgment, shock was delivered. A 3,000-cps tone was temporally coincident with each shock presentation. Each 1-hour session took place after feeding. After two sessions shock was rarely required. The infant would react to the shock by crying and the cessation of vomiting. By the third session only one or two brief presentations of shock were necessary to cause cessation of any vomiting sequence. By the sixth session the infant no longer vomited during the testing procedures. He would usually fall asleep towards the middle of the hour. . . . To vary the conditions under which learning would take place, thereby provoking for transfer of effects, the sessions were scheduled at different hours of the day, and while the infant was being held, playing on the floor, as well as lying on the bed. Nursing staff reported a progressive decrease in his ruminating and vomiting behaviour during the rest of the day and night, which paralleled the reduction observed across therapy sessions.

After three sessions, in which there was no occurrence of vomiting, the procedure was discontinued. While there was some spontaneous recovery two days later, three additional sessions successfully decreased the undesirable response and there was seen to be a steady increase in the child's weight, his activity level increased, and he exhibited a much greater interest in his environment 'enjoyed playroom experience, and smiled and reached out to be held by the nurse and other visitors'.

After a transition period, during which the mother took care of the child in the hospital, he was discharged, since he exhibited almost no ruminating behaviour. At one-month after discharge the child was found to be 21 pounds in weight and, other than slight anaemia, was fully recovered. An examination, 5 months after discharge, indicated that his appetite was good, there was no vomiting, and his weight had increased to 26 pounds. He was found to be alert and attentive. A year after treatment his parents were both pleased with their child's development and the doctor considered further treatment unnecessary.

Lang and Melamed raised a number of points about this case. For example, the antecedents of the disorder were not analysed, yet successful treatment was accomplished in an extremely short time—a little more than a week. Not only was there an absence of symptom substitution, but much pro-social behaviour such as smiling and an increased interest in his interpersonal environment took place, which seemed to substitute for the ruminating. Lang and Melamed stressed the importance of the EMG records:

which confirmed in an objective manner external observations of mouth and throat movements which seemed to precede emesis . . . [and they helped] . . . to specify those aspects of the response which were unique to the vomiting sequence, thus assuring that shock was never delivered following non-contingent behaviour. Finally, observation of the recordings during therapy probably reduced the latency of reinforcement, particularly during the early trials when the validity of external signs seemed less certain, and provided the clearest indicator of the end of the response when shock was promptly terminated.

Colitis

Lachman (1972) distinguished two main types of colitis (inflammation of the colon): (a) 'chronic ulcerative colitis, a persistent non-specific inflammatory and ulcerative condition of the colon . . . [and (b)] . . . mucous colitis, a less serious condition characterized by derangement of the motor activity and mucous-secreting activities of the colon'.

Susen (1978) reported on the treatment of a case of ulcerative colitis via conditioned relaxation. The 39-year-old female patient's condition was of four years duration. She had accepted a job as a department store cashier four years earlier, a job which she found much more difficult than she had expected. She reported symptoms of fatigue, abdominal pains, and diarrhoea. While this patient had been off work for about two weeks, after which she became more accustomed to the job, she still reported the same symptoms, and medication had not particularly helped. Susen noted that the 'illness followed a fluctuating course in which there were two-to-three-month periods of pain accompanied by bloody and slimy diarrhoea, separated by intervals without symptoms, which seldom lasted longer than two or three weeks'. The patient was apparently able to distract herself from the pain by doing housework, knitting, etc. No organic aetiology had been established.

Autogenic training with particular emphasis on abdominal relaxation was taught to the client. The client reported relaxation and warmth in the abdominal area after four weeks of such training. While the client had been monitoring her pain daily, she was not able to associate her treatment with the reduction of such pain. However, after being instructed to interrupt her non-treatment activities by practising relaxation, she was able to report after a five-week period of this treatment that her pain was being reduced on most occasions. During the last phase of treatment the patient was to think of and practise her relaxation immediately after she began to experience pain. Susen reported that the pain reduced both in intensity and duration and had disappeared after the twelfth week of treatment. Treatment effects were maintained at the one-year follow-up assessment.

Mitchell (1978) treated a 37-year-old male who suffered from spastic colitis. Mitchell notes that there are many terms which are applied to the group of gastrointestinal disorders whose aetiology is psychological. Example of these terms include intestinal neurosis, functional dyspepsia, colonic irritability, functional colitis, and spastic colitis. Mitchell placed spastic colitis in the same category as mucous colitis in terms of severity. He noted that the success of self-management techniques in treating other conditions suggested that these techniques might be used in the treatment of spastic colitis. The patient, on average, experienced three episodes of colitis per week. His condition was of four months duration and may have been precipitated by his enrolment as a part-time university student. Dietary and pharmaceutical treatment was reported as largely ineffective and had been discontinued prior to the behavioural treatment.

The patient had reported that he experienced some bouts of diarrhoea in high school before sitting examinations. He considered himself to be of a nervous disposition. Promotion required that he obtain an economics degree. Unfortunately, he was concerned over his ability to cope with both work and part-time university study. While he had done satisfactory academic work to date, he was considering prematurely terminating his studies.

The client was asked to monitor the number of attacks he experienced daily and to rate his level of muscle tension, and the frequency with which he experienced worry and other negative thoughts. Mitchell noted that an attack was defined as including abdominal cramps followed by diarrhoea. The rationale for the treatment was explained to the patient after the baseline data had been obtained. The treatment proper was divided into three stages. During Stage 1, 'the client was told that his colitis attacks were large precipitated by his own reactions of worry, tension and anxiety to events perceived as stressful in his everyday life, particularly academic-related activities and situations. The client was then trained to identify the overt and covert antecedents of tension and worry, using the events preceding his attacks in the previous three weeks as training material'.

Stage 2 consisted of two 30-minute and two 15-minute sessions of progressive muscle relaxation via audio tape over a three week period and a second three-week period during which the client was required to practise relaxation twice daily 'and to focus on reducing pre-attack tension and negative cognitions (worries, etc.)'. The client also, through the six weeks, used feedback monitor sheets by which he reviewed skill acquisition and practice.

Stage 3 included 'instruction in the procedure and application of . . . three techniques for the control of worry (thought stopping, time-out for worry, experiential focusing) and two for the management of fears and anxiety (self-desensitization, rational thinking). The aim was to increase the client's self-control over his thoughts, feelings and fantasies by providing him with the means for modifying or terminating when appropriate'.

Mitchell found that there was minimal modification of colitis attacks via self-recording and self-monitoring alone. However, the Stage 2 techniques of progressive relaxation and monitoring of skill acquisition and practice were effective in reducing muscle tension (57 per cent) and the frequency of attacks (41 per cent). The quality and frequency of intrusive cognition were not modified. The techniques used in Stage 3 were followed by considerable reductions in intrusive cognitions (59 per cent) and colitis attacks (85 per cent). A three-month follow-up indicated that there was no relapse, in that the reduction in intrusive cognitions were (60 per cent) and of colitis attacks (94 per cent).

Mitchell suggested that the combined treatment package of progressive muscle relaxation and cognitive control procedures was effective in reducing muscle tension and the worry and anxiety-type of intrusive cognitions which, in turn, resulted in a significant decrease in number of colitis attacks. He was careful to point out that while 'it is not suggested that training in self-management . . . effected a permanent cure . . . the training . . . enabled the client to modify and adapt more effectively both to his environment and his behaviour . . . and better able to cope with the academic situations perceived as stressful'.

SUMMARY

This chapter attempts to provide an overview of emotion and the psychosomatic disorders. The importance of arousal and cognitive labelling in emotion is first discussed emphasizing the importance of the autonomic nervous system, the brain stem reticular formation, and the limbic system in the regulation of the emotions. Some of the theories of the psychosomatic disorders are discussed. Most of the evidence is seen as favouring Lachman's (1972) autonomic learning theory view of the psychosomatic disorders. After an overview of Lachman's main views on the development of psychosomatic conditions, there is a selected discussion of some cardiovascular, dermatological, and gastrointestinal disorders. Relaxation training and various biofeedback procedures seem to be promising techniques in the treatment of many psychosomatic conditions. These and other treatment procedures are discussed in Part IV of this book.

The above discussion presents some of the research on selected psycho-somatic conditions. Space does not allow a more extensive discussion. However, anorexia nervosa is briefly discussed in Chapter 2. The interested reader may refer to Bachrach, Erwin, and Mohr (1965); Beumont, Beardwood, and Russell (1972); Bhanji and Thompson (1974); Button, Fransella, and Slade (1977); Pillay and Crisp (1977) for some representative articles on this condition.

Respiratory disorders such as asthma are not discussed. The interested reader may wish to consult some of the recent literature on this condition, such as: Creer, Weinberg, and Molk (1974); Khan (1977); Knapp and Wells (1978); and Philipp, Wilde, and Day (1972).

The next chapter is on pain, one of the most important subjects in the area of medicine, and includes a discussion of tension and migraine headache. Some case reports of these conditions are provided in Chapter 18.

6
The psychology of pain

Pleasure is the absence of pain
Cicero: *De finibus* II, ii

The study of pain is of great importance, particularly for the student of medicine, yet it is often inadequately covered in his training. Wexler (1976), who participated in an in-depth study of behavioural science programmes in medical education by writing detailed 'case studies' of nine major medical schools in the United States and Canada, had to conclude that only two of these nine major medical programmes paid any significant attention to the subject of pain. Wexler noted that 'If one used a well-defined model of the doctor's job as a guide to content, then all of the behavioural science groups should provide significant instruction in the study of pain.'

In the Netherlands, Groenman (1974) discussed behavioural science in the medical curriculum and reported that in the six-year medical programme, a multi-disciplinary study of pain was possible only as part of the fifth year of study, during half of which a student may choose various seminar programmes. The particular seminar on pain is of four weeks' duration and can include only 30 students per year. There is little or no evidence that the situation in the United Kingdom is any better (Rachman and Phillips 1975).

A recent British study (Vingoe 1979) which surveyed the attitude of third-year medical students to the inclusion of 24 topics in the clinical psychology course found that the subject of pain was extremely popular. In fact, the questionnaire item on pain had the highest discriminating value of the 24 items.

A number of recent books on pain are available (Bond 1979; Fordyce 1976; Melzack 1973; and Sternbach 1974). In addition, Liebeskind and Paul (1977) provide a recent review on psychological and physiological mechanisms of pain.

THE CONCEPT OF PAIN

While, like stress, pain can be discussed in terms of stimulus or response, the patient himself tends to think of his pain as feelings of distress.

As Livingstone (1953) has said 'Every feeling person knows from personal experience what pain is, yet scientists have found it extraordinarily difficult to agree on a satisfactory definition for it.'

Many would agree that pain may be usefully discussed in hedonistic terms involving feelings and emotions (Szasz 1957). Further, general agreement may be found about the effects of certain types of stimuli on the organism. Organisms tend to seek out or approach pleasurable stimuli and avoid or retreat from stimuli which cause pain. Through processes of learning, organisms may behave as if certain situations dispensed either pleasure or pain. To a great degree verbal labelling may suggest that a person or situation has negative (painful) characteristics. The nature of pain is certainly far from being simple. Its subjective characteristics are a function of the physiological characteristics of the particular individual, but, in addition, the sum total of past experience and the totality of the present situation in which the individual finds himself are modifying factors. Both the past experience and the present situation are probably largely social and psychological in nature.

Sternbach (1968) writing on pain from a psychophysiological point of view defined pain as 'an abstract concept which refers to (1) a personal, private sensation of hurt; (2) a harmful stimulus which signals current or impending tissue damage; (3) a pattern of responses which operate to protect the organism from harm. These responses can be described in terms which reflect certain concepts, i.e., in neurological, physiological, behavioural and affective languages.'

In his more clinically orientated text, Sternbach (1974) discussed somatogenic pain and psychogenic pain, and pointed out how difficult it was to make a clear differentiation between them. In Sternbach's view it was better to tell the patient that the pain experience was being described in physiological language and/or psychological language. Sternbach noted that there were practical advantages in applying this view to one's clinical work with pain patients, in that the treatment could be pursued in parallel. As is true in other areas within the health professions, it is frequently helpful to use the terms 'acute' and 'chronic' in reference to pain. Clearly, in most cases the occurrence of acute pain which results from a minor accident is of relatively little psychological interest. However, the consideration of chronic pain, whether assumed to be mainly somatogenic or psychogenic is of high priority.

TABLE 6.1
DETERMINANTS OF THE PAIN RESPONSE

1. Amount of physical damage	
2. Expectation	(Hill, Kornetsky, Flanary, and Winkler 1952)
3. Suggestion	(Hardy, Wolff, and Goodell 1952)
4. Level of anxiety	(Hardy, Wolff, and Goodell 1952)
5. Meaning of situation where injury occurs	(Beecher 1959)
6. Competing sensory stimuli	(Duncker 1937)
7. Other psychological variables	

(Modified from Melzack 1970)

Melzack (1970) also commented on the difficulty in defining pain. Traditionally, the 'concept of pain as a specific modality of cutaneous sensation has led to the psychological assumption that there is a one-to-one relationship between stimulus intensity and the intensity of pain experience'. However, much research evidence has shown that pain perception is determined by a multiplicity of factors. Table 6.1, based on Melzack's discussion of pain perception gives the determinants of the pain response. Melzack noted that pain perception was more than a function of the amount of physical damage inflicted on a person, and that since factors such as expectation, suggestion, etc., affected the total pain response, the quality and intensity of perceived pain were very much related to the brain activities underlying the various psychological processes.

If pain is thought of as only one of many sensory qualities or characteristics of stimulus objects that may be perceived, and further, if it is agreed that various central determinants of perception operate in people's everyday commerce with the external and internal environment, then it is not surprising that attitudes, expectancies, etc., as well as the total perceptual situation, affect responses to what may be consensually agreed as a painful stimulus. In general, then, a significant part of the pain response is referred to as the affective, psychological, or *reaction component* (Beecher 1959). Beecher refers to three general kinds of reaction to noxious stimulation: (1) skeletal muscle responses; (2) reactions mediated by the autonomic nervous system; and (3) the central nervous system processing of the original stimulation. Beecher stresses the importance of this central processing indicating 'that it can determine the presence or absence of suffering; it is an intimate part of the pain experience'. Thus, one may note that the reaction component of pain is that part of the total pain response that theoretically could be eliminated through the use of psychological methods.

INDIVIDUAL DIFFERENCES AND THEIR MEASUREMENT

Personality factors

When one considers the individual patient, factors such as personality and cultural background may be important in the perception of pain. For example, are extroverted people prone to have a higher tolerance for pain? In what way, if any, are the variables of neuroticism, hypochondriasis, or depression related to reported pain? A number of authors have attempted to relate Eysenck's dimensions of extroversion (E) and neuroticism (N) to pain tolerance. Levine, Tursky, and Nichols (1966) used a method of continually increasing the level of pain stimulation through an annular disc electrode placed on the dorsal surface of the forearm. This study was motivated by discrepant results obtained previously, in that Lynn and Eysenck (1961) found results supporting Eysenck's theory that extroversion and neuroticism would be directly and inversely related to pain tolerance respectively, while a study of Nichols and Tursky (1966) was unsuccessful in demonstrating a relationship between these Eysenckian variables and pain tolerance. Levine, Tursky, and Nichols (1966) used two methods of measuring pain tolerance, an 'unmotivated tolerance level', in which the subject had to indicate to the experimenter when he wished discontinuance of the stimulation, and a 'motivated tolerance level', in which the subject was motivated to allow a higher level of stimulation. A sensation threshold was determined and the difference between this threshold and the motivated and unmotivated pain tolerance levels obtained. Unfortunately, the various correlations between extroversion and neuroticism and these 'difference' measures failed to reach statistical significance. Davidson and McDougall (1969) were also interested in the relationship between extroversion and pain tolerance. Using a heat method of stimulation similar to that used by Lynn and Eysenck (1961) and a *cold-pressor test* of pain tolerance, they also failed to find any relationship between either extroversion or neuroticism and pain tolerance.

Thus, using thermal or electrical methods of experimental pain-stimulation, the relationship hypothesized by Eysenck between extroversion, neuroticism, and pain tolerance lacks firm experimental support. However Davidson and McDougall (1969) pointed out that the performance of their introverted subjects on the cold-pressor test was more variable than that of their extroverted counterparts and, therefore, the use of this test should be considered with caution. The author feels that the ability of the experimenter to control the pain stimulus is very important, and, as pointed out in other areas such as treatment via aversion therapy, the electrical method is far superior (Rachman 1965). It may be, as suggested by Sternbach (1968) that one cannot entirely equate experimental and clinical pain.

Possibly, pain patients on opposite ends of the extroversion or neuroticism continuum respond differentially to their pain. Obviously the difficulty in studying the effect of personality factors on pain tolerance in patients is greater, in that the inter-patient variability of the reaction component of pain is so high. However, a partial test of the importance of personality variables on pain response would be to demonstrate a differential response to, or demand for, treatment by patients significantly different on various personality measures. While cause and effect cannot be established, Bond's work on female cancer patients (Bond and Pearson 1969) reported on by Sternbach (1974) established that advanced cancer patients with pain were more neurotic that those without pain. In addition, while the introverted, neurotic women did not receive analgesics, the extroverted neurotic women did. Sternbach also reports on the Woodforde and Mersky (1972) article on a study of 43 chronic pain patients, 27 of whom were classed as somatogenic, and the remainder as psychogenic. While the total group obtained significantly higher N scores than normals, they were not different from other type patients who had also been referred to psychiatrists. However, no differences were found on N or E between the two subgroups of chronic pain patients.

Phillips (1976) selected a subsample of headache patients from a sample chosen randomly from the register of a British general practice unit and evaluated their scores on the extroversion, neuroticism, psychoticism, and lie scales of the Eysenck Personality Questionnaire (EPQ) (Eysenck and Eysenck 1976). She found that the scores of this group did not differ from that of their controls, the normative groups on the EPQ. However, when she divided the tension headache group into those who received high and those who received low amounts of medication, it was found that the high medication group obtained higher, but not significantly higher extroversion and neuroticism scores. This finding lends little support to Eysenck's hypothesis regarding neuroticism and extroversion. Phillips reasoned that the stereotypic view of headache sufferers held by doctors and neurologists was not supported by the data obtained on a more representative sample of headache sufferers in the general population.

Klusman (1975) obtained measures of fear and anxiety before and after a sample of mothers attended classes on childbirth and child care. The classes were found to be effective in reducing 'fears for baby' and 'irritability and tension' to a significant degree. 'Anxiety level was found to exert a significant effect on self-ratings of pain during the transition stage of labour.' The conclusion was made that anxiety enhances the perception of pain.

Thus, in summary, the evidence suggests that pain patients are more anxious or neurotic. However, they are no more neurotic than those patients referred for psychiatric consultation. In reference to the extroversion dimension, there appears to be little evidence for Eysenck's hypothesis that extroverts have a higher threshold for pain, although they may tend to complain more about their pain.

Sternbach (1974) described his use of the MMPI in the assessment of pain patients and, of great value in the treatment process, discussed the analysis of personality dynamics. Perhaps the main thrust of his discussion here is the various interactions of the MMPI scales making up the so-called 'neurotic triad', i.e. hypochondriasis (Scale I), depression (Scale 2), and hysteria (Scale 3). Sternbach attempted to make a case for the hypothesis that patients who demonstrate psychogenic pain tend to have a greater degree of hypochondriacal symptomatology relative to depressive features, i.e. suggesting that pain symptomatology may substitute for depression. On the other hand, he suggested that in psychosomatic patients without pain, that depression may be higher relative to hypochondriacal symptomatology. Sternbach reported on the Pilling, Brannick, and Swenson (1967) study which involved close to 600 patients seen at the Mayo Clinic for psychogenic pain and other psychosomatic symptoms. Essentially, a comparison between the pain and non-pain patients was carried out using a clinical interview, a checklist, and the MMPI. The results of the comparison supported the hypothesis in that Pilling *et al.* were able to conclude that 'the pain patients have significantly more hypochondriasis than those with physical symptoms other than pain . . . [Apparently,] pain may be substituted for feelings of anxiety and depression, in that pain as a symptom may be less distressing than these other feelings.'

However, from the evidence reviewed here it is not clear whether chronic pain magnifies the degree of neuroticism or anxiety already present prior to the onset of chronic pain or whether the various criteria for measuring general post-operational stress (see Chapter 4), including pain, are significantly heightened in those whose general personality structure includes a high neurotic component (trait anxiety) before chronic pain onset. While it would be helpful to have more information relating to this question, whether it is trait anxiety or state anxiety that is the major component of the global pain response, the basic treatment plan would not be affected. However, if, for example, trait anxiety was discovered to be a significant component then one would expect the treatment to be less successful.

Cultural factors

Wolff and Langley (1968) have provided us with a review on the cultural factors associated with the pain response and noted the relative lack of published reports in the anthropological literature and the failure of pharmacological studies to take into account the cultural and psychosocial characteristics of patients. A number of studies which used the radiant heat method of pain stimulation suffered from the fact that they failed to control for skin temperature. Mersky and Spear (1964) found that the differential pain reactions of white versus Afro-Asian male medical students were non-significant. A study by Sternbach and Tursky (1965) which investigated the pain response and palmar skin potentials to repeated strong electric shocks in four ethnic housewife groups of Yankee, Irish, Jewish, and Italian parentage was also summarized by Wolff and Langley. Sternbach (1968) noted that in carrying out this study (Sternbach and Tursky 1965) they were following Zborowski's (1952) report based on interviews of surgical patients who were of the same ethnic backgrounds. Sternbach (1968) indicated that Zborowski's findings were essentially replicated in that it was found that 'Old Americans† (Yankees) have a phlegmatic, matter-of-fact, doctor-helping orientation; Jews express a concern for the meaning and implications of the pain and distrust palliatives; the Italians express a desire for immediate pain relief.' Since Zborowski's (1952) research is probably considered the best of its kind available and because he has since produced a

† According to Zborowski (1969, p. 6) 'The term *Old American* is used to refer to patients of Anglo-Saxon origin, usually of protestant creed, whose ancestors have dwelt in the United States for more than three generations . . . Old American denotes the social group that seems to set the cultural model of our society as reflected in its values and structure.'

book discussing the cultural factors relating to the expression of pain, Zborowski (1969), an overview of his investigations will be presented here.

During the exploratory phase of Zborowski's research doctors were interviewed whose practice included a high proportion of three ethnic minorities: Irish, Italians, and Jewish patients. The doctors noted that both Italian and Jewish patients tended to exaggerate their pain and were more emotional than other ethnic groups, while those of Anglo-Saxon background (Old Americans) had a more accepting attitude to pain, and the Irish were found to be more stolid in their approach to pain. It was noted that the Old Americans were selected because their attitudes and behaviour patterns represented those of the majority of Americans. Consequently, the four groups of male patients selected for intensive study of their pain responses were of Irish, Italian, Jewish, and Old American origin. Zborowski noted that those patients served as cultural informants during informal, non-structured recorded interviews. Data collected during these interviews were supplemented and 'cross-validated' by obtaining information from family members, doctors, and nurses. In view of the fact that different types of pain response tend to be related to different underlying pathology, patients of the same diagnoses but different cultural backgrounds were studied in order to control for this important variable. In addition, those with both different diagnoses and different cultural background were studied.

A structural questionnaire was administered to another group of patients, the items of which had been taken from the interviews previously completed. These questionnaires were then subjected to statistical analyses. The possible biasing effects of the fact that the patients were male patients of the lower-middle and lower classes were pointed out by Zborowski (1969). Many of the observations made by doctors in the course of their contact with patients of these different ethnic groups were verified by the statistical analyses of the questionnaire. For example, the Italians and Jewish patients tended to be more emotional than the Old Americans when experiencing and expressing pain. While the Italians and Jewish tended to emphasize or heighten their perception of pain the Irish and Old Americans tended to de-emphasize it. Anxiety and worry were most frequently expressed by the Jewish patients who were concerned about the meaning or significance of the pain and were future-orientated. In contrast, the Old Americans tended to externalize their pain and tended to 'suffer alone'. The Italian group were quite present-orientated and wanted immediate pain relief. While education and socio-economic status were unrelated to the pain patient's tendency to consult his doctor upon the perception of pain, the particular attitude toward the doctor seemed to be strongly related to the patient's cultural background. The Irish and Old Americans appeared to be confident of their doctor's ability to treat them compared to the relative distrust of their doctor held by the Italian and Jewish patients. It was also reported that in spite of the high degree of worry expressed by the Irish, they tended to provide vague descriptions of their pain, in contrast to the Old Americans who were precise in their comments.

The analysis of the questionnaire completed by that group of patients in which the nature of the pathology was kept constant, revealed that the Irish and the Old Americans considered as one group, compared to the Italian and Jewish patients together, tended to show their pain less frequently. The Italian and Jewish patients tended to be much more emotional and dramatic. Thus, Zborowski noted that while the nature of the pathology plays a major role in a patient's response to pain, 'the cultural background of the individual appears to be most important, if not the determining factor in shaping his behaviour in pain and illness.' In support of the importance of cultural variables in the experience of pain, Zborowski quotes from Tursky and Sternbach (1967) who assessed physiological responses of Yankee, Irish, Italian, and Jewish housewives. Resting mean heart rate, palmar skin resistance, and skin potential levels were significantly correlated to pain thresholds. In addition, Sternbach (1968) noted that: 'The differences among the groups in physiological activity seemed to parallel the culturally acquired attitudinal sets towards pain.'

After reviewing the experimental studies which have been concerned with the effect of ethnic background on the pain response, Wolff and Langley (1968) concluded that 'cultural factors in terms of attitudinal variables, whether explicit or implicit, do indeed exert significant influences on pain perception'. Wolff and Langley also drew attention to two of Zborowski's most important conclusions, which are really behavioural principles that apply to many situations in addition to those of pain. These conclusions are: '(1) similar reactions to pain demonstrated by members of different ethnocultural groups do not necessarily reflect similar attitudes to pain, and (2) reactive patterns similar in terms of their manifestations may have different functions in different cultures.' Finally, discussing the work of Opler (1961) who had noted the differential behaviour of matched male schizophrenic groups who differed in ethnic background, the recommendation was made that 'any attempt to delineate cultural factors in the pain response should be made within the wider context of cultural attitudes toward sickness and health'.

In concluding this section on personality and cultural factors the reader is reminded of the discussion on methods of coping with conflict and stress, in the last section of Chapter 4. In particular the discussion concerning the reactions to frustration and the locus of control variable is recommended. We turn now to a brief discussion of the placebo effect.

The placebo effect

The placebo effect usually refers to the tendency to respond to an inactive medication as if it were, in fact, physiologically active. In double-blind studies, which are typically carried out to ascertain the effects of a new drug, a placebo group is used in order to control for the non-specific factors in the situation. All of the implicit, non-defined factors common to the drug group and the placebo group are implicated in the placebo effect. In the double-blind procedure, it is important to recall that neither patient nor any of the staff who deal directly with the patient are aware of which patients have been administered the active drug or which patients have been administered the inactive medication. It is clear that in the normal doctor–patient relationship, in which a drug may be prescribed, that factors such as expectation and suggestion, degree of rapport between doctor and patient, etc., have an influence on the patient's perception of the potency and general value of the drug in diminishing or alleviating the patient's symptoms.

The use of the term *placebo effect* has, of course, been extended far beyond its reference to an inactive medication to include various forms of psychological treatment in which drugs are frequently not prescribed. Many of the uncontrolled variables in psychotherapy research might be subsumed under the term placebo. Shapiro and Morris (1978) noted that 'In psychotherapy research, the placebo has become synonymous with the search for the appropriate control group against which therapies are compared'. The most recent comprehensive review of the placebo effect in medical and psychological treatment is that provided by Shapiro and Morris, while Fish (1973) has produced a book *Placebo therapy*, which emphasizes the active implementation of 'non-specific' factors in various psychological therapies.

Comaroff (1976) has written a very interesting sociological analysis of the doctor as a placebo prescriber in general practice. The data was gathered via open-ended interviews in a variety of medical settings in South Wales. Comaroff concluded her report by noting that 'placebo use is to be seen primarily as a function of the way in which doctors have come to use the prescription, and its attendant ritual to solve fundamental problems inherent in their social situation and in their relations with their patients'.

Shapiro and Morris proposed the following definition: 'A *placebo* is defined as any therapy or component of therapy that is deliberately used for its nonspecific, psychological, or psychophysiological effect, or that is used for its presumed specific effect, but is without specific activity for the condition being treated'.

There has been a widespread notion among doctors and others that patients could be differentiated into *placebo-reactors* and non-placebo reactor (i.e. that 'placebo-reactiveness' was, in fact, a personality trait, being expressed in varied situations and remaining an enduring mode of response). However, as noted by Evans (1969) there 'is no consensus about the existence of a "placebo reactor"—an individual who responds consistently to placebo in a variety of situations'. Evans carried out an interesting study to test the widely held believe that the placebo response is a special characteristic of suggestibility or hypnotizability. This belief was not supported in that there were no strong relationships between placebo response and suggestibility or hypnotizability. Shapiro and Morris also concluded that the concept of a consistent placebo-reactor is not supported by the evidence.

The importance of the doctor's or psychologist's attitude in treatment cannot be overstressed. If one considers the patient's expectation regarding treatment to be an important aspect of the placebo effect, then one must also consider the expectations of the therapist, which, if not verbalized, may nevertheless be communicated to the patient via non-verbal channels. Thus, for example, if a doctor does not have much faith in the mode of treatment he is using, yet remains 'silent' about this, the patient may 'sense' the doctor's attitude which may very well decrease the probability that treatment will be effective and result in a 'negative placebo effect' (see Shapiro and Morris (1978) pp. 388–30). On the other hand, if the therapist has positive expectations or beliefs regarding the effectiveness of a particular treatment, this may be instrumental in maximizing a positive placebo effect which will contribute to a successful outcome.

Before discussing treatment methods we will briefly consider the measurement of the pain response in the clinical setting.

Measurement of the pain response

As is true in other areas of measurement, the assessment of the pain response may vary from the use of a simple self-rating scale to a fairly complex measurement device.

Bond and Pilowski (1966) used a simple graphic rating scale (a ten centimetre line) for patient self-recording of pain. The line is anchored with the statement 'I have no pain at all' at the exteme left and the statement 'My pain is as bad as it could possibly be' at the extreme right of the line. The patient simply makes a mark on the line corresponding to the intensity of his pain.

Another example of a self-rating scale is that used by Sternbach (1974) in his pain clinic. Sternbach asked his patients to estimate their own pain by marking a point on a line, marked off from 0 to 100 to form a subjective scale. However, Sternbach went further by using a tourniquet on the patient's non-dominant arm to produce ischaemic pain. This procedure was used to obtain three measures of pain response. First, the patient was asked to say when the tourniquet or ischaemic pain matched his current clinical pain level. Secondly, the patient was asked to match the degree of ischaemic pain with his worst clinical pain. Thirdly, Sternbach obtained a maximum tolerance level by asking the patient to report when he could no longer stand the ischaemic pain produced in the tourniquet test. Sternbach found that the discrepancy between the subjective self-rating of pain and the tourniquet-matched current clinical pain level to be important in his assessment of the patient. For example, if a patient's subjective self-report of pain was in the severe range, but he indicated that the ischaemic pain matched his current clinical pain level when it was in the slight range, Sternbach might consider the difference between these two measures to be the amount of 'neurotic overlay' or to demonstrate communication difficulties. Sternbach was able to assess the range of ischaemic pain response by referring to the average latency of the responding of a specific category of pain patients of which the patient currently being assessed was a member. For example, Sternbach indicated that the average maximum tolerance time for patients with low-back pain is 7 minutes. Sternbach's use of the MMPI to assess personality factors has already been mentioned above.

Melzack (1975) used a simple 5-point self-rating scale on the McGill Home Recording Card. Graham (1975) in his report on two cases of migraine headache had patients use a home recording chart, which allowed the reporting of the frequency, intensity, and duration of migraine attacks. In addition, the patient reported if any warning signals or auras were experienced. Andreychuk and Skriver (1975) made use of a 'headache index' based on self-report in their study of migraine patients. An example of a 'daily pain record chart' (Vingoe and Lewis 1979) is seen below in Table 6.2, followed by the instructions that accompany the chart (Table 6.3).

TABLE 6.2

DAILY RECORD CHART

NAME: ....

DATE: ....

	(A) Morning	(B) Afternoon	(C) Evening
1. Sleep last night.*			
2. Situation provoking headache			
3. Prior warning of headache			
4. Time of onset			
5. Intensity +			
6. Duration of headache			
7. Medication taken: Name, amount, time taken			
8. Location of headache			

(Pain intensity scale modified from Melzack 1970).

+ **Pain intensity scale**
1. No pain
2. Extremely mild pain
3. Mild pain
4. Discomforting pain
5. Distressing pain
6. Horrible pain
7. Excrutiating pain

* **Sleep scale**
1. Excellent
2. Very good
3. Good
4. Neither particularly good or bad
5. Poor
6. Very poor
7. Extremely poor

Please note

If you find you do not have sufficient space to complete your answer in any box, please turn the chart over and indicate which box you wish to extend. To do this merely note if the box is (A), (B), or (C) and which number it is, i.e. 1–8.

For example, if you find you do not have enough room to write the situation that provoked the headache you had in the afternoon, write (B) 2, and finish describing the situation.

TABLE 6.3

Home recording chart instructions

Please indicate on the recording chart quality of sleep the previous night, the situation provoking the headache, any prior warning which indicated the onset of a headache, the time of onset, the intensity of the headache, the duration of the headache, the name, time, and amount of medication taken, if any, and the specific location of the headache. Each of these variables will be explained further below.

(A) *Sleep last night*

For this a scale has been constructed from 1 to 7. Would you please place in the box the number of the statement that most closely describes your previous night's sleep.

1. Excellent.
2. Very good.
3. Good.
4. Neither particularly good or bad.
5. Poor.
6. Very poor.
7. Extremely poor.

(B) *Situation provoking headache*

This category includes any situations that you consider to have triggered off your headache: an example being—going shopping and forgetting your shopping list.

(C) *Prior warning of headache*

This category includes any experiences that you find occurring before getting a headache. An example could be dizziness, 'spots before the eyes', etc.

(D) *Time of onset*

Please indicate as accurately as possible the exact time of the onset of your headache.

(E) *Intensity*

For this variable a scale has been constructed ranging from 1 to 7. This can be seen next to the daily recording chart. Please indicate the intensity of your pain by placing the number of the descriptive statement that most adequately describes your pain.

(F) *Duration of headache*

Please indicate the diration of your headache as accurately as possible.

(G) *Medication taken*

Please note the name of any medication you have taken, the amount in mg and the time you took this medication.

(H) *Location of headache*

Finally, could you indicate the location of your headache as accurately as possible. Could you also please indicate if it feels external (E), internal (I), or both (E) and (I).

Thank you for completing this chart. Could you please remember not only to fill this in daily, but, where appropriate, in the morning, afternoon, and evening. Please try not to rely on memory, e.g. by filling all the chart in during the evening. It is important that the information is accurate. The accuracy of your information in terms of increasing the effectiveness of the treatment is most important.

Thank you for your co-operation.

In order to assess a wide range of painful conditions, the McGill–Melzack 'pain questionnaire' (Melzack 1975) may be used, which enables the verbal descriptions of pain to be placed into sensory, affective, and evaluative categories. Melzack notes that the three major measures obtained from the questionnaire are: (1) a pain rating index; (2) number of descriptive words chosen; and (3) the present pain intensity based on a five-point scale. The scale appears to be an objective and reliable instrument for assessing the degree and nature of pain in a clinical setting and is of great value in assessing the degree of change in subjective pain after treatment. A report (Melzack and Perry 1975) which utilized this scale in a comparative treatment study of chronic pain patients is discussed in Chapter 17.

We turn now to a discussion of the treatment of chronic pain. However, since a number of interesting treatment reports have used hypnosis and biofeedback, these reports are discussed in the later chapters which discuss these techniques in some detail.

TREATMENT OF PAIN

Chronic pain is one of the most serious problems within the health service. While pain has to a large extent been approached from a physical point of view, more and more psychologists and others interested in psychological approaches to pain, are forming pain clinics in which the psychological aspects of pain are considered and various psychological approaches to pain control are instigated. Baker and Mersky (1967) reported on the problem of pain in a British general practice setting. They studied 276 patients (131 males and 145 females) over a four-week period and found that more women than men reported pain. The reporting of pain was unrelated to age, and the percentage of patients reporting pain were similar to that found in psychiatric work. However, when pain was categorized as mild, medium, or severe, relatively more women were in the severe category, and those reporting severe pain tended to be older. There was a lack of relationship of severity of pain with retirement, shift work, or civil status, and no difference was found between those women employed outside the home and those who were full-time housewives. They recommend that pain should never be diagnosed as psychogenic solely by the elimination of organic aetiology. Evidence for psychiatric illness should be present. Secondly, so-called 'bizarre' descriptions of organically-based pain in which unusual metaphors and similes are used may be as much associated with the severity of pain as with psychological aetiology.

Baker and Mersky noted that 'pain of psychological origin does tend to involve more regions of the body than pain which is mainly due to organic disease, and it is most often continuous during the day, and fails to keep the patient awake at night'. Headache is more often put down to psychological factors than any other cause, in fact, the commonest first sign of pain involves the head, and included 30 per cent of those patients in this study who reported pain. Thus pain, especially headache, is a frequent sign of psychological disturbance. Obviously, chronic pain has a varied aetiology: rheumatoid-arthritis, cancer, pain from degerative conditions, phantom-limb pain, and so forth.

As indicated above, however, more pain clinics are being developed, particularly in the United States, to attempt to solve some of these problems (Sternbach 1974). The problem of pain is not only treated by trying either to reduce the amount of pain, or in some cases to eliminate it, but also by helping some patients to live with the unavoidable pain that they have. Frequently, by the time many of these patients reach the psychologically orientated pain clinic, they have been well conditioned to a passive, patient role. They have been to many doctors, taken many drugs, had a number of operations, have been unemployed from time to time, and there may be obvious psychological problems. One of them being a dependence on drugs and a demand for more. Thus, frequently one of the first problems is to re-orientate the patient and the significant others around him to a more psychological view of pain and its management.

The majority of techniques used to treat pain are described elsewhere in this book. Therefore, the main purpose of this section on treatment will be to discuss the principal therapeutic procedures not discussed elsewhere and to present some of the research findings on the treatment of pain.

It has already been pointed out that it is the reactive component of the total pain response that is modifiable via psychological procedures. While personality factors such as trait anxiety, as well as situational factors need to be taken into account (see Table 6.1), a number of treatment procedures may be helpful in reducing the reactive component of the pain reponse. Figure 6.1 shows some of these techniques. All of these techniques may lead to a similar condition of relaxed wakefulness in the individual. Certainly subjective reports from individuals exposed to these procedures would suggest that relaxation is a common component. All of these methods would involve the lowering of the general arousal level of the patient.

The discussion so far has suggested that the reactive component of pain is determined by a number of different factors. In addition, it has been suggested that relaxation may be a common aspect of many treatment procedures. However, one must not forget the obvious, that there are many kinds of pain. A toothache, for example, feels quite different from gastro-intestinal pain. A recent study, using an objective pain questionnaire, has found, moreover, that a specific constellation of verbal descriptors is associated with eight pain categories (Dubuisson and Melzack 1976). These pain syndromes are as follows: menstrual pain, arthritic pain, labour pain, disc disease pain, toothache pain, cancer pain, phantom limb pain, and post-herpetic pain. Even if many procedures are similar, somewhat different techniques may be used to treat them depending upon the nature of the pain.

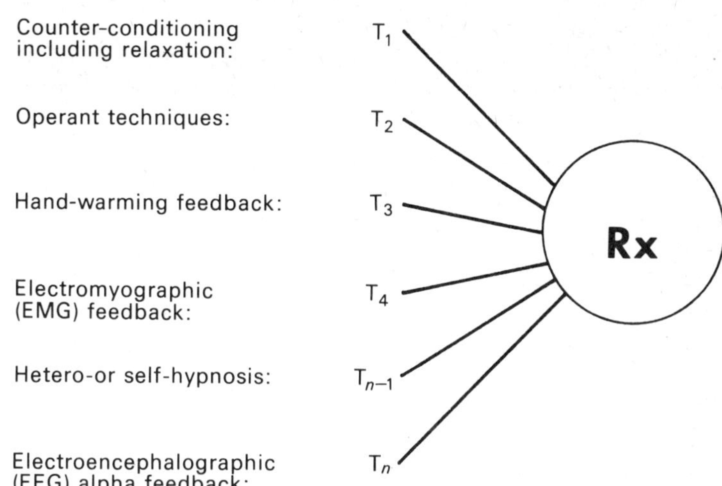

Fig. 6.1. Some potential procedures in the treatment of pain. The Ts in the figure refer to different treatment procedures, while Rx refers to the reduction of a specific type of pain (x), which in some instances may equally occur in response to different treatment strategies. It should be noted, however, that some techniques may be used for specific pain syndromes (e.g. hand-warming for migraine), whereas other techniques may be used more generally (e.g. relaxation and operant procedures) may be used for varying types of pain.

Patients may be unclear about the source of pain. For example, a patient may confuse a severe toothache with migraine, or even believe that it results from a subarachnoid haemorrhage. Pain may be felt in an area some distance from the actual lesion, a phenomenon known as *referred pain*. Obviously, consultation with a neurologist or other medical specialist is important in establishing a diagnosis.

Two relatively rare conditions involving pain should be mentioned in passing. One concerns cases of *insensitivity to pain* in situations which would evoke pain in the normal person, while the other concerns the feeling of pain in which there is an apparent lack of stimulus for pain (i.e. *phantom-limb pain*). A number of reports of congenital insensitivity to pain may be found in the literature. Kane, Downe, Marcott, and Parex-Reyes (1968) found that forty-five cases had been seriously reported, but inconsistent neurological findings related to these cases had been the rule. In addition, Rapoport (1969) indicated that there is a lack of consensus about the classification of patients with sensory deficits. Sternbach (1968) devoted a chapter to each of these rare conditions.

Referring to Figure 6.1, it may be noted that the counter-conditioning procedure is discussed in Chapter 15 while self-hypnosis, heterohypnosis and EEG alpha biofeedback are discussed in Chapters 17 and 18, together with some studies involving hypnotic and biofeedback procedures in the treatment of pain. The concept of counter-conditioning is discussed in reference to the treatment of phobic and anxiety states. The basic principles indicate that if one is able to develop a condition or state in an individual which is antagonistic to aspects of the reactive component, such as anxiety, while that person is in the presence of pain-evoking cues, then the total pain response will be decreased. Basically, the experience of relaxation, feelings of pleasure, etc., are incompatible with psychological pain. See Fig. 6.2 for the paradigm of counter-conditioning in reference to the treatment of pain.

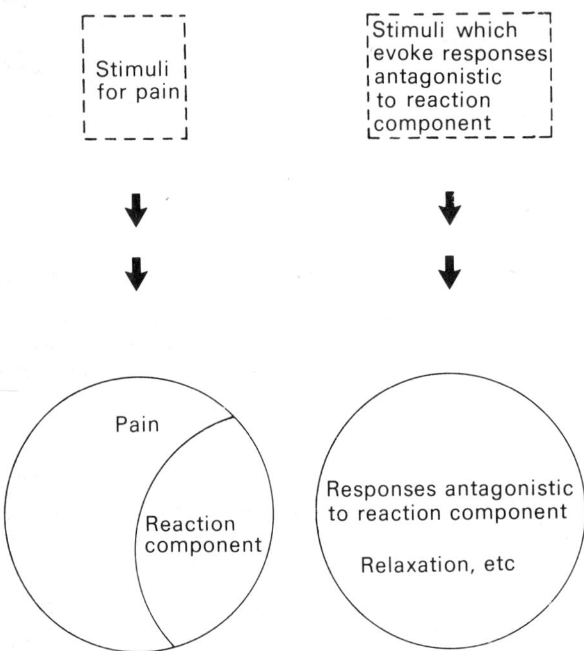

Fig. 6.2. Basic paradigm for the modification of the pain response by counter-conditioning.

Relaxation

McKechnie (1975) treated a young male patient who exhibited phantom-limb pain resulting from an amputation of his right arm owing to injuries sustained in a motor accident. Some weeks after he had been fitted with an artificial limb he began experiencing pain, which was more severe at night. The pain and some sensation in his right 'phantom' fingers was reported as 'fairly stable over the nine-and-a-half years since the artifical limb was fitted'. The patient reported the following symptoms, which had not been relieved by tranquillizers: phantom limb pain, initial insomnia, excessive smoking. An aggressive incident with his young son was instrumental in motivating him to seek help. McKechnie taught the patient to relax by asking him to imagine making a fist with his phantom hand as part of the typical Jacobson relaxation procedure (see Chapter 15). After the patient had reported an absence of pain, he was required to practise relaxation at home. There was a lack of pain for up to an hour after the completion of the active relaxation exercises. After two months he was no longer troubled by insomnia. The six-month follow-up revealed that the use of the relaxation technique allowed him pain-free periods of up to one hour, and a relaxed sleep. In addition, his cigarette consumption had been reduced by 75 per cent.

The operant approach

Operant procedures (see Chapter 15) have been used extensively by Fordyce and his colleagues (Fordyce, Fowler, and Dehateur 1968; Fordyce 1976).

The operant approach involves an assessment of the reinforcements which are maintaining the pain behaviour. Therefore, response by others, particularly significant others, to the overt pain behaviour are analysed in order to determine the consequences of overt complaints regarding pain. The typical responses to pain complaints by hospital staff are attention, solicitude, and increased administration of sedatives and analgesics. Having determined that the reported pain is not associated with any as-yet-undiscovered organic pathology, one is then in a position to modify the consequences of the reported pain and expressions of discomfort. Rather than providing extra attention and solicitude to complaints of discomfort, one can provide extra attention for behavioural responses which are antagonistic to the expression of pain. If this type of differential operant reinforcement programme were carried out, it would be expected that a gradual decrease in reports of discomfort and pain and a concomitant increase in reports indicating relative well-being would be observed.

Fordyce *et al.* (1968) report a case study using the operant approach with a married woman who complained of constant low-back pain, which resulted in an increasing inability to complete her housework. The patient reported that her back-pain increased when she engaged in any activity. She had had an herniated disc removed, and later a lumbosacral spine fusion was carried out, after which an examination failed to reveal any neurological deficit.

An operant programme was established in which treatment staff were to be socially unresponsive to complaints of pain and discomfort. On the other hand, when the patient engaged in any activity the staff were to provide positive reinforcement (social interest and praise). Increased reinforcement was contingent on increased levels of activity. Rather than receiving medication on demand, she received it on an interval schedule (see Chapter 15). Consequent upon a significant increase in her activity level, the narcotic content of her medication was decreased and then eliminated without her knowledge. An occupational therapy task was provided which demanded increased movement of her limbs. In addition, she was required to increase her walking. As Fordyce noted, the 'immediate reinforcers for the walking task were rest upon completion, social attention and praise from ward personnel both during and following her striding around the ward, and her own record, which she could observe herself and show to others'. The patient was required to monitor her scheduled and unscheduled activities and their duration. In order to decrease the possibility of relapse upon discharge, the patient's husband had been required to participate in the programme, and when the patient was at home he provided differential reinforcement and added activities to his wife's schedule. While baseline data on home non-reclining activity was about two hours daily, after treatment this rose to approximately twelve hours per day. The previous complaints of pain were reported as virtually disappeared after eight weeks of comprehensive care.

The two remaining techniques to be discussed in this chapter (i.e. handwarming feedback and EMG feedback) have typically been used to treat migraine and tension headaches respectively. While these two types of headache have historically been separated, there are cases in which symptoms of migraine may be reported by patients diagnosed as having tension headaches, and vice-versa (Bakal and Kaganov 1977).

Handwarming and migraine headache

Many specialists would accept the following British Criteria for the diagnosis of migraine: recurring throbbing headaches and two or more 'of the following five features: Unilaterial headache, associated nausea with or without vomiting, visual or other sensory aura, cyclical vomiting in childhood, and a family history of migraine' (Whitty and Hockaday 1968).

Friedman (1975) discussed migraine headache in some detail, having chaired the Ad Hoc Committee on the Classification of Headache in America (Friedman, Finley, Graham, Kumble, Ostfeld, and Wolff 1962). He pointed to the various types of migraine such as basilar artery, and hemiplegic and ophthalmophegic migraine. In reference to classic migraine, he noted that it 'occurs in approximately 10 per cent of patients with migraine. The prodromes are sharply defined contralaterial neurologic manifestations—usually visual, though in some patients the effects are sensory, motor, or a combination of these. The pain is unilateral and pulsatile, and anorexia, nausea, and vomiting are concomitant features'. One can see the close correspondence between the Whitty, Hockaday, and Whitty (1966) and the Friedman *et al.* (1962) definitions of migraine.

The generally accepted view is that a migraine attack occurs in two phases. The prodromal phase of a classical migraine attack is associated with intracranial and extra-cranial vasoconstriction followed by the painful phase of vasodilation. The pain results from the dilation of the extracranial arteries. Friedman felt, however, that this view of migraine was too simplified. However, a more complex discussion of the migraine syndrome is beyond our present scope and the interested reader is referred to Friedman (1975).

Various vasoconstricting drugs have been used in the treatment of migraine, but the most effective has been ergotamine tartrate. However, Friedman noted that there can be severe side-effects and habituation to the drug may occur. One of the most popular psychological methods used to treat migraine has been thermal training or handwarming to counteract the vasoconstriction in the first phase of a migraine attack. Sometimes autogenic phrases or suggestions directed at forehead cooling have been used concomitantly (Daniels 1976).

A number of studies have attempted to modify hand temperature using relaxation or hypnotic techniques. Reid and Curtsinger (1968) who used 20 unselected subjects found an average increase in hand temperature of 2.02 °F. after trance induction. However, the neutral hypnosis that was used would be difficult to differentiate from the instructions for deep relaxation. Peters and Stern (1973) essentially replicated the Reid and Curtisinger study using 20 highly hypnotizable subjects, but found that simply telling subjects to relax resulted in as great an increase in hand temperature as the hypnotic induction. Pulse volume measured from the left index finger verified that a tendency towards vasodilation was occurring. Peters, Lundy, and Stern (1973) selected highly hypnotizable subjects and used suggestions to increase and decrease skin temperature under two conditions: a hypnosis condition and a 'method-acting' condition. While the method-acting condition produced significant increases in hand temperature, the hypnotic condition did not. More specifically Peters *et al.* conclude 'that, regardless of the suggestion employed, Ss given "method acting" instructions display a tendency to increase in peripheral hand temperature'. Roberts, Kewman, and MacDonald (1973) selected six subjects of extremely high hypnotizability who received five to nine hours of training in which cold and hot pads placed on each hand were used to help the subjects to maintain a temperature difference between the two hands after these aids were removed. Both hypnosis and feedback regarding hand temperatures were used. The results for the six subjects combined were quite significant. Subjects were able to produce the suggested differences in skin temperature in one hand compared to the other. Roberts *et al.* (1973) concluded that while the relative effects of hypnosis and temperature feedback could not be established, that the results 'unequivocally demonstrate that some individuals are capable of achieving a high degree of control over the autonomic processes involved in peripheral skin temperature regulation'.

The role of hypnotizability in facilitating the manipulation of skin temperature is not clear. The subjects in Peters and Stern were selected for hypnotizability, yet hypnotic induction was not necessary to achieve temperature change. Likewise, the subjects in Peters *et al.* were highly hypnotizable, yet the 'method-acting' instructions were critical in effecting temperature change. Finally, Roberts *et al.* used subjects selected for hypnotizability yet suggested that hypnosis *per se* may not have been necessary. What may have been of crucial importance was some ability associated with hypnotizability, such as relaxation.

There are a number of recent reports on the treatment of migraine (Johnson and Turin 1975; Sargent, Walters, and Green, 1973; Solback and Sargent, 1977; and Turin and Johnson 1976). Sargent, *et al.* (1973) carried out a pilot study on 75 migraine patients using a temperature trainer which provided feedback on the difference in temperature between the right index finger and the subject's forehead. Autogenic phrases referred to passive concentration, body relaxation, and hand warmth were used until subjects were able to learn them and visualize the changes. Subjects were expected to practise with this trainer at home between sessions. About 80 per cent of the original 75 were followed for 150 days and were reported as having improved from a slight degree to a very good degree. Turin and Johnson (1976) trained seven migraine sufferers in finger-temperature feedback visually via a feedback thermometer. Autogenic phrases were not used. To control for expectancy, training in hand cooling was used with positive expectations for its effect. Practice was carried out at home without feedback. The results supported the use of finger temperature feedback without the use of suggestion or autogenic phrases in significantly reducing three indices of migraine activity: mean number of weekly headaches, number of tablets of medication, and number of hours of headache-associated pain.

Gainer (1978) has provided an interesting case study of a migraine patient who was treated in turn by four methods: assertion training, systematic desensitization, hand-temperature biofeedback, and temperature discrimination training. The first two methods were reported as having no lasting effect. While the temperature biofeedback produced significant temperature changes, the patient was unable to perceive these changes, and a concomitant reduction in headaches was not evident. Temperature discrimination training consists of teaching the patient to focus on sensations in her hand and providing her with very specific verbal feedback after every trial. After two sessions of discrimination training, the patient reported her ability to discriminate hand temperature changes has increased by approximately 60 per cent. A week later her migraine headaches had disappeared, and four weeks later therapy was terminated. Follow-up assessment about eight months later revealed that there had been no relapse. Gainer recommends the assessment of the ability to discriminate changes in hand temperature and suggests that some of our failures in this area may have resulted from an inability to discriminate these changes.

EMG feedback and the muscle-contraction or tension headache

There is a need to differentiate tension headache from migraine. Friedman felt that this was not a problem, although he noted that most migraine patients may exhibit tension headache between attacks of migraine. In reference to muscle-contraction headache, Friedman (1975) indicated that there were no prodromal signs, the pain was not pulsatile, and the headache usually implicated the occipital area. The patient might feel as if the head was covered by a close-fitting cap or band. In addition, symptoms of dizziness and anxiety might precede or accompany the headache. Walton (1971) reported that the aetiology was emotional tension, resulting from 'continuous partial contraction of the muscles which are attached to the scalp'. Walton also noted that there might be frontal involvement in tension headaches. Budzynski, Stoyva, Adler, and Mullaney (1973) characterized tension headache as 'a dull "band-like" pain located bilaterally in the occipital region, although it is often felt in the forehead region as well. It is gradual in onset and may last for hours, weeks, even months'.

In Blanchard and Young's (1974) review of the clinical applications of biofeedback training they found a good deal of support for the efficacy of EMG feedback in the elimination of tension headache. The typical EMG procedure involves the recording of muscle tension from the frontalis muscle site on the forehead. Feedback regarding increases or decreases in tension may be provided via an auditory signal which varies in frequency as muscle tension decreases, or a visual feedback signal may be used. Blanchard and Young reviewed the work on EMG feedback and tension headache up to 1973, including the original work of Budzynski, Stoyva, Adler, and Mullaney (1973) and that of Wickramasera (1972). The value of EMG feedback and home practice in relaxation was confirmed. However, Blanchard and Young noted that 'feedback training without home relaxation practice is not sufficient for long-lasting reduction of tension headaches. . . . Whether EMG feedback training is even necessary has not yet been determined.' A number of recent reports discuss the relative efficiency of relaxation and EMG feedback in treating tension headache (Cox, Freundlich, and Meyer 1975; Chesney and Shelton 1974; Epstein and Abel 1977; and Haynes, Griffin, Mooney, and Parise 1975). Epstein and Abel (1977), who treated six tension headache patients, obtained results which indicated that EMG feedback is insufficient 'to modify very high levels of muscle contraction'. The reports of Cox *et al.* and of Haynes *et al.* were consistent, in that they found that frontalis EMG feedback and relaxation instructions were equally effective in treating tension headache. Treatment effects were maintained at a follow-up assessment. Chesney and Shelton (1974) randomly assigned 24 tension headache patients to one of four groups: muscle relaxation, EMG feedback, combined muscle relaxation, and EMG feedback, and a no-treatment group. The relaxation and combined group used a relaxation cassette for homework. Basically the results indicated that the EMG feedback group was not effective in reducing headache symptoms as compared to the control group. However, the relaxation and the relaxation combined with EMG feedback groups were both effective compared to the control group in reducing headache frequency and severity. Chesney and Shelton noted that the 'lack of a significant difference between the Biofeedback and No-Treatment Group on any measure sheds doubt on the role of frontalis muscle feedback as a sole therapeutic agent for muscle contraction headaches'. The authors also questioned whether muscles, other than the frontalis, might have been implicated in at least some of the muscle-contraction headache patients.

The evidence suggests quite strongly then that consistent practice in muscle relaxation is an important mode of treatment and the necessity of using EMG feedback *per se* is questionable.

We will conclude this chapter by summarizing a study reported by Bakal and Kaganov (1977), which involved a psychophysiological comparison of the tension and migraine headache. Bakal and Kaganov used the Friedman *et al.* (1962) critera described above to define the two kinds of headache. Bakal and Kaganov, using 56 patients, were interested in determining whether the muscular and vascular changes hypothesized to occur with tension and migraine headaches respectively, were indeed specific to the particular headache group. The comparisons were made during headaches as well as during non-headache periods. It was concluded that, compared to control subjects, the location of pain was not related to whether the subject had been diagnosed as migraine or tension headache. Neck muscle activity for tension and migraine subjects was higher than that found in control subjects. The measurement of pulse velocities in the superficial temporal arteries revealed a high degree of similarity for both types of headache subject. Perhaps of greater interest was the finding that migraine subjects exhibited significantly higher frontalis muscle activity than did muscle-contraction headache subjects, who did not differ from controls in frontalis activity. Thus, it was suggested that there is not 'an invariable relationship between muscle contraction headache and increased EMG activity'.

Bakal and Kaganov noted that, bearing in mind that the subjects in their study were chronic headache patients and exhibited severe attacks, that their results on pain location failed to support Friedman, *et al*'s (1962) recommendations concerning the diagnosis of headache. While EMG feedback was reported as equally effective with both migraine and tension headache patients, Bakal and Kaganov recommend that biofeedback success might be improved 'if training focused on pain locations specific to each patient' [p. 214]. They emphasize that the learning of techniques of self-control may be of little value during a headache, but of use prior to attacks in preventing headache onset.

In the treatment of headache, of whatever variety, a detailed analysis of the total symptom picture is recommended, so that the patient is able to focus on those muscle groups most affected. Clearly, great emphasis should be placed on teaching patients to become aware of stimuli signalling the onset of their headache, so that self-control methods may be used at the appropriate time. Finally, it seems that, pending any contradictory research, relaxation procedures should be taught to the patient and that he should be encouraged to practise relaxation regularly. Relaxation cassettes may be tailor-made for the individual, placing particular emphasis on relaxing those muscle groups implicated in the specific headache.

Headaches can be so disturbing that they interfere with getting to sleep, although once sleep ensues there may be little disturbance from headaches which are psychogenic in aetiology. In any event, we turn now in the next chapter to a brief consideration of sleep and its disorders.

SUMMARY

While the difficulty in adequately defining pain is noted, the value of a basic knowledge of the psychology of pain for health professionals is stressed. Melzack emphasizes the importance of variables such as expectation, suggestion, level of anxiety, the meaning of the situation in which the injury occurs, competing sensory stimuli, and so forth, in determining the perception of pain. Collectively the psychological variables which affect the pain response have been labelled the *reactive component* (Beecher 1959).

The effect of individual differences in personality and cultural background on the expression of pain is discussed, and this is followed by a brief presentation on the placebo effect.

The next section concerns the measurement of pain, which is of importance in determining the effect of various treatment procedures. While many reports on pain are necessarily subjective in nature, they have been found adequate.

Various treatment methods are then discussed. Many of the treatment procedures are described in other sections of the book. These include counter-conditioning (pp. 275–8), self-and-heterohypnosis (pp. 302–33), and alpha-feedback procedures (pp. 326–31). After a brief report on the use of relaxation in treating phantom-limb pain, the operant procedures used by Fordyce (1976) and his colleagues are presented. Inexperienced staff may tend to reinforce pain complaints by their attention and through the use of medication. However, Fordyce recommends the reinforcement of patient responses which are antagonistic to pain, such as body movement and pleasant socialization.

The chapter concludes with a discussion of the treatment of migraine and tension headache. While traditionally these conditions are differentially diagnosed, the report of Bakel and Kaganov (1977) concludes that the location of head pain is unrelated to the differential diagnosis. In any case, the value of the psychological treatment of the reactive component of the pain response is emphasized. The attempt to prevent headache onset is important in using self-control procedures.

7
Sleep and its disorders

She bids you on the wanton rushes lay you down
And rest your gentle head upon her lap.
And she will sing the song that pleaseth you
And on your eyelids crown the god of sleep.
Charming your blood with pleasing heaviness
Making such difference 'twixt wake and sleep
As is the difference betwixt day and night
The hour before the heavenly-harness'd team
Begins his golden progress in the east.
Shakespeare: *Henry IV: Part I*

Sleep for the majority of humans takes up approximately one-third of the life-span. While man has thought for thousands of years that sleep functioned to restore the fatigued organism's *milieu intérieur*, and that mental activity of some sort took place during sleep, it was not until the twentieth century that these ideas could be rigorously investigated. The discovery of the importance of the brain-stem reticular formation (BSRF) in the activation of the organism (Moruzzi and Magoun 1949), the books on sleep by Kleitman (1963) and Oswald (1962), and the report on *alpha feedback* by Kamiya (1969) together with developments in electrophysiological measurement equipment all contributed to the vast expansion in sleep research.

The effect of sleep deprivation on performance has been of interest (Johnson 1975). A number of investigators have been interested in specific phases of the sleep–wake cycle (Stoyva and Kamiya 1968; Schacter 1976) and there has been a great deal of interest in responsivity and learning during sleep (Aarons 1976; Evans 1973).

There has been an increasing number of studies of disturbances of sleep, such as insomnia, catalepsy, and somnambulism or sleep-walking (Oswald 1969), and of procedures which were thought to be useful in modifying these undesirable conditions. Readable overviews of sleep may be found in Dement (1974), Kales (1969), Oswald (1966), or in Webb and Cartwright (1978).

This chapter considers the physiology of sleep, the effects of sleep deprivation, and disorders of sleep and their treatment. We will first consider the physiology of sleep.

PHYSIOLOGY OF SLEEP

The basic instrumentation necessary for classifying sleep into its various stages is a polygraph which records eye movements, muscle activity, and EEG variables (Johnson and Naitoh 1969). While the so-called International Ten-Twenty System of electrode placement (Jasper 1958) may be used in some laboratories, it is important to note that there are regional differences in terms of the placement system used. For example, Fig 7.1 shows the Maudsley system. An indication of the particular cerebral area involved is shown for the right hemisphere.

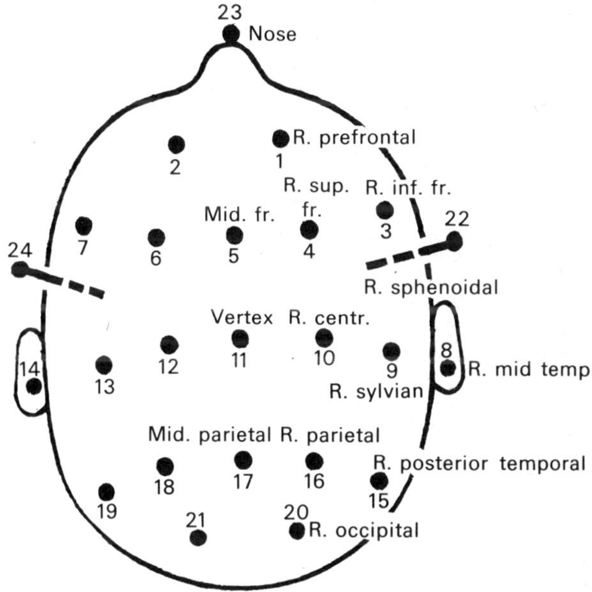

Fig. 7.1 The Maudsley system of EEG placement. (By permission of Dr M. V. Driver.)

Figure 7.2 enables the most common position of different types of EEG waves to be noted. Many of these waves are of particular importance in sleep research. Certain wave forms are found more frequently or with greater amplitude from specific cortical areas. For example, alpha rhythm is found with greater amplitude in the occipital area (see Fig. 18.2).

While until recently sleep was considered as both a passive and a static state, it is now clear that a great deal of physiological variability occurs during the typical night's sleep, and that it is neither passive nor static in nature (Koella 1974).

Figure 7.3 represents a typical night's sleep in a young adult (Hartmann 1974). It may be seen that sleep is broken down into four main stages, 1 to 4. However, there are two types of stage 1 sleep: (a) *emergent stage 1* or

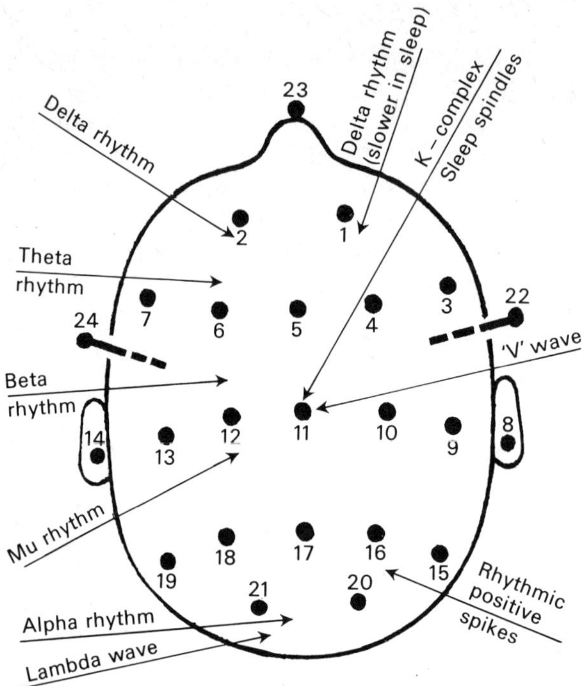

Fig. 7.2. Common positions of different types of EEG rhythms. While some activity of delta and theta frequency may be seen in computer analysis, delta and theta are not obvious features of the normal awake EEG. (By permission of Dr M. V. Driver.)

paradoxical or *rapid eye movement (REM) sleep*, which Hartmann refers to as *desynchronized* or dreaming sleep, (b) initial stage 1 (see below). *Non-REM* or *synchronized sleep* thus includes all but REM sleep. As Fig. 7.3 indicates, REM sleep emerges out of stages 3 or 4, or in some cases, particularly later in the night's sleep, stage 2.

Hartmann noted that 'the most striking features [of a night's sleep] are the regular cycling throughout the night with a cycle length of 90–100 min, and the regular alternation of synchronized (S) sleep with desynchronized (D) sleep'. It should be noted that a REM cycle is usually defined as the period from the onset of one REM period to the onset of the following REM period. Based on a 'total sleep time' (TST) of 7½ to 8 hours, anywhere from three to five REM cycles occur. Hartmann (1974) noted that 'S sleep almost always precedes D sleep, and that the deep slow-wave portions (stages 3 and 4) of S sleep occur early in the night'. The exceptions to the rule of S sleep occurring first are in: (a) the neonate where sleep may begin with REM quite naturally; (b) some cases in which a person is *sleep-deprived*; and (c) the *narcoleptic* who will go into the REM state immediately upon falling asleep.

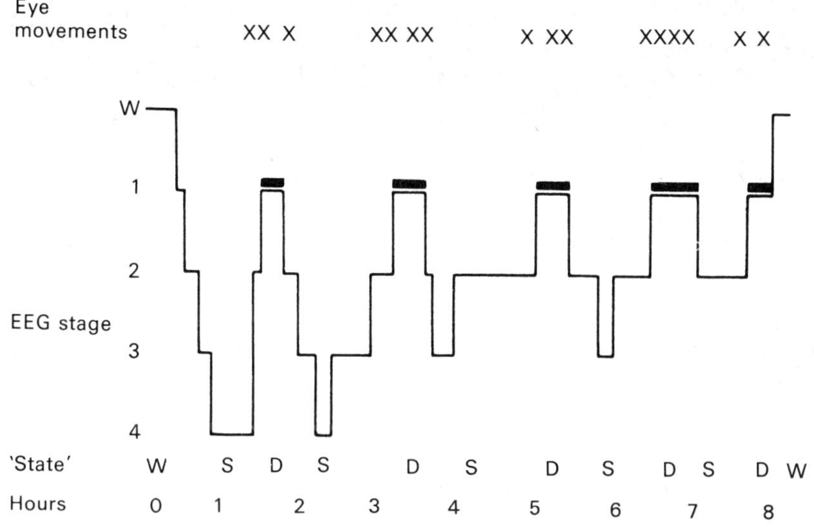

Fig. 7.3. A typical night's sleep in a young adult. The diagram actually represents a mean derived from many all-night recordings. The heavy lines indicate the D-periods, characterized by a stage-1 EEG pattern and the presence of rapid conjugate eye movements. W = waking; S= synchronized sleep; D = desynchronized or dreaming sleep. (From Hartmann 1974.)

Most sleep studies have used young adults such as naval personnel or university students. Thus, much of the quantitative information available is based upon the young adult. Table 7.1 indicates the mean percentage of time spent in each sleep stage. It can be seen that by far the greatest amount of the total sleep time is spent in stage 2, followed by REM sleep.

TABLE 7.1
MEAN PERCENTAGE OF EACH SLEEP STAGE

Sleep stage	Approximate percentage of total sleep time
1	5
2	50
3 } 4 }	20
REM	25

(Data rounded off from Williams, Agnew, and Webb (1964) who studied 16 healthy male medical students over 3 nights.)

Wake state

The basic EEG wave forms have already been defined in Table 5.1. The appearance of some of the wave forms important in sleep research is shown here in Fig. 7.4. The EEG activity found during the greatest part of the wake state mainly varies from the alpha range (approximately 8–13 Hertz) to beta activity (13 Hz and up).

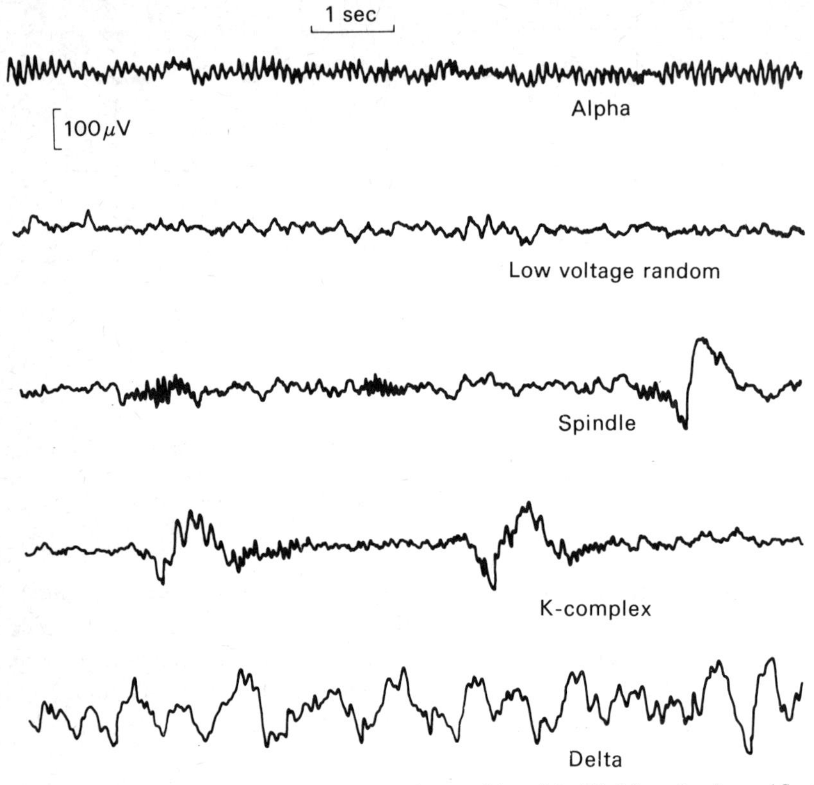

Fig. 7.4. EEG waveforms distinguishing sleep from waking. (Modified from Snyder and Scott 1972.)

Hypnagogic state

Just before, or just upon entering, regular sleep, a state of consciousness occurs which is sometimes referred to as the *hypnagogic state* (Schachter 1976). The dominant wave form here is alpha. Schachter notes that the following types of phenomena have been referred to as *hypnagogic*: 'spontaneously appearing visual, auditory, and kinesthetic images; qualitatively unusual thought processes and verbal constructions; tendencies towards extreme suggestibility; symbolic representation of ongoing mental and physiological processes; and so on'. This state is of interest to those involved in the physophysiological study of creativity.

Sleep stages

Stage 1 (initial). Fast irregular beta activity predominates with some waxing and waning of alpha rhythm. It is difficult to actually separate this stage from the hypnagogic state. Stage 1 may be referred to as the stage of light sleep. Some theta activity may also occur.

Stage 2. Sleep spindle activity at 12–14 Hz tends to occur recorded from a wide area of the cerebral cortex. Background activity is of low amplitude theta with some delta activity. Both spontaneous and external stimulus-related 'K' complexes occur here. Theta activity is increased.

Stage 3. As indicated by Dement (1974), stage 3 may be seen as intermediate stage between 2 and 4. Close to one-half of the EEG activity may now consist of delta waves of more than 100 uV. Some sleep spindles may still be seen, as well as K-complexes.

Stage 4. When more than half of the record consists of delta activity below about 2 Hz, the sleep stage is referred to as stage 4 sleep.

REM (emergent stage 1 or paradoxical) sleep. Rapid, conjugate eye-movements occur. The loss of muscle tone is signalled by a flat EMG (Koella 1974). As noted by Dement, during REM sleep, characteristic wave forms known as 'saw-tooth waves' occur. REM periods may be shown by an EEG pattern similar to 'Initial stage 1' in conjunction with a flat EMG and bilaterally-synchronous eye movements. REM sleep has been labelled as 'paradoxical' because the cortex is active, particularly the occipital area, and the blood flow through the cortex is equal to that found in the wake state (Ingvar 1973). Certain autonomic functions such as heart rate and respiration rate have shown a greater variability during paradoxical sleep (Johnson 1970), which might suggest that something unusual was occurring. However, the activity which created the greatest excitement regarding paradoxical sleep was the rapid-eye-movements (REMs) which led to the idea that dreaming might be taking place. Dement (1974) noted that 80 per cent of the times subjects were awakened during REM sleep in Kleitman's laboratory reports of vivid dreams were obtained. Figure 7.5 shows the relative percentages of dream reports obtained after REM and NREM awakening.

As Snyder and Scott (1972) noted, 'the incidence of "dream" reports from REM awakening varies between 60 and 89%, the 74% first reported being a "happy medium"'. Discussions of research on dreaming may be found in Witkin and Lewis (1967), while Cohen (1974, 1976) and Dallet (1973) discuss theoretical views of dream recall and dream function respectively. Tart (1969) also includes an interesting section on dreams.

A further interesting characteristic of REM sleep is the amount of TST during which it takes place. It has been found, for example, that in the neonate almost 50 per cent of TST is taken up by REM and that prematures show an even higher percentage of REM. Figure 7.6 indicates the relative amounts of REM versus NREM throughout the life-span. It has been suggested that since the neonate has had little visual experience from which to concoct dreams that the high percentage of TST spend in REM is related to cerebral development and is necessary to activate the growing central

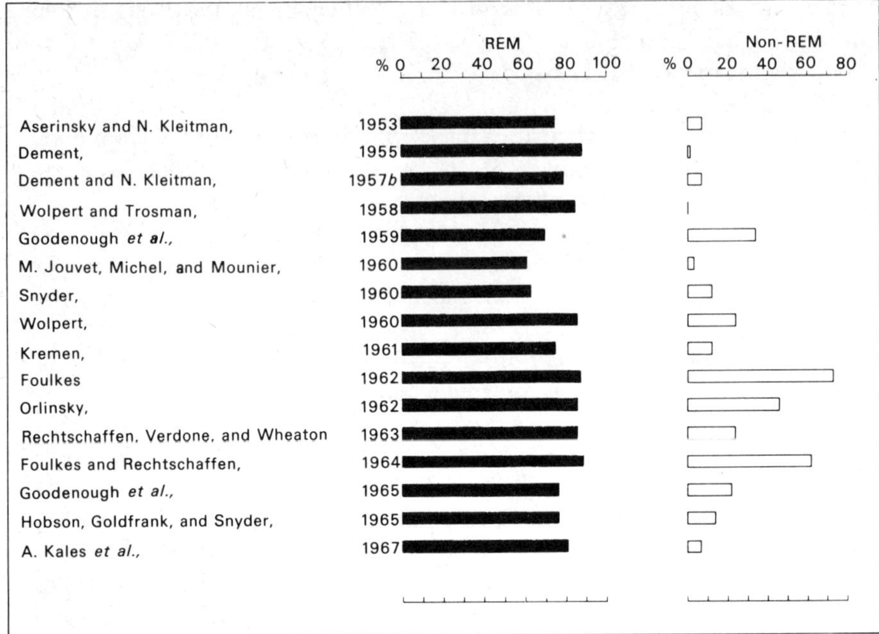

Fig. 7.5. Systematic studies of percentage dream recall after REM and Non-REM awakenings. (From Greenfield and Sternbach 1972.)

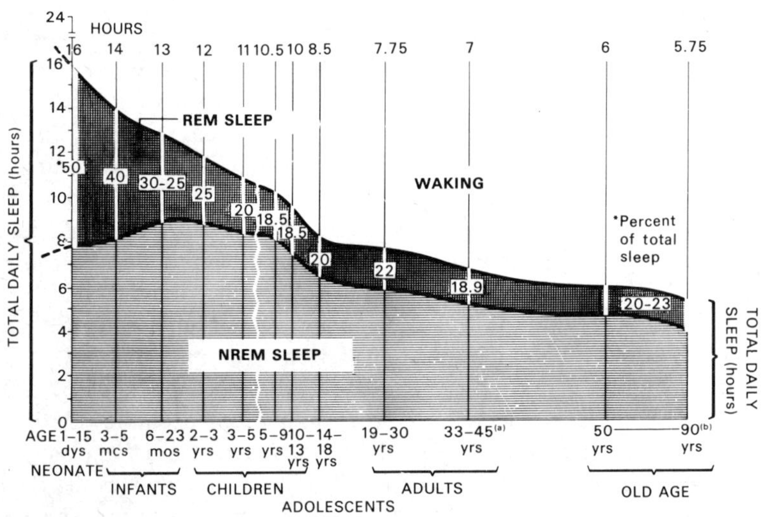

Fig. 7.6. REM/NREM sleep relationship throughout human life. (From Roffwarg 1966—later revised. Data for the 33–45 and 50–90 groups are taken from Strauch (1963), Kales *et al.* (1967), Fernberg *et al.* (1967), Khan and Fisher (1969), and Larry, Cor-Mordret, Faire, and Ridjanovic (1962), revised by the authors since publication in *Science* 604–19, 1966).

nervous system. Certainly as the child matures the proportion of REM time decreases.

We turn now to a discussion of sleep deprivation and related research.

SLEEP DEPRIVATION AND RELATED RESEARCH

A question that is frequently asked is: how much sleep does the average adult need? While the normative value that is given may be 8 hours, some would suggest that considerably less sleep is needed. For example, Webb and Agnew (1974) maintained a group of young adults on 5½ hours sleep for 60 days and found little or no decrement in performance.

Studies have been carried out on short- versus long-sleepers (Hartmann, Baekeland, and Zwilling 1972) and many reports may be found on sleep deprivation. Hartmann *et al.* differentiated long- from short-sleepers and found that while long- and short-sleepers had similar amounts of stage 3 and 4 sleep, that the long-sleepers exhibited twice as much REM sleep. Hartmann and Brewer (1976) carried out two separate questionnaire studies involving about 250 respondents, in each case, and attempted to establish what factors were associated with changes in *sleep requirement*. They noted that 'it is especially important to make certain that the person . . . meant reduced *sleep requirement*, i.e. normal functioning on reduced sleep, rather than an *inability to sleep* either because of insomniac problems or because of time pressures, i.e. a period associated with low sleep time, but with tiredness or difficulty in functioning during the day'. A certain proportion of the respondents were also interviewed in order to verify that the questions were understood. The results showed that a reduced sleep requirement was associated with 'time when everything was going well', while for a majority an increased sleep need was associated with 'times of increased physical work or exercise', a 'depressed or upset mood', or a 'stressful period'. Hartmann and Brewer noted that one important factor associated with increased sleep need 'was "mental or emotional stress" and correlated strongly with increased sleep need at times of "change of occupation", "increased mental activity", "stress", and "depressed mood". It correlated strongly in the negative direction with "times where everything is going well".' Hartmann and Brewer concluded that 'sleep and especially D-sleep [REM] may have a function in the processes of restoration after worry or stress, and perhaps after any waking reprogramming or rearrangement'.

There have been a number of studies of individuals who are quite healthy in spite of very limited sleep. One such report (Meddis, Pearson, and Langford 1973) presents a case of a 70-year-old retired district nurse who reported only one hour of sleep per night. All-night 'sleep' recordings essentially verified her verbal report in that over five nights her average TST was recorded as 67 minutes. Meddis *et al.* labelled her condition as a case of *non-somnia*, which 'refers to a reduced pressure to sleep rather than difficulty in falling and remaining asleep'. However, these cases of 'healthy insomnia' or non-somnia are relatively rare. Before discussing actual disorders of sleep, we turn to a brief overview of studies on sleep deprivation.

To what extent, it may be asked, is REM sleep necessary? What are the consequences of being deprived of stage 3 and stage 4 sleep? Johnson and his colleagues have carried out extensive work in this area (Friedmann, Globus, Huntley, Mullaney, Naitoh, and Johnson 1977; Johnson 1975; Johnson, Naitoh, Moses, and Lubin 1974; Lubin, Moses, Johnson, and Naitoh 1974; Mullaney, Johnson, Naitoh, Friedmann, and Globus 1977). In addition to the work with normal groups, De Barros-Ferreira, Golsteinas, and Lairy (1973) have studied REM deprivation in chronic schizophrenics, while Post, Kotin, and Goodwin (1976) have studied the effects of sleep deprivation in depressives.

Johnson (1975) distinguishes three types of sleep loss: (1) total sleep deprivation; (2) partial sleep loss; and (3) sleep-stage deprivation. Johnson noted that while earlier studies suggested that sleep deprivation could induce a psychotic-like state, later work made this idea quite doubtful, although prolonged sleep loss commonly leads to visual 'and to a much lesser extent, auditory hallucinations'.

Total sleep loss

Johnson found that *total sleep deprivation* up to 60 hours produced an increase in waking alpha activity while beyond 100 hours of total sleep deprivation, alpha density decreased. Delta activity was reported as 14 to 20 per cent with up to 60 hours deprivation, while beyond 100 hours, delta density increased to 44 per cent. Theta activity followed the same pattern, going up to 33 per cent beyond 100 hours deprivation: 'On the first recovery night after sleep loss, there is invariably an increase in slow-wave sleep [SWS] (stages 3 and 4) over that present before deprivation . . . REM sleep usually stays at pre-sleep loss levels or decreases on the first recovery night. If an increase in REM sleep occurs, it is usually seen on the second recovery night'.

In reference to performance changes during sleep loss, Johnson noted that 'the primary impairment . . . takes the form of lapses; the subject is unable to maintain efficient behaviour and increasingly shows short periods when performance falters or stops'. However, it is notable that alerting 'factors such as massive sensory stimulation, feedback of information as to quality of performance, and frequent task changes help to reduce the frequency and duration of lapses'. The tasks showing the greatest susceptibility to total sleep loss are experimenter-paced tasks, longer tasks, simple repetitive tasks, tasks involving 'newly acquired skills and tasks that rely upon short-term memory'. In concluding his discussion of total sleep deprivation, Johnson indicated that: 'Each subject's response to sleep loss depends upon his age, physical condition, the stability of his mental health, expectations of those around him, whether drugs or stimulants are used to maintain wakefulness, and the support he receives from his environment.'

An interesting study of a seventeen-year-old who stayed awake for 264 hours and was observed in Johnson's San Diego Sleep laboratory is provided by Dement in his extremely readable book on sleep (Dement 1974).

Partial sleep loss

Since a greater proportion of REM sleep occurs towards the end of a night's sleep, with *partial sleep deprivation*, it is to a large extent REM sleep that has been lost. Johnson reported that as partial sleep loss continued, REM sleep exhibited an earlier onset. However, he noted that 'REM sleep never replaces SWS in order of appearance, regardless of severity or duration of restriction'. Considering the effect of partial sleep loss on performance, Johnson cited Webb and Agnew (1974), who reduced the TST from 7½ to 8 hours to 5½ hours for a period of 60 days, and concluded that young adults 'can maintain 5 to 6 hours of sleep per night for as long as two months, with little or no decrement in performance for such a reduction'.

Mullaney *et al.* (1977) concluded that their data 'suggest that gradual sleep reduction may be an effective way to reduce TST by 1 to 2 hours and may permanently alter sleep habits or requirements . . . we have no indications that the TST reduction over . . . [the 1-year period of the study] posed a threat to the health of our small group of subjects'.

One of the main differences between the Mullaney *et al.* study and others relating to reducing TST is that EEG data was obtained in the subject's home so that the four couples studied were able to 'maintain their usual life styles'. The sleep reduction was accomplished by having the couples reduce their sleep by going to bed 30 minutes later every two or three weeks, depending upon their baseline TST. Friedmann *et al.* (1977) reported on the performance and mood changes which took place during the Mullaney *et al.* study. They found that throughout the sleep-reduction period that none of the moods measured by the Profile of Mood States (POMS; McNair, Lorr, and Droppleman 1977), showed any significant change. The authors noted that there 'were however, trends towards less vigor and more fatigue as sleep was reduced. Scores on both scales returned to baseline levels during the 12-month follow-up.' Performance was reported as unimpaired during the sleep-reduction period. The performance measures included an immedite memory test, a word memory test, an auditory vigilance test, and an addition test. Friedmann *et al.* discussed sleep as an adaptive process, indicating that a lengthy period of sleep was adaptive. However, they suggest that 'in an affluent society, . . . large amounts of sleep are no longer adaptive but can be considered an "evolutionary anachronism"'. On the other hand they suggested that there might be a genetic limit for most people 'beyond which sleep cannot be reduced'.

Sleep-stage deprivation

Johnson (1975) also reported on sleep-stage deprivation, and gave an account of the work of Lubin *et al.* (1974) which compared REM-deprived subjects with those deprived of stage 4 sleep. These authors were interested in the recuperative value of sleep. After being totally sleep-deprived for two nights, one group of subjects were REM-deprived for two nights, another group were stage-4-deprived for two nights. Both groups were then allowed three nights of recovery sleep. Two appropriate control groups were used. The results indicated that: 'A rebound effect for both REM and SWS was present for the appropriate groups on the first night of uninterrupted sleep, indicating that the selective sleep-stage deprivation was effective' (Johnson 1975). However, he noted that after 'sleep loss, the amount rather than the type of sleep seems to be the most important factor'.

In a second study seven subjects were first REM-deprived and seven were stage-4-deprived for three nights. Following this stage deprivation both groups were deprived of total sleep for one night and finally allowed two nights of recovery sleep. The changes in performance were found to be similar for both groups. The EEG results, however, indicated that with increased stage deprivation, there are an increasing 'number of attempts to obtain the deprived stage'. A rebound effect is also found for each type of deprivation. More consistent findings are found for stage 4 deprivation than for REM deprivation. Johnson noted that 'following two nights of total sleep loss, . . . deprivation of stage 4 required a significantly larger number of arousals than were necessary to prevent subjects from obtaining stage REM following sleep loss'.

Johnson suggested that his sleep-deprivation results enabled an argument to be made for the idea 'that recovery sleep is unitary with respect to its recuperative function, but that the various physiological and biochemical measures obtained during sleep clearly indicate that sleep is not a single state'.

De Barros-Ferreira *et al.* (1973) referred to 'intermediate sleep' (IS) stages, which are more important in schizophrenics than in normals. Whilst normals may show IS stages, they take up no more than 7 per cent of TST. However, they noted that in acute schizophrenics the percentage of IS was about 40 per cent, while in a chronic population is was about 15 per cent of TST. They reported that the differential amounts of IS in psychotics as compared to controls, 'appear to sustain the existence of relationships between disturbances of sleep and psychopathology'. Apparently, IS was found to interrupt stages 2 and 3, and to be similar in pattern to REM sleep but without eye movements, 'if REM sleep is restricted . . . to the epochs when eye movements actually appear, intermediate stages usually occur immediately before and after REM sleep periods'. In a REM-deprivation study comparing a group of chronic schizophrenics with a group of normals, De Barros-Ferreira *et al.* established that schizophrenics demonstrated more IS sleep and that in schizophrenics this stage may substitute or compensate for REM-sleep loss. The authors suggested that schizophrenics may be less able than normals to switch from one neurophysiological or neurochemical system to another.

Post *et al.* (1976) hypothesized that limited sleep deprivation might result in improvements in mood in endogenous depressives. A group of hospitalized depressives were deprived of total sleep for one night. While about half of the patients improved, the improvement was found to be only a transitory one. However, they felt that further study of selective sleep deprivation in depressives might prove valuable. Further reports on sleep loss and depression may be found in Snyder (1974) and Van Den Hooffdakker, Bos, and Van Den Burg (1974).

Having selectively discussed the research on sleep deprivation, we turn to the last section of this chapter on sleep disorders.

DISORDERS OF SLEEP

Sleep disturbances are not only characteristic for those who demonstrate psychopathology, but, in fact, are a fairly common problem, the most frequently reported being insomnia. Borkovec and Fowles (1973) indicated that of 650 beginning psychology students, 18 per cent 'felt both that they had a sleeping problem and that they would be willing to volunteer for a study of treatment techniques aimed at eliminating sleep disturbance'.

While other sleep disturbances such as sleep apnea (Dement 1974); narcolepsy (Zarcone 1973), and somnambulism (Jacobson, Kales, Lehmann, and Zweizig 1965) are much less frequent than insomnia, they have been increasingly studied, and attempts made to treat them. Zarcone (1973) feels it is helpful to divide sleep disorders into 'the insomnias, the hypersomnias, and the episodic or intermittent sleep disorders'. Disturbances in arousal mechanisms are frequently implicated in sleep disturbances (Broughton 1968). Nocturanal enuresis, somnambulism, and nightmares are discussed by Broughton, who points out that contrary to widespread views they 'occur independently of typical periods of dream activity'. The interested reader is referred to Broughton (1968) for a discussion on enuresis and nightmares. Limitations of space restrict the scope of discussion in this chapter to the sleep disorders of insomnia, somnambulism, and narcolepsy.

Insomnia

While insomnia has been mainly treated pharmacologically, behavioural methods of treatment have been increasingly applied during the last decade or so (Knapp, Downs, and Alperson 1976; Montgomery, Perkin, and Wise 1975). One of the problems that should be noted here is that there is a lack of consistency in the definition of insomnia which leads to difficulties in assessing sleep adequacy (Knapp *et al.* 1976; Montgomery *et al.* 1975). Knapp *et al.* (1976) cited Luce and Segal's (1969) fourfold system which includes 'categories for *imaginary insomnia* (the patient shows a normal number of hours of sleep in the laboratory), *situational insomnia* (those events during which sleep is highly improbable, as for example, following the death of a close friend), *pathological insomnia* (a chronic inability to get and stay asleep), and *voluntary insomnia* (extending oneself beyond one's physical capabilities, or with CNS stimulants)'. Montgomery *et al.* (1975) noted that most investigators had seemed to deal with sleep onset insomnia. For many patients who complain of insomnia the primary problem involves something else, since Knapp *et al.* (1976) cited Dement's findings which indicated 'no relationship between the complaint of insomnia and the actual hours of sleep exhibited by a patient in the laboratory'.

It is clear, as recommended by Montgomery *et al.* (1975) that an adequate behavioural analysis is necessary before embarking on treatment. As noted by both review articles, definite conclusions about the active components of various treatment procedures are difficult to draw from the literature, since many of the studies used poor control procedures or none at all. Most of the behavioural studies have not carried out EEG assessments of sleep adequacy. Naturally, this is an expensive procedure.

Knapp *et al.* (1976) divided the treatment outcome studies into the following categories: (a) case studies; (b) pre-experimental designs; (c) experimental analysis; and (d) controlled experimental studies. Treatment procedures have included progressive relaxation, stimulus control, and systematic desensitization (see Part IV for a discussion of treatment procedures). They indicated that no definite conclusions could be drawn from studies in the first two categories, above. Even the experimentally-controlled studies, with few exceptions, could demonstrate no greater results using progressive relaxation, hypnotic relaxation, single-item desensitization, than self-relaxation or a placebo condition. However, they cited a study by Tokarz and Lawrence using a stimulus control technique which seemed to offer promise. Apparently, the reduction in sleep-onset latency produced by this technique averaged 84 per cent. A five-month follow-up showed a maintenance of this decreased latency. Knapp *et al.* cited the results of Borkovec, Kaloupek, and Slama and noted that it had been shown that 'progressive relaxation with muscle tension-release produced significantly greater improvement in latency to sleep-onset than relaxation without tension-release, or the two control conditions of placebo and no treatment'.

Montgomery *et al.* (1976) came to essentially the same conclusions regarding the use of relaxation and systematic desensitization in the treatment of insomnia. However, they concluded that systematic desensitization was no more effective than muscle relaxation in the treatment of insomnia. They also reviewed studies using classical conditioning techniques, biofeedback, and electrosleep. However, the design of most of these studies make the results equivocal. They also reviewed a number of studies which suggested that the factors of expectation and attribution could be utilized to advantage in the treatment of insomnia. Davison, Tsujimoto, and Glaros found, for example, that, in support of a suggestion made by Davison and Valins reduced sleep-onset was maintained to a greater degree by those subjects who were able to attribute the behaviour change to their own efforts than those who were informed that the chloral hydrate used was the significant factor. Both Knapp *et al.* (1976) and Montgomery *et al.* (1975) made helpful suggestions for further research into and treatment of insomnia. We now turn to a discussion of somnambulism.

Somnambulism (sleep-walking)

Somnambulism, or sleep-walking, is characterized by getting out of bed at night and moving around in a somewhat confused way. However, the person's behaviour may become 'more coordinated and complex. He may avoid objects, dust tables, go to the bathroom, or utter phrases which are usually incomprehensible. It is difficult to attract his attention. If left alone, he goes back to bed' (Broughton 1968). He is usually amnesic for his sleep-walking episodes and does not remember dreaming.

Reid (1975) noted that somnambulism was not restricted to children but also occurred in young adults, although since Reid studied male military trainees he was unable to comment on the incidence of sleep-walking in the female population. That sleep-walking does occur in women can be verified on the basis of clinical experience, but the incidence is not precisely known. Broughton (1968) noted that sleep-walking typically occurred during NREM periods, specifically during arousal from stage 4 sleep. Broughton suggested that sleep-walking might arise from either psychological or physiological aetiology, although no specific causal factors had been isolated. He suggested that sleep-walking episodes might arise from daytime psychological conflicts which found expression during sleep, conflicts which could not break through repressive barriers which were standing guard during the waking state. Broughton suggested that one must entertain the possibility that the symptoms specific to somnambulism 'are due to abnormally marked physiological responses during the recurrent slow wave arousal episode . . . , i.e. the . . . sensorium impairment, leading to somnambulism'.

Reid (1975) briefly reviewed the literature on somnambulism and presented a study of six basic-combat trainees whose somnambulism was interfering considerably with the training programme. Other disabling psychiatric factors were not present. The treatment method presented to the four men in the programme was one in which the 'patient would learn to control his symptom himself . . . that for the purpose of the treatment sleep-walking was seen as happening within a "trance" and as such could be examined and treated comparably to the trances experienced in the therapist's office'. An arousal cue was taught to the patient which would enable him to achieve arousal from any trance state, including somnambulism. Initially the patients were taught to relax and to enter a trance state. A deepening of the trance procedure was also used. Positive suggestions were made about the success of the therapy, the advantages of being symptom-free, and about returning to sleep after the successful use of the arousal cue. Treatment, which took place over three weeks, was successful for four of the six men. Sleep-walking was totally absent and these men successfully completed their current military training. While long-term follow-up was not obtained, the treatment method used in Reid's (1975) study is 'suggestive', particularly when it is considered that the approach was not consistent with Reid's usual psychodynamic orientation.

We complete this section with a discussion of narcolepsy, which involves the falling into a sleep state at unusual times without volition.

Narcolepsy

It has already been noted that when narcoleptics fall into a sleep state that they enter into REM sleep in contrast to the normal pattern of sleep stage activity. Obviously, the condition may be extremely dangerous in that the person with this condition could be operating dangerous equipment or driving a car, and thus may be a danger to others as well as himself. Emotional states, such as laughing or being angry, may trigger off the lapse into sleep. Zarcone (1973) cited the criteria used to diagnose narcolepsy as presented by Yoss and Daley (1960). These are 'the presence of one or more symptoms of the tetrad—sleep attacks, cataplexy, hypnagogic hallucinations, and sleep paralysis. The last three are referred to as accessory symptoms.'

Zarcone discussed the hypersomnias in some detail, and includes a category of NREM narcolepsy. While noting that 'the relation between REM sleep attacks, episodes of NREM sleep and daytime drowsiness is not yet clear', Zarcone indicated that all 'the polygraphic studies show that a majority of patients with both sleep attacks and accessory symptoms have a disturbance of REM sleep as evidenced by the decidedly abnormal occurrence of sleep-onset REM periods in nap recording'.

Zarcone considered the theories related to narcolepsy. One point of view was that narcoleptic patients might be characterized as being REM-deprived or as needing more REM sleep. However, some of these patients were observed as needing no more than the normal amount of REM sleep per 24 hours. Zarcone also considered Kleitman's suggestion that the wakefulness system was inhibited through stimulation of the carotid sinus mechanism. Zarcone reviewed the syndrome of narcolepsy on the basis of the consensus of opinion regarding the polygraphic studies of narcolepsy 'that there is a similarity or even an identity between symptoms of narcolepsy and the phenomena of REM sleep'. He went on to discuss the complications in the condition which had come about through amphetamine abuse or habituation. After discussing the differential diagnosis of narcolepsy, he discussed management and treatment. The aetiology of the condition remained unclear and management and treatment seemed to have been mainly pharmacological in nature. For those patients who were unable to tolerate amphetamine treatment, Zarcone suggested that they should schedule naps during the day in order to reduce the frequency of sleep attacks. Zarcone counselled against shift work, since it tended to play havoc with night sleep and might increase sleep attacks. He recommended the combined use of imipramine, 25 mg three times a day, and methylphenidate, 5 or 10 mg three times a day, to control both cataplexy and sleep attacks. However, he noted that there was evidence that this combination was contra-indicated in depression.

SUMMARY

This chapter provides an outline of the physiology of sleep, including a brief indication of sleep stages with an emphasis on REM sleep, which has been associated with dreaming. This is followed by a section on three types of sleep deprivation: total sleep deprivation, partial sleep deprivation, and sleep-stage deprivation. While it is pointed out that prolonged sleep loss may lead to visual and auditory hallucinations, the earlier research suggesting that a psychotic-like state would result from extended sleep deprivation, has not been supported for the mentally healthy. Surprisingly, relatively long-term partial sleep deprivation may result in little or no performance decrement. Some of the work on intermediate sleep (IS) stages in schizophrenics is briefly discussed and a study on sleep deprivation in depressives is summarized.

The final section of the chapter considers three of the main disorders of sleep: insomnia, somnambulism, and narcolepsy. Whereas narcolepsy has been treated almost entirely by pharmacological means, insomnia has in recent years been treated by behavioural techniques. Unfortunately, most of the behavioural studies have lacked adequate controls thus prohibiting firm conclusions about the efficacy of specific behavioural methods. However, stimulus control techniques, and an incorporation of expectation and attribution factors into treatment programmes may well prove advantageous. A successful behavioural treatment programme using hypnosis and self-control methods with six somnambulists was reviewed.

Unfortunately, the vast majority of those who exhibit sleep problems receive only pharmacological treatment with its undesirable side-effects and not-infrequent drug-dependency. Therefore, the further development of behavioural methods to treat the sleep disorders should receive a high priority. While the successful treatment of narcolepsy may be other than behavioural, for the various insomnias behavioural therapy would seem to be the treatment of choice.

8
Perceptual processes and their disorders

IAN TAYLOR

There is nothing either good or bad,
but thinking makes it so
Shakespeare: *Hamlet* II, ii

The process of perception can be placed within the context of the individual's striving to adapt to his environment. The way he gains knowledge about his environment is very important. Information must be extracted from the vast array of physical energy stimulating the organism's senses. Only those stimuli which trigger some kind of adaptive action should be regarded as 'information'. Thus, *perception* could be defined as 'the process of information extraction' (Forgus 1966).

THE ORGANIZATION OF PERCEPTUAL PROCESSES

While the lower animals have perceptual programmes which are largely 'built-in' (or inherited) and therefore remain relatively unmodified with experience, higher animals have perceptual programmes very much influenced by learning. 'In the human infant, for example, the perception of light is determined by built-in programmes. This is necessary for adaptive behaviour to begin, but the programmes become modified with growth, development, and experience. Let us just think, for example, of the highly complex and abstract kind of information which has to be extracted in such diverse tasks as the aesthetic appreciation of a painting or a great musical composition, the solution of a mathematical problem, or the perception of another human being' (Forgus 1966).

Thinking might be viewed as the end result of the development of the perceptual processes. Through learning, stimuli are judged against stored information leading to the eventual development of conceptual abilities. The process becomes more abstract and involves *mediating variables* such as symbols, language, thinking, etc. Thinking will be discussed in more detail in a later section of this chapter (see p. 172).

The effects of stimulation

Before considering the specific effects of stimuli, it would be useful to look at the effects of non-specific stimulation, as there is considerable evidence that the behaviour of the organism is affected by the intensity of environmental stimulation, irrespective of the exact nature of the stimuli. Too little or too much stimulation can disrupt the organism's functioning.

The effects of non-specific stimulation

A considerable body of research in the United States and Canada has focused on the effects of sensory deprivation (e.g. Heron, Doane, and Scott 1956; Vernon and Hoffman 1956; Zubek, Pushkar, Sansom, and Gowing 1961). Procedurally, these experiments are not consistent, but most of them require subjects (often college students) to remain in isolation in sound-proofed cubicles, wearing opaque goggles and with limbs padded to reduce tactile stimuli). Lilly (1956) went so far as to immerse subjects in a tank of water to reduce stimulation even further. Wright, Taylor, Davies, Sluckin, Lee, and Reason (1970) summarized the findings of these studies as follows: 'The most general report of subjects is that after a time in isolation, it becomes harder to occupy oneself with organised trains of thought—concentration is difficult. . . . Some subjects drift further into a confused state in which they cannot tell whether they are waking or sleeping and in which they become emotionally labile. . . . Occasionally—and more often in some experimental situations than in others—visual and auditory *hallucinations* occur, ranging from fluctuations in light intensity to complex and colourful everyday scenes. There is some distortion of the alpha rhythm of the EEG, which become slower and irregular in form.'

But there have been many discrepant findings. Kubansky (1958) explained these in terms of variations in (a) conditions of deprivation; (b) subjects; (c) sensory modality preferences; and (d) response measures.

Decrements in efficiency have been shown to occur during the performance of monotonous tasks (such as long-term observation of radar screens). Vigilance tasks in the laboratory have also demonstrated such a decrement. One might distinguish between sensory deprivation, which involves drastic reduction of sensory input, and *perceptual deprivation*, in which input is made repetitive and uniform. Motorway drivers, airport pilots, and others exposed to monotonous situations have reported various perceptual abnormalities and performance deficits. It would seem that behavioural disruption is brought about by the homogeneity of stimulation rather than absolute reduction in stimulus input.

There has been less experimental work investigating the adverse effects of excessive stimulation—*sensory overload*. The effects of intense noise can cause physical damage (Allen, Frings, and Rudnick 1948).

The effects of specific stimulation

Turning now to the specific effects of stimuli, let us first consider discrimination. Organisms are able to descriminate between stimuli in the environment and respond differentially to them. The limits of discriminability are determined by two variables. First, the sensitivity of the perceptual apparatus (at a central and peripheral level) sets certain obvious limits. Only certain stimuli can be received; stimuli must be of, or above, a certain intensity and of a certain kind—i.e. visual stimuli of a wave-length falling within the visual spectrum. The sensitivity of the receptor system also limits the fineness of discrimination. Secondly, experience (practice and interest) can determine *discriminability*. For instance a trained musician is very sensitive to changes in pitch.

When discrimination is difficult, as a result of faint or ambiguous stimuli, experience is very important in determining recognition. For instance, common words are more easily identified than uncommon words of the same length (Postman and Rosenzweig 1956); words related to the subjects' interests are more readily recognized than other words (Postman, Bruner, and McGuinnies 1948); although concentrating on words presented to one ear, subjects notice the presentation of their own names to the other ear (Moray 1969; Treisman 1964). Thus it would seem that experience establishes a 'set' or readiness for some stimuli rather than others.

Instructions or the immediate context of an experimental situation have been demonstrated to establish a *perceptual set*. Siipola (1935) told subjects that they would be shown (tachistoscopically) words of a particular kind (e.g. animals). On presentation of a nonsense word, subjects often identified it as an animal name. Leeper (1935) demonstrated that the perception of an ambiguous figure can be affected by prior experimental experience of a figure stressing one aspect rather than another. Also Schafer and Murphy (1943) reported that the perception of ambiguous forms is influenced by the history of previous rewards and punishments for seeing either form.

In further consideration of the specific effect of stimuli, it will be obvious that the perception of stimuli does not always correspond exactly to the actual pattern of sensory stimulation (at the receptors and cerebral cortex). The phenomena of perceptual constancy and perceptual illusions are important examples of this non-correspondence.

Perceptual constancy

Perceptual constancy involves the perception of an object 'as it really is', even when presented under unusual or distorted conditions. This phenomenon occurs in regard to the object's colour, brightness, size, shape, and other characteristics. For example, a plate on the dinner table looks round (circular) to the individual sitting behind it, although its retinal shape is elliptical (*shape constancy*); white paper looks white whether in sunlight or in shade, despite the enormous variation in light reflected from its surface in both conditions (*brightness constancy*). The perception of depth or distance is critical in size and shape constancy. Research has shown that accuracy in estimating the size or shape of an unfamiliar object is reduced considerably if cues to its distance from the subject are eliminated (e.g. viewed through a small aperture or narrow tunnel). See Forgus (1966) for a more detailed discussion.

Forgus concluded that brightness constancy is the most primitive process phylogenetically, in that the role of learning is minimal. Shape constancy is the most advanced perceptual process, in that the effects of learning are considerable, while size constancy is intermediate, being neither as primitive as brightness constancy, nor as advanced as shape constancy. (For a more detailed review of the perceptual constancy literature, the reader is referred to Forgus (1966) Chapters 5 and 6).

Perceptual illusions

Perceptual illusions provide a further example of the non-correspondence between actual and perceived stimuli. For example there is the well-known Müller–Lyer illusion which is shown in Fig. 8.1.

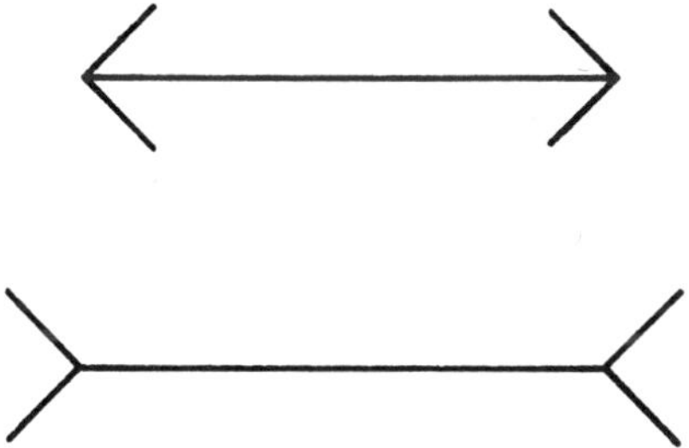

Fig. 8.1. Müller–Lyer illusion

An illusion occurring in everyday life is the '*moon illusion*'; the moon looks larger when it is nearer the horizon. Illusions may be a special case of perceptual constancy. Gregory (1966) suggested that the diverging arrowheads, in the *Müller–Lyer illusion*, are suggestive of distance or depth, while the converging arrowheads suggest the opposite. Since the two lines, retinally the same size, appear to be at different distances, the principle of *size constancy* requires that the line appearing further away should 'really be bigger'. Kaufman and Rock (1962) similarly argued, with the moon illusion, that the sky at the horizon look further away than the sky at its zenith. Thus the moon, the same size retinally at horizon and zenith, appears further away at the horizon and thus 'bigger'.

The above discussion of constancy and illusion suggest that perception is often organized in a way unrelated to actual sensory input.

Motivation

It has been suggested that the motivation of the individual is an important variable determining what is perceived. As reported above (p. 170), the recognition of stimuli is more rapid when they are related to some interest, value, or need of the perceiver. Hungry or thirsty subjects recognize words related to their needs more rapidly than other words. The identification of ambiguous stimuli appears to be particularly influenced by motivational factors. When subjects misidentify a word, they often guess in a way related to their own needs and interests. Moreover, some studies (e.g. McGuinnies 1949; Eriksen 1954) have shown that subjects take longer to recognize words which are of unpleasant connotation or are anxiety-arousing, such as 'taboo' words. This delay or 'warding off' of supposedly threatening material was commonly termed '*perceptual defence*' and was considered to be related to Freud's hypothesized mechanism of repression (the removal from consciousness of unacceptable material). However, this field of research abounds with methodological problems and difficulties in interpretation of the results, which are beyond the scope of this chapter (see Dixon (1971) for a detailed review of this area).

To summarize, stimuli have non-specific and specific effects. Non-specifically, too much or too little stimulation are disruptive to the organism's functioning. When considering the specific effects of stimulation, it becomes obvious that perception is organized in a manner which does not always correspond to external reality. The phenomena of perceptual constancy, perceptual illusions, and motivated perception are examples of this organizational process.

THINKING

As mentioned above (p. 168), thinking could be construed as a subset of perception. McKellar (1957) considered that 'thought products in general are the result of previous perceptual impressions organised into arrangements and the form of these arrangements is provided either by the original perceptual context or by relationships abstracted from other perceptual contexts'.

Forgus defined thinking as 'the act whereby already acquired content is manipulated to meet new demands on the individual'. He also stated: 'The act of thinking takes place on a broad continuum ranging from the low levels, as in reveries or dreams, to the highest levels, as in scientific creations. A high level of thinking is usually called reasoning or problem-solving because in these situations a great deal of reorganization of the present stimulation and learned context is necessary to emit the required behavioural patterns. The more uncertain the stimulus situation is for the individual, the more creative or productive his thinking must be to grasp its significance and construct a new meaningful system.'

Forgus's distinctions between low and high levels of thinking is not unlike McKellar's (1957, 1968) distinction between A- and R-thinking. A-thinking (*autistic thinking*) refers to the category of thinking including fantasy, dreams, hypnagogic imagery, hallucinations, etc. This category of thinking is reminiscent of Freud's primary process thinking (expression of unconscious needs and desires). R-thinking (*rational thinking*) refers to the category of thinking including problem-solving, logic, concept formation, critical evaluation, etc. (very much concerned with reality). Creativity and imagination would seem to involve aspects of both types of thinking.

Problem-solving

It is beyond the scope of this chapter to discuss problem-solving and concept formation in any detail. However, a brief summary of some of the important issues will be attempted. Problem-solving has been defined by Gagné (1966) as 'an inferred change in human capability that results in the acquisition of a generalisable rule which is novel to the individual, which cannot have been established by direct recall, and which can manifest itself in applicability to the solution of a class of problems'.

Maier (1930) demonstrated the importance of previous experience or '*set*' in problem-solving. The solution of a practical construction problem (building two pendulums from a limited set of materials) was very much determined by the presentation of 'direction', a clue to the manner in which the integration of the various elements of the problem takes place. Duncker (1945) showed that the spatial arrangement of components given to subjects affected the ease of solution of a construction problem. Previous experience can lead to impaired performance when skills are transferred to inappropriate situations (*functional fixation*). When an object must be used in a novel way to solve a practical problem, it is less likely to be so used if the subject has already seen it used, or used it himself for a different purpose.

Concept formation

Concept formation involves the response to stimuli as members of a class, not merely as individual events. The function of a concept is to relate present to previous experience, so that new situations and events may be dealt with without further learning. Card-sorting problems have often been used to study concept formation experimentally. A subject is given a deck of cards, each bearing certain markings. He has to sort these cards into relevant categories (i.e. learn the concepts according to which they should be sorted). Heidbreder (1946) varied the abstractness of categories in a card-sorting task and found that concrete concepts were most easily learned and abstract concepts least easily learned. Brain-damaged subjects show a greater deficit in dealing with abstract than concrete concepts (Goldstein and Scheerer 1941).

Creativity

Both problem-solving and concept formation can involve creative thinking, particularly when a task is open-ended. *Creativity* could be considered a special case of problem-solving, stressing the originality of the solution-response and usually an assessment of the value of the solution. It involves elements of both A- and R-thinking (McKellar 1957). Mednick (1963) considered that the range and strength of association to various symbols (i.e words) might be a good measure of creativity. The more creative an individual is, the more remote will be his associations to a given stimulus (word). Mednick constructed the 'remote associations test' (RAT) in order to assess this type of creative thinking. The subject is given a list of three words (wheel, electric, high) and asked to provide a fourth word which has something in common with these three (i.e. chair). RAT scores were found to correlate well with other measures of creativity (such as assessment of work produced).

There has been considerable research into the personality variables associated with creativity (e.g. Barron 1965; Getzels and Jackson 1962). Creative people are reported to be verbally fluent, flexible thinkers, independent, unconventional, often self-centred, and showing more evidence of psychopathology on clinical tests. There may be a grain of truth in the maxim 'genius is close to madness'. However, it is unwise to draw firm conclusions from such data, as both measures of creativity and personality are often poorly validated.

In considering the processes involved in creative thinking, we are very much restricted to introspective or subjective accounts by creative people. Patrick (1935, 1937) observed four stages in the creative process:

(1) *preparation*: increasing familiarity with situation and materials;
(2) *incubation*: unstructured (almost passive) assimilation of fragments and elements of task;
(3) *illumination*: goal direction established; and
(4) *verification*: results are achieved via corrections and modifications.

The process of creative thinking may be observed in the writing of a poem, the painting of a picture, and the solving of a scientific problem. McKellar (1957) described the creative process as present in many imaginative thinkers, writers, artists, and scientists.

Having mainly focused on R-thinking, it would now seem appropriate to consider A-thinking in more detail. While the majority of phenomena, which this label covers, will be dealt with in the next section on 'abnormal perceptual experience', mental imagery will be considered here.

Imagery

Imagery may be defined as an experience which revives a previous perceptual experience in the absence of the original sensory input. It is a symbolic or mediational phenomenon which represents external reality. The imager perceives the images as 'being inside his own head' and usually under conscious control. While predominantly visual, images can occur in other sense modalities. Imagery varies in vividness and in the dominance of one or other of the sense modes. McKellar (1957) categorized imagery in the following manner:

(1) *Ordinary waking images.* Imagery plays a large part in most people's everyday thinking and fantasy. There are many ways such images vary; vividness, completeness, duration, colour (with visual imagery), extent of voluntary control (autonomous → controlled).

(2) *Dream images.* These tend to be visual and strongly autonomous. They are usually reported as more vivid than waking images.

(3) *Eidetic images.* These are unusually stable and persistent images, have a quasi-perceptual character, are often three-dimensional, and have an 'out-thereness' quality unlike waking images. People vary in their ability to hold such images. Jaensch (1930) found that 60 per cent of children but only 7 per cent of adults had eidetic imagery suggesting that the skill is perhaps lost as other (perhaps verbal) thought patterns develop.

(4) *Waking–sleeping imagery.* The images occur on the borderline between wakefulness and sleep. They are often vivid and autonomous, sometimes almost hallucinogenic (see Chapter 7).

(5) *Hallucinations.* These images appear to be external and detailed. They are autonomous, as a rule. (A more detailed discussion is given on pp. 177–80.)

The above five types of images would be better conceived as forming a continuum rather than a series of rigid categories.

Imagery is, of course, of central importance in many behaviour therapy techniques such as imaginal desensitization, thought stopping, covert sensitization, and other covert control techniques (see Part IV). The manipulation of imagery in a controlled fashion is critical for successful treatment.

Thinking can be categorized in two ways: R-thinking and A-thinking. R-(rational) thinking is very much concerned with reality and includes such behaviour as problem-solving and concept formation. A-(autistic) thinking, on the other hand, involves fantasy, imagery, and hallucinations. Creativity seems to involve both types of thinking. The controlled use of the imagination is important in behaviour therapy.

ABNORMALITIES OF PERCEPTUAL EXPERIENCE

The remainder of this chapter will consider anomalous perceptual experiences generally and schizophrenia in particular.

Anomalous perceptual experience

Let us first consider anomalous imagery. We are all aware of the phenomenon of 'day dreaming', which tends to occur when we are engaged in a monotonous or repetitive task. Extreme cases of long-term stimulus deprivation can lead to more intrusive and intense imagery. The sensory deprivation research, considered on p. 169 indicated that such conditions led to an increased awareness of imagery, often in several modalaties. However, there is some controversy over whether subjects actually experience 'hallucinations'. The majority of reported hallucinatory phenomena were simple flashes and dots of light, lines, or simple patterning. Many subjects reported 'wallpaper patterns', a more complex level of perception. Few subjects reported fully integrated scenes. Strictly speaking, these phenomena should be considered as anomalous imagery rather than hallucinations, which are detailed, three-dimensional perceptions with an 'out-thereness' quality. It is possible that the subject is aware of the imagery because there is nothing else to divert his attention, and he reports it because the experimenter has asked him to do so. We probably experience many of the classical 'SD phenomena' every day, but we are rarely aware of it because we are bombarded by more interesting and relevant information.

Hypnagogic and hypnopompic imagery

Pronounced imagery often occurs as one falls asleep (*hypnagogic imagery*) and also as one wakes up (hypnopompic imagery). McKellar (1957) found that 53.18 per cent of a sample of 182 students reported hypnagogic imagery, while only 21.42 per cent reported hypnopompic imagery. Two-thirds (of those reporting such imagery) reported that it occurred only occasionally. Both types of imagery are autonomous and often vivid and realistic.

While hypnagogic images occur mainly in the visual and auditory modalities, kinaesthetic hypnagogic imagery is third in order of frequency. Two common experiences are hearing one's name called, or hearing music. Visual images can be quite bizarre and surrealistic. Unlike dream images, they appear in an illogical and disjointed sequence. They are usually unrelated to the subject's ongoing experiences.

Hypnopompic imagery is very similar to the hypnagogic variety, although less frequently reported. Its relative infrequency may be a result of its submersion by the press of early morning activities. The imagery may anticipate wakening (e.g. imagery of bell-ringing before the bell goes off).

There is some similarity between hypnagogic images and the so-called 'hallucinating' experience of SD subjects. Certainly SD would lead to drowsiness, facilitating hypnagogic imagery.

There is very little experimental work relating to such imagery. However, Foulkes, Spear, and Symonds (1966) found a correlation between personality and hypnagogic imagery. High imagers were found to have more positive personality attributes than low imagers. They were more creative, more self-accepting, more socially-poised, and less rigid. Low imagers tended to be rigid, intolerant, and conventional.

Illusions

Illusions represent a further example of anomalous perceptual experience.

We have already considered simple perceptual illusions (p. 171). More complex illusions occur in everyday life. For instance, it is not unusual, when waiting in a crowded place for a particular friend, to glimpse sight of that friend in the distance, only to find it is not that person on closer inspection. Such an illusion is due to misinterpretation which is based on:

(1) set—a predisposition to a certain kind of interpretative response related to expectations; or

(2) the ambiguity of the situation or stimulus.

Reed (1972) commented on this phenomenon: 'The stimulus, in fact, is open to a variety of interpretations and the perceiver tends to employ the one which most fits with his expectations. Perception is an hypothesis-testing activity and the hypotheses most readily available for testing are determined by our subjective probabilities about the likelihood of occurrence of any given event.' Thus, we expect to see our friend (i.e. there is a high probability of his appearance), and a distant figure is an ambiguous stimulus.

Hallucinations

So far we have considered anomalies of perception which are often experienced by most people. Hallucinations represent a very unusual perceptual response which is traditionally associated with mental disorder. Hallucinations have been defined as perceptions in the absence of a stimulus. But imagery could be similarly defined. The difference lies in the 'out-thereness' and substantiality of the hallucination, which is felt to be real. It is not a case of misinterpretation, as with illusions. Jaspers (1963) considered hallucinations to be actual false perceptions which are not distortions of real perceptions but are something quite new and occur simultaneously with and alongside real perceptions.

While in our culture hallucinations are viewed as abornmal and undesirable, other cultures have quite different attitudes. In some cultures the individual will deliberately seek hallucinations by exhausting himself or consuming toxic substances. The content of such experiences is usually related to social expectations. For instance, a young brave of the Crow Indians will isolate himself in the wilderness and submit himself to fasting, self-torture, and physical fatigue in order to perceive his guardian spirit. His future status in the tribe depends on his hallucinating appropriately. Many Eastern and South American cultures use hallucinogenic drugs to facilitate hallucinations, which form part of a striving for religious experience. Even in our own culture, LSD use has acquired a certain following and such experiences have been considered valuable and enlightening.

While hallucinations can occur in all sensory modalities, visual and auditory hallucinations remain the most common. The content is quite varied, although social (cultural) expectations often determine the type of hallucination.

Reed (1972) described several special hallucinatory phenomena.

(1) *Negative hallucinations*: the individual does not perceive a stimulus which is actually present.
(2) *Doppelganger*: an hallucination of the 'phantom double', oneself.
(3) *Pseudo-hallucinations*: the individual views the hallucination as not corresponding to external reality. It is psychologically meaningful and related to the person's situation.
(4) *Functional hallucinations*: hallucinations are associated with finite occurrences which are externally perceived (i.e. the person may hear voices whilst the bath tap is running; they stop when it is turned off).

Reed commented that 'pseudo-hallucinations and functional hallucinations were referred to as "bridges" between true hallucinations and imagery on the one hand, and illusions, on the other'.

There has been relatively little experimental work investigating hallucinations. Ellson (1941) instructed subjects to press a key when they were able to detect a faint tone, and to release the key when they could no longer hear it. The intensity of the tone was gradually increased up to the subject's threshold and then decreased again; on each trial it was preceded by a light signal. Forty subjects in the experimental group received sixty such trials, followed by 10 'test' trials in which the tone was absent. Sixty subjects in a control group received only trials without the tone. Thirty-two out of forty experimental subjects responded to one or more 'tones' on the 'test' trials, while only twelve out of sixty control subjects did. Thus, many subjects responded to a stimulus in its absence, which was perceived as being 'out there' and over which they had no voluntary control. Expectancy or set would seem to be an important element in the above phenomenon. The subject expects to perceive and respond to a certain critical stimulus. Two variables are important here:

(1) difficulty of discrimination between the presence and absence of the stimulus;
(2) motivation to perceive the stimulus.

Although the misperceptions reported in the above study might be technically defined as hallucinations, they differ in several ways from the pathological hallucinations experienced by *psychotic* individuals:

(1) they are much less complex;
(2) they are not really spontaneous, as the subject is instructed to expect them;
(3) they lack the affective component usually accompanying pathological hallucinations (their simplicity precludes any symbolic loading, and while they have hallucinatory form, they have no content); and
(4) they lack the phenomenological flavour of pathological hallucinations.

These experimentally induced phenomena seem to be more likely misidentifications than true hallucinations.

Some experimental manipulations have produced experiences which could be more validly labelled hallucinatory.

Sensory-deprivation research produced many experiences which were considered to be true hallucinations. However, as Reed (1972) commented:

In the SD condition, subjects do not usually attribute their experiences to external sources, and seldom regard them as correlates of external reality. They are almost always aware that their visual experiences are forms of imagery. . . . It seems likely that one reason why the SD subjects report imagery is that they have nothing else to do but observe their inner experiences. . . . Again, the monotony of the SD situation is naturally conducive to drowsiness and sleep, at least in the early stages. Thus, it seems likely that the complex phenomena reported are hypnagogic or hypnopompic images.

Experimental investigations of so-called 'hallucinogenic' drugs (i.e. LSD) created excitement, in that they appeared to produce true hallucinations, supposedly *psychotomimetic* in nature. However, the same criticisms apply as with SD research. The imagery is not usually perceived as real or 'out there', but is attributed to the effects of the drug.

Some research has considered the relationship between imagery and hallucination. Segal and Nathan (1964) investigated the relationship between intensity of imagery and ability to discriminate between imagery and perception of external reality. Subjects were asked to image an object while looking at a point on a blank screen. Without their knowledge, a slide of the object was projected on to the screen and its intensity was gradually increased from below threshold. It was found that those subjects who could most easily produce images were most emphatic about what were images and what were not; they were more able to discriminate imagery from real perception.

Seitz and Molholm (1947) assessed whether hallucinators were vivid imagers. They compare hallucinating schizophrenics, non-hallucinating schizophrenics, hallucinating alcoholics, and normals on a test of concrete imagery. The hallucinating subjects (schizophrenics and alcoholics) showed a lower mean percentage of imagery than did the non-hallucinating. The suggestion was that hallucinators were relatively weak imagers. Alternatively, one might speculate that hallucinators have difficulty in identifying imagery as separate from reality. There is considerable evidence to suggest that hallucinators do find it difficult to discriminate between internal and external cues. Witkin, Lewis, Hertzman, Machover, Meissner, and Wapner (1954) used the label 'field-dependence' to describe individuals dominated by cues from the environment who find it difficult as compared with 'field independent' individuals to differentiate environmental cues from internal cues. Also, SD research has suggested that field-dependent subjects are more likely to attribute imagery to external sources.

It would seem reasonable to conclude that 'the difference between imagery and hallucination cannot be defined in terms of stimulus or perceptual characteristics, but only in terms of whether the experience is believed to have an external correlate in objective existence' (Reed 1972). Hallucinations could be considered to be a result of faulty reality testing.

Many schizophrenic hallucinations are undoubtedly projections of the individual's ideas or beliefs. In other words anomalous functioning is more likely to arise from central determinants than from environmental input.

Delusions

This brings us on to discuss the anomalies of judgement and belief (or *delusions*). '*Over-valued ideas*' represent anomalies of belief and are somewhat similar to delusions. Reed (1972) defined over-valued ideas as 'beliefs of varying degrees of plausibility which are affectively loaded and tend to preoccupy the individual and to dominate his personality. They differ from true delusions primarily in the fact that they are psychologically comprehensible in terms of the individual's personality and experience.' For instance, an individual may hold a strong belief that formal education is a social evil, as a result of his own experience of the educational system. Over-valued ideas usually have some *consensual validation* (i.e. they are shared with other people). Such ideas are held with zeal and much emotion is involved in them. They can be related to personal, political, religious, humanitarian, or social issues. Naturally, over-valued ideas can only be defined in reference to a cultural norm. Very acceptable ideas in a culture are not likely to be defined as 'over-valued' even when they are maintained with zeal. Reed suggested that '*cognitive dissonance*' theory (Festinger 1957) might account for the preoccupation and proselytizing activities of people with over-valued ideas (i.e. the need to convert others to the idea). Cognitive dissonance theory states that individuals strive to maintain harmony between 'cognitive elements' (e.g. knowledge of their own and others' attitudes, feelings, and behaviour). Psychological tension results from an incompatibility of cognitive elements. The individual will strive to reduce such tension by modifying dissonant elements. The person with an over-valued idea will experience dissonance between his belief and the beliefs of others around him. Dissonance can be reduced by either dropping the idea or seeking social support. He will also seek to interpret ambiguous information as support for the idea.

How do we define delusions? According to Reed: 'A delusion is a belief which is demonstrably false by the standards of the individual's socio--cultural background, but which is held with complete conviction.' However, this definition does not seem sufficient. For instance, an individual may hold a religious belief, quite alien to the majority of his fellows, with great conviction. He would not necessarily be labelled 'deluded'. Perhaps there are areas of ideation which are allowed to remain very idiosyncratic, yet acceptable. Three further features need to be considered in more accurately defining 'delusions'.

1. *Unshakeability of belief*: the delusions remain firm despite counter-evidence and negative experience.
2. *Personalization of belief*: the content of the delusions is related to the

individual's needs, fears, or security.

3. *Extreme preoccupation of belief*: much time is spent ruminating about the delusion and noting new evidence supporting it.

In consideration of the content of delusions, cultural background is very important. Experiences shared in all cultures (e.g. hate, love, jealousy, etc.) would be expected to be common to deluded individuals generally. This is the case: *delusions of persecution* are found in most cultures. But, the more specific details of the content area vary considerably according to cultural variables. For instance, a person with delusions of persecution in a westernized scientific culture might believe that his enemies are attempting to kill him with laser beams. But, a person with a similar delusion in a 'primitive' culture might consider poisoned berries to be the instrument of persecution. Thus, as with many other psychological disorders, the form of delusion remains similar cross-culturally, while the content varies according to cultural variables. In addition to delusions of persecution, other forms of delusion include jealousy, love, *grandeur*, poverty, ill-health, and guilt. For a more detailed description of these delusional types, the reader is referred to Reed (1972, pp. 146–51).

To move beyond a descriptive analysis of delusions, it is important to distinguish between *primary* and *secondary delusions* (Reed 1972). The latter are a result of other abnormal experiences or affective states. For instance, an individual experiencing *depersonalization*, may develop a faulty explanation of this phenomenon, which is held with great conviction. The explanation may well be 'odd' because the experience itself is odd. Thus, the secondary delusion, like the over-valued idea, is psychologically comprehensible in terms of the individual's experience. The primary delusion, on the other hand, is basically the vague awareness of a *change in significance* of environmental stimuli. Things are perceived as different and uncertain. Primary delusion involves the transformation of meaning. This does not mean that information is inappropriately perceived or schematized, but that the schemators themselves have shifted interrelationships. In order to structure this unsettling situation, the individual suffering delusions seeks to explain this phenomenon (secondary delusion). The more unusual his experience of primary delusion, the more complex and idiosyncratic his explanation for the phenomenon must become. The present argument suggests that cognitive processes are not necessarily impaired, but that there has been a shift in cognitive structures. False postulation occurs as a result of this shift and the content is understandable as an attempt to account for new meanings. Experimental evidence relating to the above theoretical position of Reed will be discussed in the next section, which addresses itself to the anomalous perceptual experiences in schizophrenia.

Schizophrenic perceptual experiences

Schizophrenia can be characterized by many perceptual changes. Corbett

(1976) listed the following:

(1) changes in stimulus intensity (increased or decreased vividness of sensory stimuli);
(2) shifts in quality (changes in size, arrangement of stimuli);
(3) abnormal concomitant perceptions (stimuli are associated with secondary sensations, e.g. words are associated with pain);
(4) abnormal perceptual alienation (objects and people appear different or strange; perceptions lose their meaning);
(5) splitting of perceptions (e.g. a bird and its song are apart and separated);
(6) loss of perceptual constancy;
(7) failure of gating (too many stimuli for attention to cope with);
(8) abnormal time-perception (time speeds, slows, or stands still);
(9) abnormal spacc perception (e.g. space expands);
(10) distortion of body perception;
(11) hallucinations;
(12) changes in the perception of emotion (loss of affect, perceptions produce unusual affect).

A vast amount of experimental research has been carried out in order to investigate the nature of these perceptual changes, and to support or contradict theories developed to explain these changes. It is beyond the scope of this chapter to consider all but a small sample of this research area.

Silverman (1964) attempted to explain perceptual and attentional changes in schizophrenia in terms of extreme perceptual (or attentional) styles, of two types:

(1) extensive factors, which regulate the extent to which stimuli are sampled from the environment ('*perceptual scanning*'); and
(2) selective factors, which organize the stimulus field into relevant and irrelevant areas; the former are attended to, the latter are simultaneously inhibited ('*field articulation*').

Silverman considered that extreme forms of scanning and field articulation, minimal or excessive, characterize the perceptual functioning of most schizophrenics.

Experiments investigating perceptual constancy in schizophrenics should throw some light on the 'perceptual scanning' process. One would predict that the more intensively a subject scans the perceptual field, the greater his tendency towards over-constancy. Minimal scanning is correlated with reduced constancy or underconstancy. Experimental work (Raush 1952; Lovinger 1956; Pearl 1962) suggests that *acute schizophrenics* tend to exhibit overconstancy (i.e. they are excessive scanners) while *chronic schizophrenics* tend to exhibit underconstancy (i.e. they are minimal scanners).

Size-estimation experiments (Silverman 1964; Harris 1957; Zahn 1959) found that *reactive (good-premorbid) schizophrenics* tended to demonstrate over-constancy (i.e. excessive scanning) while *process* (*poor-premorbid schizophrenics*) tended to demonstrate underconstancy (i.e. minimal scanning). Thus, the tendency towards excessive or minimal scanning would seem to depend on both the *chronicity* and *premorbid history* of the individual schizophrenic.

Turning now to 'field articulation', research (using tests which require selective attention) suggests that *paranoids* are high field-articulators (Witkin *et al.* 1954) and that reactive schizophrenics are higher field-articulators than are process schizophrenics (Bryant 1961). Taylor (1956) found that delusional subjects demonstrated higher field-articulation than hallucinatory subjects. Witkin, Dyk, Faterson, Goodenough, and Karp (1962) suggested that the paranoid schizophrenic structures the environment by projecting his own system of ideas upon it. This is done in a highly selective fashion and tends to implicate particular people and situations. The more perceptually and conceptually articulated the paranoid is, the more systematized will be his delusional system.

Silverman (1964) considered that adoption of such extreme perceptual strategies by schizophrenics was anxiety-mediated and is related to early family experiences. For instance, the excessive scanner has learned that his most effective means of escaping or avoiding anxiety is to be hyperalert to the presence of cues which precede or occur concurrently with anxiety-provoking events. Parental communication of an ambiguous, inconsistent, or contradictory nature is considered to facilitate 'excessive scanning' (Singer and Wynne 1963; Wynne and Singer 1963). On the other hand, 'minimal scanners' are considered to avoid anxiety by directing their attention away from the environment. The parents of such individuals communicate with their offspring in a vague manner, rarely clarifying obscure perceptually-associated responses. Perception becomes more blurred, uncertain, and poorly organized. There is some evidence that institutionalization facilitates minimal scanning and articulation (Draguns 1963; Silverman, Berg, and Kantor 1965). This would make sense when one considers the low level of stimulation in institutional environments.

Many theories of schizophrenia rely on the concept of *abnormal drive or arousal*. Epstein and Coleman (1970) defined drive or arousal as 'energetic aspects of behaviour independent of directional tendencies'. It would be useful to briefly discuss a few 'drive theories' to see how well they explain the perceptual changes of schizophrenia.

Mednick (1958) suggested that schizophrenics were over-aroused or experience heightened drive. He assumed that increased drive raised the strength of all response-tendencies aroused in a situation, both dominant and competing responses. With greatly increased drive (as proposed in schizophrenia), weak response tendencies, normally well below threshold, were raised above threshold and competed with more dominant response-tendencies. This explained the response disorganization observed in schizophrenia. High arousal promoted stimulus generalization (well documented in normals) which increased the number of stimuli capable of evoking anxiety (thus increasing drive further). This spiralling effect precipitated acute schizophrenia. If the pre-schizophrenic with high drive was only exposed to limited anxiety-provoking situations, he could cope as a *schizoid personality*. But with high anxiety situations (such as life-events (Brown and Birley 1968)), the spiral began, thus precipitating an acute breakdown. The hypothesized stimulus generalization accounted for the stimulus overload, distractability, and *over-inclusive thinking*, where conceptual boundaries were loosened (see below). The acute schizophrenic learned to avoid affect-laden thoughts. Related thought tended to emerge because they are less anxiety-provoking. Long-term use of such avoidance strategies would lead to reduced drive (chronic state).

Broen and Storms (1966) also stressed the importance of drive or arousal. Instcad of a response threshold, they posited a response-strength ceiling. As drive increased, dominant responses reached a ceiling (or limit) and competing responses became more and more probable. In this way, normal response-hierarchies were destroyed and behaviour was disorganized. Three variables determined the amount of disorganization:

(1) relative initial strength of dominant and competing habit-tendencies;
(2) level of arousal; and
(3) height of response-strength ceiling.

They suggested that schizophrenics must have very low strength ceilings and/or very high levels of arousal; and also that the schizophrenic probably learnt to minimize response-disorganization by reducing his scanning of the stimulus array (i.e. he used a minimal scanning strategy).

Claridge (1972) showed that under LSD, the usual inverted U-curve representing the relationship between perceptual discrimination and arousal was reversed. Under placebo, perceptual discrimination improved to an optimum level of arousal and then deteriorated if arousal increased further (see Fig. 8.2A).

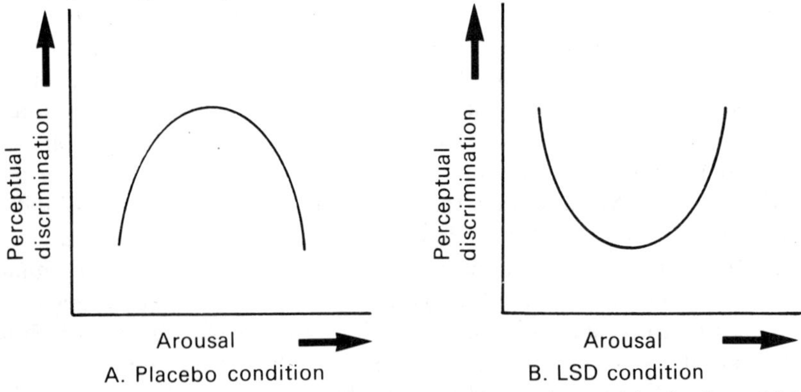

Fig. 8.2. Relationship between perceptual discrimination and arousal in placebo and LSD condtions. (Modified from Claridge 1972.)

Inhibitory mechanisms modulating the sensory input intervened once arousal had reached a critical level. However, under LSD (see Fig. 8.2B) heightened perceptual sensitivity occurred at high or low arousal and was worse at intermediate levels. The inhibiting mechanisms were inappropriately used. Claridge extrapolated these findings to schizophrenia, hypothesizing that while high arousal was associated with narrowing of attention in normals, these functions were dissociated in schizophrenia.

Epstein and Coleman (1970) also considered that the schizophrenic could not regulate the normal inhibitory mechanisms for controlling excitation. He responded in an 'all-or-none' manner, blocking excitation completely or being overwhelmed by it. Affectively-laden stimuli were particularly disorganizing. As external stimuli were often avoided to prevent overload, attention was turned towards internal stimuli, which became so intrusive as to minimize the distinction between inner and outer sense-data; both were equally compelling. It was understandable that schizophrenics might misinterpret imagery and emotional experience as external sensory experience. As the sense of 'selfness' or ego, depended somewhat on the constancy of internal and external sensory data, it followed that schizophrenics, with a loss of this constancy would be prone to an altered perception of self (i.e. feelings of strangeness, of being different, of not being at all, of being everywhere).

McReynolds (1960) emphasized the importance of anxiety in the genesis of schizophrenia. A high level of unassimilated 'percepts' (sense data and memory data) was considered to be a major source of anxiety. We have a tendency to assimilate new percepts into conceptual systems. For the schizophrenic, incongruency between the content of percepts and the systems available for assimilation becomes the major source of enduring anxiety. This 'schizophrenic' anxiety could be defended against by avoidance of new percepts (withdrawal) or inappropriate assimilation (delusions, thought disorder) by modification of existing systems. One might hypothesize that these incongruous percepts might be a result of inconsistent parental behaviour. This will be discussed later when considering the 'construct theory' approach of Bannister and Fransella (1971).

Let us now turn to research investigating schizophrenic though-processes. Early work examined 'overinclusive thinking', which may be defined as a broadening of conceptual boundaries caused by an inability to ignore distraction by irrelevant stimuli. Cameron (1939, 1944) hypothesized that overinclusive thinking resulted from the loss of organizing factors inherent in the need to communicate with others. He assumed that social motivation organized loosely-related ideas in order to communicate them to other people. There is some evidence that 'social' concepts are more disturbed than other concepts in schizophrenia (Whiteman 1954; Moriarty and Kates 1962; Brodsky 1965; Bannister and Salmon 1966), which gives some support to this position.

Bannister and Fransella (1971) applied '*personal construct theory*' (developed by George Kelly (1955)) to *schizophrenic thought disorder*. Kelly viewed man as a scientist, attempting to make sense of his perception of the world. To organize his sense data, man developed constructs which were interpretive structures (dichotomous concepts) which were continually modified. Constructs were used to predict. Confirmation strengthened the system of constructs, disconfirmation weakened the system. Bannister and Fransella considered schizophrenics to possess very loose construct systems (i.e. relationships between them were vague, inconsistent, and disorganized). To explain this *loose construing*, Bannister hypothesized a process of '*serial invalidation*' of constructs in early life. The pre-schizophrenic was unable to develop a tight construct system owing to poor validation by people around him (e.g. inconsistent parental communication). There was some experimental support for this process in normal subjects who were 'serially invalidated' on an experimental task (Bannister 1965). Thus, Bannister suggested that the early family environment was not conducive to the formation of stable construct systems. This position is not dissimilar to many researchers into family psychopathology in relation to the development of schizophrenia. Lidz, Fleck, and Cornelison (1965) suggested that the pre-schizophrenic child was reared in an environment in which meaning was confused and distorted and he learned to deny the validity of his perceptions. Bateson, Jackson, Haley, and Weakland (1956) conceived of the *double-bind* situation, where the child was faced with two incongruent communications (at different levels of communication) and was forced to respond. It was not surprising that the child learned not to trust his capacity for perceptual discrimination.

Payne and colleagues (Payne 1962; Payne, Matussek, and George 1959; Payne and Hewlett 1960) used the object classification test (OCT) which involves the sorting of cards into different categories, to assess overinclusion in schizophrenics. He found some schizophrenics to be overinclusive (usually acute paranoids with delusions and a good prognosis) and some to be retarded (usually chronic non-paranoids without delusions and a bad prognosis). *Retardation* refers to an extreme slowness in test performance. Overinclusion is considered to be a breakdown in information processing (i.e. an attentional deficit such that irrelevant stimuli are included in the consideration of a problem, so that the problem cannot be defined in a way that approaches the solution). However, two theoretical formulations are offered. Payne, *et al.* (1959) suggest that overinclusive thinking is a result of extreme stimulus generalization and a disorder of the process whereby inhibition is built up to circumscribe and define a concept (see Mednick's theory, pp. 183–4). But Payne and Hewlett (1960) argued that it is a result of a breakdown in a hypothetical selective filter mechanism which facilitates attention to relevant and not irrelevant stimuli. Chapman (1956) demonstrated that schizophrenics were very susceptible to distraction from external non-task-relevant stimuli when he presented schizophrenics and normals with a conceptual sorting task in which the number of distractor items (pictures on a card) were varied. The larger the number of distractor items, the poorer was the schizophrenic's performance.

However, the work of Payne and colleagues on overinclusion has been criticized on a number of counts:

1. There was poor reliability and validity of 'tests of overinclusion' (Kugelmass and Fondeur 1955; Payne and Hewlett 1960; Hawks 1964; Foulds, Hope, McPherson, and Mayo, 1967).
2. Incorrect classification on the OCT was automatically considered to be overinclusive thinking.
3. Correlations between overinclusiveness and (a) acuteness of the condition and (b) delusions were not replicated (Payne 1962; Goldstein and Salzman 1965).
4. The tests had no prognostic significance (Hawks 1964).
5. Two theoretical positions were offered.

Hawks and Marshall (1971) suggested that distractability and retardation were reactions to the same basic condition of information-overload. Acute schizophrenics were particularly aware of the diversity of stimulation, largely inhibited in most people. They did not appear retarded because they attempted to cope with this diverse stimulation and thus appeared distractable and thought-disordered. At some stage, they might learn to cope with this overload by reducing the rate of response. Thus, they would no longer appear distractable or overinclusive but rather retarded and slow to respond. To support this formulation Hawks and Marshall cited experimental work demonstrating that when schizophrenics could set their own pace (i.e. slow down) their performance was similar to normals (Shakow 1962). Also, it was reported that increasing time-pressure with normals produced schizophrenic-like responses (Usdansky and Chapman 1960; Flavell, Draguns, Feinberg, and Budin 1958).

Hemsley (1977, after Miller 1960) considered the many schizophrenic 'symptoms' as representing differing secondary 'adaptations' to the primary condition of information overload.

1. *Errors* (intrusion of associated responses). This represents the initial pattern of performance in acute schizophrenia, the individual attempting to respond at a rate which would have been error-free before the onset of the cognitive disturbance. Clinically observed phenomenon include inappropriate responding and incoherent speech.
2. *Omission* (lowered responsiveness, raised threshold for response). The schizophrenic learns not to respond. Much research has demonstrated this adaptation in chronic schizophrenics (e.g. Wing and Brown 1968). However, institutionalization may also contribute to the reduced responsiveness. Clinically, one might observe *under-responsiveness, poverty of speech,* and *flattening of affect.*

3. *Approximation* (simplified categorizing systems, several stimuli elicit the same response rather than individualistic responses). Stimuli are often treated as equivalent on the basis of superficial similarities. This may be crucial to the development of delusions.
4. *Escape* (reduction of exploratory responses, avoidance of 'high information' situations, e.g. social situations). Social situations are avoided as these involve response-uncertainty or information-overload. Again, social withdrawal is more prominent in chronic schizophrenics, although one cannot disentangle the effects of institutionalization (Wing and Brown 1968). *Catatonia* (a state of complete withdrawal and non-responsiveness) may represent an extreme form of this reduction of exploratory responses.
5. *Queueing* (delayed responding). Schizophrenics may slow down their rate of response to cope with information overload. Hawks and Marshall (1971) demonstrated that associative events could be reduced by slowing down the rate of response. Retardation is observed in many chronic patients.
6. *Filtering* (increased attenuation of certain classes of sensory input). A crude inhibitory system for controlling excitation of the 'all or none' kind, may well be developed.

Hemsley went on to consider the factors influencing the choice of method of adaptation.

1. *Severity of overload*
   Miller (1960) using normal subjects at high levels of overload, found 'omission' to be the most usual method of adaptation. 'The "omission" and "escape" adaptations may be the only viable methods at high levels of overload. Both are more prominent in chronic patients; it is likely that those patients who eventually become chronic are those with the greatest cognitive disturbance. At more moderate levels of disorganisation, all methods of adaptation might be attempted' (Hemsley 1977). Paranoid schizophrenics, with only moderate cognitive disorganization, may well adopt the 'approximation' adaptation. This is supported by the findings that paranoid delusions are not more prominent in chronic patients (Wing and Brown 1968) and may well be much less frequent with increased chronicity (Depue and Woodburn 1975).
2. *Personality factors*
   Personality variables may well influence the choice of method of adaptation. Narrowed scanning strategies were correlated with a measure of 'defensiveness' (Haley 1971).
3. *Environmental factors*
   There is little doubt that institutional environments facilitate withdrawal and under-responsiveness (Wing and Brown 1970). Also, relationships with family or friends may play some part in determining the method of adaptation (Brown, Monck, Carstairs, and Wing 1962).

There is some evidence that schizophrenogenic family environments exist (Lidz *et al.* 1965; Bateson *et al.* 1956; Bannister and Fransella 1971).

SUMMARY

In this section, a variety of anomalous perceptual experiences including anomalous imagery, hallucinations, and delusions are discussed. Imagery and hallucination do not appear to be perceptually distinct phenomena, but differ rather in terms of belief in external correlation with reality. Delusions seem to result from a perceived change in the significance of environmental stimuli. The distinction between primary and secondary delusions is considered. Lastly, the phenomenon of schizophrenia is examined with particular reference to perceptual and cognitive changes. Much of the research suggests that faulty information processing leading to information overload is crucial to the schizophrenic condition. A variety of theoretical models are presented which account for this breakdown and the wide variety of secondary adaptations made by the schizophrenic.

Part III
Psychological assessment and behaviour

INTRODUCTION TO PART III

This part begins with a chapter on communication and interviewing. The first two sections in this chapter discuss the basic factors in communication and multiple communication systems. The next three sections briefly discuss the dynamics of communication, levels of communication, and interviewing techniques. The final section deals with the interview as an assessment technique.

The second chapter discusses the assessment of cognitive factors. It begins by considering the main principles of psychological measurement, goes on to discuss intelligence and memory, and concludes by considering some of the errors in psychological measurement, and how to decrease or avoid them.

Chapter 11 is concerned with 'mood states' and their assessment. After discussing the nature of mood states and differentiating between 'state' and 'trait', the measurement of anxiety, depression, and hostility is considered. The chapter finishes with a discussion of the influence of response sets or styles in personality assessment.

Chapter 12 is essentially a bridging chapter relating assessment to treatment. The emphasis is on the client's motivation for treatment. However, various aspects of the therapist's role which may affect the specific behaviour of the therapist in his relationships with both clients and colleagues are discussed.

9

Communication and Interviewing

Much tongue and much judgement seldom go together.
Sir Roger l'Estrange

This chapter is one of the most important in the book, dealing as it does with various interpersonal situations, which may include the reporting of a child's test results to parents, giving a candidate for surgery the appropriate amount and type of information about his operation and recovery period, and carrying out an intense psychotherapy session. A number of sources are recommended: Bennett (1976), Ley (1977), McGuire and Rutter (1976), and Sullivan (1953). Sullivan is particularly recommended for the psychotherapeutically orientated health worker. Ivey's (1971) book on microcounselling, in conjunction with the use of videotape, is especially valuable in teaching the potential interviewer the basic components of effective interviewing. A more experimental and social–psychological discussion of communication in groups may be found in Freedman, Carlsmith, and Sears (1970) or in Zajonc (1968), and of interviewing, in Cannell and Kahn (1968). The behavioural approach to interviewing is discussed in Haynes (1978).

Clearly of great importance here are the characteristics of both the communicator and the recipient of that communication. Both the communicator and recipient tend to perceive information in a biased way depending upon those factors they tend to selectively misperceive. Both parties in an interpersonal relationship obviously have their attitudes toward different aspects of life. They may indeed have significantly different value-systems, which makes accurate communication between them somewhat difficult. In addition, particularly during psychotherapeutic interviews, the emotions of both the therapist and client may be somewhat heightened, which, at times, may make it more difficult for them to think as rationally as they might. Many assessment situations are standardized interviews. For example, the administration of the Weschler Adult Intelligence Scale (WAIS) (Weschler 1955), which is typically done in rather a formal manner can be regarded as a structured interview. The major purpose of the interview may be to establish the general level of intelligence and the specific assets and deficits of an individual in the various abilities measured. One can also note during this structured interview situation the degree to which the person assessed seems to be anxious, the degree to which he seems to be motivated to do his best under the circumstances, and whether or not he has any speech deficits or irregularities in his motor behaviour, and so forth.

Thus, the interview is considered quite important in assessment. There is general agreement that every interview is an assessment or evaluative situation, although the emphasis on evaluation tends to vary from therapist to therapist and from one session to another. The main point is that it is difficult to draw a line between an assessment and a therapy interview. Both types of situation are probably therapeutic to most clients seen by psychologists.

The interview, then, is used in the assessment of an individual's physical condition and his intellectual and emotional characteristics, and, in fact, is used in any situation in which there is an exchange of information. Since the time per patient available to most medical practitioners is limited, it is important to become proficient in interviewing, since in many ways it is the basis of the doctor–patient relationship.

BASIC FACTORS IN COMMUNICATION

A communication system can be said to consist of four units: a transmitter, a mode of communication, a medium of communication, and a receiver. Figure 9.1A shows these units.

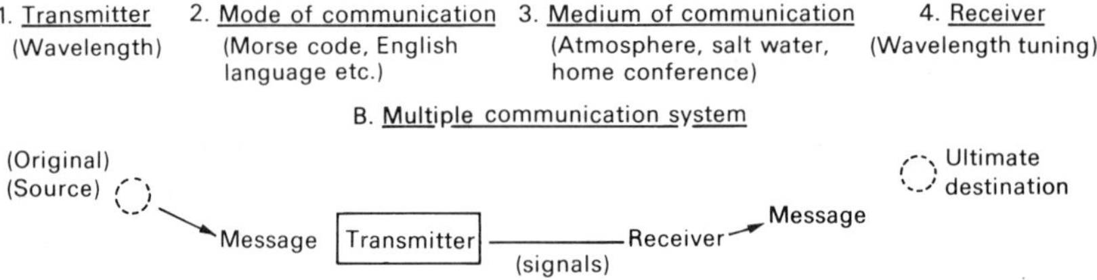

Fig. 9.1. Electronic communication system as analogous to human communication. (A) a fault (breakdown, interference) may occur in any of the above four units of a communications system, or in the human being at each end of the system. (B) multiple communications systems may increase difficulties in the transmission and reception of messages.

The terms 'transmitter' and 'receiver' are taken from electronics, and the analogy with communication between human beings is a strong one. A radio transmitter must be placed on a certain wavelength in order for the message to be received. Similarly, a human being must put himself on a certain wavelength in relation to the receiver, by making sure he has the other person's attention, has eye-contact, and is speaking loud enough and in the appropriate language or dialect.

The second unit of communication, the mode, is extremely important, even if both people use the same language or dialect, since if transmitter and receiver are of a different class or subculture within a particular society, the differences in idiosyncratic language or idiom used may produce negative attitudes, which may mean that the message received will not be the same as the message sent. Further, even if, despite the above difficulties, the message received is equivalent to the message sent, it may not then be accepted. However, if the transmitter formulates his message in a slightly different way—based on his assessment of the personality of the receiver—it is more likely that the message will be not only understood but accepted as well (see Chapter 14 for a fuller discussion of this point).

One may consider the language used by certain mental patients as being in a category of its own, for instance, the so-called "schizophrenese" used by many schizophrenic patients. Many potential receivers take the easy way out by treating this language as unintelligible nonsense, just as some people tend to reject foreigners by saying, "Why don't these people learn English", without making an effort to learn their language. While, admittedly, schizophrenese is by no means an easy language to learn, if potential receivers adopt an attitude of tolerance, acceptance and willingness to listen they can in fact learn to communicate with schizophrenic patients. Thus, the importance of the mode of communication can hardly be over-stressed.

The medium of communication depicted in Fig. 9.1A is perhaps best seen as the situation and/or emotional atmosphere in which communication occurs. In some instances, verbal communication may be carried out more effectively in the patient's home than in the health professional's office. In certain instances communication may be better carried out in a group situation, such as in the patient's family or in a ward or clinic group in which all staff involved in the case are present. While communication in groups may introduce more difficulties there are also very definite advantages.

Particularly when one is communicating in a system involving probable 'faults' in the receiver (a disturbed or emotionally involved person) then responsibility for communication may be much more in the hands of the transmitter or therapist. If the therapist is willing to vary his wavelength of transmission and his mode and possibly the medium or situation in which the communication takes place, then effective reception becomes more probable. It is not by any means suggested here that the therapist or transmitter should do all the work, however. While it is important to communicate messages to the patient and to understand the patient's 'language' behaviour, it is also important to help the patient receive on more normal frequencies, in somewhat more varied modes, and in more varied situations. Communication is not a one-way street, and this may mean that adequate communication with some patients will require more adequacy and flexibility on the part of the therapist–transmitter than is at first possible for the patient–receiver.

MULTIPLE COMMUNICATION SYSTEMS

Figure 9.1B adds two other components to the communication system, the source of the message to be transmitted, and the ultimate destination (ultimate receiver) of the message. These additions are pertinent when the source of the particular message is other than the person from whom the message is seen to originate, and the ultimate destination or receiver is one who is not the initial receiver. While one may argue that the addition of an original source and an ultimate destination or receiver simply adds two more communication systems, yet it is important to consider these additions because in human communications difficulties in transmisison and accurate reception are most likely to occur when multiple systems are involved. In many cases it is perhaps advisable not to involve more than one communication system in communicating the same message. For example, poor communication may result when a psychologist or psychiatrist asks a patient to tell his wife to behave towards him in a certain way. Clearly the patient may misinterpret the message or distort it before communicating it to his wife because of memory difficulties or because of his particular psychological needs. Even assuming that the patient is fairly intact and transmits the message accurately, there is no guarantee that the wife will perceive or accept the message adequately. It would obviously be much better to see the patient and his wife together to ensure adequate communication. It is also important to keep in mind the possibility that while one spouse is the designated patient, the other may be equally, or more, emotionally disturbed.

The types of communication situation are shown in Table 9.1.

TABLE 9.1
TYPES OF COMMUNICATION SITUATION

1. Intra-personal relations (see Freud 1964)
   Self–self (relations with self)
2. Inter-personal relations
   (see Sullivan (1953) and Haley (1963))
   (a) Self — Other (one-to-one)
   (b) Self — Others (individual to group)
   (c) Group — Group (group to group)

Note: Understanding (interpretation) is more than the reception of the message.

SOME DYNAMICS OF COMMUNICATION

Freud's very interesting and informative book *The psychopathology of everyday life* (1964) should be required reading for all those who work closely with other people. This book provides many examples of the significance of slips of the tongue, accidents, and 'forgetfulness' or distortions of memory processes. Haley's (1963) book is recommended reading for those who work with psychologically disturbed patients, especially schizophrenics and patients in marital and family units. Haley sees psychopathology as a particular set of methods used to achieve control in a relationship. From Haley's point of view, 'a symptom is the advantage it gives the patient in gaining control of what is to happen in a relationship with someone else'. Successful therapy involves the therapist gaining control of the relationship he wishes to have with his client. Therefore, the development of the tactics which may be used not only to gain this control, but also to influence the client's 'emotions and somatic sensations' is the essence of therapy in Haley's view.

Sullivan's (1953) interpersonal theory stressed the concept of participant observer. The self-awareness of the therapist is very important in analysing his reactions to his client. The therapist or interviewer not only observes the client but also himself. An analysis of his own reactions of anxiety, anger, pleasure, etc., enables the interviewer to monitor and evaluate what is taking place in the interpersonal relationship. Sullivan's approach to the interviewing situation is discussed more fully below.

LEVELS OF COMMUNICATION

Watzlawick's (1962) anthology of human communication is helpful in introducing some of the basic concepts of communication. Three main premises about communication were noted by Watzlawick. The first is that 'one cannot *not* communicate'. Obviously, one must consider non-verbal communication as important. As already mentioned above, symptomatology may be considered as a form of communication. Indeed, even silence is meaningful, particularly in situations in which it is unexpected or discouraged. Watzlawick's second premise was that 'Communication is a multilevel phenomenon'. The main point here is that communication does not occur in a vacuum—it takes place in a specific context. There are two aspects of the context: (1) the actual informational *content* of the communication and (2) the *meta-communication*, which indicates what the message concerns and the way in which the transmitter of the information perceives his relationship with the receiver. Finally, the third premise is that the 'message sent is not necessarily the message received'. The assumption is typically made by the transmitter that his view of reality is shared by the receiver. Clearly, to the extent that this assumption is unwarranted, there may be difficulty in receiving and/or accepting the actual message transmitted.

Before going on to the next section it should be noted that there is ample evidence that some form of conditioning is involved in all types of psychotherapy and counselling (Greenspoon 1955; Verplanck 1955; Krasner 1962;

Truax, Carkhuff, and Douds 1964). However, the degree to which the conditioning is knowingly and overtly used by an interviewer to achieve a particular goal with a particular client is unknown in most situations. In other words, it seems that contrary to the early statements of some client-centred therapists (see Chapter 14), evaluation and differential reinforcement of particular interview content may occur without the interviewer or client being aware of it (Vingoe 1965).

INTERVIEWING TECHNIQUES

While some interviews may be purposely arranged to induce stress in order to determine the interviewee's ability to cope with this situation, it is assumed for the purposes of this discussion that the intent of most interviews carried out by mental-health professionals is to communicate. Thus, one of the first tasks of the interviewer is to attempt to put the interviewee at his ease. However, the inexperienced interviewer may also be anxious and apprehensive. Lief and Fox (1963) found that medical students 'may be concerned lest the patient be angry or otherwise emotionally upset or uncooperative'. In many cases information about the interviewee will be available before the interview, and this can then be used to reduce the anxiety of both interviewer and client. The first phase of most interviews will be the development of rapport with the client. Watzlawick (1962) noted that 'to understand himself, man needs to be understood by another'. Thus, it is clear that there needs to be mutual understanding and trust between interviewer and interviewee.

Hetherington (1970) discussed the clinical interview in terms of the particular purpose involved. Both the attitude of the 'client' and 'therapist' are considered and there is a section concerning the structured and unstructured interview. Clearly, the 'therapist' brings his values and biases into the interview, and even if he conducts a structured interview it is likely to reflect his own point of view. Hetherington (1970) included an example of a structured psychological interview at the end of his chapter. The following relatively global areas are included: (1) attitudes, likes, and dislikes; (2) relations to others; (3) attitudes to past and future, and (4) attitude to illness.

Harry Stack Sullivan in his interpersonal theory of psychiatry regarded the interpersonal relationship as the most important concept of personality. Thus, for him, interview situations were of great importance. It has already been noted that Sullivan (1953) considered the interview as an interpersonal situation in which the interviewer came to his conclusions regarding the client through the procedure of *participant observation*. The interviewer must consider his own psychological reactions to the client in terms of assessing the factors of relevance in the interview situations. For example, he should be aware of feeling anxious from time to time, or even feeling somewhat hostile or angry towards the client. In other words, he should use his own organism as a sensitive measuring instrument of the effect of the client's manoeuvers upon his feelings and emotions. Sullivan noted that the main factor interfering with effective communication was anxiety, which he defined as 'a sign that one's self-esteem, one's self-regard, is endangered'. The three ways of handling anxiety were: (1) to avoid arousing it in the first place if possible; (2) to prevent it developing further, and (3) reassurance. Sullivan did not provide a structured questionnaire for use in the interview and, in fact, particularly in early contacts with the client, he recommended an open-ended approach. On the other hand, Sullivan did discuss the interview in four main stages: (a) the formal inception; and (2) the reconnaissance—both included as early stages of the interview; (3) the detailed inquiry; and, finally, (4) the termination. After the two initial stages, Sullivan felt that the interviewer was in a position in which he should have formulated a number of alternative hypotheses regarding the client's problem, which could consequently be tested in the detailed inquiry. Sullivan's flexible open-ended approach has much to recommend it and his book on the interview provides an excellent resource for the interviewer of any persuasion. It is difficult to do justice to Sullivan in a short space but an excerpt from his concluding chapter will give the flavour of his approach. He notes that in considering one's role as an expert that

> the interviewer is seriously interested in the problem presented by the interviewee; he is careful to avoid misunderstandings and unintentional erroneous impressions; he is ready to be corrected, yet chary of repetitive, circumstantial, or inconsequential details; he foregoes the satisfaction of any curiosity about matters into which there is no clear technical need to inquire, he eschews all procedure chiefly calculated to impress the client with the interviewer's clairvoyance or omniscience; he avoids all impractical meaningless comment, the clouding of issues, or tacit consent to dangerous delusion or error that will be difficult or embarrassing subsequently in the interview; he proceeds in general with such simple clarity that the interviewee can follow the direction of the inquiry; and from time to time he offers his impression for correction or discussion by the interviewee. And finally, the interviewer as an expert makes sure that the interviewee 'knows himself', the better for the experience.

While it is thought that Sullivan would agree that the best way to learn interviewing 'technique' is to do or experience it, yet it is advisable to read his book carefully before embarking upon experiential training.

THE INTERVIEW AS AN ASSESSMENT PROCEDURE

When the main goal of the interview is to assess the nature of a patient's problems, three principal factors are important (Sheppe and Stevenson 1963).

(1) to gain and maintain rapport;
(2) to obtain relevant information from the patient;
(3) to allow the behaviour exhibited by the patient to be observed.

These factors have been discussed in the previous section. However it must be stressed that gaining and maintaining rapport is of primary importance, for without the confidence and trust which is the essence of a good interpersonal relationship, the reliability and validity of material obtained during the interview is suspect or at least is more difficult to interpret. One of the most important tasks of the interviewer, after putting the patient at his ease, is to verify with the interviewee the purpose for which the interview is being held. It is often the case that one or more of the participants in the interview has faulty preconceptions about the purpose of the interview or is even unaware of the purpose of the interview altogether.

Clearly, non-verbal as well as verbal communication is important. Some non-verbal cues of importance include:

(1) variations in eye-contact;
(2) facial expressions;
(3) general posture;
(4) posture in relation to the interviewer; and
(5) other body movements.

It is important to correlate any of these changes with the client's verbal behaviour. In other words, are verbal and non-verbal components of the client's behaviour consistent with one another or discrepant? One of the most important points made by Haley (1963) is that an interpersonal message is accompanied by other messages which comment on the primary message. Haley noted that human messages are qualified by:

(1) the context in which they take place;
(2) verbal messages;
(3) vocal or linguistic patterns;
(4) bodily movements.

Important premises of Haley's 'level of communication theory' include the fact that 'one cannot *fail* to qualify a message [and when] . . . a message classifies or qualifies another message, it may be congruent and affirm that message, or incongruent and negate it'.

In addition to monitoring the non-verbal behaviour of the client some cues of significance to be aware of during the interview include the following.

(1) The lack of comment regarding a topic which one would expect to be mentioned, (e.g. when asked to tell the interviewer about his family, the patient makes no mention of his mother).
(2) Blocking (the patient may begin to mention something apparently significant, and without any warning, comes to an abrupt halt).
(3) Other unexpected changes in the subject being discussed.

The importance of how the interviewer is perceived by the client should be noted. For example, does the appearance or behaviour of the interviewer remind the client of an unliked or liked 'significant other'? (Sheppe and Stevenson, 1963). Positive and negative transference is discussed in Chapter 13. One must also not forget the characteristics of the interviewer. While the possession of technical skills in interviewing and treatment is important, the attitudes of the interviewer towards his client are not of lesser importance. A discussion of the four aspects of the 'psychological–examiner–therapist' (Schafer 1954) is provided in Chapter 12.

Finally, it is well to bear in mind the following dangers to which we humans may succumb:

(1) that behaviours observed during the 'initial interview' will be taken as representative;

(2) that the interviewer may tend to interpret behaviour in later interviews, so as to make it consistent with initial impressions (over generalization) (Mischel 1973).

Professionals are no more immune than others from the tendency to come to conclusions or take decisions on limited evidence. It is important to allow the client to speak in a conducive atmosphere. The interviewer or therapist must cultivate the talent of being a good listener.

The next chapter includes a discussion of the importance of obtaining a number of behavioural or test samples before coming to conclusions or taking firm decisions regarding another human being.

10
Assessment of cognitive factors

To Thales . . . the primary question was not What do we know, *but* How do we know it, *what evidence can we adduce in support of an explanation offered.*

Aristotle

Cognitive activity refers to those processes involved in learning (i.e. the registration, processing, and subsequent storage of information). Processing includes those activities known as thinking and reasoning (i.e. the comparison and forming of relationships between ideas and images). Thinking, both rational (R-thinking) and autistic (A-thinking) (McKellar 1957) are discussed in Chapter 8. The quality of cognitive activities is to a large extent a function of intellectual capacity, including memory functioning.

While the extent to which psychologists carry out assessments of general intellectual and memory functioning has decreased over the last decade or two, the assessment and understanding of these two factors, is important, especially in neuropsychological work.

Before discussing intelligence and memory it is important to outline the main principles involved in psychological measurement.

CHARACTERISTICS OF ADEQUATE PSYCHOLOGICAL SCALES

Psychologists may use measuring instruments of various levels of complexity which may satisfy the requirements of a particular *level of measurement* but not others. Siegal (1956) discussed the requirements for nominal, ordinal, interval, and ratio scales of measurement. The level of measurement is important in terms of fulfilling the assumptions of specific statistical tests. However, since the emphasis here is on concepts such as reliability and validity, rather than on statistical analysis, those interested in a more detailed treatment of the theory of measurement are referred to Siegal (1956).

Measuring instruments may vary from a simple seven-point self-rating scale to a relatively complex inventory such as MMPI. With a simple self-rating scale, the client may be given a definition of the characteristic to be rated such as extroversion, and asked to circle one of the numbers from 1 to 7 which indicate an increasing degree of extroversion.

A client may be asked to complete an inventory such as the MMPI or EPI, in which he is asked to indicate if certain statements are applicable to him. An example might be: 'I have little or no trouble getting to sleep at night'. The above are self-report scales and an examiner is not particularly necessary. On the other hand, the situation becomes more complicated when the WAIS (Wechsler 1955) or the Wechsler Memory Scale (Wechsler and Stone 1945) is administered by an examiner, in that the situation then becomes a standardized interview, in which the psychologist may use his training in *objective observation* to assess characteristics of the client which may not be directly measured by the particular scale used.

The expansion of research in the area of behaviour therapy has led to a greater interest in behavioural observation as an assessment procedure. In contrast to the administration of an intelligence test such as the WAIS, two or more observers are present in order to establish the extent of inter-observer agreement. Hayes (1978) has written an extensive text in the area of behavioural assessment. The characteristics of a measuring instrument tend to be established in different ways depending upon the type of measuring device used. In addition, some of the characteristics important in some situations may not apply in others.

As indicated by Anastasi (1976), a psychological test is essentially 'an objective and standardised measure of a sample of behaviour'. The two essential characteristics of an assessment device are reliability and validity—and you can't have one without the other. However, assuming that the test contains an adequate sample of the domain or universe of items or situations one wishes to measure, other characteristics must be satisfied before one can determine reliability and validity.

If the test is a self-report device, the instructions for responding to the items in the test should be non-ambiguous. This, of course, is equally true of an examiner-administered test. In direct observation, the behaviour to be observed must be clearly defined, a procedure set up to ensure adequate sampling of the ongoing behaviour, and observers should be rigorously trained to meet some criterion of inter-observer agreement, and frequent assessments made of the observers' performance to prevent *consensual observer drift* (Haynes 1978). The procedures in scoring the data must also be clear and non-ambiguous. Thus, in essence, the procedures used in obtaining measurement data must be standardized. As noted by Anastasi standardization implies uniformity of *procedure* in administering and scoring. Anastasi also stresses *objectivity* in administration and scoring as an important characteristic to aim for in psychological assessment. If the scale measures cognitive factors then it is important to establish the level of difficulty of the items by determining the percentage of subjects in the sample groups upon which the test is based or *normed* that pass each item.

The *reliability* of a scale refers to its *consistency*. If the scale is administered on more than one occasion are the results obtained consistent? Clearly it is assumed here that the ability or characteristic which is being measured is relatively constant, at least over short intervals of time. If fluctuating mood states are being measured (see Chapter 11) then one would not expect a great deal of consistency of response over time. In the same way one might not obtain a high degree of consistency when observing emotionally disturbed children. However, in the observation situation, good inter-observer agreement might be found. Thus, it can be seen that establishing reliability by repeated measurements is not always an appropriate method. The type of reliability established by correlating the results obtained on separate occasions is usually termed test–retest reliability. When establishing test–retest reliability the same scale may be used on different occasions, or, if available, an alternate (equivalent) form of the instrument may be used. An example of the latter would be the Stanford Hypnotic Susceptibility Scales, Forms A and B (see Chapter 17). Other methods of establishing rcliability are available, but a further discussion is beyond the scope of this book.

While *validity* is dependent upon reliability, it is generally considered to be the most important characteristic of a measuring device. Validity is a measure of the extent to which a scale measures what it is purported to measure. If a scale is constructed to measure inductive thinking it should be shown to measure inductive thinking. In fact, a question that is frequently raised is: Valid for what? It has been noted that a test or scale has multiple validities (i.e. a given scale has as many validities as it has purposes). For example, an aptitude test may be used to select people for a large number of training programmes. In this case the instrument is being used for predictive purposes, and one would expect different validities to be associated with the different training programmes. This way of using a test emphasizes prediction, and thus the validity related to this use is termed: *predictive validity*. Essentially, predictive validity is established by relating (correlating) scores obtained on the test with success in the training course. A clinical psychologist who is interested in motivation for a certain type of treament might construct a scale with this in mind. Scores on the scale would then be related to completing the course of treatment. A more detailed discussion of validity is beyond the scope of this book. Further information may be found in Anastasi (1976).

Norms are obtained before using a test in clinical or practical work. Norms simply refer to the average or typical performance of a particular group such as acute schizophrenics or obsessive patients on a particular scale. Clearly, then, norms or normative data are necessary in order to evaluate the raw scores, rating, etc., obtained by a particular client or group. Norms may be differentiated in terms of sex, age group, occupational group, and diagnosis. Frequently, test results are based on the normal curve, as shown in Fig. 10.1.

The normal curve (Fig. 10.1) shows that between ± 1 standard deviation about 68 per cent of the measurements may be found. Referring to the continuum labelled 'deviation' IQs at the bottom of Fig. 10.1 it may be seen

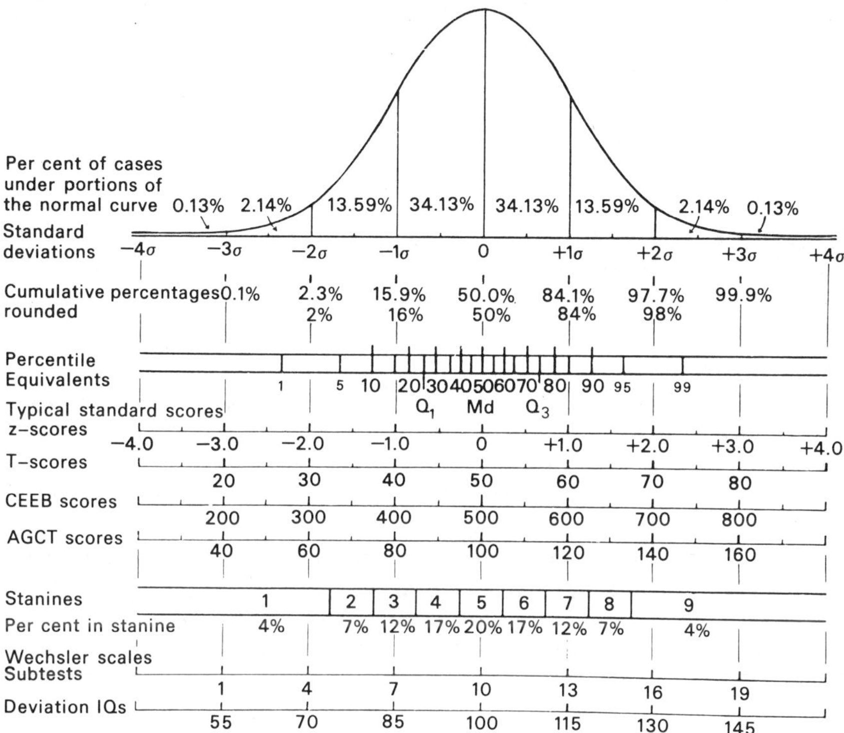

Fig. 10.1 The normal curve in test interpretation. (From the *Test Service Bulletin* of The Psychological Corportion.)

that 68 per cent of the sample upon which the Wechsler Scales were standardized obtain an IQ between 85 and 115. Thus, by the use of the normal curve, an individual's intelligence quotient may be compared to that of other people. One may note for example, that an individual who obtains an IQ of 115 is placed in the top 16 per cent of the population on this dimension.

While the use of psychological measures based upon normative groups is important, behavioural measurement (Haynes 1978) must be cognisant of specific individual differences. Haynes noted that 'Although we assume that individuals with behaviour problems in common manifest similarities in behavioural topography and maintaining factors, the topography and determinants of the target behaviour will show considerable intersubject variability. Each case, therefore, necessitates idiosyncratic intervention procedures. Behavioural assessment derives some of its importance because of the emphasis on carefully examining each case individually.'

Having considered the main principles involved in adequate psychological measurement, we turn now to a consideration of intelligence and memory, two of the principal concerns in individual assessment. Since the use of the major individual scales of intelligence has already been considered in Chapter 2 and 3, the main emphasis here will be on the nature of intelligence.

CONCEPTS OF INTELLIGENCE

There are a number of books and articles on intelligence. Many of them, for example, Cattell (1963), Guilford (1967), Hunt (1961), Jensen (1969, 1972), Matarazzo (1972), and Piaget (1963), put forward one particular theory. But a more general overview of intelligence may be found in Butcher (1975) and Butcher and Lomax (1972).

It is generally agreed that a person's ability to adapt adequately to his environment can be used as a general, albeit vague, criterion of intelligent behaviour. Obviously this does not mean that his adaptation should be so rigid that he cannot adapt to meet changing environmental conditions. However, it is doubtful that a greater flexibility of adapting to changing conditions is directly related to an increasing level on the phylogenetic scale. Nissen (1951) compared intelligence phylogenetically, suggesting that if one defined intelligence as the ability to solve tasks of increasing complexity there would probably be a fair degree of overlap between the different phyla. However, there is a lack of data on the lower mammals. A more specific and experimental view on comparative intelligence may be found in Bitterman (1965) in which a discussion on the qualitative differences in intelligence of different species may be found.

Growth of intelligence

Obviously many of the tasks which can be successfully completed by an average 18 year old are inappropriate for the average child of 2, 8, or 10 years of age. The factors which tend to be associated with intelligence are different for children at different levels of development. Bayley (1955) is one of the psychologists best known for investigations into the growth of intelligence. She points out that there are advantages in being able to accept the concept of the *constancy of the intelligence quotient* (IQ) in that one is able to compare similarly-aged children on the measure. If one could rely on the reliability or constancy of the IQ over long periods of time, the life of the teacher and others working with children would be considerably easier. Unfortunately, while little change in IQ can be demonstrated over short test–re-test intervals, this situation does not obtain when the test–re-test interval is long, when different functions are likely to be tapped by the intelligence tests used at the different age levels.

One of the problems in attempting to measure intelligence in the very young child is the very limited repertoire of behaviour exhibited. Much of the behaviour is related to sensory and motor functioning rather than being based upon higher cognitive activities. Bayley has noted that a number of studies have supported her findings, that in comparisons of repeated test scores on infants and very young children, the correlations between tests separated by a year or two are low. Two main reasons for this lack of prediction from one test occasion to another were noted by Bayley: (a) changes in cultural milieu, emotional climate, and environmental stimulation; and (b) the changes in the quality of the behaviours tested which derived from maturational changes in the child.

In summarizing the research on the growth and prediction of intelligence, Bayley noted that there was little possibility of ever being able to measure a stable and predictable intellectual factor in the very young and she saw no reason why we should continue to think of intelligence as an integrated (or simple) entity or capacity which grows throughout childhood by steady accretions. While test scores obtained from very young children are limited in their usefulness in predicting later intellectual performance, Bayley felt that children of five or six and older can be reliably classified into broad categories of normal, defective, and bright. Bayley used data from other studies on the growth of intelligence to suggest that intelligence test scores continued to increase until the age of 21 years. It was even suggested that 'intelligence' test scores might increase up to 50 years. However, it must be pointed out that the scores used which suggest this hypothesis were primarily from verbal tests such as Terman's concept mastery test. If a more global measure of intelligence were to be used the curve of growth of intelligence would be of a different nature. Matarazzo (1972) discussed this issue and pointed to the lack of adequate *longitudinal data* using the WAIS which would be useful in constructing a development curve of intelligence based on a more global measure. The growth curves based on the WAIS scores of subjects from 16 to 75 years and over show a decline in both verbal and performance IQs beginning in the early 20s. The decline in performance IQ is greater than the decline in verbal ability and deviates from the verbal curve at about age 30. It should be remembered, however, that these curves are based on *cross-sectional data* (Wechsler 1958).

Different views on intelligence

According to Freeman (1955) there are three types of definition of intelligence:

(1) definitions placing emphasis upon adjustment or adaptation of the individual to his total environment, or to limited aspects of his environment;

(2) intelligence as the ability to learn;

(3) intelligence as the ability to carry on abstract thinking . . . the effective use of symbols and concepts in dealing with situations.

Since three of the psychologists most influential in the area of intelligence are Alfred Binet, David Wechsler, and Jean Piaget, definitions from each of them are given here.

Binet defined intelligence as 'the tendency to take and maintain a definite direction; the capacity to make adaptations for the purpose of attaining a desired end; and the power of auto-criticism' (Terman 1916).

Wechsler defined intelligence as a 'hypothetical construct', and as 'the aggregate or global capacity of the individual to act purposefully, to think rationally, and to deal effectively with his environment' (Matarazzo 1972).

Piaget has noted that 'intelligence constitutes the state of equilibrium toward which tend all the successive adaptations of a sensorimotor and cognitive nature, as well as all assimilatory and accommodatory interactions between the organism and the environment' (Piaget 1963).

It can be seen that all three of these definitions of intelligence refer to *adaptation to the environment.* Clearly, modern man, of all organisms, has developed the means of living in diverse environments and thus needs to be flexible in his interactions with the outside world. Having said this, it is doubtful that modern man without his technological accomplishments would be considered as intelligent as the Australian Aborigine in his native habitat. By the same token, the Australian Aborigine would probably not be considered particularly intelligent in modern man's habitat, a cosmopolitan city. From an applied point of view, intelligence may be seen as rather a functional concept. Modern intelligence tests such as the WAIS should enable the psychologist to predict a person's ability to carry out a particular task or to succeed in a particular training programme. However, the experienced psychologist can verify that there are individuals in and out of mental hospitals who may score above average on a valid intelligence test, and yet fail to adapt to their environment.

The definitions by Binet and by Wechsler clearly refer to motivation, although this is not as obvious from Piaget's definition. However, Piaget (1963) notes that 'every action involves an energetic or affective aspect and a structural or cognitive aspect'. For Piaget, while cognition is distinct from affect, yet they are inseparable. Thus, an adequate definition of intelligence must include a motivational aspect. Both Binet and Piaget include a feedback factor which enables the individual to modify his behaviour as environmental conditions demand. This also seems to be the case with Wechsler since the intelligent individual must deal effectively with his environment, which rarely stays constant. It may be suggested that one's score on exercises in deductive logic, or one's IQ as established from the Stanford–Binet or WAIS may be based upon the factors of motivation and the ability to use feedback about one's performance. However, from the psychologist's point of view, it is far better to consider the administration of an individual intelligence test as a structured interview during which he is able to observe behaviour from which level of motivation and ability to use feedback can be inferred.

The discussion of the Aborigine and modern man above suggests that one's definition of intelligence is dependent upon the particular culture in which one finds oneself. Cattell (1965) has developed *culture-fair* tests to assess intellectual ability. These tests are reputed to be fair in that they measure factors which are common to different cultures. Cattell's basic idea is that there are two types of general ability factors. *Fluid ability* would seem to be the more innate or genetic aspect, which reaches its maximum level at about fourteen or fifteen years. Tests of fluid ability include analogies, matrices, etc., which are relatively free from educational attainment. In contrast, *crystallized intelligence* may be measured by skills based on cultural experience. Cattell (1965) noted that what 'we call crystallised intelligence is the collection of *skilled judgements* a person has acquired by applying his fluid intelligence to his school opportunities'. The growth of crystallized intelligence is seen as continuing beyond the age that fluid intelligence reaches its peak.

The traditional intelligence test, such as the WAIS is seen as measuring mainly crystallized intelligence while fluid intelligence is measured by the culture-fair test. The purported advantage of using a culture-fair (fluid) test is that it is not biased against the disadvantaged who may not have had the opportunity of acquiring the skills measured by crystallized intelligence tests, which are based on cultural-educational opportunities. Rather than measuring what a child has had the opportunity to learn in the past, the culture-fair test measures the child's capacity to learn in the future (Institute of Personality and Ability Testing 1960). The interested reader may wish to refer to Vernon (1973) who provides an extensive discussion of cultural factors and intelligence.

Space does not permit a more extensive discussion of theories of intelligence. However, the interested reader may consult the references listed at the beginning of this section.

We turn next to a discussion of memory, a factor of importance in many neurological conditions, particularly dementia.

THE MEASUREMENT OF MEMORY

It is obvious that one cannot discuss memory without referring also to learning and performance, since only by performance on some task can one assess memory, or the various factors relating to the total memory process. The main phases involved in the acquisition of material and in consequence performance are:

(1) registration
(2) encoding
(3) storage
(4) retrieval.

Thus, problems in memory may involve one or more of these phases.

In a general sense, one concludes that learning has taken place if there is evidence of increased task performance as the result of practice.

Many authors refer to 'short-term memory' (STM) and 'long-term memory' (LTM). STM refers to the holding or retention of materials for brief periods of time before either:

(1) forgetting this material, i.e. not encoding it; or

(2) encoding and storing it.

In order for material to pass from STM to LTM it must be practised or rehearsed, and may need some form of encoding. People who have been assessed as mentally backward typically have difficulty in STM tasks. Tallard (1971) noted that the difficulty this group of people had in new learning implied a failure to process and organize information. However, if the mentally backward and a group of matched controls learned materials to the same criterion they were able to retain the material equally well (pp. 110–111).

STM is considered to have a limited capacity, while LTM has an unlimited capacity. Anxiety tends to affect STM and the degree to which material goes on to long-term storage. Anxiety and other interference factors may thus result in a failure of consolidation. An example of a STM task would be the commonly used 'digit-span' (DS) test, in which the subject is asked to repeat a series of numbers which are read to him at one-second intervals. One series is required to be repeated forwards, while another series is required to be repeated backwards. The DS test is included on the Wechsler Adult Intelligence Scale (WAIS) and the Wechsler Memory Scale (WMS). Hodges and Spielberger (1969) found a decrement in DS for subjects high in 'anxiety state' but not for those high in 'anxiety trait' (see Chapter 11).

The STM system is labile, while the LTM system is quite stable once something is committed to memory. In summary 'STM is characterised by a limited capacity and short duration, and is manifested in a limited immediate memory span and rapid forgetting of information over a period of some 20–30 seconds' (Warrington 1971). A typical and much quoted study involving STM is that of Peterson and Peterson (1959) who asked subjects to remember a simple nonsense syllable of three letters. Immediately after this trigram was presented, the subject was required to count backwards by threes from a given number. Thus, the subject had little or no opportunity to rehearse the trigram. After varying intervals the subject was asked to repeat the trigram. The accuracy of recall diminished with increasing intervals of time up to about 20 seconds.

There are a number of memory scales available for the psychologist's use. For example, the Wechsler Memory Scale (WMS) (Wechsler and Stone 1945) and the Williams Delayed Memory Scale (Williams 1968). The task involved on the Williams Scale would be considered as a LTM task, in that the patient is not required to recall a series of meaningful pictures until about 10 minutes have elapsed.

Three main types of response on memory tests required of patients involve:

(1) *recall*, in which very little aid to remembering is given;
(2) *cued recall*, partial aid to remembering, such as prompting or cuing; and
(3) *recognition*, in which the patient must select from a larger number, the items learned.

The Williams Delayed Memory Scale, for example, may require all of the above three types of response.

In addition, one may establish the degree to which material is still stored by having the subject or patient relearn the material previously learned. If, for example, it took the subject 10 trials to learn a list of *paired-associates* to one errorless trial originally, and if, after relearning, it takes him only 7 trials, he has saved 3 trials. His savings score, typically expressed as a percentage, is 30 per cent.

$$\text{Percentage saved} = 100 \times \frac{\text{original number of trials} - \text{number of relearning trials}}{\text{number of original trials}}$$

While the above and other standardized memory scales are available, there may be some advantage in constructing specific tests of memory functioning for particular patients when one is working closely in the rehabilitation or management of patients with memory difficulties. In this regard, the recent book by Higbee (1977) is highly recommended as a guide.

Some of the types of error possible in memory tasks include:

(1) acoustic errors (e.g. between the letters b and d);
(2) semantic errors, i.e. errors of meaning, (e.g. chair–stool);
(3) proactive inhibition—the situation in which material previously learned interferes with the recall of more recently learned material (see Table 10.1A);
(4) retroactive inhibition—the situation in which material later learned interferes with the recall of material previously learned (see Table 10.1B).

TABLE 10.1
PARADIGM FOR PROACTIVE AND RETROACTIVE INHIBITION

A *Paradigm for proactive inhibition*			
	Presentation	*Presentation*	*Recall*
Group I	Task I	Task II	Task II
Group II	—	Task II	Task II
Task I proactively interferes with recall of Task II.			
B *Paradigm for retroactive inhibition*			
	Presentation	*Presentation*	*Recall*
Group I	Task I	Task II	Task I
Group II	Task I	(Interpolated task)	Task I
Task II retroactively interferes with the recall of Task I.			

Theories of forgetting usually implicate one or more of the four phases of aquisition–performance referred to earlier. However, some authors refer to motivated or repressive forgetting implicating dynamic personality theory. The three main theories are:

(1) decay of memory 'traces' through disuse;
(2) interference (e.g. proactive and retroactive inhibitory effects);
(3) motivated forgetting.

A more extensive discussion of memory may be found in Lezak (1976), particularly in reference to neuropsychological assessment.

SOME COMMON ERRORS IN PSYCHOLOGICAL MEASUREMENT

While the type of error may depend to some extent upon the particular psychological characteristic one is considering, there is, in fact, some similarity in the type of error which may be found in the measurement of non-cognitive qualities as well as when measuring cognitive factors. Thus, while the measurement of mood states and personality characteristics is discussed in the next chapter, much of the following discussion on error factors will be applicable to both areas of measurement.

A large number of factors affect psychological measurement, often tending to decrease the reliability and validity of the measure. Table 10.2 gives some of the factors that the psychologist must consider in the interpretation of psychological test scores in an individual test situation. To the extent that the test interpreter in unaware of these factors, he is increasingly likely to arrive at invalid conclusions concerning a client, some of which may have very adverse effects indeed.

TABLE 10.2

SOME FACTORS AFFECTING PERFORMANCE ON AN INDIVIDUAL PSYCHOLOGICAL 'TEST'

1. Degree of rapport between psychologist and client
2. Attitude to test situation
3. Differential interest in subsections of test
4. Degree of assertiveness
5. Level of motivation
6. Level of arousal or energy level
7. Degree of anxiety or other emotional state
8. Speech deficits or disturbances
9. Eye–hand co-ordination and other psychomotor factors
10. Extent of sensory deficits

Obviously, if a child has a sensory problem, such as a hearing deficit, the test results will be adversely affected. If this deficit is not suspected or detected at an early stage, the test results may be accepted as a valid indication of the child's ability and may involve the classification or labelling of the child as a slow learner, or as a person of low intelligence. This labelling may then lead to one of the constant errors typically found when rating scales are used.

Rating scales

Rating scales of various sorts may be helpful in assessing an individual's behaviour. The ratings may be based upon direct behavioural observation, or be required in a context which does not allow behavioural observation at the time of rating. In the latter situation, if the characteristic on which the ratee is to be rated is not clearly specified in behavioural terms, or if a specific definition of the characteristic to be rated is not provided, then the reliability of the rating will probably be minimal, and the usefulness of the rating is likely to be very limited.

Anastasi (1976) included the '*halo effect*', the *error of central tendency*, and the *leniency error* as constant errors in rating procedures. In order to provide an example of one of these errors we return to the example of the child with the hearing deficit. The labelling of the child as of low intelligence may lead to a negative 'halo-effect', whereby the child is rated or perceived as 'low' on many characteristics, possibly extending even beyond the cognitive realm into the area of personality. While the term 'halo-effect' has more frequently been used to describe an overgeneralization from a positive test score, rating, or personality trait description, the term may include negative overgeneralization. Anastasi defined halo effect as a 'tendency on the part of raters to be unduly influenced by a single favorable or unfavorable trait, which colors their judgement of the individual's other traits. In view of the positive connotation of the term 'halo'. Guilford (1959) prefers to use the term *rater–ratee interaction error*.

Anastasi found that one way to reduce this rater–ratee interaction error was to relate the ability or characteristic to concrete behaviour. Guilford (1959) noted that when a number of people were being rated, halo errors could be reduced by rating all the ratees in one characteristic prior to rating them on another one. Guilford also found that halo effect could be considerably reduced if a day elapsed between the rating of various characteristics.

The second constant error mentioned by Anastasi was the error of central tendency, which referred to the tendency to place persons in the middle of the scale and to avoid extreme positions.

Finally, the third constant error was the leniency error, which basically referred to a tendency to avoid giving unfavourable ratings. Anastasi noted that both the central tendency error and the leniency error reduced the descriminability of the ratings.

Guilford also referred to *logical errors* in rating, which he defined as 'the tendency to rate similarly traits that seem to the rater to be logically similar or related'. He further noted that the most disturbing result, as in the case of halo errors, was the inflation of intercorrelations of traits that were regarded as more similar or more related than they actually were.

A knowledge of the above errors and how to reduce or avoid them is important for the nursing staff and doctors who have occasion to rate others. For example, the Hospital Adjustment Scale (HAS) McReynolds and Ferguson (1955), and the Inpatient Multidimensional Psychiatric Scale (IMPS) Lorr and Klett (1966) and other rating scales are typically completed by nursing personnel.

Both Anastasi and Guilford mention that one way to reduce rating errors is to use the forced-choice rating technique, although according to Guilford it is a technique disliked by many raters. Guilford noted that the 'basic feature of the forced-choice rating method is to require the rater to choose between two favorable qualities or between two unfavorable ones when rating someone rather than to give an absolute judgement on either of them'.

Guilford made a number of technical recommendations concerning the construction of rating scales. However, he places stress on the training of raters. The use of more than one rater to establish inter-observer reliability is also important. The details concerning length and frequency of the observation periods, or the degree of acquaintance of the rater with the ratee must be considered. Guilford concluded that 'Raters should be made aware of the different kinds of errors and should be advised as to how to avoid them. They should be given instruction regarding the meaning of trait names and other pertinent terms, and they should be given supervised practice, in connection with which their errors are found and pointed out to them.'

Guilford discussed the issue of ability to judge others. Taft (1956) reported that the good judge of others was 'a serious, organized and reasonable person who apparently relies upon the use of his intelligence and conservatism in meeting successfully the hazards of life'. More recently, Vingoe and Antonoff (1968) considered the factors which made for good judgemental ability, and concluded that good judges minimize their worries and complaints, are well-adjusted, introverted, self-controlled, tolerant, and tend to present a good picture of themselves. While all of the above factors significantly differentiated good from poor judges of others, two aspects of the study should be made clear. The first is that statistical significance did not imply clinical significance, while the second is the fact that the college student judges in the study were very similar in terms of age, sex, and general background. This second factor probably made the judgemental task somewhat easier.

SUMMARY

This chapter discusses the characteristics of psychological scales, such as the use of objective procedures, the obtaining of normative data, and the reliability and validity of measurement.. It is pointed out that a scale has as many validities as uses to which it is put. However, for many purposes it may lack adequate validity. Whether or not a scale is valid for a particular purpose must be determined empirically.

The growth of intelligence is discussed, and the difficulty of predicting adult intelligence from scores obtained from very young children is indicated. It is suggested that the definitions of intelligence provided by Binet, Wechsler, and Piaget all included as components: (1) adaptation to the environment; (2) the concept of motivation; and (3) the ability to use feedback in the modification of one's behaviour.

The section on memory lists the sequence of events included in the memory process and consequent performance as: (1) registration; (2) encoding; (3) storage; and (4) retrieval. Some of the differences between short- and long-term memory are discussed, as well as the four methods of assessing memory (1) recall; (2) cued recall; (3) recognition; and (4) the savings method. Some of the errors which may be detected in assessing memory are mentioned, such as proactive and retroactive inhibition.

Finally, some of the common errors in psychological measurement are described, and some suggestions are made about overcoming or avoiding such errors. These errors included the 'halo effect' or 'rater–ratee interaction error', the 'error of central tendency', and the 'leniency error'. Two studies involving the judgement of personality characteristics are mentioned. While in certain specific situations good and poor judges of others may be differentiated, it is pointed out that a finding of statistical significance does not imply clinical significance. Better predictability is obtained when the situation from which one predicts approaches that situation towards which one is predicting.

Some of the potential error factors and response sets, etc. which influence personality measurement will be briefly discussed in the next chapter.

11
Mood states and their assessment

Alone, Alone, all, all alone,
Alone on a wide wide sea!
And never a saint took pity on
My soul in agony.

Samual Taylor Coleridge:
The Rime of the Ancient Mariner

All of us exhibit moods, at time intense ones. How we view them and respond to them is very important indeed for our mental health. While there are a multiplicity of moods, some of which are seen as positive and mentally healthy, and some as negative and not particularly beneficial, most people probably limit their attention to a few 'negative' and a few 'positive' mood states. People tend to use the terms 'mood' and 'emotion' indiscriminately, and indeed a distinction is not always made clear in the psychological literature. in fact, a large number of general psychology textbooks even fail to list the term 'mood' in their index of subjects, since moods are discussed under the topic of motivation or emotion.

Wessman and Ricks (1966) referred to moods as 'the changing states of feeling that gives our experienced world its liveliness and color'. A feeling or emotion may be characterized as a 'trait' or 'state'.

THE CONCEPTS OF TRAIT AND STATE

Typically, a 'state' refers to a feeling or emotional condition of *relatively* brief duration, while 'trait' refers to a relatively enduring condition of the organism which would be considered very difficult if not impossible to modify significantly. Guilford (1959) defined a trait as 'any distinguishable, relatively enduring way in which one individual differs from others'. A mood, as suggested above, is a state and may be relatively brief, and is well expressed when one individual says to another: 'You're in quite a state aren't you?', or 'Boy, are you in a mood'. Nowlis (1965) noted that the 'phenomena from which we infer mood have some stability through periods lasting minutes or, at the most, hours. However, when . . . the relevant state continues steadily for days other terms are used or the mood is called pathological'.

In recent years it has become obvious through personality research that the trait view of personality must be seriously questioned as more evidence supporting behavioural specificity is found (Mischel 1968, 1973). In addition, referential states seem much more pertinent than non-referential states. An example of a referential state is: 'I feel sad that my cousin has just died'. The more general statement: 'I feel sad' is an example of a non-referential state. Behavioural specificity rather than behavioural generality seems to be the rule rather than the exception.

The above comments are not meant to suggest that traits do not have some place in the area of personality. It is just that our behaviour has been found to be affected by specific situations to a greater degree than was earlier thought. To make predictions based on trait measures of personality alone may be foolhardy even if over many situations an individual might behave in accordance with predictions based upon his scores on various measures of personality traits.

Spielberger, Gorsuch, and Lushene (1970) have developed an instrument which measures both state and trait anxiety, the State–Trait Anxiety Inventory (STAI). The development of this instrument has resulted in a great deal of research, as witnessed by a recent bibliography of research articles and papers referring to the STAI of well over 600 items (Spielberger 1977). Forms of the STAI which may be used with children have also been developed. Gaudry and Poole (1975) supported the predicted sensitivity of the Anxiety-State Scale and the insensitivity of the Anxiety-Trait Scale in a study using over 400 children. Basically, success and failure on anagram problems were experimentally produced in these subjects. The two forms of the STAI for children were administered before and after the children were given the anagrams to solve. The results clearly showed that anxiety-state changes were related to the experimentally arranged conditions of success and failure, while no effect was found in relation to the trait anxiety. Spielberger (1974) discussed the issues in this distinction between trait and state anxiety.

MEASUREMENT OF MOOD STATES

We saw in Chapter 5 that emotions could be viewed as being made up of two components: a change in arousal, and the cognitive labelling of this change by the person experiencing the change in arousal. A mood state can be viewed in an analogous way. One's mood is determined to some extent by the situation in which one finds oneself. It must be remembered that our feelings are influenced by our perception, and likewise perception is influenced by our feelings. Thus, it can be seen that there is an interdependent relationship between perception and mood.

While the main dimensions to be considered in this chapter are anxiety, hostility, and depression, we will touch upon other personality dimensions or mood states. First we will discuss two scales which are very much related to level of arousal.

Measurement of arousal

Thayer (1967) developed the Activation–Deactivation Adjective Checklist (AD–ACL), which measures the following dimensions: general activation, general deactivation, high activation, and deactivation–sleep.

A revision of the AD–ACL was carried out by Clements, Hafer, and Vermillion (1976). Clements *et al.* presented the results of five studies in their report. On the basis of their study, they noted that Thayer's hypothetical continuum might be better described as one ranging from general activation through deactivation–sleep, and that what he described as high activation represented a qualitatively different and independent dimension best described as anxious tension. Clements *et al.* were successful in relating the revised activation factor of the AD–ACL to the diurnal cycle. However, a one-week test–retest reliability study produced negative results. These results were not supportive of Maddi's (1972) theory, and raised a question regarding the possible transient nature of activation level. Clements *et al.* noted that future research on reliability might focus on repeated measures within and between successive diurnal cycles. The validity of the AD–ACL activation factor was supported by substantial correlations between the activation factor and pulse-rate and respiration-rate respectively. Finally, it was found that when activation was induced psychologically, the revised activation factor scores corresponded to the induced changes. Clements *et al.* concluded that this measure of activation was related to electrophysiological variables, reflected changes in those systems, and showed points of change in the diurnal cycle and that the instrument was suitable for group administration and was easy to score.

Mackay, Cox, Burrows, and Lazzerini (1978) reported on an inventory which measured the bipolar factors of stress and arousal. Mackay *et al.* based their scale on the AD–ACL, but substituted British equivalents for some of the American adjectives used in Thayer's checklist. The new British checklist consisted of 45 adjectives to which the subject had to respond by selecting one of the following: (1) definitely feel; (2) feel slightly; (3) do not understand or cannot decide; or (4) definitely do not feel. Mackay *et al.* found that the two factors were differentially sensitive to a variety of environmental, task, and drug effects. While the British adaptation of the AD–ACL has yet to be extensively used, it is expected that its use in studies involving changes in mood state will be advantageous.

This checklist and other similar ones are very helpful in assessing changes of mood based upon psychopharmacological action or the induction of changes in level of consciousness by psychological procedures such as hypnosis, alpha training, etc.

Zuckerman (1974) also developed an instrument related to activation level. Since they were attempting to measure an individual's 'optimum stimulation level' the scale was termed the Sensation Seeking Scale (SSS). Zuckerman, Schultz, and Hopkins (1967) reported on the relationships found between sensation seeking score and volunteering for hypnosis or sensory deprivation experiments, while Zuckerman and Link (1968) reported on the subdivision of the scale into factors such as antisocial sensation seeking, visual sensation seeking, thrill sensation seeking, and social sensation seeking. The first two factors were not definable in females. Zuckerman and Link (1968) have defined the low and high sensation seeker as follows: 'The low sensation seeker seems to need order and predictability in his environment. He values social affiliation and is willing to give to, or give in to, others to maintain stability. The high sensation seeker needs change in his environment, independence from others, and probably needs others primarily as an audience to his own performance. He tends to be impulsive and labile'. It is further suggested that the high sensation seeker may share many of the traits of the creative person. In addition, he may hold 'a generalized challenging or sceptical attitude towards authority'.

Blackburn (1969) administered the SSS, the MMPI, and other scales to 83 patients in a maximum security hospital. The intelligence level of this group was average, and they were composed of 54 mentally ill (mostly schizophrenic) patients and 29 psychopaths. Psychopaths are usually seen as people who find it difficult to delay gratification (i.e. they are impulsive), to lack guilt feelings, and to be unable to form a sincere caring interpersonal relationship. They may also exhibit inappropriate aggressivity. Blackburn found that the highest correlations with sensation seeking in his sample were, in order of magnitude: hypomania, direction of hostility (extrapunativeness), impulsivity, and repression. While SSS scores were significantly related to the psychopathic deviate (Pd.) scale of the MMPI, the psychopaths and non-psychopaths were not significantly differentiated on the basis of SSS scores.

Blackburn found that his results on the SSS and other scales used suggested that many of the characteristics of psychopaths were also frequently found among paranoid schizophrenics.

We turn now to a discussion of three important dimensions of mood: anxiety, hostility, and depression.

Anxiety

Too much anxiety may lead to psychopathology; too little may also be psychopathological in that the person lacks 'drive' or motivation. A certain amount of anxiety in the modern 'civilized' world is desirable and in fact necessary for the performance of some tasks. However, the twentieth century has often been called the 'Age of Anxiety', meaning that there is far too much anxiety about for good mental health.

Anxiety has been with us since the dawn of history. It is something most of us experience from time to time. While it may facilitate desirable behaviour, it can equally well prevent desirable behaviour, and can interfere with the development and maximization of human potential. Anxiety may act as a warning signal of impending danger, enabling one to prepare for an emergency situation. However, anxiety is generally regarded as the central problem in psychoneurotic conditions. Eysenck and Rachman (1965) noted that the 'distinctive feature of a classical phobia is the presence of clearly ostensible sources of anxiety'. The presence of anxiety leads to behaviour which tends to reduce or eliminate it. In most cases anxiety leads to an avoidance of the object or situation that is perceived as evoking the anxiety.

Levitt (1967) discussed definitions of anxiety, pointing out the value of *operational definitions* of anxiety from a scientific point of view. As he said, the important consideration is whether the definition will eventually predict human behaviour, and whether it is found to be related to other partial definitions. Anxiety may be conceptualized as a hypothetical state anchored in specific stimuli and responses. The level of anxiety is inferred from specific psychological or behavioural indicants.

Physiological indicants of anxiety

Darwin (1965: originally published 1893) in his *Expression of the emotions in man and animals*, referred to a number of indicants of fear. For example, increased perspiration, dryness of the mouth, changes in voice quality, trembling, dilation of the pupils, rapid palpitations of the heart, erection of body hair, etc. Certainly, modern descriptions of anxiety are quite consistent with those of Darwin's. It may be noted that many of these indicants are observable.

Levitt (1967) suggested that it was advisable to distinguish between a psychological anxiety and a physiological anxiety. This was supported by Byrne's (1966) review of the studies on the interrelationship between anxiety as measured by the Manifest Anxiety Scale (MAS) (discussed below) and physiological indices of anxiety. The results showed there was no significant relationship. While Byrne suggested that physiological and psychological anxiety may be two different types of response, he also suggested an explanation using Lacey and Lacey's (1958) idea of *response specificity*. These authors proposed that the best index of physiological activity could be obtained by measuring an individual on a series of physiological variables and then using each subject's highest score, regardless of what the variable was. For one individual it might be GSR, for another heart rate, and so forth. Byrne cited a study by Mandler, Mandler, Kremen, and Sholiton (1961) in which eleven psychophysiological measures were obtained in addition to MAS scores. While non-significant relationships were found between MAS scores and individual psychophysiological measures, when MAS scores were correlated with each subject's highest physiological score the correlation was 0.60.

Theoretical views of anxiety

Anxiety is frequently referred to as 'bound' or having an object, and as 'free' or 'free-floating'. Levitt, however, felt that it was difficult to maintain this difference either theoretically or practically. He found that it was the free-floating anxiety that was most frequently experienced by the psychiatric patient who suffered from anxiety states. He noted that 'The person who is beset by free-floating anxiety is afraid that "something terrible is going to happen", but he does not know what it is. . . . To be afraid is painful; not to know why you are afraid can be catastrophic because you are then deprived of any avenue of escape from the threatening danger. To forestall a complete emotional collapse, the regulatory mechanisms of the personality are thought to attach the free anxiety to some object or event which then comes to be feared'.

The psychoanalytic view The three types of anxiety posited by Freud are outlined below.

1. *Reality anxiety* (some prefer to use the term 'fear'), refers to a fear of objects in the external world. The other two types are derived from this type.
2. *Neurotic anxiety* involves a fear that the instincts will be uncontrollable (involves a conflict between the id and ego). This type of anxiety involves a fear that behaviour will result from the inability to control the instincts and that this behaviour will be punished.
3. *Moral anxiety* (involves a conflict between the id and super-ego, a fear of the conscience). Even thinking about doing something contrary to the moral code produces guilt and the person may be said to feel 'conscience-stricken'.

All three types of anxiety have their basis in reality. In order to treat the patient with severe anxiety it is considered necessary to 'uncover' the underlying (unconscious) conflict through analytic procedures such as free-association.

The learning view The principles of learning suggest that a person's reinforcement history has led to the development of anxieties. We have learned to be anxious. Thus, we should be able to unlearn anxiety to the extent that it is based upon our reinforcement history. Levitt (1967) criticized the view that phobias arose from taking up free-floating anxiety. He proposed instead a learning approach. He suggested that cues, which were associated with the object or situation originally feared, might be able to evoke anxiety through this contiguity. Cues were simply characteristics of objects, or objects that were spatially or temporally associated with the object which evoked the original fear response. Secondly, Levitt noted that anxiety is extended through *stimulus generalization*. The anxious person thus responded to objects or situations similar to (i.e. in shape, colour, size, meaning, etc.) the originally feared objects which were not present at the time fear or anxiety was originally evoked.

Behaviour therapeutic approaches such as systematic desensitization, flooding, relaxation, or hypnotic procedures are used in treating phobias or anxiety states. These methods are discussed in Part IV of this text. Chapter 15 discusses stimulus generalization and other principles of learning.

Measures of anxiety

While psychophysiological measures of anxiety do not, in general, correlate well with test or psychometric measures, there is some evidence that there is a significant association between the 'most reactive' physiological measure and anxiety test scores. The concept invoked here is Lacy's concept of *response specificity*

Behaviour therapists use various fear thermometers or scales primarily to assess phobic conditions. Self-ratings of fear and anxiety are also used in conjunction with such techniques as systematic desensitization. These measures are discussed in the 'functional analysis' section of Chapter 15.

Among the paper-and-pencil measures of anxiety are the MAS, the Institute of Personality, and Ability Testing (IPAT) Anxiety Scale Questionnaire (Cattell 1965); and the State–Trait Anxiety Inventory (STAI).

Taylor (1953) developed the MAS primarily as a measure of drive or motivation for use in studies of learning. Here, the interest was in the modifying effect of different levels of anxiety on performance.

The items for the MAS are derived from the MMPI. The 50 true–false items of the MAS were determined through the agreement of clinincal psychologist judges who had been given a definition of chronic anxiety reaction (Byrne 1966).

As indicated by Levitt (1967) the MAS measures a predisposition to anxiety, not an immediate state. Most of the items in the scale call for a self-report of a general condition and none of the items requires an estimate of the respondent's emotional state at the moment of responding. Thus, the MAS is strictly a measure of anxiety trait and does not provide for the measurement of state anxiety.

The IPAT Anxiety Scale consists of 40 items, one scale for children and one for adults. Levitt noted that the IPAT scale was believed to measure anxiety-proneness. Like the MAS it was developed as a trait measure, although Cattell (1965) noted that his objective Anxiety Battery now existed in eight parallel forms so that the patient could be tested again and again in the course of diagnosis and therapy.

We have already referred to the State–Trait Anxiety Inventory, which does take into account the specificity of behaviour. Some support for the trait–state distinction in anxiety has already been presented. As noted by Levitt it is an advantage to measure both state and trait anxiety with the same inventory. In the 'today' or 'state' form of the STAI, the respondent is asked to answer the questions in terms of how he feels at the moment, while the trait form asks him to answer the questions in terms of how he generally feels. The twenty questions of each form are all quite simple statements which are responded to in terms of five degrees of magnitude.

Mischel (1968) recommended that the clinician should carry out a functional analysis with the client to discover the operations or behavioural referents for anxiousness. Mischel noted that 'the assessor enquires into just what happens when the client feels more anxious and less anxious and the changes that occur in himself and in his behaviour when he experiences the problematic anxiety. For example, the asssessor might ask, "How do you know when you are anxious?" The purpose of these probes is to obtain public referents for subjective experiences, and not to validate or invalidate the truth or falseness of the client's phenomenology. The issue here is not whether the person is "really" anxious, but rather the discovery of referents for his perceptions regardless of their accuracy'.

Thus, it may be seen that the above discussion suggests that a measure of trait anxiety is far from sufficient for clinical purposes. Most mental-health workers discover the value of the specificity approach, and through a functional analysis, with or without the use of an anxiety inventory, seek to specify the conditions under which changes in anxiety occur.

We turn now to a discussion of measures of hostility or aggression.

The feeling and expression of aggression

Clearly it is important to control the expression of aggression in the human-being. Feelings of aggression which may lead to aggressive behaviour are intermittently felt by most of us. It is not that aggression *per se* may be expressed that is of concern, but (1) the form in which it is expressed, and (2) the extent or intensity of the expression.

We have already indicated (Chapter 4) that one of the consequences of frustration is aggression (Dollard, Miller, Doob, Mowrer, and Sears 1974). Many would suggest that these authors went too far when they said that 'the occurrence of aggressive behaviour always presupposes the existence of frustration, and contrari-wise, . . . the existence of frustration always leads to some form of aggression'. Obviously, the critical words in the above statement are 'some form'. Since 'feelings of aggressivity' or an 'aggressive state', must be inferred from behaviour, and since, it may be readily agreed that the form of the 'aggressive' behaviour may be tremendously varied, it is rather difficult to test the frustration–aggression hypothesis.

While psychoanalytic theory views aggression as a basic instinct or drive, the learning view is that aggressive behaviour is learned, and since it is learned it may be unlearned. One may also argue that one many learn more 'refined' non-aggressive responses to frustration. In addition, one can argue that if an aggressive response to frustration has brought reinforcement to the individual, and behaving in non-aggressive ways, has not, that responses of aggression hold a higher position in the individual's response hierarchy. In other words, he is more likely to respond to frustrating circumstances in an aggressive manner. That aggressive behaviour may be learned operantly and via observational learning or modelling, has been supported by Bandura and his colleagues (Bandura and Walters 1963) and Berkowitz (1964). This also suggests that if non-aggressive responses to frustration have been reinforced by significant others that they will be more likely.

While a full physiological and psychological analysis of aggressive behaviour is beyond our present scope, we will review some recent reports on aggressive behaviour. We will, however, first provide a definition of aggressivity.

A definition of aggression

Freedman, Carlsmith, and Sears (1970) define aggression as 'any behaviour that hurts or could hurt others'. However, Bandura (1969) considered this definition as too limiting. He noted:

> If aggression is defined as behavior intended to produce injurious consequences, then some of the most violent interpersonal activities would be excluded from consideration. It is evident that people frequently resort to aggression because it has high utilitarian value. By aggressive behavior or dominance through physical and verbal force, individuals can obtain material resources, change rules to fit their own wishes, gain control over and extract subservience from others, terminate provocation, and remove physical barriers which block or delay attainment of desired outcomes. It is, therefore not surprising that aggressive-domineering patterns of behavior are so prevalent.

Following Bandura's comments above, it can be seen that the motivation to engage in aggressive behaviour may be very extensive indeed.

Some recent reports on aggression

Konečni (1975) assessed the relative merits of the *arousal-level* and *cognitive-labelling* (anger) interpretation of emotional (aggressive) behaviour through the use of confederates who treated the experimental subjects in a rude and insulting manner (see Chapter 5). Konečni noted that 'the knowledge of whether or not the aroused people have adopted the cognitive label of anger may be indispensable for the prediction of the amount of aggression emitted by them'.

First, the subjects were (1) insulted or (2) treated in a neutral fashion by a confederate. Eighty per cent of the subjects received either a (1) comfortably loud, simple tone; (2) comfortably loud, complex tone; (3) aversively loud, simple tone; or (4) aversely loud, complex tone, after which they had to take a decision on whether to shock the confederate. The remaining subjects were unstimulated. The results strongly supported the cognitive labelling hypothesis. Konečni noted that the cognitive-labelling hypothesis withstood an important test since even repeated exposure to aversive auditory stimulation did not enhance aggressive behaviour, unless the subjects had a good reason for considering themselves angry.

Konečni and Doob (1972) carried out a study to test the catharsis hypothesis. Freedman *et al.* defined *catharsis* as the use of 'socially acceptable aggression, vicarious aggression, or sublimation . . . [to] reduce feelings of anger and therefore subsequent aggression . . .'. Forty of eighty subjects were annoyed by a confederate while the remainder were not. In this experiment the condition was provided 'where the subject was annoyed by one person, then got a chance to hurt another, before getting a chance to behave aggressively towards the annoyer.' Konečni and Doob reasoned that if expressing anger against a 'scapegoat' is cathartic, then subjects who are given this opportunity should behave less aggressively towards their annoyer than should subjects who are not given this opportunity. Catharsis would be expected to act in such a way as to reduce agression in the subjects who were annoyed. The results showed that within the limits of this experiment that the expression of aggression against a person other than the frustrator was cathartic; such activity was actually as efficient in reducing subsequent aggression towards the frustrator as aggressivity expressed toward the frustrator himself. The authors reason that neither a retaliation nor a guilt explanation can account for the results obtained.

Measurement of aggressivity

The measurement of aggressivity is important in our understanding of a person, and in our being able to predict and modify his behaviour.

Rosenzweig in his picture frustration study (Rosenzweig 1976), categorized expressions of aggression into three main types of response, which are shown in Table 11.1. This provides a description of the three directions in

TABLE 11.1
THE DIRECTION OF EXPRESSION OF AGGRESSION

Direction of aggression	*Type of aggression ego defence*
Extra-aggression	E (extrapunative): Blame, hostility, etc., are turned against some person or thing in the environment. *E*: In this variant of E, the subject aggressively denies that he is responsible for some offence with which he is charged.
Intra-aggression	I (intropunative) Blame, censure, etc., are directed by the subject upon himself. *I*: a variant of I in which the subject admits his guilt but denies any essential fault by referring to unavoidable circumstances.
Im-aggression	M (impunative) Blame for the frustration is evaded altogether, the situation being regarded as unavoidable; in particular, the 'frustrating' individual is absolved.

(Modified from Rosenzweig 1976)

which aggression is expressed. The concepts of intropunativeness (aggression-in) and extrapunativeness (aggression-out) are important in that, in general, aggression-out is considered as the healthier response. However, this statement needs qualification since various ways of expressing anger-out would be not only unacceptable socially, but physically dangerous. Outright violent behaviour in most situations is clearly not sanctioned.

The intropunative mode of expressing anger is considered important in theoretical views on the development of psychosomatic pathology as well as in the development of depression.

Rosenzweig (1976) pointed out two fallacies in recent discussions of aggression. One of these fallacies was the equating of aggression with hostility or destructiveness. Rosenzweig noted that if aggression was 'conceived as generically or essentially *self-assertive*, aggression can be viewed as affirmative or negative, constructive or destructive in effect'. Aggression, then, is analogous to anxiety in that both too little and too much may lead to some degree of psychopathology. Obviously the common element is degree of arousal. Changes in level of arousal are, of course, common to all mood states and emotions.

The second fallacy noted by Rosenzweig was the limitation of aggression to antecedent frustration. This would seem to be clear from Bandura's definition of aggression above, which suggests that there are many incentives for aggressive behaviour.

While a detailed description of the Rosenzweig Picture Frustration (P-F) study is beyond the scope of this book a few brief comments will be made here. More extensive dicussions may be found in Rosenzweig (1960, 1976). The Rosenzweig P-F study was developed in order 'to elicit the various modes of verbal aggression induced by frustration'. This device has been referred to as 'a limited or controlled projective technique'. The subject is asked to respond to

> 24 cartoon-like pictures, each of which represents any everyday frustrating situation that involves two persons. One of the pictured individuals is shown saying something that either frustrates or helps to describe the frustration of the other individual, and this other individual is drawn with a blank balloon or caption box above his head that the subject is instructed to fill. He is to do so by writing the very first words that it occurs to him the individual might say in that situation . . . In some cases the situation is ego-blocking; some obstruction, personal or impersonal, impedes, disappoints, deprives, or otherwise directly thwarts the pictured person. In others, super-ego blocking is portrayed; the individual is accused, insulted, or otherwise incriminated by another person.

An enquiry is held with the subject after he has completed his responses to the 'cartoons' in order to clarify ambiguous responses, and so forth. The interscorer reliability of the P-F study is reported as consistently high, and most validity reports are favourable.

Zuckerman and Lubin's (1965) Multiple Affect Adjective Check List (MAACL) is a self-report inventory which includes state measures of hostility, anxiety, and depression. The subject is asked to check all the adjectives which express how he feels at the present time. While it is much easier to administer and store than the P-F study, the intercorrelations between the three scales are relatively high. Thus, the *discriminant validity* is less than desirable. On the other hand, it is a state measure, while the P-F study is not. In addition, it may be argued that there is inevitably a fair amount of communality between the three variables of anxiety, depression, and hostility. We turn now to a discussion of depression.

Depression

Lewinsohn (1974) stressed the importance of depression by noting it ranks as the second most frequent mental disorder and its association with suicide. Since it is beyond the scope of this chapter to discuss depression in any detail, the interested reader is referred to Beck (1967); Lewinsohn (1974); and Seligman (1975) for more detailed information.

Bereavement has already been discussed (pp. 57–61). Lewinsohn (1974) noted that the emphasis within psychodynamic or 'traditional approaches . . . is upon a loss which is translated into a loss of self-esteem and into the internalization of hostility with a consequent further loss of self-esteem'.

Beck (1967) presented the following as the common characteristics (or symptoms) of depression:

(1) sad, apathetic mood state;
(2) negative self-concept (feelings of worthlessness, guilt, etc.);
(3) tendency to withdraw from others;
(4) insomnia, loss of appetite and sexual desire;
(5) change in activity level either towards lethargy or towards agitation (agitated depression).

In offering an operational definition of depression, which included verbal statements of dysphoria, self-depreciation, guilt, material burden, social isolation, somatic complaints, and a reduced rate for many behaviours Lewinsohn assumed that depression was a continuous variable which could be conceptualized as a 'state' (which fluctuated over time) but also as a 'trait' (some people, 'depressives', were more prone to becoming depressed than others). Consistent with Lewinsohn's ideas concerning the presence of depressive symptomatology in other pathological conditions, is Miller's (1975) conclusion regarding the lack of evidence for deficits unique to depression. Miller reviewed studies on cognitive, motor, perceptual, and communication deficits. He noted that in severe forms of depression (manic-depressive illness and endogenous and psychotic depressions) performance deficits are found as severe as those seen in schizophrenia.

Behavioural view of depression

The behavioural view on depression stresses that the depressive lacks reinforcement. Lewinsohn cited Lazarus (1968) who conceptualized depression as a response to 'inadequate or insufficient reinforcers'. Lewinsohn presented an excellent discussion of the behavioural theory of depression: 'It is the degree to which the individual's behaviour is maintained (followed) by reinforcement that is assumed to be the critical antecedent condition for the occurrence of depression rather than the total amount of reinforcement received'.

Seligman viewed depression as a state of 'learned helplessness'. Seligman (1975) presented evidence that people tended to be labelled as depressive had developed a state of *helplessness*. He defined helplessness as 'the psychological state that frequently results when events are uncontrollable' and noted that an event is uncontrollable when we cannot do anything about it, when nothing we do matters. Laboratory experiments on helplessness produced three deficits:

(1) they undermined the motivation to respond;
(2) they retarded the ability to learn that responding works; and
(3) they resulted in emotional disturbance, primarily depression and anxiety.

Seligman suggested 'that a childhood of receiving the good things of life independently of responding can lead to a depressed adulthood, in which one is largely incapable of coping with stress'. One's ability to predict the effect of engaging in specific behaviours is important. Seligman noted that 'predictability is preferable to unpredictability; stress and anxiety are considerably greater when events occur unpredictably . . . More stomach ulcers occur, along with terror and panic . . . A person . . . is helpless with respect to some outcome when the outcome occurs independently of all of his voluntary responses.' Thus, the person felt unable to control the outcome and was said to lack controlability. Seligman concluded that in organisms from fish to man, uncontrollability produced deterioration of the organism's readiness to respond adaptively to stress.

Prociuk, Breen, and Lussier (1976) studied the relationship between locus of control, hopelessness, and depression, and found a significant relationship between hopelessness and external control and depression. The authors noted that specifically, persons who perceived reinforcements to be a function of powerful others, luck, chance, or fate, expressed greater pessimism about the future.

Measurement of depression

A number of scales are used to measure depression. Zung (1965) developed a 20-item self-report scale in which the respondent was asked to indicate on a four-point scale the degree to which a statement was true for him at the present time. Thus, Zung's measure was a state scale. Zuckerman and Lubin (1965) included a measure of state depression in the Multiple Affect Adjective Check List (MAACL). This instrument also included measures of state anxiety and hostility.

From a behavioural point of view, the determination of potentially reinforcing events may be a more profitable exercise than obtaining a score on a depression inventory. MacPhillamy and Lewinsohn's *Pleasant Events Inventory* has been 'constructed for the purpose of providing . . . information about what is potentially reinforcing for a given individual'. Validity studies on this instrument resulted in scales which were assumed to measure (1) general activity level; (2) reinforcement potential; and (3) obtained reinforcement. Lewinsohn (1974) noted that the behavioural theory of depression was strongly supported by the results of these validity studies.

We turn now to a brief discussion of response sets or styles which need to be taken into account in the interpretation of scales used in the measurement of mood and personality.

RESPONSE SETS OR STYLES

We have already referred to propensities which tend to distort a person's responses to various types of scales. An example is the tendency to avoid the extreme ratings in a simple seven-point rating scale. Anastasi (1976) noted that self-report inventories are especially subject to malingering or faking.

Clients may tend to 'fake good' or 'fake bad' when responding to a personality or mood scale. The tendency to 'fake bad' (i.e. to distort one's responses in the direction of greater pathology) may be related to a wish to receive treatment. There may be many reasons why a person may wish to 'fake good', among which may be a wish to see oneself in the best possible light. If the test results have relevance to being offered a job or in some other way are suspected as having a strong influence on the respondent's future, then 'faking good' may occur. Most personality scales such as the MMPI and the CPI have various dissimilation or lie scales built into them which detect these response sets. Response sets are greatly influenced by the content of the scale or questionnaire. One of the most investigated response sets is 'social desirability'. It is clear that most items in a questionnaire that refer to pathology are perceived as socially undesirable (Edwards 1957, 1962). Thus, a respondent's answer on an inventory such as the MMPI may be based on the social desirability value of the items or they may be based on the repondent's actual characteristics as he sees them. Unfortunately, the response may reflect both influences. As noted by Mischel (1968) it is difficult to choose between the social desirability interpretation and the characterological or trait interpretation of self-report scores on inventories. According to Anastasi social desirability may be controlled by the forced-choice technique (i.e. by forcing the respondent to choose between two statements of equal social desirability).

Another tendency is to endorse positive statements (i.e. to acquiesce). Many inventories such as the MMPI have true–false items. Citing Couch and Keniston (1960), Anastasi noted that 'Acquiescence is conceptualised as a continuous variable; at one end of the scale are the consistent "Yeasayers" and at the other end the consistent "Naysayers"'. The tendency to endorse positive statements is known as 'acquiescence response set'. It can be decreased by balancing the items (i.e. alternating negatively and positively-worded items).

In reference to these response sets, Anastasi noted that they later were referred to as *response styles* in that they came to be considered as indicators of broad and durable personality characteristics that were worth measuring in their own right.

In discussing acquiescence and social desirability response sets, Anastasi noted that the controversy over response sets was far from settled and that it might prove to be 'a tempest in a teapot', which is consistent with Mischel's (1968) conclusion that neither the generality of response tendencies across measures, nor their stable correlates, had been firmly established. A more extensive discussion of response distortions may be found in Lanyon and Goodstein (1971).

SUMMARY

This chapter is about the mood states and their assessment. While the traditional approach towards the concept of personality has been exclusively concerned with general dispositions or traits, a more reasonable view which takes account of response specificity has been in evidence over the last decade or so. Thus, the first section of the chapter discusses the concept of trait and state, pointing to some of the research on the State–Trait Anxiety Inventory of Spielberger *et al.* which supports a trait–state distinction. There is then a discussion of the measurement of various mood states, including Thayer's Activation–Deactivation Check List and its derivatives and Zuckerman's Sensation Seeking Scale.

Subsections are addressed to the concepts of anxiety, aggression, and depression. The lack of relationship between inventory and physiological measures of anxiety is pointed out. However, it is suggested that if one uses the individual's most reactive physiological measure, one is more likely to find that this relates significantly to an inventory measure. The psychoanalytic and learning views of anxiety are discussed. The behavioural point of view is that a functional analysis should be carried out whether or not an inventory measure of anxiety is used.

Some of the research on aggressive behaviour is reported, followed by a discussion on the measurement of aggression. Rosenzweig's concepts of intropunativeness, extrapunativeness, and impunativeness are discussed in reference to the Picture Frustration Study. The discussion of depression emphasized a behavioural view in which the depressed person is seen as lacking *contingent* reinforcement (following Lewinsohn) or, (following Seligman) as having developed a 'state of helplessness'. Clearly, these behavioural views are not mutually exclusive.

Finally the concern about response sets or styles is discussed, as well as methods to take them into account in the measurement of mood or personality dimensions. These response tendencies include 'faking good', faking bad', acquiescence response set, and social desirability response set. As suggested by Anastasi, there may have been more concern with these tendencies than will be found to be justified.

12
Assessment and the motivation for treatment

The Light of Lights
look always on the motive not the deed
The Shadow of Shadows on the deed alone.
Yeats: *The Countess Cathleen* Act IV

COMMUNICATING THE RESULTS OF ASSESSMENT

There has already been a discussion, in Chapter 9, of communication during an interview. While that chapter was concerned with the interviewing of patients, much of this could of course be applied to any interview such as one communicating the results of assessment and therapy to staff, patients, or relatives.

The situation in which the patient is referred for assessment is particularly important, and it must be established from the referral source not only what the purpose of the referral is but how specific conclusions arising from the assessment will affect the patient's treatment. If possible, this is best determined through personal contact with whoever made the referral. In this way, not only are the above questions answered but there is opportunity for a cross-fertilization of ideas and for a greater interdisciplinary understanding which will pave the way for improved communication in the future.

Some of the questions which need to be answered before communicating the results of an assessment are: (1) the reliability and validity of the information to be communicated (i.e. one's degree of confidence in the information); (2) the purpose of the communication; and (3) the status and characteristics of the person who is to receive the communication.

When a referral is made during a ward round or some interdisciplinary meeting, questions (2) and (3) may be more easily answered. Personal contact with whoever made the referral should help in the communication process.

(1) **Reliability and validity of the information to be communicated**

This situation may vary from one in which the psychologist can only say that the test results are unreliable and invalid, to one in which he can say that there is very little doubt about the reliability and validity of the test data. It should always be borne in mind that the psychologist is making inferences in the interpretation of test data and communicating in terms of probability statements, in the same way that research reports do. In the first situation, in which the test data is not considered valid, all is typically *not* lost if one regards the *test situation* as a standardized interview, since much valuable information may be gained by direct observation.

(2) **Purpose of the communication**

In what way might the results of an assessment be used? Is one providing a colleague with information that will help establish a diagnosis which in turn has implications for treatment? While the psychologist may be able to provide definite conclusions after assessment procedures have been carried out, at times he may be limited in arriving at definite conclusions. For example, it will not always be possible to differentiate between a diagnosis of depression and dementia in a seventy-five year old. However, a clinical opinion may be made from data obtained from the total test situation. The implications of an opinion must be considered. Will treatment for depression be ethically and rationally more desirable than suggesting that the patient demonstrates dementia? While the ultimate decisions may rest with the recipient of the tests results rather than with the psychologist, yet the psychologist may wish to give an educated guess or informed clinical impression, which will imply one sort of treatment rather than another. While this example may seem a poor one, since the EMI scan may more easily resolve the above problem in differential diagnosis, it must be remembered that such hardware is not universally available.

(3) **Specific recipient of the communication**

Is the recipient of the test results a psychological or psychiatric colleague, a general practitioner, a relative or possibly the patient himself? It is very important that the way this information is conveyed takes account of the status and personality of the recipient.

When communicating results to the patient or to a relative, it is not usual to report a specific test score. One must take into account the emotional needs of those personally involved with the patient. Does the psychologist have an ethical duty to communicate, for example, the test results of a child to his parents? Putting it in another way, do parents and other relations have the right to demand these results? Many psychologists would agree that the general answer to these questions is 'Yes'. However, it might also be added that the results should be communicated in such a way that the recipient of the information understands them, a qualification that would hardly be satisfied by the reporting of a mere test score, which, by itself, is meaningless. The meaning of the results and the degree of confidence that may be placed in them must be communicated adequately. If mental test scores are reported to parents, the Psychological Corporation would recommend the use of percentiles indicating the percentage of people whose performance the client has equalled or surpassed, and including a definite description of the norm group to whom the client is compared (Ricks 1959). On the other hand, the Test Department of Harcourt, Brace and World (Durost 1961) recommended a method which will allow a more direct comparison to be made from one test to another.

Whether results are reported to a relation, a teacher, or to a health professional it is important that the results be interpreted in terms of the behaviour of the client, and in reference to action or treatment. Test results must be made functional, and the way in which they are communicated must take into account the emotional and professional needs of those to whom the results are communicated. It is far better to over-explain than to risk the consequence of an inadequate understanding. Considering the increased involvement of parents and other non-professionals in treatment the full explanation of assessment results takes on an added importance.

SUGGESTIONS REGARDING TREATMENT

While the psychologist may engage in both the assessment and therapeutic role with a patient, he may on occasion carry out an assessment for another health professional who will act as the principal therapist. In the latter case, it is suggested that it would be best if recommendations for treatment were both included in a written report and discussed with the principal therapist. Again, by personal contact and thus feedback between different professionals, a greater understanding of each other's role would be facilitated, each professional, in essence, 'educating' the other. Obviously, increased contact would be informative in conveying the specific types of problems which particular therapists are able to undertake, as well as conveying the limitations of particular therapists and particular settings.

The use of a questionnaire such as the Edwards Personal Preference Schedule (EPPS) (Edwards 1959) may be helpful in suggesting areas of conflict to the assessor, which can be passed along to the therapist. This instrument is useful in counselling those with personality problems. An indication may be made to the client, for example, that his responses to the EPPS suggest that he has a high need to rely on others. The therapist may ask the client if this suggestion seems to be a valid one. If, after some discussion, there is acquiescence, then the therapist may wish to suggest, in turn, that: (1) this high need to rely on others may be related to his marital difficulties, and (2) may have something to do with his lack of promotion at work. While the Edwards has been used extensively (particularly in University Counselling Centres) in America, it is also beginning to be valued in the United Kingdom (Shapiro 1975).

Perhaps one of the most important factors an assessment report should discuss is the client's motivation for treatment.

THE PATIENT'S MOTIVATION FOR TREATMENT

There are a number of important questions that the therapist should pose before making definite decisions about therapy. One major question is: 'How did the client come to seek help?' Did he volunteer himself for treatment in that he felt that he had problems which required psychological help? Was he asked to see the therapist by someone else: such as his GP, his parents, or other relation, or a friend?

The client's entry into therapy is quite important in the assessment of the client's motivation for treatment. If he was referred by someone, was any degree of rejection or threat involved? Some people resent being told to seek psychological or psychiatric help. The objection or resentment may, however, be quite specific. For example, a man who feels he has an unsatisfactory sexual relationship with his wife may tell her that unless she signs up for therapy he will divorce her. This may be very threatening for the wife and, particularly if the husband refuses to receive treatment with the wife, is not very conducive to successful treatment (Masters and Johnson 1970). A father or mother may take one of their children to a child health or child guidance clinic, identifying the particular child as psychologically unwell, rather than considering the possibility of a family problem in which the total family may be involved in treatment (Haley 1963; Jackson 1970). A child or adult may be referred by the court or some organization dealing with offenders. It seems obvious that in cases like those an assessment of the potential client's willingness to undergo therapy is particularly important.

Beier 1952 (reprinted in McGowan and Schmidt 1962) noted that the most favourable situation for successful therapy is one in which the client himself volunteers for treatment. As mentioned above, some clients may not volunteer for help, and when they are referred by others, may not be particularly co-operative. Beier (1952) discussed this problem and presented a number of brief 'case histories' involving clients who were best classed as involuntary, such as juvenile delinquents, court referrals, people referred by their employers, students referred by faculty or administrators, and children. Beier defined an involuntary client as 'an individual in whom resistance toward giving up symptoms and substitute gratifications is greater than his desire for help (McGowan and Schmidt 1962).

Beier noted that the involuntary client could be dealt with in one of three ways (McGowan and Schmidt 1962):

(1) By not accepting the client for treatment initially. The therapist waits until the client is ready to seek help on his own.

(2) By accepting the client for treatment. During the initial sessions the therapist actively reflects the client's resistance to treatment.

(3) By accepting the client for treatment, but pointing out he is clearly perceived as a client, the therapist puts his cards on the table and discusses ways the client may help himself.

In the first approach the client is given a free choice regarding participation. While the client may be referred by an individual or organization regarded by the client as authoritative, the therapist tells the client that he is free to use the clinical or counselling services or not as he pleases. He emphasizes that any participation in therapy would be for the client's benefit and not a matter of 'siding' with the referral agent. Beier noted that 'Misunderstanding, misinterpretation, and the possible lack of readiness to admit and sense permissiveness are hindrances in making this pretherapeutic phase effective with some involuntatry clients. It seems to be effective with clients of a certain maturity, but fails to work where emotional factors are in the way' (McGowan and Schmidt 1962).

In the second approach, the therapist communicates his full acceptance of the client as well as his tolerance and understanding of the client's resistance. He provides a non-threatening atmosphere as recommended by the client-centred approach. Support is provided for the client's unexpressed and unrecognized needs.

Finally, in the third approach to the involuntary client, the therapist takes the risk of raising the anxiety level of the patient by communicating his perception of the client as a person who may help himself by allowing himself to talk about his problems. Beier regarded the third approach as crude but felt that it might 'be understood as an attempt . . . to support the involuntary client's own motivation towards help by motivating anxiety' (McGowan and Schmidt 1962). The problem with this approach is knowing how much anxiety is motivating, yet preventing the development of too great a level of anxiety, which may well result in premature termination of the therapeutic relationship.

It is the author's experience that a client-centred approach is very helpful in working with the involuntary patient. The therapist's position should be fully communicated to the client. Issues such as the confidentiality of information and feelings revealed during therapy, and the fact that the therapists's job is to help the client rather than act as a policeman for the referral agent, should be explicitly dealt with in the initial contact. The reflection of the client's feelings regarding his 'referral' should convey the therapists's empathic understanding (see Chapter 14 on client-centred therapy).

Some clients may give the impression of wishing help and yet not be particularly motivated for therapy. Often the patient's expectations are unrealistic. Hoehn-Saric, Frank, Imber, Nash, Stone, and Battle (1964) carried out a study involving the use of 'role-induction interview' (RII) in preparing psychiatric out-patients for psychotherapy. This interview was designed to (1) clarify the patient's expectations regarding psychotherapy, and (2) to increase the congruence between patients' behaviour and therapist's expectations of how patients should behave during therapy. Hoehn-Saric *et al.* (1964) indicated that the RII 'tried to arouse realistic expectations of improvement . . ., explain the therapist's anticipated behavior, tell the patient how he is expected to behave, and instruct him how to recognize and overcome superficial manifestations of resistance'. It was found that the group who were prepared for therapy through the use of the RII, achieved a significantly better score on the Therapy Behaviour Scale, which measures desirable therapy behaviour. In addition, the experimental group demonstrated a significantly better attendance rate, and the therapists, who were not told which group the patients belonged to, rated patients in the experimental group more favourably with respect to establishing and maintaining a therapeutic relationship. Clearly the importance of the therapists's willingness to discuss openly the type of therapy he recommends in detail with the client cannot be over-stressed. Frequently, especially if he has had no previous contact with psychologists, the client will arrive at the clinic or consulting room expecting the treatment to consist of something the psychologist does to him. The client perceives the psychologist to be the active agent of treatment, while he plays a relatively passive role. The degree to which the client may be required to participate actively in his own treatment is discussed in some detail in the chapters on behaviour therapy and Chapter 19 on self-control procedures.

If the client is perceived as a willing participant in treatment, a question that should be posed is: to what degree do the client's reported 'symptoms' match the real situation? Is the client exaggerating his problems in order to receive 'help', or in order to jump the queue for treatment? The referral statement may have to be modified in the light of the information gleaned from initial interviews before beginning therapy sessions, or referring the patient to a specialist.

If the appropriate treatment is one in which the therapist has no experience, he either refers the client to someone who is qualified or carries out the procedure himself under supervision. Clearly, the nature of the client's problems has priority, but if the treatment is incompatible with the therapists's 'personality', then even if the therapist is qualified to use the particular procedure, further referral is advisable.

THE THERAPIST'S ROLE

The previous paragraph raises the question of the therapist's motivation to treat a particular client with a particular procedure. One must ask the question: why is a particular client rejected or accepted for treatment? The therapist may be motivated by factors in addition to scientific or professional ones. Why does a particular therapist take the decision to treat a particular client? Is there something about the background of the client that could influence the therapist in accepting the client? Does the therapist basically like or dislike the client? Is the therapist interested in a client because of the nature of the problem more than a wish to help the client with his particular difficulty?

Schafer (1954) has written some interesting material on the motivation of the psychologist in the assessment situation which may equally apply to the therapeutic setting. Actually, one is hard put to differentiate clearly between one's role as assessor or evaluator and one's role as therapist, since there is a fair amount of overlap. For many patients therapy may be perceived as beginning with an assessment, and certainly with the continuous monitoring that takes place during therapy, one cannot isolate a pure therapy as distinct from assessment. Schafer noted that four constants of the psychologist's (assessor's, therapist's, etc.) role were important: (1) the voyeuristic; (2) the autocratic; (3) the oracular; and (4) the saintly. These were considered to be general aspects and not related to the motivations and circumstances that were important in bringing the therapist to his professional role, and operated regardless of the therapist's individual response to particular patients or patients in general.

The voyeuristic aspect

While the therapist is able to behave as a psychological voyeur enquiring into various facets of the client's life which are generally regarded as rather private matters, the therapist is not necessarily required to reciprocate as would be expected in normal social intercourse (see however, Jourard's (1971) work on self-disclosure). Schafer noted that 'the opportunity for voyeuristic intrusion . . . may stimulate too much inquiry, too eager pursuit of "suggestive" details of responses and verbalizations'.

The autocratic aspect

The therapist is typically in the dominant position in the therapeutic role. He is able to satisfy whatever needs for control or dominance he may have, in that there need be 'little sharing of control in the relationship'. The therapist is able to demand that the client reveal the why, when, and how of his behaviour. In this way, as Schafer noted, the therapist may bring out 'anxiety, inadequacy, compliance, rebellion and a host of other reaction tendencies. The . . . therapist is, in this respect, a psychological ringmaster'.

The oracular aspect

The therapist (particularly the relative beginner) may see himself as the interpreter *par excellence* of his client's behaviour. He may feel that the client is unable to hide anything from him—that the client cannot win. The therapist may be the type of person, for example, who notes that if the client comes to his therapy session early, he is anxious; if he comes right on time, he is compulsive; and, if he comes late, or doesn't come at all, he is demonstrating resistance. While it is hoped that most therapists have achieved some sense of proportion through the vicissitudes of life's experiences, the therapist may have to deal from time to time with those clients who 'ascribe magically insightful and influential powers to doctors, therapists and their agents'.

The saintly aspect

The typical therapist likes to see himself as a person who wishes to help the client no matter how difficult the client may be. Even if the client does not seem to appreciate that the therapist is doing his all to treat him, even if the client becomes hostile towards the therapist, as long as what he does is perceived as being right, the therapist will persist in his efforts, even going as far as to 'turn the other cheek.' Schafer asked whether the therapist did not 'implicitly promise psychological salvation? Will he not subdue his own needs and resentment and selflessly try to understand and feel the tragedy of the patient? Is not his code like that of a saint with a sinner, a slave or a leper? . . . Often patients tend to cast us in just this saintly role and they find us not altogether unprepared for it'.

Schafer noted that the therapist was able to come to terms with these four constants in an adaptive way, but that he 'is more able to do so if he is aware of the complex psychological implications of his job and of his relationships with colleagues and patients'. Having said that Schafer went on to discuss eight specific types of therapist who may experience difficulties in carrying out their roles adequately without mishandling their clients. These types include the therapist:

(1) with an uncertain sense of personal identity;
(2) who is socially inhibited or withdrawn;
(3) who is dependent;
(4) who exhibits rigid defences against dependent needs;
(5) who is rigidly intellectual in his approach;
(6) who is sadistic;
(7) who exhibits rigid defences against hostility;
(8) who exhibits masochistic behaviour.

The intent in discussing these types is not to focus on the potential abnormalities of the therapist, but to suggest that the therapist should become aware of his tendencies, which may be aggravated in a difficult therapeutic situation. If the author may act out his autocratic aspect, he would suggest that Schafer's discussion on interpersonal dynamics be required reading for all actual and would-be health workers!

SUMMARY

In summary, it is clear that both the client's motivation for treatment and the therapist's motivation in carrying out treatment in general, and with particular clients, are important variables to assess prior to, or in the early stages of, therapy. That is, the therapist should be aware of his own motives in doing therapeutic work in general, as well as the specific needs that may be satisfied in working with a particular client. Thus, a reading of Schafer's discussion of interpersonal dynamics would not be inappropriate, even for the behaviourally orientated therapist. In addition, Sullivan's (1953) ideas regarding the therapist as expert and participant observer should be helpful preparation for adequate therapeutic performance (see Chapter 9).

Part IV
Approaches to treatment

INTRODUCTION TO PART IV

This section of the book is devoted to various treatment procedures. Psychotherapy is introduced in Chapter 13 and a brief overview of the psychoanalytic approach is provided. Chapter 14 discusses the client-centred point of view and ends with a critical discussion of psychotherapy research. It is concluded that the effective components of psychotherapeutic approaches need to be established by more rigorous research.

The proliferation of research in behaviour therapy is reflected by the inclusion of two chapters covering this point of view. Chapter 15 discusses some of the learning principles upon which behaviour therapy is based, including classical conditioning, operant conditioning, and observational learning. This is followed by a discussion of the techniques used with problems of psychological deficit such as phobias, anxiety states, and problems in interpersonal relationships, etc. Chapter 16 discusses the treatment of problems of psychological excess such as the obsessive–compulsive disorders.

Chapter 17 provides an overview of hypnosis research and discusses some of the clinical applications such as the revival of forgotten memories, the treatment of pain, and the use of hypnosis in behaviour therapy. The chapter ends with a cricial discussion. Chapter 18 provides an outline of some of the research that has been carried out using biofeedback procedures, discusses clinical applications, and, like the previous chapter, ends with a critical discussion.

Finally, Chapter 19 reviews the use of self-control techniques, including self-monitoring, self-reward, self-punishment, etc. Since it is anticipated that an increasingly larger number of people will learn self-control techniques, especially as a prophylactic measure, this is considered to be a most important area of research and practice.

13
Psychotherapy and the psychoanalytic approach

1. "Know thyself"
2. "Nothing too much"
and upon these all other precepts depend.
Plutarch: *Consolations of Apollonius,*
inscribed on the Delphic oracle

INTRODUCTION TO PSYCHOTHERAPY

While the criterion of effective psychotherapy is behaviour change, the procedures which are used to promote behaviour change vary according to the therapist's particular point of view. Every psychotherapeutic approach is based upon a specific personality theory. However, a therapist may hold a point of view implicitly without being specifically aware of the basis for his approach.

Ford and Urban (1965) discuss ten approaches to psychotherapy including Freud's psychoanalysis (Freud 1956); Adler's individual psychology (Ansbacher and Ansbacher 1956); Rogers's client-centred approach (Rogers 1959), and Sullivan's theory of interpersonal relations (Sullivan 1953). A comprehensive overview of the theories underlying the major approaches to psychotherapy may be found in Hall and Lindzey (1978).

As a general clinical introduction to psychotherapy, Fromm-Reichmann's (1960) text will be found very useful. A more scientifically orientated book (Goldstein, Heller, and Sechrest 1966) presents sections on research, individual psychotherapy, and group psychotherapy.

Psychotherapy may be defined as a specific type of interaction between two or more individuals, the aim of which is to bring about a change in behaviour so that the client will be able to function more effectively in his interaction with both his external environment and with himself. While the interpersonal theory of psychiatry by H. S. Sullivan stresses a person's relationship with other people, Freud's theory emphasized intrapersonal relationships. In other words, one's intrapsychic functioning or relationship with oneself. For example, if a person is aware that he has been unjustifiably hostile towards his parents he may feel guilty (i.e. his superego may serve to punish him and he may become dejected or depressed). Thus Freud's ideas concern the relationships between the components of the personality, the id, ego, and superego, which are discussed further below.

The term 'client' as well as 'patient' is used throughout this chapter, since it is extensively used in the literature of psychotherapy, and often many of the problems brought to the psychotherapy consulting room are more psychological–sociological 'problems of living' than biologically based. Obviously the psychotherapist does not proceed with treatment without first determining whether there is some biological basis for what appears to be a psychological problem. Consultations with the GP and with specialists may be necessary at any stage of psychotherapy. If the client is taking medication, or if medication or a change in medication is indicated, then medical consultation is necessary. In working with those clients who exhibit psychosomatic-type problems, interdisciplinary liaison is particularly important.

Bandura (1961) pointed to the fact that:

> Psychotherapy rests on a very simple but fundamental assumption, i.e., human behaviour is modifiable through psychological procedures and when skeptics raise the question 'Does Psychotherapy Work?' they may be responding in part to the mysticism that has come to surround the term. Perhaps the more meaningful question, and one which avoids surplus meanings associated with the term 'psychotherapy' is as follows: can human behaviour be modified through psychological means and, if so, what are the learning mechanisms that mediate behaviour change?

If one subscribes to the idea that the aim of psychotherapy is behaviour change, then the question that one is most likely to ask is 'What does one mean by a change in behaviour?' Behaviour may refer to an individual's job or academic performance, something that may be very accurately measured. On the other hand, one may be referring to an individual's feelings about himself. One may be saying that a person's self-concept should be more positive after psychotherapy. There are many and varied aims of psychotherapy, the specific emphasis varying with the particular psychotherapeutic approach. Some therapists concentrate on symptom relief. Other therapists, particularly those who follow a client-centred approach, are involved in changing the self-concept of the individual. They are interested in increasing the individual's self mastery (see Chapter 19), so that he is able to control his emotions appropriately and prevent them from getting out of hand. These therapists feel it is important that the client should be able to regulate his life, i.e. his commerce with both his internal and external environment. Yet other therapists are interested in teaching the individual to become more independent (Snyder 1963). In Western cultures there is great emphasis on independence. One of the problems of adolescence involves the change from a relatively dependent role to a more independent status in society. Lastly, some therapists wish to change the client's behaviour to make it more in accordance with society's prescriptions and prohibitions. This is especially the case in working with those who have exhibited consistent criminal behaviour. There are many other aims of psychotherapy, but the above gives some idea of the various emphases in viewing psychotherapy as behaviour change.

There are two broad approaches to psychotherapy. One views psychotherapy as a *reconstructive* process, while the other sees it as more *supportive*. In the reconstructive approach, the emphasis is on changing the structure of personality to adapt the client to his environment. The therapist wishes to change the individual in some major way. In supportive psychotherapy, on the other hand, the therapist is not particularly interested in extensive changes in the individual. There may be a number of reasons for this. For example, the client may not be motivated to make extensive changes, or the therapist may have concluded that any attempt to change the client might make matters worse than they are already, and it may be much better for the patient to shore up and improve the defences he has now, rather than develop new coping mechanisms.

Steps in therapy

Data must first be collected through interview or test procedures. Then this data must be organized or synthesized in order to complete the tentative *formulation of the problem*, as described in Chapter 12 and discussed in Chapter 15. The formulation ends with recommendations for treatment, including an estimate of prognosis. During treatment there may be a need for a reformulation of the problem. The therapist must guard against the error of making later dissonant information consistent with that obtained in initial interviews. If treatment is carried out, not only should there be continuous monitoring of progress, but, in addition, follow-up procedures should be instituted and continued to at least the sixth post-therapy month. Follow-up procedures are important in determining the extent to which any behaviour change has been maintained, or if indeed a relapse has occurred. Unfortunately, if the client does not return or telephone, the therapist cannot legitimately assume that all is well.

While the above suggests clearly defined steps, in fact initial evaluative interviews may in fact imperceptibly shade into more specific treatment interviews, and treatment may continue during the follow-up period. In order that behaviour changes produced in the consulting room or hospital generalize to the home and work environments, the therapist often enlists the help of relatives, friends, or workmates to continue certain therapeutic procedures or to motivate the client to activate newly learned interpersonal skills. Finally, since the ultimate aim of psychotherapy is to teach the client methods of self-control, significant others may be helpful in monitoring the client's behaviour in his home environment until he has become autonomous or self-sufficient. In summary, then the main steps in therapy may be listed as:

(1) the collection of the data concerning the 'complaint' from the client;
(2) the organization or synthesis of the data obtained in order to construct a tentative formulation of the problem;
(3) the treatment proper, including monitoring of progress; and

(4) the use of follow-up procedures.

We turn now to an overview of the psychoanalytic approach to treatment, including some discussion of the more recent emphasis on ego processes.

THE PSYCHOANALYTIC APPROACH

A good introduction to Freud and his ideas may be gained by first reading C. S. Hall's (1964) *Primer of Freudian psychology* followed by Freud's (1956) *General introduction to psychoanalysis*, his *Psychopathology of everyday life* (Freud 1964), and his *Interpretation of dreams* (1970). These books are among the more popular books on psychoanalysis. Additionally, Thompson (1950) and Mullahy (1955) are helpful as background reading on psychoanalytic theories. Finally, Menninger (1958) serves as an excellent text on psychoanalytic technique.

Freudian theory divides an individual's mental life into different levels of awareness: the *unconscious, preconscious,* and *conscious*. Mullahy (1955) noted that the theory 'holds that powerful mental processes exist outside conscious awareness which can produce in the mind all the effects which ordinary ideas can, including the effects which then become conscious as ideas, without these processes themselves becoming conscious'. Thus, processes of which one is totally unaware and which would require specific techniques to bring to one's level of awareness are referred to as unconscious. On the other hand, there are processes of which one is unaware at a particular moment, but which may be recalled at any time. These ideas are preconscious, and exist in an 'intermediate state between consciousness and the unconscious'. Unconscious processes (ideas and impulses), however, tend to be dynamic and to be expressed in some form (as symptoms, for example) which is indicative of what essentially remains, for the time, unconscious. The essential procedure of psychoanalysis is to make what is unconscious, conscious. Therapy, according to this analytic theory, cannot be successful in symptomatic relief alone. The therapist must deal with the underlying conflicts by inducing the unconscious impulses, feelings, and ideas to become conscious through free-association and, consequently, desensitizing the client by the 'working through' process. If the therapist engaged in symptom removal alone, then symptom substitution will probably occur. The terms unconscious, preconscious, and conscious are descriptive, then, of different degrees of availability or awareness of ideas and feelings.

Freud postulates that each individual in his development proceeds through various psychosexual stages. Associated with each stage are certain characteristics related to the erogenous zones (mouth, anus, genitals). An individual may, however, become fixated at, or regress to, a particular stage of development, a situation that may lead to psychopathology. These stages are shown in Table 13.1. The first three stages (in the first five or six years

TABLE 13.1
FREUDIAN PSYCHOSEXUAL STAGES

Stage	*Age range*	*Characteristics*
Oral (a) incorporation (b) sadism	0–1	Pleasure through sucking Oral sadism through biting (ambivalence attutide)
Anal	1–3	Expulsive (destructive) Retentive (possessive)
Phallic	3–5	Focus on penis and equivalent in girl Oedipal complex
Latency	5–puberty	Strengthening of ego Development of super-ego Resolution of Oedipal complex
Genital	Late adolescence Early adulthood	Development of maturity Emphasis on ego processes (see. p. 45 Chapter 3)

of life) are considered most important for the formation of the adult personality.

Freud's psychoanalytic theory is hedonistic in nature. It stresses what is known as the *pleasure principle*, the idea that people tend to behave in such a way as to maximize pleasure and to avoid pain. According to Freudian theory, the personality structure is made up of three components: the *id*, the *ego*, and the *super-ego*. Basically, the pleasure principle is fulfilled by the id, which is the most basic component. The id is referred to as the reservoir of instinctual or psychic energy. During the childhood years the expression of sexual and aggressive impulses from the developing child has been punished or there has been a threat of punishment. Therefore, in order to avoid the uneasy feelings of tension or anxiety which have come to be associated with the forbidden impulses, the child has learned to *repress* ideas and feelings associated with these impulses. Repression is the process by which a person avoids the awareness of impulses. *Repression* is an unconscious process caused by anxiety. *Suppression* is similar to repression, with the exception that one is aware of pushing ideas associated with anxiety into the unconscious. Both repression and suppression, then, are a form of avoidance of a feared object or situation. A more extensive discussion of the ego defence mechanisms may be found in Hall (1964*b*), while Gleser and Ihilevich (1969) discuss an instrument for measuring the mechanisms. Thus, by this means an unconscious psychological conflict is formed which continues to draw on the reservoir of psychic energy or libido and to influence the individual's behaviour, even though the individual is quite unaware of the conflict. Impulses from the id demand immediate gratification. Should no thought be given to the reality situation in attempting to gratify these impulses, then consequences follow in the form of punishment or threatened punishment from the representatives of society (i.e. people in authority such as parents, teachers, law enforcers, etc.).

The second component of personality structure, the ego, has most commerce with the environment and is the most rational component. It is related to the environment through the *reality principle*. The ego basically forces one to face the particular reality one finds oneself in, in order to satisfy one's basic impulses (i.e. to take into account the environment). One cannot just behave on the basis of the id. There is then a basic opposition between the pleasure principle and the reality principle. The unconscious conflict between id and ego, or between id and super-ego (see below) may lead to the formation and expression of symptoms. Symptomatology is said to represent the unconscious conflict. If the ego is unable adequately to control the impulses from the id through the use of defence mechanisms then the person expends much of his energy in maladaptive ways, such as in using inhibitory mechanisms designed to prevent repressed material from breaking into consciousness. The psychoanalyst refers to this as *resistance*. In addition to the use of repression the individual may use *denial*. Denial involves the use of thoughts which oppose any admission to one's self that certain anxiety-provoking thoughts are threatening to occur, thus preventing the anxiety from reaching consciousness. The reader may remember the discussion of denial in Chapter 4, in reference to the stress associated with surgery. Even if symptoms are removed, the underlying conflict or neurosis remains. It is only by making the unconscious material conscious and desensitizing the client to it ('working through' the previously unconscious material) that the neurosis is cured.

Primary process thinking is associated with the id and the pleasure principle. On the other hand, *secondary process thinking* is associated with the ego and the reality principle. One may noted that primary process thinking tends to be the sort of thinking engaged in to an excessive degree by schizophrenics and by autistic children. It lacks reality contact so it is an autistic sort of process, whereas the sort of thinking associated with the ego is rational. From an analytic point of view a person may be assessed in terms of the extent to which primary process thinking is present relative to the degree that secondary process thinking can be demonstrated. The defence mechanism of *regression* may be seen as relatively non-adaptive. If one regresses, one goes back to a previous level of adjustment, adaptation, or development. On the other hand, the ego-psychologists have referred to '*regression in the service of the ego*'. A person may be fairly rationalistic in most of his behaviour, with an emphasis on secondary process thinking. However, one may need from time to time to take a rest from this. On occasion one may, at a party or in another situation, behave in ways which may be considered as a characteristic of a much younger person, forgetting the realities of life and one's responsibilites. This regression may be very necessary for all of us from time to time. This may be a form of recuperation, and some (Kris 1952) would argue that regression in the service of the ego may increase the probability of maintaining mental health and developing more creative ideas. It should be recalled here that the utilization of defence mechanisms is not considered pathological unless they are used to an extreme degree.

The third component of personality structure is the super-ego. Some people simply call it the *conscience*. This is the aspect of the personality into which one has incorporated the values of the society in which one lives. These values are passed on to the child by his parents or parent surrogates. One is said to develop a conscience, so that if one behaves in a way inconsistent with the principles or rules of society, one is expected to feel guilty. When the individual realizes that he has broken the moral code he feels an anxiety which Freud referred to as 'moral anxiety'. Actually, the super-ego involves two factors—the conscience and the *ego-ideal*. The ego-ideal is that aspect of the super-ego which has incorporated desirable or idealistic behaviour as a model. One might ask: 'In what way does the ideal doctor or ideal psychologist behave?' How should he behave? In the process of developing one's ego-ideal one may, if one is a serious student of medicine or psychology, focus on well-known doctors or psychologists and attempt to emulate them. In other words, they are used as models. One uses here then the defence mechanism of *identification*. This identification with various figures as one grows up, is, in fact, a very positive sort of mechanism because it helps one to direct one's attention to the sort of person one wants to become, to determine the sort of factors or characteristics one would like to develop.

Anxiety is an important aspect of Freudian theory. It is a painful emotional experience that arises from either external or internal stimulation. Freud differentiated three different types of anxiety, but he did not actually differentiate anxiety from fear. Fear for Freud was equivalent to realistic or objective anxiety. This first type of anxiety is based on a realistic situation which would be expected to induce fear. The second type of anxiety is neurotic anxiety, which is considered irrational in nature. There is no real basis for the fear, certainly as perceived by others. In Freudian terms there is a conflict between impulses from the id and the reality principle of the ego. There are two subtypes of neurotic anxiety: one type is referred to as 'free-floating anxiety', which basically means that one cannot attach it to anything. One feels genuinely anxious, but cannot say why. The second sub-type of neurotic anxiety has an object, although Freudian theory would postulate that the actual situation feared underlies the conscious object feared. This type of anxiety is strong and is referred to as a phobia. The third type of anxiety is *moral anxiety* and refers to a conflict between impulses from the id and the prescriptions and prohibitions of the super-ego.

Moral anxiety is an experience of shame or guilt. The original fear, according to Freud, from which the moral anxiety is derived, is an objective one. It is a fear of punitive parents, or of the representatives of society. It is clear that the person cannot escape from feelings of anxiety or guilt by running away. Guilt feelings then are the price that is paid: (a) by the idealistic person for being overly moralistic and (b) by the normal person for transgressing the rules he has incorporated from the society of which he is a member. The so-called psychopath is a person who is reputed not to have developed a conscience. He does not feel guilt or shame. On a simple 7-point rating scale a psychopath might rate himself as 1 in moral anxiety. On the other hand, a person who is very rigid in morals, who has set very high standards for himself might rate himself as 7 on this moral anxiety scale. This person may be so strict about everything that even a thought about wrong-doing might lead to feelings of guilt or shame.

Methods used by psychoanalysis

The prime method, or so-called *basic rule of psychoanalysis* is the method of *free association*. The individual is required to tell the analyst everything that comes to his mind, without censoring it. The psychoanalytic view assumes that the anxiety felt by the client has originated from some repressed conflict. For example, the conflict between a boy wanting to engage in some behaviour which is typically of a sexual or aggressive nature and which the parents frown upon. If the child is aggressive towards his sister, his parents typically tell him to stop this behaviour. In stopping the behaviour the actual feeling of wanting to aggress against the sister is not eliminated, but only repressed. The boy represses the conflict between his aggressive feelings and the expected punishment from his parents. This process occurs unconsciously—in other words, the boy is unaware of it because, as it approaches awareness, he gets feelings of apprehension and anxiety.

The basis of free association is to bring material that is unconscious into consciousness. The basic concept is that all ideas are associated in one's mind. Through free association one can gradually come to express ideas that have been buried in the unconscious. The basic rule is to say everything that comes to mind without hesitating and without selecting out anything.

While Freud was, at first, interested in the use of hypnosis, he later abandoned it because he had found the results 'capricious and unpredictable' (Ford and Urban 1965), although other therapists have found this procedure helpful with certain patients. In discussing psychoanalysis, Ford and Urban noted that 'The power of an emotional transference may be just as effective a media for producing responses in the patient through suggestion as hypnosis.'

The client may find it difficult to use free-association effectively, since he is likely to feel threatened by the return of the repressed material in consciousness. He may become very resistive to allowing this repressed material into his consciousness. Therefore, part of the job of the therapist is to overcome this '*resistance*', in other words, to overcome the threatening nature of the client's thoughts. It should become clear to the client after a while that the therapist is not going to morally condemn him for expressing thoughts which the client himself may find threatening because they remind him of the prohibitions and threats from his parents. The therapist and client work together in overcoming this resistance.

The *transference relationship* is seen as extremely important. In Chapter 9, it was mentioned that the client might perceive the interviewer as very much like somebody he knew in the past or knows at the time therapy is underway. For example, the therapist may appear to be very much like the client's father, mother, etc. The therapist may be perceived as somebody who is quite positive or quite negative. Thus, two types of transference are distinguished; *positive transference* and *negative transference*. The psychoanalytic method of '*working through*', is used to clarify the client's relationships with significant others in his life by assuming that the transference relationship reveals much of importance regarding the client's interpersonal relationships in general, but particularly with significant others. 'Working through' is a process whereby the client is helped to face his conflicts repeatedly so that they lose their power over him and are thus no longer conflict situations.

The transference then is something that must be worked through with the patient. The therapist can begin to perceive whether the client is looking at him as a very positive father or mother figure or as a negative figure, and begin to examine his own feelings about this. Thus, the '*counter-transference*' (Fromm 1968) is also important in terms of analysing what is going on in the psychotherapeutic relationship. The importance of analysing the main relationships in a person's life, even though they may involve parents or significant others who have subsequently died, cannot be overestimated. Potentially these relationships have an influence on the client's interactions with others during the time he is undergoing therapy. By working through the transference and the counter-transference, the therapist can obtain material that is very valuable in understanding the nature of the individual as a person, and why he has developed the particular problems he exhibits. Therefore, the interpretation of the transference is very important. By helping the patient to understand his relationship with the analyst, he helps him to understand his relationships with others. *Interpretation* of the client's defences is crucial to successful therapy.

Another technique that is sometimes used in analytic therapy is '*abreaction*'. This refers to the free expression of repressed emotion. It is a re-living of an intense emotional experience. This release may, in fact, come from the transference—the client in therapy may become so emotional that he begins to act this out against the therapist—and the therapist, provided there is no real danger involved, may allow and even encourage this to happen, thereby creating this abreaction experience.

Finally, *dream analysis* is utilized in the psychoanalytic method. The dream is created by the primary process. While the reporting of dreams is an extension of the method of free-association, potentially it is likely to produce material which is more basic than that produced normally, in that the dream report will be closer to the basic motives and desires of the client. According to Menninger (1964), 'The seventh chapter of *The interpretation of dreams* is the Magna Carta of psychoanalysis.' Menninger noted that analysts who had not become acquainted with this chapter were, in his view, incompletely trained.

In summary, psychoanalysis is past-oriented and postulates disturbances in psychosexual development to account for psychopathology which is only represented, or indicated, by surface symptomatology. The client is unaware of his actual conflicts, which are unconscious. Therefore, the main aim of psychoanalysis and psychotherapy is to make unconscious material conscious through free-association and similar techniques, to work through this material, emphasizing the transference and counter-transference relationships, so that the client finally achieves insight into his psychological difficulties. The person who is well adapted is one who is able to maintain a flexible balance between the three components of personality. The ego acts as the executive, maintaining control over the id and super-ego.

Psychoanalytic ego psychology

During the last two or three decades there has been an increasing interest in ego processes and correspondingly less emphasis on the id. Hartmann (1958) in contrast to Freud, who felt that the ego developed from the id, theorizes that the id and ego are parallel developments in personality structure. Although there is obviously still much disagreement between ideas in general psychology and psychoanalysis (Hall and Lindzey 1970), some psychologists see the developments in psychoanalytic ego psychology as providing a bridge between the two disciplines. A second trend in recent psychoanalytic literature is the reporting of the increased research with children. While there has been some modification in Freudian ideas concerning the stages of development, there is still an emphasis on the developmental stages by many authors, in particular by those who emphasize ego processes. While Freud and the ego psychologists are consistent in stressing the importance of the first five or six years of life for future development, the ego psychologists are not so limiting as Freud in terms of the possibilities for modification in personality structure during the later stages of development (Ford and Urban 1965). Erikson (1963) is also considered to follow an ego-orientated psychoanalytic approach. His 'Eight Ages of Man' have already been referred to in Chapter 2, p. 42. A good discussion of the 'ego-analysts' may be found in Ford and Urban (1965).

Criticisms of the psychoanalytic approach

Psychoanalytic psychotherapy has come under some rather severe criticism. Hall and Lindzey (1970) noted a number of criticisms which are frequently made of psychoanalysis:

(1) the uncontrolled nature of Freud's observations and the consequent shortcomings in his validation of hypotheses;

(2) the lack of criteria other than a patient's self-report (i.e. lack of any form of consensual validation by relatives, work records, psychological test data. etc.);

(3) the practical impossibility of other investigators' being able to replicate Freud's findings since there are no systematic records, qualitative or quantitative, of Freud's empirical findings;

(4) the relative lack of ability to make predictions based on psychoanalytic theory;

(5) the fact that the theory is consequently not supported by scientifically acceptable procedures.

In spite of these criticisms, psychoanalysis has led to a fair amount of research (see, for example, Glucksberg and King 1967; Hall 1964*b*; Miller 1948; Sears, Maccoby, and Levin 1957). However, because of the vagueness or ambiguity in psychoanalytic concepts, the theory has proved difficult to test. Pervin (1970) noted that 'The question for psychoanalytic theory is whether it can be developed for specific tests, or whether it will, in the future, be replaced by another theory that is equally comprehensive . . . but more open to systematic empirical investigation.' It is not only psychoanalytic theory that has come under scientific attack, but also the effectiveness of psychotherapy in general (Eysenck 1952). A discussion of this issue will, however, be deferred to the next chapter which presents an overview of a second major approach to psychotherapy, the client-centred view.

14
The client-centred approach and the effectiveness of psychotherapy

This above all: to thine own self be true,
And it must follow, as the night the day,
Thou canst not then be false to any man
Shakespeare: *Hamlet*

THE CLIENT-CENTRED APPROACH

The client-centred approach to psychotherapy was developed by Carl Rogers who formulated the idea in 1940 when he was asked to deliver a talk entitled 'Newer Concepts in Psychotherapy' (Rogers 1974) at the University of Minnesota. Rogers noted that the four elements which were included in this paper were: (1) a strong reliance on 'the individual drive toward growth, health, and adjustment; (2) a much greater emphasis on the feeling as contrasted with the intellectual aspects of the situation; (3) a greater emphasis on the 'here and now' as compared with the past; and (4) an emphasis on the relationship during therapy as a 'growth experience'. Some of the original sources on client-centred therapy are Rogers (1942, 1951, 1961). However, a more concise view of the client-centred approach may be found in Rogers (1959). While client-centred therapy has been mainly restricted to the less disturbed, the experience of using the client-centred approach with schizophrenics at the University of Wisconsin is discussed in Rogers, Gendlin, Kiesler, and Truax (1967).

Client-centred therapy has also been referred to as non-directive therapy, in that the client is expected to take the lead in determining the direction of the therapeutic interaction. The approach is a *phenomenological* one in the sense that the therapist is not so much concerned with objective reality as with reality as perceived by the client. One's behaviour is a consequence of one's idiosyncratic perceptual experience. The individual's experiences of the moment make up his reality (Snygg and Combs 1949). During therapy there is an emphasis on the observation of behaviour from the observed person's (client's) self-report of his idiosyncratic perceptions. There is an emphasis on non-judgmental understanding. The therapist attempts to provide a psychological atmosphere which will enable the client gradually to realize that it is safe to discuss his innermost thoughts and feelings, to which many significant others may have responded in a punitive or moral fashion, thus inhibiting behaviour which might have ultimately increased the client's psychological well-being.

The necessary and sufficient conditions for effective therapy

According to Rogers (1957) the psychological conditions which are both necessary and sufficient to result in effective psychotherapy are:

(1) two people are in psychological contact;
(2) the client is in a state of incongruence, being vulnerable or anxious;
(3) the therapist is congruent or integrated in the relationship;
(4) the therapist experiences unconditional positive regard for the client;
(5) the therapist experiences an accurate empathic understanding of the client;
(6) the therapist's unconditional positive regard and accurate empathic understanding are successfully communicated to the client.

The first psychological condition simply means that each person should be in the other's experiential or psychological field. This is an assumption that is typically made by the therapist. The incongruence mentioned in the second psychological condition refers to the discrepancy between the client's *self-concept* and his actual experience. The client is assumed to be vulnerable to the development of anxiety and possible personality disorganization, to the extent that he in unaware or only vaguely aware of the discrepancy. The third condition means that the therapist must be true to himself. He must behave in a genuine manner. If he feels a bit angry towards the client, he should accept this; if the client makes him feel uneasy, he should admit this in some way. The acceptance of these feelings is important. *Therapist congruence*, or *genuineness*, is basic to conditions (4), (5), and (6), in that any dishonesty in the therapist is sooner or later perceived by the client.

Unconditional positive regard means that first, the therapist perceives the client as another human being, with his frailties, his assets, etc., and respects him and does not devalue or criticize him in any way, neither the client's behaviour outside of therapy nor what is said during the therapy hour. There are no strings attached to this positive regard. The client is perceived as a human being who sincerely wants help.

The fifth and sixth conditions are fairly complex. They mean that the client's communication—verbal and non-verbal—must be clearly perceived. The therapist must be able to enter the client's phenomenal world—to perceive, to feel as the client is perceiving and feeling. The therapist must both receive and understand what the client is saying. Following the reception and understanding, the therapist has successfully to communicate his understanding in an appropriate way (i.e. so the client receives, understands, and accepts) to the client. In other words, the therapist must be *empathic*—he must be able to feel as if he were in the client's shoes, and he must be able to communicate this empathy back to the client. Obviously, this can be a tricky business. For example, if the therapist wishes to communicate a positive feeling back to the client, he might say something positive, such as, 'You give me the warm feeling that I associate with a close relation such as a son'. However, the client may be a person who has very great difficulty in accepting positive statements about himself, and the therapist would then have to spend some time in formulating a statement which the client would be able to accept.

The characteristics needed to fulfil the last three conditions are better acquired experientially than through academic instruction. This suggests, of course, that non-professionals should be as successful in carrying out client-centred therapy as the professionally trained (see Chapter 3 for a discussion of non-professional therapists).

In a later article, Rogers (1958) discussed the characteristics of a helping relationship, psychotherapeutic or otherwise. He noted that if one can be sensitively aware of and acceptant towards one's own feelings—then the likelihood is great that one can form a helping relationship toward another. Thus, Rogers related the variables of *self-awareness* and *self-acceptance* to effective interpersonal relationships. To the extent to which one could bc self-aware and self-acceptant, one could be a helpful therapist. Becoming more self-aware could be compared with achieving *insight*, which was a goal of psychoanalysis. In contrast, a significant lack of self-acceptance suggested a disturbed, neurotic personality. Rogers concluded by hypothesizing that 'the degree to which one could create relationships which facilitated the growth of others as separate persons was a measure of the growth one has achieved in one's self.

Basically, the goal of client-centred therapy has been seen as the growth of the self through an atmosphere which releases the natural potentiality for psychological growth. In order to provide this conducive atmosphere there is a lack of *overt* diagnosis or evaluation. Interpretation is not considered as a useful technique. In many ways the therapist acts as a sounding-board, reflecting feelings back to the client. *Reflection of feeling* is one of the dominant response-modes used by the therapist. By reflecting, the therapist attempts to clarify the client's statements about himself, to verify that he does understand what has been communicated and to demonstrate his empathy to the client. Gradually, in the atmosphere of complete acceptance, the client becomes able to express feelings he has until now been unable to express. Through being permitted to express himself in this atmosphere, free from evaluation, criticism, and interpretation, the client gradually is able to clarify to himself the nature of his very personal feelings and to behave more congruently with these feelings, to essentially 'be what he is'. It can thus be seen that Rogers's ideas concerning psychological growth are similar to those of Maslow (1962), who emphasizes *growth motivation* and *self-actualization* as key concepts in his *Towards a psychology of being*.

More extensive discussions of client-centred theory and therapy may be found in Hart and Tomlinson (1970) and (Wexler and Rice (1974). The use of the client-centred (existential) approach in group therapy, including encounter groups, may be found in Bebout (1974), Beck (1974), Rogers

(1973), and Truax, Carkhuff, and Kodman (1965). Some of the research generated by the client-centred approach will now be considered.

RESEARCH ON CLIENT-CENTRED THERAPY

In contrast to analytic psychotherapy, the client-centred approach has stimulated a great deal of research. Much of the earlier research (e.g. Rogers and Dymond 1954) was based on sampling of therapeutic interactions which had been recorded. These extracts could be analysed and rated in terms of the client's self-concept, etc. Seeman (1949) in analysing recordings of therapy found that as therapy progressed a decreasing number of negative self-references and an increasing number of positive self-references occurred. In general, many studies have suggested that the major changes produced by client-centred therapy are changes in self-concept, although not necessarily in behaviour. Rating scales which measure various aspects of the self have been used, and more recently scales constructed to measure the last three necessary and sufficient conditions for effective psychotherapy (p. 255), have been developed.

Reports about the degree of congruence between the present self-concept and the *ideal-self-concept* have been used as measures of self-acceptance. These self-reports may be obtained by using simple *rating scales* or by using *Q-sorts*. Some investigators have preferred to use the term self-esteem in reference to the congruence between self and ideal ratings or sorts, although Coopersmith (1968) has also used teachers' reports and psychological tests to assess children's level of *self-esteem*. Various personality traits may be used in asking subjects to rate their self and ideal-self concepts. For example, using a seven-point scale subjects may be asked to indicate the degree of dominance: (1) he feels he exhibits (self-concept), and (2) he would like to be able to exhibit (ideal concept). The Q-sort technique consists of sorting a large number of cards with statements relating to the self typed on them. An example of such a statement is 'I am dominant'. The *self-sort* is obtained by asking the subject to sort the cards into groups to describe himself as he sees himself today from those least like himself to those most like himself. Analogously, the *self-ideal sort* is obtained by asking the subject to sort the cards to describe himself as he would most like himself to be (i.e. his ideal person).

Medinnus and Curtis (1963) investigated the relationship between self-acceptance of mothers and acceptance of their children and found that self-acceptant as compared to non-self-acceptant mothers were more likely to accept their children. Results such as these may be of some help to those concerned over child-abuse. Although there has been some negative evidence (Gordon and Cartwright 1954) the bulk of the evidence supports the hypothesis of the positive relationship between self-acceptance and acceptance of others (Omwake 1954; Suinn 1961). Vingoe (1968, 1973) followed

Rogers's (1958) suggestion that both self-awareness and self-acceptance were positively related to good interpersonal relationships. Vingoe was primarily interested in establishing relationships between self-acceptance, self-awareness, and neuroticism, as measured by The Eysenck Personality Inventory (EPI) (Eysenck and Eysenck 1963). The subjects were 66 first-year female university students who were asked to rate themselves and their dormitory peers on six personality variables, in addition to completing the EPI and the California Personality Inventory (CPI) (Gough 1964). It was assumed that good interpersonal relationships would be inversely related to a degree of neuroticism. Each subject's self-awareness was established by determining the *degree of congruence* between her self-rating and the *mean peer rating* on the six personality variables, while self-acceptance was established by determining the degree of congruence between the six self-ratings and the *social-desirability* (ideal-self) *ratings* for the six variables. The social-desirability ratings were obtained by asking each subject how she would like to be rated on the personality variables by her dormitory peers. Thus, in this situation, the social-desirability rating is seen as equivalent to the *ideal sort technique* in which clients are asked to sort cards with descriptive statements on them in terms of how they would really like to see themselves. The results were supportive of Rogers's position, in that stable subjects were found to be significantly more self-acceptant than neurotics. However, the stable and neurotic groups were not significantly different in self-awareness. The results also supported the construct validity of the EPI Neuroticism Scale.

The use of Q-sorts, where it has been hypothesized that the better adjusted should show a significant correlation between self-sort and ideal-sort, has produced some apparently contradictory results. A good discussion of many of the difficulties in interpreting Q-sorts is provided in Hall and Lindzey (1970). As Hall and Lindzey pointed out, the anticipated increase in correlation between self and ideal-sorts with psychotherapy may come about in various ways (i.e. 'a change of the self-concept in the direction of the ideal, or of a change in the ideal in the direction of the self-concept, or of changes in both directions'). Hall and Lindzey provided some evidence which suggested that change could occur in both directions. Obviously, changes in either direction could be seen as psychological growth. For example, one might argue that a client's ideal sort might be analogous to an unrealistic *level of aspiration* in some area of achievement such as one's career. With experience and a greater appreciation of the real situation, one's ideal sort and level of aspiration might become more realistic in terms of one's assets, liabilities, and environmental conditions.

Hall and Lindzey also mentioned the fact that some disturbed client groups, such as schizophrenics, had presented the investigators with a higher self–ideal-sort correlation than that found among normals. In addition, they cited Cole, Oetting, and Hinkle's (1967) study of adolescent girls with behaviour problems. In this study it had been found that some of the subjects had rated the self *higher* than the ideal self. They noted that this seemed to be an indication of defensive sorting.

It has been argued that if one finds too high a correlation between self and ideal sorts or ratings, this may in fact be an unhealthy situation indicative of psychological stagnation. One might ask if such a person would be able to grow psychologically or to self-actualize. There are a number of other technical criticisms regarding the use of Q-sorts which also apply to other measuring devices. We turn now to a brief discussion of the research on the scales developed to measure the therapeutic conditions of 'genuineness', 'unconditional positive regard' (non-possessive warmth), and 'accurate empathy'. It is important to note Rogers's (1957) view that if one or more of these conditions are not present, constructive personality change will not occur.

Scales to measure these therapeutic conditions have been developed (Truax 1961) and used in a number of studies (Truax 1966); Truax, Carkhuff, and Kodman 1965), although the reliability and validity of the 'accurate empathy scale' has been questioned (Chinsky and Rappaport 1970), and contradictory results have been obtained in measuring these conditions (Beutler, Johnson, Neville, and Workman 1973; Parloff, Waskow, and Wolfe 1978).

It is logical that when the empathic relationship is optimal the other therapeutic conditions of genuineness and non-possessive warmth are satisfied. Parloff *et al.* (1978) suggested that a good empathic relationship included the other therapeutic conditions. In any case, empathy is seen as all important. Rogers (1975) noted that: '*The ideal therapist is first of all empathic.* When psychotherapists of many different orientations describe their concept of the ideal therapist, the therapist they would like to become, they are in high agreement in giving empathy the highest ranking out of twelve variables.' Rogers based this statement initially on Fiedler's (1950*a*, 1950*b*) early work (also reprinted in McGowan and Schmidt 1962) on a comparison of therapists of different therapeutic persuasions who were found to agree on their concept of an ideal therapeutic relationship (Fiedler 1950*a*). Fiedler's conclusions were essentially replicated and supported by research which emphasized the prime importance of empathy.

Unfortunately, the meaning of empathy, at least as defined by Truax and Carkhuff 1967) has been seriously questioned by Chinsky and Rappaport (1970). 'Accurate empathy' (AE) was defined by Truax and Carkhuff as: 'both the therapist's *sensitivity to current feelings* and his *verbal facility* to *communicate this understanding* in a language attuned to the client's current feelings'. Chinsky and Rappaport suggested that raters of empathy who used the Truax and Carkhuff scale might be 'responding to some quality other than that which the scale defines as AE. They also questioned the reliability of the AE scale and recommended that a large number of raters or therapists should be used in reliability studies.

Beutler *et al.* (1973) found that there was evidence of a significant relation between the therapeutic conditions of empathy, warmth, and genuineness and *depth of client self-exploration*. However, rated improvement was not related to the therapeutic conditions in spite of the relatively long post-graduate experience of the therapists, who had been differentiated into those who tended to be most successful with schizophrenics (A-types) and those most likely to be most successful with neurotic clients (B-types). Parloff *et al.* (1978) reviewed the evidence with regard to the value of accurate empathy, non-possessive warmth, and genuineness in effective psychotherapy, as well as discussing the value of dichotomizing therapists into A and B-types. Basically, Parloff *et al* expressed their agreement with the conclusions of Mitchell, Bozarth, and Krauft (1977) who noted that 'The recent evidence, although equivocal, does seem to suggest that empathy, warmth, and genuineness are related in some way to client change but that their potency and generalizability are not as great as once thought.' While this statement considerably modified the degree to which Rogers's (1957) psychological conditions were thought to be effective therapist variables in psychotherapy, one cannot dispute the degree to which Rogerian ideas have led to more rigorous research in the area of psychotherapy. We turn now to the last section in this chapter concerning the general issue of the effectiveness of psychotherapy.

CRITIQUE OF PSYCHOTHERAPY

Gottman and Markman (1978) note that three questions have been prominent in psychotherapy research: (1) Is psychotherapy effective? (2) What kind of therapy or therapeutic system is most effective? and (3) What therapeutic processes lead to the most change? Gottman and Markman suggested that the first question as it stands is not very meaningful, and Strupp (1978) believed that the question was inappropriate and non-fruitful. In spite of these recent comments about the first question, it would be helpful to review the history of this issue.

Up to the mid-1950s, psychotherapy of various persuasions was being carried out with little rigorous research available to support its effectiveness. Many reports on psychotherapy lacked any form of adequate control. Thus, any progress attributed by the therapist to the treatment might equally well have resulted from extra-therapeutic or extraneous factors. Too many psychotherapists succumbed to the '*hello–goodbye effect*' (i.e. accepted the client's plea for help by providing treatment, and later accepted the client's assertion that the therapist had been a great deal of help, even if the therapist sometimes retained some inner doubt about how effective his interventions had been). In addition, the criteria used to establish the efficacy of treatment lacked specificity, relying on broad categories such as 'slightly improved' or 'much improved' without necessarily pointing out the particular dimension to which the improvement applied. Many of the measures used to assess change were based upon trait theory. However, more recently the main assumption of trait theory has been seriously questioned (Mischel 1968) (see also p. 217). Further, non-objective measures such as the Rorschach and other projective techniques were frequently used to determine personality change. The reliability and validity of the measurement devices used were often inadequate or even unknown.

Eysenck reported his findings on the effectiveness of psychotherapy with adult neurotics after reviewing the literature on the subject. He concluded that the 'data fail to prove that psychotherapy, Freudian or otherwise, facilitates the recovery of neurotic patients. They show that roughly two-thirds of a group of neurotic patients will recover or improve to a marked extent within about two years of the onset of their illness, whether they are treated by psychotherapy or not.' (Eysenck, 1952; reprinted in Berenson and Carkhuff 1967). Eysenck's report was threatening to many therapists whose main occupation was psychotherapy, and was certainly challenging to those who believed that psychotherapy was effective and who wanted to seek evidence from research to support their theories. Eysenck concluded that the percentage of clients who had successfully undergone intensive psychotherapy was no higher than the degree of improvement reported for untreated neurotic adults. That is, the *spontaneous remission rate* was as high as the rate of improvement with psychotherapy. To add to the general consternation among therapists, Eysenck's report on adult neurotics was followed by an analogous report on children (Levitt 1957) with essentially the same conclusions. Even in Eysenck's (1960) report, in spite of the somewhat better research designs used by those investigating psychotherapy outcome, essentially the same conclusions were made, except that Eysenck placed rather more confidence in them. Eysenck noted that 'With the single exception of the psychotherapeutic methods based on learning theory, results of published research with military and civilian neurotics, and with both adults and children, suggest that the therapeutic effects of psychotherapy are small or non-existent, and do not in any demonstrable way add to the non-specific effects of routine medical treatment, or to such events as occur in the patient's everyday experience'.

Barron and Leary (1955) had carried out a study on the effect of 'brief ego-oriented' individual and group psychotherapy using out-patient neurotics, all of whom had been accepted for treatment. The MMPI was used to assess outcome. It was established that treatment and control groups were essentially comparable in educational background, diagnosis, prognosis, severity of condition, and on the MMPI scales selected as criteria. Unfortunately, the results showed that the treated patients improved no more than the waiting-list controls. In fact, on the so-called *neurotic-triad* (i.e. the depression, hysteria, and hypochondriasis scales of the MMPI) the average decrease was found to be somewhat greater for the controls than for the group therapy patients. Commenting on their unexpected results, Barron and Leary raised the question of whether the waiting-list controls were, in fact, untreated. They recommended the use of 'non-waiting-list' controls in future research on outcome. A discussion of various types of control groups is discussed by Gottman and Markman (1978). Bergin (1963) discussed six of the more adequately designed studies on outcome with particular emphasis on the studies of Barron and Leary and of Cartwright and Vogel (1960), pointing out that in both studies the treatment group exhibited a significantly greater variability in criterion scores at the conclusion of psychotherapy than did the controls. He added another important point that when the therapists were divided into those who were experienced and those who were inexperienced, it was found that the experienced therapists were effective in producing positive change in their clients, while the inexperienced produced negative change. Bergin also noted that the Wisconsin client-centred studies on schizophrenia suggested that those therapists who were high in empathy, positive regard, and congruence were significantly more effective with their clients than those therapists rated low in these conditions. Thus, Bergin suggested that the apparent lack of effectiveness of psychotherapy could be accounted for by the combination of the negative results of 'inexperienced' therapists and the positive results of the 'experienced' therapists. A further point made by Bergin was that evidence was available which strongly suggested that many control-group clients sought help from the clergy, friends, and others, and therefore were in reality members of a treatment group. Bergin hypothesized that many people functioned as positive change agents without specific training and suggested that it was the personal qualities of the 'therapist' that were most important. Finally, Bergin stressed the need for greater specificity in the measurement of antecedent and consequent variables in psychotherapy research.

The third question noted by Gottman and Markman concerned the therapeutic processes which led to change. The main influences in the process of psychotherapy include therapist variables, client variables, and the interaction between them. Bergin's report suggested that the qualities of effective therapists should be examined more closely. Truax and Carkhuff 1967), following Rogers (1957), suggested that the essential qualities of a successful therapist were: (a) therapist genuineness or authenticity; (b) non-possessive warmth; and (c) empathic understanding. However, benefiting from later research, Parloff *et al.* (1978) noted that the evidence regarding these qualities was not as potent nor as generalizable as once thought, and further research needed to be done to clarify their importance. However, Truax and Carkhuff suggested that a fourth variable was important in therapeutic encounters. This client variable was known as *depth of self-exploration*, and was hypothesized as being at least partially related to the influence of the therapist. This hypothesized relationship was later supported by Beutler *et al.* (1973). Patterson (1969*a*) commenting on the value of self-exploration, noted that *self-disclosure* is the first step in self-exploration, while self-exploration itself is probably initiated by first revealing negative aspects of the self following which more positive aspects become expressed. He felt that 'The later stages of the process lead to increasing self-awareness, which makes possible the development of the characteristics of the fully-functioning person. A qualification regarding the usefulness of self-exploration is mentioned by Truax (1969) who developed a scale to measure this dimension. According to Truax self-exploration develops late in life and is peculiar to the upper middle class. He said that it had been an almost universal experience of therapists that lower class patients did not even know what was meant by self-exploration and considered it bizarre to be asked to engage in it. Patterson (1969*b*) agreed with Truax's comment on self-exploration and suggested that lower class individuals could be encouraged to develop this ability, which was based on experience. Obviously, client variables such as social class are important in psychotherapy, as pointed out by Garfield (1978).

Garfield noted the wide individual differences in the selection of clients by different psychotherapy clinics. He found, for example, that one clinic rejected those potential clients who fell outside the 20–34 year age range. Social class criteria have frequently been related to client selection for psychotherapy. Psychoanalytically oriented clinics are reported to select clients on the basis of education, intelligence, verbal ability, and motivation for therapy. Owing to selection factors lower-class individuals have been relatively neglected, although some attempts to provide therapy for them have been made (Goldstein 1973; Lorion 1978).

The second question, regarding the most effective kind of therapy, needs reformulation, together with the other questions, to produce the question reiterated by Strupp (1978): 'What specific therapeutic interventions produce specific changes in specific patients under specific conditions?' This question thus involves both process and outcome variables and reminds us to do more than call a control group a control group, for example, but to specify as precisely as possible the way in which the 'control' group differs from the experimental group(s). Bergin (1971) discussed in some detail the nature of control groups and questioned the high rate of 'spontaneous' recovery reported by Eysenck. Barron and Leary (1955) had noted that when one referred to spontaneous remission, one was admitting to an ignorance, a lack of understanding as to why a change had occurred. In recent years a number of articles have appeared regarding the 'spontaneous' remission controversy (Subotnik 1972*a*, 1972*b*, 1975), followed by a review article in this area (Lambert 1976). These reports throw considerable doubt on the validity of earlier statements regarding the percentage of clients exhibiting spontaneous remission, as well as statements that psychotherapy is not effective. Lambert noted that *minimal treatment outcome* results would suggest a figure of 53 per cent. Based on a *no treatment* condition, a median remission rate of 43 per cent was discovered (Lambert 1976).

Eysenck (1960) and Rachman (1973) suggested that the behavioural approach to therapy was more effective than the psychotherapeutic. Rachman reviewed the evidence for the effectiveness of psychotherapy and found no reason to change Eysenck's statement regarding a two-thirds spontaneous remission rate. More specifically, he noted that 'there is still no acceptable evidence to support the claim that psychoanalysis is therapeutically effective' (Rachman 1973). Rachman was, however, more positive in his comments regarding Rogerian or client-centred therapy. He suggested that client-centred therapy should be recast in terms of learning theory, more specifically, reinforcement procedure. Rachman concluded that an alliance between the recast Rogerian procedures and behavioural techniques might be helpful. The general *Zeitgeist* seems to favour the behaviour approach to psychotherapy, although there are some dissenting voices who would question how far the behavioural approach has been successful as compared to a more psychodynamic therapy. However, consistent with the greater emphasis on specificity, we turn now to two chapters on behaviour therapy. After briefly presenting some of the principles of learning in Chapter 15 we go on to discuss the effectiveness of many of the individual techniques used to treat problems of psychological deficit. Chapter 16 discusses those behavioural techniques used to treat problems of psychological excess.

15
Behaviour therapy: introduction and treatment of problems of psychological deficit

Were a man's sorrows and disquietudes summed up at the end of his life, it would generally be found that he had suffered more from the apprehension of evils that never actually happened to him than from those evils which had really befallen him.
Addison

The critiques of psychotherapy by Eysenck (1952, 1960) and others discussed in the last chapter were instrumental in encouraging research into therapeutic procedures and their components, and led to an increasing interest in behaviour therapy, which was reputed to be firmly based on the learning or behavioural model (see Chapter 1). The basic assumption underlying behaviour therapy is that just as adaptive behaviour is learned, so also is maladaptive behaviour. Experiments using behaviour therapy have shown that if maladaptive behaviour is learned, then it can be unlearned or extinguished. It should be kept clearly in mind here that learning is generally said to have taken place only if there is evidence of a change in some behavioural performance. That is, learning is inferred from performance. Since behaviour therapists are interested in increasing a client's behaviour repertoire, and since children often need psychological treatment, both the influence of maturation, i.e. better performance based on biological development, and the influence of drugs, must be ruled out in accounting for changes in behaviour.

Eysenck's (1959) definition of behaviour therapy was as follows:

> From the point of view of learning theory, treatment is in essence a very simple process. In the case of surplus conditioned responses, treatment should consist in the extinction of these responses. In the case of deficient conditioned responses, treatment should consist in the building up of the missing stimulus–response connections.

While this definition may seem to suggest an exclusively environmentalist point of view, the biological basis of behaviour including the neurophysiology of the organism was by no means thrown overboard (Eysenck 1967; Eysenck and Rachman 1965), no more than the influence of genetic factors on behaviour (Eysenck 1956). Certainly, the probability of developing certain maladaptive responses may be higher in some people than in others owing to genetic or biochemical factors.

Symptoms, which Eysenck suggested should be called 'conditioned maladaptive responses' (CMRs), include both skeletal and autonomic responses (Eysenck and Rachman 1965). To put it simply, if one eliminates the maladaptive responses one has 'cured' the neurosis.

While the term 'symptom' continues to be used, Bandura (1969) commenting on the symptom substitution issue, noted that neither the concept of symptom or mental disease were pertinent to behavioural dysfunctions. In commenting on the social learning point of view Bandura (1968) noted that:

> When the actual social learning history of maladaptive behavior is known, the basic principles of learning provide a completely adequate interpretation of many psychopathological phenomena, and explanations in terms of symptoms with underlying disorders become superfluous.

Thus, expressions such as maladaptive behaviour or responses are preferable terms for the behaviour therapist.

In general, this early work in what later became known as 'behaviour therapy' (Eysenck 1959), was based on respondent or classical (Pavlovian) conditioning, as was much of the later work on the modification of phobic conditions. However, Skinner (1938), basing his work on that of Thorndike, who is well known for his 'law of effect', introduced the term 'operant conditioning'. In cases in which one wished the patient to acquire new behaviour, operant procedures were more likely to be used. While methods based on classical conditioning or Guthrie's counter-conditioning were used to treat mainly neurotic disorders, methods based on operant conditioning were found useful in the treatment of psychotic conditions and in training the mentally retarded. Actually, the application of operant methodology has been, and continues to be, very extensive indeed.

While during the 1940s and 1950s there was a great emphasis on learning theory, today there is a greater emphasis on principles of learning, such as generalization, extinction, spontaneous recovery, etc. Most psychologists would certainly agree that much of our learning occurs through:

(1) Pavlovian or respondent conditioning;
(2) operant or instrumental conditioning; and
(3) imitation or observation learning.

It is clear that many psychologists feel that a simple conditioning model is inadequate to account for all learned behaviour, pathological or otherwise. In recent years there has been more emphasis on cognitive factors in behaviour therapy (Bandura 1977; Ledwidge 1978; Mahoney 1974). This increased emphasis on cognitive factors has led to the development of *cognitive behaviour modification* (CBM). The stress in CBM methods is on the modification of mediating variables, such as attitudes, thoughts, and imaginal processes.

The consideration of mediating processes in learning is not particularly new (Osgood 1953), but there appears to be an increasing emphasis on what takes place between external stimulus and observable response. This increasing cognitive focus is further discussed in Chapter 16. Davison (1968) has noted that Wolpe's principle regarding reciprocal inhibitions is indistinguishable from Guthrie's view of counterconditioning (Guthrie 1952).

CLASSICAL CONDITIONING

The respondent (Pavlovian) conditioning paradigm

It is generally accepted that the organism responds to certain specific stimuli with specific *inevitable* responses. For example, one responds to a bright light trained on the eye by pupil constriction. If one is hungry one responds to the presence of food in the mouth by salivation. In the first example above, the 'unconditional stimulus' (UCS) is the light shining in the eye and is referred to as the reinforcement, while the pupil constriction is the 'unconditional response' (UCR). Similarly, in the second example, the food in the mouth is the UCS while the salivation is the UCR. Through temporal or spatial association the organism associates other (initially neutral) stimuli with a particular UCS, so that the organism eventually responds to these previously neutral stimuli, known as 'conditional stimuli' (CS), as if they were UCS. The response to a CS is known as a 'conditioned response' (CR). A specific point, discussed in Osgood (1953), is that the CR seen from a more global organismic point of view is not *in toto* the same as the UCR.

Paradigm for respondent (Pavlovian) conditioning

	light (UCS)		⟶▷	Pupil constriction (UCR)
Learning trials				
	tone (CS)	Sight of light (UCS)	⟶▷	**Pupil constriction (UCR)**
Outcome				
	tone (CS)		⟶▷	Pupil constriction (CR)

Extinction occurs when reinforcement is removed, i.e. by omitting the UCS. Thus, while pupil constriction would occur during a certain number of initial trials in which the UCS has been omitted, it would gradually diminish in magnitude and finally not occur at all. Clearly, then, if one wishes to eliminate a specific behavioural act one must first establish the idiosyncratic reinforcement which serves to reinforce or maintain that act, and then remove it (see discusssion of 'functional analysis, below).

Spontaneous recovery

When a response which has previously been extinguished recurs without any intervening training trials to account for it, spontaneous recovery is said to have taken place (see Chapter 2 for an example of the spontaneous recovery of temper tantrums in a young child).

Generalization

Watson and Raynor (1920, reprinted in Ulrich, Stachnik, and Mabry 1966) have established that at least one way of developing a phobic condition or 'conditional emotional reaction' (CER) can be explained by the respondent conditioning paradigm. An eleven-month-old child, Albert, was conditioned to be afraid of a previously neutral stimulus (a tame white rat), when this CS was paired with a loud, unexpected noise (UCS). Watson and Raynor also demonstrated the principle of *stimulus generalization* by showing that not only did Albert learn to fear the white, furry rat, but also learned to fear similar objects which included a rabbit, a seal-fur coat, and cotton wool. He was also observed to respond negatively to a dog and a Father Christmas mask (Jones 1974). Watson and Raynor noted that the number of transfers resulting from an experimentally produced emotional reaction may be very large (Ulrich, Stachnik, and Mabry 1966). One may readily imagine the extent to which fear of a particular object or situation in non-experimental settings may generalize to other similar stimuli. For a more extensive presentation of respondent conditioning, the texts by Atkinson, Atkinson, and Hilgard (1975), or Kimble (1968) are recommended. The next section provides an overview of operant conditioning.

OPERANT CONDITIONING

The operant conditioning paradigm

Following Reynolds (1975) 'operant conditioning refers to a process in which the frequency of occurrence of a bit of behaviour is modified by the consequences of the behaviour'. The basic idea of operant or instrumental conditioning follows from Thorndike's Law of Effect, which basically stated that an act may be altered in its strength by the consequences of that act. Today we might prefer to state that an act's probability or frequency of occurrence is modified by its consequences.

Acquisition

Wheras in classical conditioning a response is *elicited* by the UCS and in turn by the CS, in operant conditioning the behaviour act is *emitted*. Emitted behaviour has an effect upon some aspect of the organism's environment. A girl's success in passing an examination in ballet may result in much social approval (social reinforcement) from parents and others, in addition to a certificate or diploma. These reinforcements will probably maintain and even increase the amount and/or frequency with which the young lady practises various ballet sequences.

Practising ballet		*Social/self reinforcement*	
R	⟶	S	(S is the reinforcement)

All stimuli which serve to raise the probability of the occurrence of behavioural acts which occur just before the 'presentation' of the stimuli may be termed reinforcers.

If a person's behavioural repertoire already includes the desired response, then it is only necessary to follow occurrences of the response with a reinforcing stimulus (Reynolds 1975). On the other hand, if the desired response is not in the individual's repertoire, we must somehow arrange the environment so that the response has some probability of being emitted. Typically, the desired response may not occur in the specific form or the degree of complexity required. One then uses a procedure called *shaping* in order to create the required response. Shaping involves a procedure in which responses which are part of, or approximations to, the total complex response required are reinforced, while other responses are not reinforced. Some workers refer to this as a procedure of *successive approximations* (i.e. successive approximations of the required response are shaped by reinforcement). In a sense, then, the shaping procedure includes simultaneous training in stimulus generalization and stimulus discrimination. Reinforcement should follow immediately upon a partial or approximation response. 'The careful and systematic application of the shaping procedure with an effective reinforcer is sufficient to teach any organism any operant behavior of which it is physically capable' (Reynolds 1975).

Extinction

While in the case of classical conditioning removal of the UCS or reinforcement results in extinction, so too does removal of the S or reinforcement lead to extinction in the operant conditioning paradigm. Interestingly, resistance to extinction may be greater under an intermittent as compared to a continuous reinforcement schedule (i.e. under environmental conditions in which only a proportion of a particular type of response is reinforced). The term 'reinforcement schedule' refers to the specific manner in which reinforcement is scheduled by the environment. The particular schedule may relate to a time interval or to a specific number of responses. In the first instance, one speaks of an *interval schedule* and in the second of a *ratio schedule*. Chapter 2 provides an overview of a case study (Williams 1959) in which extinction procedures were used to eliminate tantrum behaviour.

Schedules of reinforcement

Much of everyday behaviour is controlled by intermittent reinforcement. A child in school often has to complete a number of mathematical problems before he is reinforced for this problem-solving behaviour. Migrant agricultural workers are paid at the end of every day, i.e. after a fixed interval of 10 hours. The idea of administering reinforcement only after the 'desired' behaviour, whether based on an interval or ratio schedule is usually referred to as 'contingent reinforcement'. In everyday life much reinforcement is provided in an indiscriminate way, or non-contingently. In the first example a certain number of responses are required before reinforcement is forthcoming. This is a specific example of a ratio schedule. If 10 problems must be completed before reinforcement on a consistent basis this would be referred to as a *fixed-ration 10* (FR 10) schedule. Thus, the ratio referred to in a ratio schedule is the total number of responses emitted per reinforcement. Thus, in the FR 10 example, ten responses are emitted before a reinforcement appears.

On the other hand, if the child is reinforced for problem-solving in a less rigid or fixed way, which is frequently the case in everyday life (i.e. a pupil might be reinforced after 10, then 6, and then after 2 problems are solved) one speaks of a *variable ratio* (VR) schedule. While the reinforcement is irregular, one is able to designate how it varies by averaging the number of trials required for each reinforcement made available. Thus, in the simple example above concerning mathematical problem-solving, the designation would be VR 6, based on the average number of problems solved before reinforcement is obtained. In our second example, in which the migrant worker is paid at the end of a designated day of 10 hours, for example, the period of time being fixed, we speak of a *fixed-interval* (FI) schedule.

A *variable-interval* (VI) schedule is one in which the reinforcement is presented after varying intervals of time. For example, a lecturer in physiology tells his students that in addition to the examination at the end of the course, whose value is 40 per cent of the marks, there will be continuous assessment for 60 per cent of the marks, which will be based on 30-minute tests at various intervals throughout the term. Tests might be given after a 10-day interval, then a 35-day interval, and a 15-day interval in a 10-week term. This would represent reinforcement on a VI 20 schedule. Thus, the precise time at which reinforcement will occur is unpredictable. As indicated by Bachrach (1963), this unpredictability of the VI schedule tends to produce a stable response, which is more resistant to extinction. Having been a student in such a course, the author can verify that the response of studying was more regular and consistent in physiology than it was in other coursework in which the 'reinforcement' was predictable.

OBSERVATIONAL LEARNING

The importance of imitation or observational learning, particularly in children, is difficult to over-emphasize. Bandura and Walters (1963) stressed the importance of imitation in children for social and personality development. Mischel (1968) noted that learning could occur in the absence of any direct reinforcement to the learner: 'People learn through their eyes and ears by noting the experiences of others and not merely from the outcomes they get directly from their own behaviour. Learning without direct reinforcement is sometimes called "perceptual", sometimes "cognitive", sometimes "vicarious", and sometimes "observational" or "modelling". All these labels refer to an individual's acquiring new behaviour through observation with no direct external reinforcement'. It might also be noted that specific types of behaviour may be extinguished through observing the negative consequences of engaging in the behaviour. Mischel noted that the principles of generalization and discrimination also apply to responses acquired through observational learning.

Modelling, then, is another term for observational learning or imitation. Bandura (1969) noted that 'virtually all learning phenomena resulting from direct experiences can occur on a vicarious basis through observation of other person's behavior and its consequences for them'.

The behaviour exhibited by a mother and observed by her child can have quite important consequences for the mental health of the child. For example, if the mother tends to be excessively emotional (i.e. to over-react to life's stresses by exhibiting withdrawal, psychosomatic symptoms, or by emotional disorganization), the chances are that the child will learn to respond in a similar manner. On the other hand, if the mother appears calm, and demonstrates adequate coping techniques in spite of exposure to relatively stressful situations, it is probable that the child too will learn to behave adaptively in difficult situations.

It has been established that the observational learning of adaptive or non-adaptive behaviour is related to certain variables such as the characteristics of the model or the observer and certain environmental contingencies. Some of the important variables in modelling are:

(1) the characteristics of the model, for example his social status and competence, and similarity to the observer (Bandura 1969);
(2) the characteristics of the client, for example his degree of dependency (Jakubczak and Walters 1959);
(3) the consequences of the model's behaviour, for example direct or vicarious positive or negative reinforcement (Bandura, Ross, and Ross 1963).

Clearly, however, the specific characteristics of the model which would be most facilitating are best determined on the basis of a functional analysis, including an assessment of the client's characteristics and the behaviour to be acquired or extinguished.

Before discussing 'systematic desensitization' and other behavioural procedures, it is necessary to consider *functional analysis* which is the basis from which a formulation for treatment is derived.

FUNCTIONAL (BEHAVIOURAL) ANALYSIS

The main assumption underlying a behavioural analysis is that both adaptive and maladaptive behaviour may be learned. Therefore, deficits in behaviour may be corrected through some learning procedure such as behavioural rehearsal or modelling (see pp. 280–4). Analogously, maladaptive or surplus undesirable behaviour may be corrected through some form of extinction procedure.

In contrast to assessing the client in terms of his: (a) unconscious motivation and his use of defence mechanisms; or (b) his self-concept as measured by self–ideal discrepancy, etc., a functional or behavioural analysis (Kanfer and Saslow 1969), stresses the importance of determining the variables which control the problematic behaviour. Not only is behaviour seen as a function of the environment, but environment is also seen as a function of behaviour. Thus, the consequences of specific types of behaviour may be as important as, or more important than, antecedent or eliciting factors. Kanfer and Saslow (1969) note that their approach should serve as a basis for making decisions about specific therapeutic interventions, regardless of the presenting problem. While sacrificing the use of diagnostic categories as provided by psychiatric classification systems, Kanfer and Saslow suggested that the behaviour-analytic approach led to a much more adequate formulation of specific treatment strageties for individual clients. They listed seven main areas for inclusion in an adequate behavioural analysis:

(1) an initial analysis of the problem situation including (a) behavioural excesses; (b) behavioural deficits; and (c) behavioural assets;
(2) a clarification of the problem situation;
(3) a motivational analysis;
(4) a developmental analysis including biological, sociological, and behavioural changes;
(5) an analysis of self-control;
(6) an analysis of social relationships; and
(7) an analysis of the social–cultural–physical environment.

High priority is given to determining the specific conditions under which deficit or surplus (excessive) behaviour is evident. While clearly a client may demonstrate both deficit and excessive behaviour, his problem may be initially conceptualized in terms of one or the other. For example, the alcoholic is likely to be categorized as a person who exhibits excessive behaviour. However, he may also lack social skills. If this is the case, then the client may be characterized as demonstrating a behavioural deficit. Therefore, his treatment may include the building up of adequate social skills in addition to eliminating or decreasing the excessive (drinking) behaviour. In fact, adequate treatment of the majority of problems is best carried out by the concurrent development of 'new' functional responses

established maladaptive responses. The
be useful in establishing the type and
Fear Survey Schedule, Wolpe and Lang
common fears, was developed to assess
sed before and after therapy to assess
ntly been standardized by Fischer and
ionnaires measuring assertive behaviour
ucted. Among these are the Wolpe and
thus's Assertiveness Scale (Rathus 1973)
ory (McFall and Lillesand 1971) which is
to specific requests which may be found
er assertiveness questionnaires, are re-
ler (1973) and by Jakubowski and Lacks

stablish multiple baselines of response
this way it is possible to establish the
sirable response, how intense it is, how
its occurrence. For example, if the client
hand-washing, it is important to establish
onse occurs. Do specific covert or overt
surplus response? Does the response
circumstances? While there may be an
carrying out the surplus response, one
can be demonstrated, such as sympathy
or affectional responses from significant others? Is the response maintained by others who may, in addition, allow the client to avoid behaviour, such as his work, which he may otherwise be expected to continue?

If one considers a deficit, in social skills for example, which involves complex sequences of behaviour, one must determine the particular elements which are missing in order that training can proceed successfully. In addition, the generality of the deficit behaviour must be established. Does the client exhibit a lack of social skills only in relation to the opposite sex, or is his problem a very general one? Were adequate social skills once present, or were they never a part of the client's behavioural repertoire? An assessment of the individual's assets, talents, or competences is usually undertaken, since these factors may be used as motivational or incentive factors in the treatment process.

It may be seen that motivational aspects of behaviour are important in the maintenance of both desirable and undesirable behaviour. When it is necessary to develop new responses in a client it is particularly important to become aware of the client's idiosyncratic reinforcements so that these reinforcing events or factors may be utilized in developing new responses. Thus, a significant part of a behavioural analysis is the assessment of reinforcements or pleasurable and aversive stimuli. The use of the Reinforcement Survey Schedule (Cautela and Kastenbaum 1967) may be of value in the motivational analysis.

The developmental analysis is concerned with factors which may limit the individual's behaviour. Has there been development delay or severe illness or accident during childhood which has had implications for the individual's behaviour? The client's self-concept may have been significantly affected by developmental problems. Sociological changes might involve the client's attitude towards his socio-cultural environment. Are his attitudes congruent with his socio-cultural environment or do they stand in stark contrast to those attitudes he finds around him? Are there limitations in the client's environment which tend to decrease his level of reinforcement? An assessment of behavioural change involves a determination of the congruence or lack of congruence between the client's behaviour and developmental and social norms.

An analysis of self-control concerns assessing the degree to which the client has attempted to control his problematic behaviour. To what degree has he been successful? Obviously, this aspect of the behaviour analysis has significant implications for teaching the client self-control procedures (see Chapter 19).

The analysis of social relationships establishes the significant others in the client's environment and what part they play in his problematic behaviour. To what degree do they facilitate constructive or destructive behaviour?

Finally, an analysis of the social–cultural–physical environment helps establish what aspects of the environment facilitate adaptive or non--adaptive behaviour. Is the client's problematic behaviour a function of specific aspects of his environment or is his problematic behaviour general to his total environment? What aspects of the environment might be utilized to facilitate change towards more adaptive behaviour?

Phillips (1978) criticized the relatively recent popularization of the behavioural approach which tends to omit an adequate behavioural analysis. As Phillips noted, 'the behavioral analysis must show a functional relationship between the behavior and its stimulus antecedents and consequents. . . . Assessments focussing on behavior alone or on any number of intra-personal factors such as affect, imagery, cognition and the like, cannot achieve the power of the behavioral analysis because they do not bear such a one-to-one relationship of treatment'. Phillips concluded: 'whatever the field of applied behavioral methods, a thorough behavioral assessment is called for in every case and treatment should be guided throughout by continuously charted data'.

APPLICATIONS TO TREATMENT

While both deficits and excesses may be treated concurrently in the same client, the methods of treatment discussed in this and the following chapter are divided into two groups in terms of their emphasis on deficit behaviour (e.g. phobias, relative lack of social skills) or on surplus or excess behaviour (e.g. ritualistic behaviour based on obsessional thinking, alcoholism, or excessive drinking).

Some methods of treating problems of psychological deficit

A large percentage of clients referred to behaviour therapists exhibit one or more phobic conditions, perhaps in addition to other problems. A phobia is typically defined as an intense *irrational* fear. Following the experimental work of Watson and Raynor (1920), and the assumptions of the behavioural approach, a phobia was formulated as a 'conditioned emotional response' (CER). An interesting comparison of the psychoanalytic and behavioural theories of phobias may be found in Rachman and Costello (1961). The main method which has been used to diminish or eradicate phobic conditions is the method of reciprocal inhibition or systematic desensitization, developed by Wolpe (1958). Additional methods used to treat phobias or anxiety states include: 'flooding-in-imagination', 'flooding-*in-vivo*', Modelling, and assertion training'.

Systematic desensitization

The traditional method of systematic desensitization is essentially a procedure in which, during a relaxed or hypnotized condition, the client is asked to imagine scenes which are part of the anxiety or phobic dimensions and which evoke differing degress of anxiety in the client. The client is, therefore, brought into imaginal contact with an anxiety-provoking scene and the relaxed or hypnotized 'state' is considered to be instrumental in counteracting or reciprocally inhibiting the anxiety that would normally be evoked.

Figure 15.1 presents the basic paradigm for systematic desensitization. The paradigm indicates that counterposed to the stimulus for anxiety, and present at the same time, must be a stimulus for non-anxiety, or for some condition that would counteract or inhibit the anxiety. Bandura (1961), who along with Davison (1968) preferred the term 'counter-conditioning' to 'reciprocal inhibition', noted that the method of counter-conditioning involved the following principle: 'if strong responses which are incompatible with anxiety reactions can be made to occur in the presence of anxiety-evoking cues, the incompatible responses will become attached to these cues and thereby weaken or eliminate the anxiety responses.' Davison noted that Wolpe's view of reciprocal inhibition (paraphrased above by Bandura) was indistinguishable from Guthrie's view of counterconditioning. It is important to note here that responses other than relaxation may be used to counteract anxiety. For example, affectional stimuli and preferred foods (Jones 1924). In some cases, where a person is highly anxious, methohexi-

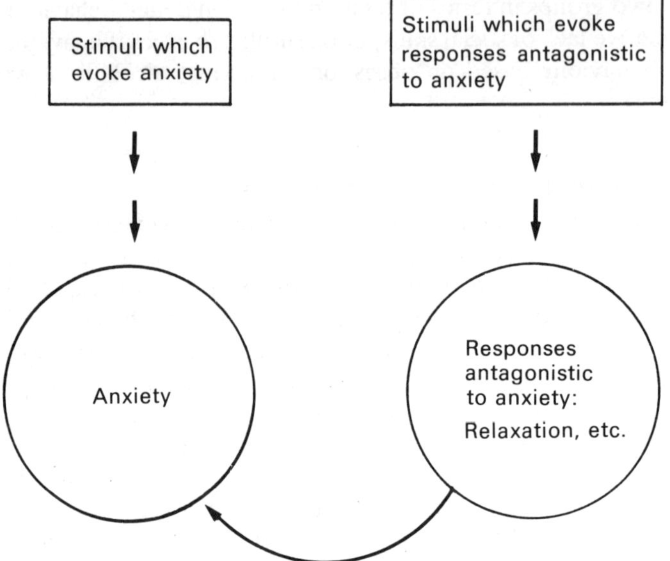

Fig. 15.1. Basic paradigm for systematic desensitization (counterconditioning).

tone sodium may be used as a means of inducing relaxation (Worsley and Freeman 1967). In some cases this drug has been used alone, and in other cases its use in conjunction with hypnosis or relaxation instructions has been recommended, so that eventually the depth of relaxation induced by the drug may generalize to the particular instructions used with it (Brady 1967). Specific advice regarding procedures in desensitization is provided by Lazarus (1964).

According to Wolpe and Lazarus (1966), the technique of systematic desensitization included the following three 'sets of operations':

(1) training in deep muscle relaxation;
(2) the construction of anxiety hierarchies;
(3) counterposing relaxation and anxiety-evoking stimuli from the hierarchies.

Thus, before carrying out the trials of systematic desensitization, the first two sets of operations must be carried out. The procedures of alternately inducing tension and relaxation in the various muscle groups as described as Wolpe and Lazarus may be used or, if preferred, another relaxation or hypnotic procedure (Weitzenhoffer and Hilgard 1959; Vingoe 1968). Jacobson (1977) discussed the development of his progressive relaxation technique (originally published in Jacobson (1938)).

Table 15.1 gives an example of an 'anxiety hierarchy' developed with a client who exhibited a spider phobia. The items are arranged in the order of their anxiety-evoking power from low to high. For example, it can be seen that the third item in the above hierarchy simply involves a picture of a spider taken from a book (Graham 1967) and is a stimulus which would be expected to evoke a low level of anxiety. On the other hand, item 12 involves very close contact with the feared insect. In this case, the client is asked to imagine picking up a real spider and to allow it to crawl up her arm.

TABLE 15.1
ANXIETY HIERARCHY DEVELOPED IN THE TREATMENT OF A SPIDER PHOBIA

Rank order	*Item*
1	The word SPIDER typed or a card
2	Reading the book *Be nice to spiders* to a young child
3	A picture of a spider at rest
4	A moving picture of a spider moving slowly away from her
5	Seeing a spider in her garden 10 metres away at rest
6	Seeing a spider in her garden 5 metres away at rest
7	Watching a spider move rapidly towards her from about 2 metres away
8	Seeing a spider building a web in the garage
9	Allowing a small spider crawl over her gloved hand
10	Allowing a small spider crawl over her bare hand
11	Allowing a large spider crawl over her bare hand
12	Picking up a large spider and allowing it to crawl up her arm

TABLE 15.2
OUTLINE OF TRADITIONAL SYSTEMATIC DESENSITIZATION PROCEDURE

Relaxation induction	Description of scene from hierarchy to be imagined	Signal from patient when scene vividly in mind	Self-report of anxiety 0–10 scale
		Scene in mind —30s—	

1 Traditionally, training in deep-muscle relaxation takes place before trials in systematic desensitization. Wolpe and Lazarus (1966) devote about six, 20-minute sessions to it and the patient is requested to practise relaxation for 15 minutes twice daily at home.
2 Trials in which the same anxiety hierarchy is imagined are repeated until a 0 anxiety-rating is obtained. After a 30-second inter-trial interval trials involving another item from the hierarchy commence.

Table 15.2 gives an outline of the traditional systematic desensitization procedure. Notice first there is a relaxation induction, after which items are taken from the anxiety hierarchy, typically beginning with the items which evoke a low amount of anxiety. The patient is asked to visualize the scene relating to the stimulus evoking a low amount of anxiety. Upon a signal from the patient that the scene is vividly in mind, the therapist allows a period of approximately thirty seconds and then asks for a self-report of anxiety on a scale from 0 to 10, or in some cases 0 to 100. If the patient indicates there is no anxiety, the therapist moves on to the next item on the hierarchy.† On the other hand, if some anxiety is expressed, another trial involving the same imaginary scene will be presented. When the client has been successfully desensitized to all of the items on the hierarchy, treatment for the particular phobia may be considered complete.

Although there are many uncontrolled and poorly designed studies of systematic desensitization in the literature, Paul (1969) has reviewed the literature up to 1967 and concluded that the findings in the well controlled experiments 'were overwhelmingly positive, and for the first time in the history of psychological treatments, a specific therapeutic package reliably produced measurable benefits for clients across a broad range of distressing problems in which anxiety was of fundamental importance'.

Systematic desensitization procedures can be relatively time-consuming and therefore some thought has been invested into automating the method (Lang, Melamed, and Hart, 1970; Evans and Kellam 1973). In addition, there has been increasing applications of desensitization in group situations (Lazarus 1961, 1968; Paul 1968; Suinn and Hall 1970).

Common sense may lead many people to believe that the procedure of systematic desensitization is limited in that one cannot be sure what is happening in the client's imagination when he imagines a feared situation or object. Additionally, one may wonder if an elimination of anxiety to an imaginal stimulus is an effective, or the most effective, method of treatment. These issues are discussed later in the chapter.

*Flooding-in-imagination and flooding-*in-vivo

Two other methods used in treating phobic conditions are not normally graded procedures. In other words, both procedures emphasize the immediate exposure of the client to the most anxiety-evoking stimuli or situations. These two methods are: (a) flooding-in-imagination and (b) flooding-*in-vivo*. Table 15.3 compares systematic desensitization, and the two flooding procedures. In addition to being used to combat phobias and anxiety states, flooding has been used to treat obsessive–compulsive disorders (Rachman, Hodgson, and Marks 1971).

Table 15.3 shows that relaxation may or may not be used in conjunction with the three methods outlined. This is discussed later in the chapter. Table 15.3 also indicates that in all three methods there is a confrontation with the feared object. However, while in the systematic desensitization and flooding-in-imagination procedures, the confrontation is 'in imagination', there is an actual confrontation with the feared situation or object in the flooding-

† Frequently, in order to determine the reliability of a particular trial, a second trial involving the same scene is carried out even when the client indicates an absence of anxiety.

TABLE 15.3
COMPARISON OF SYSTEMATIC DESENSITIZATION (SD) AND FLOODING

	Procedure	*Systematic desensitization*	*Flooding-in imagination*	*Flooding-* in-vivo
COMPONENTS	Relaxation induction	Varies	Varies	Varies
	Confrontation with feared object	Yes In imagination may be graded	Yes In imagination most feared aspect	Yes *In vivo* most feared aspect
	Changes in anxiety (arousal) level	Decrease	Increase	Increase
	Massed or spaced trials	Spaced	Massed	Massed

in-vivo procedure.

In the flooding-in-imagination procedure, the therapist induces high anxiety levels by giving the client verbal instructions to imagine scenes to which he is aversive. The method is considered as an extinction procedure. As shown in Table 15.3, the anxiety or arousal level is purposely raised in both flooding procedures. In addition, a massed or continuous procedure is used rather than the sort of discrete trials used in systematic desensitization. During the imaginative situation the client is encouraged to picture himself in the actual phobic situation, and to maintain a high level of anxiety until extinction occurs. The basic idea is that when no real harm occurs (lack of reinforcement) that extinction will ultimately take place.

Flooding-*in-vivo*, although similar to flooding-in-imagination in confronting the client with the most feared aspects of the phobic stimulus, differs in that the client must confront the phobic situation *in vivo* with little or no preparation. Rachman (1966) in an analogue study involving spider phobic subjects attempted to compare systematic desensitization and flooding. He used ten flooding-in-imagination sessions which, unfortunately, did not produce any decrease in the subject's fear of spiders. However, it is doubtful if Rachman's procedure should be called flooding, since the exposure time of anxiety stimuli was restricted to 2 minutes per trial.

Marks (1972) noted in reference to flooding-*in-vivo* that 'Flooding is not a fixed technique but comprises of a range of procedures that merge into one another. Flooding is at one end of a continuum of approach to distressing situations, at the opposite end of which is desensitization. . . . The more sudden the confrontation, the more it is prolonged, and the greater the emotion that accompanies it, the more apt is the label *flooding* for that procedure'. He stated that there were many types of flooding but there were common elements in most forms—rapid confrontation of the patient with the stimuli that distress him until he gets used to them, the evocation of intense emotion during treatment, or a combination of both. Since the distinction between imaginal treatment and treatment *in vivo* is important, imaginal treatment should be referred to as flooding-in-imagination (Marks 1972).

Marks pointed out that it was not until 1968 that systematic studies on flooding were carried out. It is quite clear that there was much confusion in the literature concerning the differentiation between flooding-in-imagination and flooding-*in-vivo*. Rachman's (1966) 'flooding' sessions were certainly not far removed from trials in systematic desensitization.

After reviewing some of the earlier uncontrolled studies on flooding Marks went on to report on the controlled investigations carried out at the Maudsley Hospital. He suggested that flooding-*in-vivo* seemed to be more effective than flooding-in-imagination in the treatment of phobias. However, he noted that further research was needed in order to verify this hypothesis. In addition, longer durations of exposure were hypothesized as more effective than shorter periods. Finally, Marks pointed out that contingent social reinforcement and therapist-modelling could facilitate progress. Mark's first suggestion above has been since subjected to experimental test by Stern and Marks (1973) and by Watson, Mullett, and Pillay (1973). While flooding-*in-vivo* was found to be clearly superior to flooding-in-imagination, a tape recorder rather than a 'live' therapist was used for flooding-in-imagination. This raised a question regarding the possible greater effectiveness of using a therapist for the flooding-in-imagination sessions. Emmelkamp and Wessels (1975) used a 'live' therapist and used a 90-minute period for each imagination procedure. After using four different procedures: (a) prolonged flooding-*in-vivo*; (b) flooding-in-imagination; (c) combined (flooding-in-imagination and *in-vivo*); and (d) self-observation, they concluded that prolonged exposure *in-vivo* proved to be superior to flooding-in the imagination both on the phobic anxiety scales (CER) and on the phobic avoidance scales (Conditioned Avoidance Response).

Marks stressed the importance of patient motivation by noting that:

> Patients need to be well motivated and to understand what is required of them in flooding treatment; otherwise they might terminate treatment prematurely and enhance future tendencies to escape. Their commitment to face unpleasantness in treatment has to be obtained beforehand.

Emmelkamp and Wessels (1975) believed that the prolonged *in-vivo* treatment might be too stressful for some individuals and suggested that prolonged exposure *in vivo* in groups or with medication might offer a solution.

Specific instructions, behavioural rehearsal, and modelling

A number of additional techniques which may be useful to people who exhibit interpersonal fears or social anxiety may be used alone or in combination. For example, assertion training may include: (a) specific instructions from the therapist; (b) behavioural rehearsal or role playing; and (c) different types of modelling.

Specific instructions Bandura (1969) noted that once a person has developed sufficient language skills, he relies upon *verbal modelling cues* for guiding his behaviour, as, for example, in following instructional manuals. Bandura distinguishes the instructional control of behaviour from verbal modelling:

> In investigating the process of verbal control it is essential to distinguish between the instigational and modelling functions of instructions. Instructions are most likely to result in correct performance when they both activate a person to respond and describe the appropriate responses and the order in which they should be performed. . . . both types of influences produce their effects through verbal modelling and they differ only in the explicitness with which the required responses are defined. As might be expected, greater performance gains are achieved when the desired behaviour is clearly specified than when it must be inferred from a few examples.

Behavioural rehearsal While role playing or behavioural rehearsal was discussed by Wolpe and Lazarus (1966), it was Lazarus (1966, 1971) who appeared to stress the efficacy of this technique. Piaget and Lazarus (1969) indicated the importance of rehearsal-desensitization (see below). Basically, the term 'behavioural rehearsal' or 'role playing' is self explanatory. Specific interpersonal situations which are anxiety-provoking or in which the client has demonstrated non-assertive behaviour are determined and used as material for behaviour-rehearsal sessions. The client usually role-plays himself while the therapist or other 'expert' role-plays the other person in the situation. However, before receiving specific instructions for changes in assertive behaviour, the client may be asked to perform as he usually does in interaction with the therapist who plays the part of his colleague, superior, etc. If video-tape facilities are available, the client has the opportunity of receiving video and auditory feedback of his performance in the rehearsal situation. He may then be asked to comment not only on his feelings in the situation, but also on his interpersonal performance. After some discussion, the therapist may give verbal instructions for a more assertive performance or may reverse roles with the client, demonstrating or modelling how an assertive person should behave in the specific circumstances. Depending upon the extent of behavioural deficit, non-verbal components of assertive behaviour may first be modelled (see below).

Modelling As noted earlier, modelling is another term for observational learning or imitation. Modelling is often used successfully in the training of social skills (Edelstein and Eisler 1976) and has been used to increase independent behaviour in out-patient neurotics and in-patient schizophrenics. Participant modelling (see below) has been successful in treating compulsive neurotics (Roper, Rachman, and Marks 1975).

Modelling is often a component of treatment, although it may not be made explicit and the therapist may not be aware of using the technique. For example, when the client is accompanied by the therapist during a flooding session, the therapist is responding to a situation 'feared' by the client in a way he would wish the client to emulate (i.é. without anxiety). One may even argue that the therapist is modelling a non-anxiety response during a psychotherapy hour, when material which is anxiety-evoking for the client is discussed. However 'modelling' is more commonly used to refer to activities carried out by the therapist which are explicitly defined as modelling by both client and therapist. In essence, the therapist is role-playing a behavioural sequence which he instructs the client to imitate. It can be seen that instructions, behavioural rehearsal, and modelling are not necessarily mutually exclusive.

Bandura and his colleagues have published extensively on imitation or modelling (Bandura 1965, 1969, 1971, 1977; Blanchard 1970; Bandura, Grusec, and Menlove, 1966, 1967; Grusec and Mischel 1966; Kazdin 1973, 1974, 1976).

Modelling is used not only in the treatment of phobias and anxiety states, but is effective in the acquisition of responses that have never been in the individual's repertoire. While in the neurotic and schizophrenic, treatment may entail the re-acquisition of responses which had been performed some time in the past, treatment of the autistic child or the mentally retarded involves the learning and performance of new responses (Marlatt and Perry 1975). Bandura (1969) argued that reinforcement might be unnecessary for the learning of responses through modelling. However, he noted that many studies 'had shown that *performance* of matching responses was substantially increased by rewarding such behaviour in either the model or the subjects.' It is important to remember that one may learn how to do something, yet if the particular task learned is unexpressed behaviourally (i.e. is not performed), an observer has no way of inferring that the learning has occurred.

Modelling may involve a live model or a symbolic model presented via film or video-tape. While, in general, the live modelling situation may be perceived as superior to the use of filmed models, the advantage of using film or tape is that one may use editing and re-use the materials for other clients. When a film or video-tape is used one uses the term *vicarious modelling*, while the *in vivo* use of a model is termed *live modelling*.

Participant modelling. Participant modelling or (contact desensitization) (Ritter 1969) is a technique which, after some live modelling, involves the client in a combined performance with the therapist or model. The therapist ensures that the client will be successful by structuring the environment in such a way as to gradually reduce the degree of threat that the environment evokes in the client. The client is thus gradually led to engage in the necessary behaviour alone (Bandura 1969, 1977; Bandura, Jeffrey, and Wright 1974). One may also speak of *vicarious reinforcement* if the client is exposed to a model or client on film or tape who receives a punishment or reward. The re-establishment of old or the acquisition of new responses then may take place through a process of *vicarious conditioning* including vicarious reinforcement. Analogously *vicarious extinction* can be demonstrated. Cognitive, social, and emotional responses may be conditioned and extinguished vicariously (Bandura 1969).

Bandura (1969) reported on the Bandura, Blanchard, and Ritter (1969) study which used a matched design, in which the relative efficacy of live modelling with participation, symbolic modelling, and desensitization were compared with a control group in producing affective, attitudinal, and behaviour changes associated with snake phobics. A fear inventory, attitudinal ratings, and a behaviour avoidance test were used as criterion measures, the subjects being individually matched on the basis of their snake-avoidance scores. The live-modelling with participation group were exposed to the model who demonstrated the desired behaviour under secure observational conditions, after which subjects were aided through further demonstration and joint performance to execute progressively more difficult responses. Whenever subjects were unable to perform a given behaviour after demonstration alone, they enacted the feared activities concurrently with the model. The physical guidance was then reduced until they were about to perform the behaviour alone. The symbolic modelling group were shown how to self-administer their treatment, which involved the progressive presentation of increasingly threatening views of interactions with a large snake. Additionally, they were taught to relax themselves and to use this relaxation during stimulus exposure. The rate of treatment was under each subject's control, in that she was able to stop and reverse the film whenever anxiety was provoked. The desensitization group received standard desensitization treatment in which deep-relaxation was paired with imaginal stimuli. Finally, the control group were merely assessed on the behavioural and attitudinal variables.

The results indicated the clear superiority of the participant-modelling procedure; the effects of the symbolic modelling and desensitization being approximately equal. Ninety-two per cent of the subjects of the participant-modelling group were free of their previous snake phobias, and both modelling groups were treated successfully since avoidance responses of long standing were extinguished. In addition, the phobic stimuli no longer evoked anxiety in the client. While the systematic desensitization treatment resulted in reduced emotional arousal during snake-approach behaviour, the degree of reduced fear was less in this group than in the two modelling groups. Bandura noted that:

> Participant modelling . . . effected widespread fear reductions in relation to a variety of threats involving both interpersonal and non-social events. The transfer obtained reflects the operation of at least two somewhat different processes. The first involves generalization of extinction effects from treated stimuli to related anxiety sources. The second entails positive reinforcement of a sense of capability through success,

which mitigates emotional responses to potentially threatening situations. Having successfully overcome a phobia that had plagued them for most of their lives, subjects reported increased confidence that they could cope effectively with other fear-provoking events.

Following up on the ideas expressed above, Bandura proposed an interesting self-efficacy theory (Bandura 1977) in which four main sources of information contribute to personal efficacy. These sources are listed as performance accomplishments, vicarious experience, verbal persuasion, and physiological states. Modelling and vicarious factors are seen as quite important in the development of efficacy through psychological procedures. For those who wish to pursue a discussion of modelling in greater detail than is possible here, Bandura (1969, 1977) and Marlatt and Perry (1975) are recommended. We turn now to a discussion of assertiveness training.

Assertiveness training

In addition to systematic desensitization, assertiveness training has been emphasized as a method which leads to behaviour which is antagonistic to anxiety responses (Wolpe 1958). One is assertive when one stands up for one's rights and demonstrates control over situations in which one justifiably should exert control. In self-theory language, one behaves in a way which reflects an adequate self-concept, preventing others from treating one unjustly. One is able to relate to others in an open way, being able to express one's feelings, whether negative or positive, to others. One tends to feel rewarded when assertive behaviour results in success. Thus, one is able to congratulate oneself or to provide positive reinforcement, in addition to receiving reinforcement from the environment, whether personal or non-personal.

A non-assertive person tends to lack spontaneity, to behave in a way which reflects an inadequate self-concept, to demonstrate social anxiety to a debilitating degree, and to lower the probability of his receiving reinforcement from the environment. His ability in making decisions may be abdicated. Wolpe (1969) believes that suppression of feeling may lead to a continuing inner turmoil which may produce somatic symptoms and even pathological changes in predisposed organs. While many reports on assertive training have been analogue studies treating students with limited interpersonal problems, e.g. Twentyman and McFall (1975), assertion training has been used in treating those who exhibit marital difficulties (Eisler and Hersen 1973; Fensterheim 1972), depression (Bean 1970; Lazarus and Serber 1968), sexual problems (Edwards 1972), and self-mutilating behaviour (Robach, Frayn, Gunby, and Tuters 1972).

Assertive responses are responses which are desirable in an interpersonal context. Thus, while an individual may stress his shyness and his high social anxiety, may exhibit self-belittling behaviour, and in general may behave in a way which suggests he has a low opinion of himself, treatment must, in due course, be applied in an interpersonal situation. While homework assignments involving one-to-one and group interactions may be desirable as soon as feasible, some individuals will not be ready for much *in vivo* practice until a certain amount of preliminary training involving the non-verbal components of assertive behaviour are practised or until a certain amount of interpersonal competence is demonstrated in behaviour rehearsal sessions which may also include some modelling of desirable responses by the therapist. Serber (1972) discussed the teaching of the non-verbal components of assertive reponses, and recommended the use of video-tape feedback. Serber noted that ineffectual people lack a command of style. He defined style as 'the ability to master appropriate non-verbal, as well as verbal, components of behaviour'. Noting the limitations of 'non-directive' psychotherapy, he indicated that after defining the behaviour which needed to be changed, the therapist must use specific instruction, modelling, role playing and the behavioural rehearsal of alternative behaviour. The above methods, together with audio-visual feedback, provided adequate means by which to shape non-verbal behaviour.

Serber listed six non-verbal variables of importance in treating non--assertive people:

(1) loudness of voice;
(2) fluency of spoken words;
(3) eye contact;
(4) facial expression;
(5) body expression; and
(6) distance from person with whom one is interacting.

Serber noted that with limited training these behaviours may be reliably rated by the clinician. Basically, it is best to work with one variable at a time, to use modelling techniques, and to provide much positive reinforcement for improvement. It is clearly important, as already mentioned in Chapter 9 (p. 200), to avoid any inconsistency between verbal and non-verbal behaviour.

Piaget and Lazarus (1969) note that sometimes behavioural rehearsal and assertive training techniques cannot be used because the client's level of anxiety is heightened and he becomes evasive and over-defensive. If systematic desensitization is also contraindicated owing to the client's inability to produce clear visual images or failure to make an affective response to imaginary situations, then a procedure referred to as 'rehearsal-desensitization' is recommended. This procedure involves a graded role-playing stage in which the client is first asked to perform in non-threatening situations, followed by interactions of a mildly threatening nature. After explaining the procedure to the client and verifying that he is agreeable to following this treatment (phase 1), an anxiety hierarchy is constructed involving situations which can be used in behavioural rehearsal (phase 2). The third phase involves the reversal of roles by client and therapist for the first presentation of each item. Thus, the behaviour required from the client is first modelled by the therapist. Social reinforcement is, of course, provided for progress. The method proceeds much as ordinary desensitization. Piaget and Lazarus suggested that compared to the traditional desensitization procedure generalization had a higher probability of occurring and was usually more extensive.

Hersen, Eisler, and Miller (1973) in their review of the literature, discussed some of the difficulties in carrying out research on the effectiveness of assertion training. The generalization of assertive training to the real-life setting is of particular concern. Hersen *et al.* (1973) referred to the relative lack of research on helping clients to express feelings of love, affection, and other positive feelings. In addition there is a relative lack of studies of assertive training using clinical groups. In spite of the above criticisms, assertion training, together with specific instructions and modelling, appears to be an effective procedure in helping a variety of individuals of diverse symptomatology if it can be demonstrated that they exhibit moderate to severe interpersonal deficits. Hersen *et al.* noted that:

> Most striking is the extent to which an active process takes place between the therapist and his patient. Indeed, the relationship approximates that of teacher and student. The therapist instructs, models, coaches and reinforces appropriate verbal and non-verbal responses. Concurrently, the patient first practises his newly developed repertoire in the consulting room and then in actual situations requiring assertive responses.

While earlier studies were unable to determine which particular component of a treatment programme involving assertive training was the active agent in successful behavioural change, a number of more recent studies have attempted to determine the effective components of treatment. McFall and Twentyman (1973), who reported on four experiments on assertion training, compared the effects of rehearsal, modelling, and coaching to treatment success. Symbolic modelling was found to play a small role in the effectiveness of treatment, while both rehearsal and coaching were effective components singly and additively. Treatment effects were not enhanced by audio-visually presented models. The addition of modelling to either rehearsal or rehearsal combined with coaching added little to the efficacy of treatment. The authors were, however, unable to explain the lack of results from observational modelling. Whether or not the addition of reinforcing consequences immediately after the modelling would have facilitated the effect of modelling alone was unanswered by the research reported. As the authors noted, their studies were only experimental analogues of fully developed clinical procedures, dealt only with refusal responses as measured by the 'conflict resolution inventory' (CRI) and used a non-clinical (student) population as a subject pool. Thus, McFall and Twentyman's (1973) results do not conflict with the more positive findings of Bandura (1969).

Melnick and Stocker (1977) also used the CRI to select student subjects and to assess treatment effects in a project on assertiveness training. A behavioural measure using simulated refusal situations was also used as a criterion. The purpose of their study was to determine the relative contribution of behavioural feedback to assertiveness training whose components were behavioural rehearsal and feedback. The effect of knowledge of recording was also assessed. Thirty-three subjects participated in two sessions of assertiveness training. One group was unaware that it was being recorded and received no feedback, while the other groups were aware of being recorded, although one group received no feedback. Neither knowledge of being recorded nor feedback were significantly effective variables as measured by the CRI or the behavioural measure. It was suggested that feedback and the awareness of being recorded are not particularly influencial in situations where high levels of self monitoring are already in operation. For those wishing to follow up research in this area in more detail, a review of research issues in the area of assertiveness training is provided by Rich and Schroeder (1976).

SUMMARY

The experimental basis of behaviour therapy is discussed including an outline of classical and operant conditioning, and a brief discussion of observation learning, which can occur without the provision of direct reinforcement to the learner. The seven main areas of functional analysis are then discussed, and the behavioural techniques which are mainly applied to problems of behavioural deficit are given. The main procedures discussed included systematic desensitization, flooding-in-imagination, flooding-*in-vivo*, behavioural rehearsal, modelling and assertiveness training.

16
Behaviour therapy: treatment of problems of psychological excess

Learning is not child's play; we cannot learn without pain.
Aristotle: *Politics*

The purpose of this chapter is to discuss the methods which are used to treat problems involving excessive behaviour, such as alcoholism, sexual 'deviation', and obsessive thinking or other intrusive experiences. The emphasis is placed on the procedures of thought stopping, response prevention, aversion therapy, and covert sensitization. The chapter ends with a critical discussion of the research in the area of behaviour therapy, and, in essence, comments on much of the material in Chapters 15 and 16.

OBSESSIONAL CONDITIONS

Beech edited a book on obsessional states, which included an interesting psychophysiological theory of these conditions (Beech and Perigault 1974). Carr (1974*b*) reviewed the literature on compulsive neurosis, and defined a compulsion as 'a recurrent or persistent thought, image, impulse, or action that is accompanied by a sense of subjective compulsion and a desire to resist it'. The feeling that he has lost control over his own behaviour is disturbing to the client. Carr considered it more logical to use the term 'compulsion' to include both thoughts and action, although he recommended that 'cognitive' or 'motor' be used as adjectival terms. The client's subjective feeling of compulsion and his wish to resist the behaviour help to differentiate the client with compulsive psychopathology from the client who exhibits stereotyped and repetitive behaviour based on organic pathology and from the so-called 'compulsive personality'. Carr presented evidence that autonomic arousal was heightened during the performance of compulsive behaviours and was also thereby reduced to baseline levels. There was no adequate evidence for genetic aetiology for the compulsive disorders. Carr supported the view that compulsions were developed and maintained through their reinforcing consequences, a view for which he had some physiological support (Carr 1974*a*). Carr pointed out that Walton and Mather (1964) concluded that in chronic compulsive conditions the motor reactions had become functionally autonomous. This conception is supported by Metzner's (1963) view that compulsive behaviours were avoidance responses. Carr did not accept the view that compulsive states were based on traumatic learning, because the various rituals performed by an individual, such as hand washing and turning off switches, could not be placed on a dimension of stimulus similarity. However, Carr did not seem to consider the idea of semantic generalization. For example, many compulsive neurotics feel that 'somebody will be hurt' if they do not continue to engage in their many rituals. Rachman's (1971) discussion of obsessional ruminations seems to support this idea. Carr (1974*b*) proposed a multifaceted model in which 'the compulsive neurotic always makes an abnormally high subjective estimate of the probability of the undesired outcomes . . . [because] all situations that have any potentially harmful outcome, however minimal, will generate a relatively high level of threat with its consequent anxiety'.

Rachman (1971) discussed *obsessional ruminations* which he defined as 'repetitive, intrusive and unacceptable thoughts . . . In content, they generally comprise thoughts of harming others . . . causing accidents to occur, swearing or distasteful sexual or religious ideas'. Behaviour which the client felt would reduce the likelihood of others being harmed was frequently carried out. For example, the client might need to keep checking under his car to reassure himself that he had not run over someone. Rachman compared ruminations with phobic stimuli.

Obsessional ruminations are considered as noxious stimuli to which the client has difficulty adapting, and to which he is particularly sensitized, especially during disturbance of mood such as agitated depression. According to Rachman, the therapist needs to facilitate a process of habituation which will not, or has not, occurred spontaneously'. Based upon his habituation model of obsessive ruminations Rachman predicted that desensitization, flooding, and modelling could all be used in the treatment process. Since the publication of the Rachman article, Rainey (1972) has reported on the treatment of an obsessional condition using flooding, while Roper, Rachman, and Marks (1975) have successfully used both passive and participant modelling to treat obsessional patients. Meyer, Levy, and Schnurer (1974) reviewed the behavioural treatment approach to the obsessive–compulsive disorders. As these authors noted: 'it is generally agreed that treatment is extremely difficult and the results are often unrewarding.'

In addition to the methods indicated above, thought-stopping and response prevention have often been used to treat those with obsessional disorders.

THOUGHT STOPPING

Wolpe and Lazarus (1966) described a thought-stopping procedure for use in treating obsessional ruminations. Basically, the client may be asked to relax as the therapist requests that he think, imagine, or ruminate about the thoughts that bother him. He is told to shout 'Stop!' when the therapist does, and to stop ruminating. The client signals when he has the 'thoughts' clearly in mind and at that instant both therapist and client shout 'Stop!' while the therapist also produces some novel, and preferably unexpected loud stimulus. This may vary from slamming a heavy book on the desk or using a gong, to using a recording of a dentist's drill or other 'noxious' stimulus. This procedure produces a startle response which tends to distract the client from his ruminations. The number of trials used for this first stage is based upon an analysis of changes in the latency between the request to 'think the thoughts' to the client's signal that he has the thoughts clearly in mind. If the latency increases and the client has difficulty in 'thinking the thoughts' it is probable that the treatment is effective. During the second stage the novel stimulus is omitted from the procedure, while during the third stage the shout 'Stop!' from the therapist is omitted. During the fourth stage, the client whispers 'Stop' while during the fifth and final stage the client tells himself to 'Stop' *sotto voce*. The criterion for moving from one stage to the next is as indicated above. However, since there is a carry-over effect it is best to carry out 20 trials or so during each stage to verify the effectiveness of the procedure with each omission. Yamagami (1971) has incorporated variations to the thought-stopping procedure, such as pleasant scenes to lengthen intervals during which the patient is not ruminating, and an electric shock which substituted for the therapist shouting: 'Stop!' Yamagami successfully eliminated a colour-naming obsession in a young male whose daily activities were disrupted by this problem. Wartnaby (1972) has suggested that a hair roller which has a large number of prickly projections on its outer surface could be gripped at the therapist's command to 'Stop', after which a pleasant scene is used to induce relaxation (see also Daniels (1976) for modifications in thought-stopping technique).

While the author has found thought-stopping to be effective when an electric shock is substituted for the therapist's command 'Stop', controlled studies (Stern, Lipsedge, and Marks 1973; Stern 1978) of the basic thought-stopping procedure do not support its effectiveness. Hackmann and McLean (1975) found that flooding and thought-stopping were about equally effective when given twice weekly on an out-patient basis. Finally, Olin (1976) discussed contraindications for the use of thought-stopping and gives a careful evaluation of those who might benefit from this technique. It seems clear that while little evidence is available to suggest that thought-stopping is the treatment of choice for obsessional neurotics, more research is needed, together with a willingness to carry out controlled studies using modifications of the basic technique.

A number of other techniques have been used to treat obsessional behaviour, among which are response prevention (Meyer, Levy, and Schnurer 1974), electrical aversion therapy (Kenny, Solyom, and Solyom 1973), and covert sensitization (Cautela 1967).

RESPONSE PREVENTION

The term *response prevention* is self-explanatory in that in some way the undesirable response (ritual) must be prevented or reduced. While the term 'response prevention' has been associated with the flooding technique in which the client is prevented from escaping from or avoiding the feared situation (Thoresen and Mahoney 1974), in the present context, the response refers to the excessive (ritualistic) behaviour. For example, a client who feels compelled to wash her hands over fifty times daily in situations in which the average person might wash her hands five times, is engaging in excessive behaviour and one might use response-prevention techniques, usually combined with other procedures, to help her to reduce her hand-washing frequency to a normal range. If the patient is in hospital, one may withdraw specific reinforcements, making these reinforcements contingent upon the successful reduction of hand-washing. However, it may be necessary, with the client's 'co-operation', to restrain her at times from performing the ritual. Obviously, ethical considerations are important here. However, as indicated by Meyer *et al.* (1974), it is important that the rituals be prevented for a long period of time while the patient is required to remain in the situations which normally evoke anxiety and ritualistic activities. In this way the obsessional should learn that the feared consequences of not performing the ritual do not occur, thus resulting in a decrease in anxiety and an eventual extinction of the ritualistic behaviour. Vingoe (1980) has reported the successful use of response prevention, together with the use of reinforcement contingent upon significant reductions in frequency of ritualistic behaviour in a middle-aged male.

AVERSION THERAPY

Aversion techniques may be used to treat those with sexual disorders, alcoholism, and obsessional conditions, and to alleviate other intrusive (cognitive) experiences. Since the procedures do involve the administration of a painful or other generally unpleasant stimuli these techniques are usually used as a last resort, when all else has failed. Obviously, informed consent is necessary and ethical considerations are of prime importance.

While three general aversive procedures have been used (i.e. chemical, electrical, and imaginative) the use of the latter two have been most frequent. The use of chemical aversive stimuli entailed a relative lack of control regarding the latency between administration and effect, as well as much variation due to differences in personal characteristics of the clients, and the fact that the chemical aversion was contraindicated for those with gastric or cardiac complaints (Rachman 1965). Thus, from an experimental point of view the chemical approach left much to be desired. However, it is probable that ethical considerations were more important in thc change from chemical to electrical aversion procedures. Rachman compared chemical and electrical aversion therapy. He noted that up to 1965 the cases reported in the literature mainly involved chemical aversion. However, he went on to point out the advantages of the electrical method. He noted that precise control was possible with electrical stimulation since individual differences in response to shock could be more easily dealt with, and the monitoring of treatment was easier. Rachman concluded by discussing the disadvantages of aversive therapy, and the importance of ethical considerations.

Thus, aversion therapy involves the use of some painful or noxious stimulus, which is paired with the undesirable behaviour in such a way that the 'thought' of engaging in the particular behaviour comes to evoke the painful or nauseous feeling itself. The procedure is probably best interpreted on the basis of operant conditioning. The painful or noxious stimulus is one that is made a consequence of the operant response of drinking or other undesirable behaviour. The reinforcement (shock or nauseous scene) results in pain, nausea, or emesis. The operant paradigm for aversion therapy is thus as seen in Table 16.1

TABLE 16.1
OPERANT PARADIGM FOR AVERSION THERAPY

	Response	*Stimulus*
I Pre-treatment:	Consummatory behaviour (e.g. drinking a glass of beer).	Basic or learned positive reinforcement and self-reinforcement (e.g. 'I feel better now').
II Treatment trials:	Consummatory behaviour (e.g. drinking a glass of beer).	Basic or learned negative reinforcement shock or other noxious stimulus or nauseous scene as in covert sensitization and self-reinforcement (e.g. 'I feel horrible').

Referring to Table 16.1, it may be seen that in the pre-treatment situation the consumption of alcohol results in positive reinforcement. The drinker may also provide self-reinforcement by saying, for example: 'Now I feel better.' In contrast, after a number of aversive treatment trials, he may say, for example, 'I feel horrible', and the sight and smell of the alcoholic drink as well as the taste will take on negative reinforcing properties.

There are a number of factors which may serve to increase the success of aversive procedures, particularly electric shock:

1. The 'shock' should be contingent on the occurrence of the undesirable behaviour.

2. The treatment should be continued until the undesirable behaviour is not evident.
3. The stimulus employed as aversive should be validated in the particular circumstances as definitely aversive and as remaining aversive.
4. There should be encouragement and reinforcement for alternative responses (i.e. responses essentially antagonistic to those to be reduced or eliminated).
5. *Fading procedures* should be employed (i.e. the situation or circumstances under which the reduction of unwanted responses occur should be gradually changed). This increases the probability of the generalization of treatment effects.
6. The schedule of reinforcement should be changed (e.g. after a period of continuous reinforcement the shift to a fixed ratio schedule should increase the durability of the response reduction).
7. The use in the treatment process of significant others such as the client's father or husband should be encouraged (see Chapter 2 on the use of non-professionals in therapy).
8. The responsibility for therapeutic change should be gradually shifted from the therapist to the client; see also Chapter 19 on self-control. (Sandler 1975).

COVERT SENSITIZATION

There has been an increasing interest in cognitive techniques in recent years. The method of 'covert sensitization' or 'aversive imagery' is a cognitive method in which disturbing scenes are described by the therapist for the client to imagine. These aversive (frequently nausea-inducing) scenes are paired appropriately with the description of the undesirable behaviour as shown in Table 16.1.

Rachman and Teasdale (1969) discussed the development of the covert sensitization technique by Gold and Neufeld (1965) and its extension by Cautela (1966, 1967). Cautela (1967) reported the successful use of covert sensitization in treating alcoholism, conduct disorders, homosexuality, and obesity. In treating obesity, for example, images of eating specific types of 'fattening' foods are paired with scenes involving nausea and emesis. Rachman and Teasdale were optimistic about the effectiveness of covert sensitization in treating surplus behaviours such as over-eating, alcoholism, addiction, sexual disorders, and compulsive behaviour, basing their conclusions on a report by Anant (1966) who apparently successfully treated 26 alcoholics by asking them to visualize themselves drinking, followed by feelings of nausea and the need to vomit.

Cautela (1969) saw covert sensitization as a self-control procedure. In his treatment the client was first trained to relax as in systematic desensitization, after which the technique was fully explained to him. After being requested to visualize the undesirable object, such as a cigarette or glass of beer, the client was required to image the sequential behavioural components which led up to the consummatory act. Just as the client visualized the last behavioural component prior to carrying out the undesirable behaviour, it was suggested that he was feeling more and more nauseous, etc. Cautela also made use of 'relief scenes' during which the client imagined himself in pleasant situations. Some of these scenes included the client's refusal to drink and the subsequent elimination of the nauseous feeling. Cautela recommended that 10 to 20 trials be included in each session, which should take place bi-weekly over several months. In addition, clients were advised to practise at home between treatment sessions with the therapist, so that, eventually, taking into consideration appropriate precautions and varying the negative scenes, the client was able to carry out his own treatment. Among conditions recently treated by covert sensitization are trichotillomania (Levine 1976); sexual deviation (Callahan and Leitenberg 1973); obesity (Janda and Rimm 1972); and drug addiction (Wisocki 1973).

In addition to the three main types of aversive stimuli used, cigarette smoke was used by Morganstein (1974) as an aversive stimulus to treat an obese client. Other possibilities exist, such as aversive noise stimuli, and odours and gustatory stimuli with aversive characteristics. Although it is recognized that the conditions which provide an atmosphere in which aversion therapy may be carried out may vary from region to region, it is suggested that there may be a decrease in the utilization of aversive methods or possibly a change in the specifics of applying aversion therapy. Some of the reasons offered for this hypothesized change are as follows:

(1) a much greater concern over the ethics of aversive techniques;
(2) a decrease in the number of homosexuals, transvestites, and others who volunteer to change their sexual orientation; and
(3) the change in orientation in reference to treating the alcoholic (i.e. to a controlled social drinking, rather than an elimination of the alcohol-drinking response) (Lloyd and Salzburg 1975).

Aversion therapy has been used to treat a wide variety of conditions, including compulsive gambling (Barker and Miller 1968) and shoplifting (Kellam 1969). Chapter 19 discusses much of the therapeutic work concerned with smoking, obesity, and alcoholism from a self-control point of view. A report on treating homosexuality is provided by Feldman and MacCulloch (1971). Lloyd and Salzburg (1975) review behavioural approaches in teaching alcoholic clients to engage in controlled drinking in contrast to total abstinence.

While aversion techniques may sometimes be seen as controversial they can be the treatment of choice in long-standing disorders, particularly in cases which are considered critical and where all else has failed. For example, see p. 124 for a discussion of Lang and Melamed's treatment of a young child with chronic ruminative vomiting. Aversion treatment has sometimes been found necessary in treating self-injurious behaviour. Thus, while there has been some concern expressed over the use of aversive techniques, there has been and continues to be good justification for their use in a significant number of selected cases.

It had not been possible to discuss all of the techniques that may be subsumed under behaviour therapy, particularly those most likely to be classed as 'cognitive behaviour modification' (CBM) procedures (Mahoney 1974; Ledwidge 1978). However, some of these are taken up in Chapter 19 on 'self-control techniques'. In addition, a number of these techniques will be briefly mentioned in the final section of this chapter to which we now turn for a brief critical discussion of behaviour therapy.

CRITICAL DISCUSSION

There has been much controversy over the definition of behaviour therapy (Yates 1970*a*; Meyer 1970; Yates 1970*b*). Yates (1970*a*), for example, would find Eysenck's definition (p. 265) to be too narrow, in that it refers only to surplus or deficient conditioned responses. Yates has argued that there are many maladaptive behaviours which would not fit into Eysenck's (1959) conception of maladaptive behaviour. There continues to be some controversy over the range and types of methods which should be included as behaviour therapy, especially since an increase in cognitive methods has been evident. In contrast to many non-human organisms, man is able to engage in cognitive activity. Man is not restricted to previous conditioning, but is able to think, to plan, and to manipulate his own environment in ways much more dependent upon central activities than is true of other organisms. While many may accept this view, there has been some reluctance to utilize explanatory mechanisms involving mediational processes in the behavioural therapy area.

Ledwidge (1978), who reviewed the development of 'cognitive behaviour modification' (CBM), expressed concern over the trend toward CBM, and asked if it is warranted in terms of the effectiveness of CBM procedures such as cognitive restructuring (Goldfried and Goldfried 1975); self-instruction (Meichenbaum 1975); coverant control (Homme 1965); and rational emotive therapy (Ellis 1969). Studies using some of these techniques are discussed in Chapter 19 on self-control methods.

During the early stages of its development some of the criticisms of behaviour therapy were:

1. Behaviour therapy exerts control over (directs) the client. This control is anti-humanistic and bad (Bandura 1961).
2. The client has very little, if any, say in his treatment.
3. Symptom removal is dangerous (i.e. symptom substitution will occur).
4. There is a relative lack of good interpersonal relationships (i.e. an I–thou relationship) (Vingoe 1965).

There is now little doubt that these criticisms have been adequately dealt with and that only a very small proportion of people would subscribe to them today. The first sentence of criticism (1) above is true and, in fact, research by Greenspoon (1962) and Verplank (1955) suggests that control is exerted by all therapists, although it may differ in degree of explicitness or subtlety. However, the second sentence does not follow, since criticism (2) above is clearly false, in that most clients are able to accept or reject the treatment offered after a full explanation and rationale is given to them. In specific cases the client's informed consent may not be possible (see, for example, Lang and Melamed (1969) discussed in Chapter 5). The symptom substitution criticism has been quite adequately answered by Bandura (1969); Lazarus (1965); and Yates (1970*c*). Bandura, for example, provided a strong argument that neither the concept of symptom or mental disease were pertinent to behaviour dysfunction. He noted that 'the symptom substitution hypothesis could never be systematically tested because it fails to specify specifically what constitutes a "symptom", when the substitution should occur, the social conditions under which it is most likely to arise and the form that the substitute symptom will take'.

The major issues in behaviour therapy today include the following, which are obviously not mutually exclusive:

1. To what extent are the particular procedures subsumed under a behavioural therapy approach actually firmly based on principles of learning? Should CBM techniques be classed as behaviour therapy?
2. There is a lack of agreement among behavioural therapists about the necessary components of the procedures used in behaviour therapy. Thus, a second issue is, to what extent do behaviour therapists use surplus components in their treatment techniques? While some of these components may merely be a waste of the patient's and therapist's time, some may tend to neutralize the effective components of treatment.
3. A third major issue is: to what extent are factors such as expectancy, suggestion, and placebo important in treatment success as compared to the clearly specified components of a particular technique?

It seems clear that some behaviour therapists do not find a great deal of support for the assumption that all behaviour therapy methods are firmly based on principles of learning or laboratory research. For example, many would question the degree to which the cognitive techniques are based on learning or basic research.

In recent years CBM techniques have proliferated and, because of the emphasis on treating mediating variables rather than treating the actual maldaptive behaviour, there has been a great deal of concern about these techniques. Returning to Ledwidge's (1978) review, he noted in reference to the trend toward CBM, that it was important to question the effectiveness of these cognitive methods 'since a wholesale conversion to cognitive methods on insufficient evidence could rob behavior therapy of its distinctiveness and lead to the abandonment of the more traditional behavioural techniques, the success of which have afforded therapy the reputation it enjoys today.' Ledwidge noted that purely cognitive or behaviour therapists do not exist 'because we don't treat behaviors or cognition, we treat people'. He indicated that 'The labels *cognitive* or *behavioral* . . . when used to describe a treatment specify only the conscious focus of the therapist in his intervention, but do not rule out other modalities of intervention.'

Ledwidge pointed out that the main question he wishes to answer is: 'Which are more efficient at changing behavior—cognitive or behavioral techniques?' He used three sources of data to make this comparison. First, he found thirteen journal articles which allowed him to make a comparison between behavioural techniques and CBM techniques. The CBM technique in six of the studies was rational emotive therapy or cognitive restructuring; in three studies self-instruction training was used, while two studies used coverant-control techniques. The remaining two reports used anxiety-management training and re-education training for study habits and skills. It should be noted that the subjects used in all thirteen of these studies were college students and the behavioural pathology was limited to : test anxiety (4 cases); speech anxiety (2 cases); small animal phobics (3 cases); and one case each of college failure, smoking, obesity, and interpersonal anxiety.

An analysis of these thirteen studies showed that behavioural and cognitive techniques were equally effective. However, in view of the restrictions in client population and the limited degree of pathology treated, one may question the extent to which cognitive (mainly verbal) methods would be effective in a clinical population which included a greater variability in intellectual ability, and a more varied, multiple, and severe type of psychopathology.

Secondly, Ledwidge referred to the research in which techniques including behavioural and cognitive aspects had been compared, which tended to support a more behavioural approach. For example, the fact that *in vivo* confrontation of a feared situation tended to be superior to the desensitization technique, in which the feared situation was confronted only in the imagination (Barlow, Leitenburg, Agras, and Wincze 1969; Litvak 1969). In addition, the Bandura *et al.* (1969) study on snake phobics, discussed in some detail in the previous chapter, which compared participant modelling, symbolic modelling, and systematic desensitization techniques, found the participant modelling procedure to be far superior to the other approaches. It should be stressed that in the Bandura *et al.* study, the criterion of effectiveness was behavioural 'as the subjects became less fearful the experimenter gradually reduced his participation and control over the snake until subjects were able to hold the snake in their laps without assistance, to let the snake loose in the room and retrieve it, and to let it crawl freely over their bodies.'

The third source of data used by Ledwidge was the social–psychological research which did not support the hypothesis that consistent attitude change could come about through cognitive approaches. Rather, the research suggested that if the therapist changed behaviour first, then a change in feelings and attitudes was likely to follow. Ledwidge found that 'comparisons of the cognitive variants of various behaviour therapy procedures with their behavioral counterparts have shown that the more cognitive the technique, the less effective it is; and research in other areas of psychology has indicated that attitudes and perceptions are altered by changes in behavior.'

Ledwidge concluded that he would prefer that the term *cognitive therapy* be used for CBM procedures. In this way should cognitive therapy be found no more effective than traditional psychotherapy, the good reputation of behaviour therapy would be preserved. While Ledwidge's conclusions suggested that behavioural techniques are more effective, he was careful to point out that the relative effectiveness of CBM and behaviour therapy could not be adequately judged until these techniques were used with more clinical populations.

The exigencies of the clinical situation lead many behaviour therapists to use a 'treatment package' in helping their clients, and while these 'package treatments' may be successful (Shepherd and Durham 1977), it is usually impossible to conclude which components of the package were the active ingredients of the mix.

Factors such as expectancy and suggestion have been specifically varied in a number of studies whose intent is to determine the effective components of a treatment package. Therefore, the second and third issued indicated on p. 296 will be discussed together.

Although controlled analogue studies are important in establishing the effectiveness of a specific technique, there remains the question of the degree to which generalization of the results of these studies to clinical populations can be expected. While Paul (1969) found support for the effectiveness of systematic desensitization, most of the well-controlled studies involved students as clients. Lazarus (1969), some of whose research was discussed by Paul (1969), noted that 'most controlled studies of systematic desensitization (except student volunteers as opposed to clients or patients seeking therapy of their own accord) are very disappointing'. He concluded that all in all his former enthusiasm for desensitization techniques had diminished in view of the higher number of relapses that his follow-ups had unearthed. Marks (1969) also questioned the efficacy of systematic desensitization, believing that its usefulness in a psychiatric population was limited. The point made by Lazarus is a particularly important one. The vast majority of studies of behaviour therapy and CBM have involved students whose problems are relatively minor. For example, anxieties associated with speech; small-animal phobias; test or examination anxiety, etc. These studies are hardly comparable to studies involving clinical populations, in which the particular phobic states or other conditions seriously interfere with the life of the patient. Unfortunately, many of these analogue studies have been used to support the point of view of a particular behaviour therapist and, therefore, it is especially important when reading the literature to note whether or not an analogue study is being reported. The degree to which the subjects used in a study are representative of a clinical population must be considered in drawing conclusions about the efficacy of a particular technique.

In regard to the components of a particular treatment package, one of the problems has been the degree of procedural variation used in studies which purport to use the same technique. Paul (1969) summarized the variation in reference to the earlier systematic desensitization studies. He noted that a careful definition of procedures was of major importance, since the procedures define the independent variables. Yates (1975) pointed out that different therapists had found systematic desensitization to be effective regardless of: (1) the presence or absence of relaxation; (2) the use or non-use of a graded presentation of hierarchy items; (3) whether the anxiety associated with a particular hierarchy item was reduced or not before moving on to the next hierarchy item; and (4) whether spaced or massed trials were used. Some of the reports supporting Yates's conclusions are Farmer and Wright (1971) on relaxation; Cohen (1969); McGlynn (1973), and Suinn, Edie, and Spinelli (1970) on graded presentations of anxiety items; Miller and Nawas (1970) on the lack of the necessity of reducing the anxiety associated with a particular item before going on to the next one, and Suinn, Edie, and Spinelli (1970) on the massed trials as opposed to spaced trials issue. Thus, according to Yates, not one of the specific components of systematic desensitization has been found to be necessary. However, before over-generalizing this conclusion, the client population—including the limited type and severity of psychopathology upon which this conclusion is based—must be taken into account.

Wilkins (1971) concluded that the only necessary component of the systematic desensitization technique was instructed imagination and that the effectiveness of the procedure may be related to expectation, feedback, training in attention, and to various social variables. For an extended discussion of Wilkins's ideas regarding the important (i.e. active) components in the systematic desensitization package, the interested reader is referred to Wilkins (1972, 1973, 1974, 1976); Wilkins and Domitor (1973); and Esse and Wilkins (1978). McReynolds and Tori (1972), who compared systematic desensitization and relaxation in the treatment of phobic college students, noted that their results suggested that the previously 'demonstrated' superiority of systematic desensitization over relaxation treatments may result from general behaviour change influences rather than specific treatment procedures. They recommended further investigation of placebo and related phenomena in desensitization. A later study on the efficacy of systematic desensitization (McReynolds, Barnes, Brooks, and Rehagan 1973) determined that a 'compelling attention–placebo control treatment' was as effective as systematic desensitization in reducing subclinical fears of harmless snakes. Emmelkamp (1974) reviewed the literature on client expectations in both systematic desensitization and flooding and concluded that expectation played an important part in both techniques.

Finally, Lick and Bootzin (1975) after reviewing expectancy factors in the treatment of fear, concluded that instructions constructed to induce expectancies that treatment would be effective as well as placebo manipulations, could result in significant 'treatment' effects. The part played by non-specific variables in many treatment techniques is considerable, as we have noted. However, according to Foreyt and Hagen (1973) the role which these non-specific factors played in many newly-developed techniques remained to be established. They assessed the degree to which a placebo control (suggestion) technique would be effective as compared to a covert sensitization procedure in treating obese college students. The change in the palatability of favourite foods for both groups was found to be greater than that found in a control group. However, no significant difference was found between the two 'treatment' groups. Foreyt and Hagen thus concluded that the reported effectiveness of covert sensitization is a function of the client's expectations as opposed to a conditioning process.

On the basis of the above discussion of some of the research on the effectiveness of non-specific variables, such as expectation, suggestion, and placebo, it must be concluded that it is highly likely that such factors are as important in behaviour therapy as elsewhere. However, rather than being unaware of the degree of their importance they deserve further study, so that actual placebo instructions may be maximized as treatment variables in their own right.

What, then, may we conclude regarding behavioural therapy?

1. It seems that behaviour therapists are quite varied in their orientations. Some believe their therapeutic endeavours are firmly based on laboratory work and the established principles of learning, while others (e.g. Lazarus 1961) are willing to bring ideas into their clinical work which have no demonstrated basis in experimental research. This diversity is not necessarily inimical to the development of behaviour therapy, although the concern expressed by Ledwidge (1978) and Wolpe (1976*a*, *b*) must be seriously considered.
2. It is surprising that, with all the criticisms aimed at behaviour therapy, particularly systematic desensitization, there is general agreement regarding its effectiveness. However, one should be aware that non-specific components of the treatment package may have contributed to this success.
3. There does seem to be increasing evidence that techniques which include an actual confrontation with the feared situation (i.e. *in vivo*

procedures) are more effective than techniques which emphasize the imagination of scenes and other cognitive techniques, particularly when treating clients in a clinical setting. There would seem to be great promise in modelling techniques, especially participant modelling. Bandura's (1977) new theory on self-efficacy, to a large extent based on the results of modelling procedures, is an encouraging sign.

The directions for further research in behaviour therapy should include the following:

1. There should be a greater involvement with clinical populations in addition to analogue work which has used college students, many of whom exhibit relatively minor complaints such as test anxiety, small-animal phobias, etc.
2. An evaluation of the non-specific factors in behaviour research, such as expectancy, suggestion, and placebo effect, should always be carried out. In other words, research designs should take these factors into account.
3. Thus, more concerted and integrated efforts might be made to answer many of the problems concerning the essential components of our behavioural and cognitive techniques.

17
Hypnosis

With thy rod of incantation
Charm my imagination.
John Gay: *Polly*, II, i.

Although during the past twenty-five years there has been a significant increase in hypnosis research, many mental health professionals still regard the concept of hypnosis as controversial and refrain from using hypnotic techniques in their clinical work. However, hypnosis research has led to a more reasonable approach in research design and in interpreting the results of this research. Sheehan and Perry (1976) noted that researchers were much more careful in their inferences than heretofore, and the 'once easy, sweeping generalizations of old are no longer viable'. The reader who is interested in hypnotic theory and research methodology should consult Sheehan and Perry's book in which six contemporary paradigms of hypnosis are discussed.

The controversy concerning hypnosis is to some degree related to the *state versus non-state* issue (Hilgard 1965) which was actively debated during the 1960s. However, later, Spanos and Barber (1974) expressed their opinion that there had been a convergence between the two views, and that both state and non-state researchers would in the future focus 'on the role of imaginal processes in hypnotic performance'. As indicated in Vingoe (1981) the accumulated research evidence is inconsistent with the concept of hypnosis as a *physiological* state. Frankel, Apfel, Kelly, Benson, Quinn, Newmark, and Malamaud (1979) noted that only 'altered perceptions and alterations in memory are currently conceptualized as essential aspects of hypnosis'. Hilgard (1975) provided an overview of hypnosis research carried out during the previous decade.

WHAT IS HYPNOSIS?

The term 'hypnosis' may be used to refer to a specific procedure (an induction), a set of procedures or phases which are included in a hypnosis session, or a 'state' or trance condition that the hypnotic subject is expected to be in after being exposed to a particular procedure. It is the author's view that hypnosis is best conceptualized as a psychological 'state' of heightened attention in which the subject is better able to focus upon suggestions made by the hynotist and to use his imagination to visualize and otherwise sense or feel aspects of stimuli or situations from the past, present, or future.

Since the late 1950s a number of scales which measure hypnotizability have been developed. Many of them, such as the well-standardized and valid Stanford scales: Stanford Hypnotic Susceptibility Scales SHSS: A and B (Weitzenhoffer and Hilgard 1959); and SHSS: C (Weitzenhoffer and Hilgard 1962) have been used for more experimental purposes. However, there has recently been a great deal of support for assessing hypnotic responsivity in the clinical situation, prior to treatment intervention. Frankel, *et al.* (1979) have recommended that hypnosis scales be more extensively used in the clinical setting. However, references to sleep should be omitted and shorter scales should be used. In reference to the use of shorter scales, Spiegel's Hypnotic Induction Profile (HIP) may be used by those who do not need the more extensive information provided by a multi-item scale. The HIP is discussed in some detail in Spiegel and Spiegel (1978), a text which has recently been reviewed by Vingoe (1980*b*). However, J. R. Hilgard and E. R. Hilgard (1979) have discussed the advantages of using a short *multi-item* hypnotic scale, and recommend the use of the Stanford Hypnotic Clinical Scale: Adult (SHCS: Adult) E. R. Hilgard and J. R. Hilgard (1975). This scale, although taking somewhat longer to administer than the 10-minute HIP scale, does not suffer from some of the disadvantages of single-item scales such as the HIP. The administration of the Stanford scales tend to divide the hypnosis session into four or five main phases. The hypnosis session in the clinical setting, in which a standardized hypnotic scale may or may not be used, may also be usefully divided into four or five phases. These phases are:

- Phase I Rapport—the establishment of a good interpersonal relationship with the client.
- Phase II (Optional) pre-induction task—application of suggestions prior to the induction.
- Phase III The induction procedure.
- Phase IV The assessment of the client's ability to perform various tasks after the hypnotic induction.
- Phase V The post-hypnotic enquiry.

Phase I

The importance of the rapport phase cannot be over-stressed. Most clients who are considering, or being considered for, hypnosis have many misconceptions about it. A significant proportion are anxious, and some may fear losing control over themselves, or are perhaps concerned lest they reveal more about themselves than they wish. It should be pointed out that the assessment of hypnotizability using the Stanford Scales does not involve any investigation into the private emotional life of the client (Weitzenhoffer and

Hilgard (1959). While the dangers associated with hypnosis have sometimes been overstressed (Kaim 1963; Marcuse 1959), a small proportion of college student subjects (approximately 3–5 per cent) report some undesirable after-effects, such as a slight headache or dizziness, a short-term lack of spontaneity or lethargy, and occasionally, a slight depressive effect. Obviously, in working with the disturbed patient certain fears may be exaggerated, or in contrast hypnosis may be regarded as a panacea for all problems. During the rapport phase, it is important to assess the client's attitudes and feelings towards hypnosis, as well as his expectations regarding its effects. While typically hypnosis can be induced successfully with the average college-student subject during a single session, it may be advisable when treating disturbed patients to postpone induction. Thus, the rapport phase may be comparatively long because of the client's exaggerated fears of losing control, a lack of trust in the hypnotist, and so on.

Phase II

While many of the hypnotic susceptibility scales include a pre-hypnotic task, this phase is optional in the clinical setting. The task often used is the postural-sway task in which the client is asked to imagine himself falling backwards or forwards. Whereas, the correlation between postural-sway and total hypnotizability scale is relatively low, some therapists may use postural-sway, or some other pre-hypnotic task, such as the Vividness of Visual Imagery Questionnaire (VVIQ) Marks (1973), as a predictor of hypnotizability.

Phase III

The induction procedure *traditionally* includes suggestions of lethargy, drowsiness, and sleep. The eye-fixation technique requires the client to focus on some object within his immediate environment and listen to what the hypnotist is saying. In general, as the induction proceeds, the client may be asked to focus his attention on certain muscles of his body, to listen to nothing else but the hypnotist's voice, and to let happen whatever will happen. In this way, if the client 'lets himself go' he will gradually experience what it is like to be hypnotized (Weitzenhoffer and Hilgard 1959). Many would agree that a traditional hypnotic induction has much in common with deep-relaxation procedures. However, hypnotic procedures may place a greater emphasis on the focussing of attention, which tends to lead to a heightened awareness of a restricted area of consciousness. More recently (Vingoe 1981) eye-fixation has been omitted and the patient is simply requested to close his eyes.

Phase IV

The main Stanford Scales include suggestions on carrying out various hypnotic tasks, such as *arm rigidity*, in which it is suggested that one of the client's arms will feel as rigid as a bar of iron (Weitzenhoffer and Hilgard 1959), or *positive hallucination*, in which the client is led to believe that another person is present, who wishes to ask him a number of questions (Weitzenhoffer and Hilgard 1962). *Amnesia* for everything that took place during the hypnotic induction and state may be suggested as well as a *post-hypnotic suggestion*. Both amnesia and post-hypnotic suggestion are assessed after the client returns to the 'non-hypnotic state' or during the enquiry. In a clinical setting, the patient may be tested on his ability to make a specific part of his body numb, to increase the temperature of his hands or to regress to a certain age.

Phase V

The enquiry is important in order to obtain the client's subjective impressions regarding his feelings and his state of consciousness and the degree to which certain ideas suggested to him were experienced as real.

Hypnosis as a psychological state

If hypnosis is a state, one may ask: What are the defining characteristics of this state? More than fifteen years ago Hilgard (1965) indicated that highly hypnotizable subjects exhibit the following main characteristics following induction:

(1) subsidence of the planning function (subject loses initiative);
(2) redistribution of attention (selective attention and inattention);
(3) availability of visual memories from the past, and heightened ability for fantasy production;
(4) reduction in reality testing and a tolerance for persistent reality distortion;
(5) increased suggestibility;
(6) role behaviour (subject is more readily able to play various roles);
(7) amnesia for what transpired within the hypnotic state.

Many of these characteristics are considered important in behaviour therapy. An additional factor, suggested in many induction procedures, is relaxation. Factor (3), a heightened ability for fantasy production, is particularly useful in cognitive procedures in which the client is required to imagine positively reinforcing or aversive-type scenes. Factor (6), increased facility in role playing, is obviously important in behavioural rehearsal and in assertive training. The factor most generally associated with hypnosis is that of suggestibility, which is assumed to be facilitated by the first two characteristics above: the loss of initiative by the hypnotic subject and the factor of selective attention. Both of these characteristics tend to increase the ability of the hypnotic subject to 'tune-in' to what the hypnotist is suggesting, and to carry out these suggestions both during and after the trance. However, research has shown that the degree to which suggestions are enhanced following a hypnotic induction has been over-estimated. Factor (4), reduction in reality testing, is clearly useful in the facilitation of the subject's cognitive or imaginative activity in which suggestions may be made which are at variance with the present objective reality situation. While there is much controversy over the nature of hypnotic amnesia, many clinicians suggest post-hypnotic amnesia to their clients, since it is thought that post-hypnotic suggestions will be more readily followed if the client is unaware that suggestions have been made. Since spontaneous amnesia cannot be guaranteed, suggestions to the effect that the client will probably have difficulty remembering what has taken place during the trance state may be made. Clearly, memories which have been revived under hypnosis may be quite upsetting for the client. If this is the case, it may be considered best to suggest amnesia, whether or not post-hypnotic suggestions are made.

MEASUREMENT OF HYPNOTIC SUSCEPTIBILITY

It is clear that hypnotic-type procedures have a long history (Pattie 1967). During the nineteenth century there were attempts to measure the 'depth' of hypnosis (Hilgard 1967). In recent years, the greatest amount of work on the measurement of hypnosis has come from Hilgard's Stanford laboratory (Hilgard 1965, 1967). After finding previous scales of hypnotic susceptibility inadequate for various reasons, the Stanford Hypnotic Susceptibility Scale, Forms A and B (SHSS: A and B), (Weitzenhoffer and Hilgard 1959) was developed. These scales were developed for experimental purposes as two equivalent forms. The (SHSS: A and B) and the later Stanford Hypnotic Susceptibility Scale; Form C (SHSS: C), Weitzenhoffer and Hilgard (1962) have been found to be quite reliable and valid measures of hypnotic susceptibility. A total of 12 points is possible on the main Stanford Scales. Considering a high score to be 8–12, a medium score to be 5–7, and a low score to be 0–4, the original Stanford normative data indicate that approximately 25 per cent are highly hypnotizable, 30 per cent moderately hypnotizable, and 45 per cent hypnotizable to a low degree.

The norms for the induction associated with the SHSS: A and B indicate a mean score for 533 college student subjects of 5.62 on these 12-point equivalent scales. Clinicians are interested in the distribution of hypnotizability in psychotics, neurotics, and other patient groups. Table 17.1 presents the results of some of the research concerning the hypnotizability of various groups.

Unfortunately, little objective data on the hypnotizability of neurotic patients is available. Weitzenhoffer (1953) noted that 'If we define neuroticism in terms of the results of a standard psychiatric examination, then the evidence strongly favours the conclusion that neurotics are more suggestible than normal individuals.' There are no SHSS norms available on a neurotic

TABLE 17.1
HYPNOTIZABILITY OF NORMALS, NEUROTICS, AND PSYCHOTICS

N	*Scale*	*Mean*	*Standard deviation*	*Group*	
533	SHSS: A	5.62	3.27	Normal students	Hilgard (1967)
24	SHSS: A, B, or C	8.08	2.12	Phobics	
	or				Frankel and Orne
24	HGSHS: A	6.08	2.98	Smoking controls	(1976)
25	SHSS: A	7.64	—	Acute female schizophrenic	Kramer and Brennan (1964)
15	SHSS: A	6.53	2.42	Chronic females w/o brain damage	Vingoe and Kramer (1966)
56	French translation SHSS: A	4.80	1.84	Psychotic male w/o brain damage	Lavoie, Sabourin and Langlois (1973)

population. Recently Frankel (1976) and Spiegel and Spiegel (1978) have stressed the importance of relating hypnotic responsivity to diagnosis. Frankel and Orne (1976) have suggested that phobic patients obtain significantly higher hypnotizability scores compared to a control group of smokers presenting for the elimination of the smoking hàbit. Both groups of patients were highly motivated for hypnotic treatment. The mean hypnotizability score of 8.08 for the phobic patients was significantly higher than for the smoking controls. These results with phobics need to be replicated. In addition, obtaining analogous data on other neurotic groups would be helpful.

In reference to the hypnotizability of psychotic patients, Kramer and Brennan (1964) using the SHSS: A, found a mean hypnotizability of 7.64 using 25 female acute schizophrenic patients, in contrast to the mean of 5.62 reported for Stanford students. A number of questions were raised regarding this unexpected result. The two main questions raised were: (a) did the medication received by these patients facilitate the hypnotic induction? and (b) did the fact that both Kramer and Brennan, who were respectively ward psychologist and ward psychiatrist and were in a position to recommend special treatment and privileges for these patients, influence their response to the various suggestions? The study by Vingoe and Kramer (1966) attempted to answer these questions by hypnotizing patients who were subjects in a double-blind study regarding the effects of phenothiazines. The hypnotist was not a member of the ward treatment team. While uncooperativeness and other attrition problems reduced a potential pool of 60 subjects to 15 who completed the SHSS: A, it was possible to conclude that phenothiazines did not facilitate the induction of hypnosis. In addition, it could be concluded that of 60 randomly selected chronic psychotic patients, 15 were fairly hypnotizable, 12 to a medium or better level. Table 17.1 shows that the final group of 15 subjects obtained a mean score of 6.53 on the SHSS: A. In terms of the number of subjects, random selection from a chronic psychotic population, and the procedures used, the study carried out by Lavoie, Sabourin, and Langlois (1973) is by far the best in this area. Lavoie and his colleagues used two objective observers as well as the hypnotist in an attempt to improve scoring procedures. The results, which may be seen in Table 17.1, indicate a somewhat lower mean score than that obtained by Vingoe and Kramer (1966). A mean score of 4.80 indicates a moderate level of hypnotic susceptibility. While this mean was found to differ significantly from the normal group's mean of 5.62, one can be optimistic regarding the use of hypnosis with psychotics, in that, as previous studies had shown, Lavoie *et al.* found that, as contrasted to normal subjects, a much higher percentage of psychotics obtained moderate hypnotizability scores. Table 17.1 shows the lower variability (standard deviation) found for the psychotic groups compared with normals.

In summary, while there is limited objective data on the hypnotizability of neurotic patients, it is felt that, by bearing in mind that the establishment and maintenance of rapport is essential, there may be good potential for using hypnosis as an aid in psychological treatment with this patient group. With more disturbed patients, if the therapist can be assured that the patient is in good contact with his environment as well as *en rapport* with the hypnotist, he can be optimistic that with selected patients hypnosis may be a useful procedure in the treatment or rehabilitation of both acute and chronic psychotic groups. However, Spiegel and Spiegel (1978) should be consulted for a different view on the hypnotizability of psychotics. Furthermore, Orne's (1979) caution that 'the relationship between hypnotizability and the likelihood of a positive response to therapeutic suggestions is by no means clear-cut' must still be taken into account.

Group hypnosis

In order to assess hypnotizability in a group situation the Harvard Group Scale of Hypnotic Susceptibility (HGSHS: A) (Shor and Orne 1962), based on the individually administered SHSS: A, was developed. Perhaps its most important use is in the selection of subjects for experimentation. Typically, however, one or more individual scales may then be used for more accurate selection. While it is best to test subjects in relatively small groups of six to eight people, one can test very large groups, if necessary, and save a great deal of effort and time. The administration of the Harvard Scale involves approximately the same procedure as in the individual hypnosis session, with adaptations to the group situation and takes, on average, 70 minutes. In the use of HGSHS: A, subjects report on their own responses to the suggestions made, rather than leaving the hypnotist to do the scoring for each individual. However, Bentler and Hilgard (1963) have obtained a highly significant correlation (0.89) between subject self-report on the

Harvard and the more objective hypnotist report in individual sessions using the SHSS: A. These results have been replicated in a Dutch sample (Vingoe 1974).

HYPNOSIS AS AN ALTERED STATE OF CONSCIOUSNESS

While not everyone would agree, a sizable proportion of those who carry out research or clinical work in the area of hypnosis would accept that hypnosis may be validly considered as an 'altered state of consciousness' (ASC). Ludwig (1966), defined an ASC 'as any mental state(s) induced by various physiological, psychological, or pharmacological manoeuvres or agents, which can be recognized subjectively by the individual himself (or by an objective observer of the individual) as representing a sufficient deviation in subjective experience or psychological functioning from certain norms for that individual during alert, waking consciousness'.

He discussed the production of ASC under five main categories, which are summarized in Table 17.2.

TABLE 17.2
FACTORS PRODUCING ALTERED STATES OF CONSCIOUSNESS

1. Reduction of exteroceptive stimulation and/or motor activity. Includes reduction of sensory input, . . . constant exposure to repetitive, monotonous stimulation.
2. Increase of exteroceptive stimulation and/or motor activity. Includes . . . excitatory mental states resulting primarily from sensory overload or bombardment.
3. Increased alertness or mental involvement. Mental states which appear to result primarily from focused or selective hyperalertness with resultant peripheral hypoalertness over a sustained period of time—prolonged vigilance, reading, writing, problem-solving, etc.
4. Decreased alertness or relaxation of critical faculties, includes passive state of mind, floating on water, etc.
5. Presence of somatopsychological factors. Included here are mental states primarily resulting from alterations in body chemistry or neurophysiology . . . may be deliberately induced or may result from conditions over which the individual has little or no control. Includes sleep-deprivation, dehydration, drug effects, narcolepsy, auras preceding migraine or epileptic seizures.

(Modified from Ludwig 1966)

It may be seen from this table that an ASC may be produced by psychological procedures which either increase or decrease the subject's level of alertness or arousal. While factors 1 and 4 in Table 17.2 are consistent with the components of the traditional hypnotic induction procedure, factors 2 and 3 seem, at first glance, to include activities or procedures that would be counter-productive in inducing a hypnotic state. However, a number of authors have referred to waking hypnosis or waking suggestibility. This type of suggestibility typically involves the giving of suggestions to subjects who are in the wake state and receive no hypnotic induction. An excellent review article in the area of waking suggestibility is provided by Evans (1967). More recently, Kratachvíl (1970) found that a high degree of suggestibility can be obtained during waking hypnosis.

Some authors have referred to an active hypnotic state or active hypnosis. Some more recent papers refer to hypnosis as involving a higher level of arousal than seems to have been characteristic of traditional hypnotic procedures. For example, Ludwig and Lyle (1964) used a method of hypnotic induction in which tension and alertness were stressed in contrast to suggestions of drowsiness, lethargy, and sleep. Ludwig and Lyle found that they were successful in inducing a trance state in drug-addict patients using an hyperalert procedure. Oetting (1964) recommended the use of alert hypnosis with students who experienced study difficulties. Liebert, Rubin, and Hilgard (1965) in a paired-associate learning study found that subjects obtained significantly fewer errors in learning, and learned the material more quickly, under an alerting instructions condition as compared to the condition of being exposed to a traditional hypnotic induction. Based on the instructions used in the Liebert *et al.* (1965) experiment, Vingoe (1968*a*) developed an alert induction procedure and a short scale referred to as the Group Alert Trance Scale (GAT). Preliminary results with this scale were presented in Vingoe (1968*b*). This procedure emphasized the maintenance of mind alertness in addition to body relaxation. No reference to sleep or sleep-like states was induced. A counterbalanced comparison of HGSHS: A and the GAT was reported in Vingoe (1973*a*). While it was found that the response to the Communication Inhibition item (shaking one's head for 'No') was significantly higher after the traditional (HGSHS: A) induction, the response on the post-hypnotic amnesia item was significantly higher after the alert procedure. Whereas a higher percentage of the subjects passed the post-hypnotic suggestion item after the GAT induction, this was not significantly higher than after the HGSHS: A procedure. As indicated by Vingoe (1975), it seems highly likely that the alert technique would be one of choice in those therapeutic techniques which emphasize cognitive processes such as thought-stopping, flooding, and other types of covert behaviour therapy. The last section of this chapter discusses the relationship between hypnosis and imaginative activity. Hilgard, Atkinson, and Atkinson (1975) suggested that the sleep metaphor, compared with the idea of greater alertness, is becoming increasingly more inappropriate.

The above discussion has been consistent with the idea of hypnosis as an ASC. However, many of the phenomena associated with hypnosis may be produced in the so-called weak state. One may speak of alert-hypnosis, and waking suggestion as well as hypnotic suggestion.

MODIFIABILITY OF HYPNOTIC SUSCEPTIBILITY

Whereas hypnosis is not contraindicated for patients low in hypnotic susceptibility, therapists find that patients exhibiting high susceptibility may be easier to treat, thus there has been a great deal of interest in determining if hypnotic susceptibility can be increased. While Hilgard considered hypnotizability as a reliable personality trait, this does not preclude the idea of maximizing hypnotizability. It may be that certain psychological factors in the individual patient serve to interfere with the expression of his potential on this dimension. Diamond (1974), who reviewed a large number of studies on the modifiability of hypnotizability, has shown that hypnotizability can be increased by various training procedures. For example, Engstrom, London, and Hart (1970) reported success in significantly increasing hypnotizability through training subjects to increase the period during which they manifested alpha rhythm. However, Hilgard (1975) has indicated that the degree of improvement is relatively limited. Supporting the stability of hypnotizability as a trait, Morgan, Johnson, and Hilgard (1974) used test–retest intervals of eight to ten years, with eighty-five subjects, and obtained a correlation of 0.60 between the two hypnotizability scores.

It has been suggested that drugs may facilitate hypnotic induction procedures, or that a specific drug might be as effective as an hypnotic induction in increasing a subject's level of suggestibility. However, Vingoe (1973*b*) concluded that while suggestibility may be increased by a few psychodelic-type drugs, there is no evidence that any drug increases hypnotizability, or indeed results in a greater change in suggestibility than a typical hypnotic induction. While the above experimental group studies suggest that hypnotizability can only be increased to a limited extent, the therapist treating an individual patient can determine whether there are any factors which could interfere with the full development of rapport, such as an unwillingness to trust the hypnotist, and remove or at least diminish these undesirable factors.

THE PREDICTION OF HYPNOTIZABILITY

Clinicians in particular would find it advantageous if they were able to predict a person's hypnotizability within a brief interval of time. In addition, the determination of personality variables or other factors related to hypnotizability would be useful from a theoretical point of view in order to further elucidate the nature of hypnosis. Weitzenhoffer (1957) has recommended the use of waking suggestions as predictors and indicated that the most frequently used predictor has been the highly reliable postural sway test. However, if predictions are simply based on passing or failing the postural sway task, then the predictability of total hypnotizability score will be poor. However, a recording device can be used by which the amount of sway is accurately measured, and it may be that the extent of sway will be found to be a good predictor of total hypnotizability.

Weitzenhoffer (1957) recommended the combined use of postural sway, hand clasping (finger lock), and eye-catalepsy suggestions in order to estimate the degree of hypnotizability. However, as indicated by Weitzenhoffer, Meares (1954) objected to the use of these predictors with patients, partly because the therapist must demonstrate an authoritarian attitude prior to the actual treatment which may be inappropriate and detrimental in some cases. Meares used a more subtle approach, assessing suggestibility during a physical examination (Weitzenhoffer 1957).

Many experimenters and clinicians have hypothesized that a good hypnotic subject would be someone who is extroverted, neurotic, or good in interpersonal relations, etc. However, in spite of a vast amount of research, the quest for a *specific* personality variable predictive of hypnosis has been largely unsuccessful (Hilgard 1965). To some degree attitudes towards hypnosis have been useful predictors of hypnotizability. Seven-point rating scales on (a) 'willingness to be hypnotized' and (b) 'scepticism toward the phenomena of hypnosis' were found to be significantly correlated with hypnotizability. Scepticism was the better predictor. When the 82 subjects were dichotomized into introverts and extroverts, it was found that the correlation between scepticism and hypnotizability for the extroverts ($N=55$) rose to -0.52, a moderately significant relationship. Thus, the lower the self-rating on scepticism, the higher the hypnotizability (Vingoe 1969).

J. R. Hilgard (1965, 1970) was interested in childhood experiences in subjects of varying hypnotizability and suggested that there were alternative pathways to hypnosis. The two main factors suggested were: (a) an adventuresome type; and (b) a fantasy-involvement type (e.g. persons highly involved in reading, music, religion, etc. had vivid imaginations). As indicated by Hammer (1972) in his review of J. Hilgard's (1970) book, a multiple correlation of various developmental factors with hypnotizability was 0.53. These factors, which were 'correlated with hypnotizability . . . were a childhood history of severe punishment, similarly of temperament to the parents of the opposite sex, and some aspects of a generally "normal" and "outgoing" personality'. In general, there would seem to be no simple quick method of predicting hypnotizability, although further research may be helpful. It is best not to 'rush into hypnosis' in that the development of rapport is essential for good results in the clinical setting.

SOME CLINICAL APPLICATIONS OF HYPNOSIS

This section will present some of the research on the clinical applications of hypnosis. Rather than presenting these research reports in terms of the particular technique used, this section will be divided into reports concerning the (a) recovery of forgotten memories; (b) use of hypnotic analgesia; and (c) use of hypnosis in behaviour therapy. However, I will first mention some other excellent articles and books which emphasize a more analytic or psychotherapeutic approach.

Milton H. Erikson has written exclusively in the area of clinical hypnosis and is well-known for his unique hypnotic techniques. Haley (1967) has written a book on Erikson's therapeutic approach including the use of hypnosis. Gill (1972) discusses hypnosis as an altered state, with particular emphasis on regression in the service of the ego. Gill also compares his point of view with the findings of J. Hilgard (1970) on personality and hypnosis. An interesting and lucid article on transference and counter-transference in hypnoanalysis is provided by Erika Fromm (1968). Frankel (1975), writing from an ego-psychological point of view, has published an interesting article on the use of trance involvement in coping with symptoms by substituting one kind of symptom for another. Frankel (1976) has also written a recent book on clinical hypnosis in which the nature and clinical usefulness of the trance experience is discussed. The recent book by Spiegel and Spiegel (1978) is a highly readable and informative text in which a good deal of emphasis is placed on the relationships between hypnotic responsivity and diagnosis. Finally, Gibbons (1979) provides a useful collection of hypnotic procedures which should be found helpful, especially to those of limited to moderate experience in using hypnotic-type techniques.

The recovery of forgotten memories

'Age regression' has been useful in the retrieval of forgotten information, which may be associated with a traumatic event in the individual's past. Arvid Ås (1962), a Norwegian at Stanford University, reported an interesting case of the recovery of a forgotten language through hypnotic age regression. The subject, an 18-year-old male freshman at Stanford, was born in Helsinki, Finland, but the language spoken in the home was Finnish-Swedish. He moved to America when he was 5 years old, and after he was 8 years old only English was spoken in the home. At 18, the subject's memory of events before 8–10 was remarkably poor. Any memories he had prior to 10 years of age were rather vague and he had forgotten all of his mother-tongue, except for a few words. The subject was a rather inhibited and introverted person, and on a pre-hypnosis test he obtained an extremely low score, but after age regression training, in which he was asked to imagine himself as much younger, he was significantly more successful. A person who was fluent in the Finnish-Swedish dialect used by the subject when he was a young child in Finland, was brought in and it was found that the student could, under hypnosis, both understand and speak in the forgotten language. In this particular case, a traumatic event was not associated with the failure to recall.

In Yugoslavia, Remic Miloš (1975) used hypnotic techniques with patients who had sustained cerebral injuries in an attempt to reduce or eliminate retrograde or anterograde amnesia. While in 7 of the 20 cases, residual amnesia appeared to be eliminated during the hypnotic state, this condition was not maintained after the hypnosis sessions.

Raginsky (1969) in Canada, and Schafer and Rubio (1978) in the United States, have worked with people, or in settings, in which the recall of forgotten memories might incriminate the client. Raginsky (1969) used hypnosis in working with an airline pilot involved in a crash. The pilot had sustained a cerebral concussion and retrograde amnesia of a few minutes duration.

Raginsky's aim was to compare the value of hypnotic recall with other methods such as psychiatric interviews, sodium pentothal injections, etc., which had been used unsuccessfully by well-qualified mental health workers over a period of two years, although Raginsky admits that these earlier methods may have facilitated the later successful hypnotic techniques. Raginsky first had the client hallucinate, under hypnosis, a 'terrifying and worrisome' situation followed by a 'very satisfying' scene. This procedure was found to be very helpful in aiding the hypnotist in the assessment of the stimuli or situations the client found highly fearful, and in determining the mode of defence used to counteract or avoid anxiety. A second technique, suggested by Fromm (1968), was to ask the client under hypnosis to imagine he was someone else, observing himself during the traumatic situation prior to the aircrash. This procedure 'a dissociation of the observing ego from the experiencing ego' was helpful in the retrieval of additional information. Raginsky was successful in aiding the pilot in his recall of what transpired during the interval of retrograde amnesia. The author provides an excellent discussion of the ethics concerning a situation in which information retrieved by a client may be self-incriminating and may lead to recommendations contrary to the client's expectations and wishes. In connection with the use of hypnosis in the recovery of crash details from a helicopter-pilot, Raginsky noted that the Civil Aeronautics Board was so impressed with hypnosis as a technique that in preference to using narcosynthesis, hypnosis would in future be the treatment of choice.

Schafer and Rubio (1978) reported their experience over a twelve-month period in using hypnosis with witnesses to a crime to obtain additional information which could be helpful in identifying the criminal or in leading to evidence obtained outside of hypnosis which leads to a conviction or an exoneration. These authors provide a number of case-studies in which hypnosis was extremely helpful in bringing a criminal to justice.

Finally, Hanley (1969) has discussed the use of hypnosis in the courtroom in cases of amnesia. Hanley referred to the controversy regarding this use of hypnosis by discussing a case of a lady on trial for the murder of her husband. The judge involved in the case disallowed any direct questioning of the defendant while she was hypnotized, but allowed the hypnotist to use post-hypnotic suggestion as an *aide memoire* after the trance-state. Hanley stressed that one must avoid too much publicity since this would make an objective evaluation of the use of hypnosis in the courtroom more difficult. An interesting court case concerning the potentiality of hypnosis in coercing subjects to engage in non-consenting sexual behaviour has recently been published by Perry (1979).

Hypnotic analgesia

Since the pain response may involve a large 'reaction-component' (see Chapter 6), suggestions applied to a patient while he is in the hypnotic state may be successful in a certain percentage of cases in reducing or eliminating the 'subjectively felt pain'. An example of experimental work on pain is provided by Lenox (1970), who induced ischaemic pain in eight subjects selected for high hypnotic susceptibility. The pain induction resulted in considerable increases in heart rate and systolic blood pressure, and subjective self-ratings of pain. During the second phase of the experiment suggested hypnotic analgesia was accompanied by low or zero pain state reports. These subjective reports were validated by the much lower measured heart rate and blood pressure changes. Lenox concludes that 'all of the variables taken together support the validity of hypnotic analgesia in selected Ss and imply that, in situations and Ss where it is applicable, hypnosis can be a highly effective method of controlling pain'. It should be noted that LeCron (1956) indicated that hypnotic analgesia may be used for major surgery in only 20 per cent of potential patients (cited by Melzack 1973).

In obstetrics, Rock, Shipley, and Campbell (1969) carried out a study of labour management using hypnotic techniques. The 40 untrained, volunteer patients during active labour were hypnotized using a 20-minute induction procedure. A control-group of patients received similar medical care and an equivalent amount of staff contact. The results showed that the hypnotized patients obtained greater pain relief and required less medication than the control-group. The authors concluded that, using only 45 minutes more with the hypnotic group than with the controls, the use of hypnosis with untrained patients in active labour could be carried out even in an adverse (noisy) environment, without particular difficulties.

Some interesting work using hypnotic and feedback techniques, separately or in combination, has been carried out in the treatment of headaches. These are discussed in the next chapter. Since space does not permit further discussion, the interested reader is referred to Dahinterova (1967), who related some of her experience in using hypnosis in treating burns; Marmer (1969), who reported on applications of hypnosis in anaesthesiology; Sacerdote (1970), who discussed pain control in malignant illness; and Zane (1966), who reported on hypnosis and ulcer pain.

Acupuncture and hypnosis

Acupuncture is an ancient Chinese surgical procedure in which fine needles are placed into various body sites according to acupuncture charts. After the needles are placed into the body, they may be twirled around vigorously, or alternatively electric current may be passed through them.

While, at first glance, acupuncture may be perceived as a physical technique, a considerable number of professionals have espoused a psychological or partial psychological explanation for its effectiveness. Some have explained its effectiveness in terms of suggestion or hypnosis (Kroger, 1972*a*, *b*). Kroger noted that acupuncture is a form of hypnosis. He pointed out that the majority of patients who undergo acupuncture in China are also treated with chemical analgesia such as morphia. Therefore, one is unable to determine the effect of acupuncture as a separate independent variable. Kroger (1972*a*) carried out major surgical procedures, such as caesarian hysterectomy and thyroidectomy, with hypnosis as the sole anaesthesia. The surgical procedures to be used were rehearsed when acupuncture was used (Dimond 1971), and when using hypnosis as the sole anaesthetic. Kroger noted that the rehearsal 'of the entire surgical procedure with the patient in the deep hypnotic state apparently blocks the neurophysiological pathways involved in the transmission of pain impulses.' In commenting on the patient's ability to respond to acupuncture, Kroger (1972*b*) noted that the 'ceremonial or ritualistic-like approach is a hypnotic procedure per se and mobilizes powerful auto-suggestive factors induced by prior indoctrinations. These motivate the patient's beliefs that acupuncture anaesthesia will be successful.'† Spiegel and Spiegel (1978) also interpreted acupuncture as hypnotic in nature and interestingly cited a number of studies which failed to find a superior effect for those patients stimulated at 'real' compared with those stimulated at 'placebo' points.

Melzack (1973) discussed acupuncture in terms of his gate-control theory of pain, finding it difficult to accept an hypnotic interpretation. In support of his view he compared the 90 per cent surgical success reported for acupuncture anaesthesia to the 20 per cent reported success for hypnotic analgesia (LeCron 1956). Melzack (1973), while mentioning the wide use of chemical anaesthetic in connection with acupuncture surgery as indicated by Dimond (1971), tended to understate any effect it may have had. However, he did raise an important question, which, if answered positively, could be subsumed under a suggestion or hypnotic theory of acupuncture. Melzack asked whether faith in acupuncture was necessary for the method to work. Both Melzack and Kroger (1972*a*, *b*) would agree that a full explanation of acupuncture awaits further research. However, Kroger (1972*a*) was of the

†An interesting film: *Hypnosis as sole anaesthesia in Caesarean section*' may be obtained for appropriate audiences from Upjohn Ltd. This can be a useful aid to discussing the rituals which may be associated with hypnosis and acupuncture.

opinion that the specific 'factors reponsible for acupuncture anaesthesia are: the antecedent variables, such as the generalized stoicism of the Chinese, the ideological zeal, the evangelical fervor, the prior beliefs shared by the *acupuncteurists* and the patients, all compound belief and faith into conviction. Conviction of pain relief results in pain relief!'

Hypnosis and behaviour therapy

There have been a number of reports concerning the use of hypnotic techniques in behaviour therapy in the last decade (Dengrove 1973; Lazarus 1973; and Weitzenhoffer (1972).

While Weitzenhoffer (1972) felt that most behaviour therapists were unaware of the extent to which hypnotic techniques could be useful adjuncts in therapy, Lazarus (1971), not only recommended the use of hypnosis, but other imaginative-type procedures as well. Basically, Weitzenhoffer recommended that 'hypnotherapists' should become much more aware of the principles of learning, and that behaviour therapists should become much more aware of the potential value of using hypnotic techniques, which could be understood in terms of learning principles. A marriage between hypnosis and behaviour therapy (including its learning basis) was seen as mutually beneficial.

Dengrove (1973) discussed hypnosis as used in systematic desensitization and aversion therapy. Dengrove noted that treatment was facilitated through hypnosis by: (1) relaxing the client; (2) preparing the way for visual imagery to be used; and (3) making available techniques which were helpful in the management of more difficult patients. Dengrove indicated that hypnosis could accelerate the relaxation process and through suggestion, which was heightened in the hypnotic state, a signal might be taught to the client enabling him to enter the hypnotic state more quickly on future occasions. Dengrove suggested that the therapist could use time-distortion techniques and hypnotic dreams in helping the client to imagine being in a previously anxiety-evoking situation and being able to do things which previously he felt unable to do because of the high degree of anxiety elicited by the situation. Throughout the pleasant and relaxed state of hypnosis the anxiety previously evoked by the feared situation is counteracted. The use of post-hypnotic suggestion in facilitating the effect of aversion therapy may be helpful. If one considers that suggestibility and the ability to vividly imagine pleasant or unpleasant scenes may be heightened through hypnosis, then for the interested and motivated client, hypnosis may be the technique of choice as compared to relaxation.

Lazarus (1971) made wide use of hypnosis and other imaginative techniques in the clinical setting. Lazarus (1973) felt that one must ask specific questions about the use of hypnosis. He noted that rather than asking 'Is hypnosis effective?' one needed to ask: 'Effective for whom, for what, and under what particular conditions?' Lazarus was particularly interested in those clients who requested hypnosis. He wished to determine if 'behavior therapy techniques are enhanced by the addition of hypnotic suggestions in clients who request to be hypnotized' (Lazarus 1973). Realizing that a certain proportion of those who requested hypnosis might perceive hypnosis as a panacea or a magical solution, Lazarus hypothesized that those clients who believed that hypnosis would help them were in possession of 'a self-fulfilling prophesy that can be advantageously activated'. Twenty clients who had requested hypnosis were assigned either to a relaxation group or a hypnosis group, and six other clients neutral to hypnosis and relaxation, were exposed to both procedures in counterbalanced order. Clients who received the hypnosis treatment were instructed to think the word 'hypnotism' as they exhaled, and the expression 'hypnotic relaxation' was used rather than 'relaxation' in the relaxation group. With this exception, the instruction for the hypnosis and relaxation conditions were essentially the same. Lazarus (1973) found that the six 'neutral' clients reported no difference between the two procedures. However, it was found that those ten clients who were exposed to hypnosis after requesting it, reported deeper levels of relaxation, more vivid images, and greater anxiety-relief than their counterparts treated by regular relaxation. Lazarus also reported that, in general, therapeutic techniques were enhanced after the 'hypnotic relaxation' as compared to the 'relaxation' condition. Lazarus was careful to point out that he considered these findings as clinical impressions rather than experimental evidence.

CRITICAL DISCUSSION

This final section to the chapter is restricted to a discussion of the role of hypnosis in (1) producing deep relaxation and (2) facilitating visual imagery.

In comparison to relaxation procedures, hypnosis is seen by many as the technique of choice in behaviour therapy, in that, not only is a hypnotic induction reputed to be better than relaxation procedures in developing a state of deep relaxation, but it results in a 'state' in which the individual is better able to use his imagination in fantasy production and in visualizing scenes from an anxiety hierarchy.

What evidence can be provided in support of these assumptions? Paul (1969*a*, 1969*b*); Paul and Trimble (1970) in a series of articles have compared hypnosis and relaxation effects.

The role of hypnosis in producing deep relaxation

Paul (1969*a*) stressed the communality of hypnotic-induction procedures and the abbreviated relaxation typically employed in systematic desensitization. Citing Gill and Brenman (1959), Paul referred to those factors which hypnotic induction procedures tended to have in common, and which were also found in relaxation training. These common factors were:

(1) extensive limitations on sensory intake;
(2) limitations on bodily activity;
(3) a restriction of attention;
(4) a narrow and monotonous form of stimulation; and
(5) an alteration in the quality of bodily awareness.

Paul was interested in the differential effects of progressive relaxation training and hypnotic suggestion. Sixty female university students served as subjects and were assigned to one of three groups; (a) abbreviated relaxation training; (b) hypnotic induction, and (c) self-relaxation control. The baseline and criterion measures used included a self-report anxiety scale, heart-rate, respiratory-rate, skin conductance, and forearm-muscle tension.

Two experimental sessions, one week apart, were used in the study. The progressive relaxation procedures involved an alternate tensing and release procedure first developed by Jacobsen (1938).

While the hypnotic induction used was developed by Kline (1953), a well-known hypnotist, who used 'hypnotic imagery', it was also described as 'an "all-purpose" relaxation induction for initial training of clinical students'. The arm-immobilization item from the SHSS (Weitzenhoffer and Hilgard 1959) was used as a challenge test.

Finally, the self-relaxation control group were asked to sit quietly for fifteen minutes with their eyes closed. They were admonished, however, not to fall asleep. The two experimental groups were asked to practise relaxation and imagery respectively at home twice daily for fifteen minutes between experimental sessions.

The results verified that the three groups were well matched on the anxiety and the four physiological measures prior to treatment. Paul (1969*a*) noted that over each session, the relaxation group consistently produced a highly significant average change from the pre-treatment baseline levels in the direction of greater relaxation. The relaxation subjects showed 'significantly greater decreases in heart rate and tonic muscle tension than hypnotic suggestion'. Paul stressed that these variables were not under direct voluntary control. This was found for both sessions. Skin conductance was not used in the analysis, since it did not show significant treatment effects. While the hypnotic-suggestion group when compared with the control group were found to have significant decreases only in anxiety and respiration rate in the first session; it was found that the second session produced significant change for the hypnosis as compared to the control group on all variables. Paul noted:

> Thus it seems clear that both hypnotic suggestion and relaxation training did produce significant cognitive and physiological changes within the brief training sessions, and that relaxation training resulted in effects over and above those attributable to hypnotic suggestion.

In attempting to find out the components of the treatment techniques that were effective in the study, Paul suggested that 'Restricted attention, narrow and monotonous stimulus input, and suggested ease of response . . . [and] either direct or indirect suggestions of relaxation, are sufficient to alter the cognitive experience of distress, while the results of physiological measures suggest that the differential content of stimulus input and attentional focus were of prime importance in the alteration of somatic responses'.

Paul concluded his comments regarding the role of hypnosis by noting that his findings were consistent with 'the interpretation of hypnotic effects within a learning framework in which suggestions may first lead to voluntary compliance, but, as restricted attention results in operator-emitted stimuli becoming more central and relevant, previously learned responses would be more likely elicited upon continued presentation of the verbal stimuli'.

Paul (1969*b*) also determined the relative effectiveness of the two experimental treatment procedures of relaxation training and hypnotic suggestion discussed above in inhibiting physiological response or arousal to stressful imagery. Both techniques were found to be effective in this regard.

Mather and Degun (1975) also compared the effect of hypnosis and relaxation. Subjects underwent a counterbalanced relaxation and hypnosis session. Suggestions to have a specific dream, awaken, and carry out a particular action were made in each condition, ten minutes and twenty minutes after the beginning of a session. Mather and Degun found that significantly more suggestions were carried out in trance than during the relaxation condition. However, no differences in heart-rate between conditions were found. There were significant changes in attitude towards hypnosis after experiencing the hypnotic condition. Unfortunately, their relaxation procedure was limited to asking the subject to 'lie on the couch and relax', as compared to an hypnotic induction of five minutes. Therefore, their results are much more limited than those of Paul (1969*a*, *b*). Considering this limitation the results regarding heart-rate do not conflict with Paul's (1969*a*) conclusions regarding the relative effect of relaxation and hypnosis on heart rate.

The role of hypnosis in facilitating vividness of imagery

One of the other factors of major importance in many behavioural techniques is the ability to visualize a scene, to utilize one's imagination. Clearly, systematic desensitization, flooding in imagination, covert sensitization, and thought stopping are techniques which require the client to make use of his imagination. Leaving aside for a moment the anxiety associated with many of the scenes that clients are asked to visualize, it has been found both clinically and psychometrically that there are individual differences in people's ability to utilize such imagery (Sheehan 1967). Investigators have anticipated that certain traits or conditions might be associated with a person's visualization abilities (Marks 1973). One of these traits has been hypnotizability (Hilgard 1965). Sheehan (1972) has reviewed the work in the area which has generally resulted in significant, although relatively low, correlations between hypnotic susceptibility and vividness of imagery. J. Hilgard's (1965, 1970, and 1974) work on imaginative involvement and hypnosis has already been referred to above and lends support to this idea. If a person's vividness of imagery is significantly related to his hypnotizability, then those who demonstrate high hypnotizability would be expected to respond more readily to treatment techniques in which imagery is an important component. In fact, some investigators suggest that regardless of degree of hypnotizability, a hypnotic induction may facilitate consequent vividness of imagery.

Starker (1974), after criticizing previous research, set out to determine the effect of a hypnotic induction on visual imagery. Thirty-six subjects were placed into one of three groups on the basis of their attitudes and expectations regarding experiments, hypnosis, psychodelics, and unusual experiences. Unfortunately, not even the name of the questionnaire, let alone reliability and validity data, is mentioned. Three groups of twelve subjects were used, each consisting of four subjects with high, four with medium, and four with low attitudes, as indicated above. The three groups were categorized as hypnotic induction, task motivation, and control. The subjects received instructions regarding rating their visual images on a 5-point vividness scale. Two lists of 15 words were used in a counterbalance design. The hypnosis, task motivation instruction and control 'task' (listening to music) were all tape recorded. Starker was mainly interested in the differences between pre- and post-vividness of imagery ratings as related to the specific procedures. Analysis of covariance regarding the ratings failed to yield significance. Starker did point to some of the possible limiting factors in his design, such as the small number of subjects, the use of unselected subjects, etc. He concluded that 'one cannot attempt to read specific conclusions about the experience of a "good hypnotic subject" in a vastly different interpersonal context, e.g., hypnotherapy'.

Interestingly enough, if one analyses the data of the 'high attitude' group in Starker's Table 1, one obtains the following mean imagery scores: hypnosis 5.75, task motivation 1.25, and control 0.25. While the lack of information regarding the attitude scale used has already been mentioned, Starker did report that it was significantly correlated with the modified Bett's Vividness of Imagery Scale (Sheehan 1967), and response to this scale may be related to hypnotizability (Sheehan 1972). In any case, these means are suggestive.

't Hoen (1978) selected subjects for both visualizing ability and hypnosis and was interested in determining if highly hypnotizable subjects 'would learn more words from a list in a specified time under imagery mediated instructions than the low hypnotizable subjects.'

Highly hypnotizable subjects were assumed to be good visualizers and it was predicted that good visualizers as compared to poor visualizers would succeed better with low imagery words than high imagery words. Twenty-eight subjects, half of whom were highly hypnotizable and half of low hypnotizability on the SHSS were used. Subjects were also selected on the basis of Marks's (1973) Vividness of Visual Imagery Questionnaire for high or low visualizing ability. The correlation between these two scales for the 110 subjects who formed the subject pool for this study was 0.28, which was statistically significant. 't Hoen's selection resulted in four subgroups: (1) one high in both hypnotizability and visualizing ability; (2) one low on both variables; and (3) two groups high on one variable and low on the other. The criterion task involved the learning of two lists of paired-associates. The stimulus and response words were of high or low imagery or concreteness respectively. 't Hoen gave *joy* as an example of a high-imagery word and *charlatan* as an example of a high concrete word. Thus, the paired-associates were categorized into four groups. Imagery-mediation instructions wcrc given to maximize recall.

The results indicated that while there was a non-significant main effect for hypnotizability, the interaction between hypnotizability and imagery-

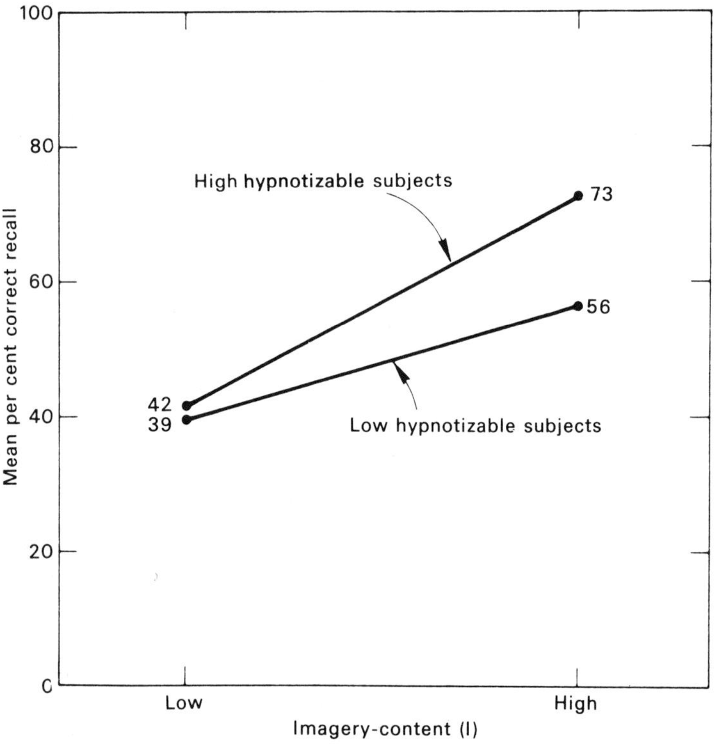

Fig. 17.1. Mean per cent correct responses by subjects with high and low response to hypnotism to words varied in imagery-content (I). (From 't Hoen 1978.)

content of the words was significant. Figure 17.1 shows this interaction graphically.

A significant interaction between hypnotizability and concreteness-content was not found.

In summary, the highly hypnotizable subjects recalled the high imagery words better than those low in hypnotizability. The advantage hypothesized that good visualizers would learn more low-imagery words was not found. It would seem then that hypnotizability is significantly related to visualizing ability, as indicated in 't Hoen's (1978) well-controlled study. Starker (1974) failed to measure hypnotizability, and his data on those subjects with highly positive attitudes towards hypnosis and enjoyment of unusual experiences tends to be consistent with the results later obtained by 't Hoen. A more extensive survey of research on imaginative involvement and hypnotizability may be found in Sheehan (1979).

SUMMARY

In summary, while there is some doubt regarding the best technique to use in producing deep relaxation, there does seem to be an advantage in using hypnosis to facilitate visual imagery. Again, while the cautions mentioned earlier in terms of using hypnosis with disturbed clients must be taken into account, it would seem reasonable to use hypnosis with the client who exhibits a belief in its effectiveness. From the strictly clinical point of view whether a defined specific component of treatment is effective or a vague 'placebo effect' may not be considered important.

We turn now to the chapter on biofeedback, which includes a number of research reports in which hypnosis and biofeedback are combined in a particular treatment package.

18
Biofeedback

There is no joy but calm
Tennyson: *The Lotus-Eaters*

Feedback is a naturally occurring phenomenon and is an integral process in biological systems. It is intimately related to the concept of homeostasis or physiological balance. Should the body become too cold, for example, it responds by behaving in such a way as to increase body temperature. Should an endocrine gland, such as the thyroid, produce an over-abundance of its particular hormone, again the *healthy* organism will respond appropriately. Figure 18.1 shows the feedback system between the pituitary and thyroid glands which ensures in the healthy organism that an over-abundance of thyroxine is not produced.

While we are not conscious of the normal, automatically controlled feedback which occurs in the endocrine system, there are some kinds of feedback

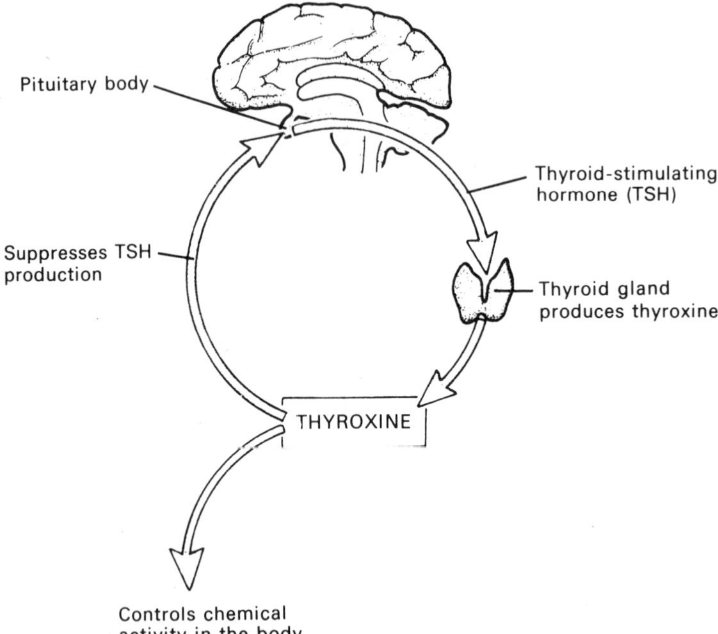

Fig. 18.1. Feedback system between the pituitary and thyroid glands. (From Mackean 1973.)

which we find more noticeable. For example, in learning to serve in tennis one receives proprioceptive feedback through the muscles, together with visual information as to one's performance in serving. One is then able to learn to relate the position of the ball when it hits the court with one's muscular-skeletal activity, and to make the necessary corrections.

Many physiological changes take place in the organism, particularly small changes, of which the person is unaware. However, when malfunctioning occurs, as in a person who demonstrates essential hypertension, and whose blood pressure therefore tends to become elevated, it would be helpful if that person could detect relatively small changes in his blood pressure. If this were possible, then the sufferer might be able to modify his physiological functioning, especially if the malfunctioning were detected at an early stage of its development.

During the past two decades a great deal of research has been undertaken to help man gain control over various bodily processes. To a large extent this has been possible through the development of sensitive electronic monitors. The procedures which have been used in this type of research have been termed biofeedback procedures.

Biofeedback procedures

Biofeedback is defined by Birk (1973) as 'the use of monitoring instruments (usually electrical) to detect and amplify internal physiological processes within the body, in order to make this ordinarily unavailable internal information available to the individual and literally to feed it back to him in some form'. Feedback studies have been carried out with cortical variables such as alpha rhythm, and autonomic variables such as heart rate, blood pressure, skin temperature, etc. The medically orientated person in particular can readily imagine the clinical significance of techniques by which a patient may be able to control such variables. Kamiya's (1969) seminal report on the feedback of alpha rhythm attracted many investigators to this area of research. He was succcessful, via feedback procedures, in increasing the preponderance of alpha rhythm in human subjects. A prepondernace of alpha rhythm is accepted as indicative of a state of relaxed wakefulness. However, alpha rhythm is also seen during REM sleep (see Chapter 7).

Budzynski (1973) listed three goals for biofeedback training:

(1) the development of increased awareness of the relevant internal physiological functions or events;
(2) the establishment of control over these functions; and
(3) the transfer or generalization of that control from the training site to other areas of one's life.

Autonomic feedback

The autonomic functions of the organism, such as blood-pressure level and heart-rate, have been typically referred to as *involuntary* in nature. However, psychologists and others have been led to reconsider this concept of the involuntary nature of certain bodily functions. Some 'conditioning' experiments in animals led to the belief that some organisms were able to control such autonomic parameters as heart-rate, blood-pressure, and salivation. This work, together with further studies with human subjects (Blanchard and Young 1974; Schwartz 1973) have led to the consideration of biofeedback techniques in helping patients to learn to control their autonomic functioning. People who exhibit cardiac arrhythmias, essential hypertension, Raynaud's disease, etc., may be helped by training in the control of heart-rate, blood-pressure, skin temperature, etc. (Blanchard and Miller 1977).

In addition, biofeedback techniques might help neurotic patients by teaching them to control their heart-rate, respiration-ratc, swcating response (galvanic skin response), etc., which are all affected during emotional states. It may be remembered that one characteristic of a neurotic individual is his tendency to over-react in an emotional (thus autonomic) sense. In addition, Lader (1975) has shown that in the anxious (neurotic) individual, deviations from base-line of autonomic measures, such as heart-rate and galvanic skin reponse, are much slower or sluggish in their return to base-line level.

The above feedback studies required the human subject to modify the particular physiological function, while being given a visual or auditory indication of when he was meeting the criterion response, by decreasing heart-rate, decreasing blood volume, or increasing hand temperature, etc. The visual signal may vary in brightness or extent, while the auditory signal may vary in frequency or loudness. Visual and auditory signals may also be used in combination. Lang (1970) reported that he had taught subjects to control the variability of their heartbeat by using a screen upon which a light stimulus was placed, whose position indicated if the particular subject was meeting the criterion of a one-second inter-beat interval. If the interval was less than, or more than, this requirement, then the light moved to the left or right respectively. With practice, subjects became quite skilled at this task.

Cortical (alpha) feedback

While there had been some earlier work on the conditioning of the alpha rhythm, it was Kamiya's (1969) report on successfully training human subjects to increase percent-time alpha, together with the availability of more sophisticated electronic monitoring equipment, which led to the increased interest in the various electroencephalic rhythms measurable from electrodes placed on the surface of the scalp. Table 5.2, p. 106, present the main EEG waves of interest. Apart frm the work on sleep, discussed in Chapter 7, and some interest in theta rhythm (Budzynski 1976; Schacter 1976), the main interest in the biofeedback of cortical activity has been in alpha rhythm usually considered to be within the EEG range of 8–13 Hertz (c.p.s.) and 25–100 microvolts in amplitude.

The so-called alpha state is considered to be a state of relaxed wakefulness. Kamiya also related changes in mood to 'turning on alpha'. Usually, alpha rhythm is more easily demonstrated in the eyes-closed condition, generally attenuating when the eyes are opened, during visual and other sensory stimulation, and during focused attention. The three of the most frequent reports associated with turning alpha on are: (a) relaxation; (b) 'letting go'; and (c) floating. In contrast, three of the most frequent reports associated with keeping alpha off were: (a) being vigilant; (b) static, holding-on attitude; and (c) tension, agitation (Nowlis 1968).

The alpha rhythm is most easily monitored from the occipital-parietal areas, its amplitude decreasing from occipital to pre-frontal area, as indicated in Figure 18.2. Greenfield and Sternback (1972) reported that the mean density of alpha activity differed between the cerebral hemispheres in about 30 per cent of normal adults, in whom a greater amplitude is frequently obtained from the right hemisphere. Lynch, Paskewitz, and Orne (1974) carried out a reliability study and found that stable measures of alpha densities could be obtained from session to session, provided that situational effects were considered.

The nature of alpha activity has been of great interest to many investigators. Andersen and Andersson (1968) concluded that the evidence strong-

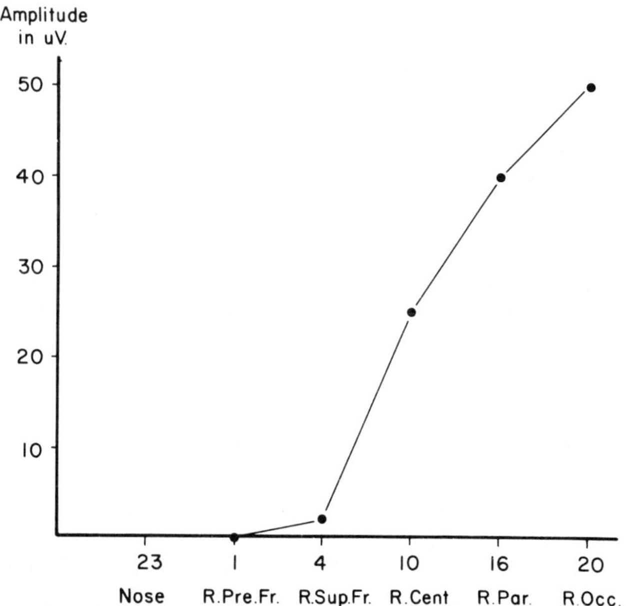

Fig. 18.2. Distribution of alpha over scalp, using nose as reference. (Data from exercise developed by Dr M. V. Driver.)

ly indicates that the thalamus is the prime mover of the thalamo-cortical rhythmic activity. In contrast, Lippold (1973) was convinced that alpha rhythm was really a rather sophisticated occular artefact. Kennedy (1959) viewed alpha as a recording artefact. However, Miller (1968) noting that Kennedy had accumulated little experimental evidence for his position, found the traditional view which considered alpha rhythms as representative of cellular metabolic processes more acceptable.

From a psychological point of view the development and maintenance of an alpha state is of great importance in that is is a good indicant of a state of relaxation, which is antagonistic to anxiety. One of the main problems of the majority of neurotic and psychosomatic patients is the presence of high levels of anxiety which they are unable to control. If one is able to teach these patients to develop an 'alpha state', then alpha training would be an important component in many treatment procedures. Many subjects who have 'turned-on' alpha report that, in addition to the 'physical' relaxation that accrues from being in the alpha state, they experience feelings of euphoria, happiness, and contentment. A number of investigators were able successfully to train subjects to control their alpha activity since Kamiya's (1969) report. For example, Brown (1970) successfully used a light signal which appeared upon the production of a defined alpha state to teach subjects control over their alpha rhythm. Nowlis and Kamiya (1970) used an audio feedback loop in their alpha-training research. This audio signal served to inform the subject that he was producing the frequency and amplitude of alpha that made up the criterion response. In essence, the particular feedback loop is controlled by the subject's own alpha rhythm. Before discussing the clinical applications, it will be useful to note some of the research work on the relationship between alpha rhythm and hypnotizability.

Hypnosis and alpha rhythm

London, Hart, and Leibovitz (1968) administered the HGSHS:A scale (Shor and Orne 1962) to 125 subjects, after which the EEG was used to obtain duration of alpha rhythm during two conditions, an operant condition, and a condition of visual imagery. In general, it was found that the percentage of alpha rhythm was directly related to degree of hypnotizability. This relationship between hypnotizability and percentage of alpha was replicated by Nowlis and Rhead (1968) in 21 subjects, using the summed scores from the Stanford A and C scales of hypnotic susceptibility. A correlation of 0.70 was found between a measure of the presence of EEG alpha rhythm during a resting condition and the separately gathered scores of hypnotic susceptibility. Table 18.1 presents the mean alpha rhythm duration per 120 seconds in relation to the total hypnotizability scores from the SHSS: A and SHSS: C (Weitzenhoffer and Hilgard 1959, 1962).

TABLE 18.1
MEAN EEG ALPHA DURATIONS (S/120S) BY HYPNOTIC SUSCEPTIBILITY SCORES

SHSS Forms A+C	*N*	*Duration EEG alpha operant*
0–9	8	22.2
10–15	2	50.0
16–23	11	74.0
24	–	–

(Based on scatterplot from Nowlis and Rhead 1968.)

It can be seen that those subjects who obtained a hypnotizability score in the range of 16–23 demonstrated more than three times the duration of alpha rhythm achieved by subjects gaining a hypnotizability score in the range 0–9. Thus, based on these studies, it may be hypothesized that the more hypnotizable person exhibits more baseline alpha rhythm per unit time.

Finally, Engstrom, London, and Hart (1970) and London, Cooper, and Enstrom (1974) reported on the use of alpha training to increase hypnotic susceptibility. Subjects were selected who had not more than 25 per cent base-rate alpha and whose average Harvard Group scale and Stanford A scale hypnotizability score was less than or equal to 7. The subjects received six alpha training sessions over a period of 1–2 weeks. It was found that alpha training was significantly effective in both increasing alpha production and in increasing hypnotic susceptibility. Interestingly enough, the control-group used who were treated exactly like the experimental group except for receiving *non-contingent* feedback, rather than their own *contingent* feedback, also increased somewhat in both alpha rhythm duration (significantly) and hypnotic susceptibility (non-significantly). However, the increase in hypnotic susceptibility and alpha rhythm increase for the experimental group was significantly greater than that for the control. London *et al.* (1974) reasoned that more consistent learning took place in the experimental or contingent feedback group, in that while alpha production during the feedback part of each training session correlated significantly with pretraining base-rate alpha production for the experimental group, this was not found for the control group. It should be pointed out that there is some dispute regarding the validity of these findings (Evans 1972).

SOME CLINICAL APPLICATIONS OF HYPNOSIS AND BIOFEEDBACK

Since research efforts using various types of feedback are discussed in several other places in this book, the discussion will be somewhat limited here. Chapter 5 includes a discussion of feedback procedures which have been used in treating cardiovascular disorders, while Chapter 6 discusses the use of EMG feedback and temperature feedback in treating tension and migraine headache respectively. The following reports are of interest because three of them used both hypnosis and feedback as treatment procedures.

Alpha feedback in treating headache

Gannon and Sternbach (1971) reported a case-study in which alpha training was used in the treatment of headache. They based their treatment on a study of yoga meditators which demonstrated that while in the meditation state subjective pain responses were eliminated and alpha-blocking avoided. The results of this single case-study were quite encouraging. In the eyes-open condition alpha increased from an initial value of being 25 per cent to approximately 45 per cent. The patient reported that throughout treatment his headaches decreased in number and intensity and that he was able to concentrate for longer periods of time and to go for a swim and attend 'rock' concerts, while before the treatment he was unable to engage in these activities. The authors concluded that their study did provide some evidence that it was possible for a patient to learn to prevent the onset of pain by means of operant alpha conditioning techniques.

Biofeedback and hypnosis in treating headache

Graham (1975) reported on two case-studies. Both patients were reported to have moderate hypnotic susceptibility. Before the actual treatment, a one-month baseline period was used in which patients kept a daily log of the frequency, intensity, and duration of migraine attacks and any warning signal (auras) that an attack was soon to commence. Treatment involved the eye-fixation method of hypnotic induction and suggestions that patients were to increase the temperature of the dominant hand. Instructions for self-hypnosis were given and between the five treatment sessions patients were asked to practise the hand-warming technique daily. Additionally, if warning signals (pre-headache phenomena) occurred, patients were to begin the hand-warming exercises immediately.† Results using the hand-warming and self-hypnotic procedures may be interpreted with some optimism, although the relative contributions of hypnosis and hand-warming remain to be demonstrated. Initially, the first patient had 15 headaches per month, mean intensity 9 (on a 10-point scale), and mean duration of 10

† The hand-warming technique is based upon the vascular theory of migraine headache. While occlusive vasoconstriction of cerebral arteries precedes the actual headache, during the migraine attack there is a vasodilation of the cranial arteries, which results in the head-pain, and a vasoconstriction periphally which typically results in cold extremities. Warming of the hands has been found to be successful in some patients in alleviating or reducing the intensity of a migraine episode (Sargent, Walters, and Green 1973).

hours. The second patient had 10 headaches per month, mean intensity 10, and mean duration 5 hours. On follow-up, the first patient was completely headache free between the third and ninth month after treatment, while the second patient was completely headache free during a full year of follow-up.

Andreychuk and Skriver (1975) were interested in treating migraine patients and selected 33 migraine sufferers from a volunteer group of 50 patients and randomly assigned them to three treatment conditions: (1) biofeedback for hand-warming; (2) biofeedback for alpha enhancement; and (3) training in self-hypnosis. The relationship between hypnotizability and success of treatment was of interest for these investigators. The authors hypothesized that treatment would be more effective for those of greater hypnotizability. A 'headache index' based on daily self-report was compiled for 6 weeks prior to the treatment programme and also for the last 5 weeks during treatment. Hypnotizability was assessed through the use of the 'Hypnotic Induction Profile' (Speigel and Bridger 1970).

The self-hypnosis group utilized procedures which included instructions for relaxation, visual imagery, verbal reinforcers, and direct suggestions for dealing with pain. The subjects in each group were urged to practise at least twice a day between sessions with the therapist. Significant improvmeent was found for each group. However, significant differences in improvement between groups was not found. These authors reported a significant difference in improvement between those groups high and low in hypnotizability, i.e. 71 per cent and 41 per cent respectively. Regardless of the specific treatment the high hypnotizability group responded to treatment significantly better than the low group.

Melzack and Perry (1975) carried out an extensive study involving 24 pain patients. The pain syndromes and number of patients treated in each group were: back pain (10); peripheral nerve injury (4); cancer pain (3); arthritis (2); phantom limb and stump pain (2); post-traumatic pain (2); head pain (1). The treatment was a combined use of hypnosis and alpha feedback. Basically, the combined-treatment group responded significantly better than the other two groups which used either hypnosis or alpha feedback training. However, Melzack and Perry stressed that the results of their research could be interpreted to a large extent on the basis of placebo reaction. In fact, a number of other projects in this general area could be interpreted in a similar way. Thus, a great deal of caution is needed when interpreting the results of such studies.

Biofeedback in treating other disorders

Biofeedback procedures have been used in treating many disorders (Birk 1973; Blanchard and Young 1974). Blanchard and Young reviewed studies using EMG feedback; cardiovascular responses, including control of heart-rate, blood pressure, and peripheral vasodilation; EEG feedback including treatment for seizure disorders; skin-temperature feedback; electrooculargram (EOG) feedback; and even stomach-acid pH. These authors conclude that the strongest evidence for the efficacy of biofeedback treatment is in the area of EMG feedback, although there are encouraging results in other areas.

Reavley (1975) reported a case study on the successful use of 'galvanic skin response' (GSR) and EMG feedback in the treatment of writer's cramp. EMG feedback was used in conjunction with progressive writing exercises, although it was not possible to determine which component of the treatment package was the significant variable. For example, it may have been the relaxation produced through the EMG feedback, the writing exercises, or 'placebo effect'.

Blanchard and Young reviewed a number of sensorimotor rhythm (12–14 Hz) feedback studies which may be helpful in treating seizure-type disorders such as *petit mal* epilepsy. Reversal designs were used with some patients and the results indicated significant improvements in clinical state. Blanchard and Young concluded that the 'results were highly encouraging since beneficial effects had been found in several types of seizure disorders. Johnson and Meyer (1974) reported success using sequential relaxation, EMG feedback as well as feedback of alpha and theta rhythms in the treatment of an 18-year-old female who had suffered from *grand mal* seizures for ten years. The frequency of her seizures was decreased to almost 50 per cent of the pre-treatment rate and a three-month follow-up indicated continued maintenance of the low seizure frequency. A discussion of sensorimotor EEG feedback can be found in Sterman (1973).

EVALUATION OF FEEDBACK PROCEDURES

Lynch (1974) noted that Dr Neal Miller and Dr Leo V DeCara 'now acknowledge that they are unable to replicate any of their previously reported research on the operant conditioning of visceral activity under curare. . . . Dr Miller suggested at the Psycho-physiological Meetings held in Boston in November, 1972, that his original findings may have been due to the curare they used at Yale, which may have been "witches' brew".'

Driessen, Knopper, Krogten, and Werre (1974) reported on attempts to replicate experiments where subjects were able to increase alpha through feedback. The results were negative whether alpha was monitored from frontal or occipital sites. These authors concluded that in view of these results and the methodological weaknesses of previous research it was too early to assume that by use of the feedback method, one could learn to elicit alpha rhythm at will. Paskowitz and Orne (1973) in a study of visual effects on alpha feedback training concluded their article by noting that 'The popular view that alpha feedback training somehow permits individuals to increase alpha densities significantly above those obtained during a comfortable baseline with eyes closed in a non-drowsy, relaxed state cannot be supported by our data'. This conclusion rests on the differential results obtained in total darkness as compared to 'dim ambient illumination'. While systematic increases were found during the latter condition, increases were not evident during darkness.

Paskewitz, Lynch, Orne, and Costello (1969) in a study of alpha feedback, used a group of controls in which false feedback was presented. They found no essential difference between those given contingent and those given false feedback. The study of Engstrom *et al.* (1970) on the effect of alpha training on hypnotic susceptibility found that the group receiving non-contingent feedback increased both their hypnotizability and their alpha production.

Lynch (1973) noted that 'Current applications of biofeedback techniques range from outright opportunism and charlatanism, to a rather widespread non-critical acceptance, by both the public and scientific community alike, of naive explanations for the most complex psychophysiological phenomena, all the way to some very interesting and promising clinical applications. There have been exceptions to the uncritical acceptance of this field, . . . but until recently their protests have been voices crying in the wilderness'. Stroebel and Glueck (1973) pointed to the debate regarding biofeedback: 'Is the subject really learning biofeedback control, is he merely altering his cognitive set, or is he responding to a suggestion–placebo effect by whatever means?' Paskewitz and Orne (1973) noted that the 'subjective experience reported to be associated with alpha training . . . may be understood as a consequence of acquiring skill in disregarding stimuli in the external and, perhaps, internal environment which would ordinarily inhibit alpha activity'.

This skill referred to by Paskewitz and Orne is clearly important in that the internal or external stimuli that the client learns to disregard are those which elicit anxiety. Thus, any control of these may be viewed as a therapeutic gain. In any case, the vast number of psychologists who use alpha training feel that it can be helpful in working with many types of patient because of the accompanying subjective feelings of relaxation and pleasantness, feelings which are antagonistic to anxiety. Clinically, there is evidence that clients who respond poorly to relaxation and hypnotic procedures may learn to lower their anxiety via EMG or EEG alpha-feedback training.

Therefore, while there is still controversy regarding the nature of biofeedback mechanisms, many therapists subscribe to the selective use of these techniques in the clinical setting. M. B. Evans (1977) argues for an integration between behaviour therapy and biofeedback procedures.

19
Self-control procedures

IAN TAYLOR

No man is free who cannot control himself
Pythagoras

Throughout history man has strived to control and change himself as he has controlled and changed his environment. Many philosophies and religions have emphasized the value and desirability of self-control. The perennial 'free-will' versus 'determinism' argument demonstrates man's preoccupation with his control over himself (or the lack of it!). Only recently has the self-control phenomenon undergone scientific analysis and application. Research has been directed towards the identification of its component processes and into the development of effective means of teaching self-control. The therapeutic advantages of individuals with psychological problems learning to control their own difficulties are obvious.

In order to change or control his own behaviour the individual must have some understanding of the factors influencing his own actions. He needs to be able to discriminate patterns and causes in the behaviour he wants to regulate. For example, the over-weight individual should appreciate the cues or stimuli that frequently precede over-eating. Thoresen and Mahoney (1974) reconstrued the old Greek maxim 'know thyself' as 'know thy controlling variables'. This process of self-observation or self-monitoring will be discussed in more detail later in the chapter.

Having gained some knowledge of the variables influencing his behaviour, the individual is now in a position to manipulate or change these variables in order to bring about desirable change in his behaviour. These manipulations form the basic strategies of self-control. The individual becomes a sort of personal scientist. He first observes what is going on (recording and analysing 'personal data'), then uses certain techniques to change specific aspects of his environment, which, in turn, modifies his own behaviour, and finally decides if the desired change in behaviour has occurred (by looking at his data).

Central to the study of self-control is the interdependence of behaviour and environment. Not only is a person's behaviour a function of his environment, but also his environment is a function of his behaviour. In other words, the individual engages in certain behaviours which change his environment in ways that, in turn, systematically modify his behaviour.

Skinner (1953) distinguished between controlled and controlling behaviour. The former was the behaviour to be changed (or the target behaviour). This change was effected by manipulating environmental variables. This manipulation was the controlling behaviour. Skinner emphasized that controlling behaviour, like controlled behaviour, must be appropriately rewarded (externally) if it was to be maintained. For instance, the maintenance of controlled eating would be dependent on the reinforcing comments of other people.

When considering self-control, the role of mediating (or symbolic) factors is very important. Bandura (1969) considered that most human behaviour resulted not only in environmental consequences but also in self-evaluation, such as self-approval or self-criticism. These cognitive mediating variables could maintain behaviour in the immediate absence of external reinforcement or punishment.

How might we then define self-control? Goldfried and Merbaum (1973) stated that: '*Self-control represents a personal decision arrived at through conscious deliberation for the purpose of integrating action which is designed to achieve certain desired outcomes or goals as determined by the individual himself*'. A less 'mentalistic' (or more behavioural) definition was given by Thoresen and Mahoney (1974): '*A person displays self-control when in the relative absence of immediate external constraints, he engages in behavior whose previous probability has been less than that of alternatively available behaviors* (involving lesser or delayed reward, greater exertion or aversive properties, and so on). Essentially, there are two forms of self-control strategy: *environmental planning* and *behavioural programming*.

Environmental planning (or stimulus control, see Reynolds 1975) involves the self-controlling individual manipulating relevant situational or environmental variables *prior* to the execution of a controlled (or target) behaviour. Such variables will be initiating or antecedent stimuli associated with the behaviour to be controlled. Consider, for instance, the person who overeats. Many environmental cues are associated with eating behaviour. To control eating behaviour, many such cues must be eliminated (i.e. the individual eats only at the table, in a certain room, at a certain time). In a similar manner, the smoker might restrict his smoking to a certain room of the house in order to reduce the number of cues associated with smoking.

Contingency contracting represents another form of environmental planning. A social agreement (or contract) is made regarding the requirements (contingencies) for reward or punishment. For example, money might be deposited with the therapist, who then rewards or fines the individual according to his self-regulatory performance. Although such procedures place less emphasis on the actual alteration of environmental variables (or cues), they do involve some modification of the environment prior to the execution of a target behaviour. Similarly, strategies where tempting cues are eliminated or altered (such as not buying cigarettes, or having less food in the refrigerator) are also instances of environmental planning. Also, self-instructions can have stimulus controlling effects, where internal cues precede the behaviour to be controlled. By modifying such self-instructions ('I am going to fail' — 'I will succeed') more desirable behaviour might well follow.

Behavioural programming (or self-presented consequences) involves a modification of the consequences of a behaviour (rather than changing its eliciting cues, as with environmental planning). Self-administered consequences represent a change in the environment that *follows* the behaviour to be controlled. Self-reward and self-punishment can be applied systematically in order to increase or reduce the frequency of the controlled behaviours. Such reward (or punishment) could involve the self-presentation of special treats (or self-denial of treats) as a consequence of certain behaviour. However, *cognitive self-evaluation* (self-praise or self-criticism) may also play a large part in the maintenance of *self-controlled behaviour*.

Thoresen and Mahoney (1974) listed the following behavioural programming techniques:

1. *Self-observation*: the recording, charting, and/or display of information relevant to a controlled response (e.g. charting one's weight).
2. *Positive self-reward*: the self-administration or consumption of a freely available reinforcer only after performance of a specific, positive response (e.g. treating oneself to a special event for having lost weight).
3. *Negative self-reward* the avoidance of, or escape from a freely avoidable aversive stimulus only after performance of a specific, positive response (e.g. removing an uncomplimentary pig poster from one's dining room whenever a diet is adhered to for a full day).
4. *Positive self-punishment*: the removal of a freely available reinforcer after the performance of a specific negative response (e.g. tearing up a dollar bill for every 100 calories in excess of one's daily limit).
5. *Negative self-punishment*: the presentation of a freely avoidable aversive stimulus after the performance of a specific, negative response (e.g. presenting oneself with a noxious odour after each occurrence of snacking).

SELF-MONITORING BEHAVIOUR

Everyone, to some degree, participates in self-observation. Few people, however, observe their behaviour in an organized systematic manner. Most people have a vague idea as to their actions, remembering some things and forgetting many others. As mentioned earlier, self-monitoring is an important part of self-control, as it provides the individual with an on-going record of the behaviour to be controlled and other relevant data (situational factors, etc). The individual not only attends to certain behaviours and events but also keeps a written record of them. Self-control would be almost impossible without such systematic data.

Many methods of self-monitoring (SM) have been applied (including record sheets, booklets, graphs, wrist counters, etc.). The possibilities of SM devices are limited only by the ingenuity of the prospective users. At the present time little is known about the specific effects of different methods of SM, although it is probably reasonable to assume that the method could interact with the environment to influence the behaviour being monitored.

Some studies have shown that SM can have a dramatic effect on behaviour. McFall (1970) asked sixteen college-student smokers, during class sessions to monitor either the number of cigarettes smoked in class or the number of times they considered smoking, but in fact did not smoke. Sixteen non-smoking students were asked to unobtrusively record the smoking frequency of the smokers over three experimental phases (baseline, self-monitoring, return to baseline). The smokers were instructed to smoke as usual. The subjects who monitored their actual smoking significantly increased their rate of smoking, while those who monitored their resistance to temptation decreased in smoking (although not significantly). However, the difference between the two groups (in smoking frequency) was significant at 'return to baseline'. Despite several methodological problems, this study demonstrated the marked effect of SM on the target behaviour. The findings suggest that monitoring an antecedent of the behaviour in question (urge to smoke) may be a more effective self-change strategy than monitoring a behaviour after it has occurred. The suggestion is that, for those subjects who actually wanted to reduce smoking, the self-recording of a desired response (not smoking) may have been more effective than the self-recording of its less desirable alternative (smoking). This hypothesis was given some support in a single-case study reported by Rozensky (1974). Self-monitoring behaviour before each cigarette was consumed was more effective in reducing smoking frequency than SM after cigarette consumption.

Broden, Hall, and Mitts (1971), in an impressive single-case study, examined the effects of SM on the study behaviour of an eighth-grade student, Lisa. Throughout the study an observer recorded the frequency of studying behaviour during class. After a baseline period of 7 days Lisa began to monitor her own studying using a record sheet to indicate every few minutes with a + or a − whether she had been studying. 'Study' (+) and 'non-study' (−) behaviours were well-defined for her. During the SM phase (7 days) her average rate of studying rose from 30 per cent to about 80 per cent. Then Lisa was informed that the record sheets were not available and the amount of study time dropped to 27 per cent over the next 4 days. Re-introduction of SM returned the study behaviour to 80 per cent. This ABAB (reversal) design clearly demonstrated that SM was the critical variable responsible for the change in her study behaviour.

Another investigation concerned with the effect of SM on study behaviour was that of Johnson and White (1971), who compared the following 3 groups of students: (1) SM of study behaviour group: subjects recorded their daily study behaviour, plotting graphs and awarding themselves points for certain study activities. SM data was returned by postcard weekly to the experimenter; (2) SM of dating behaviour group: subjects were given the same instructions except that they were asked to record the time spent in dating activities; and (3) no-contact control group. The results revealed that the SM study group received significantly higher grades than the control group over a period of ten weeks. But the difference between the two SM groups was not significant. It was suggested that SM dating students became more aware of time spent in dating, which perhaps should have been spent studying, which led to an increase in study time. However, no data is offered to support such an hypothesis.

Romaneczyk (1974) compared SM with behaviour management in a study on weight loss. Five groups of subjects were compared: (1) no treatment control; (2) daily SM of weight; (3) daily SM of weight and calorie intake; (4) behaviour management instructions without SM; (5) behaviour management instructions with SM of weight and calorie intake. In terms of weight loss, there was no difference between the 'no treatment control' and the 'daily SM of weight' group. But, SM of weight and calorie intake was as effective as both behaviour management groups. These findings suggest that SM of calorie intake was of some significance. However, the brief period of treatment (4 weeks) leads to some difficulty in interpreting these findings. A longer period of treatment might have allowed differences to emerge.

A number of single-case studies have attempted to demonstrate the reactive (or therapeutic) effects of SM with a variety of behaviours. Frederiksen (1975) reduced and eventually eliminated ruminative thoughts in a 25-year-old woman using SM procedures. Self-monitoring was presented as an assessment procedure rather than 'therapy' in order to reduce positive expectation of change. In addition, social reinforcement was given for carrying out SM as instructed (rather than for improvement), thus minimizing the effects of external reinforcement. However, the covert nature of the target behaviour prevented independent observation, and so precluded a check on the reliability of SM and the instigation of an ABAB design. Jason (1975) found that SM was effective in reducing insomnia in a 24-year-old student. As with the above study, SM was presented as an assessment procedure in order to minimize positive expectation. Although independent observation was feasible in this study, it was not carried out. The frequency of head jerking and vocal barks was successfully reduced by Hutzel, Platzel, and Logue (1974) in a 11-year-old boy with Giles de la Tourette's syndrome, using an SM procedure. A *multiple baseline design* was utilized. Following a baseline period, head-jerking was first monitored, following by vocal barks. Each behaviour was reduced in turn.

Although the above studies show the effect of SM on target behaviour, several others indicate that such effects can be short-term. For example, in a second single-case study, Broden *et al.* (1971) attempted to modify the 'talking-out' behaviour of an eighth-grade boy, Stu, utilizing a SM technique. (Stu exhibited a tendency to talk out of turn thus disrupting the classroom. It was found that SM reduced talking-out only during the experimental phase. It returned to baseline level very quickly. However, Stu had not requested help, unlike Lisa in the previously discussed study, and his motivation for change was, therefore, likely to be limited.)

Another study demonstrating the importance of motivational factors on SM effectiveness in changing behaviour is that of Fixsen, Phillips, and Wolf (1972). In this study the effect of SM on the room-cleaning behaviour of delinquent boys was examined. An observer made independent observations of such behaviour. Following a baseline of 'no SM' a minimal improvement in room-cleaning occurred, which quickly dissipated over time. This actual change (or lack of it) contrasted considerably with the SM data, which indicated very high levels of room-cleaning during the SM period. It seems reasonable to assume that these boys were not particularly motivated to change this particular type of behaviour.

Mahoney (1974) also found SM to have a short-term effect. However, unlike the above two studies, this one utilized motivated individuals who wanted to lose weight. Self-monitoring was compared with two types of self-reinforcement. Subjects in all three experimental groups showed dramatic weight loss (during a baseline SM period in which they monitored body weight and eating habits) over a control-group. However, the SM-alone group failed to continue to reduce weight compared with the other two experimental groups (self-reinforcement). This study suggests that SM can have a dramatic but short-lived effect on behaviour, but needs to be supplemented by other strategies (such as self-reinforcement) for effective long-term management.

A very large number of studies have shown that SM combined with other procedures can bring about effective change. However, it has usually proved impossible to demonstrate the relative effect of SM as an isolated procedure. Rutner (1967) compared five procedures, including SM, in reducing cigarette smoking. The SM procedure was that every time they smoked the subjects had to ask someone present to initial their record card. After 21 days all groups significantly reduced their smoking. The SM treatment was not by any means the most effective technique, but it did result in a significant reduction in smoking. However, the procedure of asking someone else to sign a card adds certain confounding variables to the SM process. One might assume that smoking could become awkward, embarrassing, even aversive, depending on the situation the individual was in. There would also seem to be an element of stimulus control here (i.e. smoking is restricted to certain social situations).

Rehm and Marston (1968) attempted to reduce social anxiety in men, using SM as a part of the therapeutic procedure. Three treatment conditions were examined: self-reinforcement (SR), non-specific therapy (NST), or no therapy (NT). Subjects in the SR group monitored their social interactions with women and awarded themselves points depending on their performance. In therapy sessions, the therapist reinforced appropriate social behaviour (depending on the number of points) and encouraged further interactions. Subjects in the NST group were provided with contact with the therapist, but did not engage in SM or reinforcement. This contact involved essentially non-directive therapy (e.g. reflection of feelings, clarification, etc.), with no direct positive or negative evaluations of the clients' behaviour. Self-reinforcement led to greater improvement on several measures compared with the two control conditions (effective at 7–9 month follow-up). As SM was combined with self-reinforcement and therapist feedback and reinforcements, the specific causal agent of change remains unclear.

Kolb, Winter, and Berlow (1968) asked graduate students to set goals for modifying their own behaviour. They observed behaviours relevant to that goal and kept daily charts (SM). All subjects attended a series of weekly meetings during the 10-week period of the study. Half of them were encouraged to report back on progress and provide one another with feedback, while the other half were told not to discuss their projects. Not surprisingly, there was more change for those subjects who received feedback (social reinforcement?) on their self-reported progress. However, as with the above studies, the effects of SM are obscured by other variables; in this case goal setting and social reinforcement. Also, there is no appropriate control-group.

In a study reported by Fisher, Green, Fielding, Levernkron, and Porter (1976) on weight reduction, goal-setting was combined with SM. A weight-graphing technique was utilized. The 11 subjects were instructed to plot their weight daily on a graph and to try to keep their weight below a diagonal line representing their ideal rate of weight loss. No further advice regarding self-management of eating behaviour was given. On average, 9.6 lb was lost in 39 days. However, follow-up data (14.5 and 19 months) was presented for only 2 subjects. Further problems with this study were:

(a) the subjects were relatives, friends, and students of the authors; and
(b) no control group was used.

Rutner and Bugle (1969) attempted to reduce the frequency of auditory hallucinations of a schizophrenic patient using SM. The patient recorded the frequency of hallucinations and after three days this data was displayed publicly on the ward. The staff praised daily records of no hallucinations. In the three days of SM alone (before display of data), the reported frequency of hallucinations decreased dramatically from 181 to 10. They had decreased to zero by the sixteenth day. But, after the first three days, it was not, of course, possible to distinguish the influence of public display and staff reinforcement from the effects of SM. Also, we do not know for sure that the self-reported data accurately reflected 'actual' instances of hallucination.

Whenever covert responses (such as hallucinations), which are naturally unobservable to the experimenter, are self-monitored, this is a considerable problem (see the discussion of Frederiksen's (1975) study p. 338). Social reinforcement was contingent upon low rates of 'recorded' hallucinations not their 'actual' reduced occurrence. However, the initial dramatic effect during the three days of SM alone does suggest that SM can be effective.

McFall and Hammen (1972) looked at four kinds of SM in an attempt to reduce smoking behaviour (1) SM: subjects were told to monitor their cigarette consumption daily. (2) Negative SM: subjects recorded on a wrist-counter a negative point each time they proved unable to resist smoking a cigarette. While recording the point, they said to themselves 'I do not want to smoke.' (3) Positive SM: subjects used the wrist-counter in successfully resisting the urge to smoke; also saying 'I do not want to smoke.' (4) Fixed-positive SM: identical to (3) except subjects had to earn at least 20 points on the wrist-counter each day. If, on any day, they experienced a decreased urge to smoke, making them unable to earn their 20 points, then they were to 'conjure up the desire, resist it and record a point'. All subjects were told to stop smoking at an initial group meeting. They were given record sheets to be returned twice weekly and were asked to buy all their cigarettes at the 'smoking clinic'. After three weeks no significant differences between the four groups were found; all groups showed a significant decrease in reported smoking. Again, there are a considerable number of confounding factors:

(1) there were instructions to stop smoking;
(2) cigarettes had to be purchased at the clinic;
(3) there was contact with the clinic and experimenter twice per week;
(4) evaluative self-reinforcement was utilized in 3 groups;
(5) imagery was used in the fixed-positive SM group.

However, the authors noted that self-monitored smoking was significantly lower during the three days of baseline than during the pre-baseline estimates of normal smoking. This does indicate that SM may have led to change before other treatment variables were introduced.

Thomas, Abrams, and Johnson (1971) used SM to reduce multiple tics in a young male adult. He counted his tics and reported them every 15 minutes to an observer who followed him about. Praise was given for low rates. However, desensitization was also utilized. Although the tics were successfully reduced, this cannot be attributed to SM alone, as both reinforcement and/or desensitization could have played a part in effecting change.

While the above studies have shown the effectiveness of SM (albeit perhaps short-term and confounded with other variables, in some cases) some research has produced negative results. Stollak (1967) compared SM with other procedures in the reduction of weight over an eight-week treatment period. The SM group kept a diary of foods eaten (How much?

What? When?). Another group (SM and reinforcement) kept the diary and also met the experimenter weekly and was reinforced (verbally) for reports of moderate eating. It was found that SM and reinforcement led to significant reduction in weight, while SM alone did not.

McNamara (1972), in a four-week study attempting to modify nail-biting, had some subjects record actual instances of nail-biting and other subjects record other incompatible behaviours (e.g. finger tapping, etc.). A further group of subjects did not engage in SM at all. It was found that all groups demonstrated a significant increase in nail-length after four weeks and that there were no significant differences between the groups. This result underlines the importance of demand characteristics (Orne 1962, 1969) and expectancy, which may account for some of the therapeutic attributes of SM reported in the literature.

SM was compared with self-reward (SR) and self-punishment (SP) in a study by Mahoney, Moura, and Wade (1973) on the modification of eating behaviour. All subjects were given a booklet describing stimulus control strategies for controlling eating behaviour (see p. 344). Subjects in the experimental groups (SM, SR, SP) weighed themselves twice weekly and recorded their weight and eating habits. A control group received the booklets but did not participate in SM. Compared with SR and SP groups, SM individuals demonstrated the least weight reduction. In fact, they were no more successful than the control group. The results of this study suggest that, to be effective, SM must be supplemented by other treatment strategies (such as SP or SR).

Bellack (1976) also found SM to be less effective than SR in reducing weight. However, he concludes:

> A direct comparison between SM and SR is not possible. Subjects instructed to administer SR must SM first. Subjects instructed to SM can freely administer covert SR. It seems highly likely that subjects in a weight reduction programme would occasionally administer positive self-reinforcement after monitoring resistance to temptation and self-criticism after eating inappropriately . . . While it cannot be concluded that SR in isolation is more effective than SM in isolation, the clinically applicable differentiation of the two procedures seems clear. The explicit use of SR critically augments whatever effects SM has . . . The question of whether SM affects behaviour directly or simply allows for the occurrence of SR cannot be fully answered until and unless there is adequate control over the administration of covert SR.

Several further studies examining the effectiveness of SM in reducing certain target behaviours have produced negative results:

(1) Bayer (1972): hair-pulling (single case);
(2) Berecz (1972): smoking;
(3) Hall (1972): eating (weight reduction);
(4) Mitchell and White (1977*b*): migraine headaches.

There is some evidence that change resulting from SM does not depend upon accurate or reliable recording on the part of the subject. Lisa's self-monitoring of study behaviour, in Broden *et al.* (1971), (see p. 337) correlated poorly with the observer's records. On 4 out of 9 days during the second SM phase and on 5 out of 8 days of the final SM phase (where teacher's praise was added), Lisa failed to fill out her record sheet. Yet, her study behaviour remained at a high level as indicated in the observers' data. It is possible that self-observation had acquired the power of a discriminitive stimulus (or cue) which facilitated study behaviour without the necessity of counting the behaviour. In other words, study behaviour came under the control of the record sheet, whether it was used or not.

In a study by Herbert and Baer (1972), where two mothers counted their episodes of attention to appropriate behaviour in their deviant children, agreement between SM and observers' data averaged only 46 per cent and 43 per cent. Yet consistent increases in maternal attention resulted from this unreliable SM.

In the above two studies, knowledge by the subject(s) of independent observation could have had a reactive effect and contributed to the behaviour change. This is less likely in the Broden *et al.* (1971) study, as a return-to-baseline period (i.e. no SM), with the observer present, led to a considerable worsening in study behaviour. The reactive effect of the observer would seem to have been minimal here. Nelson, Lipinski, and Black (1976) investigated the relative reactive effects of SM and external observation on face-touching behaviour. It was found that SM was more effective in reducing face-touching than external observation.

In a large proportion of the studies investigating the therapeutic effectiveness of SM, the role of expectancy has not been considered. Nelson, Lipinski, and Black (1975) investigated the importance of this variable in SM reactivity. Four groups of subjects self-monitored face-touching behaviour:

(1) subjects were told to expect a decrease in frequency of behaviour;
(2) subjects were told to expect an increase in frequency of behaviour;
(3) subjects were told to expect no change in frequency of behaviour;
(4) subjects were told nothing (no expectancy group).

All subjects, in fact, reduced the frequency of such behaviour and there were no significant differences between the groups. Thus, expectancy would appear to have had a negligible effect on the reactivity to SM. However, one might infer that the direction of reactivity (increase or decrease) might be influenced by an implicit value judgement as to the desirability or undesirability of such behaviour.

To summarize, SM is a crucial preliminary stage in eventual self-management. The self-controlling individual needs accurate data on both his own behaviour and relevant environmental variables controlling his behaviour before he can initiate an effective self-control programme. In consideration of the therapeutic effects of SM, they would appear to be variable and often short-term. Unless SM is supplemented by other strategies (e.g. social reinforcement, and other self-control strategies, etc.), it is unlikely to demonstrate long-term maintenance of behaviour. Motivation for change, covert self-reaction, and goal setting may be important variables determining the effectiveness of SM.

SELF-CONTROL TECHNIQUES AS PREVENTATIVE MEASURES

A great deal of research into the effectiveness of self-control procedures has focused on behaviours associated with health-risk, such as smoking and overeating. It is assumed that such behaviours are no longer under the individual's control and that he needs to learn to control them in order to prevent long-term poor health. The problem with such behaviour is that the short-term rewards very often outweigh the long-term aversive consequences. The smokers urge for a 'satisfying smoke' overrides worries concerning his health, which may take a considerable time to deteriorate.

As was discussed on p. 335 there are two forms of self-control strategy; environmental planning and behavioural programming. Perhaps, we could first consider environmental planning as a preventative technique. Ferster, Nurnberger, and Levitt (1962) first considered applying environmental planning (stimulus control techniques) in the self-management of weight. These workers suggested that eating behaviour is often associated with a large number of environmental stimuli or cues which eventually gain control over the responses and can set the occasion for its occurrence. Many people eat not only at the dinner table, but also while watching TV, studying, reading, working, or in bed. Having associated all these cues with eating over a long period of time, the individual may well engage in eating whenever he encounters them. To the average person, the kitchen, comfortable chairs, restaurants, and food shops frequently elicit eating. It is suggested that overeating might be controlled by selectively decreasing the number of environmental cues associated with eating. Eating is restricted to a few relatively infrequent situations (at meal times, at the table, in the dining room, etc.). No other distracting or rewarding activities (e.g. reading, TV, etc.) are to be engaged in at the same time. The above procedures were utilized to treat eight obese women by Stuart (1967). Over a twelve-month period, these women lost between 26 and 47 lbs. Many studies have since replicated these impressive results using stimulus control techniques.

Thoresen and Mahoney (1974) summarized the stimulus control (or environmental planning) approach to eating self-management as follows:

1. *Limit the cues you associate with eating*. Eating is to be separated from other activities that could gain stimulus control over it and/or reinforce it. (For instance, eat in a specific room, at a specific place in that room.)
2. *Do not eat to avoid waste*. Many people feel that it is a crime to leave food, and this can lead to forced eating. Get into the habit of leaving small quantities of food (particularly when given a large plateful in a restaurant) so that the cue for meal termination will not be a clean

plate.

3. *Restrict your food intake ahead of time.* A large spread of food is a cue for overeating. Prepare smaller quantities and arrange it so that it looks larger. Put other food away.
4. *Make fattening foods less available and non-fattening foods more available.* Don't purchase high-calorie snacks. Never shop on an empty stomach. Keep a supply of 'safe' (i.e. low calorie) food available at all times.
5. *Alter the eating process.* Eat slowly to reduce consumption. Swallow one bite of food before putting the next on your fork. Chew slowly and take more time before swallowing. Reduce the quantity of a bite or mouthful.
6. *Modify the physiological cues for eating.* Eat high-bulk low calorie foods to produce a sensation of fullness. Eat high-protein foods to maintain an appropriate blood-sugar level and to avoid craving for sweet foods.
7. *Arrange social cues that encourage appropriate eating.* Arrange to eat only with people who eat moderately. Do not eat with 'big-eaters', who model inappropriate eating habits.
8. *Develop non-fattening responses to emotional upset.* People often report that they eat in response to anxiety or depression. To reduce this association between emotion and food, develop alternative behaviour, where possible incompatible with eating, to reduce such emotional reactions. Do relaxation exercises in order to reduce anxiety. Engage in anti-depressant behaviour (such as socializing, reading, etc.) when depressed.

McReynolds, Lutz, Paulsen, and Kohrs (1976) found that a simple stimulus-control programme was as effective in reducing weight as a complex self-control package (involving behavioural programming strategies, to be discussed shortly). In fact, the stimulus-control treatment was superior at the 3- and 6-month follow ups. As previously discussed (p. 335), contingency contracting represents a form of environmental planning where a social agreement is made regarding the requirements for reward or punishment. An example of the application of this technique is Mann (1972), who asked overweight subjects to deposit personal valuables with an experimenter, who then returned or kept them, depending on each subject's progress in losing weight.

Stimulus-control procedures have also been applied in an attempt to control cigarette smoking. Nolan (1968) and Roberts (1969), in single-case studies, reported a simple stimulus-control strategy involving the restriction of smoking to a certain chair placed in non-entertaining surroundings. In order to smoke, the individual had to retire to this chair (located in the garage, for instance), have a cigarette alone and then return. In both of these studies, smoking was successfully reduced. However, in one study the subject was the author himself and, in the other, his wife, which places certain limitations on the validity of the results.

Several studies, including Shapiro, Tursky, Schwartz, and Shnidman (1971), have attempted to reduce smoking by having individuals associate smoking with a novel environmental stimulus (or cue). Subjects were typically asked to carry portable timers and to smoke only when given an audible cue from their timer. Initially, the smokers average period between cigarettes (pre-assessed) determined the intervals after which the timer went off. In this way, the smokers were able to break previous associations between smoking and everyday cues, such as completing a meal or consuming a cup of coffee. These novel stimuli (timer cues) became the sole cues for smoking and they were under the smoker's control. Subjects were told to gradually increase the timer intervals, thus increasing the periods between cigarettes and reducing daily smoking frequencies. Despite encouraging short-term results, long-term follow-up data, where available, is rather disappointing.

It has also been suggested that stimulus-control techniques might be applied to the problem of insomnia. Bootzin (1972) considered that the sleeping behaviour of insomniacs might be under inadequate control of relevant environmental stimuli (e.g. bed, bedroom). These stimuli associated with sleep for most people, became associated for the insomniac with sleep-incompatible behaviours, such as eating, watching TV, reading, etc.—and not sleeping! These associations understandably decrease the likelihood that sleep will occur when the individual retires to bed. It was suggested that, to increase the association between 'going to sleep' and the relevant stimuli of bed and bedroom, the insomniac should not engage in sleep-incompatible behaviours in the bedroom, he should remove himself from the bedroom when unable to sleep and he should sleep only in his bed. Bootzin obtained good results with a single case. Haynes, Price, and Simons (1975) tested out the above ideas more systematically using an ABAB design with four insomniacs. All subjects considerably reduced length of time required to fall asleep after using the above stimulus control procedures. A nine-month follow-up showed maintained improvement in all subjects.

The research into stimulus-control procedures as preventative measures suggests that they are very effective in weight reduction, of limited value in reducing cigarette consumption, and promising in the management of sleep problems.

Turning now to techniques of behavioural programming as preventative measures, we shall consider the usefulness of such techniques as self-reward (SR) and self-punishment (SP). In consideration of self-reward (SR), Bandura, Kanfer, and their colleagues (Kanfer 1970; Bandura 1969) have directed their research efforts at the understanding of SR processes in laboratory settings. Although not directly relevant to SR as a preventative measure in a clinical setting, this body of research gives us some basic insights into the validity of SR as a change strategy. Kanfer and his colleagues, employed a 'directed learning paradigm' in which subjects (usually college students) are initially trained with external (experimenter-controlled) reinforcement and then instructed to assume responsibility for presenting their own rewards. Usually the experimental work involved ambiguous verbal or perceptual learning tasks where the correctness of the subject's response is difficult to ascertain. The reward or reinforcer is often a symbolic one (e.g. a green light with 'correct' writen on it). Some of the more important findings of these workers are as follows:

1. SR can enhance the maintenance of a response, although it is more variable compared with external reward.
2. Social reinforcement, quality of modelling, and leniency of instructions can all influence the rate and quality of SR.
3. SR rates usually parallel previous rates of external reinforcement.
4. Actual SR and verbal self-evaluation are not well related.
5. Training schedules affect SR rates (as with external reinforcement). Kanfer (1970) provides a useful review of this area.

Bandura and his colleagues used a 'social learning paradigm', in which subjects (usually young children) initially observe an adult or peer model displaying SR procedures and are later placed in a situation where they are able to reward themselves. The performance task usually involved discrete motor responses, where non-ambiguous feedback is supplied. The reward was generally sweets or redeemable tokens. The important findings of this group include:

1. Behaviour maintained by SR may be established through exposure to models.
2. Self-imposed standards of reinforcement are affected by previous modelling experiences.
3. Consistency between models facilitates modelled SR standards.
4. The effects of SR are basically equivalent to those of external reinforcement in maintaining performance.
5. When allowed to choose their own SR standard, subjects will impose very high work requirements on themselves.
6. SR behaviour itself needs to be backed up eventually with external reinforcement or it could well extinguish.

Bandura (1969) reviews much of this literature.

SR has been applied clinically in the treatment of both obesity and smoking. For example, Penick, Filion, Fox, and Stunkard (1971) compared a self-control programme (including SR) with psychotherapy in a weight-reduction study. The self-control group engaged in self-monitoring and stimulus-control strategies, as well as SR. The SR procedure involved subjects' awarding themselves points for adaptive eating behaviour. Points were converted into money, which was presented at the group meetings to be donated to charity. Monitoring of weight was infrequent, as frequent weighing can be meaningless owing to short-term fluctuations. An interesting aspect of this study was the designing of individual strategies of self-reinforcement for weight loss. A popular and effective method involved placing large quantities of suet in the refrigerator and removing it according to weight loss (negative self-reward). After three months of treatment the self-control group had lost considerably more weight than the control (psychotherapy) group. While 53 per cent of the self-control group had lost more than 20 lbs, only 24 per cent of the control-group had done so. This weight-loss was maintained over a three- to six-month follow-up period. This study has, however, the following drawbacks:

1. The effects of SR are confounded with SM and stimulus control strategies.
2. The study lacks a no-treatment control group.
3. The donation of money to charity is a questionable reinforcer.
4. Social reinforcement in the group meeting could have been an important variable, particularly with individuals reporting back their points (to exchange for money).

Hall, Hall, DeBoer, and O'Kulitch (1977) also compared self-control therapy with psychotherapy (in a weight-control study) overcoming some of the inadequacies of the above study. They used a no-contract control-group and attempted to control for external reinforcement by running three behavioural treatment groups:

(a) self-control therapy alone;
(b) self-control therapy and external reinforcement; and
(c) external reinforcement alone.

After 10 weeks of treatment, the three behavioural groups lost equal amounts of weight, but significantly more than either the psychotherapy or control-groups. However, at follow-up (3 and 6 months), there was no significant difference between any of the treatment groups.

Mahoney *et al* (1973) designed a study to compare the relative effects of SR, SP, and SM (already discussed on p. 342) on weight. All groups received information on stimulus-control strategies. An SR group reinforced themselves with money (to purchase special items and entertainment) depending on weight-loss. An SP group imposed fines on themselves for lack of weight-loss. An SM group just monitored weight and eating habits (as did SR and SP groups). Control subjects only received the information on stimulus-control strategies. The results indicated that SR was more effective than SM, SP, or control treatments. These results conflict with those of McReynolds *et al*. (1976, p. 345) who found stimulus-control alone as effective as a complex self-control package (involving SR).

Mahoney (1974) compared overweight subjects divided into four groups as follows: (1) SM of weight loss and habit improvement; (2) SR with money or gift certificates contingent upon weight-loss (SRW); (3) SR contingent upon habit improvement (SRH); (4) no-treatment control. As described on

p. 339, both SR groups were superior to SM and control-groups. Also, the SRH procedures proved superior to the SRW procedures. It would seem that it is more important to reinforce adaptive eating behaviour rather than weight loss, which is very gradual and fluctuating. Bellack (1976) (see p. 342) found SR to be more effective than SM in reducing weight. However, he also pointed out the difficulties in directly comparing these two procedures.

A drawback in many of the above studies (attempting to assess the effectiveness of SR) is the complicating factor of external contact and reinforcement. Some researchers have looked at the importance of external control in relation to self-control effectiveness. As considered above (p. 348) Hall *et al.* (1977) compared external reinforcement (ER) with self-control therapy (SC) in a weight reduction study. Adding ER to SC did not increase weight loss either at post-treatment or follow-up (3–6 months).

Bellack, Schwartz, and Rozensky (1974), in an 8-week weight-reduction programme, compared three groups of subjects who either:

(a) met weekly with the experimenter and received mild social reinforcement;

(b) were contacted only through the post; or

(c) received no contact.

All subjects carried out the same self-control programme. The two contact groups (a) and (b) lost more weight than the no-contact group (although there was no significant difference between these two groups). Similarly, Bellack (1976) compared a mailed-contact with a no-contact group and found a significant difference in weight-loss between the two groups.

In another weight-control study, Hanson, Borden, Hall and Hall (1976) compared three degrees of contact on a self-control programme with attention-placebo and no-treatment controls. At post-treatment (after 10 weeks) the three self-control groups did not differ in weight loss, but all three had lost significantly more weight than the two control groups. It is of interest that it was the lowest contact group which had maintained most weight loss at follow-up (1 year). It might be hypothesized that the low-contact group were less dependent on therapist contact when it came to treatment termination and, therefore, were more successful in 'going it alone'. This result is not discrepant with the results of Bellack (1976) and Bellack *et al.* (1974) when one considers that the low-contact group in the present study had more contact than the mailed-contact groups in the former studies. However, the Hanson, *et al.* (1976) study had a high drop-out rate leaving small sample sizes, which makes their findings more suspect.

To summarize the research on SR:

(a) SR is often confounded with other techniques, such as SM and stimulus-control strategies, which makes it difficult to assess the specific effectiveness of SR alone.

(b) SR seems to be superior to SM, but, as Bellack (1976) points out, a direct comparison is not really possible (see p. 342).

(c) A certain amount of therapist contact seems necessay for behaviour change. The importance of external reinforcement here is difficult to ascertain.

Self-punishment offers a further variety of behavioural programming. Mees (1966) compared the effects of three treatment conditions on smoking behaviours: (a) self-presented shock; (b) breath-holding (intended to be mild self-punishment); (c) placebo procedure in which subjects self-presented 'subliminal electrical impulses' that could not be felt. After three weeks of treatment it was found that the placebo treatment had been slightly more effective than self-shock. This disappointing result with respect to negative self-punishment (e.g. self-shock) has been replicated by several other researchers (including Rutner 1967; and Ober 1968).

Powell and Azrin (1968) developed a special cigarette box that delivers a painful electric shock when opened. By conscientiously using this device a smoker can pre-arrange the consequences of reaching for a cigarette. Some preliminary data suggested that smoking frequency did not change as a result of using this technique, probably because smokers do not consistently use the device. Morganstein (1974), using a multiple baseline design, instructed an obese non-smoker to inhale cigarette smoke following the eating of sweets, biscuits, and doughnuts. The data indicated a fairly specific response to treatment, with each eating behaviour dropping out in response to the self-punishment. This procedure led to a weight loss of 53 lbs over 24 weeks.

Berecz (1976) instigated 'cognitive conditioning therapy' with 10 smokers. This treatment involved the self-presentation of shock in association with imagining: (a) early cognitions (or thoughts) leading up to smoking and (b) cognitions occurring simultaneously with smoking. Only 3 subjects had successfully given up smoking at follow-up (6 months to 2 years after treatment). It is of some interest that these three subjects were all in the triggering cognition (a) group. (This result is reminiscent of McFall's (1970) findings (see p. 337), which suggested that monitoring an antecedent of the target behaviour may be a more effective self-change strategy.)

Levine (1978) reported the successful elimination of psychogenic seizures (in a single-case) by self-administered lemon juice, swished in the mouth for 15 seconds at the time of the seizure. Unfortunately, this result could quite easily be considered a result of expectation or other non-specific factors. A reversal or ABAB design would have been a useful control.

The above research suggests that negative self-punishment, on the whole, is not very effective nor enduring for behaviour change. While most of the research on negative self-punishment has been concerned with smoking behaviour, there is little evidence to support the generalization that negative self-punishment is an effective clinical technique.

There is little research exploring the usefulness of positive self-punishment. Axelrod, Hall, Weis, and Rohrer (1971) offered two case histories in which subjects punished themselves by withdrawing reinforcement in order to reduce smoking frequency. In the first case the smoker recorded a baseline smoking frequency followed by an imposition of a daily limit of cigarettes. The subject was instructed to tear up a dollar bill for each cigarette over the limit. This limit was decreased by one cigarette every five days. After 50 days, smoking frequency had decreased to zero. At the two-year follow-up it had remained zero. It is of interest that the subject never exceeded the limit and thus never experienced the self-punishment. It seems likely that it was the limit setting (or a self-imposed contingency) rather than positive self-punishment which caused this reduction in smoking. In the second case-study, after recording baseline data, the subject fined herself for each cigarette smoked by contributing 25 cents to charity. Environmental planning instructions (involving the non-purchase of cigarettes) were later introduced. One year later, she was only smoking occasionally but, as the baseline rate was only 8.4 per day, the follow-up data does not indicate a marked change.

In a study already discussed (p. 348) Mahoney *et al.* (1973) compared the effectiveness of SR, SP, and SM in the treatment of obesity. A four-month follow-up indicated that subjects who used only positive self-punishment improved no more than the no-treatment control subjects. Thus, the results of positive self-punishment are not very inspiring either. However, there is a lack of research in this area.

COVERT SELF-CONTROL

So far in discussing self-control procedures we have only considered manipulation of external variables. Yet internal (or covert) events play an important part in the control of behaviour and the environment. Although Skinner (1953) warned against the pitfalls of circular 'mentalistic' concepts in the analysis of behaviour, he considered that an adequate science of behaviour must consider events taking place within the skin of the organism.

Homme (1965) considered thoughts to be 'covert operants' (or 'coverants'), in an attempt to 'behaviourize' them. Exclusion of cognitive processes limits the scope of behavioural science. Private behaviours are qualitatively no different from public ones. Thoughts, images, and feelings are neurochemical responses and, therefore, may be brought within the realm of behavioural science. In that a thought can be perceived by an individual, it is not completely 'unobservable'. Thoresen and Mahoney (1974) consider that

> By training the individual to be a personal scientist, covert events can be studied and controlled in much the same manner as overt behaviours . . . many of the behaviourist's fears about delving into cognitive processes are unjustified. By anchoring one's inference in observable criteria, adhering to direct inferences, and establishing operationally testable methods for evaluating covert phenomena, cognitive variables

can become justifiable elements in behaviour analysis. Moreover, the early exclusion of mental phenomena was argued on the basis of their lack of utility in predicting, controlling and explaining behaviour. A good practical criterion for evaluation of covert behaviours, then, is whether they prove useful in understanding behavior.

Let us first consider *covert behaviours as antecedents of overt behaviour*. A large amount of human learning is mediated by cognitive processes (Bandura 1969). Phobic individuals not only get anxious in the presence of the critical phobic stimuli, but also when imagining such stimuli or remembering past experiences of them. Desensitization, one of the most frequently employed behavioural treatments, depends on these covert events. Taking the procedure further along self-control lines, some researchers have examined self-desensitization, in which the client works through his own hierarchy while relaxing. (Phillips, Johnson, and Geyer 1972; Baker, Cohen, and Saunders 1973; Marshall, Presse, and Andrews 1976).

Many relaxation techniques not only involve muscular relaxation exercises but also cognitive relaxation exercises (or imagining a 'peaceful scene'), which enhances 'mental' relaxation. The client imagines perhaps a quiet rural scene with picturesque scenery to suit his own needs. Such self-control procedures as relaxation training have been applied to a multitude of anxiety and anxiety-related problems. For instance, many studies (including Steinmark and Borkovec 1974, and Mitchell and White 1977*a*) have examined the effectiveness of relaxation techniques in the management of insomnia (see Chapter 7). The results have been very encouraging.

Covert control has been useful in the management of sexual problems. Davison (1968) used a 'masturbatory conditioning' technique to modify a client's responses to inappropriate sexual imagery. By pairing appropriate sexual cues (*Playboy* pictures) with masturbation (or rather orgasm), the arousal capacities of sadistic sexual fantasies were successfully reduced. It was considered that the thoughts and images occurring just prior to orgasm could gain control over sexual arousal.

Extending the above research ideas, it is possible to see *covert responses as target behaviours*. Much of the work on covert self-control was stimulated by Homme's (1965) article: 'Coverants, the operants of the mind'. He suggested a technique for 'coverant' control, which employed self-reward based on the *Premack Principle* (i.e. that high probability behaviours are reinforcing events). Using smoking as an example, he suggested that an early response chain element (urge to smoke) could be followed immediately by an incompatible coverant ('smoking causes cancer' or 'my food will taste better if I don't smoke'), which is then reinforced by a high probability behaviour (HPB). He recommended the coverant control sequence given in Table 19.1.

Horan and Johnson (1971) applied the coverant control technique to overeating. Obese subjects developed lists of negative thoughts about being

TABLE 19.1
COVERANT CONTROL SEQUENCE

Covert	*Covert*	*Covert*	*Overt*
(1) Urge to smoke—	(2) Antismoking— thought (e.g. 'Smoking causes cancer'	(3) Pro-non-smoking— thought (e.g. 'My food will taste better')	(4) Reward (e.g. coffee drinking)
HPB	LPB	LPB	HPB

LPB = Low Probability Behaviour HPB = High Probability Behaviour
Modified from Homme (1965)

obese and positive thoughts about being slimmer. One group of subjects repeated these coverant pairs to themselves several times a day, while another group rewarded them with an HPB. After 8 weeks only the latter group had reduced weight significantly compared to a control group. Horan, Baker, Hoffman, and Shute (1975) found that positive coverants cued to reinforce desirable eating behaviour were significantly more effective than negative coverants dealing with aversive aspects of obesity.

Epstein and Hersen (1974), in a single case-study utilizing a multiple baseline design, successfully reduced finger picking, lip biting, and cigarette smoking by utilizing coverant-control procedures. These behaviours were self-monitored, but no reliability check was carried out. SM itself could well have contributed to the reduction in frequency of these behaviours. Vasta (1975) asked a subject who was depressed and interpersonally anxious to supply coverant-positive self-evaluations (PSEs) whenever spontaneous PSEs fell below a certain frequency. It was found that spontaneous PSEs increased and interpersonal functioning improved. However, no objective measure of interpersonal functioning was presented to support this statement.

Meichenbaum and Cameron (1974) reported a series of studies dealing with cognitive factors in behaviour modification. Individuals were trained to self-monitor 'internal monologues' (i.e. self-verbalizations) in critical stress situations. For example, a client with anxiety about public speaking might well discover he is engaging in self-arousing and counter-productive thoughts (such as 'I'm going to make a mess of this', 'God, I'm really shaky', etc.). Now, the client is trained to modify these destructive covert statements into constructive adaptive self-instructions (e.g. 'If I take my time and relax I'll do just fine, 'I'm doing O.K., no sweat'). This technique has been applied to a wide variety of problems in addition to anxiety-management.

'Thought-stopping' is a covert control technique developed by Wolpe (1958) to terminate obsessive thoughts. The client is instructed to engage in the thought to be controlled and, when he signals its presence, the therapist shouts 'Stop!' This startling stimulus usually disrupts the thought. The client is then trained to shout 'Stop!' (first aloud and then covertly in order to terminate the thought himself (see Chapter 16 for further details on thought-stopping).

Covert responses as consequences have already been mentioned as an integral part of behavioural programming. Self-praise and self-criticism are everyday covert activities and are the consequences of desirable or undesirable behaviours. Ferster *et al.* (1962) considered that many self-control problems (e.g. overeating) were related to maladaptive consequence gradients: i.e. immediately rewarding but with delayed aversive consequences. They suggested that people who overeat should reduce this delay by imagining these 'ultimate aversive consequences' early in the response chain (before eating fattening foods).

Cautela (1966) developed a technique called covert sensitization (see Chapter 16) which is rather like the reverse of imaginal desensitization. Nauseous images are paired with the problem behaviour as indicated in Table 16.1, p. 292. For instance, the smoker would imagine vomiting all over the place when reaching for a cigarette. The imagery can, of course, be tailored to meet individual needs—after all, the nauseousness of a particular stimulus will vary from person to person. An individual might well have his 'pet nausea'. In addition, the smoker might imagine feeling much better when refusing the cigarette or turning away, thus covertly reinforcing a more adaptive response.

While coverant control offers some exciting possibilities therapeutically, most research findings remain speculative, at this stage. Individual cases provided the bulk of the data. There are several methodological problems. Perhaps one of the most important is the unobservability of covert events. When covert events are target behaviours, it is impossible to check on the reliability of SM. However, this problem could be overcome where there is some observable behaviour related consistently to the covert behaviour.

SUMMARY

(a) Self-control involves the individual, directed by the therapist, learning to observe his own behaviour, to identify certain relevant variables, and then manipulate these variables to bring about a desirable change in his behaviour.

(b) Self-monitoring is a necessary part of self-control. However, its therapeutic (reactive) effects have been found to be variable and often short-term. Many other variables (expectancy, motivation, goal-setting, and covert self-reaction) can contribute to its reactivity.

(c) Stimulus control procedures have much to offer, particularly in the area of weight control.

(d) Self-reinforcement procedures probably play a significant part in self-control. SR could well occur at a covert level in all self-control procedures. The experimental literature often confounds SR with other variables. Some therapist contact appears to be necessary for behaviour change.

(e) Self-punishment procedures have proved very disappointing. More research is required in this area.

(f) Covert self-control offers many therapeutic possibilities, whether covert events are viewed as stimuli or responses. The reliable observation of covert events in an important problem. Much research is needed to demonstrate the effectiveness of such procedures.

The final chapter stresses the continual importance of research, particularly in clinical, interdisclipinary settings. Various suggestions are made concerning the future involvement of clinical psychologists in the fields of both physical as well as mental health.

20
Research and the future of clinical psychology

Not yet has man learned how to celebrate his highest attainments
Nietzsche

While the profession of clinical psychology has grown by leaps and bounds during the last twenty years, the practice of clinical psychology as a profession still lags behind the body of knowledge accumulated by research. Clearly, however, the findings of psychological research may not be as clear-cut as they are in many other scientific areas. And in any case a lag between the research findings and the application of those findings is to some degree unavoidable.

When it is remembered that clinical psychology is scarcely out of its infancy and suffers from problems of identity (Albee 1970), then it is easy to see why progress has been so slow.

The application of psychological methods to general medical problems as compared to psychiatric problems has been slow to develop. The concern with the identity of clinical psychology has led some psychologists to reject the medical model outright and to suggest that a divorce should take place between clinical psychology and psychiatry (Albee, as cited by McKeachie 1967). Unfortunately, while some sort of marriage may have taken place between clinical psychology and psychiatry, there is a great deal of circumstantial evidence that that marriage has never been consummated. However, I see no particular reason why clinical psychologists and psychiatrists cannot remain friendly toward one another and able to supplement each other's involvement in facilitating physical and mental health.

There is no reason why the two main mental health professions cannot co-operate to the mutual benefit of all concerned. Graham (1977) in discussing the tension that has developed between the professions of psychiatry and psychology, concludes his interesting article by noting: 'Rather than divorce we must surely learn together, train together and practice together . . . we must learn to trust our related professions.'

That benefits are accruing from clinical psychology's relationships with various medical specialities may be seen from the increasing number of publications which indicate the value of applying behavioural methods to medical and nursing problems (Knapp and Peterson 1976; Knapp and Peterson 1977; Knapp 1977). While an increasing number of uncontrolled case studies demonstrate clinical psychology's greater involvement in the treatment and management of problems of general medicine, etc. there is a need for more refined studies.

The continued need for research

A number of chapters in this book have indicated that there is a great need for well-designed research which will produce unambiguous results. Behaviourally orientated clinical psychologists feel that an adequate functional analysis should be completed before formulating a treatment programme. Many of the scales used in behavioural analysis can be used successfully even though the therapist may not know beforehand how valid they are for the type of patient he is treating. Many of the instruments used in behavioural procedures were developed using relatively normal persons as subjects. There is thus a great need to validate these instruments on clinical populations. A related problem is that the construction and content of some of these scales reflects their development with normal populations.

It has already been mentioned in Chapter I that there has been an increasing emphasis on systematic case studies in treatment research. In this connection, it is not particulary important to use normative (*nomethetic*) assessment devices, but quite important that an adequate period is devoted to obtaining baseline data, after, or as part of, the functional analysis, and prior to any treatment intervention proper. Chapters 14 and 16 emphasized the fact that many treatment programmes are successful. However, it was also pointed out that it was often impossible to isolate the active components of the treatment package, and it was suspected that success was in many cases due to demand characteristics, expectations regarding the outcome, or to placebo factors. It is clearly highly desirable that future research be designed in such a way as to allow the effective independent variables to be identified. At present therapists use certain treatments for certain conditions without any firm evidence that such treatments are effective. The fact that no adequate treatment for certain disorders has been found is also of concern. It has been suggested that because of the traditional emphasis on treating people as members of a diagnostic or 'symptomatic' group, and applying a specific treatment to that group, we are forgetting that all those in the group are not alike, but differ in many dimensions not particularly related to their 'diagnosis' or classification. However, these variables may be important in our treatment of the individual patient.

Admittedly, individual treatment can be quite time-consuming. While the use of group treatment procedure has not been discussed in this book, clearly it is of importance, and some references to the literature have already been given. Obviously, in theory, the use of group treatment procedures may be quite cost-effective. However, it should be remembered that in research projects in which group psychological treatment is used, 'subjects' are carefully selected to meet specific criteria, and frequently group treatment alone may not be enough. The author's own experience would suggest that the use of group treatment is best supplemented with limited individual treatment, carried out concurrently. However, Hawks's (1971) point in regard to research is considered to be a valid one. He notes that 'In many areas it would appear that what is needed is not more research . . . but the application of existing knowledge.' Hawks noted that within the institutional setting, the psychologist should be able to 'advise on such matters as the selection and training of nursing staff, the employment of patients, the regime of the ward and, hopefully, can ameliorate the many depersonalizing influences which large institutions cultivate'. Torpy (1972) in an interesting study regarding the relationship between fluctuations in staffing level and episodes of patient disturbed behaviour, obtained evidence supporting Hawks's recommendation concerning the clinical psychologist's involvement in training nursing staff.

While Hawks attempted to broaden the clinical psychologist's view of the aetiology of the individual patient's problems, his recommendations have in many cases fallen on deaf ears. In reference to Lickorish and Sims's (1971) article in which it was suggested that the extent to which the psychologist could ameliorate psychological problems was very restricted, Hawks pointed out that the clinical psychologist could be employed in a much more economical manner. Hawks, concerned about after-care facilities and the frequency of relapse, stresses the importance of the community outside the hospital in treatment and rehabilitation.

Whereas Hawks does not deny the need for research, he does suggest that clinical psychologists should 'pursue those avenues of research of potentially the greatest generality'. The support of carefully designed research may prove to be more cost-effective than continuing to use untested procedures or following a party-line which has little justification. It is clear, however, that clinicians cannot wait to treat their patients until the active components of their treatment package have been determined. It would be better however if the practising clinician were willing to conduct more research with his patients. The inclusion of environmental variables in the research design would increase the *ecological validity* of the results achieved.

One of the problems with much of the research in behaviour therapy has been the extensive use of college students to the relative exclusion of patients with problems that seriously interfere with their functioning at work, at home, or while engaged in leisure activities. The relative infrequency of considering the environmental and social variables which may be important in the aetiology of psychological and psychosomatic problems must also be noted.

While the clinical psychologist may be well trained in research activities, collaborative research with his medical colleagues may not only increase his understanding of research concerning general medical patients, but will also facilitate interdisciplinary conceptualization for all members of the research team.

It has already been noted that the involvement of the clinical psychologist in general medicine has been a slow process. How can interdisciplinary research be encouraged?

Increasing collaboration between clinical psychologists and various medical specialists is taking place. Non-research types of interdisciplinary interactions will probably facilitate co-operation on research programmes.

Most, if not all, health workers have a common purpose: to provide a service to the patient. Obviously, this common purpose may be served rather indirectly. What are some of the factors relating to the degree to which this purpose is served? Certainly, we all hope to be reinforced for our work, but the particular means of obtaining that reinforcement may differ considerably from person to person. It may, for example, be obtained by serving the patient directly in a one-to-one relationship or in a group, or indirectly by teaching trainees, by being involved in administrative activities, or by interdisciplinary co-operation of some sort such as in a clinical research project. Obviously, inter-disciplinary co-operation may be necessary in many activities. In fact, it is suggested here that the more interdisciplinary contact there is, the more probable is interdisciplinary research. However, some factors may tend to interfere with good interprofessional relationships.

If one's reinforcement is intimately bound up with ambitions for promotion, conflicts may be evident between one's perception of how best to provide a service to patients and how to carry out those activities that are perceived as necessary in order to receive promotion. For some individuals there may be difficulty in reconciling teaching and/or research activities with treatment endeavours. It is not suggested that these various activities need conflict, it is only that the various activities of the health professional may be seen to conflict by the individual carrying them out, by others in the same profession, or by people in another related profession. The internal structure or lines of authority within a profession may be quite important in the development of individual conflict as well as in interprofessional conflict. Power relationships may tend to foster or hinder the degree to which interprofessional co-operation takes place. Particularly within the mental health field, many professionals may carry out very similar functions. There may be much overlapping of role function, which may lead in some individuals in some professions to 'feelings of territoriality'. However, for some, a problem of role diffusion may result. Certain individuals may find it disturbing to lack a well-structured professional identity.

In the United Kingdom, the recent publication of the Trethowan Report (1977) on the role of psychologists in the health services, notes that clinical psychology should not be regarded as an adjunct to any other profession. It is now considered to be an independent profession within the Health Service. However, it is pointed out that 'A close working relationship is needed between psychologists and others working in this wide range of medical specialities and other professions. The danger of a comprehensive department of psychology becoming remote from the operational needs of the service, will only be obviated if lines of responsibility are drawn up so as not to conflict with the responsibilities of psychologists to their colleagues in the multidisclipinary teams'.

Many activities of clinical psychologists and psychiatrists are similar in nature, and even among health professionals these two professions are confused. Social workers, occupational therapists, and possibly others, may carry out psychotherapy, group therapy, or may use behavioural procedures in their professional activities. These overlapping functions may potentially lead to various tensions and interprofessional, and even intraprofessional, conflict as already suggested above.

One can still agree with the conclusions of the American Psychological Association, drawn up a quarter of a century ago, when it was noted that 'When a Psychologist's contribution is supplementary and distinctive, he is usually welcomed, and interprofessional relations are harmonious. In the instances in which psychological research, teaching, or practice duplicates or overlaps the areas of other professions, misunderstandings may sometimes arise. The effectiveness of the psychologist's contribution, as well as his opportunity to make it, is determined at least in part by the sort of relations he establishes with people possessing the interests, competences, and methods of other professions' (American Psychological Association 1954).

It is clear from the above that in working with a particular patient on the ward, or in ward-management programmes, etc., co-ordination of activities is very necessary in order that all professionals concerned will have a consensus of opinion as to the activities to be carried out by each individual. In addition, it is obviously important that some professional be designated as the co-ordinator or catalyst for the management of the particular programme.

Historically, most professions have engaged in activities which tend to facilitate an individual's ability to identify with his particular profession. Unfortunately, at times, the so-called 'guild functions' of a profession are antithetical to the development of good interpersonal relationships, particularly amongst those professionals who carry out very similar tasks. While it can be argued that certain activities should be the sole province of the clinical psychologist, the occupational therapist, or the psychiatrist, etc., the present and anticipated future lack of mental-health manpower suggests that psychologists and other should be more willing than some of them have been heretofore in the acceptance of different health workers carrying out the same or similar functions.

The above discussion suggests that while an increasing degree of interprofessional co-operation is taking place, that there is a great need for more interdisciplinary research, which would enable the speciality knowledge of the doctor and the research, training, and experience of the psychologist to be combined to maximize the research effort.

In today's rapidly changing environment, it is necessary to plan ahead so as to be prepared for future needs in the health professions. This is not an easy task. Scientists and health professionals of many persuasions have, in the last few decades, become more specialized, and this may make it increasingly difficult for one professional to design and carry out a good piece of clinically important research. Thus, it is the author's opinion that there is a need for more interdisciplinary training. While a great deal of the more didactic type of training would be difficult to arrange, it is felt that future educational programmes should attempt to foster more interdisciplinary contact during the clinical years or during in-service training.

The degree to which clinical psychologists have taken part in interdisciplinary training varies from region to region. It is during training that the seeds of mutually beneficial relationships are most likely to be sown. It is suggested that a greater collaboration between health professionals, particularly between doctors and psychologists, is highly desirable, and mutually beneficial, not only in the treatment process, but in the research endeavour.

The importance of research has been stressed throughout this book, and while it may be argued that research only indirectly helps the patient in need, it is only through further research that maximum progress will be made so that the various health professionals can continue to provide the maximum help for the greatest number.

References

[References marked with an asterisk are recommended for further reading]

CHAPTER 1

*Agnew, N. and Pyke, S. W. (1978). *The science game: an introduction to research in the behavioral sciences* (2nd edn). Prentice-Hall, Englewood Cliffs, New Jersey.
*Bandura, A. (1969). *Principles of behavior modification.* Holt, Rinehart, and Winston, New York.
*Barber, T. X. (1976). *Pitfalls in human research.* Pergamon, New York.
Blanchard, E. B. and Miller, S. T. (1977). Psychological treatment of cardiovascular disease. *Archs gen. psychiat.* **34**, 1402–13.
—— and Young, L. D. (1974). Clinical applications of biofeedback training. *Archs gen. psychiat.* **30**, 573–89.
*Boring, E. G. (1950). *A history of experimental psychology.* Appleton-Century-Crofts, New York.
British Psychological Society (1974). *Regulations for the British Psychological Society Diploma in Clinical Psychology.*
—— (1976). *Postgraduate qualifications and courses in Psychology.*
*Davison, G. C. and Neale, J. M. (1974). *Abnormal psychology: an experimental clinical approach*. Wiley, New York.
*—— —— (1978). *Abnormal psychology: an experimental clinical approach* (2nd edn). Wiley, New York.
Keller, F. S. (1973). *The definition of psychology* (2nd edn). Appleton-Century-Crofts, New York.
Lachman, R. (1963). The model in theory construction: In *Theories in contemporary psychology* (ed. M. H. Marx). Collier-Macmillan, London.
*Leitenberg, H. (1973). The use of single-case methodology in psychotherapy research. *J. abnorm. Psychol.* **82**, (1), 87–101.
McKeachie, W. J. (1967). The case for multiple models. *Clin. Psychol.* **20**, 108–10.
Shapiro, M. B. (1966). The single case in clinical psychological research. *J. gen. Psychol.* **74**, 3–23.
Steward, H. and Harsch, H. (1966). The psychologist as a ward administrator: current status. *J. clin. Psychol.* **22**, 108–11.
Simon, H. A. and Newell, A. (1963). The uses and limitations of models. In *Theories in contemporary psychology* (ed. M. H. Marx). Collier-Macmillan, London.

CHAPTER 2

Allen, G. (1961). Intellectual potential and heredity. *Science, N.Y.* **113**, 378–9.
American Medical Association (1965). *Mental retardation: a handbook for the primary physician.* Reprinted from *J. Am. med. Ass.* **3**.
American Psychiatric Association, Committee on Nomenclature and Statistics (1968). *Diagnostic and statistical manual of mental disorders* (DSM-II) (2nd edn). American Psychiatric Association, Washington DC.

Ammons, R. B. and Ammons, H. S. (1948). *Full range picture vocabulary test.* Psychological Test Specialists. Missoula, Montana.

Baer, D. M. and Wright, J. L. (1974). Developmental psychology. In *Ann. Rev. Psychol.* (ed. M. R. Rosenzweig and L. W. Porter) **25**, Annual Reviews, Inc, Palo Alto, California.

Bayley, Nancy (1969). *Bayley scales of infant development.* Psychological Corporation, New York.

Blaine, G. B. Jnr., McArthur, C. C., *et al.* (1966). *Emotional problems of the student.* Doubleday-Anchor, Garden City, New York.

Blakemore, C. and Cooper, G. F. (1970). Development of the brain depends on the visual environment. *Nature, Lond.* **228**, 477–8.

Blashfield, R. K. and Draguns, J. G. (1976). Toward a taxonomy of psychopathology. The purpose of psychiatric classification. *Br. J. Psychiat.* **129**, 574–83.

Bojar, S. (1966). Psychiatric Problems of Medical Students: In *Emotional problems of the student* (ed. G. B. Blaine, Jnr. C. C. McArthur, *et al.*) Doubleday-Anchor, Garden City, New York.

Brown, W. F. (1942). Heredity in the psychoneuroses. *Proc. R. Soc. Med.* **35**, 785–90.

Campbell, Magda, Dominijanni, Cristina, and Schneider, B. (1977). Monozygotic twins concordant for infantile autism: follow-up. *Br. J. Psychiat.* **131**, 616–22.

Cattell, R. B., Beloff, H., and Coan, R. W. (1958). *Handbook for the IPAT high school personality questionnaire.* Institute of Personality Ability Testing, Champaign, Illinois.

Claridge, G., Canter, S., and Hume, W. I. (1973). *Personality differences and biological variations: A study of twins.* Pergamon, Oxford.

*Clarke, A. M. and Clarke, A. D. B. (1974) (eds). *Mental deficiency—the changing outlook* (3rd edn). Methuen, London.

Clements, J. C., Bidder, R., Gardner, S., Bryant, G., and Gray, O. P. (1980). A home Advisory service for pre-school children with developmental delays. *Child Care Hlth Dev.* **6**, 25–33.

Coleman, J., Burtenshaw, Wendy, Pond, D., and Rothwell, Bernice (1977). Psychological problems of pre-school children in an inner urban area. *Br. J. Psychiat.* **131**, 623–30.

*Conger, J. J. (1973). *Adolescence and youth.* Harper and Row, New York.

Conrad, W. G. and Tobiessen, J. (1967). The development of kindergarten behavior rating scales for the prediction of learning and behavior disorders. *Psychol. Schools* **4**, (4), 359–63.

Crisp, A. H. (1973). The nature of primary anorexia nervosa. In Symposium—*Anorexia nervosa and obesity* (publication no. 42). Royal College of Physicians, Edinburgh.

—— (1974). Primary anorexia nervosa or adolescent weight phobia. *The Practitioner* **212**, 525–35.

Dahlstrom, W. G., Welsh, G. S., and Dahlstrom, L. E. (1972). *An MMPI handbook: Volume 1. Clinical interpretation.* (revised edn). University of Minnesota Press, Minneapolis.

Davidson, A. N. (1977). The biochemistry of brain development and mental retardation. *Br. J. Psychiat.* **131**, 565–74.

Davison, G. C. (1964). A social learning therapy programme with an autistic child. *Behav. Res. and Ther.* **2**, 149–59.

—— (1965). An intensive long-term social-learning treatment program with an accurately diagnosed autistic child. *Proc. Am. psychol. Assoc.* 203–4.

Doll, E. A. (1953). The measurement of social competence: *A manual for the*

Vineland Social Maturity Scale. Educational Testing Bureau, Washington DC.

Douvan, Elizabeth (1970). New sources of conflict in females at adolescence and early adulthood: In Bardwick, Judith M., Douvan, Elizabeth, Horner, Matina S., and Gutmann, D. *Feminine personality and conflict* (pp. 30–43). Brooks/Cole, Belmont, California.

Dunn, K. M. (1959). *Peabody picture vocabulary test.* American Guidance Service, Inc., Minneapolis, Minnesota.

Ellis, N. R. (1963). *Handbook of mental deficiency*. McGraw-Hill, New York.

*Erikson, E. H. (1963). *Childhood and society* (2nd edn). Norton, New York.

Eysenck, H. J. (1971). *Race, intelligence, and education.* Temple Smith, London.

Ferster, C. B. (1961). Positive reinforcement and behavioural deficits in autistic children. *Child Dev.* **32**, 437–56.

Foxx, R. M. and Azrin, N. H. (1973). The elimination of autistic self-stimulatory behavior by overcorrection. *J. appl. Behav. Analysis* **11**, 35–48.

Froese, A. P. (1975). Adolescence. *Can. ment. Hlth* **23**, (1), 9–12.

Fuhrmann, W. and Vogel, F. (1969). *Genetic counseling.* (Heidelberg Science Library, Vol. 10). Longmans, Springer-Verlag.

General Register Office (1968). *A glossary of mental disorders: studies on medical and population subjects,* No. 22. HMSO, London.

Gesell, A. (1954). *The first five years of life.* Methuen, London.

Gottesman, I. I. (1963). Hereditability of personality: a demonstration. *Psychol. Monogr.* **77**, (9), 572.

—— and Shields, J. (1973). Genetic theorizing and schizophrenia. *Br. J. Psychiat.* **122**, 15–30.

Griffiths, R. (1971). *The abilities of young children.* Privately printed, London.

Gunzburg, H. C. (1969). *Progressive evaluation index (PEI).* London: National Society for Mentally Handicapped Children.

—— (1974*a*). *The P.A.C. manual* (3rd edn). National Society for Mentally Handicapped Children, London.

—— (1974*b*). Educational planning for the mentally handicapped. In *Mental deficiency: the changing outlook* (3rd edn) ed. Ann M. Clarke and A. D. B. Clarke, pp. 628–52. Butler and Tanner, London.

Harlow, H. F. and Harlow, M. K. (1972). The young monkeys. *Readings in psychology today.* CRM Books, Delmar Publishers, New York.

—— and Novak, M. A. (1973). Psychopathological perspectives. *Perspect. Biol. Med.* **16**, 461–78.

*Hetherington, E. Mavis and Parke, R. D. (1975). *Child psychology: a contemporary viewpoint.* McGraw-Hill, New York.

Hewett, F. M. (1965). Teaching speech to autistic children through operant conditioning. *American Journal of Ortho-psychiatry* **35**, 927–36.

Hirsch, H. V. B. and Spinelli, D. N. (1970). Visual experience modifies distribution of horizontally and vertically oriented receptive fields in cats. *Science N.Y.* **168**, 869–71.

*Horrocks, J. E. (1976). *The psychology of adolescence.* (4th edn). Houghton-Mifflin, Boston.

Hutt, S. J. (1975). An ethological analysis of autistic behaviour. In *On the origin of schizophrenic psychoses* (ed. H. M. Van Praag). De Erven Bohn BV, Amsterdam.

—— and Hutt, C. (ed.) (1970). *Behavior studies in psychiatry.* Pergamon, Oxford.

—— and Ousted, C. (1966). The biological significance of gaze aversion with particular reference to the syndrome of infantile autism. *Behavl Sci.* **11**, 346–56.

Jensen, A. R. (1969). How much can we boost I.Q. and scholastic achievement? *Harv. educat. rev.* **39**, 1–123.

Kanfer, F. H. and Saslow, G. (1969). Behavioral diagnosis. In *Behavior therapy: appraisal and status* (ed. C. M. Franks) McGraw-Hill, New York.

Kanner, L. (1943). Autistic disturbances of affective contact. *Nerv. Child* **2**, 217–40.

—— and Eisenberg, L. (1956). Early infantile autism: childhood schizophrenia symposium. *Am. J. Orthopsychiat.* **26**, 556–64.

Kinsbourne, M. (1977). Why investigate autistic behavior? *Contemp. Psychol.* **22**, 112–13.

Kordinak, S. T., Vingoe, F. J., and Birney, S. D. (1968). Head start—who needs it?—That is the question. Paper presented at the Western Psychological Association Meetings, March, 28–30. San Diego, California.

Lejeune, J. (1970). Chromosomes in trisomy 21. *Ann. N.Y. Acad. Sci.* **171**, (2), 381–90.

Levine, S. (1960). Stimulation in infancy. *Scient. Am.* Reprint No. 436. Freeman, San Francisco.

Littlefield, J. W. (1970). Introductory remarks Part II Chromosomal studies. *Ann. N.Y. Acad. Sci.* **171**, 379–80.

McCarthy, J. J. and Kirk, S. A. (1961). *The Illinois test of psycholinguistic abilities.* The Institute for Research on Exceptional Children, Urbana, Illinois.

*Margolies, P. J. (1977). Behavioral approaches to the treatment of early infantile autism: a review. *Psychol. Bull.* **84**, (2), 249–64.

Milgram, S. (1963). Behavioural study of obedience. *J. abnorm. soc. Psychol.* **67**, 371–8.

*Mittler, P. (ed.) (1970). *The psychological assessment of mental and physical handicaps.* Methuen, London.

Mussen, P. H. (1970) (ed.). *Carmichael's manual of child psychology.* Vol. I. Wiley, New York (London).

Peniston, E. (1975). Reducing problem behaviours in the severely and profoundly retarded. *J. behav. Ther. exp. Psychiat.* **6**, 295–9.

Piaget, J. (1952). *The origins of intelligence in children.* International Universities Press, New York.

Queenan, J. T. (1970). Intrauterine diagnosis of Down's syndrome. *Ann. N.Y. Acad. Sci.* **171**, (2), 617–26.

Raven, J. C. (1956): *Manual for the standard progressive matrices.* NFER, Windsor.

Reisinger, J. J. (1976). A service delivery system for consumer implementation and evaluation. *J. ment. Hlth Admin.* **5**, (1), 23–38.

—— and Ora, J. P. (1977). Parent–child clinic and home interaction during toddler management training. *Behav. ther.* **8**, (5), 771–86.

—— —— and Frangia, G. W. (1976). Parents as change agents for their children: a review. *J. Commun. Psychol.* **4**, (2), 103–23.

Reynell, J. K. (1969). *The Reynell developmental language scales.* NFER, Windsor.

—— (1970). Children with physical handicaps. In *The psychological assessment of mental and physical handicaps* (ed. P. Mittler), pp. 443–69. Methuen, London.

Riesen, A. H. (1965). Effects of early deprivation of photic stimulation. In *The biosocial basis of mental retardation.* (ed. S. F. Osler and R. E. Cooke). Johns Hopkins Press.

Riley, C. M. and Epps, F. M. J. (1967). *Head start in action.* Parker Publishing Co, New York.

Rimland, B. (1964). *Infantile autism.* Appleton-Century-Crofts, New York.

Rosenthal, D. (1970). *Genetic theory and abnormal behavior.* McGraw-Hill, New York.

*—— (1971). *Genetics of psychopathology.* McGraw-Hill, New York.

*Rosenzweig, M. R., Bennett, E. L., and Diamond, M. C. (1972). Brain changes in

response to experience. *Scient. Am.* **26**, (2), 22–9.
Rutter, M. (1972). *Maternal deprivation reassessed.* Penguin, Harmondsworth.
Savage, R. D. (1970). Intellectual assessment. In *The psychological assessment of mental and physical handicaps* (ed. P. Mittler), pp. 29–81. Methuen, London.
Schadé, J. P. and Ford, D. H. (1973). *Basic neurology.* (2nd revised edn). Elsevier Scientific, London.
Schneider, H. C., Ross, J. S. G., and Dubin, W. J. (1979). A practical alternative for the treatment of tantrum and self-injurious behavior. *J. behav. Ther. exp. Psychiat.* **10**, 73–5.
*Seligman, M. E. P. (1975). *Helplessness: on depression, development and death.* W. H. Freeman, San Francisco.
Sheridan, Mary D. (1975). *Children's developmental progress: from birth to five years: the Stycar sequences.* NFER, Windsor.
Skeels, H. (1966), Adult status of children with contrasting early life experiences. *Monogr. Soc. Res. Child Dev.* **31**, 3.
Slater, E. and Cowie, V. A. (1971). *The genetics of mental disorders.* Oxford University Press.
—— and Shields, J. (1969). Genetic aspects of anxiety. In *Studies of anxiety.* (ed. M. H. Lader). *Br. J. Psychiat. Spec. Publ.* No. 3. Headley, Ashford, Kent.
Stevenson, A. C. and Davison, B. C. Clare (1970). *Genetic counselling.* Heinemann, London.
Terman, L. M. and Merrill, Maud A. (1960). Stanford-Binet Intelligence Scale. *Manual for the Third Revision, Form L–M.* Houghton Mifflin, Cambridge, Massachusetts.
Tobiessen, J., Duckworth, Barbara, and Conrad, W. G. (1971). Relationships between the Schenectady kindergarten rating scales and first grade achievement and adjustment. *Psychol. Schools* **VIII**, (1), 29–36.
Ullmann, L. P. and Krasner, L. (ed.) (1965). *Case studies in behavior modification.* Holt, Rinehart, and Winston, New York.
Vingoe, F. J., Birney, S. D., and Kordinick, S. T. (1969). Note on the psychological screening of preschool children. *Percept. Mot. skills* **29**, 661–2.
Ward, A. J. (1970). Early infantile autism: diagnosis, etiology, and treatment. *Psychol. Bull.* **43**, (5), 350–62.
Watson, J. B. (1930). *Behaviorism* (2nd edn). Norton, New York.
*Watson, L. S. Jnr. (1975). *Child behaviour modification: a manual for teachers, nurses and parents.* Pergamon, Oxford.
Wechsler, D. (1949). *Wechsler intelligence scale for children manual.* Psychological Corporation, New York.
—— (1955). *Wechsler adult intelligence scale manual.* Psychological Corporation, New York.
—— (1967). *Manual of the Wechsler preschool and primary scales of intelligence.* Psychological Corporation, New York.
Williams, C. D. (1965). The elimination of tantrum behavior by extinction procedures. In *Case studies in behavior modification* (ed. L. P. Ullmann and L. Krasner). Holt, Rinehart, and Winston, New York.
*Wing, Lorna (1976). *Early childhood autism: clinical, educational and social aspects* (2nd edn). Pergamon, Oxford.
World Health Organization (1957). *Manual of the international statistical classification of diseases, injuries and causes of death.* Geneva.
Young, F.R. (1977). Cardiac arrhythmia and behaviour in subnormal, self-stimulating children and its relevance to the behavioural treatment. *Dissertation for the B.P.S. Diploma in Clinical Psychology.*

Yule, W., Berger, M., and Howlin, Patricia (1975). Language deficit and behavior modification. In *Language, cognitive deficits and retardation.* (ed. N. O'Connor), p. 209–23. Butterworths, London.

CHAPTER 3

Allport, G. W. (1955). *Becoming: basic considerations for a psychology of personality.* Yale University Press, New Haven; Oxford University Press.

*Averill, J. R. (1978). The functions of grief. In *Emotions, conflict and defense* (ed. C. E. Izard). Plenum Press, New York

*Bayne, J. R. D. (1978). Management of confusion in elderly persons. *J. Can. med. Ass.* **118**, 139–41.

Bluestein, Venus (1976*a*). Coming to terms with the only certainty. *Change* **8**, (2), 64.

—— (1976*b*). Notes and observations on teaching 'the psychology of death'. *Teach. Psychol.* **3**, (3), 115–18.

Blum. G. S. (1953). *Psychoanalytic theories of personality.* McGraw-Hill, New York.

Boylin, W., Gordon, Susan K., and Nehrke, M. F. (1976). Reminiscing and ego integrity in institutionalized elderly males. *The Gerontologist* **16**, (2), 118–24.

*Bromley, D. B. (1974). *The psychology of human aging.* (2nd edn). Pelican, Harmondsworth.

*Butler, R. N. (1973). The life review: an interpretation of reminiscence in the aged. In *Middle age and aging* (ed. Bernice L. Neugarten), p. 486–96. University of Chicago Press.

Cattell, R. B., Eber, H. W., and Tatsuoka, M. M. (1970). *Handbook for the sixteen personality factor questionnaire.* NFER, Berkshire.

Carpenter, Hazel A. and Simon, R. (1960). Effect of several methods of training on long-term, incontinent, behaviorally regressed hospitalized psychiatric patients. *Nursing Res.* **3**, 17–22.

Diesfeldt, H.F.A. and Diesfeldt-Groenendijk, Herma (1977). Improving cognitive performance in psychogeriatric patients: the influence of physical exercise. *Age and Ageing* **6**, 58–64.

Dittes, J. E. (1969). Psychology of religion. In *Handbook of social psychology* (ed. G. Lindzey and E. Aronson). (2nd edn), Vol. 5, pp. 602–59. Addison-Wesley, London.

Erikson, E. H. (1963). *Childhood and society*, (2nd edn). Norton, New York.

Eysenck, H. J. (1967). Single-trial conditioning neurosis and the Napalkov phenomenon. *Behav. Res. Ther.* **5**, 63–5.

Eysenck, M. W. (1977). *Human memory: theory, research and individual differences.* Pergamon Press, Oxford.

Folsom, J. C. (1968). Reality orientation for the elderly mental patient. *J. geriat. Psychiat.* **1**, 291–307.

French, Vera V. (1947). The structure of sentiments. *J. Personality,* **15**, 247–82; **16**, 78–108, 209–244. (Quoted in Dittes (1969).)

Getzels, J. W. (1969). A social psychology of education. In *Handbook of social psychology* (ed. G. Lindsey and E. Aranson), (2nd edn), Vol. 5, pp. 459–537. Addison-Wesley, London.

Gibson, A. J. and Kendrick, D. C. (1979). *The Kendrick Battery for the detection of dementia in the elderly*. NFER, Windsor.

*Goffman, E.(1961). *Asylums.* (Anchor Books) Doubleday, New York.

*—— (1963). *Stigma.* Prentice-Hall, Englewood Cliffs, New Jersey.

Goldfarb, A. I. (1953). Psychotherapy of aged persons. Orientation of staff in a home for the aged. *Ment. Hyg.* **37**.

Gorer, G. (1965). *Death, grief, and mourning.* Cressent Press, London.
Gough, H. B. (1957). *Manual for the California psychological inventory.* Consulting Psychologists Press, Palo Alto, California.
Grosicki, J. P. (1968). Effect of operant conditioning as modification of incontinence in neuropsychiatric geriatric patients. *Nursing Res.* **17**, 304–11.
Grotjahn, M. (1951). Some analytic observations about the process of growing old. In *Psychoanalysis and social science* (ed. G. Roheim), Vol. 3. International Universities Press, New York.
Guilford, J. P. and Zimmerman, W. (1955). *Manual for the Guilford–Zimmerman temperament survey.* Sheridan Supply Company, Beverly Hills, California.
Havighurst, R. J. and Glasser, R. (1972). An exploratory study of reminiscence. *J. Gerontol.* **27**, 245–53.
*Heath, D. (1965). *Explorations in maturity.* Appleton-Century-Crofts, New York.
Hersen, M. and Barlow, D. H. (1976). *Single-case experimental designs: strategies for studying behavior change.* Pergamon, New York.
Jenkins, Judith, Felce, D., Lunt, B., and Powell, Liz (1977). Increasing engagements in activity of residents in old people's homes by providing recreational materials. *Behav. Res. Ther.* **15**, 429–34.
Kendrick, D. C. (1972). The Kendrick battery of tests: theoretical assumptions and clinical uses. *Br. J. soc. clin. Psychol.* **11**, 373–86.
—— (1975). Personal communication.
—— Gibson, A. J. and Moyes, I. C. A. (1979). The revised Kendrick Battery: Clinical Studies. *Br. J. Soc. clin. Phychol.* **18**, (3), 329–40.
Kris, E. (1952). *Psychoanalytic explorations in art.* International Universities Press, New York.
Larner, S. (1977). Encoding in senile dementia and elderly depressives: A preliminary study. *Br. J. soc. clin. Psychol.* **16**, 379–90.
Lavin, D. E. (1965). *The prediction of academic performance: a theoretical analysis and review of research*, Russell Sage Foundation, New York. (Quoted in Getzels (1969)).
Looft, W. R. (1973). Reflections on interaction in old age: motives, goals and aspirations. *Gerontologist* **13**, 6–10.
Mandelbaum, D. G. (1959). Social uses of funeral rites. In *The meaning of death* (ed. H. Feifel). McGraw-Hill, New York.
Maslow, A. H. (1962). *Towards a psychology of being.* Van Nostrand, Princeton, New Jersey.
Matarazzo, J. D. (1972). *Wechsler's measurement and appraisal of adult intelligence* (5th enlarged edn). Williams and Wilkins, Baltimore.
Miller, E. (1977). The management of dementia: a review of some possibilities. *Br. J. soc. clin. Psychol.* **16**, (1), 77–83.
Neugarten, Bernice L. (1971). Grow old along with me! The best is yet to be. *Psychol. Today* **5**, (7), 45–8, 79.
*—— (1973). The awareness of middle age. In *Middle age and aging* (ed. Bernice L. Neugarten). University of Chicago Press, London.
Parkes, C. M. (1971). The first year of bereavement: a longitudinal study of the reaction of London widows to the death of their husbands. *Psychiatry* **33**.
*—— (1972). *Bereavement: studies of grief in adult life.* Tavistock, London.
Pathy, M. S. (1978). Clinical presentation and management of neurological disorders in old age. In *Textbook of geriatric medicine and gerontology* (ed. J. C. Brocklehurst) (2nd edn). Churchill Livingstone, London.
Pearce, J. and Miller, E., (1973). *Clinical aspects of dementia.* Baillière Tindall, London.
Peck, R. C. (1973). Psychological developments in the second half of life. In *Middle*

age and aging (ed. Bernice Neugarten). University of Chicago Press, London.
Post, F. (1965). *The clinical psychiatry of later life*. Pergamon, Oxford.
Preston, Caroline E. (1973). Behaviour modification: a therapeutic approach to ageing and dying. *Postgrad. Med.* **54**, 64–8.
Ramsay, R. W. (1977). Behavioural approaches to bereavement. *Behav. Res. Ther.* **15**, (2), 131–6.
Raphael, Beverley (1977). Preventive intervention with the recently bereaved. *Arch. gen. Psychiat.* **34**, 1450–54.
Raven, J. C. (1958*a*). *Mill Hill vocabulary scales: manual* (2nd edn). H. K. Lewis, London.
—— (1958*b*). *Guide to the Standard Progressive Matrices.* H. K. Lewis, London.
Rogers, C. R. (1951). *Client-centred therapy: current practices, implications and theory*. Houghton Mifflin, Boston.
—— (1959). A theory of therapy, personality, and interpersonal relationships as developed in the client-centred framework. In *Psychology: a study of a science* (ed. S. Koch) pp. 184–256. McGraw-Hill, New York.
*Sachs, D. A. (1975). Behavioral techniques in a residential nursing home facility. *J. behav. Ther. exp. Psychiat.* **6**, 123–7.
*Saltz, R. (1971). Aging persons as child-care workers in a foster-grandparent program, psychosocial effects and work performance. *Aging hum. Devel.* **3**, 314–40.
Savage, B. (1974). Rethinking psychogeriatric nursing care. *Nursing Times* **70**, 282–4.
Savage, R. D. (1971). Psychometric assessment and clinical diagnosis in the aged. In *Recent developments in psychogeriatrics:* a symposium (ed. D. W. K. Kay and A. Walk), pp. 51–61. *Br. J. Psychiat.* Special Publication No. 6.
Savage, R. D., Gaber, L. B., Britton, P. G., Bolton, N., and Cooper, A. (1977). *Personality and adjustment in the aged.* Academic Press, London.
Schafer, R. (1958). Regression in the service of the ego: the relevance of a psychoanalytic concept for personality assessment. In *Assessment of human motives* (ed. G. Lindzey), pp. 119–48. Rinehart, New York.
Seligman, M. E. P. (1975). *Helplessness: on depression, development and death.* Freeman, San Francisco.
Talland, G. A. (1971). *Disorders of memory and learning.* Penguin, Harmondsworth.
Turner, R. T. and Vanderlippe, R. H. (1958). Self-ideal congruence as an index of adjustment. *J. abnorm. soc. Psychol.* **57**, (2), 202–6.
Vingoe, F. J. (1968). Rogers' self theory and Eysenck's extraversion and neuroticism. *J. consult. clin. Psychol.* **32**, (5), 618–20.
Wechsler, D. (1955). *Manual for the Wechsler adult intelligence scale.* Psychological Corporation, New York.
Wolff, K. (1971). Individual psychotherapy with geriatric patients. *Psychosomatics* **12**, 89–93.
Woods, R. T. and Britton, P. G. (1977). Psychological approaches to the treatment of the elderly. *Age and Ageing* **6**, 104–13.

CHAPTER 4

*Appley, M. H. and Trumbull, R. (ed.) (1967). *Psychological stress.* Appleton-Century-Crofts, New York.
Barker, R. G., Dembo, Tamara, and Lewin, K. (1941). Frustration and regression: An experiment with young children. *Univ. Iowa Stud. Child Welf.* **18**, (1), 1–314.

Beecher, H. K. (1959). *Measurement of subjective responses: quantitative effects of drugs.* Oxford University Press, New York.

Bourne, P. G. (ed.) (1969). *The psychology and physiology of stress.* Academic Press, New York.

Butterfield, E. C. (1964). Locus of control, test anxiety, reaction to frustration, and achievement attitudes. *J. Personality* **32**, 298–311.

Byrne, D. (1961). The Repression-sensitization scale: rationale, reliability, and validity. *J. Personality* **29**, 334–49.

—— (1964). Repression-sensitization as a dimension of personality. In *Progress in personality research* (ed. B. A. Maher), pp. 170–220, Vol. 1. Academic Press, New York.

Chapman, C. R. and Cox, G. B. (1977). Anxiety, pain, and depression surrounding elective surgery: A multivariate comparison of abdominal surgery patients with kidney doners and recipients. *J. psychosom. Res.* **21**, 7–15.

Child, I. L. and Waterhouse, I. K. (1952). Frustration and the quality of performance: I. A critique of the Barker, Dembo and Lewin experiment. *Psychol. Rev.* **59**, 351–62.

—— —— (1953). Frustration and the quality of performance: II. A theoretical statement. *Psychol. Rev.* **60**, 127–39.

*Cochrane, R. and Robertson, A. (1973). The life events inventory: A measure of the relative severity of psycho-social stressors. *J. psychosom. Res.* **17**, 135–9.

Cofer, C. N. and Appley, M. H. (1967). *Motivation: theory and research.* Wiley, New York.

*Cohen, Frances and Lazarus, R. S. (1973). Active coping processes, coping dispositions, and recovery from surgery. *Psychosom. Med.* **35**, (5), 375–89.

Davitz, J. R. (1952). The effects of previous training on post-frustration behavior. *J. abnorm. soc. Psychol.* **47**, 309–15.

—— (1969). The effects of previous training on post-frustration behavior. In *Readings in social development* (ed. R. D. Parkes), pp. 411–22. Holt, Rinehart, and Winston, New York.

Dollard, J., Miller, N. E., Doob, L. W., Mowrer, O. H., and Sears, R. R. (1974). *Frustration and aggression.* Yale University Press, New Haven, Connecticut.

*Egbert, L. D., Battit, B. E., Welch, C. E., and Bartlett, M. K. (1964). Reduction of postoperative pain by encouragement and instruction of patients. *New Eng. J. Med.* **270**, 825–7.

Erickson, R. C., Smyth, L., Donovan, D. M., and O'Leary, M. R. (1976). Psychopathology and defensive style of alcoholics as a function of congruence–incongruence between psychological differentiation and locus of control. *Psychol. Rep.* **39**, 51–4.

*Fenz, W. D. and Epstein, S. (1967). Gradients of physiological arousal of experienced and novice parachutists as a function of an approaching jump. *Psychosom. Med.* **29**, 33–51.

Gough, H. G. and Heilbrun, A. B. (1965). *The adjective check list manual.* Consulting Psychologists Press, Palo Alto.

Gutkin, T. B. (1977). The modification of locus of control among lower class, minority, elementary school students: An operant approach. Doctoral Dissertation; University of Texas at Austin (1975). *Diss. Abstr. Int.* **36**, (10), 6551–A.

Hersch, P. D. and Scheibe, K. E. (1967). Reliability and validity of internal–external control as a personality dimension. *J. consult. Psychol.* **31**, (6), 609–13.

Janis, I. L. (1958). *Psychological stress.* Academic Press, New York.

—— (1971). *Stress and frustration.* Harcourt Brace Jovanovich, New York.

*Langer, Ellen, Janis, I. L., and Wolfer, J. A. (1975). Reduction of psychological stress in surgical patients. *J. exp. soc. Psychol.* **11**, 155–65.

Lao, R. C. (1970). Internal–external control and competent and innovative behavior among Negro college students. *J. Personality & soc. Psychol.* **14**, 263–70.

Lazarus, R. S. (1966). *Psychological stress and the coping process.* McGraw-Hill, New York.

Lefcourt, H. M. (1972). Recent developments in the study of locus of control. In *Progress in experimental personality research* (ed. B. A. Maher), Vol. 6. Academic Press, New York.

Lewin, K. (1948). *Resolving social conflicts.* Harper, New York.

Luria, A. R. (1932). *The nature of human conflict.* Liveright, New York.

Maier, N. R. F. (1949). *Frustration: The study of behavior without a goal.* McGraw-Hill, New York.

—— (1956). Frustration theory: Restatement and extension. *Psychol. Rev.* **63**, 370–88

Miller, N. E. (1944). Experimental studies of conflict. In *Personality and the behavior disorders* (ed. J. McV. Hunt), pp. 431–65. Ronald Press, New York.

—— (1959). Liberalization of basic S–R concepts: extensions to conflict behavior, motivation and social learning. In *Psychology: a study of a science* (ed. S. Koch), Vol. 2, pp. 196–292. McGraw-Hill, New York.

—— (1961). Some recent studies of conflict behavior and drugs. *Am. Psychol.* **16**, 12–24.

—— (1964). Some implications of modern behavior theory for personality change and psychotherapy. In *Personality change* (ed. P. Worchel and D. Byrne). Wiley, New York.

—— and Kraeling, D. (1953). Displacement: greater generalization of approach than avoidance in a general approach–avoidance conflict. *J. exp. Psychol.* **43**, 217–21.

—— and Murray, E. J. (1952). Displacement and conflict: Learnable drive as a basis for the steeper gradient of avoidance than of approach. *J. exp. Psychol.* **43**, 227–31.

Monroe, R. R. (1970). *Episodic behavioral disorders.* Harvard University Press, Cambridge, Mass.

Parke, R. D. (ed.) (1969). *Readings in social development.* Holt, Rinehart, and Winston, New York.

Plutchik, R., Hyman, I., Conte, Hope, and Karasu, T. B. (1977). Medical symptoms and life stresses in psychiatric emergency-room patients. *J. abnorm. Psychol.* **86**, (4), 447–9.

Rosenzweig, S. (1943). An experimental study of 'repression' with special reference to need-persistive and ego-defensive reactions to frustration. *J. exp. Psychol.* **32**, 64–74.

Rotter, J. B. (1966). Generalized expectancies for internal versus external locus of control of reinforcement. *Psychol. Monogr.* **80**.

*—— (1975). Some problems and misconceptions related to the construct of internal versus external control of reinforcement. *J. consult. & Clin. Psychol.* **43**, (1), 56–67.

——, Chance, June E., and Phares, E. J. (1972). *Applications of social learning theory to personality.* Holt, Rinehart and Winston, New York.

Schmale, A. H. (1958). Relationship of separation and depression to disease. A report on a hospitalized medical population. *Psychosom. Med.* **20**, 259–77.

*Seligman, M. E. P. (1975). Helplessness: *On depression, development and death.* W. H. Freeman, San Francisco.

Selye, H. (1952). *The story of the adaptation syndrome.* Acta, Inc., Montreal.

—— (1956). *The stress of life.* McGraw-Hill, New York.

Torrence, E. (1965). Constructive behavior. *Stress, personality, and mental health.* Wadsworth, Belmont, California.

Walk, R. D. (1956). Self-ratings of fear in a fear-evoking situation. *J. abnorm. Psychol.* **52**, 171–8.

Worchel, P. and Byrne, D. (1964). *Personality change.* Wiley, London.

CHAPTER 5

Ax, A. (1953). The physiological differentiation between fear and anger in humans. *Psychosom. Med.* **15**, (5), 433–42.

Bachrach, A. J., Erwin, W. J., and Mohr, J. P. (1965). The control of eating in an anorexic by operant conditioning techniques. In *Case studies in behavior modification* (ed. L. P. Ullman and L. Krasner). Holt, Rinehart, and Winston, New York.

Beumont, P. J. V., Beardwood, C. J., and Russell, G. F. M. (1972). The occurrence of the syndrome of anorexia nervosa in male subjects. *Psychol. Med.* **2**, 216–31.

Bhanji, S. and Thompson, J. (1974). Operant conditioning in the treatment of anorexia nervosa: a review and retrospective study of 11 cases. *Br. J. Psychiat.* **124**, 166–72.

*Birk, L. (1973) (ed.). *Biofeedback: behavioral medicine.* Grune and Stratton, New York.

Blake, R. R. and Ramsey, G. V. (1951). *Perception: an approach to personality.* Ronald, New York.

Blanchard, E. B. and Haynes, Mary R. (1975). Biofeedback treatment of a case of Raynaud's disease. *J. behav. Ther. & exp. Psychiat.* **6**, 230–4.

*—— and Miller, S. T. (1977). Psychological treatment of cardiovascular disease. *Archs gen. Psychiat.* **34**, 1402–13.

*—— and Young, L. D. (1974). Clinical applications of biofeedback training. *Archs gen. Psychiat.* **30**, 573–89.

Button, E. J., Fransella, F., and Slade, P. (1977). A reappraisal of body perception disturbance in anorexia nervosa. *Psychol. Med.* **7**, 235–43.

Claridge, G. (1973). Psychosomatic relations in physical disease. In *Handbook of abnormal psychology* (2nd edn) (ed. H. J. Eysenck), pp. 689–717. Pitman Medical, London.

Cochrane, R. and Robertson, A. (1973). The life events inventory: a measure of the relative severity of psycho-social stressors. *J. psychosom. Res.* **17**, 135–9.

*Creer, T. L., Weinberg, E., and Molk, L. (1974). Managing a hospital behavior problem: malingering. *J. behav. Ther. exp. Psychiat.* **5**, 259–62.

Dunbar, H. (1943). *Psychosomatic Diagnosis.* Hoeber-Harper, New York.

Eason, R. G. and Dudley, L. M. (1971). Physiological and behavioural indicants of activation. *Psychophysiology*, **7**, (2), 223–32.

Engel, B. T. (1973). Clinical applications of operant conditioning techniques in the control of the cardiac arrhythmias. In *Biofeedback: behavioral medicine* (ed. L. Birk). Grune and Stratton, New York.

Evans, B. (1976). A case of trichotillomania in a child treated in a home token program. *J. behav. Ther. exp. Psychiat.* **7**, 197–8.

Eysenck, H. J. (1967). *The biological basis of personality.* Charles C. Thomas, Springfield, Illinois.

Fiske, D. W. and Maddi, S. R. (ed.) (1961). *Functions of varied experience.* Dorsey Press, Homewood, Illinois.

Funkenstein, D. H. (1955). The physiology of fear and anger. *Scient. Am.* (Reprint No. 428).

*Gardner, E. (1968). *Fundamentals of neurology*. Saunders, Philadelphia.

Gottlieb, A. A., Gleser, Goldine C., and Gottschalk, L. A. (1967). Verbal and physiological responses to hypnotic suggestion of attitudes. *Psychosom. Med.* **29**, 172–83.

Graham, F. K. and Kunish, N. O. (1965). Physiological responses of unhypnotized subjects to attitude suggestions. *Psychosom. Med.* **27**, 317–29.

Greenfield, N. S. and Sternbach, R. A. (ed.) (1972). *Handbook of psychophysiology*. Wiley, New York.

Ham, M. W. and Edmonston, W. E. Jr. (1971). Hypnosis, relaxation and motor retardation. *J. abnormal Psychol.* **77**, 329–31.

Hare, R. D. and Schalling, D. (ed.) (1977). *Psychopathy and behavior*. Wiley, New York.

Hebb, D. O. (1966). *A textbook of psychology*. Saunders, Philadelphia.

Jacob, R. G., Kraemer, Helena C., and Agras, W. S. (1977). Relaxation therapy in the treatment of hypertension. *Archs gen. Psychiat.* **34**, 1417–27.

Jacobsen, A. M., Hackett, T. P., Surman, A. S., and Silverberg, E. L. (1973). Raynaud phenomenon: treatment with hypnotic and operant techniques. *J. Am. med. Ass.* **225**, 739–40.

Kaufman, M. R. and Heiman, M. (1964). *Evolution of psychosomatic concepts. Anorexia nervosa: a paradigm*. International Universities Press, New York.

Khan, A. U. (1977). Effectiveness of biofeedback and counter-conditioning in the treatment of bronchial asthma. *J. psychosom. Res.* **21**, (2), 97–104.

*Knapp, R. J. and Wells, Linda A. (1978). Behavior therapy for asthma: a review. *Behav. Res. & Ther.* **16**, 103–15.

Knight, A. (1979). Personal communication.

Konečni, V. J. (1975). The mediation of aggressive behavior: arousal level versus anger and cognitive labeling. *J. personality soc. Psychol.* **32**, (4), 706–12.

*Lachman, S. J. (1972). *Psychosomatic disorders: a behaviouristic approach*. Wiley, London.

Lang, P. J. and Melamed, Barbara G. (1969). Case report: avoidance conditioning therapy of an infant with chronic ruminative vomiting. *J. abnorm. Psychol.* **74**, (1), 1–8.

*Leon, Gloria, R. (1976). Current directions in the treatment of obesity. *Psychol. Bull.* **83**, (4), 557–78.

—— and Roth, Lydia (1977). Obesity: psychological causes, correlations, and speculations. *Psychol. Bull.* **84**, (1), 117–39.

Levine, B. A. (1976). Treatment of trichotillomania by covert sensitization. *J. behav. Ther. & exp. Psychiat.* **7**, 75–6.

Lindsley, D. B. (1950). Emotions and the electroencephalogram: In *The Second International Symposium on Feelings and Emotions* (ed. M. L. Reymert). McGraw-Hill, New York.

—— (1951). Emotion. In *Handbook of experimental psychology* (ed. S. S. Stevens). Wiley, London.

*Lynch, J. J. (1977). *The broken heart: the medical consequences of loneliness*. Harper and Row, New York.

McLaughlin, Julia G. and Nay, W. R. (1975). Treatment of trichotillomania using positive coverants and response cost: a case report. *Behav. Ther.* **6**, 87–91.

Maddi, S. R. (1968). *Personality theories: a comparative analysis*. Dorsey Press, Homewood, Illinois.

Maher, B. (1966). *Principles of psychopathology: an experimental approach*. McGraw-Hill, London.

Martin, Irene (1973*a*). Somatic reactivity: methodology. In *Handbook of abnormal psychology* (2nd edn), (ed. H. J. Eysenck). Pitman Medical, London.

—— (1973*b*): Somatic reactivity: interpretation. In *Handbook of abnormal psychology* (2nd edn), (ed. H. J. Eysenck). Pitman Medical, London.

Mischel, W. (1968). *Personality and assessment.* Wiley, New York.

*Mitchell, K. R. (1978). Self-management of spastic colitis. *J. behav. Ther. & exp. Psychiat.* **9**, 269–72.

Morgan, C. T. (1965). *Physiological psychology.* McGraw-Hill, New York.

Moruzzi, G. and Magoun, H. W. (1949). Brain stem reticular formation and activation of the EEG. *Electroenceph. clin. Neurophysiol.* **1**, 455–73.

Oken, D. (1967). The psychophysiology and psychoendocrinology of stress and emotion. In *Psychological Stress* (ed. M. H. Appley and R. Trumbull). Appleton-Century-Croft, New York.

Peters, J. E. and Stern, R. M. (1971). Specificity of attitude hypothesis in psychosomatic medicine: a re-examination. *J. psychosom. Res.* **15**, 129–35.

Philipp, R. L., Wilde, G. J. S., and Day, J. H. (1972). Suggestion and relaxation in asthmatics. *J. psychosom. Res.* **16**, 193–204.

*Phillips, Clare (1976). Headache and personality. *J. psychosom. Res.* **20**, 535–42.

Pillay, M. and Crisp, A. H. (1977). Some psychological characteristics of patients with anorexia nervosa whose weight has been newly restored. *Br. J. med. Psychol.* **50**, 375–80.

Plutchik, R. and Ax, A. F. (1967). A critique of determinants of emotional state by Schachter and Singer (1962). *Psychophysiology* **4**, 79–82.

Routtenberg, A. (1968). The two-arousal hypothesis: reticular formation and limbic system. *Psychol. Rev.* **75**, 1, 51–80.

Schachter, S. (1964). The interaction of cognitive and physiological determinants of emotional state. In *Advances in experimental social psychology* (ed. L. Berkowitz), Vol. 1. Academic Press, New York.

—— (1971). Some extraordinary facts about obese humans and rats. *Am. Psychol.* **26**, 129–44.

—— and Singer, J. E. (1962). Cognitive, social and physiological determinants of emotional state. *Psychol. Rev.* **69**, 379–99.

Schadé, J. P. (1968). *Het Zenuwstelsel.* De Tijdstroom Lochem, Amsterdam.

Shagass, C. (1969). Neurophysiological studies. In *The schizophrenic syndrome* (ed. L. Bellek and L. Loeb). Grune and Stratton, New York.

Schwartz, G. E. and Shapiro, D. (1973). Biofeedback and essential hypertension. Current findings and theoretical concerns. In *Biofeedback: behavioral medicine* (ed. Lee Birk), pp. 133–43. Grune and Stratton, New York.

Stainbrook, E. (1952). Psychosomatic medicine in the nineteenth century. *Psychosom. Med.* **14**, 211–27. Reprinted (1964). In *Evolution of psychosomatic concepts* (ed. M. R. Kaufman and M. Heiman), pp. 6–35. International Universities Press, New York.

Stunkard, A. J. and Fox, S. (1971). The relationship of gastric motility and hunger. *Psychosom. Med,* **33**, 123–34.

Surwit, R. S. (1973). Raynaud's disease. In *Biofeedback: behavioral medicine* (ed. Lee Birk), pp. 123–30. Grune and Stratton, New York.

Susen, G. R. (1978). Conditioned relaxation in a case of ulcerative colitis. *J. behav. Ther. & exp. Psychiat.* **9**, 281–2.

Weiss, T. and Engel, B. T. (1973). Operant conditioning of heart rate in patients with premature ventricular contractions. *Biofeedback: behavioral medicine* (ed. L. Birk), pp. 79–100. Grune and Stratton, New York.

White, J. D. and Taylor, D. (1967). Noxious conditioning as a treatment for rumination. *Ment. Retard.* **5**, 30–3.

Worchel, P. and Byrne, D. (1964). *Personality change.* Wiley, London.

CHAPTER 6

Andreychuk, T. and Shriver, C. (1975). Hypnosis and biofeedback in the treatment of migraine headache. *Int. J. exp. Hypn.* **23**, (3), 172–83.

*Bakal, D. A. and Kaganov, Judith A. (1977). Muscle contraction and migraine headache: psychophysiologic comparison. *Headache* **17**, (5), 208–14.

Baker, J. W. and Merskey, H. (1967). Pain in general practice. *J. psychosom. Res.* **10**, 383–7.

Beecher, H, K. (1959). *Measurement of subjective responses: quantitative effects of drugs.* Oxford University Press, New York.

Blanchard, E. B. and Young, L. D. (1974). Clinical application of biofeedback training: a review of evidence. *Archs gen. Psychiat.* **30**, 573–89.

*Bond, M. R. (1979). *Pain, its nature, analysis and treatment.* Churchill-Livingstone, Edinburgh.

—— and Pearson, I. B. (1969). Psychological aspects of pain in women with advanced cancer of the cervix. *J. psychosom. Res.* **13**, 13–19.

—— and Pilowsky, I. (1966). Subjective assessment of pain and its relationship to the administration of analgesics in patients with advanced cancer. *J. psychosom. Res* **10**, 203–8.

Budzynski, T. H., Stoyva, J. M., Adler, C. S., and Mullaney, D. J. (1973). EMG biofeedback and tension headache: A controlled outcome study. *Psychosom. Med.* **35**, 484–96.

Chesney, M. A. and Shelton, J. L. (1974). A comparison of muscle relaxation and electromyogram biofeedback treatments for muscle contraction headache. *J. behav. Ther. & exp. Psychiat.* **7**, (3), 221–3.

Comaroff, J. (1976). A bitter pill to swallow: placebo therapy in general practice. *Sociol. Rev.* **24**, 79–96.

Cox, D. J., Freundlich, A., and Meyer, R. G. (1975). Differential effectiveness of electromyograph feedback, verbal relaxation instructions, and medication placebo with tension headaches. *J. consult. clin. Psychol.* **43**, (6), 892–908.

Daniels, H. (1976). The effects of automated hypnosis and hand warming on migraine: a pilot study. *Am. J. clin. Hypn.* **19**, (2), 91–4.

Davidson, P. O. and McDougall, C. Evalynne A. (1969). Personality and pain tolerance measures. *Percept. motor. Skills* **28**, 787–90.

Dubuisson, D. and Melzack, R. (1976). Classification of clinical pain descriptions by multiple group descriminant analysis. *Exp. Neurol.* **51**, 480–7.

Duncker, K. (1937). Some preliminary experiments on the mutual influence of pains. *Psychol. Forsch.* **21**, 311–26.

Epstein, L. H. and Abel, G. G. (1977). An analysis of biofeedback training effects for tension headache patients. *Behav. Ther.* **8**, (1), 37–47.

Evans, F. J. (1969). Placebo response: relationship to suggestibility and hypnotizability. *Proceedings of the 77th Annual Convention, American Psychological Association, Part II,* pp. 889–90.

Eysenck, H. J. and Eysenck, S. B. G. (1976). *Manual of the Eysenck personality questionnaire.* Hodder and Stoughton, London.

Fish, J. M. (1973). *Placebotherapy.* Jossey-Bass, London.

*Fordyce, W. (1976). *Behavioral methods for chronic pain and illness.* Mosby, St Louis.

Fordyce, W. E., Fowler, R. S., and DeLateur, B. (1968). An application of behavior modification techniques to a problem of chronic pain. *Behav. Res. Ther.* **6**, 105–7.

Friedman, A. P. (1975). Migraine. *Psychiat. Ann.* **9**, (7), 271–8.

—— Finley, K. H., Graham, J. R., Kunkle, E. C., Ostfeld, A. M., and Wolff, H. G.

(1962). Classification of headache. *J. Am. Med. Ass.* **179**, 717–18.

Gainer, J. C. (1978). Temperature discrimination training in the biofeedback treatment of migraine headache. *J. behav. Ther. & exp. Psychiat.* **9**, 185–99.

Graham, G. W. (1975). Hypnotic treatment for migraine headache. *Int. J. clin. & exp. Hypn.* **23**, (3), 165–71.

Groenman, N. H. (1974). Gedragswetenschappen in het medisch onderwijs programma. *Medisch Cont.* **29**, 1137–41.

Hardy, J. D., Wolff, H. G., and Goodell, H. (1952). *Pain sensations and reactions.* Williams and Wilkins, Baltimore.

Haynes, S. M., Griffin, P., Mooney, D., and Parise, M. (1975). Electromyographic biofeedback and relaxation instructions in the treatment of muscle contraction headaches. *Behav. Ther.* **6**, (5), 672–8.

Hill, H. E., Kornetsky, C. H., Flanary, H. G., and Winkler, A. (1952). Studies of anxiety associated with anticipation of pain. I. Effects of morphine. *Archs. Neurol. Psychiat.* **67**, 612–19.

Johnson, W. G. and Turin, A. (1975). Biofeedback treatment of migraine headaches: a systematic case study. *Behav. Ther.* **6**, (3), 394–7.

Kane, F. J. Jnr., Downie, A. W., Marcotte, D. B., and Perez-Reyes, M. (1968). A case of congenital indifference to pain. *Dis. nerv. Syst.* **29**, 409–12.

Klusman, L. E. (1975). Reduction of pain in childbirth by the alleviation of anxiety during pregnancy. *J. consult. & clin. Psychol.* **43**, 162–5.

Levine, F. M., Tursky, B., and Nichols, D. C. (1966). Tolerance for pain, extraversion and neuroticism: failure to replicate results. *Percept. mot. Skills* **23**, 847–50.

Liebeskind, J. C. and Paul, Linda A. (1977). Psychological and physiological mechanisms of pain. In *Ann. Rev. Psychol.* (ed. M. R. Rosenzweig and L. W. Porter) **28**, 41–60.

Livingston, W. K. (1953). What is pain? *Scient. Am.* **88**, 59–66.

Lynn, R. and Eysenck, H. J. (1961). Tolerance for pain, extraversion and neuroticism. *Percept. mot. Skills* **12**, 161–2.

McKechnie, R. J. (1975). Relief from phantom limb pain by relaxation exercises. *J. behav. Ther. exp. Psychiat.* **6**, 262–3.

*Melzack, R. (1970). The perception of pain. In *Perception and its disorders.* Research Publication of The Association for Research in Nervous and Mental Disease **48**, 272–85.

*—— (1973). *The puzzle of pain.* Penguin, Harmondsworth.

—— (1975). The McGill Pain Questionnaire: major properties and scoring methods. *Pain* **1**, 277–99.

*—— and Perry, C. (1975). Self-regulation of pain: the use of alpha-feedback and hypnotic training for the control of chronic pain. *Exp. Neurol.* **46**, 452–69.

Mersky, H. and Spear, F. G. (1964). The reliability of the pressure algometer. *Br. J. soc. & clin. psychol.* **3**, 130–6.

Nichols, D. C. and Tursky, B. (1966). Body image, anxiety, and tolerance for experimental pain. *Psychosom. Med.* **29**, 103–10.

Opler, M. K. (1961). Ethnic differences in behavior and health practices. in *The family: a focal point for health education* (ed. I. Galdson). New York Academy of Medicine.

Peters, J. E. and Stern, R. M. (1973). Peripheral skin temperature and vasomotor responses during hypnotic induction. *Int. J. clin. exp. Hypn.* **22**, (2), 102–8.

—— Lundy, R. M., and Stern, R. M. (1973). Peripheral skin temperature response to hot and cold suggestions. *Int. J. clin. & exp. Hypn.* **21**, (3), 205–12.

Philips, Clare (1976). Headache and personality. *J. psychosom. Res.* **20**, (6), 535–42.

Pilling, L. F., Brannick, T. L., and Swenson, W. M. (1967). Psychologic characteristics of psychiatric patients having pain as a presenting symptom. *Can. Med. Ass. J.* **97**, 387–94.

Rachman, J. and Phillips, C. (1975). A new medical psychology. *New Scient.* **65**, No. 938, 518–20.

Rachman, S. (1965). Aversion therapy: chemical or electrical? *Behav. Res. & Ther.* **2**, 289–99.

Rapoport, Judith L. (1969). A case of congenital sensory neuropathy diagnosis in infancy. *J. Child Psychol. & Psychiat.* **10**, 63–8.

Reid, A. F. and Curtsinger, G. (1968). Physiological changes associated with hypnosis: the effect of hypnosis on temperature. *Int. J. clin. & exp. Hypn.* **16**, (2), 111–19.

*Roberts, A. H., Kewman, D. G., and MacDonald, H. (1973). Voluntary control of skin temperature: unilateral changes using hypnosis and feedback. *J. abnorm. Psychol.* **82**, (1), 163–8.

Sargent, J. D., Walters, E. D., and Green, E. E. (1973). Psychosomatic self-regulation of migraine headaches. *Semin. Psychiat.* **5**, 415–28.

Shapiro, A. K. and Morris, L. A. (1978). Placebo effects in medical and psychological therapies. In *Handbook of psychotherapy and behaviour change: an empirical analysis* (2nd edn), (ed. S. L. Garfield and A. E. Bergin), pp. 369–410. Sternbach, R. A. (1968). *Pain: a psychophysiological analysis.* Academic Press, New York.

Solbach, Patricia and Sargent, J. D. (1977). A follow-up evaluation of the Menninger pilot migraine study using thermal training. *Headache.* **17**, (5), 198–208.

Sternbach, R. A. (1968). *Pain: a psychophysiological analysis.* Academic Press, New York.

*—— (1974). *Pain patients traits and treatment.* Academic Press, New York.

—— and Tursky, B. (1965). Ethnic differences among housewives in psychophysical and skin potential responses to electric shock. *Psychophysiology* **1**, 241–6.

*Szasz, T. S. (1957). *Pain and pleasure: a study of bodily feelings.* Basic Books, New York.

Turin, A. and Johnson, W. G. (1976). Biofeedback therapy for migraine headaches. *Archs gen. Psychiat.* **33**, (4), 517–19.

Tursky, B. and Sternbach, R. A. (1967). Physiological correlates of ethnic differences in response to shock. *Psychophysiology* **4**, 67–74.

Vingoe, F. J. (1979). Attitudes of medical students to various psychological topics in the psychology curriculum. Unpublished paper. Dept. *Psychol. med. Welsh National School of Medicine.*

—— and Lewis, Rita (1979). An investigation of EMG feedback, alpha rhythm and relaxation in the treatment of tension headache. Unpublished paper. University Hospital of Wales.

Walton, J. N. (1971). *Essentials of neurology* (3rd edn). Pitman Medical, London.

Wexler, M. (1976). The behavioral sciences in medical education: a view from psychology. *Am. Psychol.* **31**, (4), 275–83.

Whitty, C. W. M. and Hockaday, J. M. (1968). Migraine: a follow-up study of 92 patients. *Br. med. J.* **1**, 735–6.

—— —— and Whitty, M. M. (1966). The effect of oral contraceptives on migraine. *Lancet* **i**, 856–9.

Wickramasekera, I. (1972). Electromyographic feedback training and tension headache: preliminary observations. *Am. J. Clin. Hypn.* **15**, 83–5.

Wolff, B. B. and Langley, Sarah (1968). Cultural factors and pain response: a review. *Am. Anthrop.* **70**, 494–501.

Woodforde, J. M. and Mersky, H. (1972). Personality traits of patients with chronic

pain. *J. Psychosom. Res.* **16**, (3), 167–72.
Zborowski, M. (1952). Cultural components in responses to pain. *J. soc. issues* **8**, 16–30.
—— (1969). *People in pain.* Jossey-Bass, San Francisco.

CHAPTER 7

Aarons, L. (1976). Sleep assisted instruction *Psychol. Bull.* **83**, 1–40.
Aserinsky, E. and Kleitman, N. (1953). Regularly occurring periods of eye motility, and concomitant phenomena, during sleep. *Science, N.Y.* **118**, 273–4.
Borkovek, T. D. and Fowles, P. C. (1973). Controlled investigation of the effects of progressive and hypnotic relaxation on insomnia. *J. abnorm. Psychol.* **82**, 153–8.
*Broughton, R. J. (1968). Sleep disorders: disorders of arousal? *Science, N.Y.* **159**.
Cohen, D. B. (1974). Theories of dream recall. *Psychol. Bull.* **81**, (2), 138–54.
—— (1976). Dreaming: experimental investigation of representational and adaptive properties. In *Consciousness and self-regulation: advances in research* (ed. G. E. Schwartz and D. Shapiro) Vol. 1, pp. 313–60. Wiley, London.
Dallett, Janet (1973). Theories of dream function. *Psychol. Bull.* **79**, (6) 408–16.
Davison, G. C., Tsujimoto, R. N., and Glaros, A. G. (1973). Attribution and the maintenance of behavior change in falling asleep. *J. abnorm. Psychol.* **82**, (1), 124–33.
—— and Valins, S. (1969). Maintenance of self-attributed and drug-attributed behavior change. *J. Personality & soc. Psychol.* **11**, 25–33.
De Barros-Ferreira, M., Goldsteinas, L., and Lairy, G. C. (1973). REM sleep deprivation in chronic schizophrenics: effects on the dynamics of fast sleep. *Electroenceph. clin. Neurophysiol.* **34**, 561–9. Elsevier Scientific Publishing Co., Amsterdam.
Dement, W. C. (1955). Dream recall and eye movements during sleep in schizophrenics and normals. *J. nerv. ment. Dis.* **122**, 263–9.
—— (1974). *Some must watch while some must sleep.* W. H. Freeman, San Francisco.
—— and Kleitman, N. (1957). The relation of eye movements during sleep to dream activity: an objective method for the study of dreaming. *J. exp. Psychol.* **53**, 339–6.
Evans, F. J. (1973). Hypnosis and sleep: techniques for exploring cognitive activity during sleep. In *Hypnosis: research developments and perspectives* (ed. Erika Fromm and R. E. Shor). Elek (Scientific Books), London.
Feinberg, I., Koresko, R. L., and Heller, N. (1967). EEG sleep patterns as a function of normal and pathological aging in man. *J. psychiat. Res.* **5**, 107–44.
Foulkes, D. (1962). Dream reports from different states of sleep. *J. abnorm. soc. Psychol.* **65**, 14–25.
—— and Rechtschaffen, A. (1964). Presleep determinants of dream content: The effect of two films. *Percept. mot. Skills* **19**, 983–1005.
Friedmann, J., Globus, G., Huntley, A., Mullaney, D., Naitoh, P., and Johnson, L. (1977). Performance and mood during and after gradual sleep reduction. *Psychophysiology* **14**, (3), 245–50.
Goodenough D. R., Lewis, H. B., Shapiro, A., and Sleser, I. (1965). Some correlates of dream reporting following laboratory awakenings. *J. nerv. ment. Dis.* **140**, 365–73.
—— Shapiro, A., Holden, M., and Steinschriber, L. (1959). A comparison of "dreamers" and "non-dreamers": Eye movements, electroencephalograms and the recall of dreams. *J. abnorm. soc. Psychol.* **62**, 295–302.
Greenfield, N. S. and Sternbach, R. A. (1972). *Handbook of psychophysiology.* Holt, Rinehart, and Winston, New York.

Hartmann, E. (1974). The effects of drugs on sleep. In *Brain and sleep* (ed. H. M. van Praag and H. Meinardi). De Erven Bohn, Amsterdam.

—— and Brewer, Valerie (1976). When is more or less sleep required? *Compr. Psychiat.* **17**, (2), 275–84.

—— Baekeland, F., and Zwilling, G. R. (1972). Psychological differences between long and short sleepers. *Archs gen. psychiat.* **26**, 463–8.

Hobson, J. A., Goldfrank, F., and Snyder, F. (1965). Respiration and mental activity in sleep. *J. psychiat. Res.* **3**, 79–90.

Ingvar, D. H. (1973). Localized blood flow and REM sleep changes, *Acta neurol. scand.* **49**, 233–44.

Jacobson, A., Kales, A., Lehmann, D., and Zweizig, J. R. (1965). Somnambulism: all night EEG studies. *Science, N.Y.* **148**, 975–7.

Jasper, H. H. (1958). Report of the committee on Methods of Clinical Examination in Electroencephalography. *Electroenceph. clin. neurophysiol.* **10**, 370–5.

*Johnson, L. C. (1970). A psychophysiology for all states. *Psychophysiology* **6**, 501–16.

*—— (1975). The effect of total, partial, and stage sleep deprivation on EEG patterns and performance. In *Behavior and brain electrical activity* (ed. N. Burch and H. L. Altshuler). Plenum, New York.

—— and Naitoh, P. (1969). Instrumentation for sleep research. *Am. Psychol.* **24**, 233–5.

—— Naitoh, P., Moses, J., and Lubin, A. (1974). Interaction of REM deprivation and stage 4 deprivation with total sleep loss: experiment 2. *psychophysiology* **11**, (2), 147–59.

Jouvet, M., Michel, F., and Mounier, D. (1960). Analyse electroencephalographique comparée du sommeil physiologique chez le chat et chez l'homme. *Rev. Neurol. (Paris)* **103**, 189–204.

Kahn, E. and Fisher, C. (1969). Some correlates of rapid eye movement sleep in the normal aged man. *J. nerv. ment. Dis.* **148**, 495–505.

Kales, A. (ed.) (1969). *Sleep: physiology and pathology*. Lippincott, Philadelphia.

—— Hoedemaker, F. S., Jacobson, A., Kales, J. D., Paulson, M. J., and Wilson, T. E. (1967). Mentation during sleep: REM and NREM recall reports. *Percept. mot Skills* **24**, 555–60.

—— Wilson, T., Kales, J. D., Jacobson, A., Paulson, M. J., Kollar, E., and Walter, R. D. (1967). Measurements of all night sleep in normal elderly persons: effects of aging. *J. Am. geriat. Soc.* **15**, 404–14.

Kamiya, J. (1969). Operant control of the EEG alpha rhythm and some of its reported effects on consciousness. In *Altered states of consciousness* (ed. C. T. Tart), pp. 509–17. Wiley, New York.

Kleitman, N. (1963). *Sleep and wakefulness* (2nd edn). Chicago University Press.

*Knapp, T. J., Downs, D. L., and Alperson, J. R. (1976). Behavior therapy for insomnia: a review. *Behav. Ther.* **7**, (5), 614–25.

Koella, W. P. (1974). The temporal qualitative and quantitative structure of sleep and its electrophysiological indicators. In *Brain and sleep* (ed. H. M. van Praag and H. Meinardi) pp. 7–21. De Erven Bohn, Amsterdam.

Kremen, I. (1961). Dream reports and rapid eye movements. Unpublished doctoral dissertation. Harvard University.

Lairy, G. C., Cor-Mordret, M., Faure, R., Ridjanovic, S. (1962). *Rev. Neurol.* **107**, 188.

Lubin, A., Moses, J. M.. Johnson, L. C., and Naitoh, P. (1974). The recuperative effects of REM sleep and stage 4 sleep on human performance after complete sleep loss: experiment I. *Psychophysiology* **11**, (2), 133–46.

Luce, G. G. and Segal, J. (1969). *Insomnia: the guide for troubled sleepers.* Doubleday, New York.

McNair, D. M., Lorr, M., and Droppleman, L. (1977). *Profile of mood states (POMS).* Educational and Industrial Testing Service, San Diego, California.

Meddis, R., Pearson, A. J. D., and Langford, G. (1973). An extreme case of healthy insomnia. *Electroenceph. clin. Neurophysiol.* **35**, 213–14.

*Montgomery, I., Perkin, G., and Wise, Deidre (1975). A review of behavioral treatments for insomnia. *J. behav. Ther. & exp. Psychiat.* **6**, 93–100.

Moruzzi, G., and Magoun, H. W. (1949). Brain stem reticular formation and activation of the EEG. *Electroenceph. clin. neurophysiol.* **1**, 455–73.

Mullaney, D. J., Johnson, L. C., Naitoh, P., Friedmann, J. K., and Globus, G. G. (1977). Sleep during and after gradual sleep reduction. *Psychophysiology* **14**, (3), 237–44.

Orlinsky, D. E., (1962). Psychodynamic and cognitive correlates of dream recall. Unpublished doctoral dissertation. University of Chicago.

Oswald, I. (1962). *Sleeping and waking: physiology and psychology.* Elsevier, Amsterdam.

*—— (1966). *Sleep.* Pelican, Harmondsworth.

*—— (1969). Sleep and its disorders. In *Handbook of clinical neurology,* pp. 80–111. North Holland, Amsterdam.

Post, R. M., Kolin, J., and Goodwin, F. K. (1976). Effects of sleep deprivation on mood and central amine metabolism in depressed patients. *Archs gen. psychiat.* **33**, (5), 627–32.

Rechtschaffen, A., Verdone, P. and Wheaton, J. (1963). Reports of mental activity during sleep. *Can. psychiat. Ass. J.* **8**, 409–14.

*Reid, W. H. (1975). Treatment of somnambulism in military trainees. *Am. J. Psychother.* **29**, (1), 101–6.

Roffwarg, H. D. *et al.* (1966). *Science N.Y.* **152**, 604–19.

Schacter, D. L. (1976). The hypnagogic state: a critical review of the literature. *Psychol. Bull.* **83**, (3), 452–81.

Snyder, F. (1960). Dream recall, respiration variability, and depth of sleep. Paper presented at the Round Table on Dream Research. Annual Meeting of the American Psychiatric Association, Atlantic City, N.J., May, 1960.

—— (1974). Unresolved questions concerning the interrelation of sleep loss and depression. In *Brain and sleep* (ed. H. M. van Praag and H. Meinardi). De Erven Bohn, Amsterdam.

—— and Scott, J. (1972). The psychophysiology of sleep. In *Handbook of psychophysiology* (ed. N. S. Greenfield and R. A. Sternbach), pp. 645–708. Holt, Rinehart, and Winston, London.

Stoyva, J. and Kamiya, J. (1968). Electrophysiological studies of dreaming as the prototype of a new strategy in the study of consciousness. *Psychol. Rev.* **75**, (3), 192–205.

Strauch, I. H. (1963). Paper presented to the Association for Psychophysiological Study of Sleep, March, 1963.

*Tart, C. T. (1969). *Altered states of consciousness: a book of readings.* Wiley, New York.

Tokarz, T. P. and Lawrence, P. S. (1974). An analysis of temporal and stimulus factors in the treatment of insomnia. Paper presented at the 8th Annual Meeting of the Association for the Advancement of Behaviour Therapy. Chicago, Illinois.

Van Den Hoofdakker, R. H., Bos, K. H. N., and Van Den Burg, W. (1974). In search of a depressive sleep syndrome. In *Brain and sleep* (ed. H. M. van Praag and H. Meinardi). De Erven Bohn, Amsterdam.

Webb, W. B. and Agnew, H. W. Jnr. (1974). The effects of a chronic limitation of sleep length. *Psychophysiology* **11**, 265–74.
—— and Cartwright, Rosalind D. (1978). Sleep and dreams. *Ann. Rev. Psychol.* **29**, 223–52.
Williams, R. L., Agnew, H. W. Jnr., and Webb, W. B. (1964). Sleep patterns in young adults: an EEG study. *Electroenceph. clin. Neurophysiol.* **17**, 376–81.
Witkin, H. A. and Lewis, Helen B. (ed.) (1967). *Experimental studies of dreaming.* Random House, New York.
Wolpert, E. A. (1960). Studies in psychophysiology of dreams: II. An electromyographic study of dreaming. *Archs gen. Psychiat.* **2**, 231–41.
—— and Trosman, H. (1958). Studies in psychophysiology of dreams: I. Experimental evocation of sequential dream episodes. *Archs neurol. Psychiat.* **79**, 603–6.
Yoss, R. E. and Daly, D. D. (1960). Narcolepsy. *Med. Clins N. Am.* **44**, 953–68.
*Zarcone, V. (1973). Narcolepsy. *New Engl. J. Med.* **288**, 1156–66.

CHAPTER 8

Allen, C. H., Frings, H., and Rudnick, I. (1948). Some biological effects of high frequency airborne sound. *J. Acoust. Soc. Am.* **20**, 62–5.
Bannister, D. (1965). The genesis of schizophrenic thought disorder—a retest of the serial invalidation hypothesis. *Br. J. Psychiat.* **113**, 377–82.
—— and Fransella, F. (1971). *Inquiring man.* Penguin, Baltimore.
—— and Salmon, P. (1966). Schizophrenic thought disorder—specific or diffuse? *Br. J. med. Psychol.* **39**, 215–19.
Barron, F. (1965). The psychology of creativity. *New directions in psychology* (ed. T. H. Newcomb), Vol. 2. Holt, Rinehart, and Winston, New York.
Bateson, G., Jackson, D. D., Haley, J., and Weakland, J. H. (1956). Towards a theory of schizophrenia. *Behav. Sci.* **1**, 251–64.
Brodsky, M. (1965). Interpersonal stimuli as interference in a sorting task. *J. Personality* **31**, 517–33.
Broen, W. E. and Storms, L. H. (1966). Lawful disorganisation: the process underlaying a schizophrenic syndrome. *Psychol. Rev.* **73**, 265–79.
Brown, G. and Birley, J. (1968). Crises and life changes and the onset of schizophrenia. *J. Hlth soc. Behav.* **9**, 203–14.
—— Monck, E., Carstairs, G., and Wing, J. (1962). Influence of family life on the course of schizophrenic illness. *Br. J. prev. soc. Med.* **16**, 55–68.
Bryant, A. R. P. (1961). An investigation of process-reactive schizophrenia with relation to perception of visual space. Unpublished doctoral dissertation, University of Utah.
Cameron, N. (1939). Deterioration and regression of schizophrenic thinking, *J. abnorm. soc. Psychol.* **34**, 265–70.
—— (1944). Experimental analysis of schizophrenic thinking. In *Language and thought in schizophrenia* (ed. J. Kasanin). University of California Press, Berkeley California.
Chapman, L. J. (1956). Distractibility in the conceptual performance of schizophrenics. *J. abnorm. soc. Psychol.* **53**, 286–91.
Claridge, G. (1972). The schizophrenias as nervous types. *Br. J. Psychiat.* **121**, 1–17.
*Corbett, L. (1976). Perceptual dyscontrol: a possible organising principle of schizophrenia research. *Schizophrenia Bull.* **2**, 249–65.
Depue, R. A. and Woodburn, L. (1975). Disappearance of paranoid symptoms with chronicity. *J. abnorm. Psychol.* **84**, 84–6.

*Dixon, N. F. (1971). *Subliminal perception. The nature of a controversy.* McGraw-Hill, London.

Draguns, J. G. (1963). Responses to cognitive and perceptual ambiguity in chronic and acute schizophrenics. *J. abnorm. soc. Psychol.* **66**, 24–30.

Duncker, K. (1945). On problem solving. *Psychol. Monogr.* **58**, No. 270.

Ellson, D. G. (1941). Hallucinations produced by sensory conditioning. *J. exp. Psychol.* **28**, 1–20.

Epstein, S. and Coleman, M. (1970). Drive theories of schizophrenia. *Psychosom. Med.* **32**, 113–40.

Eriksen, C. W. (1954). The case for perceptual defense. *Psychol. Rev.* **61**, 175–82.

Festinger, L. (1957). *A theory of cognitive dissonance.* Row-Peterson, New York.

Flavell, J. H., Draguns, J., Feinberg, L. D., and Budin, W. A. (1958). A microgenetic approach to word association. *J. abnorm. soc. Psychol.* **57**, 1–7.

*Forgus, R. H. (1966). *Perception: the basic process of cognitive development.* McGraw-Hill, New York.

Foulds, G. A., Hope K., McPherson, F. M., and Mayo, P. R. (1968). Paranoid delusions, retardation and overinclusive thinking. *J. clin. Psychol.* **24**, 177–8.

Foulkes, D., Spear, P. S., and Symonds, J. D. (1966). Individual differences in mental activity at sleep onset. *J. abnorm. Psychol.* **71**, 280–6.

Gagné, R. M. (1966). Human problem solving: internal and external events. In *Problem solving: research, method and theory* (ed. B. Kleinmuntz). Wiley, New York.

Getzels, J. W. and Jackson, P. O. (1962). *Creativity and intelligence.* Wiley, New York.

Goldstein, K. and Salzman, L. F. (1965). Proverb word counts as a measure of overinclusiveness in delusional schizophrenics. *J. abnorm. Psychol.* **70**, 244–5.

—— and Scheerer, M. (1941). Abstract and concrete behaviour: an experimental study with special tests. *Psychol. Monogr.* **53**, No. 2.

*Gregory, R. (1966). *Eye and brain: the psychology of seeing.* Weidenfeld and Nicolson, London.

Haley, G. A. (1971). Relations among chronicity, diagnosis, premorbid adjustment, defensiveness, and two measures of perceptual scanning. *Percept. mot. Skills* **33**, 1163–70.

Harris, J. G. (1957). Size estimation of pictures as a function of thematic content for schizophrenic and normal subjects. *J. Personality* **25**, 651–71.

Hawks, D. and Marshall, W. (1971). A parsimonious theory of overinclusive thinking and retardation in schizophrenia. *Br. J. med. Psychol.* **44**, 75–83.

Hawks, D. V. (1964). The clinical usefulness of some tests of overinclusive thinking in psychiatric patients. *Br. J. soc. clin. Psychol.* **3**, 186–95.

Heidbreder, E. (1946). The attainment of concepts; I: Terminology and methodology. II: The problem. *J. genet. Psychol.* **35**, 173–89, 191–223.

*Hemsley, D. R. (1977). What have cognitive deficits to do with schizophrenic symptoms? *Br. J. Psychiat.* **130**, 167–73.

Heron, W., Doane, B. K., and Scott, T. H. (1956). Visual disturbances after prolonged perceptual isolation. *Can. J. Psychol.* **10**, 13–18.

Jaspers, K. (1963). *General psychopathology* (7th edn). Manchester University Press, Manchester.

Jaensch, E. R. (1930). *Eidetic imagery.* Kegan Paul, London.

Kaufman, L. and Rock, I. (1962). The moon illusion. *Scient. Am.* **207**, 120–32.

Kelly, G. A. (1955). *The psychology of personal constructs.* Norton, New York.

Kubansky, P. E. (1958). Methodological and conceptual problems in the study of sensory deprivation. Paper presented at APA Meetings. Washington DC.

(Referred to in Forgus (1966). *Perception: the basic process in cognitive development*, p. 163. McGraw-Hill, New York).
Kugelmass, S. and Fondeur, M. R. (1955). Zaslow's test of concept formation: reliability and validity. *J. consult. Psychol.* **19**, 227–9.
Leeper, R. (1935). A study of a neglected portion of the field of learning: The development of sensory organisation. *J. genet. Psychol.* **46**, 42–75.
Lidz, T., Fleck, S., and Cornelison, A. (1965). *Schizophrenia and the family.* International Universities Press, New York.
Lilly, J. C. (1956). Mental effects of reduction of ordinary levels of physical stimuli on intact, healthy persons. *Psychiat. Res. Rep.* **5**, 1–9.
Lovinger, E. (1956). Perceptual contact with reality in schizophrenia. *J. abnorm. soc. Psychol.* **52**, 87–91.
Maier, N. R. F. (1930). Reasoning in humans—I: On direction. *J. comp. Psychol.* **12**, 115–43.
McGinnies, E. (1949). Emotionality and perceptual defense. *Psychol. Rev.* **56**, 244–51.
*McKellar, P. (1957). *Imagination and thinking.* Basic Books, New York.
—— (1968). *Experience and behaviour.* Penguin, Harmondsworth.
*McReynolds, P. (1960). Anxiety, perception and schizophrenia. In *The etiology of schizophrenia* (ed. D. D. Jackson), pp. 248–92. Basic Books, New York.
Mednick, S. A. (1958). A learning theory approach to schizophrenia. *Psychol. Bull.* **55**, 316–27.
—— (1963). The associative basis of the creative process. In *Research in personality* (ed. M. T. Mednick and S. A. Mednick). Holt, New York.
Miller, J. G. (1960). Information input overload and psychopathology. *Am. J. Psychiat.* **116**, 695–704.
Moray, N. (1969). *Listening and attention.* Penguin, Harmondsworth.
Moriarty, D. and Kates, S. (1962). Concept attainment of schizophrenics on materials involving social approval and disapproval. *J. abnorm. soc. Psychol.* **65**, 355–64.
Patrick, C. (1935). Creative thought in poets. *Archs Psychol.* No. 178.
—— (1937). Creative thought in artists. *J. Psychol.* **4**, 35–73.
Payne, R. W. (1962). An object classification test as a measure of overinclusive thinking in schizophrenic patients. *Br. J. soc. clin. psychol.* **1**, 213–21.
—— and Hewlett, J. H. (1960). Thought disorder in psychotic patients. In *Experiments in personality* (ed. H. J. Eysenck), Vol II. Routledge, London.
—— Matussek, P., and George, E. (1959). An experimental study of schizophrenic though disorder. *J. ment. Sci.* **105**, 627–52.
Pearl, D. (1962). Stimulus input and overload in relation to classifications of schizophrenia. *Newsl. Res. psychol.* **4**, 44–56.
Postman, L., Bruner, J. S., and McGuinnies, E. (1948). Personal values as selective factors in perception. *J. abnorm. soc. Psychol.* **43**, 142–54.
—— and Rosenzweig, M. R. (1956). Practice and transfer in the visual and auditory recognition of verbal stimuli. *Am. J. Psychol.* **69**, 209–26.
Raush, H. L. (1952). Perceptual constancy in schizophrenia. *J. Personality* **21**, 176–87.
*Reed, G. (1972). *The psychology of anomalous experience: a cognitive approach.* Hutchinson, University Library, London.
Schafer, R. and Murphy, G. (1943). The role of autism in a visual figure–ground relationship. *J. exp. Psychol.* **32**, 335–43.
Segal, S. J. and Nathan, S. (1964). The Perky effect: incorporation of an external stimulus with an imagery experience under placebo and control conditions.

Percept. mot. Skills **18**, 385–95.
Seitz, P. F. D. and Molholm, H. B. (1947). Relation of mental imagery to hallucinations. *Archs Neurol. Psychiat., Chicago* **57**, 469–80.
Shakow, D. (1962). Segmental set: a theory of the formal psychological deficit in schizophrenia. *Archs gen. Psychiat.* **6**, 1–17.
Siipola, E. (1935). A group study of some effects of preparatory sets. *Psychol. Monogr.* **46**, 27–38.
Silverman, H., Berg, P. S., and Kantor, R. (1965). Some perceptual correlates of institutionalisation. *J. nerv. ment. Dis.* **141**, 651–7.
*Silverman, J. (1964). The problem of attention in research and theory in schizophrenia. *Psychol. Rev.* **71**, 352–79.
Singer, M. T. and Wynne, L. C. (1963). Differentiating characteristics of parents of childhood schizophrenics, childhood neurotics and young adult schizophrenics. *Am. J. Psychiat.* **120**, 234–43.
Taylor, J. N. (1956). A comparison of delusional and hallucinatory individuals using field dependency as a measure. Unpublished doctoral dissertation. Purdue University. (Referred to in Silverman. J. (1964). The problem of attention in research and theory in schizophrenia. *Psychol. Rev.* **71**, 366.)
Treisman, A. M. (1964). Selective attention in man. *Br. med. Bull.* **20**, 12–16.
Usdansky, G. and Chapman, L. J. (1960). Schizophrenic-like responses in normal subjects under time pressure. *J. abnorm. soc. Psychol.* **60**, 143–6.
Vernon, J. and Hoffman, J. (1956). Effect of sensory deprivation on learning rate in human beings. *Science, N.Y.* **123**, 1074–5.
Whiteman, M. A. (1954). The performance of schizophrenics on social concepts. *J. abnorm soc. Psychol.* **49**, 266–71.
Wing, J. K. and Brown, G. W. (1970). *Institutionalism and schizophrenia.* Cambridge University Press.
Witkin, H. A., Dyk, R. B., Faterson, H. F., Goodenough, D. R., and Karp, S. A., (1962). *Psychological differentiation.* Wiley, New York.
—— Lewis, H. B., Hertzman, M., Machover, K., Meissner, P. B., and Wapner, S. (1954). *Personality through perception.* Harper, New York.
*Wright, D. S., Taylor, A., Davies, D. R., Sluckin, W., Lee, S. G. M., and Reason, J. T. (1970). *Introducing psychology.* Penguin, Harmondsworth.
Wynne, R. C. and Singer, M. T. (1963). Thought disorder and family relations of schizophrenics. *Archs. gen. Psychiat.* **9**, 191–206.
Zahn, T. P. (1959). Acquired and symbolic affective value as determinants of size estimation in schizophrenic and normal subjects. *J. abnorm. soc. Psychol.* **58**, 39–47.
Zubek, J. P., Pushkar, D., Sansom, W., and Gowing, J. (1961). Perceptual changes after prolonged sensory isolation (darkness and silence). *Can. J. Psychol.* **15**, 85–100.

CHAPTER 9

*Bennett, A. E. (1976). *Communication between doctors and patients.* Nuffield Provincial Hospitals Trust.
Cannell, C. F. and Kahn, R. L. (1968). Interviewing. In *Handbook of social psychology* (ed. G. Lindzey and E. Aronson), Vol. 2, (2nd edn), pp. 526–95. Addison-Wesley, Reading, Massachusetts.
Freedman, J. L., Carlsmith, J. M., and Sears, D. O. (1970). *Social psychology*, Prentice-Hall, Englewood Cliffs, New Jersey.

Freud, S. (1964). *The psychopathology of everyday life.* New American Library, New York.

Greenspoon, J. (1955). The reinforcing effect of two spoken sounds on the frequency of two responses. *Am. J. Psychol.* **68**, 409–11.

Haley, J. (1963). *Strategies of psychotherapy.* Grune and Stratton, New York.

Haynes, S. N. (1978). *Principles of behavioral assessment.* Gardner Press, New York.

Hetherington, R. R. (1970). The clinical interview. In *The psychological assessment of mental and physical handicaps* (ed. P. Mittler), pp. 157–74. Methuen, London.

Ivey, A. C. (1971). *Micro-counselling—innovations in interview training.* Charles C. Thomas, Springfield, Illinois.

Krasner, L. (1962). Behavior control and social responsibility. *Am. psychol.* **17**, 199–204.

*Ley, P. (1977). Psychological studies in doctor/patient communication. In *Contributions to medical psychology*, Vol. 1 (ed. S. R. Rachman). Pergamon Press, Oxford.

Lief, H. I. and Fox, Renée C. (1963). Training for 'Detached Concern'. In *The psychological basis of medical practice.* (ed. H. I. Lief *et al.*). Harper and Row (Hoeber Medical Division), London.

McGuire, P. and Rutter, D. (1976). Training medical students to communicate. *Communication between doctors and patients* (ed. A. E. Bennett), Chapter 3. Nuffield Provincial Hospitals Trust.

*Mischel, W. (1973). Towards a cognitive social learning reconceptualization of personality. *Psychol. Rev.* **80**, (4), 252–83.

Schafer, R. (1954). *Psychoanalytic interpretation in Rorschach testing.* Grune and Stratton, New York.

Sheppe, W. M. Jr. and Stevenson, I. (1963). Techniques of interviewing. In *The psychological basis of medical practice* (ed. H. I. Lief *et al.*). Harper and Row, London.

*Sullivan, H. S. (1953). The psychiatric interview. In *The collected works of Harry Stack Sullivan*, Vol. 1. Norton, New York.

Truax, C. B., Carkhuff, R. R., and Douds, J. (1964). Toward an integration of the didactic and experiential approaches to training and psychotherapy. *J. counselling Psychol.* **11**, 240–7.

Verplank, W. S. (1955). The control of content of conversation: reinforcement of statements of opinion. *J. abnormal. soc. Psychol.* **51**, 668–76.

Vingoe, F. J. (1965). Counseling and behavior therapy—incompatible? Paper read before the Department of Psychological Counseling. University of Oregon, Eugene, Oregon.

Watzlawick, P. (1962). *An anthology of human communication.* Science and Behavior Books, Palo Alto, California.

Wechsler, D. (1955). *Wechsler adult intelligence scale manual.* Psychological Corporation, New York.

Zajonc, R. B. (1968). *Social psychology: an experimental approach.* Brooks/Cole, Belmont, California.

CHAPTER 10

*Anastasi, Anne (1976). *Psychological testing* (4th edn). Collier MacMillan, London.

Bayley, Nancy (1955). On the growth of intelligence. *Am. Psychol.* **10**, 805–18.

Bitterman, M. E. (1965). The evolution of intelligence. *Scient. Am.* **212**, (1), 92–100.

*Butcher, H. J. (1975). *Human intelligence*. Methuen, London.
—— and Lomax, D. E. (1972). *Readings in human intelligence*. Methuen, London.
Cattell, R. B. (1963). Theory of fluid and crystallized intelligence: a critical experiment. *J. educ. psychol.* **54**, 1–22.
—— (1965). *The scientific analysis of personality*. Aldine, Chicago.
Freeman, F. (1955). *Theory and practice of psychological testing* (revised edn). Holt, New York.
Guilford, J. P. (1959). *Personality*. McGraw-Hill, New York.
—— (1967). *The nature of human intelligence*. McGraw-Hill, New York.
*Haynes, S. N. (1978). *Principles of behavioral assessment*. Gardner Press, New York.
*Higbee, K. L. (1977). *Your memory: how it works and how to improve it*. Prentice-Hall Inc., Englewood Cliffs, New Jersey.
Hodges, W. F. and Spielberger, C. D. (1969). Digit span: an indicant of trait or state anxiety. *J. consult. clin. Psychol.* **33**, (4), 430–4.
Hunt, J. McV. (1961). *Intelligence and experience*. Ronald Press, New York.
Institute of Personality and Ability Testing (1965). *Manual for the culture fair intelligence test, Scale 2*. Champaign, Illinois.
Jensen, A. R. (1969). How much can we boost I.Q. and scholastic achievement? *Harvard educ. Rev.* **39**, 1–123.
—— (1972). *Genetics and education*. Methuen, London.
*Lezak, M. D. (1976). *Neuropsychological assessment*. Oxford University Press.
Lorr, M. and Klett, C. J. (1966). *Inpatient multidimensional psychiatric scale (IMPS)* (revised edn). Consulting Psychologists Press, Palo Alto, California.
Matarazzo, J. D. (1972). *Wechsler's measurement and appraisal of adult intelligence* (5th edn). Williams and Wilkins, Baltimore.
McKellar, P. (1957). *Imagination and thinking*. Basic Books, New York.
McReynolds, P. and Ferguson, J. T. (1955). *Manual for the hospital adjustment scale*. Consulting Psychologists Press, Palo Alto, California.
Nissen, H. W. (1951). Phylogenetic comparison. In *Handbook of experimental psychology* (ed. S. S. Stevens), pp. 347–86. Wiley, New York.
Peterson, L. R. and Peterson, M. J. (1959). Short-term retention of individual verbal items. *J. exp. Psychol.* **30**, 93–113.
Piaget, J. (1963). *The psychology of intelligence*. Littlefield, Adams and Co, Paterson, New Jersey.
Psychological Corporation. Methods of expressing test scores. Test Service Bulletin No. 48, New York.
Siegal, S. (1956). *Nonparametric statistics for the behavioral sciences*. McGraw-Hill, New York.
Taft, R. (1956). Some characteristics of good judges of others. *Br. J. Psychol.* **47**, 19–29.
Tallard, G. A. (1971). *Disorders of memory and learning*. Penguin, Harmondsworth.
Terman, L. M. (1916). *The measurement of intelligence*. Houghton Mifflin, Boston.
Vernon, P. E. (1973). *Intelligence and cultural environment*. Methuen, London.
Vingoe, F. J. and Antonoff, S. R. (1968). Personality characteristics of good judges of others. *J. counseling Psychol.* **15**, (1), 91–3.
*Warrington, Elizabeth K. (1971). Neurological disorders of memory. *Br. med. Bull.* **27**, (3), 243–7.
Wechsler, D. (1955). *Wechsler adult intelligence scale manual*. Psychological Corporation, New York. (English versions available from NFER Publishing Company Limited, Windsor.)
—— (1958). *The measurement and appraisal of adult intelligence* (4th edn). Williams

and Williams, Baltimore.
—— and Stone, C. P. (1945). *Wechsler memory scale manual.* Psychological Corporation, New York.
Williams, Moyra (1968). The measurement of memory in clinical practice. *Br. J. soc. clin. Psychol.* **7**, (1), 19–34.

CHAPTER 11

Anastasi, Anne (1976). *Psychological testing* (4th edn). Collier MacMillan, New York.
Bandura, A. (1969). *Principles of behavior modification.* Holt, Rinehart, and Winston, New York.
—— and Walters, R. H. (1963). *Social learning and personality development.* Holt, Rinehart, and Winston, New York.
*Beck, A. T. (1967). *Depression: clinical, experimental and theoretical aspects.* Harper and Row, New York.
Berkowitz, L. (1964). Aggressive cues in aggressive behavior and hostility catharsis. *Psychol. Bull.* **69**, 450–66.
Blackburn, R. (1969). Sensation-seeking, impulsivity and psychopathic personality. *J. consult. clin. Psychol.* **33**, 571–4.
Byrne, D. (1966). *An introduction to personality: a research approach*, Prentice-Hall, Englewood Cliffs, New Jersey.
Cattell, R. B. (1965). *The scientific analysis of personality.* Aldine, Chicago.
Clements, P. R., Hafer, Marilyn D., and Vermillion, Mary E, (1976). Psychometric, diurnal and electrophysiological correlates of activation. *J. Personality soc. Psychol.* **33**, 387–94.
Couch, A. S. and Keniston, K. (1960). Yea-sayers and nay-sayers: agreeing response set as a personality variable. *J. abnorm. soc. Psychol.* **60**, 151–74.
*Darwin, C. (1965). *Expression of the emotions in man and animals.* University of Chicago Press (Originally published in 1873.)
Dollard, J., Miller, N. E., Doob, L. W., Mowrer, O. H., and Sears, R. R. (1974). *Frustration and aggression.* Yale University Press, New Haven.
Edwards, A. L. (1957). *The social desirability variable in personality-assessment and research.* Dryden, New York.
—— (1962). The social desirability hypothesis: theoretical implications for personality measurement. In *Measurement in personality and cognition* (ed. S. Messick and J. Ross), pp. 91–108. Wiley, New York.
Eysenck, H. J. and Rachman, S. (1965). *The causes and cures of neurosis.* Knapp, San Diego, California.
Freedman, J. L., Carlsmith, J. M., and Sears, D. O. (1970). *Social psychology.* Prentice-Hall, Englewood Cliffs, New Jersey.
Gaudry, E. and Poole, C. (1975). A further validation of state–trait distinction in anxiety research. *Aust. J. Psychol.* **27**, (2), 119–25.
Guilford, J. P. (1959). *Personality,* McGraw-Hill, New York.
Konečni, V. J. (1975). The mediation of aggressive behaviour: arousal level versus anger and cognitive labeling. *J. Personality & soc. Psychol.* **32**, (4) 706–12.
—— and Doob, A. N. (1972). Catharsis through displacement of aggression. *J. Personality & soc. Psychol.* **23**, 379–87.
Lacy, J. I. and Lacy, B. C. (1958). Verification and extension of the principle of autonomic response-stereotypy *Am. J. Psychol.* **71**, 50–73.
*Lazarus, A. A. (1968). Learning theory and the treatment of depression. *Behav. Res. & Ther.* **6**, 83–9.

Lanyon, R. I. and Goodstein, L. D. (1971). *Personality assessment.* Wiley, New York.

*Levitt, E. E. (1967). *The psychology of anxiety.* Bobbs-Merrill, New York.

Lewinsohn, P. M. (1974). Clinical and theoretical aspects of depression. In *Innovative treatment methods in psychopathology* (ed. K. S. Calhoun, H. E. Adams, and K. M. Mitchel), pp. 63–120. Wiley, New York.

Mackay, C., Cox, T., Burrows, G., and Lazzerini, T. (1978). An inventory for the measurement of self-reported stress and arousal. *Br. J. soc. clin. Psychol.* **17**, 283–4.

MacPhillamy, D. J. and Lewinsohn, P. M. (1976). *Manual for the pleasant events schedule.* University of Oregon, Eugene, Oregon.

Maddi, S. R. (1972). *Personality theories: a comparative analysis.* (Revised edn). Dorsey Press, Homewood, Illinois.

Miller, R. (1975). Psychological deficit in depression. *Psychol. Bull.* **82**, (2), 238–60.

*Mischel, W. (1968). *Personality and assessment.* Wiley, New York.

—— (1973). Toward a cognitive social learning reconceptualisation of personality. *Psychol. Rev.* **80**, (4), 252–83.

Nowlis, V. (1965). Research with the mood adjective checklist. In *Affect cognition and personality* (ed. S. S. Tomkins and C. E. Izard). Springer, New York.

Prociuk, T. J., Breen, L. J., and Lussier, R. J. (1976). Hopelessness, internal–external locus of control and depression. *J. clin. Psychol.* **32**, (2), 229–30.

Rosenzweig, S. (1960). The Rosenzweig picture-frustration study, children's form. In *Projective techniques with children* (ed. A. I. Rubin and M. Haworth). Grune and Stratton, New York.

—— (1976). Aggressive behavior and the Rosenzweig picture-frustration (P-F) study. *J. clin. Psychol.* **32**, 885–91.

*Seligman, M. E. P. (1975). *Helplessness: on depression, development and death.* Freeman, San Francisco.

Spielberger, C. D. (1974). The measurement of state and trait anxiety: conceptual and methodological issues. In *Emotions: their parameters and measurement* (ed. L. Levi), pp. 713–26. Raven Press, New York.

—— (1977). *Bibliography for the state–trait anxiety inventory* (STAI). University of South Florida, Tampa, Florida.

—— Gorsuch, R. L., and Lushere, R. E. (1970). *STAI manual for the state–trait anxiety inventory.* Consulting Psychologists Press, Palo Alto.

Taylor, Janet A. (1953). A personality scale of manifest anxiety. *J. abnorm. soc. Psychol.* **48**, 285–90.

Thayer, R. E. (1967). Measurement of activation through self-report. *Psychol. Rep.* **20**, 663–78.

Wessman, A. E. and Ricks, D. V. (1966). *Mood and personality.* Holt, Rinehart, and Winston.

Zuckerman, M. (1974). The sensation seeking motive. In *Progress in experimental personality research* (ed. B. A. Maher), pp. 79–148. Academic Press, New York.

—— and Link, Kathryn (1968). Construct validity for the sensation-seeking scale. *J. consult. & clinical Psychol.* **32**, (4) 420–6.

—— and Lubin, B. (1965). *Manual for the multiple affect adjective check list (MAACL).* Educational and Industrial Testing Service, San Diego, California.

—— Schultz, D. P., and Hopkins, T. R. (1967). Sensation seeking and volunteering for sensory deprivation and hypnosis experiments. *J. consult. Psychol.* **31**, (4) 348–63.

Zung, W. W. K. (1965). A self-rating depression scale. *Archs gen. Psychiat.* **12**, 63–70.

CHAPTER 12

Beier, E. G. (1952). Client-centred therapy and the involuntary client. *J. consult. Psychol.* **16**, 332–7. Reprinted in *Counseling: readings in theory and practice* (ed. J. F. McGowan and L. D. Schmidt), pp. 263–71. Holt, Rinehart, and Winston, New York (1962).

Durost, W. N. (1961). how to tell parents about standardized test results. *Test service notebook* No. 26. Harcourt, Brace, and World, Test Department, Dunbarton, New Hampshire.

Edwards, A. L. (1959). *Edwards personal preference schedule.* Psychological Corporation, New York.

*Haley, J. (1963). *Strategies of psychotherapy.* Grune and Stratton, New York.

*Hoehn-Saric, R., Frank, J. D., Imber, S. D., Nash, E. H., Stone, A. R.. and Battle, Carolyn C. (1964). Systematic preparation of patients for psychotherapy—I. Effects on therapy behavior and outcome. *J. Psychiat.* **2**, 267–81.

Jackson, D. (ed.) (1970). *Communication, families and marriage.* Science and Behavior Books, Palo Alto.

*Jourard, S. M. (1971). *The transparent self* (2nd edn). Van Nostrand Reinhold, New York.

*Masters, W. H. and Johnson, V. E. (1970). *Human sexual inadequacy.* Little, Brown, Boston.

McGowan, J. F. and Schmidt, L. D. (1962) (ed). *Counseling: readings in theory and practice.* Holt, Rinehart, and Winston, New York.

Ricks, J. H. Jnr. (1959). On telling parents about test results. *Test service bulletin* No. 54. Psychological Corporation, New York.

Schafer, R. (1954). *Psychoanalytic interpretation in Rorschach testing.* Grune and Stratton, New York.

Shapiro, M. B. (1975). The requirements and implications of a systematic science of psychopathology. *Bull. Br. psychol. Soc.* **28**, 149–55.

Sullivan, H. S. (1953). The psychiatric interview. In *The collected works of Harry Stack Sullivan*, Vol. 1. Norton, New York.

CHAPTER 13

Ansbacher, H. L. and Ansbacher, Rowena R. (ed.) (1956). *The individual psychology of Alfred Adler.* Basic Books, New York.

Bandura. A. (1961). Psychotherapy as a learning process. *Psychol. Bull.* **58**, 143–57.

*Erikson, E. H. (1963). *Childhood and society.* Norton, New York.

Eysenck, H. J. (1952). The effects of psychotherapy: an evaluation. *J. consult. Psychol.* **16**, 319–24.

*Ford, D. H. and Urban, H. B. (1965). *Systems of psychotherapy: a comparative study.* Wiley, New York.

Freud, S. (1956). *General introduction to psychoanalysis.* (Permabooks) Doubleday, New York.

—— (1964). *The psychopathology of everyday life.* (Mentor Book) New American Library, New York.

—— (1970). *The interpretation of dreams.* Avon Books, New York.

*Fromm, Erika (1968). Transference and countertransference in hypnoanalysis. *Int. J. clin. exp. Hypnosis* **16**, (2), 77–84.

*Fromm-Reichmann, F. (1960). *Principles of intensive psychotherapy* (Phoenix edn). University of Chicago Press.

Gleser, G. and Ihilevich, D. (1969). An objective instrument for measuring defence mechanisms. *J. consult. & clin. Psychol.* **33**, 51–60.
Glucksberg, S. and King, L. J. (1967). Motivated forgetting by implicit verbal chaining: a laboratory analogue of repression. *Science, N.Y.* 27 October, 517–19.
Goldstein, A. P., Heller, K., and Sechrest, L. B. (1966). *Psychotherapy and the psychology of behavior change.* Wiley, New York.
*Hall, C. S. (1964*a*). *A primer of Freudian psychology.* Mentor, New York.
—— (1964*b*). A modest confirmation of Freud's theory of a distinction between the superego of men and women. *J. abnorm. soc. Psychol.* **69**, (4), 440–2.
—— and Lindzey, G. (1970). *Theories of personality* (2nd edn). Wiley, New York.
*—— —— (1978). *Theories of personality* (3rd edn). Wiley, New York.
Hartmann, H. (1958). *Ego psychology and the problem of adaptation.* International Universities Press, New York.
Kris, E. (1952). *Psychoanalytic exploration in art.* International Universities Press, New York.
Menninger, K. (1958). *Theory of psychoanalytic technique.* Basic Books, New York.
*—— (1964). *Theory of psychoanalytic technique.* Harper Torchbook, New York.
Miller, N. E. (1948). Theory and experiment relating psychoanalytic displacement to stimulus response generalization. *J. abnorm. soc. Psychol.* **43**, 155–78.
Mullahy, P. (1955). *Oedipus myth and complex: a review of psychoanalytic theory.* Grove Press, New York.
*Pervin, L. A. (1970). *Personality: theory, assessment and research.* Wiley, New York.
Rogers, C. R. (1959). A theory of therapy, personality, and interpersonal relationships, as developed in the client-centered framework. In *Psychology: a study of a science, Vol. 2. General systematic formulations, learning, and special processes* (ed. S. Koch). McGraw-Hill, New York.
Sears, R. R., Maccoby, E. E., and Levin, H. (1957). *Patterns of child rearing.* Row, Peterson, Evanston, Illinois.
*Snyder, W. V. (1963). *Dependency in psychotherapy.* MacMillan, New York.
Sullivan, H. S. (1953). *The interpersonal theory of psychiatry.* Norton, New York.
Thompson, Clara (1950). *Psychoanalysis: evolution and development.* Grove Press, New York.

CHAPTER 14

Barrow, F. and Leary, T. (1955). Changes in psychoneurotic patients with and without psychotherapy. *J. consult. Psychol.* **19**, 239–45.
Bebout, J. (1974). It takes one to know one: existential-Rogerian concepts in encounter groups. In *Innovations in client-centred therapy* (ed. D. A. Wexler and Laura N. Rice), pp. 367–420. Wiley, New York.
Beck, Ariadne P. (1974). Phases in the development of structure in therapy and encounter groups. In *Innovations in client-centred therapy* (ed. D. A. Wexler and Laura N. Rice), pp. 421–63. Wiley, New York.
*Berenson, B. G. and Carkhuff, R. R. (ed.) (1967). *Sources of gain in counseling and psychotherapy: readings and commentary.* Holt, Rinehart, and Winston, New York.
Bergin, A. E. (1963). The effects of psychotherapy: negative results revisited. *J. counsel. Psychol.* **10**, 244–55.
—— (1971). The evaluation of therapeutic outcomes. In *Handbook of psychotherapy and behavior change: an empirical analysis* (ed. A. E. Bergin and S. L. Garfield). Wiley, New York.

Beutler, L. E., Johnson, D. T., Neville, E. W., and Workman, S. N. (1973). The A-B therapy-type distinction, accurate empathy, non-possessive warmth, and therapist genuineness in psychotherapy. *J. abnorm. Psychol.* **82**, (2), 273–7.

Cartwright, Rosalind D. and Vogel, J. L. (1960). A comparison of changes in psychoneurotic patients during matched periods of therapy and no-therapy. *J. consult. Psychol.* **24**, 121–7.

Chinsky, J. M. and Rappaport, J. (1970). Brief critique of the meaning and reliability of 'accurate empathy' ratings, *Psychol. Bull.* **73**, (5), 379–82.

Cole, C. W., Oetting, E. R., and Hinkle, J. E. (1967). Non-linearity of self-concept discrepancy: the value dimension. *Psychol. Rep.* **21**, 58–60.

Coopersmith, S. (1968). Studies in self-esteem. *Scient. Am.* Reprint No. 511. W. H. Freeman, San Francisco.

Eysench, H. J. (1952). The effects of psychotherapy: an evaluation. *J. consult. Psychol.* **16**, 319–24.

—— (1960). The effects of psychotherapy. In *Handbook of abnormal psycholoy* (ed. H. J. Eysenck), pp. 697–725. Pitman Medical, London.

—— and Eysenck, S. B. G. (1963). *Manual for the Eysenck personality inventory.* Educational and Industrial Testing Services, San Diego, California.

Fiedler, F. E. (1950*a*). The concept of an ideal therapeutic relationship. *J. consult. Psychol.* **14**, 239–45.

—— (1950*b*). A comparison of therapeutic relationships in psychoanalytic, non-directive, and Adlerian therapy. *J. consult Psychol.* **14**, 436–45.

*Garfield, S. L. (1978). Research on client variables in psychotherapy. In *Handbook of psychotherapy and behavior change* (ed. S. L. Garfield and A. E. Bergin) (2nd edn). Wiley, New York.

*Goldstein, A. P. (1973). *Structured learning therapy: toward a psychotherapy for the poor.* Academic Press, New York.

Gordon, T. and Cartwright, D. (1954). The effect of psychotherapy upon certain attitudes towards others. In *Psychotherapy and personality change: coordinated studies in the client centred approach* (ed. C. R. Rogers and Rosalind F. Dymond), pp. 167–95. University of Chicago Press.

Gottman. J. and Markman, H. J. (1978). Experimental designs in psychotherapy research. In *Handbook of psychotherapy and behavior change: an empirical analysis* (ed. S. L. Garfield and A. E. Bergin), (2nd edn), pp. 23–62.

Gough, H. B. (1964). *Manual for the California psychological inventory.* Consulting Psychologists Press, Palo Alto, California.

Hall, C. S. and Lindzey, G. (1970). *Theories of personality* (2nd edn). Wiley, New York.

Hart, J. T. and Tomlinson, T. M. (ed.) (1970). *New directions in client-centred therapy.* Houghton-Mifflin, Boston.

*Lambert, M. J. (1976). Spontaneous remission in adult neurotic disorders: a revision and summary. *Psychol. Bull.* **83**, (1), 107–19.

Levitt, E. E. (1957). The results of psychotherapy with children. *J. consult. Psychol.* **21**, 189–96.

Lorion, R. P. (1978). Research on psychotherapy and behavior change with the disadvantaged. In *Handbook of psychotherapy and behavior change* (ed. S. L. Garfield and A. E. Bergin), (2nd edn), pp. 903–38. Wiley, New York.

McGowan, J. F. and Schmidt, L. D. (1962). *Counseling: readings in theory and practice.* Holt, Rinehart, and Winston, New York.

Maslow, A. H. (1962). *Towards a psychology of being.* Van Nostrand, New York.

Medinnus, G. R. and Curtis, F. J. (1963). The relationship between maternal self-acceptance and child-acceptance. *J. consult. Psychol.* **27**, 542–4.

Mischel, W. (1968). *Personality and assessment.* Wiley, New York.
Mitchell, K. M., Bozarth, J. D., and Krauft, C. C. (1977). A reappraisal of the therapeutic effectiveness of accurate empathy, non-possessive warmth, and genuineness. In *Effective psychotherapy: a handbook of research* (ed. A. S. Gurman and A. M. Razin). Pergamon, New York.
Omwake, K. T. (1954). The relationship between acceptance of self and acceptance of others as shown by three personality inventories. *J. consult. Psychol.* **18**, 443–6.
*Parloff, M. B., Waskow, Irene E., and Wolfe, B. E. (1978). Research on therapist variables in relation to process and outcome. In *Handbook of psychotherapy and behaviour change: an empirical analysis* (ed. S. L. Garfield and A. E. Bergin), (2nd edn). Wiley, New York.
Patterson, C. H. (1969*a*). A current view of client-centred or relationship therapy. *Counsel. Psychol.* **1**, (2), 2–25.
—— (1969*b*). Rejoinder and commentary. *Counsel. Psychol.* **1**, (2), 63–8.
Paul, G. L. (1967). Insight versus desensitization in psychotherapy two years after termination. *J. consult. Psychol.* **31**, 333–48.
*Rachman, S. J. (1973). The effects of psychological treatment. In *Handbook of abnormal psychology* (ed. H. J. Eysenck), (2nd edn), pp. 805–61. Pitman Medical, London.
Rogers, C. R. (1942). *Counseling and psychotherapy.* Houghton Mifflin, New York.
—— (1951). *Client-centred therapy.* Houghton Mifflin, Boston.
—— (1957). The necessary and sufficient conditions of therapeutic personality change. *J. consult. Psychol.* **21**, 95–103.
—— (1958). The characteristics of a helping relationship. *Personn. Guidance J.* **37**, 6–16.
—— (1959). A theory of therapy, personality, and interpersonal relationships, as developed in the client-centred framework. In *Psychology: a study of a science, Vol. 2. General systematic formulations, learning, and special processes* (ed. S. Koch). McGraw-Hill, New York.
*—— (1961). *On becoming a person: a therapist's view of psychotherapy.* Houghton Mifflin, Boston, Massachusetts.
*—— (1967). The conditions of change from a client-centred viewpoint. In *Sources of gain in counseling and psychotherapy: Readings and commentary* (ed. B. G. Berenson and R. R. Carkhuff). Holt, Rinehart, and Winston.
*—— (1973). *Encounter groups.* Penguin, Harmondsworth.
*—— (1974). Remarks on the future of client-centered therapy. In *Innovations in client-centered therapy* (ed. D. A. Wexler and Laura Rice). (Wiley Interscience) Wiley, New York.
—— (1975). Carl Rogers on empathy. *Counsel. psychol.* **5**, (2), 2–10.
—— Gendlin, E. T., Kiesler, D. J., and Truax, C. B. (ed.) (1967). *The therapeutic relationship and its impact: a study of psychotherapy with schizophrenics.* University of Wisconsin Press, Madison, Wisconsin.
—— and Diamond, Rosaline F. (1954). *Psychotherapy and personality change: coordinated studies in the client-centred approach.* University of Chicago Press.
Seeman, J. A. (1949). A study of the process of non-directive therapy. *J. consult. Psychol.* **13**, 157–68.
Snygg, D. and Combs, A. W. (1949). *Individual behavior.* Harper, New York.
Strupp, H. H. (1978). Psychotherapy research and practice: an overview. In *Handbook of psychotherapy and behavior change* (ed. S. L. Garfield and A. E. Bergin), (2nd edn). Wiley, New York.
Subotnik, L. (1972*a*). "Spontaneous remission" of deviant MMPI profiles among college students. *J. consult clin. Psychol.* **38**, 191–201.

—— (1972*b*). Spontaneous remission: fact or artifact? *Psychol. Bull.* **77**, 32–48.
*—— (1975). Spontaneous remission of emotional disorder in a general medical practice. *J. nerv. ment. Dis.* **161**, (4), 239–44.
Suinn, R. M. (1961). The relationship between self-acceptance and acceptance of others: a learning theory analysis. *J. abnorm. soc. Psychol.* **63**, 37–42.
Truax, C. B. (1961). The process of group psychotherapy: Relationships between hypothesized therapeutic conditions and intrapersonal exploration. *Psychol. Monogr.* **75**, (7), 511.
—— (1966). Therapist empathy, warmth, and genuineness and patient personality change in group psychotherapy: a comparison between interaction unit measures, time sample measures, patient perception measures. *J. clin. Psychol.* **22**, 225–9.
—— (1969). Critique of 'A current view of client-centred or relationship therapy': Today psychotherapy, tomorrow the world. *Counsel. Psychol.* **1**, (2), 61–3.
—— and Carkhuff, R. R. (1967). *Towards effective counseling and psychotherapy: training and practice.* Aldine, Chicago.
—— —— and Kodman, F. (1965). Relationships between therapist-offered conditions and patient change in group psychotherapy. *J. clin. Psychol.* **21**, 327–39.
Vingoe, F. J. (1968). Rogers' self theory and Eysenck's extraversion and neuroticism. *J. consult. & clin. Psychol.* **32**, (5), 618–20.
—— (1973). Rogers' self theory and Eysenck's extraversion and neuroticism. In *Theories of personality: primary sources and research* (ed. G. Lindzey, C. S. Hall, and M. Manosevitz), (2nd edn). Wiley, New York.
Wexler, D. A. and Rice, Laura N. (1974) (ed.). *Innovations in client-centered therapy.* (Wiley Interscience) Wiley, New York.

CHAPTER 15

Atkinson, R. C., Atkinson, Rita L., and Hilgard, E. R. (1975). *Introduction to psychology* (6th edn). Harcourt, Brace, and Javanovich, New York.
Bachrach, A. J. (1963). Operant conditioning and behavior: some clinical applications. In *The psychological basis of medical practice* (ed. H. I. Lief *et al.*), pp. 94–108. Harper and Row (Hoeber Medical Division), London.
Bandura, A. (1961). Psychotherapy as a learning process. *Psychol. Bull.* **58**, 143–59.
—— (1965). Behavior modification through modeling procedures. In *Research in behavior modification* (ed. L. Krasner and L. P. Ullmann), pp. 310–40. Holt, Rinehart, and Winston, New York.
—— (1968). A social learning interpretation of psychological dysfunctions. In *Foundations of abnormal psychology* (ed. P. London and D. Rosenhan). pp. 293–344. Holt, Rinehart, and Winston, New York.
*—— (1969). *Principles of behavior modification.* Holt, Rinehart, and Winston, New York.
*—— (ed.) (1971). *Psychological modeling: conflicting theories.* Aldine-Atherton, Chicago.
—— (1977). Self-efficacy. toward a unifying theory of behavioral change. *Psychol. Rev.* **84**, (2), 191–215.
*—— Blanchard, E. B., and Ritter, B. (1969). Relative efficiency of desensitization and modeling approaches for inducing behavioral, affective and attitudinal changes. *J. Personality & soc. Psychol.* **13**, 173–99.
—— Grusec, J. E., and Menlove, F. L. (1966). Observational learning as a function of symbolization and incentive set. *J. Child dev.* **37**, 499–506.
—— Jeffrey, R. W., and Wright, C. L. (1974). Efficacy of participant modeling as a

function of response induction aids. *J. abnorm. psychol.* **83**, 56–64.

—— Ross, D., and Ross, S. A. (1963). Vicarious reinforcement and imitative learning. *J. abnorm. soc. Psychol.* **67**, 601–7.

Bean, K. L. (1970). Desensitization, behavior rehearsal, then reality: a preliminary report on a new procedure. *Behav. Ther.* **1**, 542–5.

Blanchard, E. B. (1970). Relative contributions of modeling, informational influences, and physical contact in extinction of phobic behavior. *J. abnorm. Psychol.* **76**, 55–61.

Brady, J. P. (1967). Comments on methohexitone-aided systematic desensitization. *Behav. Res. & Ther.* **5**, 259–60.

Cautela, J. R. and Kastenbaum, R. (1967). A reinforcement survey schedule. *Psychol. Rep.* **20**, 1115–30.

Davison, G. C. (1968). Systematic desensitization as a counterconditioning process. *J. abnorm. Psychol.* **73**, 91–9.

*Edelstein, B. A. and Eisler, R. M. (1976). Effects of modeling and modeling with instructions and feedback on the behavioral components of social skills. *Behav. Ther.* **7**, (3), 382–9.

Edwards, N. B. (1972). Case conference: assertive training in a case of homosexual pedophilia. *J. behav. Ther. & exp. Psychiat.* **3**, 55–63.

Eisler, R. M. and Hersen, M. (1973). Behavioral techniques in family-oriented crisis intervention. *Archs. gen. Psychiat.* **28**, 111–16.

*Emmelkamp, P. M. G. and Wessels, Hemmy (1975). Flooding in imagination or flooding *in-vivo*; a comparison with agoraphobics. *Behav. Res. & Ther.* **13**, 7–15.

Evans, P. D. and Kellam, A. M. P. (1973). Semi-automated desensitization: a controlled clinical trial. *Behav. Res. & Ther.* **11**, 641–6.

Eysenck, H. J. (1952). The effects of psychotherapy: an evaluation. *J. consult. Psychol.* **16**, 319–24.

—— (1956). The inheritance of extroversion–introversion. *Acta Psychol.* **12**, 95–110.

—— (1959). Learning theory and behaviour therapy. *J. ment. Sci.* **105**, 61–75.

—— (1960). The effects of psychotherapy. In *Handbook of abnormal psychology* (ed. H. J. Eysenck), pp. 697–725. Pitman Medical, London.

—— (1967). *The biological basis of personality.* Charles Thomas, Springfield, Illinois.

—— and Rachman, S. (1965). *The causes and cures of neurosis.* Robert R. Knapp, San Diego, California.

Fensterheim, H. (1972). Assertive methods and marital problems. In *Advances in behavior therapy* (ed. R. D. Rubin, H. Fensterheim, J. D. Henderson, and L. P. Ullmann). Academic Press, New York.

Fischer, S. C. and Turner, R. M. (1978). Standardization of the fear survey schedule. *J. behav. Ther. & exp. Psychiat.* **9** (2), 129–33.

Graham, Margaret B. (1967). *Be nice to spiders.* Harper and Row, New York.

Grusec, J. E. and Mischel, W. (1966). The model's characteristics as determinants of social learning. *J. Personality & soc. Psychol.* **4**, 211–15.

Guthrie, E. R. (1952). *The psychology of learning* (revised edn). Harper, New York.

*Hersen, M., Eisler, R. M., and Miller, P. M. (1973). Development of assertive responses: clinical measurement and research considerations. *Behav. Res. & Ther.* **11**, 505–21.

Jacobson, E. (1938). *Progressive relaxation.* University of Chicago Press.

—— (1977). The origins and development of progressive relaxation. *J. behav. Ther. & exp. Psychiat.* **8**, 110—23.

Jakubczak, L. F. and Walters, R. H. (1959). Suggestibility as dependency behavior. *J. abnorm. soc. Psychol.* **59**, 102–7.

Jakubowski, Patricia A. and Lacks, Patricia B. (1975). Assessment procedures in assertion training. *Counseling Psychol.* **5**, (4), 84–90.

Janda, L. H. and Rimm, D. C. (1972). Covert sensitization in the treatment of obesity. *J. abnorm. Psychol.* **80**, 37–42.

Jones, Mary Cover (1924). The elimination of children's fears. *J. exp. Psychol.* **7**, 382–90.
—— (1974). Albert, Peter, and John B. Watson. *Am. Psychol.* **29**, (8), 581–3.
Kanfer, F. H. and Saslow, G. (1969). Behavioral diagnosis. In *Behavior therapy: appraisal and status* (ed. C. Franks). McGraw-Hill, New York.
*Kazdin, A. E. (1973). Covert modeling and the reduction of avoidance behavior. *J. abnorm. Psychol.* **81**, (1), 87–95.
—— (1974). Covert modeling, model similarity, and reduction of avoidance behavior. *Behav. Ther.* **5**, 325–40.
—— (1976). Effects of covert modeling, multiple models, and model reinforcement on assertive behavior. *Behav. Ther.* **7**, 211–22.
Kimble, G. A. (1968). *Hilgard and Marquis' conditioning and learning.* Appleton-Century-Crofts, New York.
Lang, P. J., Melamed, B. G., and Hart, J. (1970). A psycho-physiological analysis of fear modification using an automating desensitization procedure. *J. abnorm. Psychol.* **76**, 220–9.
Lazarus, A. A. (1961). Group therapy of phobic disorders by systematic desensitization. *J. abnorm. & soc. Psychol.* **63**, 504–10.
—— (1964). Crucial procedural factors in desensitization therapy. *Behav. Res. & Ther.* **2**, 65–70.
—— (1966). Behaviour rehearsal vs non-directive therapy vs advice in effecting behaviour change. *Behav. Res. & Ther.* **4**, 209–12.
—— (1968). Behavior therapy in groups. In *Basic approaches to group psychotherapy and counseling* (ed. G. M. Gazda), pp. 149–75. Charles C. Thomas, Springfield, Illinois.
—— (1971), *Behavior therapy and beyond.* McGraw-Hill, New York.
—— and Serber, M. (1968). Is systematic desensitization being misapplied? *Psychol. Rep.* **23**, 215–18.
Ledwidge, B. (1978). Cognitive behavior modification: a step in the wrong direction? *Psychol. Bull.* **85**, (2), 353–78.
McFall, R. M. and Lillesand, D. B. (1971). Behavior rehearsal with modeling and coaching in assertion training. *J. abnorm. Psychol.* **77**, 313–23.
—— and Twentyman, C. T. (1973). Four experiments on the relative contributions of rehearsal, modeling, and coaching to assertion training. *J. abnorm. Psychol.* **81**, (3), 199–218.
*Mahoney, M. J. (1974). *Cognitive and behavior modification.* Ballinger, Cambridge, Massachusetts.
Marks, I. M. (1972). Flooding (implosion) and allied treatments. In *Behavior modification: principles and clinical applications* (ed. W. S. Agras), pp. 151–213. Little, Brown, and Co., New York.
Marlatt, G. A. and Perry, Martha A. (1975). Modeling methods. In *Helping people change* (ed. F. H. Kanfer and A. P. Goldstein), pp. 117–58. Pergamon, New York.
Melnick, J. and Stocker, R. B. (1977). An experimental analysis of the behavioral rehearsal with feedback techniques in assertiveness training. *Behav. Ther.* **8**, 222–8.
*Mischel, M. (1968). *Personality and assessment.* Wiley, New York.
Osgood, C. E. (1953). *Method and theory in experimental psychology.* Oxford University Press, New York.
Paul, G. L. (1968). A two-year follow-up of systematic desensitization in therapy groups. *J. abnorm. Psychol.* **73**, 119–30.
—— (1969). Outcome of systematic desensitization II: Controlled investigations of individual treatment, technique variations, and current status. In *Behavior*

therapy: appraisal and status (ed. C. M. Franks). McGraw-Hill, New York.

Phillips, Laura W. (1978). The soft underbelly of behavior therapy: popular behavior modification. *J. behav. Ther. & exp. Psychiat.* **9**, 139–40.

*Piaget, G. W. and Lazarus, A. A. (1969). The use of rehearsal-desensitization. *Psychotherapy: theory, research and practice* **6**, 264–6.

Rachman, S. (1966). Studies in desensitization—II: Flooding. *Behav. Res. & Ther.* **4**, 1–6.

—— and Costello (1961). The aetiology and treatment of children's phobias: a review. *Am. J. Psychiat.* **118**, 97–105.

—— Hodgson, R., and Marks, I. M. (1971). Treatment of chronic obsessive–compulsive neurosis. *Behav. Res. & Ther.* **9**, 237–47.

Rathus, S. A. (1973). A 30-item schedule for assessing assertive behavior. *Behav. Ther.* **4**, 398–406.

Reynolds, G. S. (1975). *A primer of operant conditioning* (2nd edn). Scott, Foresman, Palo Alto, California.

Rich, A. R. and Schroeder, H. E. (1976). Research issues in assertiveness training. *Psychol. Bull.* **83**, (6), 1081–96.

Ritter, B. (1969). The use of contact desensitization, demonstration-plus-participation, and demonstration alone in the treatment of agoraphobia. *Behav. Res. & Ther.* **7**, 157–64.

Robach, H., Frayn, D., Gunby, L., and Tuters, K. (1972). A multifactorial approach to the treatment and ward management of a self-mutilating patient. *J. behav. Ther. & exp. Psychiat.* **3**, 189–93.

Roper, G., Rachman, S., and Marks, I. (1975). Passive and participant modeling in exposure treatment of obsessive–compulsive neurotics. *Behav. Res. & Ther.* **13**, 271–9.

Serber, M. (1972). Teaching the nonverbal components of assertive training. *J. behav. Ther. & Exp. psychiat.* **3**, 179–83.

Skinner, B. F. (1938). *The behavior of organisms.* Appleton-Century-Crofts, New York.

*Stern, R. and Marks, I. (1973). Brief and prolonged flooding: a comparison in agoraphobic patients. *Archs gen. Psychiat.* **28**, 270–6.

Suinn, R. M. and Hall, R. (1970). Marathon desensitization groups: an innovative technique. *Behav. Res. Ther.* **8**, 97–8.

Twentyman, C. T. and McFall, R. M. (1975). Behavioral training of social skills in shy males. *J. consult. & Clin. Psychol.* **43**, (3), 384–95.

Ullmann, L. P. and Krasner, L. (1965). *Case studies in behavior modification.* Holt, Rinehart, and Winston, New York.

Ulrich, R., Stachnik, T., and Mabry, J. (ed.) (1966). *Control of human behavior.* Scott, Foresman, Chicago.

Vingoe, F. J. (1968). The development of a group alert-trance scale. *Int. J. Clin. & exp. Hypn.* **16**, 120–32.

Watson, J. B. and Raynor, R. (1920). Conditioned emotional reactions. *J. exp. Psychol.* **3**, 1–14.

Watson, J. P., Mullett, G. E., and Pillay, H. (1973). The effects of prolonged exposure to phobic situations upon agoraphobic patients treated in groups. *Behav. Res. & Ther.* **11**, 531–45.

Weitzenhoffer, A. M. and Hilgard, E. R. (1959). *The Stanford hypnotic susceptibility scale. Forms A & B.* Consulting Psychologists Press, Palo Alto, California.

Wolpe, J. (1958). *Psychotherapy by reciprocal inhibition.* Stanford University Press, Stanford, California.

—— (1969). Foreword In *Behavior therapy: appraisal and status* (ed. C. M. Franks).

McGraw-Hill, New York.
—— and Lang, P. (1969). *Fear survey schedule.* Educational and Industrial Testing Service, San Diego, California.
—— and Lazarus, A. A. (1966). *Behavior therapy techniques: a guide to the treatment of neurosis.* Pergamon, London.
Worsley, J. L. and Freeman, H. (1967). Further comments on the use of methohexitone sodium as a means of inducing relaxation. *Behav. Res. & Ther.* **5**, 258.

CHAPTER 16

Anant, S. S. (1966). The treatment of alcoholics by verbal aversion techniques: a case report. *Manas* **13**, 79–86.
Bandura, A. (1961). Psychotherapy as a learning process. *Psychol. Bull.* **58**, 143–59.
—— (1969). *Principles of behavior modification.* Holt, Rinehart, and Winston, New York.
*—— (1977). Self-efficacy: towards a unifying theory of behavioral change. *Psychol. Rev.* **84**, (2), 191–215.
Barker, J. C. and Miller, M. E. (1968). Aversion therapy for compulsive gambling. *J. nerv. & ment. Dis.* **146**, 285–302.
Barlow, D. H., Leitenberg, H., Agras, W. J., and Wincz, J. P. (1969). The transfer gap in systematic desensitization: an analogue study. *Behav. Res. & Ther.* **7**, 191–6.
*Beech, H. R. (ed.) (1974). *Obsessional states.* Methuen, London.
—— and Perigault, J. (1974). Towards a theory of obsessional disorders. In *Obsessional states* (ed. H. R. Beech). Methuen, London.
Callahan, E. J. and Leitenberg, H. (1973). Aversion therapy for sexual deviation: contingent shock and covert sensitization. *J. abnorm. Psychol.* **81**, (1), 60–73.
Carr, A. T. (1974*a*). Compulsive neurosis: two psychophysiological studies. *Bull. Br. Psychol. Soc.* **24**, 256–7.
—— (1974*b*). Compulsive neurosis: a review of the literature. *Psychol. Bull.* **81**, (5), 311–18.
Cautela, J. R. (1966). Treatment of compulsive behavior by covert sensitization. *Psychol. Rec.* **16**, 33–41.
—— (1967). Covert sensitization. *Psychol. Rec.* **20**, 459–68.
—— (1969). Behavior therapy and self control: techniques and implications. In *Behavior therapy: appraisal and status* (ed. C. M. Franks). McGraw-Hill, New York.
Cohen, R. (1969). The effects of group interaction and progressive hierarchy presentation on desensitization of test anxiety. *Behav. res. & Ther.* **7**, 15–26.
Daniels, L. K. (1976). An extension of thought-stopping in the treatment of obsessional thinking: letter to the editor. *Behav. Ther.* **7**, 131.
Ellis, A. A. (1969). A cognitive approach to behavior therapy. *Int. J. Psychiat.* **8**, 896–900.
Emmelkamp, P. M. G. (1974). Effects of expectancy on systematic desensitization and flooding. *European J. Behav. Analysis & Modification* **1**, 1–11.
Esse, J. T. and Wilkins, W. (1978). Empathy and imagery in avoidance behavior reduction. *J. consult. & clin. Psychol.* **46**, 202–3.
Eysenck, H. J. (1959). Learning theory and behavior therapy. *J. ment. Sci.* **105**, 61–75.
Farmer, R. G. and Wright, J. M. C. (1971). Muscular reactivity and systematic desensitization. *Behav. Ther.* **2**, 1–10.
Feldman, M. P. and MacCulloch, M. J. (1971). *Homosexual behaviour: therapy and*

assessment. Pergamon Press, Oxford.

Foreyt, J. P. and Hagen, R. L. (1973). Covert sensitization: conditioning or suggestion. *J. abnorm. Psychol.* **82**, (1), 17–23.

Gold, S. and Neufeld, I. A. (1965). A learning theory approach to the treatment of homosexuality. *Behav. Res. & Ther.* **2**, 201–4.

Goldfried, M. R. and Goldfried, Anita P. (1975). *Cognitive change methods.* In *Helping people change* (ed. Frederick H. Kanfer and Arnold P. Goldstein), pp 89–116. Pergamon, New York.

Greenspoon, J. (1962). Verbal conditioning and clinical psychology. In *Experimental foundations of clinical psychology* (ed. A. J. Bachrach), pp. 510–53. Basic Books, New York.

Hackmann, A. and McLean, Carole (1975). A comparison of flooding and thought-stopping in the treatment of obsessional neurosis. *Behav. Res. & Ther.* **13**, (4), 263–9.

Homme, L. E. (1965). Perspectives in psychology: XXIV. Control of coverants, the operants of the mind. *Psychol. Rec.* **15**, 501–11.

Janda, L. H. and Rimm, D. C. (1972). Covert sensitization in the treatment of obesity. *J. abnorm. Psychol.* **80**, 37–42.

*Kanfer, F. H. and Goldstein, A. P. (ed.) (1975). *Helping people change: a textbook of methods.* Pergamon, Oxford.

Kellam, A. M. P. (1969). Shoplifting treated by aversion to a film. *Behav. Res & Ther.* **7**, 125–7.

Kenny, F. T., Solyom, L., and Solyom, C. (1973). Faradic disruption of obsessive ideation in the treatment of obsessive neurosis. *Behav. Ther.* **4**, 448–57.

*Lang, P. J. and Melamed, B. G. (1969). Case report: avoidance conditioning therapy of an infant with chronic ruminative vomiting. *J. abnorm Psychol.* **74**, 1–8.

Lazarus, A. A. (1961). Group therapy of phobic disorders by systematic desensitization. *J. abnorm. & soc. Psychol.* **63**, 504–10.

—— (1965). Behavior therapy, incomplete treatment, and symptom substitution. *J. nerv. ment. Dis.* **140**, (1), 80–6.

—— (1969). Behavioral counseling: some pros. and cons. *Counseling Psychol.* **1**, (4), 60–2.

*Ledwidge, B. (1978). Cognitive behavior modification: a step in the wrong direction? *Psychol. Bull.* **85**, (2), 353–78.

Levine, B. A. (1976). Treatment of trichotillomania by covert sensitization. *J. behav. Ther. & exp. Psychiat.* **7**, (1), 75–6.

*Lick, J. and Bootzin, R. (1975). Expectancy factors in the treatment of fear: methodological and theoretical issues. *Psychol. Bull.* **82**, (6), 917–31.

Litvak, S. B. (1969). A comparison of two brief group behavior therapy techniques on the reduction of avoidance behavior. *Psychol. Rec.* **19**, 329–34.

Lloyd, R. W. and Salzburg, H. C. (1975). Controlled social drinking: an alternative to abstinence as a treatment goal of some alcohol abusers. *Psychol. Bull.* **82**, (6), 815–42.

McGlynn, F. D. (1973). Graded imagination and relaxation as components of experimental desensitization. *J. nerv. & ment. Dis.* **156**, 377–85.

McReynolds, W. T. and Tori, C. (1972). A further assessment of attention-placebo effects and demand characteristics in studies of systematic desensitization. *J. consult. & clin. Psychol.* **38**, (2), 261–4.

*—— Barnes, A. R., Brooks, S., and Rehagen, N. J. (1973). The role of attention-placebo influences in the efficacy of systematic desensitization. *J. consult. & clin. Psychol.* **41**, (1). 86–92.

Mahoney, M. J. (1974). *Cognition and behavior modification.* Ballinger, Cambridge,

Massachusetts.
Marks, I. M. (1969). *Fears and phobias.* Heinemann, London.
Meichenbaum, D. (1975). Self-instruction methods. In *Helping people change* (ed. F. H. Kanfer and A. P. Goldstein). Pergamon Press, New York.
Metzner, R. (1963). Some experimental analogues of obsession. *Behav. Res. & Ther.* **3**, 1–7.
Meyer, V. (1970). Comments on A. J. Yates' "Misconceptions about behavior therapy": a point of view. *Behav. Ther.* **1**, 108–12.
—— Levy, R., and Schnurer, A. (1974). The behavioural treatment of obsessive–compulsive disorders. In *Obsessional states* (ed. H. R. Beech). Methuen, London.
Miller. H. R. and Nawas, M. M. (1970). Control of aversive stimulus termination in systematic desensitization. *Behav. Res. & Ther.* **8**, 57–61.
Morganstein, K. P. (1974). Cigarette smoke as a noxious stimulus in self-managed aversion therapy for compulsive eaters. *Behav. Ther.* **5**, 255–60.
Olin, R. J. (1976). Thought-stopping: some cautionary observations. *Behav. Ther.* **7**, (5), 706–7.
Paul, G. L. (1969). Outcome of systematic desensitization II: Controlled investigations of individual treatment, technique variations and current status. In *Behavior therapy: appraisal and status* (ed. C. M. Franks). McGraw-Hill, New York.
Rachman, S. (1965). Aversion therapy: chemical or electrical? *Behav. Res. & Ther.* **2**, 289–300.
—— (1971). Obsessional ruminations. *Behav. Res. & Ther.* **9**, 229–35.
—— and Teasdale, J. D. (1969). Aversion therapy. An appraisal. In *Behavior therapy: appraisal and status* (ed. C. M. Franks). McGraw-Hill, New York.
Rainey, C. A. (1972). An obsessive–compulsive neurosis treated by flooding *in vivo*. *J. behav. Ther. & exp. Psychiat.* **3**, 117–21.
Roper, G., Rachman, S., and Marks, I. (1975). Passive and participant modeling in exposure treatment of obsessive–compulsive neurotics. *Behav. Res. & Ther.* **13**, 271–9.
Sandler, J. (1975). Aversion methods. In *Helping people change* (ed. F. H. Kanfer and A. P. Goldstein), pp. 273–307. Pergamon, New York.
Shepherd, G. and Durham, R. (1977). The multiple techniques approach to behavioral psychotherapy: a retrospective evaluation of effectiveness and an examination of prognostic indicators. *Br. J. med. Psychol.* **50**, 45–52.
Stern, R. J., Lipsedge, M. S., and Marks, I. M. (1973). Obsessive ruminations: a controlled trial of thought-stopping technique. *Behav. Res. & Ther.* **11**, 659–62.
Stern, R. S. (1978). Obsessive thoughts: the problem of therapy. *Br. J. Psychiat.* **132**, 200–5.
Suinn, R. M., Edie, C. A., and Spinelli, P. R. (1970). Accelerated massed desensitization: innovation in short-term treatment. *Behav. Ther.* **1**, 303–11.
Thoresen, C. E. and Mahoney, M. J. (1974). *Behavioral self-control.* Holt, Rinehart, and Winston. New York.
Verplank, W. S. (1955). The control of the content of conversation: reinforcement of statements of opinion. *J. abnorm. & soc. Psychol.* **51**, 668–76.
Vingoe, F. J. (1965). *Counseling and behavior therapy—incompatible?* Paper presented to the Psychological Counseling Department. University of Oregon.
—— (1980). Treatment of a chronic obsessive via reinforcement contingent upon success in response prevention. *Behav. Res. Ther.* **18**, 212–17.
Walton, D. and Mather, M. D. (1964). The application of learning principles to the treatment of obsessive compulsive states in the acute and chronic phases of illness. In *Experiments in behaviour therapy* (ed. H. J. Eysenck). Pergamon Press, Oxford.

Wartnaby, Kathleen M. (1972). Thought-stopping techniques. *Br. J. Psychiat.* **120**, 125.

Wilkins, W. (1971). Desensitization: social and cognitive factors underlying the effectiveness of Wolpe's procedure. *Psychol. Bull.* **76**, (5), 311–17.

—— (1972). Desensitization: getting it together with Davison and Wilson. *Psychol. Bull.* **78**, (1), 32–6.

—— (1973). Desensitization: a rejoinder to Morgan. *Psychol. Bull.* **79**, (6), 376–7.

—— (1974). Parameters of therapeutic imagery: directions from case studies. *Psychotherapy: Theory, Res. & Pract.* **11**, (2), 163–71.

—— (1976). Imagery-based decisions. *Psychotherapy: Theory, Res. & Pract.* **13**, (3), 253–4.

—— and Domitor, P. J. (1973). Role of instructed attention shifts in systematic desensitization. *Proceedings, 81st Annual Convention, American Psychological Association,* 553–4.

Wisocki, P. A. (1973). The successful treatment of a heroin addict by covert conditioning techniques. *J. Behav. Ther. & exp. Psychiat.* **4**, 55–61.

*Wolpe, J. (1976*a*). Behavior therapy and its malcontents—I Denial of its bases and psychodynamic fusionism. *J. behav. Ther. & Exp. Psychiat.* **7**, 1–5.

—— (1976*b*). Behavior therapy and its malcontents—II Multimodal eclecticism, cognitive exclusivism and "exposure" empiricism. *J. behav. Ther. & exp. Psychiat.* **7**, 109–16.

—— and Lazarus (1966). *Behaviour therapy techniques: a guide to the treatment of neurosis*, Pergamon, London.

Yamagami, T. (1971). The treatment of an obsession by thought-stopping. *J. behav. Ther. & exp. Psychiat.* **2**, 113–5.

Yates, A. J. (1970*a*). Misconceptions about behavior therapy: a point of view. *Behav. Ther.* **1**, 92–107.

—— (1970*b*). Misconceptions about behavior therapy: a rejoinder to Meyer. *Behav. Ther.* **1**, 113–14.

—— (1970*c*). *Behavior Therapy.* Wiley, New York.

—— (1975). *Theory and practice in behavior therapy.* Wiley, New York.

CHAPTER 17

As, A. (1962). The recovery of forgotten language knowledge through hypnotic age regression: a case report. *Am. J. clin. Hypn.* **5**, 1, 24–9.

Bentler, P. M. and Hilgard, E. R. (1963). A comparison of group and individual inducation of hypnosis with self-scoring and observer-scoring. *Int. J. clin. exp. Hypn.* **11**, 49–54.

Dahinterova, Jeanette (1967). Some experience with the use of hypnosis in the treatment of burns. *Int. J. clin. exp. Hypn.* **15**, (2), 49–53.

Dengrove, E. (1973). The uses of hypnosis in behaviour therapy. *Int. J. clin. exp. Hypn.* **21**, (1), 13–17.

Diamond, M. J. (1974). The modification of hypnotizability: a review *Psychol. Bull.* **81**, 180–98.

Dimond, E.G. (1971). Acupuncture anaesthesia. *J. Am. Med. Ass.* **218**, 1558.

Engstrom, D. R., London, P., and Hart, J. T. (1970). Hypnotic susceptibility increased by EEG alpha training. *Nature, Lond.* **227** (No. 5264), 1261–2.

Evans, F. J. (1967). Suggestibility in the normal waking state. *Psychol. Bull.* **67**, 114–29.

*Frankel, F. H. (1975). Physical symptons and marked hypnotizability. *Int. J. clin. exp. Hypn.* **23**, (4), 227–35.
—— (1976). *Hypnosis: trance as a coping mechanism.* Plenum Medical, London.
—— and Orne, M. T. (1976). Hypotizability and phobic behavior. *Archs. gen. Psychiat.* **33**, 1259–61.
—— Apfel, R. J., Kelly, S. F., Benson, H., Quinn, T., Newmark, J., and Malmaud, R. (1979). The use of hypnotizability scales in the clinic: a review after six years. *Int. J. clin. exp. Hypn.* **27**, (2), 63–73.
Fromm, Erika (1968). Tranference and counter-transference in hypnoanalysis. *Int. J. clin. exp. Hypn.* **16**, 77–84.
Gibbons, D. E. (1979). *Applied hypnosis and hyperempiria.* Plenum Press, New York.
Gill, M. M. (1972). Hypnosis as an altered and regressed state. *Int. J. clin. exp. Hypn.* **20**, (4), 224–37.
—— and Brenman, Margaret (1959). *Hypnosis and related states: pyschoanalytic studies in regression.* International Universities Press, New York.
Haley J. (1967) (ed.). *Advanced techniques of hypnosis and therapy: selected papers of Milton H. Erickson, M.D.* Grune and Stratton, New York.
—— (1973). *Uncommon therapy: the psychiatric techniques of Milton H. Erikson, M.D.* Norton, New York.
Hammer, A. G. (1972). Review of Hilgard, J. R. (1970). Personality and hypnosis: a study of imaginative involvement. University of Chicago Press. *Int. J. clin. exp. Hypn.* **20**, (4), 264–7.
Hanley, F. W. (1969). Hypnosis in the court room. *Can. Psychiat. Ass. J.* **14**, 351–4.
*Hilgard, E. R. (1965). *The experience of hypnosis.* Harcourt, Brace, and World, New York.
—— (1967). Individual differences in hypnotizability. In *Handbook of clinical and experimental hypnosis* (ed. J. Gordon). Macmillan, New York.
—— (1975). Hypnosis. In *Annual review of psychology* **26**, (ed. P. H. Mussen and M. R. Rosensweig), pp. 19–44. Annual Reviews, Palo Alto, California.
—— and Hilgard, J. R. (1975). *Hypnosis in the relief of pain.* Kaufmann, Los Altos, California.
—— Atkinson, R. C., and Atkinson, Rita L. (1975). *Introduction to psychology* (6th edn). Harcourt, Brace, and World, New York.
Hilgard, J. R. (1965). Personality and hypnotizability: inferences from case studies. *In The experience of hypnosis* (ed. E. R. Hilgard), pp. 269–323. Harcourt, Brace, and World, New York.
—— (1970). *Personality and hypnosis: a study of imaginative involvement.* Chicago University Press.
—— (1974). Imaginative involvement: some characteristics of the highly hypnotizable and the non-hypnotizable. *Int. J. clin. exp. Hypn.* **22**, 138–56.
—— and Hilgard, E. R. (1979). Assessing hypnotic responsiveness in the clinical setting: A multi-item clinical scale and its advantages over single-item scales. *Int. J. clin. exp. Hypn.* **27**, 134–50.
Jacobsen, E. (1938). *Progressive relaxation.* Chicago University Press.
Kaim, B. T. (1963). Some dangerous techniques of hypnotic induction. *Am. J. clin. Hypn.* **5**, 171–6.
Kline, M. V. (1953). A visual imagery technique for the introduction of hypnosis in certain refractory subjects. *J. Psychol.* **35**, 227–8.
Kramer, E., and Brennan, E. P. (1964). Hypnotic susceptibility of schizophrenic patients. *J. abnorm. Soc. Psychol.* **69**, 657–9.
Kratochvíl, S. (1970). Sleep hypnosis and waking hypnosis. *Int. J. Clin. Exp. Hypn.*

18, 1, 25–40.
Kroger, W. (1972*a*). More on acupuncture and hypnosis. *Newsl. Soc. clin. exp. Hypn.* **13**, (4), 2–4.
*—— (1972*b*). Hypnotism and acupuncture. *J. Am. med. Ass.* **220**, 1012–13.
Lavoie, G., Sabourin, M., and Langlois, J. (1973). Hypnotic susceptibility, amnesia, and I.Q. in chronic schizophrenia. *Int. J. clin. exp. Hypn.* **21**, 157–68.
Lazarus, A. A. (1971). *Behavior therapy and beyond.* McGraw-Hill, New York.
—— (1973). "Hypnosis" as a facilitator in behavior therapy. *Int. J. clin. exp. Hypn.* **21**, (1), 25–31.
LeCron, L. M. (ed.) (1956). *Experimental hypnosis.* Macmillan, New York.
Lenox, J. R. (1970). Effect of hypnotic analgesia on verbal report and cardiovascular responses to ischemic pain. *J. abnorm. Psychol.* **75**, 199–206.
Liebert, R. M., Rubin, Norma, and Hilgard, E. R. (1965). The effects of suggestions and alertness on paired-associate learning. *J. Personality* **33**, 605–12.
*Ludwig, A. M. (1966). Altered states of consciousness. *Arch. gen. Psychiat.* **15**, 225–34. (Also reprinted in C. T. Tart (ed.) (1969). *Altered states of consciousness: a book of readings,* pp. 9–22. Wiley, New York.)
—— and Lyle, W. H. Jnr. (1964). Tension induction and the hyperalert trance. *J. abnorm. soc. Psychol.* **69**, 70–6.
Marcuse, F. L. (1959). *Hypnosis: fact and fiction.* Penguin, Harmondsworth.
Marks, D. F. (1973). Visual imagery differences in the recall of pictures. *Br. J. Psychol.* **64**, 17–24.
Marmer, M. J. (1969). Unusual applications of hypnosis in anaesthesiology. *Int. J. clin. exp. Hypn.* **17**, 199–208.
Mather, Marcia D. and Degun, G. S. (1975). A comparative study of hypnosis and relaxation. *Br. J. med. Psychol.* **48**, 55–63.
Meares, A. (1954). The clinical estimation of suggestibility. *J. clin. exp. Hypn.* **2**, 106–8.
Melzack, R. (1973). *The puzzle of pain.* Penguin, Harmondsworth.
Miloš, R. (1975). Hypnotic exploration of amnesia after-cerebral injuries. *Int. J. clin. exp. Hypn.* **23**, (2), 103–10.
Morgan, A. H., Johnson, D. L., and Hilgard, E. R. (1974). The stability of hypnotic susceptibility. *Int. J. clin. exp. Hypn.* **22**, 249–57.
Oetting, E. R. (1964). Hypnosis and concentration in study. *Am. J. clin. Hypn.* **7**, 148–51.
Orne, M. T. (1979). Editorial Note. *Int. J. clin. exp. Hypn.* **27**, (2).
Pattie, F. (1967). A brief history of hypnosis. In *Handbook of clinical and experimental hypnosis* (ed. J. Gordon). Macmillan, New York.
Paul, G. L. (1969*a*). Physiological effects on relaxation training and hypnotic suggestion. *J. abnorm. Psychol.* **74**, 425–37.
—— (1969*b*). Inhibition of physiological response to stressful imagery by relaxation training and hypnotically suggested relaxation. *Behav. Res. and Ther.* **7**, 249–56.
—— and Trimble, R. W. (1970). Recorded vs "live" relaxation training and hypnotic suggestion: comparative effectiveness for reducing physiological arousal and inhibiting stress response. *Behav. Ther.* **1**, 285–302.
Perry, C. (1979). Hypnotic coercion and compliance to it: A review of evidence presented in a legal case. *Int. J. clin. exp. Hypn.* **27**, (3), 187–218.
Raginsky, B. B. (1969). Hypnotic recall of aircrash cause. *Int. J. clin. exp. Hypn.* **17**, (1), 1–19.
*Rock, N. L., Shipley, T. E., and Campbell, C. (1969). Hypnosis with untrained non-volunteer patients in labour. *Int. J. clin. exp. Hypn.* **18**, (3), 160–80.
Sacerdote, P. (1970). Theory and practice of pain control in malignant and other

protracted or recurrent painful illness. *Int. J. clin. exp. Hypn.* **18**, 160–80.
*Schafer, D. W. and Rubio, R. (1978). Hypnosis to aid the recall of witnesses. *Int. J. clin. exp. Hypn.* **26**, 81–91.
Sheehan, P. W. (1967). A shortened form of the Bett's questionnaire upon mental imagery. *J. clin. Psychol.* **23**, 386–9.
—— (1972). Hypnosis and the manifestations of 'imagination' In *Hypnosis: research developments and perspectives* (ed. E. Fromm and R. E. Shor) pp. 293–319. Aldine-Atherton, Chicago.
—— (1979). Hypnosis and the processes of the imagination. In *Hypnosis: developments in research and new perspectives* (2nd edn) (ed. E. Fromm and R. E. Shor) pp. 381–411. Aldine, New York.
*—— and Perry, C. (1976). *Methodologies of hypnosis.* Wiley, London.
Shor, R. and Orne, Emily C. (1962). *Harvard group scale of hypnotic susceptibility. Form A.* Consulting Psychologists Press, Palo Alto, California.
Spanos, N. P. and Barber, T. X. (1974). Toward a convergence in hypnosis research. *Am. Psychol.* **29**, 500–11.
Spiegel, H. and Spiegel, D. (1978). *Trance and treatment: clinical uses of hypnosis.* Basic Books, New York.
Starker, S. (1974). Effects on hypnotic induction upon visual imagery. *J. nerv. ment. Dis.* **159**, (6), 433–7.
't.Hoen, P. (1978). Effects of hypnotizability and visualizing ability on imagery-mediated learning, *Int. J. clin. exp. Hypn.* **26**, (1), 45–54.
*Upjohn Limited. *Hypnosis as sole anaesthesia in Caesarian section.* A film available upon request from Upjohn Ltd., for appropriate professional or student audiences.
Vingoe, F. J. (1968*a*). Development of a group alert trance scale. *Int. J. clin. exp. Hypn.* **16**, 120–32.
—— (1968*b*). *The utilization of a group alert trance technique in facilitating human performance.* Paper presented at the Western Psychological Association Convention. San Diego, California.
—— (1969). Introversion-extraversion, attitudes toward hypnosis, and susceptibility to the alert trance. *Proc. Am. psychol. Ass.* Part II, 902–3.
—— (1973*a*). Comparison of the Harvard Group Scale of Hypnotic Susceptibility, Form A and the Group Alert Trance Scale in a University population. *Int. J. of clin. exp. Hypn.* **21**, 169–79.
—— (1973*b*). More on drugs, hypnotic susceptibility and experimentally controlled conditions. *Bull. Br. Psychol. Soc.* **26**,95–103.
—— (1974). Unpublished Project Report. Clinical Psychology Department, University of Groningen.
—— (1975). The effect of different hypnotic induction procedures in research and therapy. *Proc. Br. Psychol. Soc.* (Abst.), p. 37.
—— (1980). A review of Spiegel, H. and Spiegel, D. (1978). Trance and treatment: clinical uses of hypnosis. *Bull. Br. Soc. exp. clin. Hypn.* **3**, 23–5.
—— (in press). Clinical hypnosis and behaviour therapy: a cognitive emphasis in the eighties? *Bull. Br. Soc. exp. clin. Hypn.* **3**.
—— and Kramer, E. (1966). Hypnotic susceptibility of hospitalized psychotic patients: a pilot study. *Int. J. clin. exp. Hypn.* **14**, 47–54.
Weitzenhoffer, A. M. (1953). *Hypnotism: an objective study in suggestibility.* Wiley, New York.
—— (1957). *General techniques of hypnotism.* Grune and Stratton, New York.
—— (1972). Behavior therapeutic techniques and hypnotherapeutic methods. *Am. J. clin. Hypn.* **15**, (2), 71–82.

—— and Hilgard, E. R. (1959). *Stanford hypnotic susceptibility scales, Forms A and B*. Consultant Psychologists Press, Palo Alto, California.
—— (1962). *Stanford hypnotic susceptibility scale, Form C*. Consulting Psychologists Press, Palo Alto, California.
Zane, M. D. (1966). The hypnotic situation and changes in ulcer pain. *Int. J. clin. exp. Hypn.* **14**, (4), 292–304.

CHAPTER 18

Andersen, P. and Andersson, S. A. (1968). *Physiological basis of the alpha rhythm*. Appleton-Century-Crofts, New York.
Andreychuk, T. and Skriver, C. (1975). Hypnosis and biofeedback in the treatment of migraine headache. *Int. J. clin. exp. Hypn.* **24**, (3), 172–83.
*Birk, L. (ed.) (1973). *Biofeedback: behavioral medicine*. Grune and Stratton, New York.
*Blanchard, E. B. and Miller, S. T. (1977). Psychological treatment of cardiovascular disease. *Arch. Gen. Psychiat.* **34**, 1402–13.
—— and Young, L. D. (1974). Clinical applications of biofeedback training. *Arch. gen. Psychiat.* **30**, 573–89.
Brown, Barbara (1970). Recognition of aspects of consciousness through association with EEG alpha activity represented by a light signal. *Psychophysiology* **6**, 442–52.
Budzynski, T. H. (1973). Biofeedback procedures in the clinic. In *Biofeedback: behavioral medicine* (ed. L. Birk), pp. 177–87. Grune and Stratton, New York.
—— (1976). Biofeedback and the twilight states of consciousness. In *Consciousness and self-regulation: advances in research.* (ed. G. E. Schwartz and D. Shapiro), Vol. 1, pp. 361–85. Wiley, London.
Driessen, M. H. D., Knoppers, M., van Kroten, I. A. M. H., and Werre, P. F. (1974). Beheersing van alfa activiteit of: de nieuwe kleren van de keizer? *Dutch J. Psychol.* **28**, 649–68.
*Engstrom, D. R., London, P., and Hart, J. T. (1970). Hypnotic susceptibility increased by EEG alpha training. *Nature, Lond.* **227** (No. 5264), 1261–2.
Evans, F. J. (1972). Hypnosis and sleep: Techniques for exploring cognitive activity during sleep. In *Hypnosis: research developments and perspectives* (ed. Erika Fromm and R. E. Shor), pp. 43–83). Aldine-Atherton, Chicago.
Evans, M. B. (1977). Biofeedback training: some clinical considerations. *Behav. Ther.* **8**, (1), 101–3.
Fromm, Erika and Shor, R. E. (ed.) (1979). *Hypnosis: research development and perspectives.* Aldine-Atherton, Chicago.
*Gannon, L. and Sternbach, G. (1971). Alpha enhancement as a treatment for pain. a case study. *J. behav. Ther. exp. Psychiat.* **2**, 209–13.
Graham, G. W., (1975). Hypnotic treatment for migraine headaches. *Int. J. clin. exp. Hypn.* **23**, 165–71.
Greenfield, N. S. and Sternbach, R. A. (ed.) (1972) *Handbook of psychophysiology*. Holt, Rinehart, and Winston, New York.
Johnson, R. K. and Meyer, R. G. (1974). Phased biofeedback approach for epileptic seizure control. *J. behav. Ther. exp. Psychiat.* **5**, 185–7.
Kamiya, J. (1969). Operant control of the EEG alpha rhythm and some of its reported effects on consciousness. In *Altered states of consciousness: a book of readings* (ed. C. T. Tart), pp. 509–17. Wiley, New York.
Kennedy, J. L. (1959). A possible artifact in electroencephalography. *Psychol. Rev.* **66**, 347–52.

Lader, M. (1975). *The psychophysiology of mental illness.* Routledge and Kegan Paul, London.
Lang, P. J. (1970). Autonomic control or learning to play the internal organs. *Psychology Today,* October, 37–41, 86.
Lippold, O. (1973). *The origin of the alpha rhythm.* Churchill Livingstone, Edinburgh.
London, P., Cooper, L. M. and Engstrom, D. R. (1974). Increasing hypnotic susceptibility by brain wave feedback. *J. abnorm. Psychol.* **83**, (5), 554–60.
—— Hart, J. T., and Leibovitz, M. P. (1968). EEG alpha rhythms and susceptibility to hypnosis. *Nature, Lond.* **219**, 71–2.
Lynch, J. J. (1973). Biofeedback: some reflections on modern behavioral science. In *Biofeedback: behavioral medicine* (ed. Lee Birk), pp. 191–202. Grune and Stratton, New York.
—— (1974). Review of Barber, T. X., DiCara, L. V., and Kamiya, J. (ed.) (1972). Biofeedback and self-control. Aldine-Atherton, Chicago. *J. nerv. ment. Dis.* **158**, 394–5.
—— Paskewitz, D. A. and Orne, M. T. (1974). Inter-session stability of human alpha rhythm. *EEG & clin. Electroencephalogr.* **36**, 538–40.
Mackean, D. G. (1973). *Introduction to biology,* Murray, London.
*Melzack, R. and Perry, C. (1975). Self-regulation of pain: the use of alpha-feedback and hypnotic training for the control of chronic pain. *Exp. Neurol.* **46**, (3), 452–69.
Miller, H. L. (1968). Alpha waves — artifacts. *Psychol. Bull.* **69**, (4), 279–80.
Nowlis, D.P. (1968). Early observations on a system providing EEG alpha feedback training. *Hawthorne House Research Memorandum,* No. 78.
—— and Kamiya, J. (1970). The control of electroencephalographic alpha rhythms through auditory feedback and the associated mental activity. *Psychophysiology* **6**, 476–84.
—— and Rhead, J. C. (1968). Relation of eyes-closed resting EEG alpha activity to hypnotic susceptibility. *Percept. Mot. Skills.* **27**, 1047–50.
Paskewitz, D. A., Lynch, J. J., Orne, M. T., and Costello, J. G. (1969). The feedback control of alpha activity-conditioning or disinhibition! Paper presented at Annual *Meeting of the Society for Psychophysiological Research,* Monterey, California, also in Psychophysiology (1970), **6**, 637–8. (Abstract).
—— and Orne, M. T. (1973). Visual effects on alpha feedback-training. *Science N.Y.* **181**, 360–3.
Reavley, W. (1975). The use of biofeedback in the treatment of writer's cramp. *J. behav. Ther. exp. Psychiat.* **6**, 335–8.
Sargent, J. D., Walters, E. D., and Green, E. E. (1973). Psychosomatic self-regulation of migraine headaches. In L. Birk (ed.) *Biofeedback: behavioral medicine.* Grune and Stratton, New York.
Schacter, D. L. (1976). The hypnagogic state: a critical review of the literature. *Psychol. Bull.* **83**, (3), 452–81.
Schwartz, G. E. (1973). Biofeedback as therapy: some theoretical and practical issues. *Am. Psychol.* **28**, 666–73.
Shor, R. and Orne, Emily C. (1962). *Harvard group scale of hypnotic susceptibility Form A.* Consulting Psychologists Press, Palo Alto, California.
Speigel, H. and Bridger, A. A. (1970). *Manual for hypnotic induction profile: eye-roll levitation method.* Soni Medica, New York.
Sterman, M. B. (1973). Neurophysiologic and clinical studies of sensorimotor EEG biofeedback. In *Biofeedback: behavioral medicine* (ed. Lee Birk), pp. 147–65. Grune and Stratton, New York.
Stroebel, C. F. and Glueck, B. C. (1973). Biofeedback treatment in medicine and

psychiatry: an ultimate placebo? *Biofeedback: behavioral medicine* (ed. Lee Birk), pp. 19–33. Grune and Stratton, New York.

Tart, C. T. (1969). *Altered states of consciousness.* Wiley, London; also (1972) Doubleday, Garden City, New York.

Weitzenhoffer, A. M. and Hilgard, E. R. (1959). *Stanford hypnotic susceptibility scales, Forms A and B.* Consulting Psychologists Press, Palo Alto, California.

—— (1962). *Stanford hypnotic susceptibility scale, Form C.* Consulting Psychologists Press, Palo Alto, California.

CHAPTER 19

*Abramson, E. E. (1977). Behavioural approaches to weight control: an up-dated review. *Behav. Res. & Ther.* **15**, 355–63.

Axelrod, S., Hall, R. V., Weis, L., and Rohrer, S. (1971). Use of self-imposed contingencies to reduce the frequency of smoking behavior. Paper presented at the meeting of the Association for the Advancement of Behavior Therapy, Washington, DC.

Baker, B. L., Cohen, D. C., and Saunders, J. T. (1973). Self-directed desensitization for agoraphobia. *Behav. Res. & Ther.* **11**, 79–89.

Bandura, A. (1969). *Principles of behavior modification.* Holt, Rinehart, and Winston, New York.

Bayer, C. A. (1972). Self-monitoring and mild aversion treatment of trichotillomania. *J. behav. Ther. & exp. Psychiat.* **3**, 139–41.

Bellack, A. S. (1976). A comparison of self-reinforcement and self-monitoring in a weight reduction program. *J. behav. Ther. & exp. Psychiat.* **5**, 245–9.

—— Schwartz, J. and Rozensky, R. H. (1974). The contribution of external control to self-control in a weight reduction program. *J. behav. Ther. & exp. Psychiat.* **5**, 245–50.

Berecz, J. (1972). Modification of smoking behavior through self-administered punishment of imaginal behavior: a new approach to aversive therapy. *J. consult. & clin. Psychol.* **36**, 244–50.

—— (1976). Treatment of smoking with cognitive conditioning therapy: A self-adminstered aversion technique. *Behav. Ther.* **7**, 641–8.

Bootzin, R. R. (1972). Stimulus control treatment for insomnia. Paper presented at the 80th annual meeting of the American Psychological Society, Honolulu.

Broden, M., Hall, R. V., and Mitts, B. (1971). The effect of self-recording on the classroom behavior of two eighth grade students. *J. appl. Behav. Analysis* **4**, 191–9.

Cautela, J. R. (1966). Treatment of compulsive behavior by covert sensitization. *Psychol. Rec.* **16**, 33–41.

Davison, G. C. (1968). Elimination of a sadistic fantasy by a client-controlled counter-conditioning technique: a case study. *J. abnorm. Psychol.* **73**, 84–9.

Epstein, L. H. and Hersen, M. (1974). A multiple baseline analysis of coverant control. *J. behav. Ther. & exp. Psychiat.* **5**, 7–12.

Ferster, C. B., Nurnberger, J. I., and Levitt, E. B. (1962). The control of eating. *J. Mathetics* **1**, 87–109.

Fisher, E. B., Green, L., Frielding, C., Levenkron, J., and Porter, F. L. (1976). Self-monitoring of progress in weight-reduction: a preliminary report. *J. Behav. Ther. & exp. Psychiat.* **7**, 363–5.

Fixsen, D. L., Phillips, E. L., and Wolf, M. M. (1972). Achievement place: the reliability of self-reporting and peer-reporting and their effects on behavior. *J. appl. Behav. Analysis* **5**, 19–30.

Frederiksen, L. W. (1975). Treatment of ruminative thinking by self-monitoring. *J. behav. Ther. & exp. Psychiat.* **6**, 258–9.

*Goldfried, M. R. and Merbaum, M. (1973). *Behavior change through self-control.* Holt, Rinehart, and Winston, New York.

Guttman, M. and Marston, A. (1967). Problems of S's motivation in a behavioral program for the reduction of cigarette smoking. *Psychol. Rep.* **20**, 1107–14.

Hall, S. M. (1972). Self-control and therapist control in the behavioural treatment of overweight women. *Behav. Res. & Ther.* **10**, 59–68.

—— Hall, R. G., DeBoer, G., and O'Kulitch, P. (1977). Self and external management compared with psychotherapy in the control of obesity. *Behav. Res. & Ther.* **15**, 89–95.

Hanson, R. W., Borden, B. L., Hall, S. M., and Hall, R. G. (1976). Use of programmed instruction in teaching self-management skills to overweight adults. *Behav. Ther.* **7**, 366–73.

Haynes, S. N., Price, M. G., and Simons, J. B. (1975). Stimulus control treatment of insomnia. *J. behav. Ther. & exp. Psychiat.* **6**, 279–82.

Herbert, E. W. and Baer, D. M. (1972). Training parents as behavior modifers: self-recording of contingent attention. *J. appl. Behav. Analysis* **5**, 139–49.

Homme, L. E. (1965). Perspectives in psychology, XXIV: Control of coverants, the operants of the mind. *Psychol. Rec.* **15**, 501–11.

Horan, J. J., Baker, S. B., Hoffman, A. M., and Shute, R. B. (1975). Weight loss through variations in the coverant control paradigm. *J. consult. & clin. Psychol.* **43**, 68–72.

—— and Johnson, R. G. (1971). Coverant conditioning through a self-management application of the Premack Principle: its effect on weight reduction. *J. behav. Ther. & exp. Psychiat.* **2**, 243–9.

Hutzell, R. R., Platzek, D., and Logue, P. E. (1974). Control of symptoms of Gilles de la Tourette's syndrome by self-monitoring. *J. behav. Ther. & exp. Psychiat.* **5**, 71–6.

Jason, L. (1975). Rapid improvement in insomnia following self-monitoring. *J. behav. Ther. & exp. Psychiat.* **6**, 349–50.

Johnson, S. M. and White, G. (1971). Self-observation as an agent of behavioral change. *Behav. Ther.* **2**, 488–97.

Kanfer, F. H. (1970). Self-regulation: research, issues and speculations. In *Behavior modification in clinical psychology* (ed. C. Neuringer and J. L. Michaels), pp. 178–220. Appleton, New York.

Kolb, D. A., Winter, S. K., and Berlow, D. E. (1968). Self-directed change: two studies. *J. appl. behav. Sci.* **4**, 453–71.

Levine, B. A. (1978). The use of a self-administered gustatory stimulus in the elimination of a seizure disorder. *J. behav. Ther. & exp. Psychiat.* **9**, 77–9.

Mahoney, M. J. (1974). Self-reward and self-monitoring techniques for weight control. *Behav. Ther.* **5**, 48–57.

—— Moura, N. G. M., and Wade, T. C. (1973). The relative efficacy of self-reward, self-punishment and self-monitoring techniques for weight loss. *J. consult. & clin. Psychol.* **40**, 404–7.

—— and Thoresen, C. E. (1974). *Self-control power to the person.* Holt, Rinehart and Winston, New York.

Mann, R. A. (1972). The behavior-therapeutic use of contingency contracting to control an adult behavior problem: weight control. *J. appl. behav. Analysis* **5**, 99-109.

Marshall, W. L., Presse, L., and Andrews, W. R. (1976). A self-administered behavior program for public speaking anxiety. *Behav. Res. & Ther.* **14**, 33–9.

McFall, R. M. (1970). The effects of self-monitoring on normal smoking behavior. *J. consult. clin. Psychol.* **35**, 135–42.

—— and Hammen, C. L. (1972). Motivation, structure and self-monitoring: the role of non-specific factors in smoking reduction. *J. consult. & clin. Psychol.* **37**, 80–6.

McNamara, J. R. (1972). The use of self-monitoring techniques to treat nail-biting. *Behav. Res. & Ther.* **10**, 193–4.

McReynolds, W. T., Lutz, R. N., Paulsen, B. K., and Kohrs, M. B. (1976). Weight loss resulting from two behavior modification procedures with nutritionists as therapists. *Behav. Ther.* **7**, 283–91.

Mees, H. L. (1966). Placebo effects in aversive control. Paper presented at the Joint Meeting of the Oregon–Washington State Psychological Association.

Meichenbaum, D. O. and Cameron, R. (1974). The clinical potential of modifying what clients say to themselves. *Psychotherapy: Theory, Res. & Pract.* **11**, 103–17.

Mitchell, K. R. and White, R. G. (1977*a*). Self-management of severe predormital insomnia. *J. behav. Ther. & exp. Psychiat.* **8**, 57–63.

—— and White, R. G. (1977*b*). Behavioral self-management: an application to the problem of migraine headaches. *Behav. Ther.* **8**, 213–21.

Morganstein, K. P. (1974). Cigarette smoke as a noxious stimulus in self-managed aversion therapy for compulsive eaters. *Behav. Ther.* **5**, 255–60.

Nelson, R. O., Lipinski, D. P., and Black, J. L. (1975). The effects of expectancy on the reactivity of self-recording. *Behav. Ther.* **6**, 337–49.

—— —— —— (1976). The relative reactivitiy of external observations and self-monitoring. *Behav. Ther.* **7**, 314–21.

Nolan, J. D. (1968). Self-control procedures in the modification of smoking behavior. *J. consult. & clin. Psychol.* **32**, 92–3.

Ober, D. C. (1968). Modification of smoking behavior. *J. consult. & clin. Psychol.* **32**, 543–9.

*Orne, M. T. (1962). On the social psychology of the psychological experiment: with particular reference to demand characteristics and their implications. *Am. Psychol.* **17**, 776–83.

—— (1969). Demand characteristics and the concept of quasi-control. In *Artifact in behavioral research* (ed. R. Rosenthal and R. L. Rosnow), pp. 143–79. Academic Press, New York.

Penick, S. B., Filion, R., Fox, S., and Stunkard, A. J. (1971). Behavior modification in the treatment of obesity. *Psychosom. Med.* **33**, 49–55.

Phillips, R. E., Johnson, G. D., and Geyer, A. (1972). Self-administered systematic desensitization. *Behav. Res. & Ther.* **10**, 93–6.

Powell, J. and Azrin, N. (1968). The effects of shock as a punisher for cigarette smoking. *J. appl. behav. Analysis* **1**, 63–71.

Rehm, L. P. and Marston, A. R. (1968). Reduction of social anxiety through modification of self-reinforcement: an instigation therapy technique. *J. consult. & clin. Psychol.* **32**, 565–74.

Reynolds, G. S., (1975). *A primer of operant conditioning* (2nd edn). Scott, Foresman, Palo Alto, California.

Roberts, A. M. (1969). Self-control procedures in the modification of smoking behavior: replication. *Psychol. Rep.* **24**, 675–6.

Romanczyk, R. G. (1974). Self-monitoring in the treatment of obesity: parameters of reactivity. *Behav. Ther.* **5**, 531–40.

Rozensky, R. H. (1974). The effect of timing of self-monitoring behavior on reducing cigarette consumption. *J. Behav. Ther. exp. Psychiat.* **5**, 301–3.

Rutner, I. T. (1967). The modification of smoking behavior through techniques of self-control. Unpublished Master's Thesis. Wichita State University.

—— and Bugle, C. (1969). An experimental procedure for the modification of psychotic behavior. *J. consult. & clin. Psychol.* **33**, 651–3.

Shapiro, D., Tursky, B., Schwartz, G. E., and Shnidman, S. R. (1971). Smoking on cue: a behavioral approach to smoking reduction. *J. Health & Soc. Behav.* **12**, 108–13.

Skinner, B. F. (1953). *Science and human behavior.* Macmillan, New York.

Steinmark, S. W. and Borkovec, T. D. (1974). Active and placebo treatment effects on moderate insomnia under counter-demand and positive demand instructions. *J. abnorm. Psychol.* **83**, 157–63.

Stollak, G. E. (1967). Weight loss obtained under different experimental procedures. *Psychotherapy: Theory, Res. & Pract.* **4**, 61–4.

*Stuart, R. B. (1967): Behavioral control over eating. *Behav. Res. & Ther.* **5**, 357–65.

Thomas, E. T., Abrams, K. S., and Johnson, J. B. (1971). Self-monitoring and reciprocal inhibition in the modification of multiple tics of Giles de la Tourettes Syndrome. *J. behav. Ther. & exp. Psychiat.* **2**, 159–71.

Thoresen, C. E. and Mahoney, M. J. (1974). *Behavioral self-control.* Holt, Rinehart, and Winston, New York.

Vasta, R. (1975). Coverant control of self-evaluations through temporal cuing. *J. behav. Ther. & exp. Psychiat.* **7**, 35–7.

Wolpe, J. (1958). *Psychotherapy by reciprocal inhibition.* Stanford University Press, Stanford, California.

CHAPTER 20

Albee, G. W. (1970). The uncertain future of clinical psychology. *Am. Psychol.* **25**, 1071–80.

American Psychological Association (1954). *Psychology and its relations with other professions.* Washington, DC.

*Graham, P. (1977). Psychology and psychiatry. *Bull. Br. psychol. Soc.* **30**, 76–9.

*Hawks, D. V. (1971). Can clincial psychology afford to treat the individual? *Bull. Br. psychol. Soc.* **24**, 133–5.

Knapp, T. J. (1977). Behavior management procedures for diabetic persons. Paper presented at the Third Annual Meeting of the Midwest Association of Behaviour Analysis, Chicago, May, 1977.

—— and Peterson, Linda W. (1976). Behavior management in medical and nursing practice. In *Behavior modification: principles, issues, and applications* (ed. W. E. Craighead, A. E. Kazdin, and M. J. Mahoney). Houghton Mifflin, Boston.

—— (1977). Behavior analysis for nursing of somatic disorders. *Nursing Res.* **26**, (4), 281–7.

Lickorish, J. R. and Sims, C. A. (1972). Social psychologist or clinical scientist? *Bull. Br. psychol. Soc.* **25**, (87), 111–12.

McKeachie, W. J. (1967). The case of multiple models. *Clin. Psychol.* **20**, 108–10.

Torpy, D. M. (1972). The individual and the clinical psychologist. *Bull. Br. psychol. Soc.* **25**, (89), 309–10.

*Trethowen Report (1977). *The role of psychologists in the health services.* Department of Health and Social Security.

Glossary

Abreaction: The release of emotions which occur during the recall of stressful experiences.

Accepted message: Implies more than the reception, registration, and understanding of the message. The message is credible and is registered and perceived with little or no distortion (*see also* Empathy).

Acquiescence response set: The tendency to endorse positive statements in personality tests and questionnaires.

Acupuncture: An ancient Chinese procedure in which needles are placed into specific body sites and rotated vigorously in order to diminish or eliminate pain.

Activity theory: Postulates that the maintenance of activity is necessary in maintaining life satisfaction.

Acute schizophrenia: Schizophrenia of recent onset.

Age-regression: A hypnotic procedure in which the subject is asked to go back in time and to imagine himself as a younger person of a specific age.

Agoraphobia: Phobia of open or public places.

Alert hypnosis: Refers to an hypnotic induction in which suggestions are made to maintain, or even increase, general arousal or alertness. May also refer to a 'state' of alert hypnosis.

Allocentricity: An interest in other people.

Alopecia areata: Sudden loss of hair in specific area, usually scalp or face—may follow extreme stress.

Alternate activities: *see* Incompatible activities.

Amniocentesis: A procedure in which a sample of amniotic fluid is taken from a pregnant woman in order to test for the likelihood of birth defects, such as spina bifida.

Analogue study: A study which has therapeutic implications, carried out to test a specific hypothesis about behaviour. Normal subjects are used because of the greater flexibility and control possible in experiental design.

Angina pectoris (anginal syndrome): Sudden and severe thoracic pain, typically substernal. May be precipitated by emotional factors.

Anorexia nervosa: An eating disorder characterized by amenorrhea, loss of appetite, and consequent weight loss which cannot be attributed to any primary physical or psychiatric condition.

Antagonist activities: *see* Incompatible activities.

Anxiety: Physiological and psychological reaction to perceived threat to organism's well-being (*see also* Free-floating, Neurotic, Moral, and Realistic anxiety).

Anxiety hierarchy: A rank-order listing of those situations related to a client's phobia which evoke varying degrees of anxiety. Used particularly in systematic desensitization.

Arousal: The degree to which the organism is mobilized to defend itself from actual or potential harm, or to prepare itself for activities which require relatively high levels of energy.

Assertion training: Training aimed at counteracting feelings of inadequacy, especially in interpersonal situations. Learning to assert one's rights.

Attitude: A learned emotional tendency to respond in a specific way to a particular group, person, philosophical position, etc.

Attribution theory: Postulates that the variable to which one attributes the effectiveness of behavioural change is important. For many people if the effectiveness of a specific behavioural change can be attributed to their own efforts, the change is more reinforcing and more resistant to extinction or relapse.

A-type therapists: Therapists who tend to be most successful with schizophrenics.

Aura: Change in body sensation which serves as a warning that a migraine headache or epileptic fit is about to occur. Examples of an aura include 'spots in front of the eyes, flushing of the head, etc.

Autistic thinking: A category of thinking related to a loose flow of ideation (i.e., fantasy, dreams, etc.) supposedly reflecting unconscious needs and ideas.

Autogenic phrases: Statements meant to affect the physiological functioning of the organism which the client repeats to himself (e.g.: 'My forehead is becoming pleasantly cool').

Autogenic training: A psychophysiological type of therapy which stresses concentration on specific types of physiological and mental functioning.

Autonomic learning: Learning largely based on emotional stimulation via the autonomic nervous system. Genetic and other non-emotional factors may also play a part.

Aversive therapy: Consists of behavioural procedures in which an aversive stimulus, such as an electric shock, is administered at the same time as maladaptive behaviour, including unwanted thoughts and imagery occurs.

Baseline data: Data which may be expressed as frequency of, or time spent in, some pathological or undesirable activity and/or adaptive or desirable behaviour. This data is obtained prior to treatment intervention. The progress of treatment may then be measured as changes from this baseline. the changes may involve either a decrease or an increase in a specific type of behaviour, depending on whether the therapist is dealing with excessive behaviour or deficit behaviour.

Becoming: Refers to the self-actualization process (q.v.).

Behavioural model (*see also* Model): This model views disturbed behaviour or psychopathology as resulting from a failure to learn adaptive behaviour or as resulting from the learning of the actual maladaptive behaviour. While this model does not deny the reality of organic aetiology where there is evidence for it, the emphasis is on the development of psychopathology through the principles of learning. Maladaptive behaviour is learned just as adaptive behaviour is learned.

Behavioural programming (self-presented consequences): A modification of the consequences of a behaviour by the individual himself (i.e., self-reward or self-punishment).

Behavioural rehearsal (role playing): A technique frequently used in assertive training, in which the client is required to play a specific role in an interpersonal situation which is closely associated with his particular problem.

Brightness constancy: An example of perceptual constancy whereby brightness remains perceived as constant despite 'retinal' brightness.

B-type therapists: Therapists who tend to be most successful with neurotics.

Catatonia: State of extreme unresponsiveness to the environment sometimes present in schizophrenia; a sub-type of schizophrenia.

Catelepsy: A sudden decrease or loss of muscle tone which may cause the person to fall to the floor quite unable to move.

Catharsis: (a) Release of aggressive feelings through socially acceptable means; (b) Discharging of tension relating to earlier stressful material which had been repressed.

Central determinents of perception: Factors such as beliefs and attitudes one has about oneself and others. They tend to be relative enduring characteristics which influence our perception of ourself and others. Thus, if a particular patient perceives himself as strong and masculine, and believes that those health professionals who are treating him also have the same concept of him, his pain threshold is likely to be higher than would otherwise be the case.

Challenge-test (item): An item on an hypnotizability scale where the subject is challenged to perform some action after it has already been suggested that the action will be found impossible to perform.

Chronicity: Refers to a disorder of relatively long duration.

Chronic schizophrenia: Long-standing schiozophrenia.

Classical conditioning: Refers to the conditioning procedure developed by Pavlov, in which an organism is taught to make a specific response to a previously neutral stimulus. The required response was initially only elicited by the unconditional stimulus, which inevitably brings forth this response.

Cognitive behaviour modification (cognitive therapy): Refers to that type of therapy in which the modification of mediating variables such as attitudes, beliefs, fantasies, and imaginery productions is the goal.

Cognitive dissonance theory: A theory developed by Festinger (1957) concerning the strategies individuals use to maintain harmony between conflicting ideas and beliefs.

Cognitive labelling: The characterization of an arousal state as a specific emotion may be, to some degree, dependent upon the context in which the arousal takes place. In other words, the labelling of the arousal state as indicative of a paricular emotion is determined partially by situational factors.

Cognitive mediating variables: Symbolic processes, such as self-approving thoughts, which maintain behaviour in the immediate absence of external reinforcements.

Cognitive restructuring: A behavioural method in which the focus of attention is on cognitive variables, such as attempts to modify attitudes or beliefs.

Cognitive self-evaluation: Mediating variables (such as self-praise or self-criticism); *see* Cognitive mediating variables.

Cold-pressor test: A test of pain tolerance in which the subject is required to place his hand in ice-water.

Colitis: Inflammation of the colon.

Communication system: Includes the units involved when communication takes place between two persons. These units are a transmitter, mode of communication, medium of communication, and a receiver.

Complex hand-movements: A form of stereotypic behaviour in which the hands are moved in an apparently meaningless, non-functional way. Typically found in the autistic children and in some mental retardates.

Compulsion: A recurrent irresistable tendency to engage in irrational behaviour.

Compulsive ritual: Ritualistic irrational behaviour, the performance of which is irresistible (e.g., having to cook the dinner by time-consuming counting procedures).

Computerized axial tomography (CAT): A computerized procedure which allows the investigator to vizualize structures in the brain and to assess the degree of cortical atrophy and the dilation of the cerebral ventricles.

Conditioned emotional response (CER): An emotional response such as fear, which is learned through the process of conditioning.

Conditioned maladaptive responses: *see* Conditioned emotional response.

Conflict: The simultaneous presence of two or more incompatible intentions or goal strivings, so that one is unable to carry out the behaviour necessary to attain the various goals at the same time.

Conflict (approach–approach): The presence of two or more desirable goals which cannot be attained simultaneously.

Conflict (approach–avoidance): Refers to a situation or goal which appears to be characterized by an equal number of desirable aspects and undesirable aspects.

Conflict (avoidance–avoidance): Finding oneself in the presence of two undesirable situations, one of which must, at least at first glance, be accepted (*see also* Leaving the field).

Confusional state: A state whose aetiology is usually organic, characterized by delirium, restlessness, stuper, disorientation, and memory impairment.

Congruent message: A message (verbal or non-verbal) which is consistent with or confirms another message. An incongruent message negates or disconfirms another message. For example, if one person says to another: 'Glad to have you aboard', but neglects to look the recipient of that message in the eye and does not shake his hand, there is an incongruence.

Consciousness: A descriptive term referring to being aware. One is aware of ideas and imaginings at the 'conscious' level of awareness.

Consensual observer drift: Refers to the situation in which there is a drift away from some agreed criterion which sets the limits for the behaviour to be observed, yet a high degree of interobserver agreement is maintained. This usually occurs when the different observers know one another well.

Consensual validation: Belief shared with others.

Contingency contracting: A form of environmental planning where a contract is made with another person regarding the requirements for rewards or punishment.

Contingent positive reinforcement: Reinforcement which is contingent upon adaptive, desirable behaviour.

Controlled behaviour: The behaviour to be modified.

Controlling behaviour: The manipulation of environmental variables by the individual in order to modify his own behaviour.

Controlling variables: The variables which control or regulate behaviour.

Conversion reaction: A condition frequently involving the sensory or motor apparatus, which results from the conversion of anxiety into physical symptomatology (e.g., functional blindness).

Counterbalancing: A design meant to compare the effect of two independent variables A and B by eliminating the effect of order by matching two groups on procedure, and requiring 50 per cent of the subjects in each group to follow an A–B order while the other 50 per cent follows a B–A order.

Counterconditioning (reciprocal inhibition): A procedure in which a stimulus which results in a pleasant response is presented simultaneously with a stimulus which, through conditioning, brings forth an unpleasant emotional response. Eventually, the effect of the pleasant response eliminates the other emotional, maladaptive response.

Countertransference: Emotional relationship of the therapist with the client. Most likely to occur unconsciously after the expected transference relationship has developed.

Coverants: Covert operants—thoughts as discrete behaviours, which can be controlled in the same manner as overt behaviours.

Coverent control techniques: Cognitive behaviour modification techniques aimed at increasing the frequency of adaptive self-statements by arranging for high-probability behaviours to follow them.

Covert sensitization (aversive imagery): A cognitive procedure in which behaviour to be reduced or eliminated is associated imaginatively with an aversive situation, such as nausea and vomiting.

Creativity: A form of thinking laying emphasis on the originality of solution to a problem-solving situation.

Critical period: A stage in maturation during which the organism is structurally and physiologically prepared to learn (perceive) on the basis of specific types of stimulation.

Cross-sectional data: Samples of data obtained at the same time from different individuals or groups.

Cultural-fair tests: Tests designed to be fair to individuals from diverse cultures or with varied educational opportunity.

Cutaneous hypochondriasis: an excessive concern with the condition of the skin.

Crystallized ability (intelligence): The component or aspect of intelligence most related to cultural experience.

Delirium: A condition of cognitive confusion including disorientation, excitement, agitation, clouding of consciousness, and frequently hallucinations.

Delusion: A belief, false by society's standards, which is held with complete conviction by the individual.

Delusion of grandeur: A delusion involving the belief that one is a powerful, famous, or influential person.

Delusion of persecution: A delusion involving the belief that others are attempting to harm the individual in some way.

Dementia: An organic process characterized by a significant deterioration in higher cognitive functioning, including severe memory deficits, problems in orientation and, frequently, significant changes in affect.

Denial: A defence mechanism which enables a person to prevent anxiety-provoking thoughts and feelings from reaching consciousness.

Depersonalization: A loss of feeling of the reality of oneself or of one's body; a feeling as if dead.

Depression: A dampened or sad, apathetic mood, including feelings of worthlessness and guilt, insomnia, decreased appetite and sexual drive. The behavioural view is that depression arises from a perceived lack of reinforcement.

Depression (endogenous): A depressive condition, usually chronic, which is hypothesized as having a biological aetiology or as arising from within the organism.

Depression (reactive): A depressed state clearly precipitated by some significant (stressful) life event, such as the death of a loved-one.

Dermatitis artefacta: Self-inflicted skin lesions.

Determinants of perception: *see* Central determinants of perception.

Diabetes mellitus: an organic disorder of carbohydrate metabolism related to disturbed insulin production.

Discriminability: The relative ability to discriminate between stimuli in the environment.

Discriminant validity: Indicates that a measure is statistically discriminable from another measure and thus specific (e.g., Dominance and Intelligence would probably be discriminable, i.e., would not correlate significantly).

Disorientation: Cognitive confusion in reference to person, place, or time.

Diurnal cycle: The daily physiological cycle involving fluctuations in arousal level.

Double-bind situation: Hypothetical situation where individual is faced with inconsistent and incongruent communication.

Double-blind study: A study designed to determine the effects of a drug or treatment procedure as compared to a placebo, in which the patients and those who evaluate the effects of the drug are unaware until the completion of the study, which patients have received the active treatment, and which the placebo.

Down's syndrome (mongolism): A form of mental retardation in which the facial characteristics are similar to those of the 'mongolian' race.

Drive or motive: A specific state of the organism which includes a quantitative dimension or strength and a direction (i.e., it is related to a particular goal or set of goals). A drive may be basically innate (e.g., sexual drive) or learned (need for power).

Early infantile autism (EIA): a disorder present from birth characterized by mutism, a lack of object relations, including interpersonal indifference, repetitive stereotypic behaviour, and no evidence of neurological dysfunction.

Echolalic: A person characterized by the repetitive verbalization of whatever is said to him, no matter how meaningless it is.

Ego: That component of the person which acts as the executive (the self).

Electromyographic (EMG) feedback: The feedback of information to a person regarding muscle activity in a specific area.

Emergent stage one sleep: (*see* REM sleep).

Emotional redintegration: Occurs when an element or part of an experience results in the remembering of the total emotional experience or situation.

Empathy (accurate empathic understanding): Includes an awareness of the feelings of a person which can be adequately communicated back to that person.

Encoding: To relate information that has been registered to material in long-term storage or to translate information into such a form as to enable it to be integrated into long-term storage.

Environmental planning (stimulus control): The manipulation of environmental variables *prior* to the controlled behaviour in an attempt to modify that behaviour.

Error of central tendency: The tendency to rate people in the middle and to avoid extreme ratings or judgments.

Essential (functional) hypertension: Chronic high blood pressure lacking organic aetiology.

Ethological analysis: An analysis of an organism's actual behaviour via systematic recording, and quantification procedures in naturalistic settings. The aim is to determine the aetiology and function of specific types of behaviour.

Evoked cortical potentials: Cerebral electrical potentials produced via visual or auditory stimulation techniques.

Experimental intervention: The introduction of a new treatment procedure.

External personality: *see* Locus of control.

Extinction procedure: The withdrawal of reinforcement from previously reinforced behaviour.

Extrapunativeness: A tendency to externalize hostility or feelings of aggressivity.

Extraversion: A dimension of personality characterized by outgoing behaviour (sociability) and impulsiveness.

Fading procedures: A gradual change in stimulus conditions after treatment in a specific environment (e.g. hospital) has been successful. The purpose of these procedures is to generalize the effects of treatment so as to prevent relapse under different stimulus conditions (e.g. the home).

Faking (bad): Presenting oneself (usually on personality questionnaires) as a person very much in need of treatment, perhaps to be considered as an 'emergency' case, so as to avoid being placed on a long waiting list.

Faking (good): Presenting oneself (usually on personality questionnaires) as a person with highly desirable characteristics, in an effort to obtain a job, promotion, or to avoid treatment.

Field articulation: The extent to which stimuli are selectively attended to or ignored.

Filtering: A process of selective attention.

Flattening of affect: Little display of emotion, positive or negative.

Flooding: (a) (*In vivo*): A behavioural method in which the client is confronted with the most anxiety-evoking situation related to his problem. (b) (In-imagination): In contrast to the *in vivo* treatment, the client is asked to *imagine* the most anxiety-evoking situation.

Fluid ability (intelligence): The more innate or genetic component or aspect of intelligence.

Forced-choice rating technique: This technique requires the rater to choose between two equally favourable or unfavourable qualities or situations.

Free-association: The reporting to the therapist of everything that comes to mind without censor. (Basic concept of psychoanalysis.)

Free-floating anxiety: Anxiety which has no obvious object. The cause of the anxiety is unknown.

Frustration: Occurs when one is prevented from attaining a particular goal.

Frustration tolerance: The ability to tolerate frustration (may be specific to a particular class or category of behaviour).

Functional (behavioural) analysis: An assessment procedure which determines a client's assets, deficits, and excesses, and attempts to determine the precipitating and maintaining factors in relation to the specific maladaptive behaviour demonstrated. This analysis leads to a formulation of a treatment programme.

Functional autonomy: A principle which postulates that a specific type of behaviour can become an end or goal in itself, although some other factors may have initiated it.

Functional disorder: A disorder of psychological aetiology. There is no organic basis for the condition.

Functional fixation: the negative effect of 'set' on a problem-solving situation whereby objects tend to be utilized according to previous experience rather than in a novel manner, which may be required by the situation.

Gate-control theory: A comprehensive theory of pain which postulates that somatic input is modulated at the dorsal horns of the spinal cord, like a gate which can increase or decrease the passage of neural impulses from the periphery to the central nervous system.

General adaptation syndrome (GAS): Postulated by Selye as including three stages which the organism goes through in response to stress (i.e., the alarm reaction, resistance, and exhaustion). The GAS is invoked when adaptations to the particular form of the stressor are ineffective, or in situations in which the stressor is non-specific.

Generalization: The making of a similar, if not equivalent, response to a stimulus or situation which is similar to the stimulus or situation which originally elicited the response.

Genital stage: The stage of late adolescnece or early adulthood, during which there is an emphasis on ego processes.

Genotype: The genetic template which determines, together with the environment, the way in which a particular characteristic or disorder will be expressed.

Genuineness (congruence): A condition of openness in which the therapist must be honest and behave in a way which is congruent with his feelings.

Good premorbid status: Good adjustment by individual in social and interpersonal relationships prior to onset of schizophrenia.

Grief work: The repetitive worry regarding the loss of a loved-one, in which there is a preoccupation with thoughts of the lost person.

Hallucinations: A perception in the absence of stimulus, which is believed to be real (or 'out there').

Halo effect (rater–ratee interation error): Refers to an overgeneralization based upon limited evidence such as a person's appearance, a favourable or unfavourable personality or intelligence test score.

Headache (tension or muscle contraction): A headache typically elicited by emotional tension, characterized by a band-like pain around the head, usually in the occipital area but also occurring frontally. There are no prodromal signs and the pain is located bilaterally.

Helplessness (hopelessness): Similar to externality, in that one who exhibits helplessness believes that, no matter what he does, he is unable to control his reinforcements. In Seligman's view, the depressed person is one who feels helpless and lacks reinforcements to a large degree. He gets very little, if any, pleasure in life.

Hives (urticaria): A skin disorder of psychological aetiology, characterized by itching facial eruptions.

Hopelessness: *see* Helplessness.

Huntington's chorea: An hereditary disorder characterized by progressively severe choreiform movements and mental deterioration.

H-value (hereditability): A value, usually expressed as a decimal fraction, which indicates the percentage of the variance in a particular variable or characteristic, which may be attributable to genetic factors.

Hyperhydrosis: An excessive perspiration (overactivity of the sweat glands).

Hypnagogic imagery: Pronounced imagery occurring around sleep onset.

Hypnagogic state: A state of consciousness which occurs as one is falling asleep. The occurrence of mental imagery in a number of sensory modes, and a tendency to experience unusual and relatively loose thought processes is characteristic of this state.

Hypnopompic imagery: Pronounced imagery occurring around waking.

Hypnosis: a trance state or subjectively altered state of consciousness, tending to facilitate suggestibility, attention and imaginal processes.

Hypnotherapy: The use of hypnosis in treatment by therapists of an analytic persuasion.

Hypnotic amnesia: Amnesia produced specifically by hypnotic suggestion or occurring spontaneously, apparently through expectation of the subject, after an hypnotic induction.

Hypnotic induction A procedure, usually verbal, used to produce a 'state' of hypnosis, either by an operator (heterohypnosis) or via the subject himself (self or autohypnosis).

Hypnotizability (hypnotic responsiveness): Refers to the degree of hypnotic responsiveness as measured by an hypnotic susceptibility scale, and based on the number of items (suggestions or tasks) passed following a hypnotic induction.

Hypochondriasis: A neurotic condition in which a person is excessively preoccupied with his health, leading to frequent somatic complaints in the absence of organic pathology. Also a scale of the MMPI.

Hypothetical construct: Refers to a hypothetical state or condition, such as a drive of the organism which is linked to antecedent and consequent variables (stimuli and responses).

Hysteria: A rather obsolete term referring to conversion reactions in which symptoms of apparent organic disorder are present although no organic pathology is evident (*see* Conversion reaction).

Id: That component of personality associated with primative impulses.

Identification: A defence mechanism, usually adaptive, in which the individual relates himself emotionally (identifies) with another person, group, or movement (*see* Delusions of grandeur for an exaggerated use of this mechanism).

Idiosyncratic reinforcements: The specific rewards and punishment (aversive situations) which are particularly effective in modifying a specific person's behaviour.

Illusion: A false perception, based on ambiguity and set.

Impunativeness: Refers to the characteristic of evading the placement of blame when frustrated. Neither self nor other is blamed, but the situation producing the frustration is regarded as unavoidable.

Incompatible activities: Activities which are reinforced in behaviour therapy because they are desirable and prevent the carrying-out of maladaptive or undesirable behaviour simultaneously.

Insight: (a) The perception of meaningful relationships in a problem-solving situation. (b) In psychotherapy the realization of meaningful relationships between feelings and behaviour (i.e., understanding the dynamics or motivating factors in one's behaviour).

Insomnia: A disturbance of sleep characterized by an inability or relative inability to get off to sleep or to stay asleep.

Institutionalization: Refers to the 'conditioning' process or regimentation that an individual is exposed to in an institution. The individual is said to be institutionalized or to exhibit an 'institutional neurosis' when he becomes apathetic and habit-bound, and mentally deteriorated.

Institutional neurosis: *see* Institutionalization.

Intermediate sleep stages: Found to be significantly higher in acute schizophrenics. Similar in pattern to REM sleep, but without eye-movements. This stage usually occurs immediately before and after REM sleep, and interrupts stages 2 and 3.

Internal personality: *see* Locus of control.

Interobserver agreement: Agreement between two or more objective observers.

Interpretive therapy: Psychotherapy in which an emphasis is placed on an interpretation of the client's defensive manoeuvres.

Inter-rater reliability: Reliability established by measuring the agreement between raters.

Intrapersonal conflict: Refers to a conflict between the major components of personality (i.e., the id, ego, and superego).

Intrasubject correlation: A correlation between measures (e.g., self-rating on fear and skin conductance measures) obtained from the same subject.

Intropunativeness: A tendency to internalize hostility or feelings of aggressivity.

Intrusive experiences (cognitions): Unwanted thoughts or imaginings, usually of a negative nature.

K-complex: An EEG wave form indicative of an inner or outer stimulation occurring typically during stage 2 sleep.

Klinefelter's syndrome: Hypofunction of the gonads, specifically seminiferous tubular dysgenesis.

Learned helplessness: *see* Helplessness.

Leaving the field: The avoidance of two or more undesirable situations by removing oneself from the domain or area in which the negative situations are located.

Leniency error: Refers to the tendency to avoid giving unfavourable ratings or opinions.

Level of aspiration: The level or degree of success in a particular area that a person aims at achieving (i.e., an individual's standard of success).

Level of measurement: Refers to the assumptions made about the basic measurements obtained which subsequently are important in the type of statistical test that may logically be used to draw conclusions related to that data. The basic scales of measurement include nominal, ordinal, interval, and ratio scales.

Lichen planus: A chronic pruritic inflammatory eruption which may result in rough scaly skin on extremities or genital aras. This condition may occur following stress.

Life review: An inner introspective-like process in which the individual reminisces over his past life.

Limbic system: A ring of grey matter around and above the corpus collosum which is considered to be particularly involved in emotional reactions.

Locus of control: Refers to the degree to which the individual believes he has control of his reinforcements. The individual who believes that his behaviour is significantly related to his achievements, rewards, or the reinforcements he receives is termed an *internal*, or is said to exhibit an internal locus of control. The individual who believes that his behaviour has no relationship to the reinforcements he receives is termed an *external*.

Logical error: The tendency to rate people similarly on what are judged to be logically similar dimensions or qualities.

Longitudinal data: Samples of data obtained from the same individual or groups over a period of time.

Loose construing: Outcome of disconfirmation (invalidation) of constructs concerning the world around an individual.

Malingering: The simulation or faking of the symptoms of some physiological or psychological condition with conscious intent.

Material reinforcements: May be money, chocolate, etc., or tokens which may later be exchanged for some idiosyncratic 'reward'.

Maturation: Structural and physiological development of the organism necessary before certain sequences of behaviour may be learned.

Mediating variables: Hypothesized processes which occur between stimulus and response and, although not observable, have explanatory properties.

Medical model: This model of psychopathology sees non-adaptive or disturbed behaviour as symptomatic of some underlying disease process. One needs to determine the underlying disease (psychopathology) and to treat it. If one treats only the symptoms, one is not actually treating the disease or basic problem (underlying conflict) and symptom substitution is anticipated.

Mental retardation: Characterized by low intelligence (usually below 70 I.Q.) which may severely restrict the degree to which the individual is able (without training) to engage in self-help skills, etc.

Meta-communication: Refers to the concern of the message other than the actual content *per se*, and the way in which the transmitter of the information perceives his relationship with the receiver.

Method-acting condition: An experimental procedure in which subjects are asked to behave 'as if' something, such as an increase in skin temperature, were occurring.

Milieu treatment: Treatment procedures which involve a manipulation of the physical and social environment in order to facilitate rehabilitation.

Model: Sometimes used as a synonym for *theory* or *paradigm*. A model may be expressed in mathematical language, a diagram, or in some other structural form. However, a model is typically separate from the particular theory to which it applies, but may contribute to the construction, application, and interpretation of a theory. A model may derive from a non-psychological field (e.g. computers) and be used analogously to apply to a psychological area (e.g. central nervous system).

Modelling: Behaviour procedures based on observational learning or imitation. Modelling involves the therapist in 'role-playing'—a behavioural sequence which he instructs the client to imitate. (a) *Vicarious modelling* procedures involve the client observing the desired behaviour on film or television. If the model has a good interpersonal relationship with the client and he is reinforced for the desired behaviour, the client is more likely to engage in that behaviour; (b) *Participant modelling* (contact desensitization) involves the client in a combined performance with the therapist or model.

Mood: A person's relatively-enduring emotional tone.

Moon illusion: An illusion whereby the moon is perceived larger when it is nearer the horizon.

Moral anxiety: Involves a conflict between impulses from the id and the prescriptions and prohibitions of the superego.

Müller–Lyer illusion: An illusion whereby two lines of equal length are perceived as of unequal length.

Multiple baseline design: Refers to an approach in which baseline measures are taken on a number of variables. In the multiple baseline design first there is an intervention which is expected to modify one variable, following which each of the variables to be modified is treated in turn. The expectation is that only the specific behaviour being treated will change, while the other to-be-treated behaviours will not change until treatment is initiated with each of them.

Narcolepsy: Sleep disturbance characterized by one or more of the following: REM sleep at sleep onset, cataplexy, hypnagogic hallucinations, and sleep paralysis.

Narcosynthesis: Psychotherapy which is aided by the use of some narcotic drug, such as sodium amytal.

Negative reinforcer: A reinforcer which has negative or aversive consequences and is administered after maladaptive or undesirable behaviour.

Neurosis (psychoneurosis): A relatively mild group of disorders, such as phobic conditions and obsessional reactions, which usually do not require hospitalization.

Neurotic anxiety: An apparently irrational response which includes: (a) Bound-anxiety, attached to a definite object or situation and; (b) *Free-floating*, which has no object. There appears to be no realistic basis for these types of anxiety.

Neurotic (functional) overlay: That component of 'pain behaviour' which may variously be termed psychogenic, psychological, or operant in nature.

Neurotic triad: Refers to the MMPI scales of hypochondriasis, depression, and hysteria.

Nondisjunction: The failure of homologous chromosomes to separate during anaphase, so that both pass to the same daughter cell.

Non-specific factors: Those factors in a treatment situation which are not usually labelled as active components of the treatment, such as expectancy, suggestion, and placebo effects.

Normal curve: A mathematically defined curve which represents the distribution of biological variables, such as height and body weight among the population. Many psychological test score distributions, such as for example, intelligence, follow the normal curve

Norms: Refers to the average or typical performance of a particular group of people on a particular measuring instrument. Norms may be based on age, sex, occupational group, diagnostic group, etc. Thus, one would anticipate that the average short-term memory of a representative sample of 70–80 years olds would be significantly different from the average short-term memory of a representative sample of 16–20 year olds.

Obesity: Refers to the condition in which an individual is 50 per cent or more above ideal body weight.

Objective observation: Includes a definition of the behaviour to be observed and rating scales by which the observer is able to indicate the frequency, extent, duration, and intensity of the specific behaviour. Using these objective procedures two independent observers would be able to find a high degree of inter-observer reliability in their ratings.

Observational learning (imitation, modelling) (*see also* modelling): Learning which occurs through the observation of others (referred to as social imitation in children). Demonstrated through behavioural performance which has either (a) never been in the observer's repertoire, or (b) dropped out of the individual's repertoire because of anxiety or other factors. The procedure used in behaviour therapy in which active use is made of observation learning is termed modelling. The therapist models the behaviour.

Obsessional (obsessive–compulsive) condition: A condition characterized by persistent irrational thoughts which tend to result in compulsive acts or rituals.

Obsessional ruminations: Noxious internal stimuli, especially thoughts and imaginings that continuously appear in consciousness during mood disturbances.

Open-ended interview: A relatively unstructured interview situation in which the interviewee may largely determine the direction in which the interview will go.

Operant procedures: Procedures based on the principle that behaviour is governed by its consequences.

Operational definition: A definition in which the salient characteristics of the trait to be defined are elucidated by the operations (procedures) which are necessary to arrive at a measure of the trait (e.g., hypnotizability is measured (defined) by following the specified procedures in using a scale of hypnotizability).

Organic condition: A disorder of organic aetiology.

Overcorrection: A procedure useful in eliminating self-stimulatory and disruptive or aggressive behaviour. Foxx and Azrin (1973) list two main aspects of overcorrection: (a) to overcorrect the environmental effects of an inappropriate act, and (b) to require the disruptor to intensively practise correct forms of relevant behaviour. Where disruption does not occur, only the positive practice is required.

Overinclusive thinking: Thought disorganization brought about by a loosening of conceptual boundaries.

Overprotective: Refers to behaviour (usually parental) which serves to encourage dependency.

Over-valued ideas: Strongly held beliefs which preoccupy the individual and dominate his personality.

Pain: The subjective experience of being hurt. The experience of pain is a function of physiological and personality factors, and is affected by the individual's past experience as well as the specific situation in which the 'painful stimulus' occurs.

Pain-operant: That part of the total pain response that can be accounted for by the principles of operant learning.

Pain (psychogenic): That part of the total pain-response that is based on psychogenic factors, such as anxiety and depression (*see also* Neurotic overlay).

Pain-reaction component: The affective or psychological component of the total pain response. The reaction component includes expectancies, suggestion, level of anxiety, and the meaning of the situation in which the 'injury' occurs. Theoretically, the reaction component is that part of the total pain response which may be eliminated by psychological treatment.

Pain tolerance: The degree to which one can tolerate pain. Usually determined experimentally using the cold-pressor, test, electric shock, etc.

Paired associate learning: A learning task in which pairs of nonsense syllables or words have to be associated.

Paradigm: Refers to a set of interrelated assumptions or beliefs which serve to integrate the evidence in a particular field, which in turn serves as a guide to therapeutic procedures or further research. These assumptions and beliefs are shared by a number of workers in the field. While a paradigm may be consensually validated, it may be superseded in time in that another paradigm may be found to account for the evidence more satisfactorily.

Paradoxical sleep: *see* REM sleep.

Paranoid schizophrenia: Subtype of schizophrenia characterized by persistent delusions but otherwise intact cognitive structures.

Participant observer: A term coined by the psychiatrist H. S. Sullivan to describe the interviewer's *modus operandi* in the interview situation. Sullivan views the interviewer as an expert who not only observes the behaviour of the client, but also uses himself as a sensititve measuring instrument in detecting changes in his own anxiety and other feelings or emotions. The interviewer is not just a relatively passive listener but actively responds to the client's and his own emotions.

Perception: The process by which the organism extracts information from its environment.

Perceptual constancy: The phenomenon whereby, under certain conditions, perception will remain constant and objectively accurate despite 'retinal' variations.

Perceptual defence: A hypothetical phenomenon whereby supposedly anxiety-provoking or threatening stimuli are not perceived or are perceived with increased delay in order to prevent anxiety.

Perceptual deprivation: The reduction of meaningful and variable stimulation impinging in the organism.

Perceptual scanning: The extent to which stimuli are sampled from the environment.

Peceptual set: A readiness to perceive some stimuli rather than others.

Personal construct theory: A psychological theory developed by Kelly (1955) relating to the way that man construes his world.

Personality dynamics: The way in which personality factors interact.

Phenomenal field: Refers to the field of one's subjective reality or idiosyncratic perceptual field.

Phenomenology: Refers to idiosyncratic perception (i.e. it is the investigation of conscious experience). The individual's subjective reality is more important than an objective consensually validated reality.

Phenothiazines: The major tranquillizing drugs which are helpful in reducing excitement and agitation.

Phenotype:The way in which a particular disorder or behaviour which has a significant genetic component is expressed. That is, the phenotype occurs as a result of the interaction of the genotype with a specific environment.

Phenylketonuria (PKU): A disorder of protein metabolism which untreated results in mental retardation.

Phobia (conditional emotional response: CER): An intense irrational fear.

Phobic: One who has a phobia (*see* Phobia).

Placebo effect: The response to an inactive medication or to the non-specific components of a treatment as if an active drug or treatment factor was present.

Placebo-reactor: An individual who responds consistently to placebo across various situations.

Pleasure principle: Associated with primary-process thinking. The basic principle is that people tend to behave in such a way as to maximize pleasure and to avoid pain. In reference to the id, the principle involves the immediate gratification of instinctual desires either directly or through fantasy.

Poor pre-morbid status: Poor adjustment by individual in social and interpersonal relationships prior to onset of schizophrenia.

Positive hallucination: An hallucination in which one 'perceives' something for which there is no sensory stimuli. An item of some hypnotizability scales.

Post-hypnotic suggestion: A suggestion made to the hypnotic subject during 'trance', to be carried out following 'trance'.

Postural sway: A test of primary suggestibility carried out without an hypnotic induction.

Poverty of speech: Reduced vocabulary and verbal expressiveness.

Preconscious: A level of awareness at which processes exist of which one is unaware at a specific moment, but which may be recalled fairly easily, such as a telephone number one has not used for some time.

Predictive validity: The adequacy with which a test score or other measure allows one to predict some criterion. An example might be the use of secondary school grades in predicting degree of university success.

Prolonged exposure: Duration of exposure to a feared situation, as in flooding (*see* Flooding *in vivo*).

Premorbid history: Status of individual prior to onset of a disorder.

Primary delusion: The altered perception of environmental stimuli due to a change in meaning.

Primary reinforcer: A reinforcer such as food, drink, or something immediately useable.

Process schizophrenia: Gradual onset of disorder with a long history of pre-psychotic psychological problems; poor prognosis.

Progressive muscle relaxations: A systematic procedure in which the major muscles of the body are alternately tensed and relaxed. There is an emphasis on becoming quite aware of the difference between the tensed and relaxed state.

Psychasthenia: One of the neuroticism scales of the MMPI. It measures phobic and obsessive–compulsive symptoms.

Psychodelic-type drugs: (*see* Psychotomimetic drugs).

Psychological homeostatis: The relative balance of psychological factors within the organism. Analogous to physiological homeostasis.

Psychomotor retardation: Reduced speed in completing motor tasks which require some cognitive processing.

Psychomotor speed: The speed of carrying-out tasks which require both cognitive and motor abilities.

Psychopath: An individual, characterized as lacking a conscience or superego, who, although tending to engage in criminal or immoral behaviour can also exhibit a very charming manner.

Psychosomatic coronary disease: Coronary disease in which the aeriology is sustained by high anxiety brought on by stress. Blood coagulation time has been correlated with anxiety, thus the higher probability of thrombosis in those subjected to persistent stress.

Psychosomatic disorder: A disorder frequently involving tissue damage which has occurred as a result of intense emotional or stressful conditions which act largely through the autonomic nervous system.

Psychotherapy: A generic term including various verbal methods for effecting changes in behaviour which will primarily aid the individual towards better adaptation to himself and his environment.

Psychotic speech: Refers to speech that superficially, at least, is illogical and incomprehensible, it apparently deriving from primary process or autistic thinking.

Psychotomimetic: Mimicking psychotic states.

Psychotomimetic drugs: Drugs which induce a state similar to a psychosis. Three of the major types are lysergic acid diethylamide (LSD 25), mescaline, and psilocybin.

Pyramidal cells: The cell bodies are found in the fifth layer of the cerebral cortex, and their axons decend to the internal capsule. Important in motor activities.

Rapid eye-movement (REM) sleep (emergent stage one or paradoxical sleep): Characterized by rapid conjugate eye movements, greater variability in heart-rate and respiration-rate, genital erection in the male, and an EEG pattern similar to initial stage one sleep, indicating a higher level of cortical arousal. Dreaming has been associated most frequently with this stage of sleep.

Rapport: The establishment and maintenance of a good interpersonal relationship including trust and confidence, which increases the probability that adequate communication will take place.

Rational-emotive therapy: A therapeutic approach which stresses rational-assertive behaviours and attempts to modify irrational attitudes and beliefs. It has been classed as a behaviour approach.

Rational thinking: A category of thinking related to a tight, organized flow of ideation (i.e., problem solving, logic, etc.) supposedly reflecting reality-testing.

Raynaud's disease: A functional disorder in which there are intermittent bilateral vasospasms of the extremities. The aetiology may be cold stimulation or emotional stress.

Reactive schizophrenia: Sudden onset of disorder with little or no history of pre-psychotic psychological problems: favourable prognosis.

Realistic anxiety (fear): Anxiety based on a realistic situation which would be expected to be perceived as threatening or dangerous to the organism.

Reality orientation: Techniques used to treat those clients with problems of disorientation. Teaching the client information that he tends to forget.

Reality principle: Refers to the adjustment or modification of instinctual urges to environmental demands.

Reconstructive therapy: A psychotherapy approach in which emphasis is placed on changing the structure and dynamics of personality.

Referential states: Involves a state (feeling) that is referred to a particular event (e.g. 'I feel happy that I have passed my law examinations').

Reflection of feeling: An important aspect of client-centred therapy characterized by the clarification of the client's communications (verbal and non-verbal) about himself. Serves to verify that the therapist understands the client and is empathic.

Regression: A return, usually temporary, to an earlier, less mature level of psychological functioning (*see also* Regression in the service of the ego).

Regression in the service of the ego: Particularly stressed by psychoanalytic ego psychology. A *temporary* return to a less mature mode of adaption in response to a stressful situation. This mechanism helps to maintain ego integrity and some hypothesize that some creative ideas may derive from this regression.

Rehearsal desensitization: A graded desensitization procedure in which role-playing by client and therapist is the major component.

Reinforcement: A stimulus which increases or decreases the probability of a particular response. In classical conditioning the unconditional stimulus is the reinforcement.

Reinforcement contingencies: Refers to the circumstances (or behaviour) after which reinforcement can be expected.

Reinforcement interval: The interval between one reinforcement and the next.

Reliability (consistency): Refers to various methods of establishing that under similar circumstances that there is a consistency of response (e.g., that one's score on a scale measuring extroversion varies very little from time to time, provided interventions which might affect one's extraversion score have not occurred between the measurements. Test–retest reliability is obtained when measurements obtained on one occasion are correlated with measurements obtained on another occasion.

REM cycle: The period from the onset of one rapid eye-movement period to the onset of the next REM period.

Reminiscence (reminiscing): The vivid remembering and ruminating of experiences. Occurs more frequently in the elderly during the life-review process.

Repression: A defence mechanism in which the individual unconsciously forgets material that would cause anxiety, feelings of guilt, or other negative emotions.

Resistance: The client's use of inhibitory mechanisms to prevent repressed material breaking through into consciousnes.

Response prevention: Procedures which function to reduce checking and other ritualistic behaviour, especially in obsessional conditions.

Response sets (styles): Tendency to respond (especially to questionnaire items) in a specific way, such as the tendency to acquiesce.

Response specificity: Postulates that the best index of physiological responsivity to stress is that measure which is most responsive, which may be blood pressure in one individual and heart-rate in another.

Retardation: Extreme slowness in test performance.

Reticular formation: An area of the brain stem important in determining the arousal level of the organism.

Retrograde amnesia: The loss of memory for experiences preceding head injury or other traumatic event.

Reversal technique: A treatment procedure which consists of four phases: (1) establishing baseline measurements; (2) treatment intervention; (3) reversal (i.e., discontinuance of treatment intervention) procedure; and (4) return to treatment intervention.

Ruminative thoughts: *see* Obsessional ruminations.

Schizoid personality: a personality type, often pre-schizophrenic, characterized by isolation and affective dissociation.

Schizophrenia: A psychotic disorder (i.e., loss of contact with reality) usually characterized by cognitive disorganization and perceptual change.

Schizophrenic thought disorder: The disorganization of thoughts and ideas which often characterizes schizophrenia.

Secondary delusion: A faulty explanation for abnormal experience or altered perception (primary delusion).

Secondary reinforcer: Analogous to secondary drives, such as the need for affiliation. Reinforcers that are learned, such as verbal approval, rather than primary, such as food.

Self-actualization: A basic tendency for the person to maintain and enhance himself.

Self-concept: The person's perception of himself.

Self-disclosure: Refers to a willingness to be open about one's self.

Self-fulfilling prophesy: Refers to a belief, the holding of which may lead to behaviour (or a perception of behaviour) which tends to support such a belief.

Self-ideal: Refers to the person one would like to be.

Self-injurious behaviour (SIB): Self-inflicted behaviour such as head-banging, eye-gouging.

Self-instruction training: The systematic presentation of material to be learned with the provision of feedback regarding accuracy of learning. Can be used to treat phobic conditions, to modify attitudes, or to teach academic content.

Self-monitoring (SM): Observation and recording of one's own behaviour and variables relating to it.

Self-presented consequences: *see* Behavioural programming.

Sensation-seeking motive: *see* Sensation seeker.

Sensation seeker: Refers to a person who seeks environmental change, tends to be emotionally labile, wishes independence from others, and tends to need others mainly as an audience to his own performance.

Sensory deprivation: The absolute reduction and/or elimination of sensory stimulation impinging on the organism.

Sensory overload: The effect of dramatically increasing sensory stimulation impinging on the organism.

Serial invalidation: Process of disconfirmation of constructs concerning the outside world, supposedly producing 'schizophrenic' loose construing (or thought disorder).

Shape constancy: An example of perceptual constancy whereby shape remains perceived as constant despite 'retinal' shape.

Shaping (successive approximation): The reinforcement of responses which are a component of the behaviour to be learned.

Size constancy: An example of perceptual constancy whereby size remains perceived as constant despite distance ('retinal' size).

Significant other: Refers to people in a person's environment who may be seen as having a significant influence on a person's development, adaptation, and adjustment. Relations, friends, teachers, may be included as significant others.

Sleep spindles: Waves of 14–16 Hertz which occur in a relatively wide area of the cerebral cortex during stage two sleep.

Sleep walking: *see* Somnabulism.

Social desirability: A response set in which the individual has a strong tendency to agree with statements about himself which are considered socially desirable.

Social learning therapy: Therapy based on the research findings of social learning which includes the application of the principles of learning in a social context. Modelling techniques and the use of social reinforcement would be important.

Social reinforcement: Social behaviour of others which has reinforcing properties.

Sodium pentathol: A narcotic drug sometimes used to promote relaxation and suggestion during psychotherapy.

Somatopsychological disorder: A psychological disturbance based upon the presence of somatic pathology. The disorder arises because of the individual's intense reaction to his somatic condition.

Somnabulism (sleep walking): A condition in which a person gets out of bed at night and moves around in a confused fashion. He is typically able to avoid obstacles in his way, but usually talks in a rather incoherent fashion. The episodes occur independently of dreaming periods, and the person is usually amnesic for his sleep-walking activities.

Specific attitudes hypothesis: Suggests that specific attitudes determine the development of particular psychosomatic conditions (e.g., it has been hypothesized that the person with hives perceives others as mistreating him and he ruminates about this).

Spina bifida: A congenital defect of the central nervous system, frequently affecting the spinal cord. The condition is caused by an interference with the normal formation and closure of the neural tube.

Spontaneous recovery: The reappearance of a response which had been extinguished without any intervening conditioning trials.

Spontaneous remission: A somewhat controversial concept which refers to the recovery from some disorder without any intervening treatment.

Stable equilibrium: The condition in which a person finds himself when caught between two situations, the one negative, and the other positive. While there may be vacillation, the individual does not move close enough to either situation to break or solve conflict.

Standardization: Refers to the specifically consistent way in which a test is administered and scored.

Standardized interview: An interview which includes a specified procedure which is usually followed by the assessor in his interaction with each client. Many psychological tests may legitimately be referred to as standardized interviews.

Startle response: A normally expected response involving an involuntary motor reaction to novel or unexpected stimuli.

State: A person's relatively temporary emotional condition.

Stimulus control: *see* Environmental planning.

Stimulus control techniques: Techniques based upon the use of environmental stimuli to control behaviour such as respiratory functioning or sleep onset (i.e., the use of previously neutral stimuli as conditional stimuli).

Storage: Refers to the information in long-term memory.

Stress: May refer to the stimulus situation an individual is exposed to, the state of the organism during such an exposure, or to the response the individual makes to the 'stressful' situation. When an individual feels stressed, he perceives that his well-being or integrity is threatened and he must use all his resources to protect himself.

Structured interview: An interview situation in which the interviewer directs the questions into definite areas, such as family background and vocational history in a systematic way.

Stupor: Lethargic, unresponsive condition.

Superego: This component of personality has two aspects:

(a) the *conscience*, which has incorporated the prohibitions or 'don'ts' of the society in which one lives, and

(b) the *ego-ideal*, which has incorporated desirable or idealistic principles of behaviour as a model.

Supportive therapy: A therapeutic approach which avoids extensively changing the client, but rather stresses the shoring-up and strengthening of the client's defences.

Suppression: The conscious inhibition of ideas associated with anxiety into the unconscious.

Symptom substitution: The *medical model* assumes that if only maladaptive *behaviour* (symptomtology) is treated then other symptoms, which are based on the underlying pathology which has not been treated, will be expressed, and take the place of the symptoms which have been removed.

Systematic case study: Includes the systematic measurement of dependent or criterion variables during and after treatment has taken place, as compared to baseline conditions. There is no control group. However, if changes in the criterion variables follow the intervention, particularly if this is consistent over a number of patients, then one has confidence that the intervention procedure was responsible for the changes observed.

Systematic desensitization: A behavioural procedure used to treat phobias and some other neurotic conditions. The procedure is characterized by the simultaneous presentation of a stimulus antagonistic to anxiety while the client is imagining an anxiety–evoking situation (*see also* counterconditioning).

Target behaviour: The behaviour that needs to be modified.

Task motivation: The use of instructions to subjects in an experiment to facilitate maximum performance. For example, the instructions may appeal to their desire to contribute to scientific knowledge.

Temperature discrimination training: Training by which a patient/subject focuses on bodily sensations (typically in his hand) and receives feedback concerning his success in discriminating between sensations of warmth and cold.

Territoriality: A concept which refers to the claiming and defence of an area or territory as one's own.

Thinking: A general category of covert behaviour (not observable) which involves the manipulation of acquired information.

Thought stopping: Procedures used to stop intrusive experiences or obsessional ruminations. Simultaneously with the occurrence of the unwanted experiences some novel stimulus is presented and the therapist shouts, 'stop', which serves to disrupt the subject's experiences or thoughts.

Time-distortion techniques: Therapeutic techniques, usually applied following an hypnotic induction, which involves suggesting to the subject or client that he imagines that it is some time in the past or future.

Time out: A procedure in which the individual who is engaging in maladaptive behaviour is removed from the situation in which the undesirable behaviour is occurring for a definite period of time. Typically used with children or the mentally backward.

Today form: Refers to an inventory or mood-scale which asks the respondent to respond to the questions in reference to how he is feeling today, or more specifically, at the moment.

Token economy: Refers to a behavioural programme involving a ward or other treatment unit or group, such as a group of delinquents, in which those clients or others in the programme receive tokens as rewards (which may be later exchanged for more idiosyncratic reinforcements, such as coffee, chocolates, etc.) for desirable, non-illness or well behaviour.

Trait: A characteristic of an individual which is considered to be relatively enduring, such as degree of extroversion.

Transference: The tendency to perceive, usually unconsciously, the therapist as some significant-other, such as a parent from the client's past.

Trichotillomania: Chronic hair pulling.

Turner's syndrome: A genetic disorder characterized by limited sexual development and short stature.

Unconditional positive regard (non-possessive warmth): a full acceptance, with no qualifications,of the client by the therapist.

Unconscious: A level of awareness at which processes exist of which one is totally unaware.

Under-responsiveness: A reduced responsiveness to the environment.

Validity: Usually refers to the extent to which a measurement procedure measures the characteristic it was constructed to measure. Predictive validity refers to the extent to which measures obtained on a particular occasion relate to some future performance, such as the degree of success in carrying-out a particular task.

Vicarious conditioning: Occurs in observational learning or modelling procedures, in which the client observes the model making a specific response which is reinforced.

Vicarious extinction: Occurs in observational learning or modelling procedures, in which the client observes the model making a particular response which is *not* reinforced.

Vicarious reinforcement: The observation, by the client in modelling procedures, of the model receiving reinforcement following a specific response.

Visual place response: Occurs in animals in which visual cortex is normal: the instinct to stand on a solid object within its field of vision.

Waking suggestibility: Procedures which involve the giving of suggestions during the waking state, in contrast to during or after a hypnotic induction.

Working through: Term used to refer to the analysis of the client's conflicts and transference relationship in psychoanalytic psychotherapy.

Zygote: Results from the union of the male and female germ cells (a fertilized egg).

Author Index

Subject Index